DATE DUE

GAYLORD 234			PRINTED IN U. S.

DOCUMENTS ON
INTERNATIONAL AFFAIRS
1958

DOCUMENTS ON
INTERNATIONAL AFFAIRS
1958

SELECTED AND EDITED
BY
GILLIAN KING

Issued under the auspices of the
Royal Institute of International Affairs

OXFORD UNIVERSITY PRESS

LONDON   NEW YORK   TORONTO

1962

Oxford University Press, Amen House, London E.C.4

GLASGOW NEW YORK TORONTO MELBOURNE WELLINGTON
BOMBAY CALCUTTA MADRAS KARACHI KUALA LUMPUR
CAPE TOWN IBADAN NAIROBI ACCRA

SET AND PRINTED IN GREAT BRITAIN
BY HAZELL, WATSON AND VINEY LTD.
AYLESBURY AND SLOUGH
REPRINTED LITHOGRAPHICALLY AT THE
UNIVERSITY PRESS, OXFORD
BY VIVIAN RIDLER
PRINTER TO THE UNIVERSITY

PREFACE

OVER the past few years the *Documents on International Affairs* and the *Survey of International Affairs* have been published as independent volumes. As the two series fall back into step again it is hoped to make the volumes complementary. The *Documents* for 1958, marking a half-way stage in this transition, forms a volume which stands in its own right. While it does not have introductions to each chapter, as did the three preceding volumes, explanatory footnotes have been added where necessary.

The material for the most part is arranged under functional headings, but occasionally other documents, which do not strictly fit the heading, have been included for convenience. For example, the Resolution of the U.S.S.R. Supreme Soviet of 31 March on the unilateral termination by the Soviet Union of atomic and hydrogen weapon tests, and the Soviet reply of 3 March to the Polish memorandum on an atom-free zone in Central Europe appear in Chapter I—East–West Exchanges.

Chapter I covers the most important topics which at one time or another formed the subject matter of numerous exchanges between East and West. An exception is the correspondence between Mr. Khrushchev and Mr. Macmillan on the crisis in the Middle East; these letters have been included in Chapter IIB, The Middle East, Landings in the Lebanon and Jordan. This well illustrates the difficulties frequently encountered in selection and arrangement. One might reasonably argue that since these nine letters form part of the repeated and almost continuous Soviet attempt throughout 1958 to arrange a summit meeting, and since they are East–West exchanges, they should be included in Chapter I. Equally, however, it could be said that since this correspondence was so inextricably bound up with local events in the Middle East and with the operations of the United Nations in that area, the letters should be placed in their local rather than in their general East–West context. On balance I have chosen the second alternative.

Chapters III and IV each document the crises, negotiations, and agreements within one of the two camps, while Chapter V is in effect an appendix which brings together the documentation on six conferences of interest. A chronological list of the documents reproduced has for the first time been included at the end of the book.

I am most grateful to Miss Elizabeth Monroe for her advice on the Middle Eastern sections, to Miss Marianne Gellner for her help with the selection of documents for the part of Chapter III which deals with the Common Market, Euratom, and the Free Trade Area, and to Professor Geoffrey Barraclough who read the whole volume in draft. Finally I should like to thank Dr. Noble Frankland for his help and advice in the earlier stages of the work, without which its remaining imperfections could not but have been far more numerous and apparent.

G. K.

Chatham House
 2 March 1961

CONTENTS

CONTENTS

III. THE WESTERN ALLIANCE

A. WESTERN RELATIONS

V. SIX CONFERENCES

A. CONFERENCE ON THE LAW OF THE SEA

SOURCE ABBREVIATIONS

Cmd., Cmnd.	Command Paper (London, H.M.S.O.).
Documents	*Documents on International Affairs* (London, Oxford University Press for Royal Institute of International Affairs).
D.S.B.	U.S.A.: *Department of State Bulletin* (Washington, U.S.G.P.O.).
G.A.O.R.	General Assembly Official Records (United Nations).
H.C. Deb., vol., col.	House of Commons Debates (bound volumes).
H.N.A.	*Hsinhua News Agency*, Daily Bulletin (London).
New Measures for Economic Cooperation	*Special Committee to study the Formulation of New Measures for Economic Cooperation, volume I: Report and Documents* (Council for the Organisation of American States, Washington, D.C., 1959).
S.C.O.R.	Security Council Official Records (United Nations).
S.W.B.	*Summary of World Broadcasts* (Monitoring Service of the British Broadcasting Corporation).
Part IIB	Hungary, Rumania, Bulgaria, Albania, Yugoslavia.
Part IV	The Arab World, Israel, Greece, Turkey, Iran.
Tanjug	*Telegraphic Agency New Jugoslavia* (London).
T.I.A.S.	United States Treaties and Other International Agreements (Washington, Department of State).
U.S. Documents	*Documents on American Foreign Relations* (New York, Council on Foreign Relations).
U.S. in World Affairs	*United States in World Affairs* (New York, Council on Foreign Relations).

I. EAST–WEST EXCHANGES

A. GENERAL: SUMMIT CONFERENCE, STRATEGIC BALANCE OF POWER, ETC.

a. Summit conference

1. Letter from Mr. Bulganin to Mr. Macmillan, Moscow, 14 March 1958[1]

Dear Prime Minister, Having carefully studied you messages of January 16 and February 8,[2] I consider it necessary to return to some questions connected with the preparation of a conference of leading statesmen of the East and West with the participation of heads of government.

First of all I would like to express my satisfaction that the desire of the Soviet government to reduce international tension and establish better relations between our countries meets with understanding on the part of the government of the United Kingdom. I was also glad to hear that you are ready to take part in a conference of leading statesmen of the East and West. The unity of views of our governments with regard to the necessity of convening a summit conference raises great hopes that the efforts now being made to convene this conference will be successful.

In your message of February 8, you stress that it would be desirable to prepare the ground thoroughly for holding a summit meeting and that in your opinion it would be preferable to have, in the preparatory stage, a meeting of Foreign Ministers of the governments represented at the Geneva Conferences of 1955. You have also expressed agreement that the appropriate preparatory work be conducted through diplomatic channels. These views, which in one form or another have also been expressed by the governments of certain other countries, have been examined and taken into consideration by us.

It is the opinion of the Soviet government that the summit conference— about the need for which the heads of all the major states have now expressed their views—requires preparation insofar as concerns a decision on its composition, the problems which, by the mutual consent of the parties, are to be included in the agenda, and also the time and place of the conference. At the same time we believe that all ways and means that could speed up the preparations for the heads of government conference

---

[1] *Soviet News*, 20 March 1958.   [2] See *Documents* for 1957, pp. 62–66.

should be used. Certain of the questions relevant to this could, we think, be agreed upon through diplomatic channels, and naturally these possibilities should be utilised.

Taking into account the wishes of the government of the United Kingdom, and also those of other western countries, the Soviet government has decided to agree that the preparations for a summit conference be entrusted to the Foreign Ministers, who will meet for this purpose.

In our opinion the Ministers should concern themselves with organisational matters connected with preparing the conference, namely: drawing up an agenda and deciding on the composition, and the place and time of the conference. It would be a good thing for the work to be carried out in the shortest possible time. It seems to us that the meeting of Foreign Ministers could take place already in April. Should you agree, then we could come to an understanding through our Ambassadors about the practical matters connected with the meeting of Ministers.

We have noted your readiness, in drawing up the agenda for the heads of government conference, to examine the problems which were set out in 'The Proposals of the Soviet Government for Reducing International Tension.'[1] It goes without saying that the Soviet government, as it has already pointed out repeatedly, is also willing to discuss at the conference, subject to mutual agreement, other constructive proposals aimed at ending the 'cold war.'

In particular, the Soviet government would be ready to discuss at the conference the question of banning the use of outer space for military purposes and dismantling foreign bases on the territories of other states. An agreement on this important issue would, without doubt, greatly reduce the danger of the sudden outbreak of war and would be a great step towards ensuring conditions for a peaceful and tranquil life for the peoples.

In our opinion the conference could also examine the question of the conclusion of a German peace treaty. The Soviet government proposes that the governments of the German Democratic Republic and the Federal Republic of Germany be invited to take part in the discussion on this question. It goes without saying that the question of the unification of the German Democratic Republic and the Federal Republic of Germany in a single state, a question which falls entirely within the competence of these two German states, cannot be, as the Soviet government has already repeatedly pointed out, a subject for discussion at the forthcoming summit conference.

The development of ties and contacts between countries, the importance of which we all recognise, could also be discussed at the conference. As

[1] Enclosed in Mr. Bulganin's letter of 8 January 1958 to Mr. Macmillan; see *Documents* for 1957, pp. 51–62.

you are well aware, the Soviet government attaches great importance to the maintenance of systematic personal contacts between leading states-men for the exchange of views on urgent international issues, in the interests of improving relations between states, of strengthening mutual trust and consolidating world peace.

Nor would we object to an exchange of views at the conference on ways and means of strengthening the United Nations.

At the same time I must make some remarks with regard to the pro-posals for the agenda of the conference put forward in the message of the United States President of January 12, proposals which, as you say in your letter, have the full support of the government of the United Kingdom.[1]

You are aware that certain American proposals relating to the pro-gramme of work for the summit conference cannot be accepted by the Soviet Union. It is desirable that there should be no obscurity about the reasons why the Soviet government objects to these · proposals being submitted to the conference.

In our opinion it would not be, for instance, in the least useful to discuss the proposal to renounce the unanimity principle among the permanent members of the United Nations Security Council in the examination of certain problems, although the authors of this proposal argue that it is aimed at strengthening the United Nations. The Soviet Union, throughout the 13 years of the United Nations' existence, has done, and continues to do, all in its power to strengthen by every means the significance of this international organisation, which is called upon to be the centre for harmonising the actions of the nations for working out mutually accept-able decisions in the interests of ensuring peace. That is why any proposal aimed at strengthening the United Nations has always had, and will continue to have the most sincere and resolute support of the government of the Soviet Union, and we would have no objection to an exchange of views on proposals of such a nature.

However, one may ask: Does the proposal aimed at doing away with the principle of the unanimity of the great powers serve the purpose of strengthening the United Nations? Indeed, it is well known that it is precisely the application of this principle in the Security Council that has prevented the adoption of certain decisions detrimental to international co-operation, which did not take into account the well-founded interests of states not belonging to the western countries' military groupings. The United Nations, as is well known, cannot claim to have the role of some kind of world government, whose decisions would be in the nature of orders binding on the sovereign states which are members of this inter-

[1] For President Eisenhower's letter to Mr. Bulganin of 12 January 1958, see *D.S.B.*, 27 January 1958, pp. 122-7.

national body. In accordance with its Charter, it is called upon to co-ordinate the positions of states and work out mutually acceptable solutions. It is clear that the carrying out of the measures proposed by the United States government could lead in practice to the Security Council being used in the interests of one state or one group of states at the expense of the rights and interests of other states. What would be the outcome of such a situation? Certainly not the strengthening of the United Nations but, on the contrary, the shattering of the very foundations of its existence, the undermining of co-operation and confidence among the great powers, which bear the main responsibility for maintaining world peace.

Nor can we agree to discuss matters which fall within the province of the internal affairs of other states and the examination of which could have no other result than a still greater exacerbation of relations between the powers. Such questions as the situation in the countries of Eastern Europe and the problem of the unification of the German Democratic Republic and the Federal Republic of Germany in a single state come precisely within this category.

In my letter to you of January 8[1] I already had occasion to express the Soviet government's point of view on these questions and it is hardly necessary to speak at length about this again. Discussion of such questions would constitute impermissible interference in the internal affairs of sovereign states to which the Soviet government will in no way agree.

The question legitimately arises as to why the Soviet government is being approached with a proposal to discuss the internal affairs of third countries which are sovereign states and with which both the United Kingdom and the Soviet Union maintain normal diplomatic relations. Indeed, if anything in the internal structure of any East European country is not clear to the government of the United Kingdom, then, as you are aware, there is the time-honoured practice of clearing up such questions through the usual diplomatic channels and not by interfering in the internal affairs of other countries. We do not consider it possible to assume the role of judge and solve problems pertaining to the internal structure of other countries. Nor can we recognise such a right for any other state, and we consider it impermissible not only to discuss such questions but even to raise them.

We have no doubt that should anyone propose that an international conference discuss the internal political situation, for example, in France, Italy, Turkey, Canada or the United Kingdom itself, such a proposal would meet with justified objections on your part. To include such issues in the agenda of a summit conference would be deliberately to doom it to failure, and that is something we do not at all want.

It can be concluded from your letter that the government of the United

[1] See *Documents* for 1957, pp. 41–51.

Kingdom and also the government of the United States are displaying an interest in the summit conference discussing the disarmament problem. This gives grounds for hoping that at the conference those taking part will exert the necessary effort to find a way, acceptable to all, to advance the solution of this most important problem of the day. We believe that if a start were to be made by ending tests of atomic and hydrogen weapons, by prohibiting the use of those weapons and by the dismantling of foreign military bases on the territories of other states, then it would be possible to create favourable conditions also for reaching agreement on other aspects of the disarmament problem.

I consider it necessary, Mr. Prime Minister, to draw your attention to certain circumstances which, I must tell you frankly, are causing some anxiety in the Soviet Union. The exchange of views between governments on holding a high-level conference, which was initiated by the U.S.S.R., has now been going on for months. Unfortunately, however, no great progress in this matter can yet be observed, since the representatives of certain western countries continue to insist that the agenda include issues which are known in advance to be unacceptable, and postpone the convening of such a conference indefinitely.

Even greater anxiety is aroused by the fact that, in addition to dragging out the settlement of the question of convening the conference, the governments of the United Kingdom, the United States and certain other member-countries of the North Atlantic Alliance are speeding up the implementation of practical measures in the sphere of military preparations, which only lead to a worsening of the international situation.

Indeed, this is borne out by the reports on the preparations being made to hold a N.A.T.O. Defence Ministers' conference in Paris this April—a conference which is to examine and take decisions concerning the question of siting bases for launching medium-range rockets in the N.A.T.O. countries, supplying atomic weapons to members of N.A.T.O. and stationing atomic warhead depots in those countries.

It is sufficient to compare the range of questions which we offer for discussion at a conference of leading statesmen of the East and West with those questions which it is planned to discuss in Paris, in order to realise that there is a complete contradiction and incompatability between the tasks and aims which are being pursued, on the one hand, by the N.A.T.O. states, in convening a conference of their Defence Ministers at the present time, and, on the other hand, by the states proposing to hold talks at the summit level in the interests of reducing international tension.

It was recently announced officially that an Anglo-American agreement had been concluded providing for the establishment on United Kingdom territory of launching sites for medium-range rockets with nuclear warheads. As can be seen from the same announcements, the implementation of this agreement is given high priority. The fact is not concealed that the rocket installations which will be built at these bases will have as their objective targets in the Soviet Union. It is no less clear either that this step by the British government—and the unpopularity of this step in Britain is generally known—can contribute neither to the betterment of relations between our countries nor to the relaxation of international tension.

Needless to say, every government is itself responsible to its people for its country's security. But I have no right to keep silent about the fact that the British government's consent to the construction of American rocket bases on the territory of its country brings a serious element of tension into the international situation, into the relations between the states of East and West. In this connection we cannot ignore the recent British government White Paper which in fact declares Britain's readiness to use atomic and hydrogen weapons against the Soviet Union first.[1]

How can one reconcile such steps of the British government with its assurances of its desire to promote the easing of international tension and improve relations between our countries?

In the present circumstances, when a certain reduction in international tension is in evidence, when new shoots of trust are springing up in relations between states and when, finally, the calling of a conference of leading statesmen of the East and West at the highest level is a matter which is not only desirable but quite within reach, any actions that are in contradiction with the efforts of the peoples and the governments of many countries in the world to put an end to the 'cold war' and reduce the danger of war breaking out, do particularly great harm to the establishment of mutual understanding between the countries of the East and West.

And if certain N.A.T.O. countries are today exerting such efforts to enlarge the field of preparations for a rocket and nuclear war and to ensure the further expansion of the N.A.T.O. armed forces and armaments, then all this is certainly not being done in order to decide the next day to cancel these measures. In the light of this, the announced meeting of the Defence Ministers of the N.A.T.O. countries, as well as the agreement between the United States and the United Kingdom with regard to rocket bases cannot be regarded as other than an attempt to hinder the

---

[1] Cmnd. 363, Report on Defence, February 1958, in which the following paragraph appeared: 'The West on the other hand, relies for its defence primarily upon the deterrent effect of its vast stockpile of nuclear weapons and its capacity to deliver them. The democratic Western nations will never start a war against Russia. But it must be well understood that, if Russia were to launch a major attack on them, even with conventional forces only, they would have to hit back with strategic nuclear weapons. In fact, the strategy of N.A.T.O. is based on the frank recognition that a full-scale Soviet attack could not be repelled without resort to a massive nuclear bombardment of the sources of power in Russia . . .' (p. 2).

convocation and the success of the summit conference, an attempt to confront this conference with certain *faits accomplis* which would remove in advance the basis for agreement on a number of issues most important from the point of view of strengthening peace.

In the opinion of the Soviet government it is now more than ever necessary to refrain from any measures of a military nature or other unilateral actions which are aimed at undermining confidence between the partners in the expected talks and which could complicate the calling of a conference of leading statesmen of the East and West or make it more difficult to reach agreed decisions on the questions proposed for discussion. As far as the Soviet Union is concerned, there is complete readiness to do everything that is necessary in order to strengthen mutual understanding and confidence between states in the interests of ensuring the success of the top-level conference of statesmen with the participation of the heads of government.

We are confident that the sooner the governments of our countries get down to immediate preparations for the summit conference the greater will be the confidence in the positive solution of international problems ripe for settlement that is so passionately desired by the peoples, who are tired of living in an atmosphere of constant alarm and anxiety for their future.

Allow me, Mr. Prime Minister, to express the hope that the Soviet government's considerations set out in this letter, concerning preparations for convening a conference of heads of government, will be favourably received by the government of the United Kingdom.

Yours respectfully,

N. BULGANIN

2. Letter from Mr. Macmillan to Mr. Khrushchev with a joint communication from the United Kingdom, United States, and France, London, 31 March 1958[1]

My dear Prime Minister: As you will be aware, the Soviet Ambassador in London delivered to me on March 17 a letter from Mr. Bulganin, about the proposed meeting of Heads of Government.

After giving careful consideration to the letter, I feel that what I wish to say in reply could not be better expressed than in the attached communication, which is a joint one from the Governments of the United Kingdom, the United States of America and France.

I sincerely hope that the Soviet Government will agree with our

[1] Cmnd. 423, pp. 7–8. On 27 March 1958, Mr. Bulganin resigned, and Mr. Khrushchev was elected to succeed him as Chairman of the Council of Ministers.

proposals. We should then be able to divert our energies from conducting a lengthy public correspondence and get down to serious preparatory work without further delay.

Yours sincerely,

HAROLD MACMILLAN

JOINT COMMUNICATION FROM THE GOVERNMENTS OF THE UNITED KINGDOM, THE UNITED STATES OF AMERICA AND FRANCE

The present international situation requires that a serious attempt be made to reach agreement on the main problems affecting the attainment of peace and stability in the world. In the circumstances a Summit meeting is desirable if it would provide opportunity for conducting serious discussions of major problems and would be an effective means of reaching agreement on significant subjects.

It is clear that before a Summit meeting can meet in these conditions preparatory work is required.

This preparation work could best be performed by exchanges through diplomatic channels leading to a meeting between Foreign Ministers.

The main purpose of this preparatory work should be to examine the position of the various Governments on the major questions at issue between them and to establish what subjects should be submitted for examination by Heads of Government. It would not be the purpose of these preparatory talks to reach decisions, but to bring out by general discussion the possibilities of agreement.

The Foreign Ministers, assuming they have concluded the preparatory work to their satisfaction, would reach agreement on the date and place of the Summit meeting and decide on its composition.

If this procedure is acceptable to the Soviet Government it is suggested that diplomatic exchanges should start in Moscow in the second half of April.

3. Letter from Mr. Khrushchev to Mr. Macmillan, 4 April 1958[1]

Dear Mr. Prime Minister, the need for suspending immediately the tests of various types of atomic and hydrogen weapons is one of the most urgent questions in present-day international relations, a question deeply agitating the minds of millions of people in all countries. It is easy to realise the anxiety which continuing experimental nuclear weapon explosions arouse among all sections of the population, from political leaders and scientists to the common folk, the working people of town and countryside and mothers of families. British public circles are also known

---

[1] *Soviet News*, 8 April 1958. A similar message was sent to President Eisenhower on 4 April 1958, and to M. Gaillard on 8 April 1958.

to be concerned over the continuing nuclear and hydrogen weapon tests because they are aware of the calamities which an atomic war could bring to Great Britain because of her geographical position alone. After all, these tests whip up the arms race and are conducive to the development of new and more destructive and deadly types of nuclear weapons thereby increasingly aggravating the danger of atomic war now overshadowing mankind.

Moreover, the systematic experimental explosions of atomic and hydrogen weapons have already now, in peacetime, become hazards to the health of unsuspecting and innocent civilians in various countries. The petition signed by 9,235 scientists from 44 countries, including many distinguished scientists of Great Britain and the Soviet Union, and handed last January to the Secretary-General of the United Nations, says that every nuclear bomb explosion increases the quantity of radioactive fall-out throughout the world, harming the health of the people everywhere and jeopardising the normal development of the generations to come.

Considering all this, the Soviet government has arrived at the conclusion that the solution of the problem of ending nuclear weapon tests brooks no delay insofar as we cannot allow the health of people to be irreparably harmed.

Today nuclear weapons are possessed by only three powers—the U.S.S.R., the United States and the United Kingdom—which makes agreement on ending nuclear weapon tests relatively easy to achieve. If the tests are not ended now, other countries may also develop nuclear weapons soon, and then agreement to end tests will, of course, be much more difficult.

In the past three years the Soviet government has repeatedly approached the governments of the United Kingdom and the United States of America with a proposal to end atomic and hydrogen weapon tests. Inasmuch as the government of the United Kingdom and the government of the United States did not agree to a final discontinuation of nuclear experiments, the Soviet Union proposed, as a start, their suspension for at least a limited period of, say, two or three years. The Soviet proposals on this score provide for appropriate international control over the ending of tests.

In spite of all this we, unfortunately, have still not reached agreement on the question of an unconditional ending without delay of all nuclear weapon tests, or even on their suspension.

Guided by the desire to make a practical beginning for the universal ending of atomic and hydrogen weapon tests and thereby take the first step towards finally ridding mankind of the danger of a devastating atomic war, the Supreme Soviet of the Union of Soviet Socialist Republics decided that tests of all types of atomic and hydrogen weapons should be ended in the Soviet Union.

On the strength of this decision of the U.S.S.R. Supreme Soviet, the Soviet government resolved to end unilaterally all tests of atomic and hydrogen weapons as from March 31, 1958.[1]

The Soviet government urges the government of the United Kingdom and also the government of the United States to follow this example.

If the governments of the powers now possessing nuclear weapons support this Soviet proposal and also decide to give up further tests, this problem which deeply agitates the minds of all peoples will be finally solved and a big step will thereby be taken to strengthen peace and confidence among states.

However, if the governments of the powers now having nuclear weapons at their disposal refuse to respond to this decision of the Soviet government and prefer to leave everything as it is, if they continue experimenting with atomic and hydrogen weapons, the Soviet Union will naturally have no other choice but to consider itself free, in the interests of its security, from its commitment to end nuclear tests. The Soviet government would not like this to happen. It hopes that the government of the United Kingdom will join the initiative of the Soviet Union thereby making possible a universal discontinuation of nuclear weapon tests for all time.

This first practical step to protect man from the hazards of modern nuclear weapons will greatly ease progress towards fulfilment of the task of delivering the peoples from the danger of atomic war. The ending of experiments with atomic and hydrogen weapons will greatly improve the international political atmosphere as a whole and create more favourable conditions for the solution of other outstanding international problems.

Allow me, Mr. Prime Minister, to express the hope that these proposals of the Soviet government will be favourably received by the government of the United Kingdom.

Sincerely yours,

N. KHRUSHCHOV

4. Soviet *aide-mémoire* to the United States, Moscow, 11 April 1958[2]

The government of the U.S.S.R. has studied with due care the joint statement of the governments of the United States of America, the United Kingdom and France of March 31,[3] made in connection with the Soviet government's proposal to speed up the preparations for a summit meeting,

---

[1] See below, p. 59.

[2] *Soviet News*, 14 April 1958. Copies of the note were handed to the United Kingdom, and French ambassadors in Moscow.

[3] See above, p. 8.

set forth in the aide-mémoire of the Soviet government of March 24, 1958.[1]

The Soviet government notes that although the governments of the three powers declare that the present international situation demands serious effort in achieving agreement on the basic international problems and the strengthening of universal peace and makes the convening of a summit conference desirable, they have actually evaded an answer to the concrete proposals of the Soviet Union to call such a conference—proposals made as far back as December, 1957.

As has been noted in the aide-mémoires of the Soviet government of February 28 and March 24 this year, the main task at the present time is to complete as early as possible preparatory work for a summit conference. In order to carry out this work, the Soviet government believed it necessary to arrange a Foreign Ministers' meeting not later than April.

It has to be stated, unfortunately, that the governments of the three powers have been seeking to drag out the talks on preparing a summit meeting.

At the present time in order to achieve the earliest completion of preparatory work for the convening of a summit meeting, the Soviet government believes it necessary, first and foremost, to agree to a Foreign Ministers' meeting not later than the end of April or in the middle of May, this year. This implies that all preparatory work through diplomatic channels should be completed by that time. That is why the Soviet government would consider it expedient to limit the exchange of opinion through diplomatic channels to a minimum of problems pertaining directly to the arrangement of a Foreign Ministers' meeting, namely, the questions about the time and place of the meeting and its composition.

Desirous of achieving the earliest completion of preparatory work for a summit meeting, the Soviet Union, as is well known, has long since introduced for the consideration of the governments of the United States, the United Kingdom and France its proposals about the agenda, the composition, place and date of a summit meeting. The Soviet government expects that the governments of the United States, the United Kingdom and France will shortly give a definite reply to these concrete proposals.

As for the Foreign Ministers' meeting, the Ministers, in the opinion of the Soviet government, should agree on the time, place and composition of a summit meeting and determine the range of problems to be discussed at such a meeting.

It is not to be precluded that the Ministers, while dealing with preparations for a summit meeting, could in case of necessity and by common agreement exchange opinions on some of the questions which the sides propose for inclusion in the summit agenda, in order to determine the

[1] See *Soviet News*, 25 March 1958.

expediency of placing this or that issue on the agenda of such a meeting.

Needless to say, the question cannot be made contingent on this or that result of the meeting of the Foreign Ministers. The Soviet government proceeds from the assumption that all those taking part in the meeting will strive to achieve positive results. For its part the Soviet government will do everything it can to achieve that aim. However, should the Ministers fail to reach the necessary agreement on questions connected with preparing a summit meeting, this would in no way signify that the need for such a conference has become any less urgent. The present tense international situation demands the earliest settlement of pressing international problems and under the circumstances it would be wrong to make the question of convening a summit conference contingent on the results of a meeting of Foreign Ministers. Obviously, the difficulties which may arise at the Minister's meeting can and should be overcome at a meeting of statesmen vested with wider powers.

The Soviet government, on the basis of what has been said above, is prepared to start, on April 17, in Moscow, an exchange of views about the preparation for a meeting of Foreign Ministers.

5. *Aide-mémoire* from the Governments of the United Kingdom, United States, and France to the Soviet Government, 16 April 1958[1]

The United States, British and French Governments have studied the *aide-mémoire* communicated to their Ambassadors in Moscow on April 11. They note that the Soviet Government has accepted their proposal that the preparatory work for a Summit meeting could best be performed by exchanges through diplomatic channels leading to a meeting between Foreign Ministers. They also note that the Soviet Government agrees that these exchanges should begin in Moscow as soon as possible. The Western Powers for their part will be ready to begin on April 17.

It is clear from the Soviet Government's *aide-mémoire* that there are still substantial differences of opinion between the Soviet Government and the Western Governments as to the precise character and scope of the preparatory work.

In the first place, our Foreign Ministers cannot absent themselves from their countries for a prolonged period. Thus, it is essential that the diplomatic talks in Moscow should be concerned not only with plans for a meeting of Foreign Ministers, but with examining the positions of the various Governments on the major questions at issue between them, and with carrying on discussions designed to bring out the possibilities of agreement on them. Even if such diplomatic talks do not result in complete

---

[1] Cmnd. 423.

agreement, they would greatly facilitate the task of the Foreign Ministers.

As regards a Summit meeting the Western Governments hold the view that such a meeting will not be fruitful unless the ground has been thoroughly prepared in advance, and it is clear from this preparatory work that there is broad agreement on the nature and order of the agenda, and a real desire, among all who participate in the meeting, to make practical progress towards a settlement of the differences between us. There must be reasonable prospect of achieving concrete results on specific issues. Satisfactory completion of the preparatory work must therefore precede arrangements for such a meeting. This approach is in consonance with the statement made by the Head of the Soviet Government on February 1, 1958, that a Summit meeting should be 'concentrated on most urgent problems, with regard to which the known positions of the States provide a certain degree of assurance as to their positive solution at this time'.[1] Up to the present, the exchange of views on this matter has been conducted solely through published correspondence, and has not yet established any degree of assurance that agreement on urgent problems could be reached. Thus, there is plainly need for preparatory work beyond mere matters of organisation.

It is the view of the Western Governments that the differences of opinion mentioned above should be the first subject of discussion between the Soviet Government and the Western Ambassadors in Moscow. Such discussion may be more likely to lead to agreement than a further exchange of public communications. That is our hope.

The Western Ambassadors will, for this purpose, make themselves available to the Soviet Ministry of Foreign Affairs on April 17.

6. Joint communication from the Governments of the United Kingdom, United States, and France, 24 April 1958[2]

In their joint communication of March 31[3] the French, United States and United Kingdom Governments proposed to the Soviet Government, in connexion with arrangements for a Summit Meeting, that the preparatory work could best be performed by exchanges through diplomatic channels, leading to a meeting between Foreign Ministers.

The Soviet Government's reply, dated April 11[4] refers to the joint communication of the three Powers and expresses readiness to begin an exchange of views in Moscow on the preparations for the Foreign Ministers' Meeting. There is nothing in this reply which suggests that the Soviet

---

[1] See Mr. Bulganin's letter to President Eisenhower of 1 February 1958, *Soviet News*, 4 February 1958.

[2] Cmnd. 469, p. 3. This note was delivered to the Soviet Ministry for Foreign Affairs, Moscow.

[3] See above, p. 8.   [4] See above, pp. 10–12.

Government had any other plan in view than dealing with the three Powers jointly in making the necessary arrangements for the Foreign Ministers' Meeting.

The three Governments were therefore surprised when, in his interviews with their respective Ambassadors, the Soviet Foreign Minister made it clear that he was not prepared to hold joint discussions with the three Ambassadors.

As the three Powers have already stated, their view is that the main purpose of the preparatory work should be to examine the position of the various Governments on the major questions at issue between them and to establish what subjects should be submitted for examination by Heads of Governments. It would not be the purpose of these preparatory talks to reach decisions, but to bring out by general discussion the possibilities of agreement.

The three Powers consider that as a matter of practical procedure the necessary preparations can be advanced more rapidly by joint meetings rather than by a series of separate interviews. In this way unnecessary complications and delay would be avoided. They wish, therefore, to suggest to the Soviet Government that joint meetings between the three Ambassadors and the Soviet Foreign Minister should begin immediately in order to make the necessary preparations for the Foreign Ministers' Meeting.

The three Governments think that such joint meetings should first discuss the agenda for a Summit Meeting for the purpose described in paragraph four and then, at the appropriate time, discuss the date and place of a Foreign Ministers' Meeting and what countries should be invited to be represented at this meeting.

In conclusion, the three Governments wish to express their hope that the Soviet Government will feel able to give favourable consideration to the above proposal as offering a prospect of early progress by means of a simple and straightforward procedure.

7. Soviet *aide-mémoire* to the Government of the United States, Moscow, 26 April 1958[1]

The Soviet government has studied the considerations of the United States government set forth in its statements of April 16 and 24 in connection with the Soviet government's proposal for the earliest completion of preparations for a summit meeting, made in its aide-mémoire of April 11, 1958.[2]

[1] *Soviet News*, 28 April 1958. This note was handed to the United States ambassador in Moscow Mr. Llewellyn Thompson; identical notes were handed to the United Kingdom and French ambassadors in Moscow.

[2] See above, p. 10.

These statements make it clear that the United States government has agreed to the Soviet proposal to begin an exchange of views in Moscow on preparing a Foreign Ministers' meeting.

At the same time, a study of the statements leads to the conclusion that the governments of the United States, the United Kingdom and France are actually acting in such a way as to delay the convening of a summit meeting indefinitely.

The Soviet government considers it necessary to draw attention to the fact that although more than four months have elapsed since the Soviet Union introduced its proposal to hold a summit conference, the United States government, like the governments of the United Kingdom and France, has not yet replied to the questions pertaining to preparations for such a conference, namely, its date, place and composition. The co-ordination of the range of questions to be discussed at the conference is in no better state. The exchange of views which has so far taken place with the western powers, including talks by the Soviet Foreign Minister with the Ambassadors of the United States, the United Kingdom and France on April 17 and 18, does not make it possible to determine what questions, in their opinion, are ripe for a discussion which could yield positive results.

As is known, the Soviet government, for its part, has not only introduced concrete proposals about a summit agenda, as well as about other issues pertaining to the convening of the conference, but has also met the wishes of the western powers half way by agreeing to carry out preparatory work for the conference through diplomatic channels and a meeting of the Foreign Ministers.

At the moment the main task is the earliest completion of the preparatory work for a summit conference, which should ensure a decisive turn towards an improvement in the international climate as a whole. In this connection the Soviet government reaffirms its considerations set forth in its aide-mémoire of April 11, on the question of speeding up the preparations for a summit meeting.

As for the exchange of views through diplomatic channels on preparations for a Foreign Ministers' meeting, what is meant is that the exchange of views should concentrate on issues pertaining directly to the organisation of that meeting, namely, the time and place of the Foreign Ministers' meeting and its composition. It is not precluded that during the meeting at ambassadorial level and in the course of the Foreign Ministers' conference an exchange of opinion may be held, in case of necessity and by common agreement, on some of the issues which the sides propose to place on the summit agenda, in order to explore the advisability of placing this or that question on the agenda of such a conference and the possibility of adopting mutually acceptable decisions on them.

As for the question touched upon in the statement of the governments of the United States, the United Kingdom and France of April 24 concerning joint talks between a Soviet representative and the three Ambassadors, that statement makes it clear that the governments of the three powers are now proposing holding joint meetings of the three Ambassadors with the Soviet Foreign Minister to carry out the necessary preparations for a Foreign Ministers' meeting.

That proposal, which, incidentally, the western powers had not advanced in any of their previous documents, cannot be considered acceptable because such a conference would be tantamount to a four-power conference in which three states of the North Atlantic Alliance and only one state of the Warsaw Treaty Organisation would be taking part. This circumstance was already pointed out by the Foreign Minister in his talks with the three Ambassadors. It was stressed that this might give rise to certain complications in the talks and therefore should be avoided.

The Soviet government considers it necessary to state that, as before, it regards a preliminary exchange of views through diplomatic channels, by means of talks between the Soviet Foreign Minister with each of the Ambassadors separately, to be most expedient and conforming to the standing practice of exchanging views through diplomatic channels in such cases.

If, however, the governments of the three powers should prefer to exchange views through diplomatic channels in some other form, in the form of a conference of Ambassadors in Moscow with the Soviet Foreign Minister, in that case the parity principle should be adhered to as the basic principle in determining the composition of a summit conference with the participation of the heads of government, which would preclude any discrimination and would guarantee their equality.

Needless to say, at the summit conference or in the course of its preparation no questions may be solved by a vote, by an adoption of decisions by a formal majority vote. But at the conference at which an exchange of views will be held for the purpose of arriving at decisions acceptable to both sides, both sides should naturally be represented equally, and only such an approach is objective and justified.

In this connection the Soviet government proposes that a conference of Ambassadors with the representative of the U.S.S.R. together with the Ambassadors of the United States, the United Kingdom and France, should also be attended by the Ambassadors of Poland and Czechoslovakia. This was announced by the Soviet Foreign Minister in his talks with the Ambassadors of Britain and France on April 18. A conference of such composition would take due cognisance of the parity principle and guarantee the equality of the sides, so necessary for a fruitful preparation of a summit meeting. The Soviet government believes that the course of preparations it has proposed facilitates the convening of a summit conference in the nearest future, if, naturally, such a conference is sincerely desired. The Soviet government should like to hope that an exchange of views through diplomatic channels would help the earliest solution of that issue.

In conformity with what has been said above, the Soviet Foreign Minister is prepared to meet the Ambassadors as soon as they are ready for it.

8. Joint communication from the Governments of the United Kingdom, United States, and France to the Soviet Government, Moscow, 3 May 1958[1]

The Governments of the United States, United Kingdom, and France have noted with regret that the Soviet Government, in its *aide mémoire* of April 26,[2] has rejected their proposal for joint meetings between the three Ambassadors and the Soviet Foreign Minister to begin the preparatory work for a Summit Meeting and, in doing so, has raised an unnecessary obstacle in the task of carrying this work forward. As the Soviet Government points out in its *aide mémoire*, no progress has been made toward agreement on the range of questions to be dealt with nor in determining what questions offer prospects for agreement.

The three Powers have not changed their view that progress could be made more rapidly by joint meetings rather than by a series of separate interviews. Since they desire to move ahead with the work itself, however, and in view of the fact that the Soviet Government agrees that the Ambassadors will discuss substantive issues, they are prepared to meet the Soviet Government's preference for separate interviews. Their acceptance of this procedure, however, does not prejudge in any way the composition of any future meetings. Following the discussion of the agenda for a Summit Meeting as proposed in the tripartite statement of April 24, the three Ambassadors will be prepared to discuss the matter of a date and place of a Foreign Ministers' Meeting and what countries should be invited to be represented at this meeting.

The three Ambassadors, therefore, stand ready to meet the Soviet Foreign Minister for this purpose.

9. Soviet *aide-mémoire* to the Government of the United States, Moscow, 5 May 1958[3]

The Soviet government, having studied the reply of the United States government, and also the replies of the governments of the United

---

[1] Cmnd. 469, pp. 5–6. [2] See preceding document.
[3] *Soviet News*, 6 May 1958. Identical *aides-mémoire* were sent to the United Kingdom and France.

Kingdom and France, to the aide-mémoire of the U.S.S.R. government of April 26, notes that the governments of the three powers agree with the Soviet government's proposal that preliminary exchanges of opinion through diplomatic channels on the necessary preparation for a Foreign Ministers' meeting should be effected in accordance with the practice generally accepted in such cases, through conversations between the U.S.S.R. Foreign Minister, on the one hand, and each of the Ambassadors on the other.

The Soviet government, like the governments of the United States, the United Kingdom and France, considers that the acceptance of such a procedure in no way predetermines the composition of the future Foreign Ministers' meeting and summit conference.

At the same time, the Soviet government expresses regret that the governments of the three powers did not agree to invite representatives of Poland and Czechoslovakia to take part in the present stage of preparation for the summit conference, as their participation would undoubtedly have helped to produce positive results.

The Soviet government does not share the United States government's view that the procedure for the exchange of opinion through diplomatic channels proposed by the Soviet Union was likely to hamper preparatory work for the summit conference. In its aide-mémoire of April 26 the Soviet government has already touched on the causes of the delay in preparing for the summit conference and would now merely like to point out that this delay has occurred through no fault of the Soviet side and contrary to its wishes.

Now that the question of the procedure for the exchange of opinion through diplomatic channels has at last been agreed upon, the Soviet government expects all the sides to exert the necessary efforts for the earliest accomplishment of this work.

As for the nature of the exchange of opinion through diplomatic channels on the question of preparing for the Foreign Ministers' meeting, the Soviet government proceeds from the need to conclude the preparatory work for this meeting as soon as possible and sees no reason for relegating to the background the discussion of questions connected with the organisation of the Ministers' meeting.

It is envisaged that during the exchange of opinion through diplomatic channels the parties will also agree on the most expedient procedure for discussing the questions, including questions connected with the organisation of a Foreign Ministers' meeting. As has already been pointed out, the Soviet government does not preclude the possibility, in case of necessity and by common consent, of an exchange of opinion taking place on some of the questions which the sides propose for the agenda of the summit conference during the meeting with the Ambassadors and during the

Foreign Ministers' conference, with the object of ascertaining the advisability of placing this or that question on the agenda of the conference and the possibility of adopting mutually acceptable decisions on them.

The Soviet government expresses the hope that the government of the United States, for its part, will exert efforts to reach agreement on a Foreign Ministers' meeting in the nearest future, which in turn should ensure the earliest convening of a summit conference with the participation of the heads of government.

Identical aides-mémoire have been handed to the Ambassadors of the United Kingdom and France in Moscow for transmission to their governments.

10. Proposals of the Soviet Government for the agenda for a summit conference, 5 May 1958[1]

On January 8, 1958, the Soviet government submitted for the consideration of the other governments its concrete proposals on questions of easing international tension. These proposals provide for discussion by a conference of leading statesmen at a high level, with the participation of heads of government, on questions whose settlement would facilitate the easing of international tension and the establishment of confidence in relations between states.[2]

The Soviet government is still of the opinion that there are a number of international problems ripe for settlement that could be solved already at the present time. It holds the view that it is necessary and possible to reach agreement among the states on disputed issues of international relations. For its part, the Soviet Union has named a number of such questions and is ready to take part in the examination of other problems that may be proposed by the participants in a summit conference, provided, of course, that these questions come within the competence of an international conference and are aimed at strengthening peace.

The Soviet government is profoundly convinced that if the heads of government take a firm decision to devote their efforts to seeking mutually acceptable decisions on international problems ripe for solution, it is possible to say with confidence that the forthcoming summit conference will secure the required turn in the development of relations among states towards an improvement in the entire international situation and the ending of the 'cold war.'

[1] *Soviet News*, 18 June 1958. These proposals were forwarded to the Governments of the United States, the United Kingdom, and France, through their ambassadors in Moscow on 5 May 1958, and they were also attached to the letters that Mr. Khrushchev wrote to President Eisenhower, Mr. Macmillan, and General de Gaulle on 11 June 1958.

[2] See *Soviet News*, 10 January 1958, for the text of these proposals which was sent by the Government of the U.S.S.R. to the Governments of N.A.T.O. countries, of members of the U.N., and the Government of Switzerland.

Taking into consideration the exchange of views that has taken place on the convening of a summit conference, and being desirous of facilitating the earliest completion of the preparatory work for this conference, the Soviet government, for its part, puts forward for examination at the conference the following questions, at the same time setting out some considerations regarding them:

1. IMMEDIATE ENDING OF TESTS OF ATOMIC AND HYDROGEN WEAPONS

The ending of tests of all types of atomic and hydrogen weapons is an urgent problem capable of practical solution. The universal ending of these tests would have beneficial results for the strengthening of peace and the stopping of a further arms race. Agreement on this question would constitute a definite obstacle to the creation of new and still more destructive types of atomic and hydrogen weapons and would be a practical step towards the complete prohibition of these weapons of mass destruction.

The necessity for an immediate solution to this question is further dictated by the fact that tests of atomic and hydrogen weapons, as the most eminent scientists testify, increase the concentration of atomic radiation in the atmosphere, in the soil and in water, already at the present time creating a serious danger to the health and lives of people living today and threatening the normal development of future generations. This danger will continue to grow in the future unless an end is put to the experimental explosions of nuclear weapons.

At the present time only three countries are producing nuclear weapons —the Soviet Union, the United States and the United Kingdom, and the ending of tests of these weapons now, with the Soviet Union having already suspended them unilaterally, depends only on two powers—on the United States and the United Kingdom. The Soviet government expects that the United States and the United Kingdom will suspend nuclear weapon tests without delay, so as to make it possible at the heads of government conference to reach agreement on the three powers reinforcing these decisions by an appropriate agreement.

Although modern technical resources for detecting nuclear explosions make it possible for an explosion of an atomic or hydrogen weapon to be registered, wherever it is carried out, and although each interested power can itself follow the way in which the other partners are carrying out an agreement on the ending of tests, the Soviet government once again confirms its agreement to the establishment of international control over the ending of nuclear weapon tests, with the establishment of international control posts, as it suggested as long ago as June, 1957. It is of the opinion that it should not be difficult to reach agreement on the concrete measures for such control, as soon as the governments of the United States and the

United Kingdom also cease further tests of these weapons. Without this, any talks on studying questions of control, at the level of experts or at any other level, must inevitably develop into barren discussion and, naturally, will bring no tangible results.

To make the ending of atomic and hydrogen weapon tests dependent on the settlement of other aspects of disarmament, on which there are still serious differences, and the resolving of which is a more complicated matter, implies in actual fact a refusal to end atomic and hydrogen weapon tests.

Although the ending of nuclear weapon tests already at the present time, immediately, by all the powers possessing these weapons, would place the countries parties to the Warsaw Treaty at a disadvantage as compared with the N.A.T.O. countries, in view of the fact that the Soviet Union has carried out far fewer test explosions of atomic and hydrogen weapons than the United States and Britain, the Soviet Union has nevertheless agreed to this, in an endeavour to make a practical start in the ending of the atomic arms race. The adoption of this proposal by the United States of America and the United Kingdom would put an end to atomic and hydrogen weapon tests everywhere and for all time.

2. RENUNCIATION OF USE OF ALL TYPES OF ATOMIC, HYDROGEN AND ROCKET WEAPONS

The Soviet government is of the opinion that the reaching of agreement on the joint renunciation by the states possessing nuclear weapons—the U.S.S.R., the U.S.A. and the United Kingdom—of the use of all types of these weapons, including bombs, rockets of all ranges with atomic or hydrogen warheads, atomic artillery, etc., would be an important step towards the removal of the danger of atomic war and towards the relaxation of tension in relations between states. Should an agreement on the renunciation of the use of nuclear weapons be concluded, any government that had the temerity to break such an agreement would expose itself in the eyes of the peoples as an aggressor, as an enemy of peace.

The great importance of such an agreement is confirmed by the experience of history. As we know, the Geneva Protocol of 1925, prohibiting the use of chemical and bacteriological weapons, played an important part in preventing the use of these weapons during the Second World War. In the Soviet government's opinion, a decision to renounce the use of atomic, hydrogen and rocket weapons could be formalised by extending the 1925 Geneva Protocol to nuclear and rocket weapons.

The Soviet government is of the opinion that an agreement among the powers to renounce the use of nuclear and rocket weapons at the present time, at this stage, would create favourable prerequisites for carrying out, in the next stage, such measures as the complete and unconditional prohibition of nuclear weapons, the prohibition of their manufacture, their removal from the armaments of states, and the destruction of all stockpiles of these weapons.

3. ESTABLISHMENT IN CENTRAL EUROPE OF A ZONE FREE FROM ATOMIC, HYDROGEN AND ROCKET WEAPONS

In Central Europe, at the present time, two groupings of states are opposing one another, and quantities of armed forces and armaments of various types are concentrated that are abnormal for peacetime. This circumstance alone creates a serious threat to peace, and we cannot shut our eyes to the fact that in such a situation, whether by evil intent or by accident, the conflagration of a new war could break out, with the most modern means of destruction—nuclear and rocket weapons—being used.

In order to preclude the danger of events developing in such a way, the Soviet government considers it advisable for the conference to examine the proposal made by the government of the Polish People's Republic, for the establishment in Europe of a zone free from atomic, hydrogen and rocket weapons, embracing the territories of the Polish People's Republic, the Czechoslovak Republic, the German Democratic Republic and the Federal Republic of Germany. If these states were to assume the obligation not to manufacture nuclear weapons of any type and not to allow the deployment on their territories of such weapons or of installations for the launching of rockets which might carry nuclear warheads, this would undoubtedly help to prevent the possibility of military conflicts breaking out in the centre of Europe.

Since the governments of the Polish People's Republic, the Czechoslovak Republic and the German Democratic Republic have already announced their willingness to enter an atom-free zone, the establishment of such a zone now depends only on the consent of the government of the Federal Republic of Germany.

Agreement among the governments of the U.S.S.R., the United States, the United Kingdom and France on the desirability of creating an atom-free zone in this area of Europe would undoubtedly assist the reaching of agreement with the government of the Federal Republic of Germany on the Federal Republic's adherence to this zone.

Agreement on the establishment of an atom-free zone in Europe will be effective if, alongside the appropriate undertakings by the states coming within this zone, those powers which possess nuclear and rocket weapons in their armaments for their part undertake to respect the status of the zone and to regard the territories of the states constituting it as being excluded from the sphere of the use of atomic, hydrogen and rocket weapons.

As far as the Soviet Union is concerned, it has already declared its readiness to assume such obligations if the governments of the United States, the United Kingdom and France do likewise.

The undertakings of the states coming within the zone, and likewise the undertakings of the great powers, could be formalised either by an appropriate international agreement or by corresponding unilateral declarations.

In order to ensure that the undertakings and their implementation would be effective, the states concerned would undertake to establish on the territory of the atom-free zone a broad and effective system of control, on the ground and in the air, with the institution of control posts by agreement among the appropriate states.

The establishment of an atom-free zone in the centre of Europe would be an important step towards ending the dangerous arms race and removing the threat of atomic war.

4. NON-AGGRESSION PACT

Desiring to facilitate the easing of international tension, the Soviet government considers that the interests of ending the 'cold war' and the arms race would be met by the conclusion in one form or another, of a pact (for agreement) on non-aggression between the member-states of the North Atlantic Treaty Organisation and the states parties to the Warsaw Treaty. The conclusion of such a pact would be an important step towards the creation of a general European system of security, towards strengthening mutual trust and co-operation among the states.

If the western powers were to show a desire to conclude such a pact or agreement, it would not, in the opinion of the Soviet government, be difficult to reach agreement on the form it should take, either on the basis of a multilateral agreement between all the countries belonging to the Warsaw Treaty Organisation and the North Atlantic Alliance, or between some of the countries belonging to these groupings, or else, lastly, in the form of non-aggression agreements on a bilateral basis between individual members of these groupings.

The Soviet government believes that the basis for such an agreement should be reciprocal renunciation by the parties to the agreement of the use or threat of force, and an undertaking to settle disputes which might arise between parties to the agreement by peaceful methods only. Provision should also be made for the desirability of mutual consultations between the parties to the agreement concerning the fulfilment of their obligations under it.

Such a pact could be open for all other states of Europe to adhere to it, with a view to facilitating the creation, at a subsequent stage, of a system of general European security and the gradual liquidation of the existing military-political groupings.

In proposing the conclusion of a non-aggression agreement the Soviet government regards this as a first step towards a radical improvement in the relations between the states belonging to the North Atlantic Alliance and the Warsaw Treaty Organisation and as a prerequisite for the conclusion, at the next stage, of a broader agreement on European security.

5. PROHIBITION OF THE USE OF OUTER SPACE FOR MILITARY PURPOSES, THE DISMANTLING OF FOREIGN MILITARY BASES ON ALIEN TERRITORIES, AND INTERNATIONAL CO-OPERATION IN EXPLORING OUTER SPACE

Scientific and technical progress in rocketry has raised the question of the lines to be followed in the use of the latest achievements of science: whether they are to serve peaceful purposes or whether they are to be used to intensify the arms race, increasing the danger of the outbreak of atomic war.

The complete and unconditional prohibition of atomic and hydrogen weapons, with their removal from armaments and the destruction of stockpiles, would constitute an effective measure totally precluding the possibility of the use of outer space for military purposes, and ensuring that the immense achievements in the creation of rockets and artificial earth satellites would be used exclusively for peaceful purposes. In view of the fact that at present, because of the attitude of the western powers, this is difficult, and will evidently have to be carried out at a subsequent stage, the Soviet government proposes that at this stage agreement be reached on prohibiting the use of outer space for military purposes, with the simultaneous dismantling of foreign bases on alien territories and, in the first place, on the territories of countries in Europe, the Middle East and North Africa. This measure is in keeping with the interests of the security of all states. As far as the states on whose territories these military bases are situated are concerned, they would only benefit from such a decision, for the dismantling of foreign bases would remove the danger to which they are subjecting themselves in providing their territories for the stationing of foreign bases.

Guided by these considerations, the Soviet government proposes that the question of concluding an international agreement on the use of outer space for peaceful purposes be discussed, with this agreement covering the following main points:

Prohibition of the use of outer space for military purposes and an undertaking by the states to launch rockets into outer space only under an agreed international programme;

The dismantling of foreign military bases on alien territories, and first of all in Europe, the Middle East and North Africa;

The establishment, within the framework of the United Nations of appropriate international control over the fulfilment of the above undertakings;

The establishment of a United Nations organ for international co-operation in the exploration of outer space.

The conclusion of such an agreement would open the way to broad international co-operation in the peaceful uses of outer space and would pave the way for joint study by scientists of all countries of problems connected with outer space.

6. REDUCTION OF THE NUMBER OF FOREIGN TROOPS ON THE TERRITORY OF GERMANY AND WITHIN THE FRONTIERS OF OTHER EUROPEAN STATES

Consistently striving for the necessary agreement with the other powers, the Soviet Union has repeatedly submitted concrete proposals for disarmament, and has also carried out a number of unilateral measures reducing its own armed forces and armaments, proceeding on the assumption that the other great powers would, for their part, follow this example. The Soviet Union is in favour of a radical solution to the disarmament problem, of a substantial reduction in the armed forces and armaments of the states, the complete withdrawal of foreign armed forces from the territories of the European member-states of both military groupings, including Germany, and the dismantling of all foreign military bases on alien territories.

However, since the western powers have so far displayed no readiness to reach agreement on all these questions, the Soviet Union proposes that at this stage the course should be followed of settling those questions on which there is already every possibility of reaching agreement now. The Soviet government proposes that a gradual reduction of foreign armed forces on alien territories be carried out, and submits the proposal that, as a first step, there should be a reduction during 1958 in the armed forces of the U.S.S.R., the United States, the United Kingdom, France and other states with troops stationed on the territory of Germany, amounting to one-third or to any other agreed amount. The contingents by which these forces are reduced are to be withdrawn from the territory of Germany to within their own national frontiers.

The question of a substantial reduction in the armed forces and armaments of the states, and of the conclusion for this purpose of an appropriate international agreement, and also of the complete withdrawal of foreign armed forces from the territories of N.A.T.O. member-states and states parties to the Warsaw Treaty, could be discussed at a later stage in the talks.

7. CONCLUSION OF A GERMAN PEACE TREATY

Whereas all the peoples of Europe drawn into the war on the side of Hitler Germany have long since been enjoying the fruits of a state of peace and are building their lives independently, the German people are still deprived of conditions of peaceful development for their country and of equality with other peoples. The absence of a peace treaty is also having a detrimental effect on the accomplishment of their common national task of unifying the country. Furthermore, the indecision on questions concerning a peace settlement in Germany is being used by those who have no regard for the fate of peace in Europe, in order to draw the western part of Germany into preparations for atomic war.

In these circumstances the Soviet government believes that the powers which bear responsibility for the development of Germany along peaceful lines must exert their efforts to achieve the speediest peace settlement with Germany. As an advocate of such a settlement, the Soviet government reaffirms its proposal that the summit conference should discuss the question of preparations for the conclusion of a German peace treaty.

However, taking into consideration the attitude displayed by the governments of the United States and the other western powers with regard to this proposal, the Soviet government would be prepared at the forthcoming conference to come to an agreement at least on the first steps in settling this question: namely, to agree at the present time on the main principles of a German peace treaty and on the procedure for preparing it. The Soviet government proceeds here from the standpoint that preparatory work for the conclusion of a German peace treaty, with the participation of German representatives from the German Democratic Republic and the Federal Republic of Germany, would provide an impetus for uniting the efforts of the German Democratic Republic and the Federal Republic of Germany with a view to their *rapprochement* and the restoration of the unity of the German people.

8. PREVENTING SURPRISE ATTACK BY ONE STATE ON ANOTHER

Since it is not possible at the present time to solve the problem of disarmament fully, and since it is a question of reaching agreement on partial measures of disarmament, the Soviet government proposes that the question of preventing a surprise attack be solved gradually, in accordance with the nature of the steps on disarmament in the first stage. Agreement should be reached on the establishment of control posts at railway junctions, at big ports and on motor highways and also on the carrying out of aerial surveys in the zone of demarcation of the main armed forces of the military groupings in Europe, at this stage in definite limited areas, to be recognised as the most important from the standpoint of removing the danger of a surprise attack.

In proposing this approach to the solution of this problem, the Soviet government proceeds from the fact that the western powers have recognised the advisability of the Soviet proposal for the establishment of control posts as a means of preventing surprise attack. This provides grounds for hoping that the conference will be able to reach agreement on this question.

The Soviet government reaffirms its proposal for the establishment in Europe of an aerial inspection zone 800 kilometres[1] deep, to the East and to the West of the demarcation line of the armed forces of the N.A.T.O. and Warsaw Treaty military groupings.

As regards the proposal for carrying out aerial surveys of extensive areas of the U.S.S.R. and the United States, or of their entire territories, this question cannot be examined in isolation from measures for the easing of international tension and the strengthening of confidence between states, and first and foremost between the great powers. In the present international situation, with the continuing arms race which is causing tension in the international situation and distrust and suspicion in the relations between the states, and with the dark shadow of the 'cold war' looming over the entire international situation, the proposal for flights on a reciprocal basis over all the territories of the two countries is unrealistic. The Soviet government, however, is of the opinion that this measure could be carried out at the concluding stage of disarmament, that is to say, after the solution of the problem of the complete prohibition of atomic and hydrogen weapons, with their withdrawal from the armaments of the states, a substantial reduction in the armed forces and armaments of the states, and the dismantling of foreign military bases on alien territories, i.e., when relations of genuine confidence between states have been established.

9. MEASURES FOR DEVELOPING INTERNATIONAL TRADE RELATIONS

The Soviet government considers that there are very real possibilities at the present time for carrying out a number of measures to develop international trade relations, as the natural and most reliable basis for peaceful co-operation among all states, regardless of differences in their social systems. The restoration and expansion of trade between the western countries and the vast market of the East, where something like 1,000 million people live, demands first and foremost the removal of the discrimination and restrictions which still exist and which hinder the expansion of international trade.

[1] About 500 miles.

As a result of industrial depression and the reduction in trade, at the present time a number of western countries are experiencing serious economic difficulties, the solution to which must also be sought in the development of international trade, and not in an arms race or in the intensification of economic warfare and blockade.

As concrete measures for the development of international trade, the Soviet government proposes the adoption of a declaration of basic principles of international economic co-operation, which should contain provisions for the observance of complete equality, mutual benefit, inadmissibility of any discrimination whatsoever in economic and trade relations among states; respect for the sovereign rights of every state to control its own wealth and natural resources; and mutual aid and assistance to underdeveloped countries for their economic development, free from all demands of a political, military or any other character incompatible with the national sovereignty of these countries.

There is also a pressing need for convening an international economic conference, at which it would be desirable to discuss the question of the further development of international trade on a long-term basis, with a view to establishing confidence and stability among the trading countries, and also the question of creating, within the framework of the United Nations, an international trade organisation open to all countries.

It would also be necessary to discuss such urgent questions as the rational utilisation of world economic resources, and aid to underdeveloped countries. An additional source of funds for such aid could be found by reducing expenditure on armaments.

10. DEVELOPMENT OF CONTACTS BETWEEN COUNTRIES

The Soviet government attaches great importance to the development of international contacts, and invariably advocates the development of contacts between East and West. The establishment of broader political, economic and cultural ties between countries, irrespective of their social systems, on the basis of mutual respect for sovereign rights and non-interference in domestic affairs, is in keeping with the vital interests of the peoples and promotes the strengthening of friendship and businesslike co-operation among them. This is borne out, in particular, by the successful conclusion of bilateral negotiations and the signing in Washington of a Soviet-American agreement in the fields of culture, technology and education,[1] and also by the successful co-operation between scientists of

---

[1] The Agreement between the United States and the Soviet Union on exchanges in the cultural, technical, and educational fields was signed on 27 January 1958 upon the conclusion of negotiations which had begun in Washington on 28 October 1957. For the joint communiqué containing the text of the agreement, see *D.S.B.*, 17 February 1958, pp. 243–7.

many countries on the programme of the International Geophysical Year.

The Soviet government likewise attaches great importance to the establishment and broadening of systematic personal contacts between statesmen and public leaders of the countries of East and West for the exchange of views on urgent international questions. The expansion of such ties and contacts in the near future could be effected through the reciprocal exchange of parliamentary delegations and delegations from public organisations; the reciprocal exchange of delegations of scientists, technologists and cultural workers; reciprocal exchange of artists, theatre companies, symphony orchestras, etc.; reciprocal exchange of scientific and technical literature and documentation, including projects and blueprints of machinery and equipment, descriptions of technical processes, etc.; free access to industrial exhibitions; reciprocal exchange of delegations of students and professors and of university delegations; the utmost encouragement of tourism, relations in the field of sport, and so on.

11. ENDING PROPAGANDA FOR WAR, ENMITY AND HATRED BETWEEN PEOPLES

Notwithstanding the fact that 10 years have gone by since the United Nations General Assembly, in October 1947, took the decision to prohibit war propaganda, this unanimous decision of the General Assembly is not being observed in a number of countries. In those countries, by means of the press, radio, television and various other means, the idea is constantly being inculcated in the peoples that a new war is inevitable, and the necessity for a nuclear arms race and a further increase in military appropriations and taxation is being insisted upon.

There can be no doubt, given good will and the mutual desire of all participants in the summit conference, that there would be no difficulty in reaching agreement to end war propaganda and in its place to conduct propaganda for friendship among the peoples.

The settlement of this question could be achieved by the adoption of a joint declaration in which the governments taking part in the conference would reaffirm their intention strictly to observe the resolution of the United Nations General Assembly of October 1947, banning all war propaganda, hostile to the cause of peace and mutual understanding, and would undertake to adopt effective measures to cut short such propaganda in their countries.

12. WAYS OF EASING TENSION IN THE MIDDLE EAST AREA

In recent years there have periodically arisen in the Middle East area centres of tension fraught with dangerous international conflicts which could lead to a breach of world peace. For the purpose of easing tension in the Middle East there must be created for the countries in this area the confidence that any breach of the peace in the Middle East area by any aggressive forces whatsoever will be decisively condemned and cut short. One such measure could be a joint delcaration by the powers condemning the use of force in settling outstanding issues in the Middle East and intervention in the domestic affairs of countries in that area. Agreement could also be reached on reciprocal undertakings by the countries taking part in the conference not to supply arms to the countries of the Middle East, and also not to deploy nuclear or rocket weapons in those countries.

In view of the economic difficulties being experienced by the Middle East countries, and in view of their desire to consolidate their independence, the need also arises to examine the question of economic co-operation with the Middle East countries, particularly as regards assistance in creating their own national industries, proceeding in this matter on the basis of the principles of complete equality and mutual benefit, without laying down any political, military or other conditions incompatible with the principles of their independence and sovereignty.

*   *   *

The Soviet government is confident that good will and a readiness to seek mutually acceptable solutions, taking due account of the interests of the parties, can ensure the success of the summit conference and create the necessary turn in the development of the international situation in the interests of strengthening peace among the nations.

11. *Aide-mémoire* and agenda regarding a summit conference submitted to the Soviet Union, by the Governments of the United Kingdom, United States, and France, 28 May 1958[1]

The Governments of the United States, United Kingdom and France, after consideration of the Soviet Government's *aide mémoire* of May 5, have concluded that the positions of the Governments with regard to the purposes of the talks between the three Western Ambassadors and the Soviet Foreign Minister and of a subsequent Foreign Ministers' Meeting are sufficiently close to permit the substantive preparatory work for a possible Summit Meeting to proceed without delay. It is their understanding that this work should go forward along the following lines:

The purpose of the preparatory work shall be to examine the position of the various Governments on the major questions at issue between them

---

[1] Cmnd. 469, pp. 16–21. The *aide-mémoire* and memorandum on the agenda were handed to the Soviet Minister for Foreign Affairs by the United Kingdom ambassador in Moscow, on 28 May 1958.

and to establish what subjects should be submitted for examination by Heads of Government; it is understood that it would not be the purpose of the preparatory work to reach decisions, but to bring out by general discussion the possibilities of agreement. When they have made progress in this work, the Ambassadors and the Soviet Foreign Ministers will also have the task of agreeing on the time, place, and composition of a Foreign Ministers' Meeting.

The special tasks assigned to the Foreign Ministers themselves shall be to establish whether they are satisfied that the preparatory work affords the prospect that a Summit Meeting would, in fact, provide the opportunity for conducting serious discussions of major problems and be the means for reaching agreement on significant subjects. If and when this has been established to their satisfaction, the Foreign Ministers will then reach agreement on the date, place, and composition of a Summit Meeting.

MEMORANDUM ON THE AGENDA HANDED TO THE SOVIET MINISTER FOR FOREIGN AFFAIRS BY THE BRITISH AMBASSADOR IN MOSCOW ON MAY 28, 1958

The Governments of the United States, United Kingdom and France believe that the present international situation requires that a serious attempt be made to reach agreement on the main problems affecting attainment of peace and stability in the world. They consider that, in the circumstances, a Summit Meeting would be desirable if it would provide opportunity for serious discussions of major problems and would be an effective means of reaching agreement on significant subjects.

They regard such settlements as constituting effective means for developing a spirit of confidence in their relations with the Soviet Union which could lead to co-operation among nations in the pursuit of a just and lasting peace.

Such settlements, if they are to serve this purpose, must take into account the legitimate interests of all the parties concerned and must embrace the necessary elements to assure their implementation.

In his letter of January 12, 1958, President Eisenhower put forward a series of proposals to Premier Bulganin.[1] The Governments of the United States, United Kingdom and France consider that they form the basis for mutually beneficial settlements at a meeting of Heads of Government. Some of the considerations which underlie this view are set forth below. In making their proposals in the field of disarmament the three Governments recall their obligations, undertaken in the United Nations Charter, not to use any weapons against the territorial integrity or political independence of any State. While a comprehensive disarmament remains their

[1] See D.S.B., 27 January 1958, pp. 122–7.

ultimate aim, they propose certain practical, balanced and interdependent measures which would mark significant progress toward controlling the arms race and thus reducing the danger of war. Progress of this sort would also create an atmosphere of confidence which could facilitate settlement of the political controversies that disturb relations between the Western Powers and the Soviet Union. Reduction in both nuclear weapons and conventional armed forces and armaments are vital for this purpose. The three Governments, therefore, consider it desirable to make clear once again what were the reasons which led them to put forward far-reaching proposals for partial disarmament in 1957.[1]

1. MEASURES TO CONTROL PRODUCTION OF FISSIONABLE MATERIALS FOR NUCLEAR WEAPONS AND TO REDUCE EXISTING MILITARY STOCKS OF SUCH MATERIALS

As for the nuclear problem, the heart of the matter is not the mere testing, but the weapons themselves. The Western Powers seek a dependable ending to the accumulation of nuclear weapons and a dependable beginning of the steady reduction of existing weapons stockpiles. Since there is no known reliable means for detecting the weapons already made, the most effective and feasible way to work toward the reduction and elimination of nuclear weapons is to halt production of fissionable materials for making them and to begin reducing weapons stockpiles by equitable transfers to peaceful uses. The Western Powers are prepared to discuss these measures and the ratios of materials to be transferred from existing weapons stocks to peaceful uses with a view to arriving at equitable proportions for such transfers by the States concerned.

2. SUSPENSION OF NUCLEAR TESTS

If there is agreement to put an end to the production of new fissionable materials for nuclear weapons, the way lies open to an immediate solution of the problem of nuclear testing. So long as unrestricted manufacture of nuclear weapons continues, and new means are being developed for delivering nuclear weapons rapidly and surely, the suspension of nuclear testing does not constitute disarmament. It is relevant to underline the fact that the existence of nuclear stocks, which are constantly growing, constitutes a much more serious danger than nuclear tests. Thus, the Western Powers propose not only the suspension of nuclear tests but the stopping of production of new fissionable materials for weapons purposes and the progressive reconversion of stocks of these materials to peaceful

[1] See *Documents* for 1957, pp. 141–6, for the 'Working paper by Britain, Canada, and the United States on partial measures of disarmament, 29 August 1957'.

uses. Testing could be stopped indefinitely if the necessary inspection system is installed, and the production of fissionable materials for weapons is also effectively ended. Both would be carried out under effective measures of international control.

3. THE REDUCTION AND LIMITATION OF CONVENTIONAL ARMS AND MANPOWER

An agreement on initial verifiable reductions of armed forces and their stocks of arms could ease the way toward settlement of problems which create international friction. In their turn, such settlements could set the stage for further reductions. This is a sound approach for developing confidence in relations between countries. On the other hand, unverified and uncontrolled unilateral measures can well be merely shifts in deployment or temporary reductions. They do not inspire confidence.

With these considerations in mind, the Western Governments propose that the Soviet Union join them in agreeing on an initial limitation of their armed forces; and on placing in storage depots, within their own territories, and under the supervision of an international control organisation, specific quantities of designated types of armaments. They will be prepared also to negotiate on a further limitation of their armed forces and armaments provided that compliance with commitments has been verified to mutual satisfaction, and that there has been progress toward the solution of political issues, and that other essential States have accepted equitable levels for their armed forces and armaments.

4. MEASURES TO GUARD AGAINST SURPRISE ATTACK

Until general controlled disarmament becomes a reality, the surest way toward the development of confidence lies in lifting fears of surprise attack. Growing capabilities of surprise attack on a massive scale underscore the importance of a prompt beginning on measures to deal with this problem. The Western Powers want to meet it on the broadest scale possible. The Governments of the United States, United Kingdom and France express their readiness to enter into discussion of this subject both from the standpoint of technical considerations of ways and means of achieving this end in the most practical way and from the standpoint of initial areas to be included in the progressive installation of such a system. In this connexion, the three Governments reaffirm their willingness as expressed in the United Nations Disarmament Sub-Committee on August 29, 1957, to consider the installation of a system of air and ground inspection as a safeguard against surprise attack on a comprehensive scale embracing all of the United States, USSR, Canada, and with the consent of the countries involved, the greater part of Europe as well. If this proposal is not acceptable to the USSR, the three Governments are also prepared to consider the establishment in the first instance of smaller zones in the Arctic and European regions, provided that the latter also included a significant part of the territory of the Soviet Union. As the United States indicated at Geneva in 1955, if agreement is reached on the installation of measures of air and ground inspection on the comprehensive scale outlined above, negotiations can be undertaken promptly both with other sovereign states involved and with the Soviet Union for the appropriate extension of such inspection on a reciprocal and equitable basis and subject to the consent of any Government concerned to bases outside of National territory.

5. USE OF OUTER SPACE FOR PEACEFUL PURPOSES

An opportunity to stop the development of new and more powerful weapons was tragically lost a decade ago, when the United States offer to renounce making atomic weapons and to make the use of atomic energy an international asset for peaceful purposes only, was not accepted. A great step forward in building confidence among peoples and in reducing danger to humanity from new and powerful weapons would have been made if this offer had been accepted. The responsible countries are faced once more with a similar decision, laden with serious consequences for mankind. The three Governments propose that the Soviet Union join in the establishment of a group of experts who would make the necessary technical studies for determining what measures are required to assure that outer space is used for peaceful purposes only.

6. REUNIFICATION OF GERMANY IN ACCORDANCE WITH THE TERMS OF THE 1955 DIRECTIVE OF THE FOUR HEADS OF GOVERNMENT TO THE MINISTERS OF FOREIGN AFFAIRS

The continued division of Germany is a major obstacle to the restoration of confidence and the creation of conditions of genuine peace and stability in Europe. Thirteen years have passed since the end of the war in Europe, yet no peace settlement has been made with Germany. A necessary prerequisite for such a settlement is the creation of a Government which truly reflects the will of the German people. Only a Government created on such a basis can undertake obligations which will inspire confidence on the part of other countries and which will be considered just and binding by the people of Germany themselves.

The Heads of Government in Geneva recognised the common responsibility of the four Powers for the settlement of the German question and the reunification of Germany. They agreed that the settlement of the German question and the reunification of Germany through free elections should be carried out in conformity with the national interests of the German people and the interests of European security. The Western Powers propose that the Soviet Union join with them in immediate steps to carry out their responsibility by agreeing to permit an all-German Government to be formed by free elections and enabling it to carry out its functions. Such an agreement would give tangible evidence of a common desire on the part of the four Governments to create the conditions of trust on which a lasting peace can be based.

7. EUROPEAN SECURITY ARRANGEMENTS

The Western Powers are aware of the fact that the Soviet Union has expressed concern that the creation of a freely-chosen all-German Government with the full attributes of sovereignty would bring about changes in the present situation in Europe which the Soviet Union would consider detrimental to its security interests. The three Governments are prepared to enter into arrangements concerning European security which would give assurances to the Soviet Union in this regard. The arrangements they envisage would involve limitations on forces and armaments. They would also involve assurances designed to prevent aggression in Europe by the exchange of undertakings to take appropriate action in the event of such aggression.

The three Governments seek no one-sided advantage in such arrangements, nor do they contemplate entering into arrangements which would give a one-sided advantage to the Soviet Union to the prejudice of their essential security interests. Confidence can be created by international agreements only if the agreements take equally into account the legitimate security interests of all the parties concerned.

The Western Powers call on the Soviet Union to enter into negotiations on the subject of European security in this spirit, with a view to concluding a treaty which would enter into force in conjunction with an agreement on the reunification of Germany. This would recognise the close link which the Powers concerned have agreed exists between the two subjects. The linked settlement of these two questions and the confidence created thereby would also permit further progress to be made in the limitation of armaments generally.

8. INTERNATIONAL EXCHANGES

Lasting peace requires a satisfactory settlement of the problems which concern the general relationship between the peoples of Eastern Europe and those of the Western countries. An important step forward along the path of mutual understanding would be made if the interested Governments agreed to remove the obstacles which still prevent peoples from knowing each other and to satisfy the common aspirations of all men by guaranteeing them objective and complete information and by promoting closer cultural ties and human relations.

In July 1955, at the Geneva Conference, the four Heads of Government rightly included this question in the directives given to the Ministers of Foreign Affairs.[1] While some progress has been made in certain fields since that date, much remains to be done to eliminate the obstacles which still hinder mutual acquaintance and understanding, the conditions for a durable and genuine peace.

9. MEANS OF STRENGTHENING THE UNITED NATIONS

The peoples of the world look upon the United Nations organisation and the pledges of its members embodied in its Charter[2] as man's best hope for peace and justice. Thus, the Western Governments cannot but welcome the recent assertion of the Soviet Union that it believes in the importance of the United Nations and its role in the maintenance of peace and security as well as in the peaceful settlement of international issues. Like the USSR they deem that efforts should be made to strengthen the United Nations by every means, so that it should be able to fulfil its tasks more effectively. One practical way in which this can be done is through an undertaking by the Governments of the United States, United Kingdom, France and USSR that they will, as a matter of policy, avoid vetoing Security Council recommendations as to how nations might proceed toward the peaceful solution of their disputes.

10. WAYS OF EASING TENSIONS IN EASTERN EUROPE

The creation of conditions of stability in Eastern Europe based on relations of independence and friendship among the countries of the area would greatly contribute to the cause of promoting a just and lasting world peace. That this should come about is thus not an aspiration of neighbouring Western Europe alone, but of all the world. This international interest found its expression in the international agreements concerning the right of the peoples of the area to choose their own Governments; the peace treaties with their provisions designed to safeguard human rights; the efforts of many countries to improve the economic welfare of the people; and efforts to eliminate interference in their internal affairs.

*   *   *

[1] For the Directive to the Foreign Ministers of 23 July 1955, see *Documents* for 1955, pp. 48–49.
[2] See Cmd. 7015.

The Western Powers believe that a serious discussion of the problem posed by the existence of tensions in Eastern Europe should be held with the aim of eliminating interference in the internal affairs of the countries of that region and the use of force in the settlement of disputes there.

The Western Governments believe that the proposals set forth above are feasible and could be put into effect now. They believe their implementation is verifiable. The proposals take into account the legitimate interests and security needs of the countries concerned. Their adoption could create a basis for the development of an atmosphere of confidence and trust that would favour the growth of more active, mutually beneficial relations between our peoples and Governments.

12. Western proposals for the agenda of a summit conference, 31 May 1958[1]

On May 31 the United States Ambassador called on Mr. Gromyko and proposed to him that the suggestions for the agenda should be considered under five general headings with an agreed list of sub-topics under each. These sub-topics would then be discussed in turn with the object of establishing which of them should be submitted for examination by the Heads of Government. The Ambassador also gave Mr. Gromyko the lists of sub-topics proposed by the Western Powers. These, and the general headings under which they appear, are reproduced below.

I.—*Disarmament*

(a) Measures to control the production of fissionable material for nuclear weapons and to reduce existing military stocks of such material.
(b) The suspension of nuclear tests.
(c) The reduction and limitation of conventional arms and manpower.
(d) Measures to guard against surprise attack.
(e) The use of outer space for peaceful purposes.

II.—*European Security and Germany*

(a) Reunification of Germany in accordance with the terms of the 1955 Directive of the Four Heads of Government to the Ministers of Foreign Affairs.
(b) European security arrangements.

III.—*International Exchanges*

(a) Cessation of jamming of foreign broadcasts.
(b) Censorship.

[1] Cmnd. 469, p. 21.

(c) Free distribution and sale to the public of books and publications.
(d) Free distribution and sale of foreign newspapers and periodicals.
(e) Freedom of travel.

IV.—*Methods of Improving International Co-operation*

(a) Means of strengthening the United Nations.

V.—*Other Topics*

(a) Ways of easing tensions in Eastern Europe.

13. Letter from Mr. Khrushchev to Mr. Macmillan, 11 June 1958[1]

Dear Prime Minister, I am impelled by the situation that has arisen at the present time over preparations for a summit conference to send you this letter.

It is now nearly two months since the start of the preliminary talks, which the western powers proposed should be conducted through diplomatic channels, in preparation for this conference. When the western powers proposed that preliminary talks be conducted through diplomatic channels, the Soviet government expressed serious doubts as to whether this procedure would be helpful in the convening of a summit conference. We never concealed our fears that we might find ourselves, in starting such talks, on the slippery slope leading to the whole affair being drawn out, to postponement of the heads of government meeting. Nevertheless, since the western powers insisted on this method of preparing for the conference, the Soviet government agreed to such talks.

Unfortunately, our fears concerning the preliminary talks are beginning to be proved right. Over the preparations for the conference we continue, as before, to mark time, and, on a number of points, are in effect even moving backwards. In these circumstances many people—and not in the Soviet Union alone—are beginning to suspect that the whole object of proposing such preliminary talks was to put additional difficulties in the way of convening a summit conference.

The Soviet government, when it called on the government of the United Kingdom and the governments of other countries, six months ago, to convene a broad international conference of leading statesmen, was guided by the desire to find means, by joint efforts, of radically altering the situation that had arisen in international relations. We were and still are of the opinion that this conference should reach agreement in order to ease tension between states, to eliminate the 'cold war,' to ensure conditions for the peaceful co-existence of states, agreement that war should

[1] *Soviet News*, 17 June 1958.

not be resorted to as a means of solving outstanding issues. We cannot reconcile ourselves to the dangerous trend followed today in the development of relations between the states, particularly between the great powers. Today, when the destructive force of the weapons at the disposal of the states knows no limit, it would be criminal to remain inactive. The time has come for vigorous joint intervention by responsible statesmen with a view to averting a terrible danger, ridding mankind of the oppressive threat of atomic war, and giving men and women that which they need most of all—lasting peace and confidence in the future.

Last February, Prime Minister, you responded to the proposal for a summit conference and stated that you would be prepared to meet the leaders of the Soviet Union and other countries.[1] The governments of the United States and France responded to the proposal in a similar way. All this strengthened our hope that such a conference would be held at an early date, and was well received by other governments and by the peoples of all countries.

In these circumstances it was natural to expect that during the preliminary talks the parties would endeavour to put forward for examination at the conference such international problems, ripe for consideration, on which, given the good will of those taking part in the talks, there was a practical possibility already now of attaining favourable results and of improving the international atmosphere. We still adhere to this view, in particular as regards preparing the agenda for the summit conference.

Permit me to enumerate once more the questions which, in the Soviet government's view, should be considered at this conference. These are the questions:

The immediate ending of tests of atomic and hydrogen weapons;

Renunciation of the use of all types of atomic, hydrogen and rocket weapons;

The establishment in Central Europe of a zone free from atomic, hydrogen and rocket weapons;

The conclusion of a non-aggression pact between the states;

Prohibition of the use of outer space for military purposes, the dismantling of foreign military bases on alien territories, and international co-operation in exploring outer space;

The reduction of the number of foreign troops on the territory of Germany and within the frontiers of other European states;

The conclusion of a German peace treaty;

The prevention of surprise attack by one state on any other state;

Measures for the extension of international trade;

The development of relations and contacts between countries;

---

[1] For Mr. Macmillan's letter to Mr. Bulganin of 8 February 1958, see *Documents* for 1957, pp. 65–66.

The ending of propaganda for war, hostility and strife between the peoples;

Ways of easing tension in the Middle East.

We put first the universal ending of atomic and hydrogen weapon tests. Why do we do this? Because already now, in peacetime, such tests are polluting the atmosphere and the soil, infecting every living thing on earth, having a pernicious effect on the health of men and women, and threatening the lives of future generations, not to mention that these tests lead to the invention of new and still more devastating types of weapons, the use of which—should war break out—would have the most dire consequences for mankind.

Agreement on the ending of nuclear tests, which is possible already now, would strengthen trust between the states, would help to create the peaceable atmosphere for which the peoples of all countries yearn so intensely, and would be a good beginning paving the way to the settlement of all major international problems. Working for the ending of nuclear tests, we have ourselves unilaterally suspended these tests, although this puts us at a disadvantage compared with the N.A.T.O. countries. It is common knowledge that Britain and the United States have carried out far more nuclear weapon test explosions than the Soviet Union, so that agreement on ending these tests would only stabilise the situation in favour of the N.A.T.O. countries. But we are doing this, sacrificing our own interests, because we are guided by the supreme interests of all mankind, and we are of the opinion that the ending of nuclear weapon tests by all the powers would not create distrust but would help achieve the main object—the avoidance of war.

In adopting this decision to end tests, we called on Britain and the United States to follow our example. To our disappointment, however, the governments of Britain and the United States have not agreed to do this. Although your letter of April 21[1] expressed your readiness to discuss this question at a summit conference, barely a week after I had received your letter the United Kingdom government had started a new series of British hydrogen bomb explosions in the Pacific. This could not fail to create a most distressing impression in the Soviet Union and in other countries. Any unbiased person is quite justified in asking what considerations guided the United Kingdom government in undertaking this dangerous step after the Soviet Union had already stopped carrying out tests. In these circumstances we consider that discussion of this question at a summit conference is particularly urgent.

---

[1] Mr. Macmillan's letter to Mr. Khrushchev of 21 April 1958 was so brief that it was not reproduced in the Cmnd. paper series on Correspondence with the Soviet Union. The note urged that experts should begin to work out a system of inspection and control for the suspension of nuclear tests. For a text see *The Times*, 22 April 1958.

And who can deny that the reaching of agreement on such points as renunciation of the use of all types of nuclear weapons, the conclusion of a non-aggression pact between the member-states of the Warsaw Treaty and of the North Atlantic Alliance, and the creation of a zone in Central Europe free from nuclear and rocket weapons, would result in a relaxation in international tension and constitute an important step towards solving the problem of disarmament as a whole?

And is it not in accordance with the interests of all countries that an end should be put to the war propaganda which is being conducted day after day in some countries and which seriously poisons relations between the states?

And would it not be sensible to discuss such a question as the free development of trade and other economic ties between the countries, so as to find mutually advantageous ways of substantially broadening such ties. It would appear to me that the business circles of most countries, including the United Kingdom, would agree that the solution of this question could be most useful.

Nor do I think I am mistaken in saying that there are now very few people bold enough to deny that it would be in keeping with the vital interests of every country, of every nation, to reach agreement on the questions we have suggested for consideration, at a summit conference.

As you are aware, Prime Minister, the Soviet government set out its considerations regarding the questions which could be discussed at this conference in the proposals handed to the British Ambassador in Moscow on May 5. We did this so as to facilitate agreement on the convening of the conference. We also took into account the considerations expressed during the exchange of views on preparations for the conference by the governments of the western powers, including the government of the United Kingdom. I append hereto the text of these proposals of the Soviet government.

Submitting its proposals for the agenda of a conference of heads of government, the Soviet Union from the very outset declared its readiness to examine also, by general agreement, other proposals that would be conducive to ending the 'cold war' and the armaments race. At the same time I should like to stress quite definitely that should the western powers not be prepared at the present time to settle all the questions which the Soviet Union has proposed for discussion at the conference, certain of these questions could be selected and agreement reached on them, which would facilitate further progress towards strengthening peace.

We had hoped that the governments of the United Kingdom, the United States and France would examine the Soviet Union's proposals with due care, defining their attitude towards them, and would also, for their part, show concern for bringing the positions of the parties as close together as possible and facilitate the preparations for the conference, especially since, in your message to the Soviet government of February 8, you declared that when the agenda for the conference was being drawn up it would be necessary to examine both the Soviet government's proposals and the proposals of other interested governments. However, on studying the documents received during the past few days from the three powers in reply to the Soviet government's proposals of May 5, we find, to our profound disappointment, that these documents once again advance questions which do not bring closer but put off the possibility of reaching agreement, questions which we have already clearly and repeatedly declared to be unacceptable. We ask ourselves: Why are the governments of the western powers acting in such a manner? Can it be that there is a desire to offend us?

The western powers' proposals which have been handed to us raise once more the 'question of the situation in Eastern Europe.' In this way an attempt is again being made to revert to something that is over and done with, to insist on discussion of a question on which the positions of the parties have long since been thoroughly clarified. The government of the United Kingdom is well aware that this question is not a subject for discussion. We have repeatedly stated that we regard the raising of such a question at an international conference to be impermissible. The Soviet Union has no intention of intervening in the internal affairs of other sovereign states and is of the opinion that no one can assume the right to such intervention.

It is not difficult to imagine the absurd situation the world would be in if international conferences dragged in questions about the internal systems of individual states which for some reason or other had incurred the dislike of other countries. There can be no question of the countries drawing closer if we engage in discussing the fundamental differences existing between the social systems. That is not the road to the relaxation of international tension. To insist on intervening in the affairs of other countries, on the discussion of their internal affairs by third countries with absolutely no authority to do this, is to take the path of flagrant violation of the United Nations Charter, which expressly forbids such intervention, is to hold up to ridicule the principles of the United Nations.

Perfectly obvious, too, is the completely forced nature of the clamour about 'tension in Eastern Europe' with which attempts are being made to justify the demand for including this question on the conference agenda. The Soviet Union has diplomatic relations with all the East European countries and maintains the most lively ties with them. And I must say that we know of no symptoms of any 'tensions' whatsoever in the area. If the British government has any doubts regarding the situation in these countries, it has its ambassadors in nearly all of them, and no one is stopping them from ascertaining questions which interest them by the normal diplomatic means. And, frankly speaking, anyone with the slightest knowledge of the present-day international situation is well aware that the tension dangerous to peace must be sought in entirely different directions.

If the governments of the western powers, who are well aware of the viewpoint of the Soviet Union and the people's democracies themselves on this question, nevertheless still consider it possible to propose it once more for examination at the conference, how else can this be understood but as proof of the intention to nip the conference of heads of governments in the bud?

Nor can any other description be given to the efforts of the three western governments to insist that the conference of heads of government consider the question of German reunification. Here again, as the Soviet government has already repeatedly had occasion to point out to the government of the United Kingdom, this is a question which does not come within the competence of an international conference. It seems to us that it is high time to recognise as an incontrovertible truth the fact that in present-day circumstances the reunification of Germany can only come about as the result of the efforts of the two sovereign states existing today on German soil. Given the desire by both parties, it would be far easier for the German Democratic Republic and the Federal Republic of Germany to agree between themselves without the intervention of third parties. After all, the Germans in the east and the Germans in the west of Germany speak the same language, and they don't even need interpreters for negotiations, let alone foreign guardians who would solve for them questions concerning the destiny of the German people.

As is known, even the Federal German government has declared that discussion of German reunification should not be regarded as a condition for the convening of a summit conference. It has apparently no inclination to assume the grave responsibility for the breakdown of the conference, a conference which the peoples have awaited so long. Are we to understand the position of the three western powers in such a way that they are prepared to assume this responsibility, and are they not using the question of German unification as a pretext for further hampering agreement on the convening of a summit conference?

In their proposals the western powers set out their views on the question of European security. The urgency of this problem, it goes without saying, is indisputable. For the strengthening of peace in Europe and to lessen the danger of an outbreak of war on the continent of Europe there is a great deal that needs to be done and can be done. But what is proposed on this question?

To speak frankly—and I think that only by complete frankness can our exchange of views be really useful—the essence of these proposals, which are presented as a plan for strengthening European security, consists of the following: The western powers wish to draw the whole of Germany into their military grouping and wish to lull the peoples of Europe with declarations about the provision of 'guarantees.'

As long ago as our meeting in Geneva we pointed out that the proposal to provide guarantees for the Soviet Union was, to say the least, strange. As we know, guarantees are usually provided by a strong state (or states) to a weak state. The fundamental prerequisite is inequality, and it is the strong state which lays down the conditions for the weak state. The state to which guarantees are given is placed in dependence upon the state providing these guarantees. There are many examples in history of the state which provided guarantees violating its undertakings and thereby creating a hopeless position for the state to whom these guarantees were given. You must agree, Prime Minister, that the Soviet Union is by no means a weak state and that consequently it has no need of guarantees, for it is itself capable of protecting its interests. Therefore, in this instance, the conditions do not exist that would justify even raising the question of guarantees. Behind the raising of the question of guarantees as applied to the U.S.S.R. there is the obvious desire to place our country in an unequal position compared with the other powers, and this in itself is proof of the groundless nature of this desire.

It would be a different matter were the great powers, including the U.S.S.R., to assume reciprocal guarantees, and consequently accept a solution of the question which would not place any of the powers in an unequal and, all the more so, a degrading position. This demand for reciprocal guarantees would be met by the conclusion of a non-aggression pact, the tremendous significance of which cannot be denied, given an objective appreciation of the situation.

The artificial nature of the whole of this proposal for providing 'guarantees' for the Soviet Union becomes especially clear if we bear in mind that it is proposed that the role of guarantors be assumed by the powers who occupy a commanding position in the North Atlantic military grouping, whose entire activity is subordinated to military preparations against the Soviet Union and the countries friendly to the Soviet Union. Thus we are being offered 'guarantees of security' by a bloc of powers which day after day proceeds to forge weapons of war, whose military leaders call practically every day for atomic war against the Soviet Union, and whose propaganda machine systematically provokes war hysteria. There may be some people who would like to close their eyes to reality and rely on words of reassurance, but we do not belong to that category. And I do not for a single moment doubt that in similar conditions the United Kingdom would adopt the same attitude.

It is our firm conviction that on the question of European security the task is not that of putting forward some kind of 'guarantees' for the Soviet Union, of which it has no need; the task consists in safeguarding the security of all European peoples, of creating a position which would make it impossible for Europe to become once more the arena of a new war.

Precisely this object would be furthered by the creation, as the government of the Polish People's Republic has proposed, of a zone in Central Europe free from nuclear and rocket weapons, and also by reducing the strength of foreign troops stationed on the territory of European states, and in the first place in Germany, with the establishment of appropriate reciprocal control.

In your message to the Soviet government of January 16, you stated, in reference to the proposal of the government of the Polish People's Republic for the establishment of a zone in Central Europe free from atom and rocket weapons, that the British government was studying it with a view to seeing whether there were elements in it which could be made the basis of some alternative proposal. This statement gave grounds for assuming that the government of the United Kingdom agreed in principle with the idea itself of creating such a zone and was working out constructive proposals to be submitted for the consideration of other interested states. These expectations, however, have not been justified.

Yet the implementation of these measures would not violate the security interests of a single state. On the contrary, it would greatly reduce the possibility of atomic war breaking out in an area where there are now concentrated, in close proximity to each other, the great masses of armed forces and armaments of the opposing groups of powers. The creation of such a zone in one area could lead gradually to similar zones being formed in other areas, removing ever greater areas of the earth from the sphere of preparations for atomic war. And this would reduce the risk of the peoples becoming involved in such a war.

It is our opinion that the conclusion of a non-aggression pact between the member-states of the Warsaw Treaty and the countries belonging to the North Atlantic Alliance is a question that has long been ripe for settlement. The conclusion of such a pact would in no way disturb the existing correlation of forces between the two groupings; at the same time it would be of enormous benefit. The so essential element of stability and reassurance would be introduced into the entire international situation.

The peoples would see that the strongest countries in the military sense had reached agreement between themselves and did not want war. Need we point out that this would immediately reduce the danger of war, for it is perfectly obvious that a new military conflagration in Europe, and not only in Europe, in present conditions could only be the outcome of conflict between the two main groupings of powers.

We were greatly encouraged, Prime Minister, that in your broadcast of January 4 you yourself put forward the idea of concluding a solemn pact of non-aggression. The Soviet government at the time welcomed your statement, hoping that on this question we would subsequently encounter not only mutual understanding but also British support. In your letter to the Soviet government of January 16 you again spoke with approval of the idea of concluding a non-aggression pact.

It was natural to expect that, in developing these proposals, the British government would make concrete suggestions, so as to carry out its intentions with regard to the conclusion of a non-aggression pact. However, such proposals, unfortunately, were not made. Moreover, in subsequent statements, and in particular the proposals for the agenda of the summit conference to which I have already referred, the British government does not even mention a non-aggression pact. The question legitimately arises— does this signify that the British government has changed its attitude as regards concluding a non-aggression pact?

I should also like to point out that since the Soviet government's proposals were handed over on May 5, the question of the conclusion of a non-aggression pact has been examined at the conference of Warsaw Treaty member-states, who worked out a draft of such a pact and made a joint proposal to the N.A.T.O. member-countries on this question. The Soviet government expresses the hope that the British government will examine this draft and let it have its views on it.

The proposals made by the governments of the United Kingdom, the United States and France, like the proposals of the Soviet government, raise other questions, pertaining to disarmament. In our view these questions deserve serious consideration. However, taking into account our experience of the protracted talks in the United Nations Disarmament Sub-Committee, about which we have already had occasion to express our views, we doubt whether these questions, in the form in which they are raised in the present proposals of the western powers, are really being put forward with a view to reaching an agreed decision, with a view to reaching agreement on complete disarmament, and to starting to carry out at least initial measures, such as the ending of nuclear weapon tests, etc.

Why do we express such doubts and uncertainties? Because the western powers—those selfsame powers who took part in the United Nations Disarmament Sub-Committee, but in reality represented N.A.T.O. on it— having received our concrete proposals on measures that are urgently required in the sphere of disarmament, have in fact given no reply to them. They continue to repeat their previous proposals, claiming that the disarmament problem can only be solved in its entirety. They are thereby trying to drive matters on to the old road, already proven worthless, and to revive the barren discussions about the problem of disarmament 'as a whole.'

Such discussion, or to be more precise, such wrangling over the problem of disarmament, lasted for more than thirteen years behind closed doors. In actual fact no talks were held, it was nothing but deceiving public opinion, which was misled into thinking that progress was being made on disarmament, but in reality not a single practical problem of disarmament was ever solved.

Furthermore, the western powers, under cover of these disarmament talks, developed an unparallelled armaments race. That is why the Soviet Union has refused to take part in the Disarmament Commission, nor shall we take part in it as long as the N.A.T.O. countries insist on their demands, insist on totally unacceptable principles in approaching the disarmament problem.

The British government is well aware that the Soviet Union has been and continues to be an advocate of a radical solution of the disarmament problem. It has made repeated proposals to the western powers to come to an agreement about an all-embracing programme of disarmament, which should include a substantial reduction in armed forces and armaments, the prohibition of atomic and hydrogen weapons and appropriate measures for international supervision. The western powers, however, have revealed no desire to reach agreement on such broad measures of disarmament.

If for thirteen years we were unable to reach agreement on the problem of disarmament 'as a whole,' because the solution of individual questions was made contingent on the solution of others, how can we expect that with the same approach this problem can be solved at a conference of heads of government within a few days? Is it not obvious that the only realistic way is first of all to separate and solve those problems which are already ripe for solution, and then to proceed to solve the more involved problems. And this is what the Soviet Union proposes.

The Soviet Union has always considered and continues to consider it to be its duty to do everything possible to further the speediest solution of the disarmament problem. We were guided by this purpose in adopting the recent decision to effect a substantial reduction in the strength of our armed forces and for the unilateral ending by the Soviet Union of tests of all types of atomic and hydrogen weapons. Desiring to hasten agreement on the universal ending of such tests, the Soviet government has met the wishes of the United States and British governments, expressed, in particular, in your letter of April 21, for the appointment of experts to study ways of detecting possible violations of an agreement to end nuclear tests.

We hope that this latest step by the Soviet Union will be properly appreciated by the western powers, and that as a result a more favourable atmosphere will be created which will facilitate the speediest convening of a summit conference.

Prime Minister, I think the time has come to ascertain finally and with complete frankness what position the parties take as regards the main question: Do all the parties really desire the convening of a summit conference? I must say that the documents presented to us by the western powers have made us seriously doubt this. It is difficult to dismiss the thought that the authors of the proposals set out in these documents were not guided by the desire to find solutions of all problems most acceptable for all the sides, but, on the contrary, were hunting out questions for the solution of which the conditions are not yet ripe, with a view to being able to declare later that they were right when they foretold the failure of the heads of government meeting.

And it is this that has impelled me to write this letter to you. We should like to know definitely whether the governments of the western powers have any serious intentions regarding the organisation of a summit meeting and the holding of talks the results of which are awaited literally by all mankind, or whether they are hoping to lull the vigilance of the peoples, to create the impression that contacts have been established, that talks are going on, while in actual fact they are putting forward questions which aim not only at upsetting the preparations for the conference but also at preventing the summit meeting from taking place, so as to accuse our country of 'intractability.' Such tactics are very familiar to us from the experience of certain previous negotiations.

The Soviet government has studied most carefully the considerations regarding a possible agenda for the summit meeting, set out in your letters, Prime Minister. We expressed our views on these proposals in detail, and informed you that we considered some of the questions proposed by the western powers to be acceptable for discussion. We are also prepared to examine the question of ways of strengthening the United Nations, which was mentioned in the correspondence between our governments, for we, too, have something to say on this point.

Prime Minister, I have set out quite frankly my considerations regarding the situation which has now arisen over the preparations for a summit conference. In this situation the responsibility which rests with the governments of the great powers is particularly great. To realise the great weight of this responsibility we need only imagine how immensely disappointed all the peoples would be if we failed to find a common language. No one could understand or justify statesmen who are unable to agree even on how to start talks between ourselves while the world is gripped by the fever of an ever-intensifying armaments race and there is not a corner where men and women are free of the oppressive fear of the danger of a new military explosion.

We are convinced that it is quite possible to achieve a radical improvement in the international situation through the joint efforts of the states, including the joint efforts of the United Kingdom and the Soviet Union. An important step towards this could be a conference of leading statesmen, with the participation of the heads of government. I express the hope that the government of the United Kingdom will examine this letter with due attention and, for its part, will take the necessary steps to prevent a breakdown of the summit conference, to clear the road to this conference of the obstacles which are being artificially created.

I am simultaneously sending messages on this subject to the President of the United States and to the Prime Minister of France.

With sincere respects,

N. Khrushchov

14. Letter from Mr. Macmillan to Mr. Khrushchev, 1 July 1958[1]

Dear Mr. Prime Minister, Your letter of June 11[2] makes it perfectly clear that you and we have two totally different objectives in view. Yours is to simply convene a Summit Conference. Ours is to negotiate a settlement of some of the differences which divide us. We want a Summit Conference because we want an effective means of making progress in negotiation.

2. But how can a negotiation be successful and result in a real *détente* if the two sides are unable even to agree on what they are to negotiate about? All our recent efforts have been bent towards trying to reach an agreement with you about this. But we have had no response.

3. You have produced your list of proposals about which to negotiate and we have produced our list. We have suggested a method of getting round the difficulties created by the fact that the two sets of proposals were divergent; but you have ignored it. The suggestion was that since all your proposals as well as ours fell under certain general headings, discussion of individual topics should take place within the framework of these headings, each side being free to include under each heading such topics as it wished to have discussed. Neither side should veto the inclusion of any topic. Whatever topics either side insisted on discussing would be included under one or other of the headings. An examination could then have been made of our respective positions on all the topics to see which ones should be submitted to the Foreign Ministers and then to the Heads of Government. Mr. Gromyko promised a reply to this proposal. But none has been forthcoming and your letter ignores it altogether. Nor do you say anything in your letter to suggest that you have any alternative idea to put forward.

---

[1] Cmnd. 469, pp. 30–31.   [2] See preceding document.

4. You simply repeat your set of proposals and criticise some of ours. But that really takes us no further.

5. Unless we can agree, by some such method as the one we have suggested, on what the negotiations are to be about, I really do not see how we can get started. To persist in refusing to consider any compromise method of reaching agreement on this is bound to create the impression that you are not really interested in the success of but only in the demand for a Summit Conference. I must add that this impression also arises from your action in publishing our confidential exchanges without even consulting us before doing so.

6. But although I must admit to feeling discouraged by your letter I have no intention of abandoning the hope that we may still be able to get the negotiations started. We shall certainly not relax our efforts and I ask you most sincerely to make your contribution by accepting our procedural proposal in a spirit of compromise or to let us hear of some alternative suggestion.

Yours sincerely,

HAROLD MACMILLAN

15. Soviet note to the United Kingdom and the draft treaty of Friendship and Co-operation among the states of Europe, 15 July 1958[1]

The Soviet government considers it necessary to approach the government of the United Kingdom on the following matter:

The Soviet government believes that the situation developing on the continent of Europe obliges the governments of all states concerned to endeavour to work out joint measures which would check the trend in Europe towards war, and to find ways of strengthening peace on the basis of developing mutual confidence and expanding general co-operation among the states of Europe.

The brunt of the two world wars which mankind has suffered fell first and foremost on the peoples of Europe. Nobody will deny that the greatest human losses and material destruction as the result of those wars was suffered by the countries of Europe. Scores of millions of Europeans were killed on the battlefields or in air raids on peaceful towns; died from wounds or disease; were tortured to death in fascist concentration camps. In the course of the hostilities many once well-built and prospering towns and villages were wiped out and irreplaceable monuments of culture were destroyed.

At the cost of losses which can never be made good to any nation or

---

[1] *Soviet News*, 21 July 1958. Identical notes and the text of the draft treaty were sent to the Governments of the countries of Europe and the United States.

family, at the cost of unbelievable physical and moral strain, the peoples of Europe won the right to live without fear for their own future or that of coming generations.

Today, however, the peoples of the countries of Europe are once more compelled to live in the atmosphere of feverish preparations for war; they live under the shadow of an even more appalling military disaster. The principles of mutual co-operation in international affairs spoken of so much during the struggle against the common enemy, are far from being respected by everybody.

One cannot fail to appreciate that such measures as the continued whipping-up of the arms race—and especially of that in atomic and hydrogen weapons—with the expansion of armies and expenditure for military purposes, the setting up of nuclear and rocket bases on foreign territories, the handing over of nuclear and rocket weapons to additional states and, first of all, to the Federal Republic of Germany, are nothing but preparations for war. This aim is also served by the propaganda carried on in some countries in order to make the peoples believe that it is impossible to safeguard peace, and in order to foster feelings of enmity, estrangement and hostility towards states and peoples outside their particular military groupings, and which have chosen a different political and social system and are shaping their life in accordance with their own ideals. The creation of opposing military groupings of states has resulted in strong distrust and a dangerous atmosphere of tension in Europe.

Each year it becomes more and more evident that a war in Europe—if, deplorably, it should be unleashed and unless timely and special steps to thwart or at least limit it are taken in advance—would be a war in which nuclear and rocket means of destruction would be used. In spite of the unilateral termination of all kinds of atomic and hydrogen weapon tests by the Soviet Union, the United States and Britain are still carrying out such tests, and are avoiding an agreement on the renunciation of the use of nuclear weapons, and at the same time are involving their allies in the North Atlantic Pact in preparations for a rocket and nuclear war.

The false claims that, by creating and stockpiling the most destructive and deadly means of annihilation, mankind is able to prevent the danger of a war in which such means of annihilation would be used, are a challenge to common sense. The more atom and hydrogen bombs in the stockpiles of states, the greater the number of states possessing atomic and hydrogen weapons, the closer the armed forces and bases of those powers to each other the more likely is the outbreak of a new war. To maintain this position is tantamount to putting a flaming torch to a powder barrel.

It is not difficult to see what would happen if the member-states of the Warsaw Treaty, instead of carrying out their measures to ease tension in Europe, began to act in the same way as the N.A.T.O. countries. It is clear that the danger of a military conflagration would increase immeasurably if they, like N.A.T.O., in their turn began to press an arms race on other states, to move their military bases on to foreign territories closer to the vital centres of states belonging to the military group opposed to them, if they began sending their own military aircraft through the skies of Europe towards those American aeroplanes which are continuously in the air carrying atom and hydrogen bombs.

As the largest European state, which twice in the lifetime of one generation has undergone invasion through its western frontiers, the Soviet Union, naturally, cannot but display unremitting anxiety for European security, which is inseparable from its own security. Millions of Soviet men and women did not lay down their lives on the battlefields of the Second World War so that, today, the Soviet people might look on, unconcerned, while the combustible materials for a new war are being accumulated in Europe.

Like other peaceloving states, the Soviet Union has always done, and continues to do, everything it can to eliminate the war danger and achieve peaceful co-operation among all the states of Europe—co-operation based on confidence, irrespective of social systems and affiliations to any given group of states.

The Soviet Union has closed down its military bases on the territories of other states. The Soviet Union is not placing stores of atomic and hydrogen weapons or preparing launching sites for rockets beyond its national frontiers. The strength of the Soviet armed forces has been reduced, by unilateral action, by a total of 2,140,000 men in the past three years. They included more than 90,000 officers and men demobilised from the Soviet armed forces stationed in the German Democratic Republic. Military expenditures and armaments have been reduced correspondingly. At the last session of the Supreme Soviet of the U.S.S.R., a decree was adopted unilaterally stopping tests of all kinds of atomic and hydrogen weapons by the Soviet Union.[1]

At a meeting of the Political Consultative Committee of states signatories to the Warsaw Treaty, which took place in Moscow at the end of May, a decision was taken to withdraw from the Rumanian People's Republic at an early date Soviet troops stationed there in accordance with that Treaty; and also to make additional reductions in the number of Soviet troops stationed on the territory of the Hungarian People's Republic.

Wishing to reduce the possibility of friction and to rule out the danger of the contradictions between the two main groups of powers in Europe developing into a military conflict, the participants of the meeting proposed that a non-aggression pact should be concluded between the states

[1] See below, pp. 59–60.

signatories to the Warsaw Treaty and the member-states of N.A.T.O. The Soviet government is convinced that the conclusion of such a non-aggression pact would be a reliable preventive measure serving to strengthen peace in Europe.

In spite of the great beneficial role such a non-aggression treaty would play, one should bear in mind, however, that such a measure would be only a first step and the least that must be done in the existing circumstances so as to establish the necessary climate of confidence among states in Europe. It would be an unforgiveable omission if, at the same time, no efforts were made to take other transitional steps, leading from the present explosive situation to the establishment of conditions of lasting peace in Europe.

The Soviet government starts from the fact that peace and security in Europe cannot be ensured without the combined efforts of all the European states, and the establishment of broad, all-sided co-operation among them. The experience accumulated in settling important international problems shows that ways and means of reaching mutually acceptable decisions contributing to peace can always be found—provided that there is goodwill among the parties concerned. In the first postwar years, for instance, peace treaties were concluded with Bulgaria, Rumania, Hungary Italy and Finland, which greatly contributed to the normalisation of the situation in Europe. Even more convincing evidence of this was the signing by the states in 1955—in an atmosphere of 'cold war' and sharpened mutual distrust—of the Austrian State Treaty, which restored political and economic independence to Austria, as a neutral state.

The government of the U.S.S.R. is well aware that certain governments of West European countries and also the United States hold views which differ from those of the U.S.S.R. regarding the reasons which have led to the existing tension in Europe, as well as about suitable ways to ease this tension in relations among European states. For all that, however, it cannot be disputed that the situation in Europe demands that the governments of the European states rise above their existing differences. A polemic itself, which is not supplemented by real constructive steps, can neither halt a falling bomb nor diminish the force of its explosion. Controversy must not be allowed to interfere with the sober facing of facts which are giving Europeans a feeling of deep anxiety and it must not hide the most important thing, the need to seek persistently and patiently for an agreement on concrete steps towards lasting peace in Europe.

It will be recalled that, in the period between the two world wars, plans for safeguarding security in Europe, plans to organise Europe-wide collaboration, ended in failure—first and foremost because there was no agreement among the leading states, which possessed the strongest armed forces and the combined efforts of which could have made aggression impossible. The Soviet government believes that this lesson of history must be learned, so as not to repeat the grave mistakes of the past.

There is no need now to point out that attempts to substitute for the solution of problems facing Europe as a whole the practice of setting up, on a limited and closed basis, various associations of individual West European states, such as the European Coal and Steel Community, the Common Market, Euratom, and so on, can lead only to such states bringing themselves into increasing opposition to the other European states, thus widening the gulf between Western and Eastern Europe.

The idea of co-operation among all European countries, bringing them together to secure Europe's peace, prosperity and wellbeing, is deeply rooted in the history and the present-day life of the peoples of Europe. In the eastern part of our continent and in the western part, the desire for the development of mutual understanding and all-sided relations among European countries is continually growing. This can be seen, for instance, from the fact that, at the 12th session of the United Nations Organisation, all European countries and the United States voted for a resolution calling for peaceful and good-neighbourly relations among states.[1]

If they wish to put an end to the dangerous trend of events in Europe, the Soviet government believes that the governments of European states, and the government of the United States should direct their efforts so as to work out, on a regional basis, Europe-wide decisions which can be put into practice even at the present stage, and which would be acceptable to all governments. In this connection, the Soviet government is putting forward a proposal for the conclusion by the states of Europe and the United States of a Treaty of Friendship and Co-operation.

In the Soviet government's opinion such a treaty should include provisions designed to prevent and deter aggression in Europe, and to reinforce the security of all European states. It would be important, for this reason, for the treaty to embody obligations by the European states and the United States not to give military or economic assistance or moral support to any state violating peace in Europe—irrespective of whether they are partners or not of the aggressor state under existing military pacts or treaties. It is well known that the idea of such an agreement has been repeatedly expressed by countries, including the United States, Britain and France, over recent years.

Appreciating that agreement on disarmament involves considerable difficulties, and that the efforts to that end exerted over many years have not brought any progress, the Soviet government suggests that such a treaty should provide for measures contributing to ending the arms race and action in Europe to reduce the armed forces of the Warsaw Treaty Organisation and of N.A.T.O. Initiative by European states seeking such

[1] Resol. 1236 (XII). See fn. 1 on p. 67, below.

partial solutions could open up the prospect for wider agreements concerning the disarmament problem.

The creation of a zone, in direct proximity to the line dividing the existing military groupings in Europe, in which the production and deployment of atomic, hydrogen or rocket weapons would be prohibited, would be of supreme importance in preventing military conflicts in Europe. The signatories to the treaty would, in that case, undertake to respect the status of that zone, and to regard the territories it included as excluded from the use of such weapons.

It is also desirable that the treaty should provide, as a first step, for the reduction in the next year or two of the strength of foreign military forces on German territory, by one-third or any other agreed amount. When carrying out this reduction it would be possible to agree upon the establishment of the necessary system of control and inspection to ensure that the obligations accepted by participants of the corresponding agreement are carried out.

The Soviet government is in favour of aerial survey within the limits of a specified zone extending on both sides of the line dividing the forces of the states signatories to the Warsaw Treaty and those of N.A.T.O., for the purpose of preventing surprise attack.

The extension of economic co-operation, mutually beneficial and with equal rights, on a basis excluding any discrimination or artificial restrictions of any kind, would undoubtedly promote the economic development of the member-states of the treaty, and promote peaceful and business-like contacts and mutual understanding between them. The inclusion of such provisions in the treaty would be especially useful, since the encouragement of unhampered world trade would render good service to a number of countries whose economies, particularly in the recent period, have been afflicted by unhealthy developments.

The Soviet government supports the development of collaboration among the European countries, and the United States as well, to solve the great problem of the peaceful use of atomic energy. It considers it desirable that the treaty express the readiness of its signatories for an exchange of experience in scientific research and industrial practice in the use of atomic energy as well as an exchange of raw materials, supplies and equipment. The joint efforts of the parties to the treaty in this field would promote increased wellbeing of the peoples, the further development of science and culture, and would extend knowledge of natural laws, and their use for the benefit of mankind.

In the Soviet government's view, the parties to the treaty could place on a firmer basis the development of contacts with one another, especially in the fields of science, technology and culture, so as to let the peoples learn of each other's national achievements.

The treaty could also include a number of other measures, realisation of which would help to reduce the danger of a war breaking out in Europe.

The Soviet government is guided by the conviction that, taken together, the measures it proposes would lead to the transformation of Europe into a zone of lasting peace and real security.

Taking into account these considerations, the Soviet government puts forward for the consideration of the government of the United Kingdom and the governments of other European countries and of the United States, a draft 'Treaty of Friendship and Co-operation among the States of Europe'; and it expresses the hope that the government of the United Kingdom will give favourable consideration to this proposal.

Draft Treaty of Friendship and Co-operation among the States of Europe

The High Contracting Parties,

Determined to promote in every way the development of friendly relations and co-operation among the states of Europe and to resolve exclusively by peaceful means whatever issues in dispute may arise among them;

Recognising that the most important task of the peoples of the European states is to create among them an atmosphere of confidence which would preclude the possibility of a new war breaking out on the continent of Europe;

Believing that the strengthening of good-neighbourly relations of friendship among the European peoples, irrespective of their chosen form of government, will help to ease international tension, to end the arms race, to develop and strengthen fruitful co-operation among the states in the political, economic, cultural, scientific and other fields;

Noting that the United Nations Charter encourages the conclusion among states of regional agreements with the object of maintaining universal peace and security;

Guided by the determination to carry out the high principles of the United Nations, and in amplification of the provisions on peaceful and good-neighbourly international relations, adopted by the 12th Session of the United Nations General Assembly—

Have resolved to conclude the present Treaty of Friendship and Co-operation among the States of Europe, and for this purpose have agreed as follows:

Article 1. The treaty is open to all states of Europe and to the United States of America, who recognise the objects and assume the undertakings provided for in the present treaty.

Article 2. The High Contracting Parties, in a spirit of sincere co-operation and mutual understanding, will develop and strengthen good-neighbourly relations of friendship among their peoples based on principles of mutual respect for territorial integrity and sovereignty, non-aggression, non-interference in one another's domestic affairs, equality and mutual benefit.

Article 3. The High Contracting Parties undertake to solve whatever disputes may arise among them by peaceful means exclusively, in accordance with the principles of the Charter of the United Nations.

In the event of a situation arising that could lead to a deterioration in the friendly relations among states, or could create a threat to peace in Europe, the High Contracting Parties shall immediately consult with one another for the purpose of taking joint measures as may be found proper to end the situation that has arisen.

Article 4. Should one or several of the High Contracting Parties be attacked by any state, the other parties to the treaty undertake not to render any military or economic aid or moral support to the aggressor, regardless of whether they are bound to the aggressor state by obligations of alliance, or by any other obligations.

Article 5. Pending the conclusion of a general agreement on the reduction of armaments and armed forces and on the prohibition of nuclear weapons, the High Contracting Parties undertake:

(a) To reduce, within the space of one to two years, their armed forces and armaments stationed on the territory of Germany by one-third or any other agreed amount; the contingents of troops thus released will have to be withdrawn from the territory of Germany behind the national frontiers of the states concerned.

Following this reduction of armed forces and armaments, consideration shall be given to a further reduction in foreign armed forces stationed on the territory of Germany, and also to the reduction of foreign armed forces stationed on the territories of other European states; in both cases, the contingents of armed forces shall be withdrawn behind the national frontiers of the states concerned.

Information shall be exchanged regularly, and at least twice a year, on the numerical strength of armed forces and quantity of armaments of the High Contracting Parties, stationed on the territories of other states in Europe.

(b) In order to prevent the possibility of surprise attack, provision must be made for carrying out aerial photographic inspection within the limits of a zone extending for 800 kilometres on both sides of the demarcation line between the armed forces of the member-states of the North Atlantic Treaty Organisation, and those of states which are parties to the Warsaw Treaty. This zone shall be established in agreement with the states whose territories are incorporated in it.

Not later than six months after the signing of this Treaty, the representatives of the High Contracting Parties will determine the boundaries of the zone referred to in point (b), and will also establish an appropriate system of control and inspection over the fulfilment of the undertakings provided for in this Article.

Article 6. The High Contracting Parties are unanimously in favour of the establishment in Central Europe of a zone free from the production and deployment of atomic, hydrogen or rocket weapons, as well as of equipment and installations for servicing such weapons. This zone, with the agreement of the respective governments, shall embrace the territories of the German Democratic Republic, the Federal Republic of Germany, the Polish People's Republic and the Czechoslovak Republic.

The High Contracting Parties pledge themselves to respect the status of this zone and to regard the territories of the states covered by it as being removed from the sphere of the use of atomic, hydrogen or rocket weapons. They recognise it as necessary that an appropriate system of control and inspection be established over the fulfilment of the agreement on the establishment of this zone.

Article 7. Proceeding from the principle that economic co-operation and contacts between states are a natural and reliable basis for the strengthening of peaceful, friendly relations with one another, the High Contracting Parties undertake:

(a) To develop economic co-operation and the exchange of experience; to give one another any assistance required in solving those most urgent economic problems that are of great importance for ensuring full employment for the population and improving their wellbeing;

To develop in every way among the parties to the treaty co-operation in the sphere of trade, on the principle of complete equality and mutual benefit;

(b) To take measures for the gradual removal of the obstacles and restrictions which still exist in the development of economic relations among states, on the basis of bilateral or multilateral agreements, including agreements within the framework and through the medium of the United Nations Economic Commission for Europe;

(c) To develop co-operation in the peaceful uses of nuclear energy, including exchange of experience in the construction of power stations, industrial transport and other installations powered by atomic energy, exchange of experts, raw materials, supplies and equipment.

Article 8. With the object of broadening international contacts and co-operation in the fields of science and culture, which promote mutual understanding among the peoples, the High Contracting Parties undertake to develop and strengthen reciprocal contacts and co-operation in the fields of science, culture, technology and education.

For this purpose they express readiness to discuss at an early date specific questions of cultural and scientific co-operation, with a view to concluding bilateral or multilateral agreements on these questions.

Article 9. This treaty is concluded for a term of ten years.

The treaty is subject to ratification in accordance with the legislative procedures of the states parties to the treaty.

Article 10. The treaty is open to all European states.

Article 11. The present treaty, the Russian, English, French and German texts of which are equally authentic, shall be deposited for custody in the care of the Secretary-General of the United Nations.

In witness whereof, the Plenipotentiaries have signed the present treaty and affixed thereto their seals.

b. Suspension of tests and prevention of surprise attack

16. Resolution of the U.S.S.R. Supreme Soviet regarding the unilateral termination by the Soviet Union of atomic and hydrogen weapon tests, Moscow, 31 March 1958[1]

As time passes the question of ending atomic and hydrogen weapon tests is assuming ever greater importance for the cause of peace and the welfare of the peoples.

Today the ending of tests is being demanded by the overwhelming majority of the people of the world. Yet although the peoples have been persistently working for the ending of these tests for many years, these weapons are still being manufactured. This has resulted in the creation of ever newer types of death-dealing nuclear weapons, in an increase in the concentration of radioactive elements in the air and the soil, and this is poisoning the human organism and is threatening the normal development of coming generations.

The Soviet Union has been exerting efforts steadily and persistently to reach an agreement with the powers possessing atomic and nuclear weapons on an immediate and unconditional termination of nuclear tests. To this end the U.S.S.R. Supreme Soviet and the Soviet government have in recent years repeatedly put forward concrete proposals to end the tests—proposals which could long ago have served as a basis for agreement on this question.

In its appeal to the United States Congress and the Parliament of Great Britain of May 10, 1957, the U.S.S.R. Supreme Soviet urged them' to work for an agreement between the governments of the U.S.S.R., the United States and Britain on the immediate termination of atom and hydrogen bomb test explosions.

---

[1] *Soviet News*, 1 April 1958. For a speech by Mr. Gromyko made at a joint session of the two Chambers of the U.S.S.R. Supreme Soviet on 31 March 1958, on the ending of nuclear tests, see ibid., pp. 3–8.

At its previous session last December, the U.S.S.R. Supreme Soviet, expressing the unswerving determination and the unanimous desire of the Soviet people for peace, proposed that the U.S.S.R., Britain and the United States pledge themselves to cease all atomic and hydrogen weapon tests as from January 1, 1958.

The United States and Britain, however, failed to react to these proposals of the Soviet Union. As a result, test explosions of atomic and hydrogen bombs are still taking place in various parts of the globe— evidence of the further intensification of the race to create ever more dangerous types of weapons of mass destruction.

Guided by its desire to make a practical beginning to the worldwide ending of atomic and hydrogen weapon tests, which would be the first step towards finally ridding mankind of the threat of devastating atomic war, the Supreme Soviet of the Union of Soviet Socialist Republics resolves:

1. To end all types of atomic and hydrogen weapon tests in the Soviet Union.

The U.S.S.R. Supreme Soviet expects that the Parliaments of other states possessing atomic and hydrogen weapons will do everything to terminate test explosions of these weapons by their countries as well.

2. To entrust the U.S.S.R. Council of Ministers with taking the necessary measures to implement Article 1 of this resolution, and to address an appeal to the governments of other states possessing atomic and hydrogen weapons, urging them to take similar steps to ensure the ending of atomic and hydrogen weapon tests everywhere and for all time.

In the event of other nuclear powers continuing these tests, the government of the U.S.S.R. will naturally act as it sees fit as regards the testing of atomic and hydrogen weapons by the Soviet Union, depending on the aforementioned circumstances and with a view to the interests of the security of the Soviet Union.

The U.S.S.R. Supreme Soviet sincerely hopes that the Soviet Union's initiative in ending nuclear weapon tests will meet with due support from the Parliaments of other countries.

The U.S.S.R. Supreme Soviet is firmly convinced that if in response to the decision of the Soviet Union other nuclear powers similarly end the testing of such weapons, this will be an important practical step towards consolidating peace and strengthening the security of all peoples. Such a step would unquestionably do much to improve the international situation as a whole, and would help to free mankind from oppressive fears for the future of peace and the fate of the generations to come.

Supreme Soviet of the Union
of Soviet Socialist Republics

17. Statement by the Department of State on the Soviet announcement regarding the termination of atomic and hydrogen weapon tests, 31 March 1958[1]

The Soviet statement about nuclear testing will, of course, be studied in detail. But some general observations can be made at once.

The Soviet statement comes on the heels of an intensive series of secret Soviet tests. They should arouse world opinion to the need to deal in an orderly and dependable way with the testing and related aspects of the disarmament problem.

Soviet official propaganda incessantly seeks to create abroad the image of a peace-loving Soviet Government. But that same Government openly defies the United Nations with respect to both the substance and the procedure of disarmament.

The charter of the United Nations gives that organization broad authority with reference to principles of disarmament and the regulation of armaments. In the exercise of that authority the United Nations General Assembly has, by an overwhelming vote, approved a comprehensive first-stage disarmament proposal and called on the nations concerned to begin at once technical studies as to how these proposals might be carried out.[2] These studies included the studies needed for a supervised suspension of nuclear testing. The United States stands ready instantly to respond to that resolution. But the Soviet Union refuses to comply.

The same General Assembly reconstituted and enlarged its Disarmament Commission. The United States wants that Commission to carry out its mandate. But the Soviet Union boycotts the Commission.

The charter makes the Security Council responsible for formulating plans for the establishment of a system for the regulation of armaments. The United States has recently proposed to the Soviet Union that this responsibility be discharged.[3] But the Soviet Union refuses to co-operate.

The Soviet Government declines to deal with the subject of armament in any of the several ways prescribed by the United Nations Charter. It prefers elusive formulations of its own.

It is elemental that free nations which want to remain free will not, and should not, forgo their indispensable collective capacity to deter and defend against aggression merely in reliance on a Soviet statement of

---

[1] D.S.B., 21 April 1958, pp. 646–7.

[2] Resol. 1148 (XII), adopted by the General Assembly at the 716th meeting on 14 November 1957, by a roll-call vote of 56 to 9 (Albania, Bulgaria, Byelorussian S.S.R., Czechoslovakia, Hungary, Poland, Rumania, Ukranian S.S.R., U.S.S.R.), with 15 abstentions (Afghanistan, Burma, Ceylon, Egypt, Finland, Ghana, India, Indonesia, Japan, Nepal, Saudi Arabia, Sudan, Syria, Yemen, Yugoslavia). See G.A.O.R., Twelfth Session, Supplement No. 18 (A/3805), pp. 3–4.

[3] See D.S.B., 31 March 1958, p. 516.

intentions for which there is no system of verification, which can be evaded in secrecy and altered at will.

The United States again calls on the Soviet Union to deal with the vital problem of disarmament in an orderly way, in accordance with the United Nations Charter, to which the signature of the Soviet Union is affixed. That charter constitutes a solemn agreement. If it is nullified by the Soviet Union, why should the world place confidence in new Soviet engagements?

18. Letter from President Eisenhower to Mr. Khrushchev regarding the suspension of nuclear tests, 8 April 1958[1]

Dear Mr. Chairman: I have your communication of April 4[2] repeating, in substance, the already widely publicized statement of the Soviet Government with reference to the suspension of nuclear testing.[3]

It seems peculiar that the Soviet Union, having just concluded a series of tests of unprecedented intensity, should now, in bold headlines, say that it will not test again, but add, in small type, that it may test again if the United States carries out its already long announced and now imminent series of tests.

The timing, wording, and manner of the Soviet declaration cannot but raise questions as to its real significance.

The position of the United States on this matter of testing is well-known. For several years we have been seeking a dependable ending to the accumulation of nuclear weapons and a dependable beginning of the steady reduction of existing weapons stockpiles. This was my 'Atoms for Peace' proposal, made in 1953 before the United Nations.[4] Surely, the heart of the nuclear problem is not the mere testing of weapons, but the weapons themselves. If weapons are dependably dealt with, then it is natural to suspend their testing. However, the Soviet Union continues to reject the concept of an internationally supervised program to end weapons production and to reduce weapons stocks. Under those circumstances of the Soviet's making, the United States seeks to develop the defensive rather than the offensive capabilities of nuclear power and to learn how to minimize the fissionable fallout.

[1] *D.S.B.*, 28 April 1958, pp. 679–80. For Mr. Macmillan's brief reply, in which he stated 'that the question of nuclear tests, . . . together with other problems of disarmament' would be discussed at a possible summit, although 'any practical agreement in this sphere must depend of course upon an agreed system of inspection and control', see *Commonwealth Survey*, 29 April 1958, p. 415.

[2] For this letter from Mr. Khrushchev to President Eisenhower, see *D.S.B.*, 28 April 1958, pp. 680–1. Mr. Khrushchev's similar letter of 4 April to Mr. Macmillan is given above, p. 8.

[3] See above, p. 59.

[4] See President Eisenhower's speech to the U.N.G.A. of 8 December 1953, *Documents* for 1953, pp. 116–21 (extracts only).

It goes without saying that these experiments, so far as the United States is concerned, are so conducted that they cannot appreciably affect human health.

Perhaps, Mr. Chairman, you recall the Joint Declaration made by the Governments of the United Kingdom and the United States at Bermuda on March 24, 1957.[1] We then declared that we would conduct nuclear tests only in such a manner as would keep world radiation from rising to more than a small fraction of the levels that might be hazardous. We went on to say that we would continue publicly announcing our test series well in advance of their occurrence with information as to their location and general timing.

We further said that we would be willing to register with the United Nations advance notice of our intention to conduct future nuclear tests and to permit limited international observation of such tests if the Soviet Union would do the same.

The Soviet Union has never responded to that invitation. Its latest series of tests was conducted behind a cloak of secrecy, so far as the Soviet Union could make it so. Nevertheless, as I recently stated,[2] it is the intention of the United States to invite observation by the United Nations of certain of our forthcoming tests.

Not only did the Soviet Union ignore our Bermuda proposal on testing, but it has persistently rejected the substance of my 'Atoms for Peace' proposal. It refuses to agree to an internationally supervised cut-off of the use of new fissionable material for weapons purposes and the reduction of existing weapons stocks by transfers to peaceful purposes. During the five years since I first proposed 'Atoms for Peace', the destructive power in our nuclear arsenals has steadily mounted, and a dependably controlled reduction of that power becomes ever more difficult.

Mr. Chairman, now that you have become head of the Soviet Government, will you not reconsider your Government's position and accept my proposal that fissionable materials henceforth be manufactured only for peaceful purposes!

If the Soviet Union is as peace-loving as it professes, surely it would want to bring about an internationally supervised diversion of fissionable material from weapons purposes to peace purposes.

If the Soviet Union is unwilling to accept 'Atoms for Peace', there are other outstanding proposals by which the Soviet Union can advance the cause of peace. You will recall, Mr. Chairman, my 'Open Skies' proposal made to you and Chairman Bulganin in Geneva in 1955.[3] You will also recall my proposals for the international use of outer space for peaceful

---

[1] See *Documents* for 1957, pp. 381–3.
[2] See President Eisenhower's statement of 26 March 1958, *D.S.B.*, 14 April 1958, p. 601.
[3] See *Documents* for 1955, pp. 39–41, for President Eisenhower's statement of 21 July 1955.

purposes emphasized in my recent correspondence with Chairman Bulganin.[1] These proposals await Soviet acceptance.

The United States is also prepared, in advance of agreement upon any one or more of the outstanding 'disarmament' propositions, to work with the Soviet Union, and others as appropriate, on the technical problems involved in international controls. We both recognize that international control would be necessary. Indeed, your present letter to me speaks of 'the establishment of the necessary international control for the discontinuance of tests'.

What is 'necessary'! The question raises problems of considerable complexity, given the present possibility of conducting some types of tests under conditions of secrecy.

If there is ever to be an agreed limitation or suspension of testing, and the United States hopes and believes that this will in due course come about as part of a broad disarmament agreement, plans for international control should be in instant readiness. Why should we not at once put our technicians to work to study together and advise as to what specific control measures are necessary if there is to be a dependable and agreed disarmament program!

The United Nations General Assembly has called for technical disarmament studies, in relation both to nuclear and conventional armaments. The United States says 'yes'. I urge, Mr. Chairman, that the Soviet Union should also say 'yes'. Then we can at once begin the preliminaries necessary to larger things.

Sincerely,

DWIGHT D. EISENHOWER

19. Statement by the Soviet Minister for Foreign Affairs, Mr. Gromyko, regarding flights by United States aircraft with H-bombs towards Soviet frontiers, Moscow, 18 April 1958[2]

The Soviet government has learned that recently aircraft of the United States air force carrying atom and hydrogen bombs have repeatedly flown across the Arctic areas in the direction of the frontiers of the U.S.S.R. on orders from their command.

It transpires from *United Press* reports, confirmed by spokesmen of the United States air force command, that such flights are made whenever the screens of American radar installations of the so-called advance warning system show vague shapes which American observers take for guided

---

[1] For President Eisenhower's letters to Mr. Bulganin of 12 January 1958 and 15 February 1958, see *D.S.B.*, 27 January 1958, pp. 122–7, and *D.S.B.*, 10 March 1958, pp. 373–6. This correspondence between the President and Mr. Bulganin was similar in content to the letters of January and February 1958 between Mr. Macmillan and Mr. Bulganin printed in *Documents for 1957*.   [2] *Soviet News*, 21 April 1958.

missiles or ballistic rockets. Subsequent checks have shown that the reasons for these actions by American bombers, unheard of in peacetime, have been either electronic interference or meteoric showers.

American generals plead that so far United States aircraft have returned to their bases from half way as soon as it has become clear that the alarm was false. But what will happen if these generals, whose nerves, as the facts show, frequently play them false, do not realise in time that the meteor they are seeing is not a guided missile, and American aircraft proceed with their mission and approach the Soviet Union's frontier? Is it not clear that the interests of security would require instant measures on the part of the U.S.S.R. to eliminate the threat to the Soviet people?

And what would happen if the Soviet air force acted as the American air force is now doing? After all, Soviet radar screens also show meteors and electronic interference. If, in these circumstances, Soviet planes carrying atom and hydrogen bombs were to fly in the direction of the United States and its bases in other states, the two air fleets, sighting each other somewhere over the Arctic wastes, would draw the natural conclusion that an enemy attack had indeed taken place, and mankind would find itself plunged into the vortex of an atomic war.

These flights by American bombers are too dangerous a game for one to agree to its continuation. The danger is all the greater since United States aircraft, carrying the same deadly load, are flying round the clock over the territories of many West European countries.

All this shows that mankind has on several occasions been on the brink of another war which could have flared up instantly through irresponsible or provocative actions on the part of the United States military command, and the peoples have not even suspected what danger has been looming over the world. It is not for nothing that it is being said with alarm, both in Western Europe and in the United States itself, that whenever American bombers have taken to the air with their load and set out on their course, they have been flying towards World War III.

The government of the U.S.S.R. regards these actions by the United States military command as a dangerous provocation against peace.

The Soviet government would not like to believe that these actions of the American air force are taken with the sanction of the government of the United States and President Eisenhower personally. Yet no one has stated the contrary; no one has stated that these actions are arbitrary acts of the military command and that the government of the United States condemns them and will not permit a repetition of them.

The Soviet people, engrossed as they are in peaceful creative labour and striving sincerely to live in peace and friendship with all other peoples, cannot but feel profoundly indignant about these actions of the American air force.

Equally understandable is the alarm and indignation of the European peoples, who see in these actions a manifestation of the 'growing madness' of the forces hostile to peace. Reckless flights by American bombers are extending the fearful shadow of atomic war to the British and the French, to the people of Western Germany, to the peoples of all countries which have been bound hand and foot by military commitments to the United States and which have allowed American atomic and rocket bases to be built on their territories.

One must be blind not to see in our time the dangerous consequences that this juggling with atomic and hydrogen bombs can have for the United States itself, for millions upon millions of Americans.

The peoples of all countries are coming to realise that certain groups in the United States are doing literally everything they can to keep the world on the brink of war and that this brink, as their actions show, may be overstepped in a matter of hours. The world is finding itself in a position in which atomic war can result from the slightest mistake on the part of an American technician, from carelessness, miscalculation or a wrong conclusion on the part of some American officer.

The Soviet government has repeatedly given warning of the danger to peace involved in the policy of an unbridled arms race and sabre rattling which is being pursued by the United States and the leaders of the North Atlantic bloc, and has insisted that the international atmosphere be cleansed of the poison of the 'cold war.' If any additional proof were required of the danger this policy presents to the peoples, it would be difficult to find a more striking example than the adventurist sorties by American planes with atom and hydrogen bombs in the direction of the Soviet frontiers.

It appears that the men shaping the policy of the United States—men who have been trying for many years to frighten the American people and their allies with a mythical threat of war on the part of socialist countries and who are doing their best to foment war hysteria—have in the end fallen victims to their own propaganda. The trouble is, however, that their measures born of war hysteria go far beyond the United States and constitute a grave threat to other peoples. It is worthy of note that all this is happening at a time when preparations are being made for a summit meeting to ease international tension and reduce the danger of rocket and atomic war.

It would seem natural to expect the governments of all nations to refrain at least from taking steps which, in this situation, can complicate the preparations and the holding of talks that can have historic importance for the destinies of the peoples. However, the United States, which is one of the great powers principally responsible for maintaining world peace, is acting in a diametrically opposite direction and in defiance of the interests of peace and international co-operation. Small wonder, therefore, that any efforts to ease tension and hasten a summit conference should be coming up against unceasing resistance from that quarter.

While the Soviet Union, desirous of contributing to the utmost to an improvement of the international situation, halting the 'cold war' and creating the necessary climate of confidence between states, is going ahead with extensive reductions of its armed forces and has not even hesitated to suspend unilaterally all atomic and hydrogen weapon tests, the United States is reacting to this noble peace move of the Soviet Union with defiant actions of its military aircraft.

If these undertakings of the United States are meant to intimidate the Soviet Union, that is a waste of effort. The Soviet people, steeled as they are in stern tests, have sufficiently strong nerves, and their armed forces have everything needed to ensure the reliable protection of the peaceful life of the Soviet people and, if need be, to deal a crushing retaliatory blow at any aggressor.

The government of the U.S.S.R., which has invariably had as the supreme aim of its foreign policy the ensuring of world peace through the progressive enforcement of the principles of the peaceful co-existence of all nations, emphatically protests against the actions of the American air force as being actions dangerous to peace, and demands that an immediate end be put to the practice of sending bombers carrying atom and hydrogen bombs towards the frontiers of the Soviet Union.

The Soviet government appeals to the governments of all other countries to raise their voices in protest and to press for the peoples to be relieved of the danger inherent in the provocative actions of American military aircraft.

Taking into account the grave threat which these flights represent to the peace of the world, the Soviet government is submitting the question of stopping them to the Security Council of the United Nations.

Last December the 12th session of the United Nations General Assembly unanimously approved a resolution on the peaceful co-existence of nations.[1] Expressing the common will of the peoples, the General Assembly drew attention to the need to ease international tension and called upon the members of the United Nations to work for the strengthening of world peace and for the promotion of friendly relations and co-operation. The United States delegation, too, voted for that resolution. Yet such acts of the United States as the dispatch of planes with nuclear weapons towards the frontiers of the Soviet Union cannot be regarded as being compatible with the obligations arising for the governments from that resolution.

[1] Resol. 1236 (XII) adopted by the General Assembly at the 731st meeting on 14 December 1957 by 77 votes to 0, with one abstention (China), see G.A.O.R., 12th Session, Supplement No. 18 (A/3805), p. 5.

The forum of the United Nations, including the latest session of the General Assembly, has more than once been used by representatives of many countries to sound the alarm and express disquiet over the fact that the sinister danger of a war catastrophe is looming larger because of the arms race and the fomenting of the 'cold war.' These fears are amply justified by the present war preparations of the United States and the N.A.T.O. countries that are following in the wake of its policies, and by its obvious intention of increasing international tension to breaking point, as it were.

It is the Soviet government's conviction that no one who has the cause of peace at heart and who is justifiably concerned over the destinies of the peoples, over the destinies of his kith and kin, can fail to add his voice to the warning of the Soviet Union and to its efforts to remove the threat of war and preserve peace.

20. Statement by the United States Department of State denying the Soviet charge of provocative flights in the Arctic, 18 April 1958[1]

It is categorically denied that the U.S. Air Force is conducting provocative flights over the Polar regions or in the vicinity of the U.S.S.R. Mr. Gromyko's charges appear to be an attempt to raise fears of mankind in the nuclear age. What we do is public knowledge; what happens behind the Iron Curtain menacing to the free world is carefully hidden by the Soviets. We will be glad to discuss this question in the United Nations, as we are always willing to discuss there any charge made against us. The United States is ready and willing to work with all nations of the world to reduce tensions and particularly the fear of sudden surprise attack. The U.S. proposals for increasing protection against surprise attack have had as their aim not merely protection of one side against the other, but also have been designed to give each side knowledge of the activity of the other so as to reduce fears and misjudgments. Until these fears are banished, the United States must take all steps necessary to protect the free world from being overwhelmed by a surprise attack.

The Strategic Air Command is the mainstay of the free world's deterrent position. It has been successful in accomplishing this mission for the past decade. It can only accomplish its mission of deterrence in the future if it is well known that it is so trained, so equipped, and so situated that it cannot be surprised and destroyed on the ground by an enemy. Therefore, it has in the past, and will continue in the future, to maintain its high state of efficiency through constant practice. All these training exercises, however, are designed to maintain the force within areas which

<hr />

[1] *D.S.B.*, 5 May 1958, pp. 728–9.

by no stretch of the imagination could be considered provocative to the U.S.S.R. So far the SAC force has never been launched except in carefully planned and controlled exercises and practices. Should there be a real alert, based on a warning of a possible attack, the force would be launched under a procedure which makes certain that no SAC airplane can pass beyond proper bounds far from the Soviet Union or its satellites without additional unequivocal orders which can come only from the President of the United States. The procedures are in no sense provocative and could not possibly be the accidental cause of war.

21. Letter from the permanent representative of the Soviet Union to the United Nations, to the President of the Security Council regarding United States provocative flights towards Soviet frontiers, 18 April 1958[1]

1. I am instructed by the Government of the Union of Soviet Socialist Republics to request you to convene an urgent meeting of the Security Council to consider the question of 'Urgent measures to put an end to flights by United States military aircraft, armed with atomic and hydrogen bombs, in the direction of the frontiers of the Soviet Union'.

2. The threat to the cause of peace which has arisen as a result of the danger arising out of the numerous cases of flights in the direction of USSR territory by United States bombers carrying hydrogen bombs makes it imperative that this question should be considered without delay.

3. The Charter of the United Nations confers on the Security Council primary responsibility for the maintenance of international peace and security of peoples. The Soviet Government therefore hopes that the Security Council will give this question the most urgent consideration and will take the necessary steps to eliminate this threat to the cause of peace.

A. SOBOLEV

22. Letter from Mr. Khrushchev to President Eisenhower regarding the suspension of nuclear tests, 22 April 1958[2]

Dear Mr. President, I have received your message of April 8[3] containing a reply to my message to you, in which, on behalf of the Soviet government, I appealed to the United States government to join the Soviet Union in ending tests of atomic and hydrogen weapons.

[1] S.C.O.R., Supplement for April, May, and June 1958, Doc. S/3990. The Security Council met on 21 April 1958 to consider this question. The Soviet representative introduced a draft resolution (Doc. S/3993), later withdrawn, which consisted of paras 1, 2, and 3 of their resolution of 28 April 1958, see below, p. 78.
[2] *Soviet News*, 24 April 1958.   [3] See above, p. 62.

Why has the Soviet Union taken this decision?

In the first place, because we consider it necessary to put an end at last to the situation in which the testing of atomic and hydrogen weapons is, yet in peacetime, causing an ever-present and ever-mounting danger to the health and life of the peoples.

In the second place, in order to put an end to the manufacture of even more horrible means of annihilation, as the production of still more destructive types of weapons is in itself increasing the nuclear war menace.

In the third place we did this because we regard the ending of atomic and hydrogen weapon tests by the powers as the first practical step which is not only entirely within the bounds of the present possibilities, but makes it possible to break the deadlock in which the disarmament problem is floundering.

There have already been more than enough declarations as to the desirability of disarmament. What is now necessary is practical action. An ending of atomic and hydrogen weapon tests by all nuclear states would constitute such action. This measure is suitable as a beginning if only for the reason that its implementation will do no harm to the defence interests of any of the nuclear powers—either the U.S.S.R., the United States, or Britain and will, on the contrary, go far towards strengthening the feeling of safety of all peoples.

Lastly, it is our firm conviction that such a step would start a real shift in international relations in general, a shift in favour of international confidence, which is so essential for the solution of other international problems and for the strengthening of peace.

The initiative taken by the Soviet Union has left the solution of the problem of ending atomic and hydrogen weapon tests dependent entirely on the governments of two powers—the United States and Britain—for it is these two powers alone who, besides the Soviet Union, possess such weapons at the present time. That is why we appeal to you and to the Prime Minister of Britain, Mr. Macmillan, to support this initiative of the Soviet Union and to call a halt to your nuclear weapon tests as well.

Your negative reply to my appeal has bitterly disappointed us. I am even leaving aside the tenor of the message and the fact that it contains a number of assertions deliberately misrepresenting the Soviet position on the disarmament problem.

The main thing is that in your reply we have failed to find any evidence of the United States government's willingness to follow the example of the Soviet Union and to end the tests of atomic and hydrogen weapons, too.

Moreover, there is an attempt made in your message to question the good faith of the Soviet step. To tell you frankly, I was surprised to learn that in a statement at your press conference on April 2 you described the decision of the supreme body of the Soviet state as a 'propaganda gesture.'[1] How can one describe as propaganda an act which is directed towards putting up the first barrier to the nuclear arms race and towards safeguarding the life and health of the peoples from radiation hazards?

You found it fit to declare in your message that the Soviet Union had taken this decision after carrying out its atomic and hydrogen weapon tests. But is it not a fact that the United States has carried out a far greater number of nuclear tests than the Soviet Union has? Has the United States not had a chance, after any of these tests, of displaying initiative in the matter of halting further tests? May I assure you, Mr. President, that should the United States have been the first to take this step, we would have sincerely welcomed it.

It is well known that the talks between the powers on the suspension of nuclear tests have so far led to no agreement. But does that mean that we should put up with the situation as it is and take no steps to get this question settled? Of course not. The peoples want us to take practical steps, and it is the duty of statesmen to do everything in their power to meet the aspirations of the peoples.

Someone had to take the first step in so important a matter as ending the tests of atomic and hydrogen weapons. We have taken this step, and we now expect the government of the United States to follow suit. If one proceeds from the interests of strengthening peace and averting the danger of nuclear war, one has to recognise unequivocally that there is no reason why the United States government should not take this step.

Indeed, can the ending of atomic and hydrogen weapon tests by the United States, following the Soviet Union, in any way harm the United States' security interests or her prestige? Certainly not. If we consider the view that the United States needs tests to perfect her atomic and hydrogen weapons, then, since the United States has already carried out a far greater number of such tests than the Soviet Union has, she does not stand to lose from ending the tests of atomic and hydrogen weapons, as the Soviet Union has already stopped them.

With atomic tests ended, all parties would find themselves on equal terms from the point of view of their security interests. One could object to the ending of nuclear tests, for instance, if one of the parties wished to gain military or strategic advantage at the expense of another. However, I think, Mr. President, you will agree that none of the parties should strive for that.

As to the considerations of prestige, I think you will agree with me if I say that a power acting in the interests of peace will never do harm to its

[1] For the transcript of President Eisenhower's press conference of 2 April 1958, see *New York Times*, 3 April 1958.

prestige. On the contrary, the peoples will only be grateful to any power for taking action to maintain peace. It is never too late to do a good thing.

In your reply you mention a possibility of some kind of tests being carried out in secrecy, thus intimating that there will be no means of checking up on the ending of tests and that there is room for deception. This view cannot be accepted because the actual state of things is entirely different. There are such apparatus, such appliances and such methods of detection available at present which can register any explosions of atomic or hydrogen weapons, wherever they may be. You have yourself spoken of this. Thus, no state can break its obligation to end atomic and hydrogen weapon tests without other states learning of this.

It remains for me to add that the Soviet government, far from objecting to the establishment of a system of control over the suspension of atomic and hydrogen weapon tests, has made its own concrete proposals to this effect. Unfortunately, the western powers have not accepted the proposals of the Soviet Union, and it has so far been impossible to reach agreement on control over the ending of atomic and hydrogen weapon tests.

There is no need for me to emphasise here the great moral and political responsibility which the states would assume by announcing the suspension of atomic and hydrogen weapon tests. Can one imagine any state nowadays breaking the obligations it has assumed, knowing in advance that it will expose itself in the eyes of the peoples?

You say further that an ending of nuclear tests must be a component part of a largescale disarmament agreement. One cannot bring oneself to accept this view, mindful of the many years of what have, in effect, been fruitless talks on disarmament. Competent scientists are already warning us of the dangerous consequences which radioactive fall-out entails for the health of people all over the world. What, then, Mr. President, is in store for us if talk of disarmament is to be accompanied by the testing of still more destructive means of annihilation? Is it not obvious that the deleterious character of radioactive fall-out resulting from nuclear tests will by no means diminish if the staging of tests is announced in advance and the tests are observed by representatives of different countries?

There is only one way of putting an end to the mounting danger to human health, and that is, by ending all kinds of atomic and hydrogen weapon tests. Such a decision by the three powers possessing these weapons would, at the same time, be a major practical contribution to reducing international tension and increasing international confidence. Should the United States and Britain follow the Soviet Union in ending the tests of atomic and hydrogen weapons, that would, beyond all doubt, contribute also to the solution of other unsettled international problems, including that of disarmament.

These are the remarks I find it necessary to make on the question of ending atomic and hydrogen weapon tests.

In your message, Mr. President, you recall—as if to counter-balance the U.S.S.R.'s proposal to end atomic and hydrogen weapon tests—your earlier proposals for the 'open skies', for the use of outer space for peaceful purposes and for stopping the production of fissile materials for military aims.

I should like to say, in this connection, that the Soviet Union's position on all of these subjects is well known.

We have declared more than once, and say it again, that flights by aircraft of one country over the territory of another, which is what the 'open skies' plan provides for, do not further in any way the solution of the disarmament problem.

The peoples of our countries will hardly feel very safe and have peace and tranquillity if, at a time of friction and distrust between us, American planes start flying up and down our land while Soviet planes will patrol the American sky. Wouldn't it be more correct to expect the opposite? In conditions when all our proposals to ban atomic and hydrogen weapons, or at least to renounce their use, are categorically rejected, when preparations for nuclear war are underway—as is attested to by the decisions of N.A.T.O.'s December session[1] and the continual and intensive construction of more and more military bases which, as openly admitted by some statesmen and military leaders of the United States and other countries of the North Atlantic Alliance, are designed for striking 'an atomic blow' at the Soviet Union—in these conditions air surveying might increase international tension and suspicion among the peoples. Far from helping to eliminate the 'cold war' and to establish friendly relations among states, this would play into the hands of the forces which are casting about for a pretext to plunge mankind into the abyss of a devastating nuclear war.

In this connection I should like to say that we in the Soviet Union could not overlook the reports saying that the United States military command had already repeatedly sent planes of the Strategic Air Force loaded with hydrogen bombs towards the U.S.S.R. According to these reports, orders for the take-off were given in view of the American radar stations' signals that Soviet guided missiles were allegedly approaching United States territory. It goes without saying that no Soviet missiles had ever threatened, or threaten the United States, and as one should have expected, American radar stations are giving wrong signals.

[1] See *Documents* for 1957, pp. 404–10, for the declaration and communiqué of the North Atlantic Council of 19 December 1957. Para. 20 declared that '. . . , N.A.T.O. has decided to establish stocks of nuclear warheads, which will be readily available for the defence of the Alliance in case of need. In view of the present Soviet policies in the field of new weapons, the Council has also decided that intermediate range ballistic missiles will have to be put at the disposal of the Supreme Allied Commander Europe.'

It is unnecessary for me to say how dangerous to the cause of peace are such flights of American planes loaded with hydrogen bombs towards the frontiers of the Soviet Union. Is it not clear that in these conditions a simple mistake in the transmission of signals might trigger off a world catastrophe.

Just imagine for a minute, Mr. President, what would happen if the Soviet command, acting in the way the American military command is doing now, sent planes loaded with atom and hydrogen bombs in the direction of the United States on the grounds that radar stations were sounding warnings of approaching American military planes, or if the Soviet military command, in reply to the provocative flights of the American aircraft, decided in its turn to send Soviet military planes loaded with hydrogen bombs in the direction of the United States. And in these conditions, such flights of Soviet planes would be perfectly justified.

It is sufficient to put the question this way and it at once becomes clear how dangerous such actions of the American command are. You might say that my definitions are too sharp when I speak about these irresponsible and provocative actions of the American military command. However, I am compelled to speak in this manner by the alarm I feel when I think that in the climate of war hysteria, so characteristic of certain circles in your country, a world tragedy, incurring the loss of millions upon millions of human lives, may occur unexpectedly to all of us.

We expect the United States government immediately to put an end to this dangerous playing with fire.

Then I would like to deal with the question of using outer space for peaceful purposes.

During the exchange of opinions in connection with the preparations for a summit meeting, you suggested that this conference discuss the problem of banning the use of outer space for warlike purposes. We attentively examined your proposal and stated that we were ready to consider at the summit meeting the question of banning the use of outer space for warlike purposes and of closing down foreign military bases on other people's territories. In doing so we proceeded from the assumption that the solution of this problem should take into account the security interests of the Soviet Union, the United States and other countries. The Soviet government's proposals on the questions of banning the use of outer space for warlike purposes, closing down foreign bases on other people's territories and international co-operation in studying outer space are in keeping with this. We are prepared to sign an agreement banning the use of outer space for warlike purposes and permitting the launching of rockets into outer space only under an agreed international research programme. At the same time we cannot ignore the fact that atomic and hydrogen weapons can be carried to targets not only by intercontinental rockets but also by intermediate and close-range missiles, as well as by conventional bombers stationed at numerous American military bases situated in close proximity to the Soviet Union.

Your proposal on the use of outer space for peaceable purposes actually envisages the prohibition of intercontinental ballistic rockets only, and leaves out other important aspects of the problem. It will be easily seen that you suggest a solution of the problem which meets the security interests of the United States alone, but contains no provisions for removing the danger to the security of the Soviet Union and of many other states arising from the existence of numerous American military bases in other countries. The point of your proposal is to ward off from yourselves a retaliatory blow via outer space through banning intercontinental ballistic rockets. It goes without saying that one cannot agree to such an unjust solution, which would place one side in a privileged position with respect to the other side. We declared, therefore, that the agreement banning the use of outer space for warlike purposes must also provide for the closing down of foreign military bases situated on the territories of other countries, primarily in Europe, the Middle East and North Africa. Such a solution would be just, in our opinion, inasmuch as it is in full accord with the security interests of the United States and the Soviet Union, and of other countries on whose territories American military bases are situated. One may say with assurance that they would only profit by such a solution of the problem, inasmuch as the closing down of bases would fully accord with the national security interests of these states by removing the deadly menace which threatens their populations in the case of war.

In your message, Mr. President, you entirely ignore our proposal and declare that you expect the Soviet government to accept your proposal. The impression is that an attempt is being made to impose upon us such a solution of the problem of utilising outer space which would be in the interests of the United States alone and would entirely ignore the interests of the Soviet Union. Such a lopsided approach is absolutely impermissible in negotiations between independent states and cannot, of course, result in an agreement.

In your letter, Mr. President, speaking about the peaceful uses of atomic energy, you are attempting to present matters in such a way as if the United States is a champion of the peaceful use of atomic energy. This does not tally with actual facts, however. Indeed, if we look at the facts, we cannot but admit that the Soviet Union resolutely advocates the use of atomic energy not for the purpose of exterminating human beings but for fully channelling it to satisfy mankind's peaceful requirements. Since the very first day when this problem emerged, the Soviet government has been consistently working in the United Nations for banning the use of atomic and hydrogen weapons of all kinds, for their removal from national armaments and the destruction of stockpiles of them, for ending the manufacture of such weapons, with international control over the implementation of these measures.

But what has prevented the acceptance of these proposals, the purpose of which was to lay the foundations for using atomic energy for peaceful purposes only? As is known, the United States, together with its western allies, also from the very first days of the emergence of this problem have been opposing these proposals and have prevented their acceptance, continuing to base its foreign policy on the use of nuclear weapons. Thus there has been a deep discrepancy between the words of the United States about its desire to channel atomic energy for peaceful uses and its deeds.

Naturally, the Soviet Union, which feels itself in sacred duty bound to relieve mankind of the menace of a devastating nuclear war, could not and cannot agree to such proposals which would lead us away from the prohibition of atomic and nuclear weapons and play into the hands of the forces which want the menace of a nuclear war to hang constantly over mankind as the sword of Damocles.

Unfortunately, your proposal of April 8 contains no proposals aimed at solving the disarmament problem and removing the danger of a nuclear war. Instead, you suggest that we study the question of necessary control measures, appointing appropriate experts for this purpose. But can technical experts do anything for the solution of the disarmament problem if no agreement on this score has been reached between governments? In the course of 13 years of disarmament talks hundreds of speeches have been made and mountains of paper covered with writing on the subject of control, but this has failed to bring us a single step nearer to the solution of the disarmament problem. It is impermissible that the solution of the disarmament problem itself be dragged out indefinitely under the pretext of studying problems of control.

Far from ever objecting to control, the Soviet Union has itself repeatedly submitted proposals for establishing a reliable control system over the implementation of concrete disarmament measures. The refusal of the western powers, however, to take any practical steps towards disarmament has made pointless the question of control, inasmuch as one cannot, naturally, control the fulfilment by states of obligations which do not exist.

The present international situation calls, not for general professions of the desirability of disarmament, but for concrete deeds in this sphere on the part of all states, above all the great powers, which bear the main responsibility for the destiny of peace.

The Soviet Union has made its contribution to the cause of relaxing international tension, to the cause of peace. From now on not a single atom or hydrogen bomb will be exploded by the Soviet Union, unless the United States and Britain compel us to do so. We appeal to the governments of the United States and Britain: Do not initiate a chain reaction of experimental explosions of atom and hydrogen bombs.

Now the decision of the question of whether nuclear tests will be ended for ever or will continue, polluting the air and increasing the danger of a devastating atomic war, depends on two powers alone—the United States and Britain—and the governments of the United States and Britain bear a great responsibility before the world.

It is possible, Mr. President, that you do not agree with all the considerations I have set forth, and yet I would like to express the wish: Is it not possible to put an end to polemics over this question, to let bygones be bygones and agree that the United States and Britain, like the Soviet Union, end tests of atomic and hydrogen weapons? I assure you, humanity would heave a sigh of relief if all three powers manufacturing atomic and hydrogen weapons ceased tests of these weapons.

It is our profound hope, Mr. President, that you will use all your authority and influence for these noble aims.

Sincerely yours,

NIKITA KHRUSHCHOV

23. United States draft resolution recommending the establishment of a zone of international inspection against surprise attack, 28 April 1958[1]

THE SECURITY COUNCIL,

Considering further the item of the Union of Soviet Socialist Republics of 18 April 1958,

Noting the development, particularly in the Soviet Union and the United States of America, of growing capabilities of massive surprise attack,

Believing that the establishment of measures to allay fears of such massive surprise attack would help reduce tensions and would contribute to the increase of confidence among States,

Noting the statements of certain members of the Council regarding the particular significance of the Arctic area,

Recommends that there be established promptly the northern zone of international inspection against surprise attack, comprising the area north of the Arctic Circle with certain exceptions and additions, that was

[1] S.C.O.R. Supplement for April, May, and June 1958, Doc. S/3995. The draft resolution was not adopted in the vote on 2 May 1958; 10 nations voted in favour of the resolution: the U.S.S.R. voted against it.

considered during August 1957 by the Sub-Committee of the United Nations Disarmament Commission, which is composed of Canada, France, the Union of Soviet Socialist Republics, the United Kingdom and the United States of America;[1]

2. *Calls upon* the five States mentioned, together with Denmark and Norway, and any other States having territory north of the Arctic Circle which desire to have such territory included in the zone of international inspection, at once to designate representatives to participate in immediate discussions with a view to agreeing on the technical arrangements required;

3. *Decides* to keep this matter on its agenda for such further consideration as may be required.[2]

24. Soviet draft resolution regarding United States provocative flights towards Soviet frontiers, 28 April 1958[3]

THE SECURITY COUNCIL,

Having examined the question submitted by the Soviet Union concerning 'Urgent measures to put an end to flights by United States military aircraft armed with atomic and hydrogen bombs in the direction of the frontiers of the Soviet Union',

Considering that the practice of making such flights increases tension in international relations, constitutes a threat to the security of nations and, if continued, may lead to a breach of world peace and the unleashing of an atomic war of annihilation,

Calls upon the United States of America to refrain from sending its military aircraft carrying atomic and hydrogen bombs towards the frontiers of other States for the purpose of creating a threat to their security or staging military demonstrations;

Mindful of the necessity for taking steps as soon as possible to avert the threat of atomic warfare and ease international tension,

1. *Notes with satisfaction* that preliminary talks are in progress between the interested States with a view to the convening of a summit conference to discuss a number of urgent problems, including the question of drawing up measures to preclude the danger of surprise attack;

2. *Expresses the hope* that the summit conference will be held at the earliest possible date.

[1] Official Records of the Disarmament Commission, Supplement for January to December 1957, Doc. DC/113, Annex 1.

[2] On 29 April 1958, Mr. Cabot Lodge, the U.S. permanent representative, elaborated on the United States proposal, see S.C.O.R., 814th meeting, especially paras 36–46. President Eisenhower in his letter to Mr. Khrushchev of 28 April, asked that a meeting of experts be set up to study 'the practical problems involved'. See facing page.

[3] S.C.O.R., Supplement for April, May, and June 1958, Doc. S/3997. The resolution was rejected on 2 May 1958, by 9 votes to one (U.S.S.R.) with one abstention (Sweden).

25. Letter from President Eisenhower to Mr. Khrushchev regarding the United States proposal for an international inspection system in the Arctic, 28 April 1958[1]

Dear Mr. Chairman: I have your communication of April twenty-second in reply to mine of April eighth. I regret that it is not an affirmative response to my proposal.

You refer in your letter to the question raised recently by the Soviet Union in the United Nations Security Council which also touches upon the disarmament question.[2] I am sure that you would agree that with the growing capabilities in the Soviet Union and the United States of massive surprise attack it is necessary to establish measures to allay fears. The United States has just asked the Security Council to reconvene in order to consider the establishment of an international inspection system for the Arctic zone.[3] The United States has submitted a constructive proposal to this end. I urge you to join with us in supporting the resolution of the United States now before the Council. Your support of this proposal and subsequent cooperation would help to achieve a significant first step. It would help to reduce tensions, it would contribute to an increase of confidence among states, and help to reduce the mutual fears of surprise attack.

The United States is determined that we will ultimately reach an agreement on disarmament. In my letter of April eighth, I again proposed an internationally supervised cutoff of the use of new fissionable materials for weapons purposes and the reduction of existing weapons stocks by transfer to peaceful purposes; an agreed limitation or suspension of testing; 'open skies', and the international use of outer space for peaceful purposes.

As an effective means of moving toward ultimate agreement on these matters and other disarmament matters, I proposed that we start our technical people to work immediately upon the practical problems involved. These studies were called for by the United Nations General Assembly. They would include the practical problems of supervision and control which, you and I agree, are in any event indispensable to dependable disarmament agreements.

The solution of these practical problems will take time. I am unhappy that valuable time is now being wasted.

[1] *D.S.B.*, 19 May 1958, pp. 811–12.
[2] The question concerned 'Urgent measures to put an end to flights by United States military aircraft, armed with atomic and hydrogen bombs, in the direction of the frontiers of the Soviet Union'. See above, p. 69.
[3] The Security Council met on 29 April and 2 May to consider a draft resolution submitted by the United States, see above p. 77, and a draft resolution submitted by the U.S.S.R., see facing page.

You say that we must first reach a final political agreement before it is worthwhile even to initiate the technical studies. But such studies would, in fact, facilitate the reaching of the final agreement you state you desire.

For example, why could not designated technical people agree on what would be required so that you would know if we violated an agreement to suspend testing and we would know if you should commit a violation?

Would not both sides be in a better position to reach agreements if we had a common accepted understanding as to feasibility of detection or as to method of inspecting against surprise attack?

Studies of this kind are the necessary preliminaries to putting political decisions actually into effect. The completion of such technical studies in advance of a political agreement would obviate a considerable period of delay and uncertainty. In other words, with the practicalities already worked out, the political agreement could begin to operate very shortly after it was signed and ratified.

I re-emphasize that these studies are without prejudice to our respective positions on the timing and interdependence of various aspects of disarmament.

Mr. Chairman, my offer to you still and always will remain open. I hope you will reconsider and accept it. In that way we both can make an important contribution to the cause of just and lasting peace.

Sincerely,

DWIGHT D. EISENHOWER

26. Letter from Mr. Khrushchev to President Eisenhower regarding the suspension of nuclear tests and the United States proposal for an international inspection zone in the Arctic, 9 May 1958[1]

Dear Mr. President, I have received your message of April 28. Unfortunately, I failed to find in it the American government's reply to our appeal on the ending of atomic and hydrogen weapon tests, which was dealt with in my letter of April 22. Yet the need for solving that problem is today all the more pressing since attempts are being made to thwart the efforts to end nuclear weapon tests once and for all. What I have in mind are the recent tests of nuclear bombs by the United States and the United Kingdom.[2]

I shall not conceal from you our feelings of regret at the fact that the governments of the United States and the United Kingdom have found it possible to hold these tests. Such actions do not in any way accord with the peaceable professions that have been repeatedly made recently by the governments of the United States and the United Kingdom. Such actions,

---

[1] *Soviet News*, 12 May 1958.   [2] See fn. 1 on p. 103, below.

constituting an open challenge to the will of the peoples, can obviously only throw the world back to its initial position on this vital issue and once again cause a chain reaction of experimental explosions of atom and hydrogen bombs. We believe that everything should be done to avoid such a course of events.

Under the circumstances, the responsibility resting with the governments of our two countries is particularly great. A decision by the American government to end nuclear weapon tests would unquestionably be duly appreciated by the peoples of the world as a great contribution to the cause of easing international tension and removing the menace of atomic war.

I must tell you frankly that we find it difficult to understand what prevents the American government from taking such a step. The ending of nuclear tests by the United States after the Soviet Union has done so would not harm in any way American security interests and would not place your country at a disadvantage with respect to other countries. Speaking of this aspect of the matter, the ending of atomic and hydrogen weapon tests by all the nuclear powers would place the Soviet Union and its allies in the Warsaw Treaty at a disadvantage compared with the United States and other N.A.T.O. members, because, as you are well aware, the U.S.S.R. has made considerably fewer test explosions of nuclear weapons than the United States and the United Kingdom have. Nevertheless we have ended our nuclear tests unilaterally, desiring to make the first practical step towards ending the atomic weapons race.

It is often said in the United States that in a situation in which the necessary confidence in relations between states is lacking, an agreement to end nuclear tests could be broken and that one of the sides could continue to make such tests in secret. There is no reason for such apprehensions. Such a possibility is precluded by the methods of detection and the pertinent devices now available to modern science. That is why it would not be difficult to control the implementation of the agreement ending tests. You are aware, Mr. President, of the Soviet government's concrete proposals about the forms of such control advanced a year ago. Problems of control over the ending of nuclear weapon tests are, generally speaking, no obstacle to halting such tests immediately.

We believe that it is necessary first of all for the United States and the United Kingdom to halt their nuclear weapon tests, as the Soviet Union has already done, and that this question of principle should be settled without delay. That is clearly the shortest route towards a solution of the problem of ending nuclear weapon tests. In my correspondence with you I have already expressed apprehension lest, in the present circumstances, when there is no unity of opinion among the nuclear powers on this crucial problem of the need for ending nuclear bomb tests without delay, the referring of this problem for study to technical experts might lead to a delay in the solution of this pressing problem. We must not blind ourselves to the fact that such a situation may be used by those who stand to gain from such a delay. And conversely, if the United States and the United Kingdom should also adopt a decision to end nuclear weapon tests, that fact itself would create a situation in which each side would see to it that all the other powers which have pledged themselves to end nuclear weapon tests fulfilled their obligations.

Your messages make it clear that you regard the work of experts as very important in studying technical details pertaining to control over the implementation of an agreement ending nuclear weapon tests. Bearing this in mind, in spite of our serious doubts, of which I have just spoken, we are prepared to try that way as well.

The Soviet government agrees to have either side appoint experts, who should start work immediately on studying the means of detecting possible violations of an agreement to end nuclear tests, with the proviso that that work should be completed in the shortest time possible, with the term agreed upon beforehand.

At the same time, I would like to call on you once again, Mr. President, to support the initiative of the Soviet Union in ending nuclear weapon tests, in order to make possible the solution of that problem once and for all, which is so ardently hoped for by the peoples of the world.

The present international situation is such that there is particular need for practical steps by the powers designed to ease the existing tension. This is adequately proved by such dangerous and, needless to say, profoundly abnormal phenomena for peacetime as the systematic flights by American Strategic Air Force planes loaded with atom and hydrogen bombs in the direction of the Soviet Union's frontiers and over the territories of other countries, a fact to which I have already drawn your attention in my previous letter. In your message, Mr. President, you intimate that a means against these dangerous actions may be the establishment of an international system of inspection for the Arctic zone, as proposed by the United States. But it must be stated that this proposal of the United States government does not in any way remove the threat to international peace represented by the current actions of the American air force.

It is true that the air route across the North Pole area is the shortest distance between the U.S.S.R. and the United States and it is therefore an important strategic area of particular significance in view of the existence of rocket weapons. That is just why the Soviet Union, desirous of preventing that area from becoming a centre of military conflict between our countries, believes it necessary that no action should be taken within its bounds which could lead to tragic consequences. That is just why we believe that the dangerous flights by American war planes with atom and hydrogen bombs in the Arctic zone must be stopped. This requires only one thing—a pertinent order on the part of the United States government.

Unfortunately, the United States government's proposal concerning the establishment of a system of inspection for the Arctic does not in any way solve this problem, for in advancing that proposal the American government has not even promised that, should it be adopted, the flights by American nuclear bombers in the direction of the Soviet Union's frontiers would be stopped. The American Secretary of State, Mr. Dulles, recently spoke indirectly of the possibility of reducing to a minimum the flights against which the Soviet Union has protested.

There is yet another important factor that we cannot ignore: The Arctic is not the only area from which an attack can be made against our country. We have to reckon also with such facts as the existence of American military bases on the territory of a number of states not far removed from the Soviet Union's frontiers, such as, for example, in Britain, France, Western Germany, Italy and Turkey. Under the circumstances we cannot avoid the inescapable conclusion that the American government's proposal to establish an inspection zone in the Arctic does not spring from its desire to ensure the interests of universal peace and security, but is designed to gain unilateral advantages for the United States of America. However, it appears obvious that a genuine solution of the problems affecting the security interests of many states can be found only if the narrow egoistical purposes of certain states are not allowed to be served to the detriment of the interests of other countries.

Allow me to remind you, Mr. President, that the Soviet Union, in its desire to meet the United States half-way, long ago proposed the establishment of zones of aerial inspection in order to preclude a sudden attack in Central Europe, as well as in the Far East and in the corresponding part of the United States. These proposals of ours were objective and took due cognisance of the security interests of all the sides concerned. However, although the United States had previously said much about the desirability of designating certain areas for aerial inspection, the Soviet Union's concrete proposals on the subject have not yet met with any positive response on the part of the United States government. I wish to emphasise that these Soviet proposals remain in force.

We must needs speak of yet another question on which we should like to have everything cleared up between us. The United States has lately been reproaching the Soviet Union for not agreeing to the American proposal to establish an inspection zone for the Arctic area although the majority of the Security Council had voted for that proposal. I must tell you frankly that the method used by the United States in the Security Council, during examination of the question tabled by the Soviet Union about the need to end the flights of American nuclear bombers in the direction of the Soviet Union's frontiers, does not, in our opinion, testify to a serious desire to reach agreement on a mutually acceptable basis, but testifies to attempts to exert pressure on the Soviet Union by using the majority in the Security Council. It is common knowledge that that majority in the Security Council is composed of the votes of countries dependent in one way or another, primarily economically, on the United States. Thus, the Security Council in its present composition cannot be regarded as an impartial arbiter, and that is why it has recently ceased to play the important role in the maintenance of international peace and security which devolves upon it by virtue of the United Nations Charter.

The Soviet government is sincerely desirous of reaching an equitable and mutually acceptable agreement with the United States and the other western countries. We wish to see peaceful relations between our states, relations that are stable and improving every day. We were guided by this when we took such a step as the unilateral ending of nuclear weapon tests and in introducing our proposal for a meeting with the participation of the heads of government.

We should like to see the United States government show a similar desire for mutual understanding and co-operation with us, in the interests of both our countries and in the interests of universal peace. Needless to say, this requires a new approach to international affairs, different from the one which was exemplified by the recent speech of the American Secretary of State in New Hampshire, in which Mr. Dulles reiterated all the old arguments and inventions of the opponents of an agreement with the Soviet Union and the opponents of a *détente*.[1] To proceed in one's foreign policy from such principles is to preclude beforehand any possibility of reaching agreement. We should not like to believe that such is the purpose of the United States government.

You have repeatedly stressed, Mr. President, that the strengthening of peace requires practical deeds. We fully share your opinion and should like to hope that the United States government would approach the solution of the problem of ending nuclear weapon tests in just such a spirit.

With sincere respect,

N. S. KHRUSHCHOV

[1] Presumably the address by Mr. Dulles to the Atomic Power Institute, sponsored by the New Hampshire Council on World Affairs at Durham, N.H., on 2 May 1958; see *D.S.B.*, 19 May 1958, pp. 799–804.

27. Letter from President Eisenhower to Mr. Khrushchev regarding the suspension of nuclear tests, 24 May 1958[1]

Dear Mr. Chairman: I have your letter of May 9, 1958. I note with satisfaction that you accept, at least partially, my proposal that technical persons be designated to ascertain what would be required to supervise and control disarmament agreements, all without prejudice to our respective positions on the timing and interdependence of various aspects of disarmament.

Your letter of May ninth states that 'the Soviet Government agrees to having both sides designate experts who would immediately begin a study of methods for detecting possible violations of an agreement on the cessation of nuclear tests with a view to having this work completed at the earliest possible date, to be determined in advance.'

Experts from our side will be prepared to meet with experts from your side at Geneva, if the Swiss Government agrees, within three weeks of our learning whether these arrangements are acceptable to you. On our side, experts would be chosen on the basis of special competence. I have in mind, for example, experts who might be contributed not only from the United States, but from the United Kingdom which, like the Soviet Union and the United States, has conducted nuclear tests, and from France, which has advanced plans for testing, and possibly from other countries having experts who are advanced in knowledge of how to detect nuclear tests. We assume that the experts on the side of the Soviet Union would be similarly chosen on the basis of special competence, so as to assure that we get scientific, not political, conclusions.

I also suggest that the experts should be asked to make an initial progress report within thirty days after convening and to aim at a final report within sixty days or as soon thereafter as possible.

In view of the Charter responsibilities of the General Assembly and the Security Council of the United Nations in the field of disarmament, we would propose to keep the United Nations and its appropriate organs informed of the progress of these talks through the intermediary of the Secretary General.

I will write you further shortly regarding your statements on the problem of surprise attack and the Arctic Zone of inspection which we have proposed.

Sincerely,

DWIGHT D. EISENHOWER

[1] D.S.B., 9 June 1958, p. 939.

28. Letter from Mr. Khrushchev to President Eisenhower
regarding the suspension of nuclear tests, 31 May 1958[1]

Dear Mr. President, I have received your message of May 24[2] in reply to my letter of May 9.

Just as in your previous message, I did not find, unfortunately, a reply to such an urgent matter—which has been the subject of my previous appeals to you—as the question of immediately discontinuing the tests of atomic and hydrogen weapons.

There is no need to reiterate that in the present conditions, when the states possessing nuclear weapons have not agreed on the question of principle—the need to put an immediate end to atom and hydrogen bomb tests—the study by technical experts of the methods of detecting possible breaches of an agreement on the discontinuation of nuclear tests may lead to a delay in settling the main issue, namely, the suspension of tests. This causes us serious anxiety. That is why it would be necessary now, when we are discussing the calling of a conference of experts, to take steps so that the work of the experts would be completed at the earliest possible date—a date fixed in advance.

We agree to your proposal that the experts should begin their work within the next three weeks, bearing in mind the need to start this work as soon as possible.

In your reply you also suggest that the experts should be instructed to draft a report on the initial results of their work within 30 days, or as soon as possible after the expiry of this period.

The Soviet government considers that, in the interests of a general suspension of nuclear weapon tests at the earliest possible moment, it would be advisable to agree that all the work of the experts be concluded within three or four weeks after the opening of the conference and that the final report of the experts, with their conclusions and opinions, should be submitted within this period to the governments of the states whose experts take part in the conference.

You also say that experts might be delegated, not only by the U.S.S.R. and the United States, but also by the United Kingdom and France and, possibly, by other countries having specialists with a good knowledge in the sphere of detecting nuclear tests.

The Soviet government has no objection to this and proposes that Czechoslovak and Polish experts should also take part in the conference of experts.

---

[1] *Soviet News*, 2 June 1958. This letter was undated, but according to *Soviet News*, 2 June 1958, it was handed on 31 May 1958 by Mr. Menshikov, U.S.S.R. ambassador to the U.S., to the Department of State. It was later referred to as the letter of 30 May 1958, see, for example, the next document.

[2] See above, p. 85.

The Soviet government believes that the work of the experts should not be confined to those countries alone. That is why it is also advisable to invite to the conference experts from India and possibly some other countries.

As for the venue of the experts' conference, we of course share the opinion that Geneva is a suitable place. However, we would prefer the conference to be held in Moscow. I can assure you, Mr. President, that in Moscow all the necessary conditions will be provided for the work of the experts.

The Soviet government agrees to the proposal that the Security Council and the United Nations General Assembly be informed through the Secretary-General about the progress of the conference of experts.

I hope, Mr. President, that my considerations will be favourably received by you.

Upon receipt of your reply, the Soviet government will communicate the list of experts from the Soviet Union for the abovementioned conference.

Sincerely yours,

N. KHRUSHCHOV

29. Letter from President Eisenhower to Mr. Khrushchev regarding the suspension of nuclear tests, 10 June 1958[1]

Dear Mr. Chairman: I have your letter of May 30 and am glad to note you have accepted my proposal that technical experts meet to study the possibility of detecting violations of a possible agreement on suspension of nuclear tests. These talks would be undertaken without commitment as to the final decision on the relationship of nuclear test suspension to other more important disarmament measures I have proposed.

I propose that these discussions begin on or about July 1 in Geneva. While we appreciate your offer to hold these talks in Moscow, we believe that Geneva would be preferable from our standpoint, and note that it would be acceptable to you. The Swiss Government has agreed to this location.

With respect to participation I suggested that initially at least we adhere to the concept expressed in your letter of May 9, 1958,[2] where you say, 'the Soviet Government agrees to having both sides designate experts.' As indicated in my letter of May 24, 1958,[3] our side at this discussion will include experts from the United States, United Kingdom, France and possibly from other countries which have specialists with a thorough knowledge in the field of detecting nuclear tests, and we note that you have no objection to this. With regard to the inclusion on your

[1] D.S.B., 30 June 1958, p. 1083.   [2] See above, p. 80.   [3] See above, p. 85.

side of experts from Czechoslovakia and Poland, we have no objection to this. With respect to experts of nationalities not identified with either side, we have no objection in principle to their joining later in the discussions if it is agreed during the course of the talks that this is necessary or useful from the point of view of the purposes of the technical talks.

It may be possible for the experts to produce a final report within three or four weeks as you suggest. However, I believe that there should be enough flexibility in our arrangements to allow a little longer time if it is needed to resolve the complex technical issues involved.

I propose that further arrangements for the meeting be handled through normal diplomatic channels.

Sincerely,

DWIGHT D. EISENHOWER

30. Soviet *aide-mémoire* to the United States regarding the conference of experts to consider the means of detecting nuclear explosions, Moscow, 13 June 1958[1]

The Soviet government notes with satisfaction that the Soviet government and the government of the United States agree that a meeting of experts should be held at an early date to study the means of detecting nuclear explosions and that the work of the experts should be concluded within three or four weeks from the opening of the meeting. The Soviet government agrees to the experts beginning their work in Geneva on July 1.

The Soviet government, as it has already declared, proceeds from the assumption that the work of the experts will be concluded within a short time and that, as a result, agreement will be reached on the suspension of nuclear weapon tests by all powers possessing these weapons.

The Soviet government takes note of the United States government's affirmative reply to the proposal that the aforementioned meeting be attended by experts from the United States, Britain and France, on the one hand, and experts from the U.S.S.R., Czechoslovakia and Poland on the other, and the question of the composition of the meeting can therefore be regarded as settled.

As regards inviting experts of other countries to take part in the meeting, the Soviet government regrets that agreement has not been reached at the present stage of the talks that Indian experts should take part in the meeting from the very beginning of its work.

It is hereby made known that the Soviet Union will be represented at the meeting by the following experts: Y. K. Fyodorov, corresponding member of the U.S.S.R. Academy of Sciences; N. N. Semyonov, aca-

[1] Soviet News, 16 June 1958.

demician; I. Y. Tamm, academician; M. A. Sadovsky, corresponding member of the U.S.S.R. Academy of Sciences; O. I. Leipunsky, professor and Doctor of Physics and Mathematics; I. P. Pasechnik, scientific worker at the U.S.S.R. Academy of Sciences; K. Y. Gubkin, scientific worker at the U.S.S.R. Academy of Sciences, and S. K. Tsarapkin, head of the U.S.S.R. Foreign Ministry's department for international organisations and member of the Ministry's collegium.

In connection with the considerations expressed by the United States Ambassador in Moscow, Mr. Thompson, in a conversation with the U.S.S.R. Minister of Foreign Affairs, A. A. Gromyko, concerning certain organisational matters relating to the holding of the meeting, the Soviet government does not object to the United Nations Secretariat being enlisted to serve the meeting of experts in a technical capacity, or to minutes being taken at the meetings. The Soviet government also agrees with the view of the American side that the expenses of the meeting should be shared equally by both sides.

31. United States *aide-mémoire* to the Soviet Union regarding the conference of experts to consider the means of detecting nuclear explosions, 20 June 1958[1]

The Government of the United States of America notes the acceptance by the Government of the USSR of the proposal by the Government of the United States of America that a meeting of experts convene at Geneva on or about July 1 to consider means of detecting nuclear explosions. With regard to duration of the meeting, the Government of the United States of America considers that there is sufficient agreement between the views of the United States and the Soviet Union as set forth in the letters of President Eisenhower dated May 24 and June 10 and the letter from Premier Khrushchev dated May 30[2] to permit commencement of work by the experts. The positions of the Governments of the Soviet Union and the United States of America regarding the relationship between this meeting and cessation of nuclear tests have also been set forth in these letters.

The Government of the United States of America has proceeded on the basis of the statement in the letter of May 9, 1958,[3] from Mr. Khrushchev that 'the Soviet Government agrees to having both sides designate experts.' We note with concern that the Aide Memoire of June 13 appears to shift from this agreed concept of a panel of experts on each side, chosen on the basis of technical competence. We consider that a useful meeting of experts can best be conducted on the basis of the original concept of a panel on each side.

[1] *D.S.B.*, 7 July 1958, p. 11.   [2] See above, pp. 85, 87, and 86.   [3] See above, p. 80.

In the letter from President Eisenhower dated June 10, 1958, he stated 'As indicated in my letter of May 24, 1958, our side at this discussion will include experts from the United States, United Kingdom, France and possibly from other countries which have specialists with a thorough knowledge in the field of detecting nuclear tests, and we note that you have no objection to this.' The panel on our side is now being formed in accordance with this principle, and will include the following experts:

Dr. James B. Fisk, Vice President of Bell Telephone Laboratories and Member of the President's Science Advisory Committee;

Dr. Robert F. Bacher, Professor, California Institute of Technology and Member of the President's Science Advisory Committee;

Sir John Cockroft, Fellow of the Royal Society;

Dr. Ernest O. Lawrence, Director, University of California Radiation Laboratory;

Sir William Penney, Fellow of the Royal Society;

Professor Yves Rocard, Director, Laboratory of Physics, Ecole Normale Superieure of Paris;

Dr. Omond Solandt, Former Chairman of the Defense Research Board of Canada.

It is assumed that, since experts from Czechoslovakia and Poland as well as the Soviet Union will participate on your side, the Government of the Soviet Union within due course will transmit the names of Polish and Czechoslovakian experts on its panel.

32. Soviet *aide-mémoire* to the United States regarding the conference of experts to consider the means of detecting nuclear explosions, 24 June 1958[1]

The Soviet government notes that agreement has been reached by the parties that the conference of experts is to begin its deliberations in Geneva on July 1, and also on the duration of the work of the conference. As for the composition of the conference, one cannot help being surprised at the contention contained in the *aide-mémoire* of the United States government of June 20 concerning an alleged departure of the Soviet side from the understanding reached in this connection. The Soviet government invariably stands by the position set forth in the messages of May 9 and May 30,[2] this year, from the Chairman of the U.S.S.R. Council of Ministers, N. S. Khrushchov, to the President of the United States, Mr. Eisenhower, according to which, along with experts from the U.S.S.R. and the United States, experts from other countries possessing a good knowledge of nuclear explosion detection may take part in the conference on both sides. In its previous documents the United States government

[1] *Soviet News*, 26 June 1958.   [2] See above, pp. 80 and 86.

raised no objections to this. The Soviet government hopes that the *aide-mémoire* of June 20 does not mean that the United States government has changed its attitude on this question.

The Soviet side has already announced its agreement that the conference of experts be attended, together with the United States representatives, by representatives of the United Kingdom and France. Nor is there any objection to the participation of a Canadian representative, as stated in the *aide-mémoire* of the United States government of June 20.

The list of participants in the conference from the Soviet Union has already been given to the United States government in the *aide-mémoire* of June 13. By agreement with the governments of the Polish People's Republic and the Czechoslovak Republic, a list of experts appointed by the governments of these countries to participate in the Geneva conference is given herewith:

> From the Polish People's Republic: Marian Mensowicz, professor and doctor, chairman of the physics commission of the Polish Academy of Sciences' Committee for the Peaceful Uses of Atomic Energy; Leopold Yurkiewicz, professor and doctor, chairman of the commission for the study of air contamination of the Polish Radiological Defence Committee; and Meczislaw Blustain, doctor, head of the Polish Foreign Ministry's department for international organisations.
>
> From the Czechoslovak Republic: Cestmir Simane, engineer, director of the Czechoslovak Academy of Sciences' Nuclear Physics Institute; Professor Frantisek Behounek, corresponding member of the Czechoslovak Academy of Sciences; Professor Alois Zatopek, corresponding member of the Czechoslovak Academy of Sciences, head of the geophysical division of the physics and mathematics department of Charles University; and Zdenek Trhlik, head of the international department of the Foreign Ministry of the Czechoslovak Republic.

An expert appointed by the government of the Rumanian People's Republic, whose name and other particulars will be made known later, will also take part in the conference.

The Soviet government continues to proceed on the basis of the fact that the work of the conference of experts should promote the ending of tests of atomic and hydrogen weapons, at the earliest possible date, by all states possessing such weapons.[1]

---

[1] For the list of United States experts at the conference, see *D.S.B.*, 14 July 1958, pp. 48–49.

33. Soviet *aide-mémoire* to the United States in reply to a statement made by Mr. Dulles on 17 June, 25 June 1958[1]

On June 17 Mr. Dulles, the U.S. Secretary of State, speaking at a press conference in Washington, made a statement concerning the role of the contemplated conference of experts from the U.S.S.R., the United States and other countries to study the ways and means of detecting nuclear explosions.[2] As can be seen from the published report of this press conference, Mr. Dulles, replying to a question as to whether an agreement by the experts on methods of inspection would lead to the parties concerned undertaking the obligation to stop nuclear weapon tests, declared that the work of the experts must be carried out without prejudice to the question whether tests would be temporarily stopped or not.

It is impossible to agree with such an attitude on the part of the U.S. Secretary of State. The conference can be fruitful only if it leads to positive results. But in what way can the positive nature of these results be determined other than by whether they do or do not ensure that in the course of the experts' work the final goal is reached—the goal of the universal and immediate discontinuation of experimental explosions of atomic and hydrogen bombs? Otherwise what sense is there, in general, in calling such a conference and what is the sense of sending experts to it? If the results of the experts' work do not lead to reaching this final goal, then all their work will become a fruitless waste of time. Moreover, there are grounds for fearing that in such an event the conference of experts would become a means of deceiving the peoples, who would entertain the false illusion that something was being done to bring nearer the ending of nuclear weapon tests, while in actual fact matters would be at a standstill.

In view of the declaration by the U.S. Secretary of State, the legitimate question arises: For what purpose was the prosposal for a conference of experts made? In the light of this statement made by the Secretary of State, the logical conclusion seems to be that this proposal was made in the hope that the Soviet government would turn it down. And as this did not happen, attempts are being made to seal the doom of the conference in advance.

It should be frankly stated that this is not a new method. This method is known from past experience, especially with regard to negotiations on disarmament problems. On numerous occasions after the proposals of the

---

[1] *Soviet News*, 26 June 1958. The American Ambassador in Moscow, Mr. Thompson, acting on instructions from President Eisenhower, delivered a message on 26 June to Mr. Gromyko in reply to the Soviet *aide-mémoire* of 25 June, in which he was authorized to state 'that the United States considers the aims of the conference of experts remain as determined in the exchange of correspondence between the Soviet Government and the United States Government'. *D.S.B.*, 14 July 1958, p. 47.

[2] For the relevant part of the news conference, see *D.S.B.*, 7 July 1958, pp. 9–10.

other side had been accepted by the Soviet Union, everything possible was subsequently done in order to prevent agreement, under the pretext that the reason for the lack of agreement was, allegedly, the intractability of the U.S.S.R.

The United States government can scarcely deny the fact that when it proposed a meeting of experts, this proposal was understood, not only in the Soviet Union but in all other countries as well, as a means of ensuring the solution of the main task mentioned, namely, the ending of nuclear tests. For this purpose the Soviet government met the U.S. government's wishes half way and agreed to President Eisenhower's proposal concerning a conference of experts. Though the Soviet government had doubts on this subject, it nevertheless put those doubts aside, being guided solely by the desire to utilise every opportunity to comply with the aspirations of the people, who are demanding the immediate and universal ending of these weapon tests. In the opinion of the Soviet government the people's will is the principal thing by which every government should be guided, if it is really striving to promote the easing of international tension, the stopping of the arms race, and the ending of the 'cold war.'

It was precisely the necessity for ending nuclear tests that was the basis for the agreement to hold a conference of experts. And this agreement has been set down in the corresponding documents which the government of the Soviet Union and the government of the United States have exchanged. From the very outset it has not been a question of a meeting of experts in general, but of a meeting with the definite purpose mentioned above.

The declaration of the U.S. Secretary of State, however, put forward another attitude which actually nullifies the position set forth in President Eisenhower's messages on the necessity for reaching agreement on control over the ending of atom and hydrogen bomb tests. One cannot but draw the conclusion that the gist of the position expounded by Mr. Dulles is to make the meeting of experts pointless and thus discredit it. If the United States government really takes such a stand, if it does not wish the experts' conference to result in ensuring the ending of tests of nuclear weapons by all the powers possessing those weapons, then there is no need to send experts to the abovementioned conference. Under such conditions the Soviet Union cannot send its experts, as it does not want to be an accomplice in deceiving the peoples.

The Soviet government would like to receive confirmation from the United States government that the meeting of experts should be convened with the aim of solving the problem of the universal and immediate ending of nuclear weapon tests and, consequently, that the purpose of this conference remains the same as was determined in the correspondence between the Soviet government and the government of the United States.

34. United States *aide-mémoire* to the Soviet Union regarding the conference of experts to consider the means of detecting nuclear explosions, 30 June 1958[1]

The Government of the United States of America notes with satisfaction the position of the Soviet Government in its aide memoire of June 28 that decision on cessation of tests of nuclear weapons must be taken by Governments themselves and not by experts. The task of the experts who are to meet in Geneva beginning July 1, as agreed by the Soviet Government in its aide memoire of June 24, has been clearly defined in the preceding correspondence between our Governments; it is to study methods of detection of possible violations of an agreement on the cessation of nuclear tests.

The position of the Government of the United States has been clearly and unequivocally expressed from the time of its initial proposal. In his letter of April 28,[2] President Eisenhower proposed to Chairman Khrushchev that technical people start to work immediately upon the practical problems of supervision and control which are indispensable to dependable disarmament agreements, and stated that:

I re-emphasize that these studies are without prejudice to our respective positions on the timing and interdependence of various aspects of disarmament.

It was in reply to this letter that Chairman Khrushchev on May 9[3] stated that the Soviet Government agreed to having both sides designate experts for the study which is now about to begin.

35. Letter from Mr. Khrushchev to President Eisenhower regarding the prevention of surprise attack, 2 July 1958[4]

Dear Mr. President, I am addressing this letter to you in order to make a proposal on joint steps towards the settlement of the problem of preventing a surprise attack.

The strained nature of international relations at the present time and the continued speeding up of the rate at which the powers are arming, especially in the sphere of the manufacture of ever more destructive types of weapons of mass annihilation, make it necessary, in our opinion—along with initial steps towards restricting the arms race, such as, for instance, the universal ending of nuclear weapon tests—to reach agreement on the adoption of measures to prevent the possibility of a surprise attack by one state on another. Attaching great importance to this question, the Soviet

---

[1] *D.S.B.*, 21 July 1958, p. 101. Delivered by the American Ambassador in Moscow to the Soviet Ministry for Foreign Affairs.
[2] See above, pp. 79–80.   [3] See above, pp. 80–84.   [4] *Soviet News*, 4 July 1958.

government, as you know, has proposed that it be included in the agenda of the conference of heads of government.

I must state that recently the problem of preventing a surprise attack has become especially acute in connection with the fact that the United States of America has begun the dangerous practice of flights by American aircraft, loaded with atomic and hydrogen bombs, over the territories of a number of West European states and in the Arctic regions in the direction of the frontiers of the U.S.S.R.

The Soviet government has already repeatedly stated its opinion of such actions on the part of the United States Air Force. It can only be added that on the day when the American government issues an order stopping such flights, the danger of an atomic war that is hanging over mankind will be greatly diminished.

We know from your messages to the Soviet government that the United States government agrees that the question of removing the danger of a surprise attack should be discussed at the summit conference. We are glad of this, for agreement by both sides on the desirability of discussing such an important question is already in itself an important thing.

There exists, however, another aspect of the problem which should not be forgotten. The problem of preventing a surprise attack can be settled, of course, only on the basis of taking just account of the interests of all parties, so that not a single state would be placed at a disadvantage from the standpoint of ensuring the interests of its security.

The United States government has been informed of the Soviet government's proposals on concrete measures to prevent the possibility of a surprise attack. The Soviet Union proposes that agreement be reached on the establishment of control posts at railway junctions, at large ports and on motor highways, in combination with definite steps for disarmament, and also on aerial surveys in regions important from the point of view of forestalling a surprise attack. In particular, we are prepared to agree on reciprocal aerial surveys in the zone in which the main armed forces of the two groupings of powers in Europe are concentrated, 800 kilometres[1] to the East and to the West of the line of demarcation of these forces. The Soviet government has suggested that in addition to the zone in Europe, an aerial inspection zone should be established which would include a part of Soviet territory in the Far East and a corresponding part of the territory of the United States.

These proposals are based on fair consideration of the security interests of the parties. They envisage, for instance, aerial control over equivalent territories of the U.S.S.R. and the United States. They also take into consideration previous proposals of the western powers, including those of the United States government. That is why it seems to us that these

[1] About 500 miles.

proposals could prove an acceptable basis for agreement. Unfortunately, so far they have not met with a favourable response on the part of the United States government.

We have studied with due attention the counter-proposals put forward by the government of the United States, jointly with the governments of the United Kingdom and France. It has to be stated, however, that the proposals of the three western powers on this question, conveyed to the Soviet government on May 28, this year,[1] do not provide evidence of a desire to seek jointly for agreement on the ways to prevent a surprise attack.

Although the document of the three powers does mention the need for pursuing a realistic course and taking into account, on a fair basis, the legitimate security interests of all the powers concerned, the proposals on the question of preventing a surprise attack which are contained in it are clearly at variance with these statements.

Thus, on the question of preventing the possibility of a surprise attack we have so far reached agreement only in the sense that both sides recognise the importance of this problem and the desirability of having it considered at the summit conference. As for concrete ways of carrying out this task, we are still far from agreement. It seems to me, however, that in this connection, too, agreement is quite possible, provided that all parties proceed on the basis of the need for taking into account the security interests of each party to the agreement and refrain from actions tending to exacerbate the situation and to increase the danger of the outbreak of war.

Taking into consideration the great importance that agreement on joint measures to prevent a surprise attack by one state on another would have for the preservation of world peace, I would like to propose to you, Mr. President, that the governments of our countries display practical initiative in this important matter.

In the Soviet government's opinion, it would be useful if appropriate representatives, including those of the Defence Ministries of both sides, for instance on the level of experts, appointed by the governments of the U.S.S.R., the United States and possibly some other states, met in the very near future in order to make a joint study of practical aspects of this problem and, within a definite time limit, worked out recommendations on measures to prevent the possibility of a surprise attack. The results of these talks could be considered at the conference of the heads of government. This preliminary work would undoubtedly make it easier to reach a decision on this question at the conference itself.

We hope that this proposal will be favourably received by the government of the United States and that joint efforts by our two countries will

---

[1] See above, pp. 30–37.

bring about the stronger confidence between states that is vital for ensuring world peace.

Yours sincerely,

N. KHRUSHCHOV

36. United States *aide-mémoire* to the Soviet Union regarding the conference of experts to consider the means of detecting nuclear explosions, 26 July 1958[1]

The Government of the United States is gratified to note the position of the Government of the USSR in its aide-memoire of July 9 that the task of the experts meeting in Geneva will be carried forward toward the objective of reaching a successful conclusion on the methods of detecting possible violations of an agreement on the cessation of nuclear tests.[2]

With respect to the question of whether the United States agrees 'that the meeting of the experts must be subordinated to a solution of the task of universal and immediate cessation of tests of nuclear weapons' President Eisenhower in his letter of April 28 to Chairman Khrushchev,[3] defined the relationship of technical studies to agreement on disarmament in the following terms:

The United States is determined that we will ultimately reach an agreement on disarmament. In my letter of April eighth, I again proposed an internationally supervised cutoff of the use of new fissionable materials for weapons purposes and the reduction of existing weapons stocks by transfer to peaceful purposes; an agreed limitation or suspension of testing; 'open skies', and the international use of outer space for peaceful purposes.

As an effective means of moving toward ultimate agreement on these matters and other disarmament matters, I proposed that we start our technical people to work immediately upon the practical problems involved. These studies were called for by the United Nations General Assembly. They would include the practical problems of supervision and control which, you and I agree, are in any event indispensable to dependable disarmament agreements. . . .

You say that we must first reach a final political agreement before it is worthwhile even to initiate the technical studies. But such studies would, in fact, facilitate the reaching of the final agreement you state you desire.

For example, why could not designated technical people agree on what would be required so that you would know if we violated an agreement to suspend testing and we would know if you should commit a violation?

[1] *D.S.B.*, 11 August 1958, pp. 235–6. Delivered by the American Embassy in Moscow to the Soviet Ministry for Foreign Affairs.

[2] For a summary of the Soviet *aide-mémoire* of 9 July 1958, see *Soviet News*, 10 July 1958.

[3] See above, pp. 79–80.

Would not both sides be in a better position to reach agreements if we had a common accepted understanding as to feasibility of detection or as to method of inspecting against surprise attack?

Studies of this kind are the necessary preliminaries to putting political decisions actually into effect. The completion of such technical studies in advance of a political agreement would obviate a considerable period of delay and uncertainty. In other words, with the practicalities already worked out, the political agreement could begin to operate very shortly after it was signed and ratified.

I re-emphasize that these studies are without prejudice to our respective positions on the timing and interdependence of various aspects of disarmament.

This remains the position of the United States. It was in reply to this letter of April 28 that Chairman Khrushchev on May 9[1] stated that the Soviet Government agreed to having both sides designate experts for the study which is now in progress.

37. United States note to the Soviet Union regarding President Eisenhower's proposal to hold technical talks on the safeguards against surprise attack, 31 July 1958[2]

The Embassy of the United States of America presents its compliments to the Ministry of Foreign Affairs of the Union of Soviet Socialist Republics and has the honor to refer to the letters of May 9, 1958 and July 2, 1958[3] from Prime Minister Khrushchev to President Eisenhower with regard to the problem of preventing surprise attack. The Prime Minister's letters commented upon the proposals of the United States on this subject and advanced certain additional proposals of the Soviet Government. The Government of the United States would like now to reply to these letters insofar as they relate to this important question.

As President Eisenhower pointed out in his letter of April 28, 1958,[4] the United States is determined that the Soviet Union and the United States ultimately reach an agreement on disarmament. As an effective means of moving toward ultimate agreement, he proposed that technical experts start to work immediately upon the practical problems involved. In this connection, he raised the question whether both sides would not be in a better position to reach agreements if there were a common accepted understanding as to methods of inspecting against surprise attack. It is noted that Prime Minister Khrushchev now suggests that appropriate representatives—including those of the military agencies of both sides, e.g., at the level of experts—designated by the Soviet Union,

---

[1] See above, pp. 80–84.　　　　　　　　　[2] D.S.B., 18 August 1958, pp. 278–9.
[3] See above, p. 80 and p. 94.　　　　　　　[4] See above, pp. 79–80.

the United States and possibly by the governments of certain other states meet for a joint study of the practical aspects of this problem. Accordingly, the United States proposes that qualified persons from each side meet for a study of the technical aspects of safeguards against the possibility of surprise attack. They should concentrate on the means and objects of control, and on the results which could be secured from these safeguards. The discussions could bear, if necessary, on the applicability of inspection measures to various areas for illustrative purposes only, but without prejudging in any way the boundaries within which such measures should be applied. It will be recalled that the United States has always favored the broadest possible application of such measures, and that in fact in President Eisenhower's initial proposal in 1955 he suggested that the entire territories of the United States and the Soviet Union be open to inspection.[1] The United States assumes, on the basis of Prime Minister Khrushchev's letter of July 2, 1958 that the Soviet Government agrees that these discussions would take place without prejudice to the respective positions of the two Governments as to the delimitation of areas within which safeguards would be established, or as to the timing or interdependence of various aspects of disarmament. The United States does not agree that the particular areas to be supervised as against surprise attack should be those indicated by Prime Minister Khrushchev's letter of July 2, 1958.

In this connection, the Government of the United States must indicate disagreement with Prime Minister Khrushchev's statement that the proposals relating to zones of inspection against surprise attack put forward by the United States, United Kingdom, and France on May 28, 1958[2] fail to strike a balance between the interests of both sides. It is the zones of inspection proposed by the Soviet Government which are subject to this criticism. This is particularly true of the European zone proposal which covers only a very limited area, scarcely touching Russian territory and far too small to cover the areas from which a surprise attack would be launched under modern conditions. Moreover, this proposal seems to be motivated by the political desire to crystalize the present dividing line in Europe since it is calculated from the 'line of demarcation' between NATO and the Warsaw Pact.

The United States believes, however, that joint technical studies would make it easier to reach agreement later at a political level on the definition of the regions in which the safeguards would apply. Accordingly, the United States proposes that during the first week of October, which is the earliest date by which preparations adequate to the significance and

[1] See *Documents* for 1955, pp. 39–41, for President Eisenhower's statement on disarmament made at the Geneva Conference on 21 July 1955.
[2] See pp. 33–34.

complexity of the task can be completed, these discussions begin in Geneva. In view of the Charter responsibilities of the General Assembly and the Security Council of the United Nations in the field of disarmament, the United States would propose to keep the United Nations informed of the progress of the talks through the Secretary General. Further arrangements for the meeting can be concluded through diplomatic channels.

In his letter of May 9, 1958 in particular, and again on July 2, 1958, Prime Minister Khrushchev also referred to the question of United States military flights especially in the Arctic area.

The United States regrets that unfounded charges continue regarding United States flights in the Arctic area and that the Soviet Union continues to reject United States proposals for a timely international inspection system in this area which would serve the end which the Soviet Union proposes, namely 'to prevent this area from becoming a hot bed of military conflict between our countries.'

It is stated that the proposal of the United States for inspection in this area, a proposal which commanded general support not only in the United Nations Security Council[1] but throughout the world, is no solution because the United States did not promise to suspend atomic bomber flights in the direction of the Soviet Union if an Arctic zone were established.

With respect to that statement, the United States desires to correct the apparent misunderstanding concerning atomic bomber operations of the United States. The greater portion of the Arctic zone air space is internationally free. There is considerable military aviation activity in that area, participated in by the United States, the Soviet Union, and other nations of the world. The statements of the Soviet representative in the United Nations Security Council, however, indicate concern that in this or other areas military aircraft of the United States armed with hydrogen and atomic bombs may have been sent in the direction of the borders of the Soviet Union as a result of a misinterpreted radar blip or other false alert. The Government of the United States gives categorical assurances that the United States has never had the need to launch nor has it in fact ever launched any atomic bomber flights of this type. Furthermore, if dependable and adequate safeguards were to be provided against surprise attack, then, of course, any United States flights entering, leaving or operating within an Arctic zone would conform to agreed control measures.

The United States believes that technical discussions of measures to reduce the possibility of surprise attack, even though made without reference to particular areas, will produce a fuller realization of the value of an

[1] For background and texts of three statements by Mr. Cabot Lodge, see *D.S.B.*, 19 May 1958, pp. 816–20.

Arctic zone, and pave the way for agreement on safeguards in this and other regions. Such technical discussions would also be helpful in determining whether a meeting of heads of government would provide opportunity for conducting serious discussions of major problems and would be an effective means of reaching agreement on significant subjects.

38. Communiqué issued on the conclusion of the conference of experts to study a possible agreement on the suspension of nuclear tests, Geneva, 21 August 1958[1]

The Conference of Experts to study the possibility of detecting violations of a possible agreement on the suspension of nuclear tests, which began its work in the Palais des Nations at Geneva on July 1, concluded its work on August 21, 1958.

2. The Conference expressed its appreciation for the good offices of the Secretary-General of the United Nations, carried out through his personal representative, Mr. Narayanan, and for the efficient services rendered by the United Nations Secretariat staff attached to the Conference.

3. In the course of the work of the Conference there was an exchange of opinions on the question of the various methods of detecting nuclear explosions.

4. The Conference came to the conclusion that the methods of detecting nuclear explosions available at the present time, viz. the method of collecting samples of radioactive debris, the method of recording seismic, acoustic and hydro-acoustic waves, and the radio signal method, together with the use of on-site inspection of unidentified events which might be suspected of being nuclear explosions, make it possible, within certain specific limits, to detect and identify nuclear explosions, and it recommends the use of these methods in a control system.

5. The Conference noted that the combined use of the various methods considerably facilitates detection and identification of nuclear explosions.

6. The Conference of Experts noted that the effectiveness of the methods considered will increase in course of time with improvement of measuring techniques and with study of the characteristics of natural phenomena which cause interference when explosions are detected.

7. The Conference has adopted an agreed conclusion regarding the technical equipment of the control system necessary for the detection and identification of nuclear explosions.

8. The Conference of Experts reached the conclusion that it is technically feasible to set up, with certain capabilities and limitations, a workable

[1] Cmnd. 551, p. 41. For the report of the conference of experts to study the methods of detecting violations of a possible agreement on the suspension of nuclear tests, see Cmnd. 551, pp. 3–26.

and effective control system for the detection of violations of a possible agreement on the world-wide cessation of nuclear weapons tests.

9. It was established in this connexion that a network of control posts which were equipped with all the necessary apparatus appropriate to the various methods of detection of nuclear explosions should be disposed on continents and on islands, as well as on a few ships in oceans.

10. The Experts came to the conclusion that the control system should be under the direction of an international control organ which would ensure the coordination of the activities of the control system and the functioning of the system in such a way that it would satisfy the necessary technical requirements.

11. On August 21, 1958, the Conference of Experts adopted a final report for consideration by Governments. The report will be made public at a time to be determined by Governments.

39. Statement by the United Kingdom Government on the conclusion of the conference of experts to study a possible agreement on the suspension of nuclear tests, London, 22 August 1958[1]

Her Majesty's Government have learnt that the conference of scientific experts at Geneva on the detection of nuclear weapon tests has reached a successful conclusion. This report represents a new and hopeful development, and Her Majesty's Government regard the outcome as a clear justification of the technical approach to problems of control and inspection in the field of disarmament which they themselves first proposed over a year ago.

It is now established that effective international control over a suspension of nuclear weapons tests is technically possible. The report of the Geneva Conference provides the essential technical basis on which to build further progress. The next task is to find solutions to the important practical and political problems relating to the organization, installation and functioning of a control organization.

Her Majesty's Government are prepared to enter into negotiations with other governments which have tested nuclear weapons with a view to solving these problems and concluding an agreement for the suspension of nuclear weapons tests under effective international control. Her Majesty's Government for their part will be ready to begin negotiations for that purpose by October 31, 1958.

Her Majesty's Government hope that such negotiations will not only lead to successful results in themselves but will also facilitate early negotiation on measures of disarmament. Her Majesty's Government have always

[1] Cmnd. 551, p. 42.

made it clear that they do not regard the suspension of nuclear tests as itself constituting a measure of disarmament. If peace and security are to be placed upon a firmer and more lasting foundation, early progress must be made towards real disarmament, both nuclear and conventional, by measures such as Her Majesty's Government have themselves proposed. Any real disarmament must also be subject to effective international control, and Her Majesty's Government hope that the precedent of expert discussion established by the Geneva Conference may be followed in other fields.

As is known, Her Majesty's Government are now beginning a short series of tests. This will be completed as soon as possible.[1] In view of the opportunities for agreement now opened up, both on the controlled suspension of nuclear tests and on measures of real disarmament, Her Majesty's Government will, from the date when negotiations are begun for the suspension of nuclear tests under effective international control, refrain from further testing of nuclear weapons for a period of one year. They will do so on the understanding that the object of the negotiations has been accepted in principle by all the Governments which have tested nuclear weapons, and so long as the Soviet Government does not resume testing in this period. Her Majesty's Government will be prepared to refrain from nuclear tests thereafter for further successive periods of one year provided that the Soviet Union will do the same, and that satisfactory progress has been made towards the installation of an effective system of international control over the suspension of nuclear tests and towards the adoption and execution of measures of real disarmament.

[1] The following nuclear tests were carried out in 1958:

U.S.S.R.:	22 February–23 March (6 known explosions)
	30 September—3 November
U.S.:	28 April–3 July (11 known explosions)
	19 September–31 October
U.K.:	28 April (H-bomb exploded in Christmas Isles)
	22 August–23 October (4 explosions)

See *Le Monde*, 14–15 February 1960.

On 31 March 1958 the U.S.S.R. announced the suspension of nuclear tests, see above, p. 59, but on 30 August the Soviet Government declared that the tests of the U.S. and U.K. had freed the U.S.S.R. of this commitment. On 3 October 1958 a *Tass* statement announced that the U.S.S.R. had resumed testing, see *Soviet News*, 3 October 1958. Mr. Zorin, in a speech on 27 October 1958, in the political committee of the U.N., said: 'The stand taken by the western powers, which reject the immediate and unconditional ending of nuclear weapon tests, entitles the Soviet Union to continue nuclear tests in the proportion of one to one with regard to the number of tests staged by the U.S. and the U.K. taken together, until the number of explosions after March 31 this year equals the number of nuclear tests staged by those powers since that date', see *Soviet News*, 28 October 1958.

40. United States note to the Soviet Union transmitting a statement by President Eisenhower offering to negotiate the suspension of nuclear weapon tests, 22 August 1958[1]

(a) *The United States note, 22 August 1958*

The Embassy of the United States of America presents its compliments to the Ministry of Foreign Affairs of the Union of Soviet Socialist Republics and has the honor to transmit the attached statement made today by President Eisenhower. It will be noted that the United States, taking account of the conclusions of the Geneva meeting of experts, is prepared to proceed promptly to negotiate an agreement, with other nations which have tested nuclear weapons, for the suspension of nuclear weapons tests and the actual establishment of an international control system on the basis of the experts report. The United States proposes that negotiations toward this end begin in New York on October 31, 1958, and that the progress and results of these negotiations be reported through the Secretary General to the United Nations General Assembly and Security Council.

(b) *President Eisenhower's statement, 22 August 1958*

The United States welcomes the successful conclusion of the Geneva meeting of experts who have been considering whether and how nuclear weapons tests could be detected. Their conclusions indicate that, if there were an agreement to eliminate such tests, its effective supervision and enforcement would be technically possible.

This is a most important conclusion, the more so because it is concurred in by the experts of the Soviet Union. Progress in the field of disarmament agreements depends upon the ability to establish effective international controls and the willingness of the countries concerned to accept those controls. The fact therefore of an agreement on technical possibilities of inspection and control opens up a prospect of progress in the vitally important field of disarmament.

The United States, taking account of the Geneva conclusions, is prepared to proceed promptly to negotiate an agreement with other nations which have tested nuclear weapons for the suspension of nuclear weapons tests and the actual establishment of an international control system on the basis of the experts' report.

If this is accepted in principle by the other nations which have tested nuclear weapons, then in order to facilitate the detailed negotiations the United States is prepared, unless testing is resumed by the Soviet Union, to withhold further testing on its part of atomic and hydrogen weapons for a period of one year from the beginning of the negotiations.[2]

[1] *D.S.B.*, 8 September 1958, pp. 378–9.   [2] See fn. on preceding page.

As part of the agreement to be negotiated, and on a basis of reciprocity, the United States would be further prepared to suspend the testing of nuclear weapons on a year-by-year basis subject to a determination at the beginning of each year that: (A) the agreed inspection system is installed and working effectively; and (B) satisfactory progress is being made in reaching agreement on and implementing major and substantial arms control measures such as the United States has long sought. The agreement should also deal with the problem of detonations for peaceful purposes, as distinct from weapons tests.

Our negotiators will be instructed and ready by October 31 this year to open negotiations with other similarly instructed negotiators.

As the United States has frequently made clear, the suspension of testing of atomic and hydrogen weapons is not, in itself, a measure of disarmament or a limitation of armament. An agreement in this respect is significant if it leads to other and more substantial agreements relating to limitation and reduction of fissionable material for weapons and to other essential phases of disarmament. It is in this hope that the United States makes this proposal.

41. Soviet note to the United States regarding the suspension of nuclear tests, 30 August 1958[1]

The Ministry of Foreign Affairs of the Union of Soviet Socialist Republics presents its compliments to the Embassy of the United States of America and, with reference to the Embassy's Note of August 22, has the honour of communicating that the government of the U.S.S.R. is prepared to begin, on October 31, this year, negotiations between representatives of the U.S.S.R., the United States and the United Kingdom for the purpose of concluding an agreement by the states on the ending of atomic and hydrogen weapon tests for all time, coupled with the institution of appropriate control over the fulfilment of such an agreement. In the opinion of the Soviet government Geneva would be the most convenient place for these negotiations. In order to avoid dragging out the negotiations, it would be expedient to agree in advance to limit them to a definite period of time. The Soviet government, for its part, suggests that this time be two or three weeks.

Appended hereto is the text of a statement by N. S. Khrushchov, Chairman of the U.S.S.R. Council of Ministers, setting out the Soviet government's point of view on the questions dealt with in President Eisenhower's statement of August 22.[2]

[1] *Soviet News*, 2 September 1958. A similar note was sent to the United Kingdom.
[2] The text of Mr. Khrushchev's replies to questions put to him by a *Pravda* correspondent published in the Soviet press on 30 August 1958, is not included here. For the text, see ibid., 1 September 1958.

42. United States note to the Soviet Union regarding the United States proposal for studies of the practical aspects of safeguards against surprise attack, 8 September 1958[1]

The Embassy of the United States of America presents its compliments to the Ministry of Foreign Affairs of the Union of Soviet Socialist Republics and has the honor to refer to the United States note of July 31, 1958,[2] regarding a study of the technical aspects of safeguards against the possibility of surprise attack.

It is noted that while the Government of the U.S.S.R. has responded to the United States proposal for negotiations on a nuclear test suspension beginning October 31, it has not yet responded to the United States proposal for studies of the practical aspects of safeguards against surprise attack beginning the first week of October. The United States hopes that it may receive an early reply to its note of July 31, since it attaches great importance to the proposed study as an effective means of moving toward agreement on meaningful measures of disarmament. Because of the delay and the necessity for careful preparations if the proposed technical talks are to be of greatest value, the United States believes that the meeting originally proposed for the first week of October should now be scheduled at a later date about two months after a reply from the Soviet Government has been received.

43. United States note to the Soviet Union regarding the talks on the suspension of nuclear weapon tests, 10 September 1958[3]

The Embassy of the United States of America presents its compliments to the Ministry of Foreign Affairs of the Union of Soviet Socialist Republics and, referring to the Ministry's Note of 30 August of this year, has the honor to state that the Government of the United States of America notes with gratification that the Government of the Union of Soviet Socialist Republics has agreed to the date of October 31, 1958 as proposed by the United States for the beginning of negotiations among representatives of the United Kingdom, the Union of Soviet Socialist Republics and the United States on the question of suspension of nuclear weapons tests and the actual establishment of an international control system on the basis of the Report of the Geneva Conference of Experts.[4] The United States further notes that the Government of the Union of Soviet Socialist Republics suggests that these discussions be held in Geneva. The United

[1] *D.S.B.*, 29 September 1958, p. 504.   [2] See above, pp. 98–1
[3] *D.S.B.*, 29 September 1958, p. 503.
[4] For the text of the report, see Cmnd. 551.

Sta.tes agrees to this location. The United States is informed by the Secretary General of the United Nations that conference facilities and secretariat services will be available at the Palais des Nations.

'The Government of the Union of Soviet Socialist Republics also proposes that a period of two to three weeks be set for the duration of the proposed discussions. The United States, of course, agrees that the negotiations should be concluded as quickly as possible, but believes that their importance requires the expenditure of whatever time may mutually be deemed necessary for their successful conclusion.

The Chairman of the United States Delegation to the conference will be Ambassador James J. Wadsworth, United States Representative on Disarmament.

With regard to the other issues raised in the note and those discussed by the Chairman of the Council of Ministers of the Union of Soviet Socialist Republics in the statement attached to the note of the Government of the Union of Soviet Socialist Republics,[1] the views of the United States Government are as set forth in the statement of President Eisenhower of August 22.[2] The United States proposes that these issues be reserved for discussion at the meetings which will commence at Geneva on October 31.

44. Soviet note to the United States regarding the conference of experts on the prevention of surprise attack, 15 September 1958[3]

The Ministry of Foreign Affairs of the U.S.S.R. presents its compliments to the Embassy of the United States of America and, in reference to the Embassy's Note No. 128 of July 31, has the honour to state the following:

The Soviet government notes the favourable attitude of the United States government to the proposal put forward in the message sent by N.S. Khrushchov, Chairman of the U.S.S.R. Council of Ministers, to President Eisenhower on July 2, this year. This message suggested that competent representatives, including representatives of the military departments of the two sides, appointed by the governments of the U.S.S.R. and the United States—and, possibly, representatives of some other states—should meet in the near future for a joint study of the practical aspects of the problem of preventing surprise attack and should draft within a certain limited period, stipulated in advance, recommendations on measures to prevent the possibility of surprise attack.

In proposing a conference at experts level, the Soviet government

---

[1] See fn. 2 on p. 105, above.   [2] See above, pp. 104–5.
[3] *Soviet News*, 17 September 1958. For the Soviet note of 10 November 1958, naming the Soviet, Polish, Czech, Rumanian, and Albanian delegations, see *Soviet News*, 12 November 1958.

proceeded from the assumption that such a conference would be useful only if its work were aimed at drafting practical recommendations on measures to prevent surprise attack in conjunction with definite steps in the sphere of disarmament.

As the United States government will recall, the message of the Chairman of the U.S.S.R. Council of Ministers of July 2 states that the Soviet Union suggests that it be agreed to set up control posts at railway junctions, major ports and motor roads, in conjunction with definite steps in the field of disarmament and aerial survey of regions which are of great importance for averting the threat of surprise attack.

Consequently, the United States government's assertions, that the Soviet government supposedly agrees that these discussions should not predetermine the corresponding positions of the two governments with regard to the timing and interdependence of various aspects of disarmament, are unfounded. It is understood that the experts will have to give serious attention to such technical problems as means and objects of control and the results which might be secured by these measures.

As the Soviet government has already stated, agreement on measures to prevent surprise attack is quite feasible provided fair consideration is given to mutual interests, and such actions as would aggravate the international situation and increase the risk of war are renounced.

Of course, the decision to set up, on reciprocal principles, a system to prevent the possibility of surprise attack must be taken by the governments and not by the experts, who will do only the preparatory work. However, the drafting by the experts of practical recommendations on specific ways of preventing surprise attack will undoubtedly facilitate a fruitful discussion by a heads of government conference of the question of preventing surprise attack.

The Note of the United States Embassy again raises the question of the flights by United States military planes in the Arctic region and of the Arctic zone of inspection.

In its Note the United States government gives the categoric assurance that the United States has never found it necessary to carry out flights by military planes loaded with hydrogen and atom bombs towards the frontiers of the Soviet Union.

However, one cannot fail to point out that the United States government's statement alleging that American atomic bombers are not flying towards the frontiers of the U.S.S.R. appears unconvincing in the light of the speeches by its representatives in the United Nations Security Council and the statement made by Mr. Dulles, the United States Secretary of State, at a press conference on May 1.[1]

[1] Presumably this refers to the opening statement made by Mr. Dulles, also issued separately as a press release by the State Department, in which he said: 'The Soviet Government has said

It will be recalled that Mr. Dulles bluntly said in this statement that if the Soviet Union agreed to the introduction of international inspection in the Arctic region, the United States would regard it safe to reduce to the minimum these flights against which the Soviet Union was protesting. When asked whether the United States would put an end to such flights if inspection in the Arctic region were established, Mr. Dulles stated that this would depend on the information obtained by the United States as a result of this inspection.

These statements by Mr. Dulles clearly confirm the fact of the flights by American planes carrying atom and hydrogen bombs towards the frontiers of the Soviet Union.

As regards the Arctic zone of inspection, which is mentioned in the United States Embassy's Note, the Soviet Union's attitude to this question has already been exhaustively explained.

As for the practical aspect of convening a conference of experts, the Soviet government does not object to the date and venue of the conference proposed by the United States in its Note of July 31. However, if the United States government would not be ready to take part in the conference by this date, we have no objection to it being convened later, as proposed in the United States Embassy's Note of September 8. Proceeding from this, the Soviet government suggests that the conference of experts should open in Geneva on November 10, envisaging that its work would be completed as soon as possible, within four or five weeks, for instance.

The Soviet government believes it would be advisable that, besides the U.S.S.R. and the United States, other countries should take part in the conference of experts. In so doing, the Soviet government considers it necessary to proceed from the principle of parity of Atlantic Pact members and Warsaw Treaty Organisation members. Taking this into consideration, the Soviet government proposes that representatives of the United States, the United Kingdom, France, Belgium, the U.S.S.R., Poland, Czechoslovakia and Rumania should take part in the conference of experts.

It goes without saying that the United Nations will be informed of the progress of the experts' talks, through the United Nations Secretary-General.

The Soviet government hopes that the United States government will carefully examine the considerations put forward in this Note, and will give an affirmative reply to the proposals made in it.

that it is worried by the flights of United States aircraft in this area [the Arctic]. We have said that we need to keep planes aloft because we are fearful that the Soviets may launch a nuclear attack against us over the top of the world'. See *D.S.B.*, 19 May 1958, particularly p. 804.

45. Soviet note to the United States regarding the talks on the suspension of nuclear weapon tests, 1 October 1958[1]

The Ministry of Foreign Affairs of the U.S.S.R. presents its compliments to the Embassy of the United States of America and, in connection with the Embassy's Note No. 262 of September 10,[2] has the honour, on the instructions of the Soviet government, to communicate the following:

Note is taken of the United States government's affirmative reply to the proposal of the Soviet government that discussions on the suspension of nuclear weapon tests by all powers possessing such weapons should be held in Geneva. Thus, the date for opening the discussions—October 31, this year—and their venue can be regarded as agreed.

As for the purpose of the forthcoming conference, the Soviet government considers it necessary to reaffirm its position, set forth in the Ministry's Note of August 30, that is, that the purpose of such a conference is the conclusion of an agreement on ending, once and for all, atomic and hydrogen weapon tests by the states, with the introduction of proper control over the fulfilment of this agreement.

At the present time, when the Geneva experts' conference has confirmed that no tests of atomic and hydrogen weapons can fail to be detected, there should be no obstacles to agreement by the powers possessing nuclear weapons on the immediate ending of tests of all types of atomic and hydrogen weapons once and for all.

Taking into consideration that the immediate and universal ending of nuclear weapon tests is a problem that brooks no delay and affects the vital interests of all mankind, the Soviet government hopes that the parties to the conference will exert every effort to agree on and sign an appropriate agreement at the earliest possible date.

Bearing this in mind, the Soviet government believes that the conference should be convened at the level of the Foreign Ministers of the Soviet Union, the United States and the United Kingdom.

The Soviet government expresses the hope that the government of the United States will carefully study this proposal of the Soviet government and will give an affirmative reply.

46. United States note to the Soviet Union regarding the technical talks on the prevention of surprise attack, 10 October 1958[3]

The Embassy of the United States of America presents its compliments to the Ministry of Foreign Affairs of the Union of Soviet Socialist Repub-

---

[1] *Soviet News*, 2 October 1958. An analogous note was forwarded to the United Kingdom.
[2] See above, p. 106.
[3] *D.S.B.*, 27 October 1958, p. 648. For the United States note of 7 November 1958, naming the experts from Canada, France, Italy, the United Kingdom, and the United States, see *D.S.B.*, 24 November 1958, pp. 815–16.

lics and has the honor to refer to note 53/OSA of September 15, 1958, regarding a meeting of technical experts to study the practical aspects of minimizing the possibility of surprise attack.

The Government of the United States believes that the primary purpose of the meeting should be to examine the methods and objects of control and to assess the results that might be obtained from the adoption of those methods in lessening the danger of surprise military attack. The study should be undertaken with a view to the preparation of a technical report which could be recommended for consideration by governments. The report would be useful in the subsequent examination among governments at an appropriate level of the problem of introducing measures against surprise attack. As stated in its note of July 31,[1] the United States considers that the discussions should take place without prejudice to the respective positions of the two Governments as to the delimitation of areas within which measures might be established, or as to the timing or interdependence of various aspects of disarmament.

With this understanding, the Government of the United States agrees to commencement of this meeting at Geneva on November 10. The United States hopes that substantial progress could be made in a meeting of four to five weeks as suggested by the Soviet Government.

With regard to the question of participation in the proposed meeting, the United States believes it would be appropriate to include experts from countries other than the United States and the U.S.S.R. in order to provide the broadest possible base of technical experience under varying conditions. After consultation with other nations the United States proposes that, for the Western countries, there will be experts from the United States, the U.K., France, Canada, Italy and possibly other countries. The names of the experts who will participate will be communicated in due course.

The comments in the United States note of July 31, with regard to the question of flights of United States aircraft carrying nuclear weapons, with which the Union of Soviet Socialist Republics takes issue in its note of September 15, were directed to the charges made by the Union of Soviet Socialist Republics' representative in the Security Council of the United Nations in April of this year.[2] At that time, the Union of Soviet Socialist Republics' representative spoke of the 'practice of regular United States bomber flights armed with atomic and hydrogen bombs which proceed towards the borders of the Soviet Union upon the giving of an alarm.' The United States reaffirms the statement contained in its note of July 31 'that the United States has never had the need to launch nor has it in fact ever launched any atomic bomber flights of this type.'

[1] See above, pp. 98–101.   [2] See, for example, Mr. Sobolev's speech of 21 April, S.C.O.R., Thirteenth Year, 812th meeting, paras. 3–27.

47. United States note to the Soviet Union regarding the suspension of nuclear weapon tests, 20 October 1958[1]

The Embassy of the United States of America presents its compliments to the Ministry of Foreign Affairs of the Union of Soviet Socialist Republics and has the honor to refer to note 58/OSA of October 1, 1958, regarding arrangements for the meeting on suspension of nuclear tests and establishment of an international control system scheduled to begin in Geneva among the U.S., U.K., and U.S.S.R. on October 31.[2]

The United States takes note of the Soviet statement that the aim of the conference would be the conclusion of an agreement to cease tests of atomic and hydrogen weapons by all states forever, and the establishment of appropriate control over the implementation of such an agreement. It is the sincere hope of the United States that the conference will make sufficient progress to justify the expectation that the final termination of all nuclear weapons test explosions may in due course be achieved. The United States has always accepted as a most desirable objective the final termination of nuclear weapons test explosions. However, the United States feels it necessary to refer once again to the terms of the statement of the President of the United States of August 22, 1958.[3] In this statement, President Eisenhower declared that the United States would be prepared to refrain from nuclear weapons tests for further successive periods of one year after the initial suspension of one year, provided that the Soviet Union would do the same, that the agreed inspection system is installed and working effectively, and that satisfactory progress is being made in reaching agreement on and implementing major and substantive arms control measures. If sufficient progress can be made at the Geneva conference which is to open on the 31st of October and if subsequently these objectives are effectively achieved without undue delays, the world could then be confident that nuclear weapons testing would never be resumed by the parties to the agreement.

The United States considers that an agreement for the suspension of nuclear weapons testing under international control should be worked out as rapidly as possible. In view of the complexities of detecting and verifying violations of an agreement on suspension of nuclear tests which are revealed in the report of the Geneva Conference of Experts,[4] careful and detailed negotiations will be required for an agreement of such importance, however, and the United States considers that this work should be initiated on October 31 at the diplomatic level. If, as the discussions at the diplomatic level proceed, the presence of Foreign Ministers seems necessary and desirable, the Secretary of State would be prepared to attend.

[1] *D.S.B.*, 10 November 1958, pp. 723–4.   [2] See above, p. 110.

[3] See above, p. 104.   [4] See fn. on p. 101 above.

48. Soviet note to the United States regarding the suspension of nuclear weapon tests, 30 October 1958[1]

In connection with the United States Embassy's Note No. 392 of October 20, concerning the Geneva talks between the United States, the U.S.S.R. and the United Kingdom on the ending of atomic and hydrogen weapon tests, the U.S.S.R. Foreign Ministry has the honour to state the following:

The Embassy's Note, as the earlier Notes of the United States government on the Geneva talks, states that these negotiations should be devoted to the question of suspending, and not ending nuclear weapon tests. This Note of the United States government again links the achievement of agreement on the universal ending of atomic and hydrogen weapon tests with the preliminary fulfilment of a number of conditions. Moreover, the Note particularly emphasises the difficulties of implementing the agreement on control over the ending of nuclear weapon tests.

It is in place to note here that the eight-power Geneva meeting of experts not only arrived at the unanimous conclusion that it was quite feasible to establish a workable and effective system of control over the implementation of an agreement to end nuclear weapon tests, but also made specific recommendations regarding the establishment of this system. It is obvious that under these conditions the attempts to link the ending of nuclear tests with the fulfilment of preliminary terms, to make reservations and to stress the complexity and difficulty of carrying out control, indicate a desire to continue to create artificial obstacles to the early achievement of an agreement on the universal ending of nuclear weapon tests once and for all.

In connection with this, the U.S.S.R. Foreign Ministry believes it is necessary to reaffirm the Soviet government's position outlined, specifically, in its Notes of August 30 and October 1, that the purpose of the forthcoming Geneva meeting of the U.S.S.R., the United States and the United Kingdom should be to conclude an agreement on ending atomic and hydrogen weapon tests for ever in conjunction with appropriate control over the implementation of this agreement.

The immediate and universal ending of nuclear weapon tests is a pressing

[1] *Soviet News*, 31 October 1958. An analogous note was sent to the United Kingdom. The conference met from 31 October to 19 December 1958. Between 31 October 1958 and July 1959 the negotiations passed through 3 phases: initial deadlock, a period of clarification, and renewed stalemate. In December the rudiments of a control system were worked out and both sides agreed to the establishment of a 7-nation control commission headed by an administrator. Voting rules within the proposed commission and the nature and composition of the inspection teams were then discussed. Three key questions remained when the conference recessed on 19 December: (1) whether or not the voting procedure in the control commission should include a veto; (2) whether the inspection teams would be permanent or created on an *ad hoc* basis; (3) the nationality of the inspectors of the 180 control posts. These questions dominated the conference from 5 January 1959 until its second recess on 19 March 1959.

problem affecting the vital interests of all mankind, and the Soviet government would like to hope that the Geneva talks, which are to start on October 31, will result in the ending of nuclear weapon tests once and for all.[1]

For its part the Soviet government will do everything it can to facilitate the achievement of this goal. It is firmly convinced that if the other parties to the talks—the United States and United Kingdom—approach the solution of this problem in the same way, this will ensure that the meeting will achieve an agreement ending the tests of all types of atomic and hydrogen weapons.

The Soviet government regrets that its proposal to hold a Foreign Ministers' meeting in Geneva was not supported by the United States government. The Soviet government continues to believe that the convening of a Ministerial conference would have created the most favourable opportunities for reaching agreement on the ending of nuclear weapon tests as soon as possible.

Considering, however, the United States government's readiness, expressed in the Embassy's Note, to send the United States Secretary of State to Geneva at a certain stage in the talks, the Soviet government proposes that the Ministers of Foreign Affairs of the U.S.S.R., the United States and the United Kingdom should join the meeting at a later date, which would undoubtedly facilitate the early achievement of the agreement necessary for ending nuclear weapon tests.

49. Statement on behalf of the western experts at the conference on the prevention of surprise attack, Geneva, 18 December 1958[2]

Today, December 18, is our concluding session. About three months ago, in a note of September 15, 1958, the Soviet Union suggested that this conference should 'complete its work in the shortest possible time, for example in four to five weeks.' We are almost at the end of the sixth week of our discussions. It now seems clear, for reasons I shall explain, that there is little purpose in carrying these present deliberations further until or unless a better understanding has been reached on their purpose.

We, on this side of the table, have tabled a number of papers. They are as follows:

---

[1] See fn., p. 103, above.

[2] U.N. Doc. A/4078, Annex 14. This statement was made by Mr. Foster, the senior United States expert, on behalf of the United States, Canadian, Italian, French, and United Kingdom representatives, at the concluding session of the conference, which took place at the European Headquarters of the United Nations from 10 November to 18 December 1958. The report of the conference was transmitted to the United Nations through the intermediary of the Secretary-General, on 5 January 1959.

GEN/SA/4 of November 18: 'A survey of the relevant technical aspects of possible instruments of surprise attack as a prerequisite for examining means of detection and systems of inspection and control.'[1]

GEN/SA/5 of November 19: 'A survey of techniques which would be effective in the observation and inspection of the instruments of surprise attack.'[2]

GEN/SA/6 of November 24: 'An illustrative outline of possible systems for observation and inspection of long range aircraft.'[3]

GEN/SA/9 of December 3: 'A paper illustrating a possible system for observation and inspection of ballistic missiles.' (Introduced by a statement on the Usefulness of Warning in the Missile Age reproduced in GEN/SA/PV. 19 of December 3.)[4]

GEN/SA/10 of December 5: 'An illustrative outline of a possible system for observation and inspection of ground forces.'[5]

GEN/SA/12 of December 17: 'An explanatory statement regarding certain factors involved in the planning of an integrated observation and inspection system for reducing the possibility of surprise attacks.'[6] (Tabled by the Western Experts on December 17 and previously read to the conference on December 9). The experts on the other side of the table have put forward certain proposals. These are as follows:

GEN/SA/3 of 17 November: 'Draft recommendation regarding the undertaking by States of an obligation not to carry out flights of their aircraft with atomic and hydrogen weapons over the territories of other States and over open seas.'[7]

GEN/SA/8 of 28 November: 'Proposal regarding the establishment of ground control posts, the taking of aerial photographs and the putting into operation simultaneously of a number of disarmament measures to reduce the danger of surprise attack.'[8]

GEN/SA/7 of 28 November: 'Statement by the Soviet Government on measures for preventing surprise attack.'[9]

GEN/SA/11 of 12 December: 'Tasks and functions of ground control posts and aerial inspection.'[10]

The contrast between these two sets of documents is self-evident. We have sought to promote technical discussion and understanding. You have sought discussion of a selection of political proposals, for the most part not susceptible of technical assessment. We have, in the later stages of our discussion, been able to achieve, in a fragmentary and restricted way, some critical discussion of various aspects of control. The difference in our approach has, however, remained so wide that it cannot be overcome in this session. The only practical course to follow is to refer to governments

[1] Ibid., Annex 5. [2] Ibid., Annex 6. [3] Ibid., Annex 7. [4] Ibid., Annex 10.
[5] Ibid., Annex 11. [6] Ibid., Annex 13. [7] Ibid., Annex 4.
[8] Ibid., Annex 9. [9] Ibid., Annex 8. [10] Ibid., Annex 12.

the task of reconciling this difference in the hope that future discussions may deal with the problem to better effect. Accordingly, we believe that the time has come to transmit a report to our governments, even though we have not been able to arrive at conclusions on the ways of reducing the possibility of surprise attack.

Because the Soviet declaration and the accompanying proposal of the experts on the other side of the table are almost entirely political in content, we Western experts have felt unable to do other than transmit them to our governments for study at the political level. We have no doubt that our governments have been considering them closely, although little in them is new. What should be done when our governments have had time to formulate their views is again a matter for the various governments concerned to decide. If, at some future date, the Soviet government wishes to advance these proposals again in some suitable political forum, we can assure the other side that our governments would be willing to discuss them, together with any proposals which our governments themselves might wish to advance, with a view to reducing the danger of surprise attack, to facilitating agreement on balanced measures of disarmament under proper control, and to reducing international tension generally. What is clear to us now is that this conference is not the appropriate forum for discussion of these proposals as presented to us.

We came here in the hope of technical discussion of the sort conducted so successfully last July and August on the detection of nuclear tests. We made extensive preparations for this conference and brought here for this purpose over a hundred scientists and experts in military technology. We hoped to follow for a second time the kind of approach which the Western governments have sought over the last two to three years and which the General Assembly of the United Nations has twice endorsed. This is the kind of approach which the Western powers proposed as early as 1956 and 1957, not only for the problem of reducing the danger of surprise attack but also for other questions in the field of controlled disarmament. This same concept inspired President Eisenhower's dual proposal of April 28, 1958 for technical discussions on both surprise attack and the detection of nuclear tests.

We believe that the merits of our approach may be summed up in four mutually related points.

1. *The Scientific Nature of Our Approach*

The first is that our plan of work would have provided an orderly and logical progression from the relevant data to sound technical conclusions. It is, as we have elaborated in statements of November 26 and December 9 particularly, a scientific approach, which called for the consideration in turn of the following questions:

(a) In seeking means to reduce the possibility of surprise attack, what instruments of warfare must we consider, and what are the general characteristics of each category of those instruments?

(b) What technical means are available to afford observations and inspection of those instruments?

(c) What techniques of observation and inspection can be applied to each category of the instruments of surprise attack, and what would those techniques tell which might be useful in preventing surprise attack?

(d) Considering all the categories of instruments of surprise attack, and all the possible techniques of observation and inspection, what would be the general technical characteristics of an overall system to reduce the possibility of a surprise attack?

(e) What agreed technical conclusion will we report to our governments as a result of our discussions?

These five points in fact constituted the plan of work which we tabled on November 11. It was to illustrate how we might go about answering these questions in a joint endeavour that we prepared for this conference the documents and statements which I cited above. If the experts across the table had agreed to this approach, we might have jointly developed these papers into a solid outline of the essentials of a system to reduce the possibility of surprise attack—into a report as scientific and soundly reasoned as that agreed upon on August 20 at the conclusion of the talks on nuclear test detection.

2. *Exclusion of Political Issues*

The second point I wish to emphasize is that our approach was designed to avoid, without prejudice to any national interests, a wide range of difficult political issues which do not admit of technical discussion and can only be handled in the give and take of diplomatic negotiation. The approach which the experts across the table have proposed would automatically raise such questions. Our own programme of work was carefully designed so that we would not get caught up in such questions and in the belief that account might more appropriately be taken of them in subsequent political negotiations which might take place following adequate technical studies.

We have sought a discussion that would first take account of all the instruments of surprise attack—not only the older weapons systems but also the most modern systems of surprise attack which can be brought to bear against any part of the globe. We believe it would be absurd to embark on a discussion of systems for reducing the danger of surprise attack in which some critically important weapons systems were arbitrarily left out of account from the outset. In opposing such an approach we have been concerned to avoid establishing huge gaps at the outset and to ensure that no country might in the future enjoy certain advantages because our study failed to take due account of these instruments.

The listing of the instruments of surprise attack in our explanatory document on Section One of our Plan of Work thus covers all the major relevant weapons systems. It does not, to be sure and for a good reason, list nuclear weapons as a separate and special category. There is instead an indication of the capability of each weapons system to deliver nuclear weapons. The main reason for this, as Dr. Kistiakowsky explained on December 9, is the difficulty of controlling nuclear weapons as such. Although the question does not concern this conference, we must note that our governments have proposed a cessation, under international control, of the production of fissionable material for weapons purposes to be followed by a transfer, in successive increments, of agreed amounts of fissionable material from past production over to supervised peaceful uses. Our scientists have been unable to discover any practical means for detecting the immediate presence or imminent use of nuclear weapons as such. We have, therefore, in our plan for examining the problem of surprise attack concerned ourselves with systems of delivery since these, in contrast to warheads, can at the present time be observed and inspected in a practical way.

We would note parenthetically that in insisting that all instruments of surprise attack should at the outset be taken into account, we have at the same time made clear our view that a complete system cannot be achieved all at once. We are not advocating an all or nothing approach. We would not prejudge what measures governments might or might not decide to institute. Our plan of work merely attempts to ensure that all the relevant factors would be studied, so that expert technical judgments could be made concerning the types of measures most likely to bring the greatest amount of security against surprise attack and also concerning measures of a more limited nature. Such judgments would not only advance our governments' understanding of the problem and of what could be done to produce the greatest reduction of the danger. They would also clarify the nature and value of various possible preliminary measures which governments might wish to institute. All we have asked here is that we prepare for governments an evaluation of these questions and let them decide on the procedures for implementation and the relationship of such implementation to measures of disarmament.

Just as we have insisted that no instrument of attack be left out of account from the outset, so we have been equally unwilling to narrow the discussion to the specific areas affected by the proposals of the experts on the other side of the table. In the absence of some acceptance by them of our plan of work, such an undertaking would have meant ruling out of the discussion automatically long range aircraft and missiles. We have always been willing to relate the discussion to geographical areas for purposes of illustration; but if discussion is to be effective such illustrative areas must take account of the range of modern weapons.

3. *Surprise Attack and Disarmament Measures*

Our third point is that we believe that our approach would have given all of us a sufficiently broad frame of reference to permit a fruitful and effective discussion of the technical aspects of reducing the danger of surprise attack. We believe that the experts on the other side of the table have not had sufficient grounds for rejecting our plan of work in their unsubstantiated claim that there can be no fruitful or effective discussion of the problem of surprise attack except in the context of a broad discussion of disarmament measures.

We do not want to go into what appears to us to be the self-evident logic of approaching the problem of surprise by considering ways of increasing our knowledge of what is about to happen. Let me just emphasize again a point which we have already made on various occasions. We have repeatedly invited you to substantiate your view that the problem of surprise attack is wholly inseparable from disarmament. We do not prejudge this question. We have sought to discuss possible systems of warning as hypotheses—to be confirmed, modified, or abandoned as the facts may require. If it is the firm conviction of the experts across the table that our hypotheses are false, we believe that they should not have declined to submit a technical demonstration of their point—the more so since such a discussion would have been without prejudice to the later decisions of governments.

Beyond this, we believe that the approach we have recommended is broad rather than narrow as the experts across the table have implied. We have stated our willingness under Section III of our plan of work to consider and make allowances for changes which might take place, by unilateral action or by mutual agreement, in the actual strength and condition of the weapons system under inspection. Thus on November 25, in introducing our explanatory document on Long Range Aircraft, we noted that the changes in question might concern force levels, the pattern of aircraft operation and aircraft types and other equipment.

4. *The Need for Objective Judgments*

Our fourth and final point is that our approach is concrete and realistic. We submit that a proposal in the field of disarmament does not become concrete until it is possible to make quantitative judgments concerning its requirements. We grant that these judgments would become even more specific as we reached the point of dealing with geographic areas, with all the political difficulties that this would entail. We believe, however, that it is both desirable and feasible to make certain measurements before reaching these political difficulties. This is what we had hoped, at the very least, to accomplish in these talks. The urgent need for these measurements represents the fourth and perhaps most compelling recommendation of our plan of work. Let me discuss first why it would have been desirable to begin with these measurements and then suggest briefly how it would have been feasible.

There are two main reasons why it would have been desirable. The first concerns our insistence that measures to reduce the danger of surprise attack, like other measures in the field of disarmament, should be dependable. We have been charged with making control, that is to say means of verification, an absolute principle and universal remedy. This is not so. We want only as much verification as may be necessary to ensure dependability. In the case of the problem of surprise attack, we seek to define certain arrangements which could increase assurance on all sides that a surprise attack is not imminent. The essence of the problem lies in the ingenuity and balance of the arrangements designed for the purpose. Any agreement to institute arrangements which are not adequate really to increase this assurance would serve no good purpose. It is inconceivable to us that we could lay an adequate technical foundation for working out arrangements for this purpose without a systematic examination of the capabilities of modern techniques of detection in the light of the technology of modern weapons. To have agreed to such an examination would have been to us an earnest of your willingness to work toward dependable measures. You were willing to go into these matters after only a few days of the technical discussions on the detection of nuclear tests last July. Your complete refusal to do so here after over a month of discussion suggests to us you may not desire any genuine or practical measure to reduce the danger of surprise attack. Our suspicion is greatly reinforced by the nature of the paper submitted by the experts on the other side of the table on December 12 on ground control posts and aerial inspections. What is described in this document is in effect self inspection. It would afford no indication—or at best only the most unreliable indication of the imminence of surprise attack.

To begin the working out of measures to reduce the danger of surprise attack by answering concrete technical questions would thus, in our view, have been an acknowledgment on all sides of the need to evolve effective and practical measures. But it would have afforded more than this basis of confidence. We believe as a general principle that one reason why disarmament negotiations have become deadlocked in the past is that they have been addressed to questions which cannot be answered in objective terms. In dealing with the problem of surprise attack for example, considerations of national interest have been viewed from both sides without the benefit of any objective estimate as to the requirements of a given kind of attack or of the relative capability of a given system in discouraging an attack. As a result both sides have in the past made proposals and counter-proposals without a precise knowledge of their implications, making an allowance for this imprecision in the conservatism of the proposals. At least partly as a result of this such proposals have been far apart and past political negotiations without issue. Our plan of work could have helped to overcome this difficulty in the case of the problem of surprise attack.

These are some reasons why we have thought concrete technical discussion would have been desirable. Let me now suggest some reasons why we have thought it would be feasible. The outcome of the talks on the detection of nuclear testing last August was in itself a clear demonstration that such technical discussions can reach agreed conclusions. Apart from this, however, let me enumerate a number of questions which we could have usefully answered here without getting into political problems:

1. In the absence of an exchange of blueprints, how much aerial survey effort, of what sort, would be required to locate, say 90 percent of the designated instruments of surprise attack within a given area and their sites, bases, etc.? How much supplemental ground inspection effort would be required to reliably locate and identify items disclosed by the aerial survey but not identified?

2. With what reliability could ground observers (assuming certain equipment, personnel, rights of access, and advantages of location vis a vis specific instruments of attack) observe indications of attack at various stages in the preparation of an attack?

3. For each instrument what is the minimum time that would be likely to elapse between a strong indication of its commitment to attack and its impact in the target area? For which instruments might the time be lengthened to include some of the period of preparation? For which might it be shortened because of ambiguities as to final commitment?

4. What are the feasible minimum communication lags from observation sites to the ultimate data processing centres? What time lags in communications are permissible and appropriate for various components of an integrated inspection system? What are the probable loads on a communications system for integrated inspection systems of various sorts in terms of total message groups sent over various circuits, etc.?

These are questions which concern measurable phenomena. For example, the minimum time lag for communicating data (or the fact of circuit interruption) from a ground control post to a data processing centre can be computed in units of time. It amounts to only a small fraction of the flight time of an intercontinental missile. We believe we have suggested over the past five weeks a wide range of questions admitting of equally objective answers; and that if we had together worked out answers to them these answers might well have added up to practical and I need not add concrete systems, and an evaluation of the contribution of each. We have, therefore, been disappointed when the experts on the other side have flatly affirmed that communications lags would exceed the flight of intercontinental missiles and then give no computation or any technical justification for their position.

So much for methodology. We regret that circumstances have not permitted us to go beyond it at this Conference.

We leave Geneva still prepared and anxious to discuss seriously and in detail the technical bases of measures that might reduce the danger of surprise attack. Our preparations for this Conference and work here will not have been a waste of time. We trust we have laid the basis for progress later. We profoundly hope so. We stand ready to resume discussions that show any signs of achieving progress on this critical aspect of the great challenge of our time; the achievement of a secure and durable peace.

I cannot conclude without expressing our sincere thanks to the Secretary-General of the United Nations through his personal representative, Mr. Narayanan, for the invaluable assistance rendered us by the secretariat staff in Geneva. We thank again the authorities of the government of Switzerland and of Geneva for granting us their permission to meet here.

50. Statement regarding the position of the eastern delegations at the conference on the prevention of surprise attack, Geneva, 18 December 1958[1]

I think it appropriate to draw a few conclusions today regarding the work of this Conference, which has been in session now for almost six weeks. The Soviet Union delegation, in consulation with the delegations of the socialist countries taking part in the Conference, has prepared the text of the following declaration on this subject and has entrusted me with the task of delivering it.

First of all it should in all seriousness be stressed that, despite the urgency of the need to solve the problem under discussion, because of the position taken by the western experts so far the Conference has not completed its basic task—it has not succeeded in drawing up recommendations to governments regarding practical measures to prevent surprise attacks. The only significance of the Conference is that it has provided an opportunity to clarify the points of view of the two sides regarding the problem of reducing the danger of surprise attacks. It must be hoped that this in its turn will make it possible to ascertain the real reasons why the Conference

---

[1] U.N. Doc. A/4078, Annex 15. This statement was made by Mr. Kuznetsov, the Soviet delegate, on behalf of the delegations of Albania, Czechoslovakia, Poland, Rumania, and the U.S.S.R.

did not achieve its object, and thus be of help for further attempts to solve the problem.

The need to come to an agreement to take measures to do away with the possibility of one State carrying out a surprise attack on another, as pointed out in the message sent by the Chairman of the Council of Ministers of the USSR, Mr. N. S. Khrushchev, to the President of the United States of America, Mr. D. Eisenhower, on 2 July, arises from the strained character of present international relations and the continuing increase in the rate of re-armament by States, especially in so far as the production of increasingly destructive types of weapons of mass annihilation is concerned.

In initiating action in connexion with convening this Conference, the Soviet Government proceeded on the assumption that the first steps towards preventing surprise attacks would be useful if they included, in addition to a number of control and inspection measures, definite disarmament measures.

Such a trend in the work of the Conference, as has been stressed by us more than once, was necessary because of the nature of the problem. The danger of surprise attack is a direct result of the 'cold war' and the policy of engaging in an armaments race, which increase distrust and suspicion between States and lead to the position of one State regarding another as its potential foe. With the armaments race in progress, particularly as regards weapons of mass destruction, the policy of aiming at 'a position of strength' and 'balancing on the brink of war' pursued by the United States of America and its partners in military blocs, make the problem of preventing surprise attacks especially acute and urgent.

From those indisputable facts, it follows that the solution of this problem is indissolubly bound up with solving the problem of disarmament and putting into operation effective measures to create trust between States.

Any analysis of the reasons why the danger of sudden attack has arisen clearly shows that reliable guarantees that this danger will be removed can only be ensured after atomic and hydrogen weapons have been banned and eliminated from the arsenals of States and the stocks of such weapons have been destroyed and after there has been a substantial reduction of conventional armaments and armed forces.

The Western Powers refuse to agree to the banning of nuclear weapons and to a serious reduction of conventional armaments; thus they do not appear to be prepared at the moment to take serious steps for preventing surprise attacks. Nevertheless, we are certain that even under present conditions we can, provided the will is there, reach an agreement about certain practical steps directed towards lessening the danger of surprise attacks.

It is clear that effective measures for preventing surprise attacks can only be worked out if the interest of all parties are taken into consideration, when no country is placed in a position of inferiority from the point of view of ensuring its safety. Another indispensable condition for the solution of the problem of preventing surprise attacks is that all countries, and above all the great Powers, should abstain from actions leading to a deterioration of international relations and to an increase of the danger of war.

During the Conference, the delegations of the Socialist countries were invariably guided by these principles which spring from the peaceful foreign policy they pursue. With a view to assisting the Conference in reaching a solution of the problems with which they were faced, the Soviet delegation, in consultation with the delegations of Albania, Czecho-slovakia, Poland and Romania, proposed a method of work designed to enable the Conference—provided the other side was willing to do so—to begin immediately to study all the practical aspects of the problem and to work out jointly and agree upon measures that could be realized in practice at the present time.

One of the reasons that necessitated the convening of the present Conference on the prevention of surprise attacks was the dangerous practice of United States planes, carrying nuclear weapons, making flights over the territories of Western European countries and also across the Arctic regions in the direction of Soviet territories.

The Soviet delegation, desiring from the outset to direct the work of the Conference towards the study of urgent measures for the prevention of the danger of surprise attacks, after consulting with the delegations of Albania, Czechoslovakia, Poland and Romania, submitted on 17 November for study by the Conference, a draft recommendation calling on the various States concerned to pledge themselves not to permit flights by their planes carrying atomic and hydrogen weapons over the territories of other countries and over the open seas.

It seems to me there is no need to dwell upon the danger and the threat to world peace of this practice by American atomic bombers. Indeed how can we speak of any prevention or limitation of the dangers of surprise attacks if the air space above the territories of other countries is constantly filled by hundreds of planes with their loads of atomic and hydrogen bombs?

The Soviet Government in its declaration of 28 November stated that 'as long as these flights continue, any agreement on measures for reducing the danger of surprise attack would be to a large extent pointless and could only create false illusions among the peoples of the world, leading them to believe that some measures for reducing the danger of surprise attack had indeed been taken while in actual fact that would not be the case at all.' If the Conference had accepted our recommendation the peoples of the world would have had visual proof that the Conference was making an effort to protect them from the danger of surprise attacks and from the threat of the outbreak of war. Such a measure would create a favourable climate in which it would be easier to regulate the problem of prevention of surprise attacks and settle other important international problems.

The Conference did not reach any positive solution of this problem because of the position taken up by the Western experts. Nevertheless, the delegations of the Socialist countries consider that the question of the prohibition of planes, carrying nuclear weapons, flying over foreign territories is still on the agenda. This question must be settled, since the security of the peoples of the world demand it.

Realizing the importance of the problem of preventing surprise attacks, the Soviet Government did all in its power to ensure that the work of the Conference did not get into an impasse and to promote the successful solution of the problems facing it. An important step in this direction was the Declaration of the Soviet Government concerning the measures to be taken to prevent surprise attack, introduced by the Soviet delegation for the consideration of the Conference on 20 November 1958. On the same day the head of the Czechoslovak delegation introduced, together with the delegations of Albania, Poland, Romania and the Soviet Union, a proposal regarding the introduction of measures for the prevention of surprise attack dealing with the region of Europe and the Near East.

We suggested the establishment on the territories of the NATO countries and of the Baghdad Pact, including the eastern coastal region of the United States of America, and on the territories of the countries of the Warsaw Pact, including the western frontier regions of the Soviet Union of ground control posts at railway junctions and in major ports and on main motor-roads, which would have the task of preventing a dangerous concentration of armed forces and technical equipment at these particular points.

At the same time it was proposed that there should be established an area of aerial photography, extending 800 kilometres east and west of the line dividing the main armed forces of the NATO and Warsaw Pact countries in Europe, as well as on the territories of Greece and Turkey and Iran. Further to this zone the Soviet Government proposed that aerial photography be carried out over equal parts of the eastern territories of the USSR and the western areas of the United States of America, including in this zone a control over Japan and the Island of Okinawa, inasmuch as the United States of America has military bases and troops on the territory of Japan.

In their desire for new constructive measures for the prevention of surprise attacks, the delegations of the Socialist countries submitted, on

21 December,[1] a proposal in which further details were given concerning the aims and functions of land control posts and of aerial inspection.

In their proposals the Socialist countries emphasized that the land control posts and aerial photography cannot *per se* lead to a decrease of the danger of surprise attacks, unless they are linked with measures directed towards a reduction of the concentrations of troops facing one another and para-military political groups in the more dangerous regions of Europe, and unless the more threatening and destructive types of modern arms were prevented from being deployed, at least to begin with, in parts of the territory of Central Europe. In this connexion, a proposal was introduced concerning agreement with the Western Powers to reduce by at least one-third the number of foreign troops stationed at present on the territories of European countries forming part of the control area, and an understanding not to keep nuclear and rocket arms on the territories of the Federal Republic of Germany and the territory of the German Democratic Republic.

As would be obvious to any unprejudiced person, the measures suggested are such that they would not prejudice the security of any country and would, on the contrary, strengthen the security of Europe and would be an important step in the normalizing of the general situation in Europe. Can there really be any doubt that such measures meet the fundamental interests of the peoples of every European country who are perturbed at the situation which has now been created in Europe and who are conscious of the catastrophic consequences of a new war waged with nuclear weapons, especially in densely populated areas of Europe.

It should be further emphasized that, given goodwill on the part of representatives of the Western Powers, the implementation of the measures described above would present no difficulty, even under present conditions.

Had the Conference followed the path recommended by the delegations of Socialist countries, it would undoubtedly have led to an agreement about the concrete and realizable measures which would have led to the reducing of the danger of surprise attack by one State against another.

Unfortunately this did not take place, because the representatives of the Western Powers adopted a negative position with regard to the suggestions which had been put forward and generally refused to make any recommendations to the governments concerned. What exactly had the delegations of those countries in mind when they came to the Conference? It must be stated bluntly that they arrived at the Conference with an aim difficult to reconcile with the problem of preventing surprise attacks.

Judging by the 'illustrative' documents which the Western experts have introduced as well as from their statements, it is clear that the Western experts have come to the Conference with instructions based on

[1] Presumably misprint (in original text) for 12 December, see p. 115 above.

the familiar policy of 'a policy of strength'. According to this policy foreign relations between countries are built not on the principle of the equality of all countries and on a mutual respect for their sovereignty and independence. The policy of action 'from a position of strength' rejects the idea that international problems should be resolved by peaceful means through negotiation by equal countries.

The Western experts made declarations at the Conference in which they stated quite openly the theory that peace could be maintained through deterrents and a further building up of means of mass destruction of human beings. There is no doubt that this conception as well as the conception of a strategic massing of nuclear weapons and of balancing on the brink of war were erected in order to justify a nuclear weapons race, in order to justify the efforts of NATO to increase the number of States possessing atomic and missile weapons.

This fact is once more clearly indicated at the current session of NATO in Paris, which according to the plan of the Western Powers must mobilize all military, scientific, economic and other resources of its members so as to encourage the race in armaments and speed up preparations for a war with nuclear weapons. This session of NATO plans to increase further the number of atomic missile bases in Western Europe as well as to augment considerably the number of West German military units provided with atomic and missile weapons.

It is easy to see that those who follow this path expect to keep ahead of others in the production of the latest types of weapons and in the stocking of such weapons, and count upon possessing a military preponderance with the object of dictating their will to the other countries, if need be by force.

It is hardly necessary to say that the policy based on 'a position of strength' is based on rather shaky foundations and will fail, however strongly its partisans attempt to convince us that this is not so, for this policy is directed—contrary to the peoples' will—towards increased tension between countries and an increased threat of war and, consequently, towards an increased danger of surprise attack. History provides us with sufficient examples of the fact that where relations between countries have been built on a policy of an armament race, on the balance of armed forces, the result has always been war. Nations who have paid dearly for such a policy with their blood and suffering—as may be seen from the history of the Second World War—refuse to live any longer in a climate of oppressive military psychosis under conditions of ever-increasing anxiety about the future and about the fate of their dear ones and humanity in general. The peoples desire that, irrespective of their social and political systems, Governments shall firmly adopt a policy of the widest possible co-operation, mutual respect for human interest, and that this shall solve all problems peacefully.

It would have been far more sensible to approach the problem of surprise attack from the point of view of promoting the security of all countries. That would have been the natural path to take and it would have led the present Conference into making a valuable contribution to the solution of such a pressing problem.

But, the representatives of the Western Powers regarded the Conference not as a means of agreement on practical steps which would have led to the diminution of the danger of surprise attack and of lessening the existing tension between various countries, but as a means for attempting to obtain one-sided military advantages for the Western Powers and to weakening the defensive power of the countries of the Socialist bloc.

This had become clear at the outset of the Conference, when Western experts presented a programme of work that was entirely subordinated to the problem of collecting information concerning the existing types of armament and more particularly the more modern type. At the same time there was not a single word in the programme about developing currently feasible measures for reducing the danger of surprise attack.

The Conference has been at work for almost six weeks but the Western experts have, by and large, failed to get beyond discussing the method of work, trying in every way to impose their programme of developing and submitting for the consideration of governments various abstract 'illustrative' schemes. They openly stated that their plans did not include the development, consideration and, still less, the approval of any concrete proposals for solving the problem before us.

Making all efforts to shun the fulfilment of the task before the Conference, the Western experts perverted the sense of the correspondence between the Governments of the USSR and the United States of America on the nature of the Conference. The Conference, which, as is in part indicated by its agreed title, should have considered currently possible measures for preventing a surprise attack, was turned by them into a highly technical Conference on exclusively technical questions pertaining to armaments and means of observation. In actual fact, the representatives of the Western Powers initiated a highly political discussion under the guise of a technical one, defending the aggressive policy of 'position of strength' and the arms race carried out by the NATO countries. This deliberately altered interpretation of the task of the Conference was necessary to the Western experts as a means of justifying their refusal to consider the proposals of the Socialist countries for reducing the danger of a surprise attack.

During the course of our labours here the Western representatives obstinately attempted to drag the Conference into a consideration of nothing but control questions, a control whose obvious purpose was to get as much military information as possible about the newest weapons such as, for example, long distance rockets. Not measures for preventing a surprise attack, but the means themselves for such an attack—that is what the representatives of the West were particularly interested in.

Striving by all means to impose their programme on the Conference, the Western experts tried to make matters appear as if the Soviet Union and all the Socialist countries did not attach importance to control and inspection. Here it is necessary to clarify our position as regards control.

The Soviet Union and all the Socialist countries have always acted and still act on the assumption that it is necessary to establish an effective control system over concrete measures and agreements designed to bring sanity into the world situation, including, first and foremost, control of all disarmament measures. The necessary control measures were also provided for in our proposals for preventing a surprise attack, which were submitted to the Conference. However, there is a fundamental difference between the approach of the Socialist countries and that of the Western Powers to control questions. The Western Powers are separating control from practical measures for preventing a surprise attack and see in control nothing but the acquisition of information about the defensive readiness of the Socialist countries. Here, as can be seen from their documents and explanations, they have in mind an unrealistic 'universal' control of all territories in the globe, at the same time refusing to adopt the only possible solution in present-day circumstances—control measures in an initially limited area—Europe and the Near East where the danger of a sudden attack is greatest.

One does not have to be experienced in politics or military matters to see that, in view of the mistrust and suspicion among the Governments, the establishment of a control and inspection system, particularly only over the types of weapons the West is interested in, without the parallel application of disarmament measures, cannot be otherwise regarded than as an attempt to take advantage of the control for purposes of reconnaissance. In present conditions, control alone, without measures for increasing confidence and developing co-operation, can only render the situation more acute and contribute to the arms race. In actual fact a Power, learning in the course of such 'universal' control that it is behind its rival, and receiving definite military technical-information, would do everything in its power to catch up. And judging by the policy of the Western Powers this dangerous rivalry can only end in a catastrophe.

It goes without saying that the socialist countries, striving, not for an arms race, but to reach an agreement on disarmament and for the consolidation of world peace, cannot agree with much so-called 'control', which can only help a would-be aggressor and which would increase the danger of a surprise attack.

The Western representatives very understandably showed particular interest in long-distance rockets and in the establishment of control over them. In their statements and 'illustrative' documents they kept on coming back to this question. But as regards ballistic rockets the Western experts were interested in only one part of this weapon, and that is the rocket as a bearer of a warhead. At the same time they refuse to concern themselves with that which transforms these rockets into dangerous weapons—atomic and hydrogen warheads. Nevertheless, it is clear to everyone that atomic and hydrogen bombs dropped from aeroplanes flying from American military bases in, for example, Europe, the Middle and Near East or in North Africa, are as dangerous for human beings as bombs borne in intercontinental rockets. Atomic and hydrogen bombs are equally capable of sowing death and destruction regardless of the means of delivering them to their destination.

It should be fully emphasized that the solution of the problem of rockets and their control is only possible on one condition, namely, that it guarantees in equal measure the security of the United States, the Soviet Union and other States. Consequently, it is impossible, in view of present relations between States, to consider the question of control over intercontinental rockets without also touching the question of prohibiting nuclear weapons and liquidating military bases on foreign territory.

The tactics of concentrating on gathering military information and establishing a control system which would facilitate the gathering of such information, are by no means new, although the Western representatives did try to put them forward as a 'fresh' approach to the problem of preventing a surprise attack.

What is fresh about this approach, when the Western Powers have for nearly thirteen years been trying to persuade States to tackle the question of classifying weapons, ammunition and war materials, instead of seeking ways to reach an agreement on disarmament? Similarly, in this Conference the Western representatives proposed a laboratory study of all means of war instead of a practical approach to the important problem of preventing war. We may well ask what is new about this so-called 'fresh' approach of the Western Powers?

A study of the course of the Conference and an objective analysis of the positions of both parties shows that the representatives of the NATO countries: the United States of America, the United Kingdom, France, Italy and Canada, as distinct from the representatives of the socialist countries, did not make any effort to find ways of solving the problem of preventing a surprise attack. Basing their approach on the interests of Western aggressive circles, they would like to impose their plans on the Conference, which have nothing in common with the interests of peace and international security.

At the same time, the delegations of the socialist countries tried very hard to make the Conference a success. They were guided by the desire to find a common basis giving equal consideration to the security of all parties. This is attested by the proposals of the delegations of the socialist countries, which do not seek to gain any advantages for themselves.

However, as a result of the unconstructive attitude of the Western representatives at the Conference, it proved impossible to prepare agreed recommendations to the governments on measures which might serve to reduce the danger of a surprise attack by one State on another.

In view of the importance and urgency of solving the problem of preventing a surprise attack, the representatives of the socialist countries preferred to continue their efforts to find mutually acceptable recommendations and to avoid interrupting the work of the Conference. However, they were forced to take account of the fact that the Western experts insisted on an interruption. At the same time, the representatives of the socialist countries consider that an interruption should be short and that the sessions should be renewed as soon as possible. They proposed a specific date for renewing the Conference—not later than 5 January 1959. Unfortunately, the Western side refused to name a date. This can only be interpreted as an attempt to shun further talks on preventing a surprise attack.

However, the present state of international relations demands that a common language be found and suitable measures be taken for strengthening peace and guaranteeing the peoples of the world a tranquil life without the perpetual depressing consciousness of the threat of a new and deadly war. The problem of preventing a surprise attack is the problem of the preservation of peace. Its solution is in the interests of all peoples.

As regards the socialist countries, they will from now on strive with might and main to see that the problem of preventing a surprise attack finds a positive solution.

If the representatives of the Western Powers were to change their present negative attitude and, like the representatives of the socialist countries, make real efforts, on the renewal of the Conference, to find a solution mutually acceptable to all States, this would enable us quickly to work out definite measures for preventing the danger of a surprise attack, and, consequently, reducing the danger of a new war. Thus, a very important step would be taken towards preservation of peace and creating favourable conditions for developing co-operation between all States.

c. Rapacki Plan

51. Soviet reply to the Polish memorandum on an atom-free zone in Central Europe, 3 March 1958[1]

In reply to the Memorandum of the government of the Polish People's Republic of February 14,[2] concerning the establishment of an atom-free zone in Central Europe, the Soviet government considers it necessary to state the following:

The Soviet government, as it has repeatedly declared, fully supports the initiative of the government of the Polish People's Republic concerning the establishment in Europe of a zone—including the territories of the Polish People's Republic, the Czechoslovak Republic, the German Democratic Republic and the Federal Republic of Germany—in which atomic, hydrogen and rocket weapons would be neither manufactured nor deployed. The implementation of this proposal would unquestionably be a major contribution to the cause of relaxing tensions and ensuring peace in the heart of the European continent, in one of the tensest areas of the world with an unusual—for peacetime—concentration of the troops of two military groupings and various modern weapons and equipment.

The establishment of an atom-free zone in Europe would fully accord with the vital interests of the peoples of the European states, who have been profoundly alarmed by the danger of a devastating war involving the use of atomic, hydrogen and rocket weapons and who realise the calamities and suffering that would result from the use of such weapons of mass destruction, particularly in the densely populated areas of Europe. The implementation of this proposal would have a most beneficial effect on the international situation as a whole and would lead to the establishment of the necessary confidence in the relations between states.

If such an atom-free zone were to be set up in Europe, all of Central Europe, embracing a territory with an area of roughly one million square kilometres[3] and a population of more than 100 million, would be freed from the manufacture and stockpiling of atomic, hydrogen, and also rocket weapons, and this would be of inestimable importance to Central Europe, where the armed forces of the two military groupings are in contact and where local conflicts can most easily grow into major ones, with all the dire consequences this would entail for the cause of peace.

---

[1] *Soviet News*, 5 March 1958.

[2] See *Documents* for 1957, pp. 155–9. The memorandum was included in the 1957 volume since the plan owed its origin to a speech by Mr. Rapacki in the United Nations in October 1957, was renewed through diplomatic channels in December 1957, and, as the House of Commons was informed by Mr. Ormsby-Gore on 16 December, was being examined by the British Government before the end of 1957. See ibid., p. 123.

[3] About 386,100 square miles.

The Soviet government has carefully studied the Memorandum of the government of the Polish People's Republic, which sets forth its considerations concerning both the obligations to be undertaken by the states within the zone as well as the obligations to be undertaken by the U.S.S.R., the United States, the United Kingdom and France, and also other states whose troops are stationed on the territories of the states within that zone.

The Soviet government fully agrees that the states within the zone should undertake not to manufacture, stockpile or receive for their own purposes, and to prevent the installation on their territories of devices and equipment to service nuclear weapons, including rocket launching ramps.

The Soviet government believes, as it has already said in its statement of February 19,[1] that the effective implementation of the proposal to set up a zone in Central Europe free from atomic, hydrogen and rocket weapons requires that, along with the corresponding obligations of the states within this zone, the powers possessing nuclear and rocket weapons should solemnly undertake to respect the status of the zone and regard the territory of the states within it as one excluded from the use of nuclear and rocket weapons. This would put these powers under the obligation not to equip their troops or the troops of other states stationed on the territory of the zone with atomic and rocket weapons, and not to transfer these weapons to the governments of states within the zone or to the armed forces stationed within it under the command of military groupings, as also not to import or build installations and military equipment to service nuclear weapons, including rocket launching installations.

Guided by the interests of consolidating peace on the European continent and throughout the world, the Soviet government, for its part, already declared on February 19 that it was ready to assume the aforementioned obligations, provided the governments of the United States, the United Kingdom and France did likewise.

The government of the U.S.S.R. notes with satisfaction the identity of viewpoints of the Soviet Union and the Polish People's Republic on this question and expresses its full agreement with the proposal of the Polish People's Republic to the effect that the U.S.S.R., the United States, the United Kingdom, and France assume the obligation not to use nuclear weapons against the territory of the zone and any objects on it, as well as the obligations:

(a) Not to maintain nuclear weapons among the armaments of their troops stationed on the territories of the states of the zone; not to maintain and not to site on the territory of the states of the zone any installations and equipment designed for servicing such weapons, including rocket launching installations;

[1] For text, see *Soviet News*, 20 February 1958.

(b) Not to transfer in any way or under any pretext either nuclear weapons or related installations and equipment to governments or any other agencies on this territory.

The Soviet Union is also in agreement with the considerations set forth in the Memorandum concerning control—to be agreed upon by the parties concerned—in the zone, and is ready to take part in effecting such control.

The Soviet government also expresses its full agreement with the proposals of the government of the Polish People's Republic relating to the procedure of preparing and giving form to the agreement on the zone.

The realisation of the proposal for setting up a zone free from atomic, hydrogen and rocket weapons would be conducive to the solution of questions relating to the reduction, by agreement between the states concerned, of the strength of foreign troops and conventional armaments in this zone and to the adoption of further broader measures both in the sphere of disarmament and in the solution of other major international problems.

The problem of the establishment in Central Europe of a zone free from the production and stationing of atomic, hydrogen and rocket weapons is one of the most pressing international problems, calling for immediate solution. It is precisely for this reason that the Soviet government has suggested that a conference of leading statesmen, with the participation of the heads of government, should consider the question of establishing a denuclearised zone, among other most important problems of our times.

The Soviet government hopes that the governments of the powers possessing nuclear and rocket weapons, and also the government of the Federal Republic of Germany, will give every support to the proposal for setting up the zone and thus contribute to the achievement of the noble aim of removing the danger of an atomic war and of using atomic energy only for peaceful purposes, for the benefit of mankind.

52. United States note replying to the Polish memorandum on an atom-free zone in Central Europe, 3 May 1958[1]

Excellency: I have the honor to acknowledge the receipt of Mr. Rapacki's note of February 14, 1958, enclosing a memorandum elaborating on the Polish Government's proposals concerning the establishment of a denuclearized zone in Central Europe.[2]

Recognizing that the initiative of the Polish Government stems from a desire to contribute to the attainment of a stable and durable peace, my

[1] D.S.B., 19 May 1958, pp. 821–2; for the United Kingdom note of 17 May 1958 rejecting the Rapacki Plan for similar reasons, see Manchester Guardian, 20 May 1958.
[2] See fn. 2 on p. 132, above.

Government has given these proposals serious and careful consideration. On the basis of this study it has concluded that they are too limited in scope to reduce the danger of nuclear war or provide a dependable basis for the security of Europe. They neither deal with the essential question of the continued production of nuclear weapons by the present nuclear powers nor take into account the fact that present scientific techniques are not adequate to detect existing nuclear weapons. The proposed plan does not affect the central sources of power capable of launching a nuclear attack, and thus its effectiveness would be dependent on the good intentions of countries outside the area. The proposals overlook the central problems of European security because they provide no method for balanced and equitable limitations of military capabilities and would perpetuate the basic cause of tension in Europe by accepting the continuation of the division of Germany.

An agreement limited to the exclusion of nuclear weapons from the territory indicated by your Government without other types of limitation would, even if it were capable of being inspected, endanger the security of the Western European countries in view of the large and widely deployed military forces of the Soviet Union. Unless equipped with nuclear weapons, Western forces in Germany would find themselves under present circumstances at a great disadvantage to the numerically greater mass of Soviet troops stationed within easy distance of Western Europe which are, as the Soviet leaders made clear, being equipped with the most modern and destructive weapons, including missiles of all kinds.

The considerations outlined above have caused the United States in association with other Western Powers to propose that nations stop producing material for nuclear weapons, cease testing such weapons and begin to reduce present stockpiles. The United States has further proposed broader areas of inspection against surprise attack, including an area in Europe, roughly from the United Kingdom to the Ural mountains. We remain willing to do this. You will recall, moreover, that the Western nations offered at the London disarmament negotiations to discuss a more limited zone in Europe.[1] With regard to missiles you will recall that over a year and a half ago the United States proposed that we begin to study the inspection and control needed to assure the exclusive peaceful use of outer space now threatened by the development of such devices as intercontinental and intermediate range ballistic missiles.

The United States, in association with other Western Powers, has also proposed that a comprehensive and effective European security arrangement be established in conjunction with the reunification of Germany. The proposed arrangements would provide for limitations on both forces

---

[1] For the text of a British, French, Canadian, and U.S. working paper of 2 August 1957 offering to discuss 'a more limited zone of inspection in Europe', see *The Times*, 3 August 1957.

and armaments, measures for the prevention of surprise attack in the area, and assurances of reaction in the event of aggression.

Your note speaks of the existence of opposing military groupings in Central Europe as being responsible for tensions in the area. It should not be necessary for me to recall that the present division of Europe stems primarily from the decision of the Soviet Union not to permit Eastern European nations to participate in the European Recovery Plan. Nor need I repeat the many assurance given as to the defensive character of the North Atlantic Treaty Organization which is reflected in its entire organizational and command structure. The entire history of its creation and development testify to this, though persistent efforts are made in some quarters to portray it otherwise.

In the absence of effective arrangements either general or regional in character which would promote real security and in view of the present policies and armaments of the Soviet Union, the countries of Western Europe along with Canada and ourselves, joined in alliance with them, have no other recourse than to develop the required pattern of integrated NATO military strength and to utilize for defensive purposes modern developments in weapons and techniques.

The views which I have presented above on behalf of my Government point out the basic reasons why the United States considers that the Polish Government's proposals for establishing a denuclearized zone in Central Europe would not serve to advance their expressed objectives. Nevertheless, the United States appreciates the initiative of the Polish Government in seeking a solution to these problems. It hopes that this exchange of correspondence will enable the Polish Government better to understand American proposals in the fields of European security and disarmament. I trust that the improved relations between Poland and the United States will serve as a basis for a better understanding between our two countries on these problems, as well as on other matters.[1]

[1] On 4 December 1958 Mr. Selwyn Lloyd told the House of Commons of Mr. Rapacki's revised proposals: 'He [Mr. Rapacki] announced them at a Press Conference in Warsaw on 4 November. From the account which I have read, it seems that he now suggests action in two phases. The first phase is to provide for a ban on the production of nuclear weapons in Poland, Czechoslovakia and the whole of Germany. It provides for an undertaking not to equip with nuclear weapons armies in those areas which do not already possess them, and it provides for an agreement not to complete installations for nuclear weapons. The second phase provides for reductions of conventional arms, which would be carried out simultaneously with the complete removal of nuclear weapons. Both phases would be subject to appropriate measures of control. It is quite clear that, in the second plan, Mr. Rapacki has tried to meet some of the earlier objections.' Mr. Lloyd then indicated briefly two United Kingdom objections to the revised plan: '. . . the "freeze" on existing equipment of armed forces with nuclear weapons' would 'seriously impair the defence capabilities of the N.A.T.O. forces', and 'involve discrimination against the troops of particular countries'. He went on: 'The complete removal of nuclear weapons . . . would have much wider consequences, because, in my view, it would involve the United States not only in leaving Germany but in leaving Europe as well.' See H.C. Deb., vol. 596, coll. 1376–8.

B. GERMANY AND THE BERLIN CRISIS

1. Note from the German Democratic Republic to the Four Powers regarding a peace treaty for Germany, 5 September 1958[1]

The Government of the German Democratic Republic deems it necessary to approach the Government of the Union of Socialist Soviet Republics in the following matter:

More than 13 years have passed since the end of the Second World War and still no Peace Treaty has been concluded with Germany. The German people calls on all those concerned to apply themselves at last fully and seriously to the solution of this problem and to become conscious of their obligations relative to the future of the German people and to the peace of Europe. The question of the peace treaty is that part of the German problem the solution of which falls within the competency of all states formerly engaged in war, the chief responsibility being upon the four Powers and the two German states. A peace treaty with Germany would be a decisive contribution to a peaceful development in Europe in accord with the interests of its peoples. The preparation of such a treaty is perfectly possible at present and would represent a further step towards the solution of the questions connected with the German problem.

In past years the Government of the German Democratic Republic has repeatedly taken steps conducive to a solution of the question of the peace treaty with Germany. These steps have not unfortunately met with the support of the Western Powers who share responsibility for the working out of a peace treaty with Germany.

In the interest of the early conclusion of a peace treaty with Germany, the Government of the German Democratic Republic proposes to the Governments of the Union of Socialist Soviet Republics, the United States of America and the United Kingdom of Great Britain and Northern Ireland and the Republic of France the immediate setting up of a commission formed of representatives of the four Powers with the task of commencing consultations relative to the preparation of a peace treaty with Germany. These terms of reference would also include the agreement to be made as to the stage at which and the form in which the two German states should be brought in as parties to the negotiations. The Government

---

[1] Translated from the German text in *Europa-Archiv*, 5–20 October 1958, pp. 11124–5. A similar note was sent on the same day to the German Federal Republic. More emphasis was placed on the inclusion in the commission of representatives of the two German states, see *Neues Deutschland*, 6 September 1958 (German text).

of the German Democratic Republic believes that the formation of such a commission would considerably accelerate the conclusion of a peace treaty with Germany and would contribute to the advancement of the solution of this urgent international and pressing German national problem.

The Government of the German Democratic Republic informs the Governments of the four Powers that in connection with the proposal put forward in this Note it has approached the Government of the German Federal Republic with the request that a commission be set up formed of representatives of the two German states which would concern itself with discussion of the questions bound up with the preparation of a peace treaty with Germany. The Government of the German Democratic Republic is of the opinion that this commission should also concern itself with such questions as are exclusively the affair of the two German states. In this connection the emphasis would be on the discussion of such steps as would serve the creation of an undivided, peace-loving and democratic German state.

The Government of the German Democratic Republic expects the Government of the German Federal Republic, in the national interest of the German people and the interests of peace of all peoples, to consent to the proposal put forward and to refrain from further attempts to take the solution of the German question outside the competency of the German Democratic Republic and the German Federal Republic and to transfer it to other powers. The resolution of the Federal Parliament instructing the Government of the German Federal Republic to call upon the four Powers to set up a Four-Power Commission for the working out of proposals for the unification of the two German states is a persistence in the standpoint that the unification of the two German states is the concern of foreign powers and not that of the German people. Such a course would exclude the German people from the solution of its most important national question—a duty incumbent upon it—and impose upon it a foreign decision relative to the ordering of its national and social affairs. Every attempt to disregard the right of the German people to self-determination is, however, doomed to failure.

The method proposed by the Federal Parliament is unrealistic and contrary both to the interests of the German people and to the interests of peace of other peoples. The resolution drawn up by the Federal Parliament is not conducive to the creation of the pre-requisite conditions for the unification of the two German states but diverts and impedes them; it therefore in no way serves the peaceful solution of the German question.

The Government of the German Democratic Republic expresses the expectation that the Governments of the four Powers will consent to the setting up as proposed of a commission of representatives of the four

Powers with the terms of reference put forward above. It hopes that the formation of the commission will take place speedily and that the commission will be able to embark on its work very soon. This would correspond with the wishes of the entire German people and would contribute beyond doubt to the achievement of further progress towards the peaceful solution of the question of Germany.

2. *Aide-mémoire* from the German Federal Republic to the United States, 9 September 1958[1]

The German Federal Parliament (Bundestag) at its meeting July 2, 1958, unanimously passed the following resolution, which was endorsed by the German Federal Council (Bundesrat) at its meeting July 18, 1958:

In order to promote the reestablishment of German unity, the Federal Government is herewith directed to request the four powers, France, the Union of Socialist Soviet Republics, the United Kingdom, and the United States, to set up, either at a future international conference (summit conference) or independently thereof, a four-power group (at least at the level of an ambassadors' conference) with a mandate to prepare joint proposals for the solution of the German problem.

The Federal Government shares the desire expressed in the Bundestag resolution, that a group of the four powers responsible for the solution of the German problem be set up either at a future international conference (summit conference) or independently thereof. It hopes that this group will study proposals concerning the reestablishment of German unity, and carry out the preparatory work necessary for final negotiations to be held at a later date.

In compliance with the mandate given to it by the Bundestag and the Bundesrat, and in view of the talks in preparation for an international conference which have been taking place in Moscow between representatives of the four powers responsible for the reunification of Germany, the Federal Government begs to direct the attention of the Government of the United States of America to the desire expressed in the above resolution.

[1] *D.S.B.*, 20 October 1958, pp. 614–15. Identical *aides-mémoire* were delivered to the United Kingdom, French and Soviet representatives in Bonn on 9 September 1958. The resolution of the Bundestag of 2 July was turned down by Mr. Khrushchev in his address to the Fifth Congress of the Socialist Unity Party of Germany in Berlin on 11 July. For a report of this speech in which Mr. Khrushchev described the Bundestag's plan for a 4-power committee as another attempt to make the German people accept the illusion of a possible 4-power solution of the German problem, see *Soviet News*, 14 July 1958.

3. Soviet note to the United States regarding the proposals of the German Democratic Republic for a German peace treaty, 18 September 1958[1]

The government of the Union of Soviet Socialist Republics presents its compliments to the government of the United States of America, and considers it necessary to make the following communication:

On September 5 last, the Soviet government received from the government of the German Democratic Republic a Note expressing anxiety regarding the intolerable delay over the preparation of a peace treaty with Germany. The Note suggested the immediate setting up of a commission of representatives of the four great powers, with the duty of holding consultations to draft a German peace treaty. The government of the German Democratic Republic announced that analogous Notes had been sent to the governments of the United States, the United Kingdom and the Republic of France. The government of the German Democratic Republic also announced that, at the same time, it suggested to the government of the Federal Republic of Germany that a commission of representatives of the two German states be set up, to examine, from the German point of view, all questions relating to the drafting of a peace treaty with Germany. According to the proposal made by the government of the German Democratic Republic, this commission would deal with matters relevant to the establishment of a single, peaceloving, democratic republic which fall within the competence of the two German states.

Bearing in mind that the drafting of a peace treaty is part of the German problem, responsibility for the solution of which rests on all countries which took part in the war and, above all, on the four great powers, the Soviet government would like to make clear to the government of the United States its point of view on the proposals of the government of the German Democratic Republic, so that joint steps may be taken, in the near future, to bring about a peaceful settlement with Germany. The action of the government of the German Democratic Republic shows how deeply the German people feel about the abnormal situation which has remained for 13 years in Germany, as a result of the absence of a peace treaty with that country. It is another reminder to the great powers—which bear the main responsibility for a peaceful settlement with Germany—of the need to discharge, at last, their duty to the German people.

The proposal of the government of the German Democratic Republic that a commission of representatives of the four powers, and an appropriate

---

[1] *Soviet News*, 22 September 1958. Similar notes were sent to the United Kingdom and France. For a summary of the notes sent to the German Democratic Republic and the German Federal Republic, see ibid.

German commission, be set up to draft a peace treaty with Germany takes into account the realities of the conditions prevailing today and paves the way for the practical solution of this problem, long since ready for solution.

Advocating the fundamental solution of the German problem, the Soviet government has more than once made proposals aimed at the immediate conclusion of a peace treaty with Germany—proposals which, however, were not supported at the time by the western powers.

It again raised this question recently, in connection with the preparations for a summit conference, believing that the question should be examined as one of the most important items on the agenda of such a conference.[1]

Everyone is aware of the undeniable fact that the absence of a peace treaty with Germany leaves unsettled many questions which profoundly disturb the whole German people, and affect most important interests of other European peoples who took part in the war against Germany, including these peoples' security. No one has the right to deprive the German people, for such a long period, of their opportunity to enjoy all the blessings of peace—all the more so since similar questions affecting all other countries involved in the war on the side of Hitler Germany have long since been settled.

The conclusion of a peace treaty with Germany would finally draw a line under the last war and its grave aftermath for the European peoples, and would undoubtedly be of great importance for easing tension and safeguarding European security. It would also make it possible to protect the domestic development of Germany from any outside interference, and to restore fully her sovereignty and independence. Germany would be placed on an equal footing with other countries in all respects, and would be admitted to the United Nations. The drafting of a peace treaty, laying down the political and economic conditions for Germany's development and military status, is also prompted by the urgent need to give the German people a clear perspective for Germany's future development.

Supporting the initiative of the government of the German Democratic Republic, the Soviet government also believes that the preparation of a peace treaty, with the participation of the two German states, would help to bring them closer together, would help them to pool their efforts with the object of restoring the unity of the German state.

The Soviet government hereby informs the government of the United States that it has conveyed to the government of the German Democratic Republic its agreement to the proposal for the setting up of a commission of representatives of the four powers, with the object of holding discussions

---

[1] Item 7 of the Soviet proposals on questions to be put forward for consideration at a summit conference of 5 May 1958, see above, p. 26.

on the drafting of a peace treaty with Germany. It also supports the proposal for the establishment of a commission of representatives of the two German states, and expresses its willingness to give such a commission any assistance it requires. The Soviet government anticipates that, in keeping with its obligations concerning a peace settlement with Germany, the government of the United States of America will also support these proposals of the German Democratic Republic, and will take the necessary steps to carry them into effect.

The Soviet government would be grateful to learn, as soon as possible, the views of the government of the United States on the matters discussed in this Note.

4. United States *aide-mémoire* to the German Federal Republic, 30 September 1958[1]

The Embassy of the U.S.A. has been instructed to inform the Federal Ministry of Foreign Affairs as follows:

The Government of the United States refers to the Aide Memoire of the Federal Government of September 9, 1958, which draws attention to a resolution passed by the German Federal Parliament and endorsed by the German Federal Council. This resolution calls for the establishment of a Four Power group composed of representatives of the powers responsible for solution of the German problem with a mandate to prepare joint proposals for the solution of the German problem. It also suggests that the group envisaged would be set up either at a future international conference of Heads of Government or independently thereof.

The Government of the United States notes that the Government of the Federal Republic shares the desire expressed in the resolution of the German Legislature and that it hopes that this group will study proposals concerning the re-establishment of Germany unity and carry out the preparatory work necessary for final negotiations to be held at a later date.

The Government of the United States welcomes the initiative of the Federal Government. As the latter is aware, the German problem is an important element in the proposals put forward by the Western Powers to the Soviet Government on May 28[2] for an agenda for a meeting of Heads of Government. The preparatory talks in Moscow for such a meeting, mentioned in the Federal Republic's Aide Memoire, have been in suspense since the end of May because of the Soviet Government's failure to reply to the Western proposal of May 31[3] for overcoming the procedural

---

[1] *D.S.B.*, 20 October 1958, pp. 613–14. Identical notes were delivered to the Federal Ministry for Foreign Affairs by the United Kingdom and French representatives at Bonn on 30 September 1958.

[2] See above, pp. 31–37, particularly pp. 34–35.   [3] See above, p. 37.

difficulty caused by the divergence in the Soviet and Western sets of agenda proposals. Additional efforts to obtain a response, made by the Western Powers on July 1 and August 22,[1] have also so far been to no avail.

The Western Powers continue to hold that a summit meeting would be desirable if it would provide opportunity for serious discussions of major problems and if it would be an effective means of reaching agreement on significant subjects. The Government of the United States hopes that the Soviet Government will now reply to the Western proposal so that the preparatory talks which would cover the important question of Germany, may continue. At the same time, in view of the crucial importance of the settlement of the German problem to the relaxation of world tensions, the Government of the United States is also prepared to discuss the German problem in a separate Four Power group to be set up in accordance with the desire of the Federal Government expressed in its Aide Memoire of September 9.

The Government of the United States has constantly sought to bring about the creation of a freely-elected all-German Government which would be truly representative of the German people and which could conclude a peace treaty. Until such a Government is created the continued division of Germany maintains a situation in which a segment of the German people is forced to suffer the oppression of a regime imposed on it from without.

For a long time, efforts to resolve German questions have been thwarted by the refusal of the Soviet Government to agree to any plan which would make reunification possible in a way which would insure the freedom of the whole German people. Once a freely-elected all-German Government truly representative of the German people has been created, it would be possible to proceed with such a Government to the conclusion of a peace treaty. The Government of the United States is informing the Soviet Government of its support of the initiative of the Federal Republic and urging the Soviet Government to give it favorable consideration.

5. United States note to the Soviet Union regarding a German peace treaty, 30 September 1958[2]

The Embassy of the United States of America presents its compliments to the Ministry of Foreign Affairs of the Union of Soviet Socialist

---

[1] Mr. Macmillan's letter to Mr. Khrushchev of 1 July is printed above, pp. 49–50. For a similar letter from President Eisenhower to Mr. Khrushchev of 2 July, see *D.S.B.*, 21 July 1958, pp. 95–6. For the United States note of 22 August see above, p. 104; identical notes were sent by the United Kingdom and France.

[2] *D.S.B.*, 20 October 1958, pp. 615–16. Identical notes were delivered to the Soviet Ministry for Foreign Affairs by the United Kingdom and French Embassies in Moscow on 30 September 1958.

Republics and on instruction of its Government has the honor to state the following:

The United States Government wishes to refer to the Soviet Government's note of September 18. It regrets that the Soviet note ignores the proposals made by the Government of the Federal Republic of Germany, which were contained in an Aide Memoire of September 9 addressed to the Governments of France, the Soviet Union, the United Kingdom and the United States. These proposals, based on an unanimous resolution of the German Federal Parliament which was endorsed by the German Federal Council, also called for the establishment of a Four Power group to discuss the German problem. The United States Government observes that instead, the Soviet note is based on proposals made by the so-called 'Government of the German Democratic Republic'.

The United States Government fully shares the view expressed in the Soviet Government's note that 'no one has the right to deprive the German people for such a long time of the opportunity to enjoy all the advantages of a state of peace'.

It also notes with satisfaction the statement that the Soviet Government is 'in favor of a fundamental settlement of the German question'. It is well known to the Soviet Government that this has long been the aim of the United States Government. It is sufficient to recall the opening words of the Berlin Declaration which was made by the Governments of France, the Federal Republic of Germany, the United Kingdom and the United States on July 29, 1957[1]:

Twelve years have elapsed since the end of the war in Europe. The hopes of the peoples of the world for the establishment of a basis for a just and lasting peace have nevertheless not been fulfilled. One of the basic reasons for the failure to reach a settlement is the continued division of Germany, which is a grave injustice to the German people and a major source of international tension in Europe.

The United States Government agrees that, as stated in the Soviet note, 'the conclusion of a peace treaty with Germany would finally draw the line below the last war', and that the German people should themselves participate in the preparation of such a treaty. An essential prerequisite for the negotiation of a peace treaty is, however, the creation of a Government which truly reflects the will of the German people. Only a Government created on such a basis could undertake obligations which would inspire confidence on the part of other countries and which would be considered just and binding by the people of Germany themselves. Moreover, German representatives at any discussions about a peace treaty which were held in advance of the reunification of Germany would, as the Soviet Government must be aware, have no power to commit a

[1] See *Documents* for 1957, p. 97.

future all-German Government to any of the conclusions reached. For these reasons, the United States Government considers that the first task in any discussion of the German problem must be the reunification of Germany and the formation of an all-German Government by means of free elections.

On the method by which such Government should be formed, the United States Government finds the proposals in the Soviet Government's note both unrealistic and unsatisfactory. According to these proposals, the question of the reunification of Germany is to be left to a commission composed of representatives of the Federal Republic and the Soviet Zone. The regime established in the Soviet Zone of Germany does not represent the will of the people of Eastern Germany. It is rightly regarded by the people of all parts of Germany as a regime imposed by a foreign power and maintained in power by foreign forces. Since this regime has no mandate from the people it purports to speak for, it would violate any genuine concern for the interests of the German people to allow such a regime to participate in any discussions involving their future Government.

In the Directive issued by the Four Heads of Government at Geneva in 1955,[1] the Soviet Government recognized its responsibility for the reunification of Germany. The Directive provides *inter alia*: 'The Heads of Government, recognizing their common responsibility for the settlement of the German question and the re-unification of Germany, have agreed that the settlement of the German question and the re-unification of Germany by means of free elections shall be carried out in conformity with the national interests of the German people and the interests of European security'. The United States Government cannot accept that the Soviet Government has the right unilaterally to evade this responsibility or this agreement. In accordance with its similar responsibility the United States Government, in conjunction with the Governments of France and the United Kingdom, has on may occasions put forward proposals designed to achieve the restoration of German unity. These Western proposals recognize the right of the German people to determine their own way of life in freedom, to determine for themselves their own political, economic and social system, and to provide for their security with due regard to the legitimate interests of other nations. They provide for the exercise of this right through the holding of free elections throughout Germany, the establishment of an all-German Government, and the negotiation with this Government of the terms of a peace treaty.

The Government of the United States is ready at any time to enter into discussions with the Soviet Government on the basis of these proposals, or of any other proposals genuinely designed to insure the reunification of Germany in freedom, in any appropriate forum. It regards the solution

[1] See *Documents* for 1955, pp. 48–49.

of the German problem as essential if a lasting settlement in Europe is to be achieved. This problem has been included as one of the subjects which the Western Powers put forward on May 28 for examination at a conference of Heads of Government.[1] Although the Soviet Government agreed that preparations for such a conference should be made between representatives of the Four Powers in Moscow, these preparations have been in suspense since the end of May because of the Soviet Government's failure to reply to the Western proposals of May 31 for overcoming the procedural difficulty caused by the divergence in the Soviet and Western sets of agenda proposals.[2] The further Western communications of July 1 and August 22 have so far also remained unanswered.[3] Since the Soviet Government has indicated in its note that it, too, attaches importance to the solution of the German problem, the United States Government hopes that the Soviet Government will now reply to the Western proposal so that the preparatory talks may continue.

In the interests of making progress on this subject, the Government of the United States is, however, prepared to discuss the German problem in a separate Four Power group to be set up in accordance with the desire of the Federal Government expressed in its Aide Memoire of September 9. The purpose of the group would be to discuss proposals connected with the German problem and to carry out the preparatory work necessary for final negotiations to be held at a later date either at a conference of Heads of Government, if one can be arranged, or otherwise.

The Government of the United States hopes that, in view of the importance of settling the German problem, not only for the German people but also as a contribution towards the relaxation of tension in Europe, the Soviet Government will agree to the procedure set out above.

A copy of the United States Government's reply to the Federal Government's Aide Memoire of September 9 is attached. The United States Government is also informing the Federal Government of the terms of this note.

6. Note from the Soviet Government to the United States regarding the question of Berlin, 27 November 1958[4]

The government of the Union of Soviet Socialist Republics is addressing the government of the United States of America, as one of the powers that

---

[1] See above, pp. 34–35.   [2] See above, p. 37.   [3] See fn. 1 on p. 143, above.
[4] *Soviet News*, 28 November 1958. Similar notes were sent to the United Kingdom and France. Mr. Khrushchev, in a speech made in Moscow on the occasion of the visit of a Polish good-will mission to the Soviet Union, on 10 November 1958, said: 'The time has obviously arrived for the signatories of the Potsdam Agreement to renounce the remnants of the occupation régime in Berlin and thereby make it possible to create a normal situation in the capital of the German Democratic Republic. The Soviet Union, for its part, would hand over to the sovereign

signed the Potsdam Agreement, on the urgent question of the status of Berlin.

The question of Berlin, which lies in the centre of the German Democratic Republic but the western part of which is severed from the German Democratic Republic as a consequence of foreign occupation, profoundly affects not only the national interests of the German people but also the interests of all peoples wishing to establish a lasting peace in Europe. There, in the historic capital of Germany, two worlds are in direct contact and barricades of the 'cold war' exist at every step. A situation of constant friction and tension has prevailed for many years in the city, which is divided into two parts. Berlin, which witnessed the greatest triumph of the joint struggle of our countries against fascist aggression, has now become a dangerous centre of contradictions between the great powers which were allies in the last war. Its role in the relations between the powers can be compared with a slow-burning fuse leading to a barrel of gunpowder. Incidents arising there, even if they seem to be of local significance, in a situation of heated passions, suspicion and mutual apprehension may cause a conflagration which it will be difficult to put out.

This is the dismal finale, reached after 13 postwar years, to the once joint, concerted policy of the four powers—the U.S.S.R., the United States, the United Kingdom and France—towards Germany.

In order to assess correctly the real importance of the Berlin problem confronting us today and in order to determine the possibilities available for normalising the situation in Berlin, it is necessary to recall the development of the policy towards Germany of the powers which were parties to the anti-Hitler coalition.

It is common knowledge that it was not by any means immediately that the United States, or the United Kingdom and France either, drew the conclusion that it was necessary to establish co-operation with the Soviet Union with the aim of resisting Hitler aggression, though the Soviet government constantly displayed willingness for this. In the capitals of the western states opposite tendencies prevailed for a long time and they became most obvious in the period of the Munich deal with Hitler. Entertaining the hope of taming German militarism and pushing it eastward, the governments of the western powers tolerated and encouraged the policy of blackmail and threats pursued by Hitler and acts of direct aggression by nazi Germany and its ally, fascist Italy, against a number of peaceloving states.

It was only when fascist Germany, upsetting the shortsighted calculations

German Democratic Republic the functions in Berlin that are still exercised by Soviet agencies. This, I think, would be the correct thing to do.' For the text of Mr. Khrushchev's speech see *Soviet News*, 11 November 1958.

of the inspirers of Munich, turned against the western powers, and when the nazi army began moving westward, crushing Denmark, Norway, Belgium and the Netherlands and breaking the back of France, that the governments of the United States and the United Kingdom had no alternative but to acknowledge their miscalculations and take the road of organising, jointly with the Soviet Union, resistance to fascist Germany, Italy and Japan. Given a more farsighted policy on the part of the western powers, such co-operation between the Soviet Union, the United States, the United Kingdom and France could have been established much earlier, in the first years after Hitler seized power in Germany, and then there would have been no occupation of France, no Dunkirk and no Pearl Harbour. In that case it would have been possible to save the millions of human lives which were sacrificed by the peoples of the Soviet Union, Poland, Yugoslavia, France, Britain, Czechoslovakia, the United States, Greece, Norway and other countries in order to curb the aggressors.

The creation of the anti-Hitler coalition was an event unprecedented in modern history, if only because states with differing social systems united in a defensive, just war against the common enemy. The Soviet government greatly appreciates the co-operation of the countries—co-operation which took shape in the struggle against fascism and was sealed by the blood of the freedom-loving peoples. The Soviet people would like to preserve and develop the sentiments of trust and friendship which marked their relations with the peoples of the United States, the United Kingdom, France and the other countries of the anti-Hitler coalition during the stern years of the last war.

When the peoples were celebrating victory over Hitler Germany, a conference was held in Potsdam between the heads of government of the Soviet Union, the United States and the United Kingdom in order to work out a joint policy towards postwar Germany. The Potsdam Agreement, to which France acceded soon after its signing, generalised the historical experience of the struggle waged by the peoples to prevent aggression by German militarism. The whole content of that agreement was directed towards creating conditions that would exclude the possibility of an attack by Germany—not for the first time—on peaceloving states, towards preventing the German militarists from unleashing another world war, towards Germany—having abandoned forever the mirage of a policy of conquest—firmly taking the road of peaceful development.

Expressing the will of the peoples who made incalculable sacrifices for the sake of smashing the Hitler aggressors, the governments of the four powers solemnly pledged themselves to extirpate German militarism and nazism, to prevent forever their resurgence and to take all measures to ensure that Germany would never again threaten her neighbours or the preservation of world peace. The participants in the Potsdam Conference expressed their determination to prevent any fascist and militarist activity or propaganda. They also pledged themselves to permit and encourage all democratic political parties in Germany. With the aim of destroying the economic foundations of German militarism, it was resolved to eliminate the excessive concentration in the economy of Germany, represented in the form of cartels, syndicates, trusts and other monopoly organisations which had ensured the assumption of power by fascism and the preparation and carrying out of Hitler aggression.

The Potsdam Agreement contained important provisions whereby Germany was to be regarded as a single economic whole during the occupation period. The agreement also provided for the setting up of central German administrative departments. The Council of Foreign Ministers, set up by decision of the Potsdam Conference, was instructed to prepare a peace settlement for Germany.

The implementation of all these measures should have enabled the German people to effect a fundamental reconstruction of their life and to ensure the establishment of a united, peaceloving and democratic German state.

Such are the main provisions of the Potsdam Agreement, which ensured a just combination of the interests both of the peoples who had fought against Germany and the fundamental interests of the German people themselves, and at the same time created a sound foundation for carrying through a concerted policy of the four powers on the German question, and consequently, for extensive and fruitful co-operation among them on European questions in general.

However, further developments did not follow the course laid down at Potsdam. The relations between the U.S.S.R. and the three western powers increasingly deteriorated and there was a growth of mutual distrust and suspicion, which have now already developed into unfriendly relations.

The Soviet government sincerely hoped that after the victorious war it would be quite possible, notwithstanding all the inevitability of ideological differences, to continue the fruitful co-operation among the great powers that headed the anti-Hitler coalition, on the basis of sober recognition of the situation created by the war.

The policy of the western powers, however, was increasingly influenced by forces hating socialist and communist ideas, but concealing, during the war, their schemes hostile to the Soviet Union. As a result, a course was set in the West towards the utmost sharpening of the ideological struggle headed by aggressive leaders, opponents of peaceful co-existence between states. The signal for this was given to the United States and other western countries by Winston Churchill in his notorious Fulton speech in March 1946.

The conflict between two ideologies—a struggle of minds and convictions

—in itself could not have done any special harm to the relations between states. The ideological struggle has never died down and it will
continue, inasmuch as different views are held on the system of society.
But the pronouncements of Winston Churchill and his associates unfortunately influenced the minds of other western statesmen, which had the most
regrettable consequences. Government agencies and armed forces joined
in the heated ideological struggle. The results are universally known:
instead of an expansion of co-operation between the main great powers,
the world was split into antagonistic military groupings and competition
began in the manufacture and stockpiling of atomic and hydrogen weapons
—in other words, war preparations were launched.

The Soviet government deeply regrets that events took such a turn,
since this prejudices the cause of peace and is contrary to the natural desire
of the peoples for peaceful co-existence and friendly co-operation. There
was a time when leaders of the United States and the United Kingdom, and
in particular Franklin D. Roosevelt, the outstanding statesman of America,
reflecting these sentiments of the mass of the people, proclaimed the
necessity of setting up a system of mutual relations between states under
which the peoples would feel secure and men and women everywhere
could live all their lives knowing no fear.

The relations of the United States, and also of the United Kingdom and
France, with the Soviet Union took a particularly sharp turn when those
powers began carrying through in Germany a policy contrary to the
Potsdam Agreement. The first violation of the Potsdam Agreement was
the refusal of the governments of the United States, the United Kingdom
and France to honour their commitments under this agreement regarding
the transfer to the Soviet Union of the agreed amount of industrial equipment from Western Germany as partial compensation for the destruction
and damage inflicted on the national economy of the U.S.S.R. by the
aggression of Hitler Germany.

But that was not all, and the governments of the United States and the
United Kingdom, with every passing year, further abandoned the
principles underlying the Potsdam Agreement.

The same road was followed by France who, though she acceded to the
Potsdam Agreement later, cannot, of course, disclaim her share of
responsibility for the fulfilment of this agreement.

Setting about the restoration of the military and economic potential of
Western Germany, the western powers revived and strengthened the very
forces that had forged the nazi war machine. Had the western powers
honoured the Potsdam Agreement, they should have prevented the
restoration of the positions of the German militarists, checked revenge-
seeking tendencies and not tolerated the building up by Germany of an
army and an industry for the manufacture of means of annihilation. It is,

however, well known that the governments of the three powers, far from doing this, on the contrary have sanctioned the setting up of a West German army and are encouraging the arming of the Federal Republic of Germany, disregarding the commitments assumed at Potsdam. Furthermore, they have included Western Germany in the North Atlantic bloc, which was set up behind the Soviet Union's back, and, as is clear to everyone, against the Soviet Union, and are now arming Western Germany with atomic and rocket weapons.

It is evident that the bitter lessons of the murderous war have been lost on some western statesmen, who are again dragging into the light of day the notorious Munich policy of instigating German militarism against the Soviet Union, recently their comrade-in-arms.

The legitimate question arises: Can those who have inspired the present policy of the western powers towards Germany themselves guarantee that German militarism, which they have nurtured, will not attack its present partners again and that the American, British and French peoples will not have to pay with their blood for the violation by the governments of the three western powers of the Allied agreements on the development of Germany along a peaceloving and democratic road? Such a guarantee could scarcely be given by anyone.

The policy of the United States, the United Kingdom and France towards Western Germany also led to a violation of the provisions of the Potsdam agreements designed to ensure the unity of Germany as a peace-loving and democratic state. And when a separate state—the Federal Republic of Germany—was set up in Western Germany, occupied by the troops of the three powers, Eastern Germany, where forces determined to prevent the plunging of the German people into another catastrophe had assumed the leadership, had no alternative but to create, in its turn, an independent state.

Two states thus came into being in Germany. Whereas in Western Germany, whose development was directed by the United States, the United Kingdom and France, a government took office whose representatives do not conceal their hatred of the Soviet Union and often openly advertise the similarity of their aspirations with the plans of the nazi aggressors, in Eastern Germany a government was created which broke forever with Germany's aggressive past. State and public affairs in the German Democratic Republic are regulated by a constitution that is fully in keeping with the principles of the Potsdam Agreement and the finest progressive traditions of the German people. The domination of the monopolies and junkers was abolished for ever in the German Democratic Republic, nazism was extirpated, and a number of other social and economic transformations were carried out which prevented the possibility of a revival of militarism and made the German Democratic Republic an important factor for peace in Europe. The government of the German Democratic Republic solemnly proclaimed that it would fulfil its commitments under the Potsdam Agreement to the letter, which, by the way, the government of the Federal Republic of Germany is obstinately avoiding doing. The inclusion of the Federal Republic of Germany in the North Atlantic bloc impelled the Soviet Union to take retaliatory measures, since the obligations binding the Soviet Union, the United States, the United Kingdom and France, had been broken by the three western powers who had united with Western Germany, and previously with Italy, against the Soviet Union, which had borne the brunt of the struggle against the fascist aggressors. This restricted military grouping likewise created a threat to other countries. Such a situation impelled the Soviet Union and a number of other European countries that had suffered from aggression by German and Italian fascism, to establish their own defensive organisation, concluding for this purpose the Warsaw Treaty, to which the German Democratic Republic also acceded.

There is only one conclusion to be drawn from the foregoing: The Potsdam Agreement has been grossly violated by the western powers. It looks now like the trunk of a tree, once mighty and fruit-bearing, but now mangled and with its core cut out. The lofty aims for which the Potsdam Agreement was concluded, have long since been thrown away by the western powers, and their practical activity in Germany is diametrically opposed to what the Potsdam Agreement envisaged.

The crux of the matter is not, of course, that the social and political systems of the German Democratic Republic and the Federal Republic of Germany are basically different. The Soviet government considers that the settlement of the question of the social structure of the two German states is the concern of the Germans themselves. The Soviet Union stands for complete non-interference in the internal affairs of the German people, just as in those of any other people. But the advance of the German Democratic Republic towards socialism has given rise to the Federal government's ill-feeling and even completely hostile attitude towards it, which is entirely supported and encouraged by the N.A.T.O. countries and, above all, by the United States. Prodded on by the western powers, the government of the Federal Republic of Germany is systematically fomenting the 'cold war' and its leaders have repeatedly made statements to the effect that the Federal Republic will pursue a 'policy of strength,' that is to say, a policy of dictating to the other German state. It follows that the government of the Federal Republic of Germany does not want the peaceful unification of the German people, who are living in two states under two different social systems, but nurtures plans for the abolition of the German Democratic Republic and for strengthening its own militarist state at the expense of the G.D.R.

The Soviet government fully sympathises with the position of the German Democratic Republic, which does not want to see the German working people's democratic and social gains destroyed, capitalist ownership and landlordism restored, the land, mills and factories taken away from the people and a militarist regime extended to the German Democratic Republic. The elections to the People's Chamber, and the local government elections which were held in the German Democratic Republic a few days ago, are yet another striking indication that the population of the German Democratic Republic is overwhelmingly behind the policy of its government, which aims at strengthening peace and reuniting Germany by peaceful and democratic means, but which is determined to defend its socialist gains. The Soviet Union expresses its complete solidarity with the German Democratic Republic, which is firmly defending its legal rights.

If the truth is to be faced, it must be recognised, too, that other countries are far from supporting the plans of the government of the Federal Republic of Germany for the forcible reunification of Germany. And this can be understood, since the peoples, including those of France and Britain, are still smarting from the wounds inflicted on them by Hitler Germany. The scars of the last war, which swept the towns and villages of France, are far from having healed. Nor has the damage done to the capital and many cities of Britain by Nazi air-raids yet been made good, while millions of Englishmen are unable to forget the tragic fate of Coventry. This feeling can also be understood by those peoples who fell victim to occupation by the Hitler army. They lost millions who were killed or tortured to death, and saw on their own soil thousands of towns destroyed and villages burnt. The Soviet people will never forget what happened to Stalingrad, nor will the Poles ever forget the fate of Warsaw or the Czechoslovak people that of Lidice. American families, too, had to taste the bitterness of bereavement, the loss of their kith and kin. Germany started both world wars and on both occasions she drew in the United States of America, whose sons had to shed their blood in lands thousands of miles away from American shores.

Mindful of all this, the peoples cannot, nor will they, permit Germany to be united on the basis of a militarist state.

There is another programme for uniting Germany, one which is put forward by the German Democratic Republic. This is a programme for uniting Germany as a peaceloving and democratic state, and it cannot fail to be welcomed by the peoples. There is only one way of carrying it out. And that is through agreement and contacts between the two German states, and through the setting up of a German Confederation. This proposal, if carried out, would channel the efforts of the two governments and parliaments into a common route of peaceful policy, and would

ensure a gradual coming together and merging of the two German states
—without affecting the social bases of either the German Democratic
Republic or the Federal Republic of Germany.

The Soviet Union, like other countries concerned to strengthen peace
in Europe, supports the proposals of the German Democratic Republic
for the peaceful unification of Germany. The government of the U.S.S.R.
is sorry to note that none of the efforts made in this direction have so far
produced any positive result, since the governments of the United States
and the other N.A.T.O. countries—and, above all, the government of the
Federal Republic of Germany—are, in point of fact, doing nothing towards the conclusion of a peace treaty, or the uniting of Germany.

Consequently, the policies of the United States, the United Kingdom
and France, directed as they are towards the militarisation of Western
Germany and involving her in the military bloc of the western powers,
have prevented the enforcement of those provisions of the Potsdam
Agreement which deal with German unity.

Of all the Allied agreements on Germany, there is, in fact, only one
which is being complied with today. That is the agreement on what is
known as the quadripartite status of Berlin. Basing themselves on this
status, the three western powers rule the roost in West Berlin, making it a
sort of state within a state, and using it as a centre from which to pursue
subversive activity against the German Democratic Republic, the Soviet
Union and the other parties to the Warsaw Treaty. The United States,
Britain and France communicate freely with West Berlin along lines of
communication passing through the territory and the air space of the
German Democratic Republic, which they are not even prepared to
recognise.

The governments of the three powers seek to retain in force a long since
obsolete section of the wartime agreements which governed the occupation
of Germany and which entitled them in the past to remain in Berlin. At
the same time, as has been said, the western powers have grossly violated
the quadri-partite agreements, including the Potsdam Agreement, which
is the most concise expression of the obligations of the powers with respect
to Germany. Nevertheless, the other four-power agreements on the
occupation of Germany, which the governments of the United States, the
United Kingdom and France invoke in justification of their rights in West
Berlin, were approved under the Potsdam Agreement or concluded in
amplification thereof. In other words, the three powers demand the
preservation, for their own purposes, of occupation privileges based on the
quadripartite agreements—agreements which they have flouted.

If the United States, Britain and France are indeed staying in Berlin in
exercise of the rights stemming from these international agreements and,
above all, from the Potsdam Agreement, then this implies their duty to

abide by those agreements. They who have grossly violated those agreements have lost all right to retain their occupation regimes in Berlin or in any other part of Germany. Furthermore, is it really possible to insist on the occupation regimes being maintained in Germany or in any part of Germany more than 13 years after the end of the war? For every occupation is an event of limited duration, which fact is explicitly stipulated in the quadripartite agreements on Germany.

It is well known that the conventional way of ending occupation is for the parties which were at war with each other to conclude a peace treaty, offering the defeated country the conditions necessary for the normalisation of its life.

The fact that Germany still has no peace treaty is, above all, the fault of the governments of the United States, the United Kingdom and France, which have never seemed to like the idea of drafting such a treaty.

It is well known that the governments of the three powers have reacted negatively to every approach the Soviet government has made to them for the preparation of a peace treaty with Germany.

At the moment, the United States, the United Kingdom and France—as follows from their Notes of September 30 last—are opposed to the latest proposals for a peaceful settlement with Germany, put forward by the Soviet Union and the Germany Democratic Republic, while making no proposals of their own on this subject, just as they have made none at any time during the postwar period. In point of fact, the recent Note of the United States government is a restatement of a position shown to be utterly unrealistic, whereby Germany's national unity would be re-established by the U.S.S.R., the United States, Britain and France, instead of by the German states which are to unite. Another fact revealed by the United States government's Note is that it is once again avoiding negotiations with the Soviet Union and the other interested countries for the drafting of a peace treaty with Germany. The result really is a vicious circle: The government of the United States objects to the drafting of a German peace treaty on the grounds of the absence of a united German state—while, at the same time, it hampers the reunification of Germany by rejecting the only feasible chance of solving this problem through agreement between the two German states.

Are not the western powers sticking to this line on the preparation of a peace treaty so as to preserve their privileges in Western Germany and to maintain the occupation regime in West Berlin interminably?

It is becoming increasingly clear that this is precisely the situation.

The Soviet government reaffirms its readiness to take part at any time in negotiations for the drafting of a peace treaty with Germany. However, the absence of a peace treaty can by no means be used as an excuse for an attempt to maintain the occupation regime anywhere in Germany.

The occupation of Germany has long since become a thing of the past, and any attempts to prevent the disappearance of special rights of foreign powers in Germany are becoming a dangerous anachronism. The occupation regime in Germany has never been an end in itself. It was established so as to help the healthy forces of the German nation to build their own new peaceloving and democratic state, on the ruins of militarist Germany.

Anxious to live in peace and friendship with the whole German people, the Soviet Union has established and is maintaining normal diplomatic relations with both German states. It maintains close friendly relations with the German Democratic Republic. These relations have been anchored in the treaty which the Soviet Union and the German Democratic Republic concluded on September 20, 1955. In conformity with that treaty, relations between the two states are based on the principles of complete equality, respect for each other's sovereignty and non-interference in one another's domestic affairs. These, too, are the principles by which the Soviet government is guided in its relations with the other German state—the Federal Republic of Germany.

The governments of the United States, the United Kingdom and France announced the end of their occupation regime in the territory of the Federal Republic of Germany, which had been under their control and administration, when they signed the Paris agreements.

The quadripartite status of Berlin came into being because Berlin, as the capital of Germany, was to be the seat of the Control Council established to run Germany in the first period of occupation. This status has been scrupulously observed by the Soviet Union until the present, although the Control Council ceased to exist as long as ten years ago, and there have long since been two capitals in Germany. The United States, Britain and France, on the other hand, have chosen to abuse in a blatant fashion their occupation rights in Berlin, using the quadripartite status of Berlin to pursue their own objective of damaging the Soviet Union, the German Democratic Republic and the other socialist countries.

The agreement on the quadripartite status of Berlin was once an equal agreement concluded by the four powers for peaceful and democratic goals which were later to become known as the Potsdam principles. At that time this agreement was in accordance with the exigencies of the day and with the interests of all the signatories the U.S.S.R., the United States, Britain and France. Now that the western powers have begun to arm Western Germany and turn her into an instrument of their policy spearheaded against the Soviet Union, the very essence of the allied agreement on Berlin has vanished. It has been violated by three of its signatories, who have been using this agreement against the fourth signatory, the Soviet Union. This being the situation, it would be ridiculous to expect the Soviet

Union or any other self-respecting state to pretend to ignore the changes which have taken place.

A patently absurd situation has arisen, therefore, in which the Soviet Union supports and maintains, as it were, favourable conditions for activity by the western powers directed against the U.S.S.R. and its Warsaw Treaty allies. It is clearly obvious that the Soviet Union, and the other parties to the Warsaw Treaty, can no longer tolerate this state of affairs. For the occupation regime in West Berlin to continue would be tantamount to recognising something like a privileged position for the N.A.T.O. countries, a privileged position for which, of course, there is no justification.

Can anyone really seriously believe that the Soviet Union will help the forces of aggression to develop subversive activities against the socialist countries, let alone to prepare an attack on them? It must be clear to everyone of sound mind that the Soviet Union cannot maintain a situation in West Berlin which is detrimental to its legitimate interests, to its security and to the security of the other socialist countries. It would be well to remember that the Soviet Union is not a Jordan or an Iran, and that it will never allow methods of pressure to be applied to it, in order to force on it conditions suiting the powers belonging to the opposing N.A.T.O. military bloc. But this is just what the western powers want from the Soviet Union, since they seek to retain their occupation rights in West Berlin.

Can the Soviet government afford to disregard all these facts, which affect the basic security interests of the Soviet Union, and its ally, the German Democratic Republic, and of all the signatories of the Warsaw Defence Treaty? Why, of course not! The Soviet government can no longer consider itself bound by that part of the Allied agreements on Germany which has assumed an unequal character and is being used for the maintenance of the occupation regime in West Berlin and for interference in the domestic affairs of the German Democratic Republic.

In view of this, the government of the U.S.S.R. hereby notifies the government of the United States that the Soviet Union regards as null and void the 'Protocol of the Agreement between the Governments of the Union of Soviet Socialist Republics, the United States of America and the United Kingdom, on the Occupation Zones of Germany and on the Administration of Greater Berlin,' dated September 12, 1944; and the associated supplementary agreements, including the Agreement on the Control Mechanism in Germany concluded between the governments of the U.S.S.R., the United States, the United Kingdom and France on May 1, 1945—that is, to say, the agreements which were to be effective during the first years following the surrender of Germany.

It is not difficult to see that all the Soviet government has done by this statement is to acknowledge the real state of affairs, which rests in the fact that the United States, Britain and France have long since abandoned the essentials of the treaties and agreements concluded during the war against Hitler Germany and following her defeat. The Soviet government is doing no more than drawing conclusions which, the Soviet Union finds, follow inevitably from the actual state of affairs. In connection with the foregoing, and also proceeding from the principles of respect for the sovereignty of the German Democratic Republic, the Soviet government will enter into negotiations with the government of the German Democratic Republic at an appropriate moment with a view to transferring to the German Democratic Republic the functions which the Soviet authorities have exercised temporarily in accordance with these Allied agreements, and also in accordance with the agreement between the U.S.S.R. and the German Democratic Republic of September 20, 1955.

The best way to solve the Berlin question would be for a decision to be taken, based on the enforcement of the Potsdam Agreement on Germany. But this would be possible only if the three western powers resumed, in common with the U.S.S.R., a policy towards Germany which would accord with the spirit and the principles of the Potsdam Agreement. In the present circumstances, this would mean the withdrawal of the Federal Republic of Germany from N.A.T.O., with the simultaneous withdrawal of the German Democratic Republic from the Warsaw Treaty Organisation, and the achievement of an agreement whereby, in accordance with the principles of the Potsdam Agreement, neither of the two German states would have any armed forces in excess of those needed to maintain law and order at home and to guard their frontiers.

If the government of the United States of America is unwilling to contribute in this way to the implementation of the basic political principles of the Allied agreements on Germany, it can have no reason, either legal or moral, for insisting on the preservation of the quadripartite status of Berlin.

There may, of course, be some ill-wishers of the Soviet Union who will try to read an urge for some sort of annexation into the Soviet government's position with regard to the occupation regime in Berlin. Such an interpretation would not, of course, have anything in common with real facts. The Soviet Union, like the other socialist countries, makes no territorial claims. It is guided undeviatingly in its policy by the principle of denouncing annexation, that is to say, the grabbing of other peoples' lands and the subjugation of other peoples. This principle was proclaimed by Lenin, the founder of the Soviet state, in the very first days of Soviet government in Russia.

The U.S.S.R. does not seek any conquests. All it wants is to put an end to the abnormal and dangerous situation which has developed in Berlin because of the continued occupation of its western sectors by the United States, the United Kingdom and France.

An independent solution to the Berlin problem must be found in the very near future, since the western powers are refusing to take part in the drafting of a peace treaty with Germany, and the government of the Federal Republic of Germany, supported by the same powers, is pursuing a policy of obstructing Germany's unification. It is necessary to prevent West Berlin from being used any longer for intensified espionage, wrecking or any other subversive activities against the socialist countries, against the German Democratic Republic, the U.S.S.R., or, to quote the leaders of the United States government, to prevent it from being used for 'indirect aggression' against the countries of the socialist camp.

Essentially speaking, the only interest the United States, the United Kingdom and France have in West Berlin consists in using this 'frontline city,' as it is vociferously called in the West, as a vantage point from which to carry on hostile activity against the socialist countries. This is the only benefit the western powers are deriving from their presence in Berlin as occupationists. The ending of the legally unjustified occupation of West Berlin would do no harm either to the United States, or to the United Kingdom, or to France. It would, on the other hand, go far towards improving the international atmosphere in Europe and setting people's minds at rest in all countries.

Conversely, the only conclusion one can draw from the western powers persisting in preserving their occupation of West Berlin is that 'indirect aggression' against the German Democratic Republic and the Soviet Union is not the only aim they are pursuing, and that there must be some plans for a yet more dangerous use of West Berlin.

The Soviet government makes this appeal to the government of the United States, proceeding from its determination to secure a relaxation of international tension; to put an end to the state of 'cold war' and to clear the way for the re-establishment of good relations between the Soviet Union and the United States, and also with the United Kingdom and France; to put out of the way everything which brings our countries into conflict and sets them at loggerheads, and to reduce the causes which give rise to these conflicts. Indeed, one cannot get away from the fact that West Berlin, with its present status, is just such a source of discord and suspicion between our countries.

The most correct and natural way to solve the problem would, of course, be for the western part of Berlin, which is virtually detached from the German Democratic Republic, to be reunited with its eastern part and for Berlin to become a single united city within the state on whose land it is situated.

However, the Soviet government, taking into account the present unrealistic policy of the United States, and also of the United Kingdom and France, with regard to the German Democratic Republic, cannot fail to see the difficulties the western powers have in contributing to such a solution of the Berlin problem. At the same time it is guided by concern to prevent the process of abolishing the occupation regime from involving anything like a painful disruption of the ways which have become entrenched in the life of the population of West Berlin.

One cannot, of course, fail to take into account the fact that the political and economic development of West Berlin, during its occupation by the three western powers, has differed from that of East Berlin and the German Democratic Republic, with the result that the way of life in the two parts of Berlin is entirely different at the present time. The Soviet government considers that upon the ending of foreign occupation, the population of West Berlin should be given the right to establish a way of life of its own choosing. Should the inhabitants of West Berlin desire to preserve the present way of life, based on private capitalist ownership, it is up to them to do so. The U.S.S.R., for its part, will respect any choice the West Berliners may make.

On the strength of all these considerations, the Soviet government finds it possible for the question of West Berlin to be settled for the time being by making West Berlin an independent political entity—a free city—without any state, including either of the existing German states, interfering in its life. It might be possible, in particular, to agree on the territory of the free city being demilitarised and having no armed forces on it. The free city of West Berlin could have its own government and could run its own economy and its administrative and other affairs.

The four powers, which shared in the administration of Berlin after the war, could, as could the two German states, undertake to respect the status of West Berlin as a free city, just as has been done by the four powers, for instance, with regard to the neutral status which has been adopted by the Austrian Republic.

For its part, the Soviet government would have no objection to the United Nations also sharing, in one way or another, in observing the free-city status of West Berlin.

It is obvious that, taking into consideration the special position of West Berlin, which lies in the territory of the German Democratic Republic and is cut off from the outside world, the question would arise of some kind of arrangement with the German Democratic Republic concerning guarantees of unhindered communications between the free city and the outside world—both eastward and westward—with the aim of free movement for passenger and freight traffic. In its turn, West Berlin would commit itself not to tolerate on its territory hostile subversive activity directed against the German Democratic Republic or any other state. That solution to the problem of the status of West Berlin would be an important step towards normalising the situation in Berlin, which, instead of being a hotbed of unrest and tension, could become a centre for contacts and cooperation between the two parts of Germany in the interests of Germany's peaceful future and the unity of the German nation.

The establishment of the status of a free city for West Berlin would make it possible to safeguard firmly the expansion of the economy of West Berlin, owing to its all-sided contacts with the eastern and western countries, and proper living standards for the population of the city. For its part, the Soviet Union declares that it will do its utmost to promote the attainment of these aims, especially by placing orders for an amount of manufactured goods that will fully ensure the stability and prosperity of the economy of the free city and also by regular systematic supplies of the necessary raw materials and foodstuffs to West Berlin on a commercial basis. Thus, West Berlin's population of over two million, far from suffering from the abolition of the occupation regime, would, on the contrary, have every possibility of raising their living standards.

If the government of the United States, as well as the governments of the United Kingdom and France, expresses its consent to examine the question of abolishing the present occupation regime in West Berlin by setting up a free city on its territory, the Soviet government would be willing, on behalf of the four powers, to enter into official contact on this question with the government of the German Democratic Republic, with which it has already held preliminary consultations before the despatch of the present Note.

It should, of course, be borne in mind that the consent of the German Democratic Republic to the setting up of such an independent political organism as the free city of West Berlin within its territory would be a concession, a definite sacrifice by the German Democratic Republic for the sake of strengthening peace in Europe, for the sake of the national interests of the German people as a whole.

The Soviet government, for its part, has resolved to carry out measures designed to abolish the occupation regime in Berlin, guided by the desire to normalise the situation in Berlin, in the interests of European peace, and in the interests of the peaceful and independent development of Germany. It hopes that the government of the United States will show a proper understanding of these motives and adopt a realistic attitude on the Berlin issue.

At the same time the Soviet government is ready to open negotiations with the governments of the United States and other countries concerned, on granting West Berlin the status of a demilitarised free city. If this proposal is not acceptable to the United States government, there is no topic left for talks on the Berlin question by the former occupying powers.

The Soviet government strives for the necessary changes in the position of Berlin to be made in a calm atmosphere, without haste and unnecessary friction, with the maximum account being taken of the interests of the sides concerned.

It is obvious that some time is needed for the powers that occupied Germany after the defeat of the nazi Wehrmacht to agree on proclaiming West Berlin a free city, provided, of course, that the western powers take a proper interest in this proposal. It should also be taken into consideration that the necessity may arise of talks between the city authorities of both parts of Berlin and also between the German Democratic Republic and the Federal Republic of Germany for a settlement of the issues that may arise.

In view of this the Soviet government proposes to make no changes in the present procedure for military traffic of the United States, the United Kingdom and France from West Berlin to the Federal Republic of Germany for half a year. It regards this period as quite adequate for finding a sound basis for a solution to the problems connected with the change in the position of Berlin and for preventing the possibility of any complications if, of course, the governments of the western powers do not deliberately work for such complications.

During this period the sides will have the possibility of proving, by settling the Berlin issue, their desire for a relaxation of international tension.

If the above period is not used for reaching an appropriate agreement, the Soviet Union will effect the planned measures by agreement with the German Democratic Republic.

It is envisaged that the German Democratic Republic, like any other independent state, must fully control questions concerning its space, that is to say, exercise its sovereignty on land, on water and in the air. At the same time there will be an end to all the contacts still maintained between representatives of the armed forces and other officials of the Soviet Union in Germany and corresponding representatives of the armed forces and other officials of the United States, the United Kingdom, and France on questions relating to Berlin.

Voices are being raised in the capitals of some western powers claiming that these powers do not recognise the Soviet Union's decision to discard the functions of maintaining the occupation status in Berlin. How can such a question be raised? Anyone who today speaks of non-recognition of the steps planned by the Soviet Union would obviously like to speak of it, not in the language of reason and well-founded argument, but in the language of brute force, forgetting that the Soviet people are not affected by threats or intimidation. If, behind the word 'non-recognition,' there really lies the intention to resort to force and draw the world into a war over Berlin, the advocates of such a policy should take into consideration the fact that they are assuming a very grave responsibility before the peoples and before history for all the consequences of that policy.

Anyone who brandishes weapons in connection with the situation in Berlin once again exposes his interest in maintaining the occupation regime in Berlin for aggressive purposes. The government of the Soviet Union would like to hope that the problem of normalising the situation in Berlin, which life itself raises before our states as an imperative necessity, will in any case be solved in accordance with the considerations of states-manship, in the interests of peace among the peoples, without any un-necessary tension or aggravation of the 'cold war.'

Methods of blackmail and reckless threats of force are least of all oppor-tune in solving such a problem as the Berlin issue. Such methods will not help to settle a single question: they can only aggravate the situation to danger point. Only madmen, however, can go to the length of unleashing another world war over the preservation of the privileges of occupationists in West Berlin. If such madmen should really come to the fore, there is no doubt that strait-jackets could be found for them.

If the statesmen responsible for the policy of the western powers are guided in their approach to the Berlin question, as well as other inter-national problems, by hatred of communism, of the socialist countries, no good will come of this.

Neither the Soviet Union nor any other socialist state can deny its existence precisely as a socialist state, nor are these states going to do so. That is why, having united in an unbreakable fraternal alliance, they take a firm stand in defence of their rights and their state frontiers, acting according to the motto, 'Each for all, and all for each.' Any violation of the frontiers of the German Democratic Republic, Poland, or Czecho-slovakia, any aggressive action against any state that is a party to the Warsaw Treaty, will be regarded by all its signatories as an act of aggres-sion against all of them and will immediately result in appropriate retaliation.

The Soviet government believes that it would be sensible to recognise the situation existing in the world and to create normal relations for co-existence between all states, to expand world trade, to build the relations between our countries on the basis of the well-known principles of mutual respect for one another's sovereignty and territorial integrity, non-aggression, non-interference in one another's internal affairs, equality and mutual benefit.

The Soviet Union, its people and its government are sincerely striving for the restoration of good relations with the United States of America— relations based on trust, which are quite feasible, as has been shown by the experience of the joint struggle against the Hitler aggressors and which, in peacetime, would offer our countries nothing but the advantages of mutually-enriched spiritual and material co-operation between our peoples, and would offer all other men and women the blessing of a tranquil life in conditions of lasting peace. Copies of the Soviet government's Note to the government of the United States have been sent to the governments of all states with which the Soviet Union maintains diplomatic relations and also the governments of other members of the United Nations.

7. Statement by the Government of the People's Republic of China supporting the Soviet proposal for Berlin, 21 December 1958[1]

The Government of the Soviet Union recently sent notes to the Governments of the United States, Britain and France, proposing the withdrawal of foreign troops from Berlin and termination of the state of occupation of Berlin. This is another important measure taken by the Soviet Government to promote a peaceful settlement of the German question and to ease tension in Europe and the world. Berlin must be returned to the German people. This is a just measure in conformity with the unanimous desire of all the German people and in the interests of world peace. This proposal of the Soviet Government is another powerful proof of the Soviet Government's noble desire and spirit of initiative to safeguard peace. The Government of the People's Republic of China fully supports this reasonable proposal of the Government of the Soviet Union.

More than 13 years have passed since the conclusion of the war against German fascism. But to this day the whole of Germany, including its capital Berlin, still remains divided under occupation. This is an abnormal situation which is extremely unreasonable. The history of the past 13 years fully shows that the blame for the protraction of such an abnormal situation rests squarely with the Governments of the United States, Britain and France, which have time and again rejected constructive proposals put forward by the Soviet Union and the German Democratic Republic for a reasonable settlement of the German question, and insisted throughout on the annexation of Democratic Germany by West Germany as the means of unifying Germany. Militarism, fostered energetically by them, particularly by the U.S. imperialists, has revived in West Germany and West Berlin. They have further misused the occupation regime in Berlin to turn West Berlin into a 'frontline city' within Democratic Germany, a base for conducting the cold war, creating tension and undertaking subversive

---

[1] *Peking Review*, 30 December 1958, pp. 17–18.

and disruptive activities against Democratic Germany and other socialist countries. All this proves that by their actions the United States, Britain and France have long since thoroughly violated the fundamental principles of the Potsdam Agreement, and that therefore they have forfeited all legal grounds for their continued occupation of West Berlin. Precisely because of this, the recent proposal of the Soviet Government on the withdrawal of foreign troops from Berlin and termination of the state of occupation of Berlin has received the warm welcome and support of the German Democratic Republic, the German people and all peace-loving people throughout the world. One can see clearly that the realization of this proposal of the Soviet Government will not only promote the normalization of the Berlin situation, but also be conducive to mutual understanding and gradual rapprochement between the two Germanys. There is no doubt that this will also benefit the consolidation of peace in Europe and the world.

But the Western countries, the United States in particular, are alarmed about the proposal of the Soviet Government. They are seeking all sorts of pretexts in an attempt to reject the Soviet Government's reasonable proposal, and are even poisoning the international climate with war cries. To cover up their design to prolong their occupation of West Berlin, they are stubbornly hanging on to the totally untenable and fallacious argument that the settlement of the Berlin question must depend on that of the unification of Germany. It is quite clear that the Soviet proposal for the termination of the occupation regime in Berlin will be of great help to the gradual rapprochement between the two existing Germanys without outside interference, thereby facilitating the peaceful unification of Germany. If the Western countries, the United States, Britain and France, should continue to persist in their stubborn attitude, it will only prove their complete lack of sincerity for the peaceful settlement of the German question and the easing of international tension. In line with its consistent stand on the German question, the Government of the People's Republic of China fully supports the proposal of the Soviet Government and firmly maintains that the occupation regime in Berlin must be abolished, Berlin must be returned to the German people, and the cancerous tumour of West Berlin, which poisons the European and world situation, must be removed. If the Governments of the United States, Britain and France are not bent on turning West Berlin into a cancerous tumour endangering Germany and the world, they have no justification to reject this fair and reasonable proposal put forward by the Government of the Soviet Union.

8. Note from the United Kingdom Government to the Government of the Soviet Union regarding Berlin, 31 December 1958[1]

I

Her Majesty's Government in the United Kingdom have received the Note addressed to them by the Soviet Government on November 27 about Germany.

2. The Soviet Government's Note contains certain passages about the events which preceded the last war. The least which can be said about these passages is that in the opinion of Her Majesty's Government they do not conform to historical fact. It is not the purpose of Her Majesty's Government to enter into polemics about the rights and wrongs of events which took place 20 years ago, in political conditions widely different from those of to-day. Nevertheless, Her Majesty's Government think it right to correct any misapprehensions which might exist as a result of the Soviet Government's comments on the European situation at the beginning of the last war.

3. The Soviet Government's Note says:—

'It is well known that it was far from at once that Great Britain and also the United States of America and France reached the conclusion that it was necessary to co-operate with the Soviet Union for the purpose of opposing Hitlerite aggression, although readiness to do this had been continuously shown on the part of the Soviet Government. For a long time in Western capitals contrary aspirations had the upper hand; these became particularly evident during the period of the Munich deal with Hitler.'

4. In this connexion Her Majesty's Government think it appropriate to recall the position which existed shortly before the outbreak of war in 1939. In May of that year, Her Majesty's Government had suggested to the Soviet Government that it should make a declaration that if France or Britain should be involved in war because of their undertakings to Poland or Roumania, the Soviet Union would help France or Britain if this assistance was called for. The Soviet Government declined to accept this proposal. However, negotiations on the proposed Anglo-Franco-Soviet pact continued and at Soviet request three-Power military negotiations began in Moscow on August 12, 1939. It was on August 23, with a suddenness which shook Europe, that the German-Soviet non-aggression pact, usually known as the Molotov-Ribbentrop Pact, was announced. It is a matter of surprise to Her Majesty's Government that the Soviet

[1] Cmnd. 634, pp. 22–27. For a similar, but shorter, note from the United States Government to the Government of the Soviet Union of 31 December 1958, see *D.S.B.*, 19 January 1959, pp. 79–81. The Department of State published a memorandum on the legal aspects of the Berlin situation on 19 December 1958, see *D.S.B.*, 5 January 1959, pp. 5–13. See also below, pp. 372–4.

Government fails to mention this pact in the historical part of its Note of November 27, since the signature of this pact is generally considered to have made the outbreak of war inevitable. Nor can it be forgotten that the negotiations for the Molotov-Ribbentrop Pact were actually taking place during the time when the Western Powers were still negotiating in good faith with the Soviet Government. Both these names, for good or ill, are part of history.

5. The attitude of the Soviet Government at this time is well illustrated by the remarks of the Soviet Minister for Foreign Affairs at the Fifth Session of the Supreme Soviet of the U.S.S.R. on October 31, 1939. At that date it will be remembered that the United Kingdom and France were already at war with Germany. M. Molotov said:—

'The ruling circles of Britain and France have been lately attempting to depict themselves as champions of the democratic rights of nations against Hitlerism, and the British Government has announced that its aim in the war with Germany is nothing more nor less than the "destruction of Hitlerism". It amounts to this, that the British, and with them the French, supporters of the war have declared what is in the nature of an "ideological" war on Germany, reminiscent of the religious wars of olden times. . . . But there is absolutely no justification for such a war. As with any other ideological system, one may accept or reject the ideology of Hitlerism—that is a matter of political views. But everybody will understand that an ideology cannot be destroyed by force, that it cannot be eliminated by war. It is therefore not only senseless, but criminal to wage such a war—a war for the "destruction of Hitlerism", camouflaged as a fight for "democracy".'

6. Such was the position at the outbreak of war in 1939. When in 1940 the Nazi armies overran Western Europe, Great Britain stood alone against Hitler, whose relations with the Soviet Government continued to be governed by the Molotov-Ribbentrop Pact until the time when his armies advanced into Soviet territory. The Soviet Government will not have forgotten the speed with which at that time Her Majesty's Government, led by Mr. Churchill, resolved to ignore past differences and conclude an alliance with the Soviet Government.

7. The Soviet Note speaks of the Munich Pact of 1938. It also speaks of:—

'the short-sighted calculations of the inspirers of Munich'.

On this point Her Majesty's Government would only observe that whatever views may now be held on the motives and actions of the British Government at that time, Her Majesty's present Government are resolved to profit by the historical lessons which were then learnt. In fact, they are determined not to pursue a policy of appeasement or to be deterred by threats, from faithfully adhering to their international engagements.

II

The Soviet Government's Note also deals at some length with the question of the Potsdam Agreement. Her Majesty's Government do not accept the argument that the status of Berlin depends upon that agreement. Their view of the purely juridical position of Berlin is set forth in later passages of this Note. Nevertheless they consider it useful to comment on certain of the observations in the Soviet Government's Note on the subject of the Potsdam Agreement.

2. As the Soviet Government correctly states, the Potsdam Agreement provided for Germany to be regarded as a single economic whole. But the Soviet Government made no attempt to fulfil this vital provision of the Agreement. From the beginning of the occupation the Soviet Government carried out an independent economic policy in its Zone, which was progressively stripped of assets and equipment for the sole benefit of the Soviet Union. In addition the Soviet Government while maintaining its own claims to reparations persistently refused to agree to any of the measures, such as common import-export programmes for Germany as a whole, which were specifically called for under the Potsdam Agreement.

3. The Soviet Government further contends that the Western Powers, in contravention of the Potsdam Agreement, 'brought to life and strengthened the very forces which had forged the Hitlerite military machine'. Her Majesty's Government would recall in this connexion the measures of re-militarisation which the Soviet Government carried out in its Zone of Germany. The most important of these was the creation of *Bereitschaften* ('Alert Squads') to which Her Majesty's Government drew the attention of the Soviet Government in a Note of May 25, 1950:—

> 'In that part of Germany subject to Soviet control, a police force has been created which, by reason of its organisation, training and equipment, has the character of an army. . . . It is known . . . to be organised on the basis of *Bereitschaften* under the control of the *Hauptverwaltung fuer Ausbildung* (Training Department) and to consist of nearly 50,000 men. They are embodied in military formations, which include artillery, tank and infantry battalions. They receive basic military training and are not employed on normal police duties. They are equipped with military weapons including, in some units, machine guns, anti-tank guns, anti-aircraft guns, mortars and tanks. A number of high-ranking German army officers are employed in the force.'

4. The Soviet Government also alleges that the Western Powers have violated those provisions of the Potsdam Agreement aimed at securing the unity of Germany as a peace-loving democratic State. The word 'democratic' would seem to-day to be susceptible of many interpretations. In the West, it still denotes a social system in which freedom of religion,

speech, voting and the press are permitted. As the Soviet Government is aware, specific provision for the establishment of such freedoms was made in the Potsdam Agreement, as well as for the formation of free trade unions. None of these freedoms exists in East Germany. If it is suggested that this is a matter of opinion Her Majesty's Government would recall that some two million Germans have left East Germany in recent years rather than endure any longer the social system which exists there. These are facts, not theories.

5. Her Majesty's Government's object in drawing attention to these considerations is simply to correct the impression presented by the Soviet Government in that part of its Note dealing with the Potsdam Agreement. As stated above, however, Her Majesty's Government do not admit the relevance of the Potsdam Agreement to the question of Berlin, which is the question immediately at issue.

III

The Berlin situation of which the Soviet Government complains and which it considers abnormal is a result of the very nature of the German problem as it has existed since 1945. When Hitler's Reich collapsed the Western allies were in military possession of more than one-third of the area which was then occupied by the Soviet authorities. The Soviet Union was in possession of Berlin. As a result of the Agreements of September 12, 1944, and May 1, 1945, the Western allies withdrew and permitted the Soviet occupation of large parts of Mecklenburg, Saxony, Thuringia and Anhalt. In consequence of the same Agreements, the three Western Powers moved into their sectors in West Berlin.

2. The Soviet Union has directly and through the régime which it refers to as the German Democratic Republic consolidated its hold over the large areas which the Western allies relinquished to it. It now demands that the Western allies should relinquish their rights in Berlin which were provided for in the above Agreements. But Agreements made by the Four Powers cannot be considered obsolete because one of them, having obtained the full advantage therefrom, now considers that the time has come to cancel them. These Agreements are binding upon all of the signatories so long as they have not been replaced by other agreements following free negotiation.

3. In any case however the right of the three Western Powers to be in Berlin rests, not on the agreements referred to above, but on the unconditional surrender of Germany and the assumption by the victorious Powers of supreme authority in Germany. They are not prepared to relinquish this right, upon the continued exercise of which the freedom of West Berlin will depend as long as there is no settlement of the German problem.

4. So far as the Potsdam Agreement is concerned, the status of Berlin

does not depend upon that Agreement and it is the Soviet Union that bears responsibility for the fact that the Potsdam Agreement was not implemented.

5. The Soviet memorandum purports formally to repudiate the Agreements of September 12, 1944, and May 1, 1945.[1] This repudiation in fact involves other and more recent engagements. Her Majesty's Government would refer in this connexion to the Four Power Agreement of June 20, 1949,[2] whereby, among other things, the Soviet Union assumed 'an obligation' to assure the normal functioning of transport and communication between Berlin and the Western zones of Germany. This 'obligation' the Soviet Union now purports to shed. Her Majesty's Government would also refer to the 'Summit' Agreement of July 23, 1955,[3] whereby the Four Powers recognised 'their common responsibility for the settlement of the German question', a phrase which necessarily includes the problem of Berlin. Apparently the Soviet Union now attempts to free itself from these agreed responsibilities and obligations.

6. Her Majesty's Government note that the Soviet Government wishes to terminate its own authority in the quadripartite régime in the sector which it occupies in the City of Berlin. However that may be Her Majesty's Government will not and do not in any way accept a unilateral denunciation of the Agreements of 1944 and 1945, nor are they prepared to relieve the Soviet Union of the obligations which it assumed in June 1949. Such action on the part of the Soviet Government would have no legal basis, since the Agreements can only be terminated by mutual consent. Her Majesty's Government will accordingly continue to hold the Soviet Government directly responsible under existing Agreements, for the discharge of its obligations undertaken with respect to Berlin. The French and United States Governments and Her Majesty's Government have the right to maintain garrisons in their sectors of Berlin and to have free access thereto. Certain administrative procedures have been agreed with the Soviet authorities and are in operation at the present time. Her Majesty's Government will not accept a unilateral repudiation on the part of the Soviet Government of its obligations in respect of that freedom of access. Nor will they accept the substitution of the régime which the Soviet Government refers to as the German Democratic Republic for the Soviet Government in this respect.

7. The continued protection of the freedom of more than two million people of West Berlin is a right and responsibility solemnly accepted by the three Western Powers. Thus Her Majesty's Government cannot consider any proposal which would have the effect of jeopardising the freedom and security of these people. The rights of the Three Powers to remain in

---

[1] For texts, see Cmd. 7534, p. 5, and Cmd. 6648, p. 7.
[2] For text, see Cmd. 7729, p. 18.   [3] For text, see Cmd. 9543, p. 28.

Berlin with unhindered communications by land and air between that city and the Federal Republic of Germany are under existing conditions essential to the discharge of that right and responsibility. Hence the proposal for a so-called 'free city' for West Berlin, as put forward by the Soviet Union, is unacceptable.

8. In the view of Her Majesty's Government there can be no 'threat' to the Soviet Government or the régime which the Soviet Government refers to as the German Democratic Republic from the presence of the French, United States and British garrisons in Berlin. The forces of the three Western Powers in Berlin number about 10,000 men. The Soviet Government, on the other hand, is said to maintain some 350,000 troops in East Germany while the régime which the Soviet Government refer to as the German Democratic Republic is understood also to maintain over 200,000 men under arms. In these circumstances, the fear that the Western troops in Berlin may 'inflict harm' appears to be wholly unfounded. If Berlin has become a focus of international tension, it is because the Soviet Government has deliberately threatened to disturb the existing arrangements at present in force there, arrangements to which the Soviet Government is itself a party. The inhabitants of West Berlin have recently reaffirmed in a free vote their overwhelming approval and support for the existing status of that city.

9. As is stated in the Soviet Government's Note of November 27, it is certainly not normal that thirteen years after the end of the war there should still remain in a part of German territory a system of occupation instituted in 1945. Her Majesty's Government deplore this fact and the fact that Germany has not yet been reunified so that Berlin might resume its rightful position as capital of a united Germany. For ten years the Western Powers have at numerous international meetings with the Soviet Union done everything in their power to bring about the signing of a Peace Treaty with a reunified Germany. But all their efforts have failed.

10. The form of government in Berlin, the validity of which the Soviet Government attempts to contest to-day, is only one aspect of the German problem. This problem, which has often been defined, involves the well-known questions of reunification of Germany and European security as well as a Peace Treaty. Her Majesty's Government made clear their readiness to discuss these problems in their Note to the Soviet Government of September 30, 1958, in which it was stated:—

> 'Her Majesty's Government are ready at any time to enter into discussions with the Soviet Government on the basis of these proposals (*i.e.*, the Western proposals for free all-German elections and free decisions for an all-German Government) or of any other proposals

genuinely designed to ensure the reunification of Germany in freedom, in any appropriate forum. They regard the solution of the German problem as essential if a lasting settlement in Europe is to be achieved.'

The Soviet Government has not yet replied to this Note.

11. Public repudiation of solemn engagements, formally entered into and repeatedly reaffirmed, coupled with an ultimatum threatening unilateral action to implement that repudiation unless it be acquiesced in within six months, would afford no reasonable basis for negotiation between sovereign states. Her Majesty's Government could not embark on discussion with the Soviet Government upon these questions under menace. It is assumed that this is not the purpose of the Soviet Note of November 27 and that the Soviet Government, like themselves, is ready to enter into discussions in an atmosphere devoid of coercion or threats.

12. On this basis Her Majesty's Government would be glad to learn whether the Soviet Government is ready to enter into discussions of all these problems between the Four Powers concerned. In that event, it would be the object of Her Majesty's Government to discuss the question of Berlin in the wider framework of negotiations for a solution of the German problem as well as that of European security. Her Majesty's Government would welcome the views of the Soviet Government at an early date.

C. THE SINO-AMERICAN AMBASSADORIAL TALKS AND THE CRISIS OVER FORMOSA

1. Statement by the Government of the People's Republic of China regarding the Sino-American ambassadorial talks, 12 April 1958[1]

It is four months since the 73rd meeting of the Sino-American ambassadorial talks held on December 12, 1957.[2] During this period, in spite of repeated prodding by the Chinese side, the United States has used its customary Panmunjom tactics to drag on, so that the Sino-American ambassadorial talks have been suspended for a long time. This state of affairs has caused dissatisfaction among the people of our country and concern among the peace-loving people of the world. To set forth the truth, the Ministry of Foreign Affairs has decided to make public the facts

[1] *Peking Review*, 22 April 1958, pp. 22–23.

[2] Meetings had taken place in Geneva between United States and Chinese ambassadorial representatives since 1955. The United States had originally opened these negotiations to obtain the release of 76 Americans detained in China. Seventy had been released, but the remaining six seemed likely to remain in China until their prison sentences had expired. Two were released in June 1958.

behind the prolonged suspension of the Sino-American ambassadorial talks.

(1) At the 73rd meeting of the Sino-American ambassadorial talks, Ambassador U. A. Johnson, representative of the American side, informed our representative, Ambassador Wang Ping-nan, that he had been transferred to a new post and would henceforth be unable to participate in the talks, and that the U.S. Government had designated his assistant Mr. Edwin W. Martin as the U.S. representative.

Ambassador Wang Ping-nan pointed out at the time that, as the Sino-American ambassadorial talks were being held as a result of consultations between China and the United States, no alteration must be made by either party at will, and that designation by the U.S. Government of Mr. Martin, who is not of the rank of ambassador, as representative was evidently inconsistent with the agreed arrangement between China and the United States.

Thus, no date was fixed or published for the next meeting.

(2) In his letter to Ambassador Johnson dated January 14, 1958, Ambassador Wang Ping-nan pointed out that the American side had long been preventing progress in the talks by various means, and that now, in attempting to relegate the talks to a lower level, it was trying to create the false impression that the Sino-American talks continue, while actually it had no intention to settle any problem. Ambassador Wang was authorized to state that the Chinese Government could not agree to a unilateral alteration by the U.S. Government of the result of consultations between the Chinese and the American sides, and that if the U.S. Government has still any intention to carry on the Sino-American ambassadorial talks, it should designate as soon as possible a representative of the rank of ambassador.

After a delay of nearly two months, Mr. Martin, on behalf of Ambassador Johnson, wrote to Ambassador Wang Ping-nan in reply on March 12, 1958. In his letter, Mr. Martin repeated statements made by Ambassador Johnson at the 73rd meeting, and indicated that the U.S. Government would continue to postpone the designation of a representative of ambassadorial rank. Moreover, Mr. Martin attempted to lay the blame on our side for the past failure of the Sino-American ambassadorial talks to fulfil the hopes place in them.

(3) Mr. Martin's reply on behalf of the U.S. Government was disappointing. Ambassador Wang Ping-nan's assistant, Mr. Lai Ya-li, was therefore instructed to reply on March 26, 1958 to Mr. Martin that the Chinese Government cannot agree to a unilateral change of the level of the Sino-American ambassadorial talks, nor can it agree to suspending the talks for long and reducing them to an empty name on the pretext of administrative reasons; and that if the U.S. Government still has any

intention of continuing the Sino-American ambassadorial talks, it should not delay further the designation of a representative of the rank of ambassador.

(4) It can be seen clearly from the above correspondence that, while the Chinese side has abided by the agreement and taken a just attitude, the United States has done everything to drag out the talks and go back on its promise in violation of agreement. In the face of the world's strong demand for relaxation of international tension, the United States dares not openly break up the Sino-American talks. On the other hand, it is afraid that such relaxation will further discomfit its cold-war policy. That is why it has prevented any progress in the talks and, moreover, tried to incapacitate the talks. Here lies the root cause why, for the past four months, the United States has been playing fraudulent tricks to stall the Sino-American talks.

(5) We now make public the letters from Ambassador Wang Ping-nan to Ambassador Johnson dated January 14, 1958, from Mr. Martin to Ambassador Wang Ping-nan dated March 12, 1958, and from Mr. Lai Ya-li to Mr. Martin dated March 26, 1958.[1]

2. Statement by the Government of the People's Republic of China regarding the Sino-American ambassadorial talks, 30 June 1958[2]

More than half a year has passed since the U.S. Government suspended the Sino-American ambassadorial talks. The Chinese Government considers that this state of affairs should not continue. The U.S. ruling circles have been playing all sorts of tricks in an attempt to create the false impression that the Sino-American talks are still continuing in order to cover up its continued occupation of China's territory of Taiwan and its activities to create world tension. Such sinister designs must not be allowed to bear fruit. The Chinese Government agreed to hold the Sino-American ambassadorial talks with the aim of settling questions. The U.S. Government must answer clearly whether it is sincere about the talks.

Since December 12, 1957, when the U.S. Government broke the agreement between China and the United States on holding talks on an ambassadorial level by refusing to designate a representative of ambassadorial rank, thereby suspending the talks, the Chinese side, on January 14 and March 26, 1958,[3] repeatedly urged the U.S. Government to designate a representative with the rank of ambassador to resume the talks. The U.S. Government, however, not only refused to do this but did not even con-

---

[1] For the texts of these letters, see *H.N.A.*, 14 April 1958.
[2] *Peking Review*, 8 July 1958, pp. 21–22.
[3] See fn. 1.

sider it necessary to reply to the March 26 letter of the Chinese side. Moreover, a spokesman of the State Department of the United States recently even remarked nonchalantly that a First Secretary of its foreign service was ready to hold talks with us at any time, as if there had never been an agreement between China and the United States on the holding of talks on an ambassadorial level. This cannot but rouse the indignation of the Chinese people.

The imperialistic attitude consistently maintained by the United States is proven by the record of nearly three years of the Sino-American ambassadorial talks. The U.S. occupation of China's territory of Taiwan created tension in the Taiwan area. This is a naked act of aggression against China and the Chinese people have every right to take any measures to repulse it. Nevertheless, the Chinese side, in order to relax the tension in the Taiwan area, expressed its willingness to sit down and talk matters over with the United States and, during the Sino-American ambassadorial talks, put forward a series of reasonable proposals for the peaceful settlement of the international disputes between China and the United States in the Taiwan area. But the American side rejected all these proposals. They attempted to confuse China's domestic affair, a matter between the Chinese Government and the Taiwan local authorities, with the international disputes between China and the United States in the Taiwan area, and demanded that China give up its right of exercising sovereignty over its own territory and recognize the right of 'self-defence' for the United States on China's territory. This demonstrates clearly that the aim of the United States is not to relax the tension in the Taiwan area at all, but to insist that China recognize the status quo of U.S. occupation of Taiwan and to maintain and heighten tension. It is due to the imperialist policy of the United States that discussion on this crucial question of Sino-American relations has bogged down since the latter part of 1956.

In order to break the deadlock and gradually improve Sino-American relations, the Chinese side further put forward a series of proposals on certain questions that are comparatively easy to settle, such as removing the trade barriers between the two countries, eliminating the obstacles in the way of mutual contacts and cultural exchange between the two peoples, exchanging correspondents for news coverage on an equal and reciprocal basis and rendering judicial assistance between the two countries. Although questions such as the entry of correspondents for news coverage and judicial assistance were first raised by those concerned on the American side to those concerned on the Chinese side, and all the proposals of the Chinese side were fully in accord with the principles of equality and mutual benefit, the U.S. Government nonetheless rejected them. What is even more intolerable is the fact that the United States, in disregard of the agreement reached in 1955 on the return of civilians of both sides, continues to detain thousands upon thousands of Chinese civilians in the United States and prevent them from returning to their motherland.

Irrefutable facts show that what the United States was after in the Sino-American ambassadorial talks was by no means a peaceful settlement of the international disputes between China and the United States on the basis of equality and mutual repsect for territorial integrity and sovereignty, but to impose its imperialist will on the Chinese people and, failing that, to make use of the ambassadorial talks to deceive the people of the world and cover up its sinister designs to continue its aggression against China and to create international tension. During the past three years, the United States has been intensifying its interference and control of all aspects of life in Taiwan, establishing on it bases for guided missiles to threaten the Chinese people[1] and utilizing the reactionary clique in Taiwan to carry out subversive activities and armed intervention against Southeast Asian countries. At the same time, the United States is endeavouring to bring about, at many international conferences and organizations, a situation of 'two Chinas,' to create eventually such a *fait accompli* in the international arena, and thereby to prolong its occupation of Taiwan. This is the crux of the reason for the failure of the Sino-American ambassadorial talks to make progress. U.S. Secretary of State Dulles recently declared that it is in the best interests of the United States to persist in its policy of enmity towards the People's Republic of China but that it will deal with China when its interest so demands. This demonstrates most clearly that, in the minds of the U.S. ruling circles, the Sino-American ambassadorial talks are but a means serving the imperialist policy of the United States. The reason China agreed to hold the ambassadorial talks was to try by peaceful means to eliminate armed aggression and the threat of force in the Taiwan area on the part of the United States. However, the Chinese people are by no means afraid of U.S. aggression, and there is no reason whatsoever why they should pine for talks with the United States. Building socialism with lightning speed, the Chinese people are perfectly strong enough to liberate their territory of Taiwan. No force on earth can stop the great cause of the Chinese people in building up and uniting their motherland. The handful of U.S. imperialists can only suffer isolation and defeat from their policy of enmity towards the 600 million Chinese people.

The Chinese Government hereby declares once again that it can neither agree to the unilateral changing of the level of the Sino-American am-

---

[1] For the announcement of 7 May 1957 by the American Embassy in Taipei, and the Foreign Office of the Republic of China on the stationing of tactical missiles in Formosa, see *Documents for 1957*, p. 112.

bassadorial talks, nor can it agree to the continued suspension of the talks on any administrative pretext. The Chinese Government demands that the United States Government designate a representative of ambassadorial rank and resume the talks within fifteen days counting from today, otherwise, the Chinese Government cannot but consider that the United States has decided to break off the Sino-American ambassadorial talks.[1]

3. Statement by Mr. Dulles, 4 September 1958[2]

I have reviewed in detail with the President the serious situation which has resulted from aggressive Chinese Communist military actions in the Taiwan (Formosa) Straits area.[3] The President has authorized me to make the following statement.

1. Neither Taiwan (Formosa) nor the islands of Quemoy and Matsu have ever been under the authority of the Chinese Communists. Since the end of the Second World War, a period of over 13 years, they have continuously been under the authority of Free China, that is, the Republic of China.

2. The United States is bound by treaty to help to defend Taiwan (Formosa) from armed attack and the President is authorized by Joint Resolution of the Congress to employ the armed forces of the United States for the securing and protecting of related positions such as Quemoy and Matsu.[4]

3. Any attempt on the part of the Chinese Communists now to seize these positions or any of them would be a crude violation of the principles upon which world order is based, namely, that no country should use armed force to seize new territory.

4. The Chinese Communists have, for about 2 weeks, been subjecting Quemoy to heavy artillery bombardment and, by artillery fire and use of small naval craft, they have been harassing the regular supply of the

---

[1] At his news conference on 1 July 1958, Mr. Dulles said, in reply to a question, that the United States was actually in the process of making arrangements to appoint an ambassador and shift the seat of the ambassadorial talks from Geneva to Warsaw. He went on: 'We do not intend to be bound by the 15-day ultimatum which is included in the Chinese Communist statement.' See D.S.B., 21 July 1958, pp. 106–7. On 28 July Mr. Martin sent a letter to Ambassador Wang Ping-nan in Warsaw saying that the American ambassador to Poland, Mr. Jacob Beam, had been appointed to continue the talks as the United States representative. This letter was not acknowledged, and on 4 August Mr. Beam tried to arrange a meeting for 7 August. In answer to another inquiry of 7 August the Chinese said the matter had been referred to Peking. For a detailed U.S. statement of 13 September recording the efforts to reach an agreement with China on the renunciation of force in Formosa, see New York Times, 14 September 1958.

[2] D.S.B., 22 September 1958, pp. 445–6. This statement was made on the authority of President Eisenhower after he and Mr. Dulles had had a conference at Newport, Rhode Island.

[3] The heavy bombardment of the Matsu and Quemoy Islands began on 23 August 1958. Air and naval clashes between the Communists and the Nationalists had become so frequent that a state of emergency was declared in Formosa on 7 August 1958.

[4] For the text of H.J. Resol. 159, 84th Congress, 1st session, see Documents for 1955, pp. 446–7.

civilian and military population of the Quemoys, which totals some 125 thousand persons. The official Peiping radio repeatedly announces the purpose of these military operations to be to take by armed force Taiwan (Formosa), as well as Quemoy and Matsu.[1] In virtually every Peiping broadcast Taiwan (Formosa) and the offshore islands are linked as the objective of what is called the 'Chinese People's Liberation Army.'

5. Despite, however, what the Chinese Communists say, and so far have done, it is not yet certain that their purpose is in fact to make an all-out effort to conquer by force Taiwan (Formosa) and the offshore islands. Neither is it apparent that such efforts as are being made, or may be made, cannot be contained by the courageous, and purely defensive, efforts of the forces of the Republic of China, with such substantial logistical support as the United States is providing.

6. The Joint Resolution of Congress, above referred to, includes a finding to the effect that 'the secure possession by friendly governments of the Western Pacific Island chain, of which Formosa is a part, is essential to the vital interests of the United States and all friendly nations in and bordering upon the Pacific Ocean'. It further authorizes the President to employ the Armed Forces of the United States for the protection not only of Formosa but for 'the securing and protection of such related positions and territories of that area now in friendly hands and the taking of such other measures as he judges to be required or appropriate in assuring the defense of Formosa'. In view of the situation outlined in the preceding paragraph, the President has not yet made any finding under that Resolution that the employment of the Armed Forces of the United States is required or appropriate in insuring the defense of Formosa. The President would not, however, hesitate to make such a finding if he judged that the circumstances made this necessary to accomplish the purposes of the Joint Resolution. In this connection, we have recognized that the securing and protecting of Quemoy and Matsu have increasingly become related to the defense of Taiwan (Formosa). This is indeed also recognized by the Chinese Communists. Military dispositions have been made by the United States so that a Presidential determination, if made, would be followed by action both timely and effective.

7. The President and I earnestly hope that the Chinese Communist regime will not again, as in the case of Korea, defy the basic principle upon which world order depends, namely, that armed force should not be used to achieve territorial ambitions. Any such naked use of force would pose an issue far transcending the offshore islands and even the

---

[1] On 27 August 1958 the Fukien Command of the Chinese army broadcast a communiqué over Peking radio in which it was stated that: 'The Chinese People's Liberation Army has determined to liberate Taiwan, a territory of the Fatherland, as well as the offshore islands and the landing on Quemoy is imminent.' For the State Department statement of 28 August 1958, see *D.S.B.*, 15 September 1958, p. 415.

security of Taiwan (Formosa). It would forecast a widespread use of force in the Far East which would endanger vital free world positions and the security of the United States. Acquiescence therein would threaten peace everywhere. We believe that the civilized world community will never condone overt military conquest as a legitimate instrument of policy.

8. The United States has not, however, abandoned hope that Peiping will stop short of defying the will of mankind for peace. This would not require it to abandon its claims, however ill-founded we may deem them to be. I recall that in the extended negotiations which the representatives of the United States and Chinese Communist regime conducted at Geneva between 1955 and 1958, a sustained effort was made by the United States to secure, with particular reference to the Taiwan area, a declaration of mutual and reciprocal renunciation of force, except in self-defense, which, however, would be without prejudice to the pursuit of policies by peaceful means. The Chinese Communists rejected any such declaration. We believe, however, that such a course of conduct constitutes the only civilized and acceptable procedure. The United States intends to follow that course, so far as it is concerned, unless and until the Chinese Communists, by their acts, leave us no choice but to react in defense of the principles to which all peace-loving governments are dedicated.

4. Statement by Premier Chou En-lai, 6 September 1958[1]

On September 4, 1958, United States Secretary of States Dulles, authorized by United States President Eisenhower, issued a statement openly threatening to extend United States aggression in the Taiwan Straits area against the People's Republic of China and carrying out war provocation, thereby aggravating the tension in this area created by the United States and seriously jeopardizing the peace of the Far East and the world. Regarding this, I have been authorized by the Government of the People's Republic of China to make the following statement.

(1) Taiwan and the Penghu Islands have been China's territories from ancient times. Following the Second World War, they were restored to China after being occupied by Japan for a period of time. It is entirely China's internal affair for the Chinese people to exercise their sovereign right to liberate these areas. This is the Chinese people's sacred and inviolable right.[2] The United States Government itself also declared formally that it would not get involved in China's civil conflict in the Taiwan area. Were it not for the fact that the United States Government

---

[1] *Peking Review*, 9 September 1958, pp. 15–16.
[2] On 4 September 1958 the People's Republic of China issued a statement extending the breadth of its territorial sea to 12 miles, see below, p. 523.

later went back on its own statement and carried out armed intervention, Taiwan and the Penghu Islands would have long been liberated and placed under the jurisdiction of the Government of the People's Republic of China. These are undeniable facts unanimously recognized by fair-minded world public opinion.

(2) United States support of the Chiang Kai-shek clique entrenched on Taiwan and the Penghu Islands, which has long been repudiated by all the Chinese people, and its direct armed occupation of Taiwan and the Penghu Islands constitute unlawful interference in China's internal affairs and infringement on China's territorial integrity and sovereignty, and are in direct conflict with the United Nations Charter and all codes of international law. All so-called treaties concluded between the United States and the Chiang Kai-shek clique and all related resolutions adopted by the United States Congress are null and void as far as the Chinese people are concerned. They can never legalize United States aggression. Much less can they be used as pretexts by the United States for extending its aggression in the Taiwan Straits area.

(3) Supported by the United States, the Chiang Kai-shek clique has for long been using coastal islands such as Quemoy which is close by Amoy and Matsu which is close by Foochow as advance bases for conducting all sorts of harassing and disruptive activities against the Chinese mainland. Recently, since the United States launched armed intervention against the Arab states, the harassing and disruptive activities of the Chiang Kai-shek clique against the Chinese mainland have become more unbridled. The Chinese Government has every right to deal resolute blows and take necessary military action against Chiang Kai-shek's troops entrenched on the coastal islands; any outside intervention would be a criminal infringement on China's sovereignty. But the United States, in order to divert the attention of the people of the world from continued United States aggression in the Middle East and procrastination in withdrawing its troops from the Lebanon, attempts to take advantage of this situation and is amassing large numbers of armed forces in the Taiwan Straits area and openly threatening to extend its aggression in the Taiwan Straits area to Quemoy, Matsu, and other coastal islands. This is a grave war provocation against the 600 million Chinese people and a serious menace to the peace of the Far East and the world.

(4) The Chinese people's determination to liberate their own territory of Taiwan and the Penghu Islands is unshakable. In particular the Chinese people cannot tolerate the presence in their inland waters along the mainland of an immediate threat posed by such coastal islands as Quemoy and Matsu. No amount of U.S. war provocations can cow the Chinese people; on the contrary, they will only arouse even greater indignation among our 600 million people, and make them even more determined

to fight American aggressors to the very end. The fact that the United States, while not yet withdrawing its forces of aggression from the Lebanon, has hastened to create a new danger of war in the Taiwan Straits area, has made the peace-loving countries and people of the world see even more clearly the brutish features of the United States aggressors bent on sabotaging peace and that the United States imperialists are the most vicious enemy of all national independence movements in Asia, Africa and Latin America and the world peace movement.

(5) In pursuance of its foreign policy of peace, the Chinese Government has always stood for peaceful co-existence of countries with different social systems in accordance with the Five Principles and for the settlement of all international disputes by the peaceful means of negotiation. Despite the fact that the United States has invaded and occupied China's territory of Taiwan and the Penghu Islands by armed force and crudely violated the minimum codes in international relations, the Chinese Government proposed to sit down to negotiate with the U.S. Government to seek relaxation and elimination of the tension in the Taiwan area. In the Sino-American ambassadorial talks which started in August 1955 the Chinese side time and again proposed that the two parties should, in accordance with the principles of mutual respect for sovereignty and territorial integrity and non-interference in each other's internal affairs, issue a statement declaring their intention to settle the dispute between China and the United States in the Taiwan area through peaceful negotiation and without resorting to the threat or use of force against each other. But, contrary to Dulles' assertion in his September 4 statement, it is precisely the United States that has refused to issue such a statement and, moreover, has later suspended unilaterally the talks themselves. After the Chinese Government demanded in July this year that the talks be resumed within a set time-limit, the U.S. Government did not make a timely reply, but it has ultimately designated a representative of ambassadorial rank. Now, the U.S. Government again indicates its desire to settle the Sino-American dispute in the Taiwan area through peaceful negotiation. To make a further effort to safeguard peace, the Chinese Government is prepared to resume the ambassadorial talks between the two countries. But the danger of war created by the United States in China's Taiwan area has not been reduced thereby. In view of the fact that the U.S. Government often acts differently from what it says and often uses peaceful negotiation as a smokescreen to cover up its actual deed of continuously expanding aggression, the entire Chinese people and the peace-loving people all over the world must not relax in the least their struggle against U.S. interference in China's internal affairs and against U.S. threat to the peace of the Far East and the world.

(6) The Sino-American dispute in the Taiwan Straits area and the

Chinese people's internal matter of liberating their own territory are two matters entirely different in nature. The United States has all along tried to confuse these two matters so as to cover up its aggression and intervention in China. This is absolutely not to be allowed. The Chinese people have every right to liberate their own territory by all suitable means at suitable time, and will not tolerate any foreign interference. Should the U.S. Government, brazenly disregarding the Chinese people's repeated warnings and the desire of the people of the world for peace, persist in their aggression and intervention against China and impose war on the Chinese people, it must bear the responsibility for all the serious consequences.

5. Letter from Mr. Khrushchev to President Eisenhower, Moscow, 7 September 1958[1]

Mr. President, I am addressing you on a very important question which, we are convinced, is gripping the minds of all those who cherish the cause of peace.

As a result of the policy pursued by the United States with regard to China, and particularly the steps now being taken by the American government in the area of the Chinese island of Taiwan and the Taiwan straits, a dangerous situation has emerged in the Far East. Mankind is again confronted with a direct threat of war.

At this crucial moment the government of the Soviet Union has decided to call on the United States government to show reasonableness, to refrain from steps which could entail irreparable consequences.

You know full well, Mr. President, that the Soviet Union stands firmly for peaceful co-existence among all states, irrespective of social or political systems, and comes out for the creation of conditions throughout the world ensuring a tranquil life for the peoples and preventing military conflicts. I believe no one will question the fact that the principles of peaceful co-existence have already received broad international recognition, and it can be said that an overwhelming majority of nations hold them to be the basis of their relations with other countries.

In the postwar years, however, an extremely abnormal situation has persisted in the Far East owing to the aggressive policy of the United States government, a policy of war. The main reason for the prevailing tension, or to put it bluntly, for this extremely dangerous situation, lies in the fact that the United States has seized by force of arms the ancient Chinese territory of Taiwan and the Penghuletao[2] Islands, is continuing the occupation of this territory—covering it up by references to its support

---

[1] *Soviet News*, 9 September 1958.   [2] Pescadores.

of the traitor to the Chinese people, Chiang Kai-shek—and is also trying to extend its aggression to Chinese off-shore islands.

As has repeatedly been stated by the Soviet government in the United Nations, and also in its correspondence with the United States government and the governments of other powers, the situation is absolutely impermissible in which such a great power as the Chinese People's Republic is deprived, because of the attitude of the United States government, of the opportunity to take part in the work of the United Nations, and when it is not represented in this organisation in spite of its lawful right to representation. You know just as well as I do that the Chinese state is one of the foundation members of the United Nations and that for this reason alone the prevailing situation is absolutely abnormal and represents a gross injustice to the Chinese people.

The situation which has developed now as a result of United States actions in the area of Taiwan and the Taiwan straits is a great worry to the Soviet government and the Soviet people. It will not be an overstatement to say that this situation alarms the whole world—every country, irrespective of the distance separating it from the area of Taiwan. If we look reality in the face, we will have to admit that the United States is striving to assume the functions of some kind of world gendarmes in this area. We believe that it is unseemly for any civilised state, no matter how strong or influential it is, to assume this role, and, what is more, that it is risky.

The United States government is staging military demonstrations in an attempt to prevent the liberation of Taiwan and to retain this Chinese island as its war base, directed, above all, against the Chinese People's Republic, and also to obstruct the lawful actions of the Chinese People's Republic to liberate the Chinese off-shore islands where the Chiang Kai-shekites have entrenched themselves. One of the biggest formations of the United States navy—the United States Seventh Fleet—is now in the area of the Taiwan straits. Hasty steps are being taken to reinforce this fleet, and warships and aircraft are being rushed to the Far East from the United States, the Mediterranean and other regions.

Moreover, it has been announced that 'joint manoeuvres' of the naval forces and the marines of the United States with the Chiang Kai-shek clique will be held in the Taiwan area shortly, and new contingents of American troops are being rushed to Taiwan under this pretext. The question arises whether these actions can be regarded, in the prevailing situation, as other than a direct provocation. We believe that no other evaluation can be given to these actions, even with the most charitable approach.

It should be pointed out that the practice of rushing United States warships from one place to another has in general become frequent of late. Indeed, it can be almost unmistakably determined where the next blackmail or provocation will occur by the movement of American naval units.

Quite recently the world has witnessed such demonstrations by the American navy in the Mediterranean, when the United States carried out its military intervention in Lebanon and when the United States Sixth Fleet trained its guns on the capital of Lebanon, and on the whole of the country for that matter. Today, when attempts are being made at sabre-rattling and threatening China, we think it is appropriate to recall that China is not little Lebanon, which has recently fallen victim to a foreign intervention overwhelmingly condemned by the latest emergency session of the United Nations General Assembly.

China's great 600 million people are strong and invincible not only by virtue of their inexhaustible resources, but also by virtue of their unity behind their government. They are advancing firmly and confidently along the road of developing and consolidating their country and increasing their well-being, a fact in which we in the Soviet Union sincerely rejoice and which cannot fail to please all those who wish the Chinese people well. But I should like to emphasise not only this aspect of the matter, but also the fact that China is not alone, that it has true friends who are ready to come to its aid at any moment in the event of an act of aggression against China, because the security interests of People's China are inseparable from those of the Soviet Union.

The practice of dispatching naval fleets and air wings from one part of the world to another—for instance, to the Middle East, the Far East, Latin America and other areas—to bring pressure to bear now on some nations, now on others, and to try to impose a foreign will on them, raises the question whether it is not time to put an end to such actions which cannot, naturally, be recognised as normal methods in international relations. It is legitimate to ask whether the United Nations should not consider this and take a decision forbidding powers to undertake such movements of their naval and air forces for the purposes of blackmail and intimidation and obliging them to keep these forces within their national frontiers.

I should like to make one more remark in connection with the use of such methods in United States foreign policy.

Does it not seem to you, Mr. President, that such dispatching of warships now in one direction, now in another, today loses much of its sense, at least with respect to countries possessing modern weapons? I do not know what your military advisers tell you, but it seems to us they cannot but know that the heyday of surface navy powers is over. In the age of nuclear and rocket weapons of unprecedented power and rapid action these once formidable warships are fit, in fact, for nothing but courtesy visits and gun salutes, and can serve as targets for the right types of rockets. This may hurt the pride of people closely connected with the navy, but these are incontestable facts one cannot ignore.

Hardly a day passes without certain political and military leaders of the United States hurling threats at People's China. This is the only meaning of the repeated statements of the United States Secretary of State, Mr. Dulles, on the United States' actions in the Taiwan area and, notably, the statement he made on your behalf and his own on September 4. This statement cannot but be strongly condemned. It represents an undisguised attempt at gross and unceremonious infringement of the soverign rights of other states. The government of the United States, having no right at all to do so, takes the liberty of arbitrarily fixing some limits of its own interests and of the spheres of operations of its armed forces on the territory of China. Such actions cannot be classed as other than aggressive, and will certainly be condemned as such by all peoples.

Nor can one assess in any other way the United States government's statement of September 6.[1]

One cannot fail to note the provocative statement by United States Minister of Defence McElroy which contains barefaced threats against the Chinese People's Republic and attempts to justify the aggressive actions of the American armed forces in the Far East and to shield the Chiang Kai-shek clique. And the commander of the American armed forces in Taiwan, Vice-Admiral Smoot, lost all sense of proportion when he proclaimed the United States' intention of joining with the Chiang Kai-shek clique in defeating communist China.

Military leaders in the United States are also trying, with the tacit agreement of the American government, to resort to atomic blackmail against China, acting, evidently, under the lingering impression of the mood that reigned in Washington during the period of the United States' shortlived monopoly of atomic weapons.

Even at that time, it will be recalled, the policy of atomic blackmail was not a success, nor could it be. It is needless to say that the attempts to frighten other nations by atomic weapons are utterly hopeless in the present circumstances, with the United States having long lost the monopoly of atomic arms.

I say this because it seems to me that there are still some people in the United States who do not want to part with the policy of intimidation and atomic blackmail, although every day seems to furnish enough evidence that such a policy is for ever doomed to failure.

It can be said with full confidence that no threats or blackmail can scare the Chinese people. This has been made obvious, too, by the statement made by Chou En-lai, Premier of the Government Council of the

[1] For text, see *D.S.B.*, 22 September 1958, pp. 446-7.

Chinese People's Republic, on September 6. The Chinese people want peace and they are upholding peace. But they do not fear war. Should a war be forced on China, whose people are determined to defend their righteous cause, we have not the least doubt that the Chinese people will strike back at the aggressor in a fitting manner.

The United States' aggressive preparations in the Far East are not, judging by all indications, confined to the Taiwan straits. There are reports that Syngman Rhee, encouraged and egged on by the United States, is again preparing for war provocations and airing his intention to 'march north.' Some people in the United States seem to have definite plans for turning Korea into a field of bloody struggle once again. Is it not for this reason, by the way, that the United States government is so adamant in its refusal to withdraw its troops from South Korea? But there must be no repetition of the Korean tragedy and Syngman Rhee's criminal designs must be curbed, There can be no doubt that, should the Syngman Rhee clique risk another 'march' of theirs, they would suffer the same fate that befell them when the Korean people and the Chinese People's Volunteers inflicted a real defeat on the aggressor and destroyed all their plans. It goes without saying that the responsibility for Syngman Rhee's provocations lies entirely with the government of the United States.

At the recent emergency session of the United Nations General Assembly you spoke, Mr. President, of an alleged threat of some indirect aggression against certain Arab countries in the Middle East from other Arab states, and called for condemnation of this non-existent indirect aggression. Now the United States is itself carrying out, not only indirect, but also direct aggression in the Far East by occupying the Chinese island of Taiwan and propping up the anti-national clique of traitors to the Chinese people who have entrenched themselves on that island under the protection of American arms and are using it as a base for piratical attacks against China.

The United States is wont to make references to certain commitments 'with regard to the defence' of the Taiwan area to justify sending its armed forces to the Taiwan straits and the adjacent waters of the Pacific. But have the Chinese people asked the American government to assume such commitments to which they now refer in obstructing China's exercise of its sovereign right to Taiwan and other Chinese islands?

The American people themselves had in the past to beat off the attempts of foreign powers to intervene in their home affairs and to impose their will on them by force of arms. It is well known that those attempts had a sad ending for those who made them. Would it not be right to draw the proper conclusions from this historical experience of the United States and end the policy of interference in China's affairs? For, indeed, if national independence is dear to the American people, why should it not be just as dear to the Chinese people, or to any other people for that matter? You will, perhaps, consider what I have said as too sharp. I beg to differ. The only thing I want to do in this letter to you, just as on other occasions, is to speak my mind and to emphasise the full gravity of the situation which has developed in the area of Taiwan and China's off-shore islands as a result of the United States' actions. If we were to clothe our thoughts in outwardly courteous diplomatic wording, we would find it, I think, more difficult to see each other's point. But we do want you, the government of the United States and the entire American people, with whom we want to have nothing but good relations and friendship, to have a correct idea of the consequences which the United States' current actions in the Far East may entail.

It would be a serious miscalculation for the United States to believe that one can make short work of China, just as some powers used to do in the past. Such a miscalculation would have grave consequences for the cause of world peace. Let us, therefore, make this quite clear, for any misunderstanding and equivocal statements are most dangerous things in such matters.

An attack on the Chinese People's Republic, which is a great friend, ally and neighbour of our country, is an attack on the Soviet Union. Loyal to its duty, our country would do everything to defend, jointly with People's China, the security of both countries and the interests of peace in the Far East and throughout the rest of the world.

Nothing could be more erroneous than to try to read in this message of mine an intention to lay the colour on too thickly, let alone any threats. All we want to do is to draw your attention to the situation which no one would be able to get out of, neither you, nor we, should a war break out in the Far East. We want to find a common language with you so as to end the present downward movement and so that the U.S.S.R., the United States, the Chinese People's Republic and other countries may join efforts in removing the tension which has now arisen in the Far East, and so that one could say that a good job for world peace had been done by combined efforts.

Of course, it is the business of the United States government to decide whether to 'recognise' or 'not recognise' the Chinese People's Republic. It can be only noted in this connection that neither the fact of the Chinese People's Republic's existence as one of the world's great powers, nor the role which this state now plays in international relations are changed by this. But at present the United States government's policy with regard to China has brought about a situation in which the question of the United States' attitude to China has transcended the bounds of purely domestic affairs of the United States.

A situation has developed which affects the interests of many countries. The tension in relations between the United States and China, artificially kept up by United States policy, and even more so the steps now being taken by the United States in the Far East, tend to aggravate the relations between all the great powers—the founders of the United Nations. It is no exaggeration to say that the present policy of the United States with regard to China complicates the solution of many important international problems and greatly hampers the normal functioning of the United Nations as an international organisation charged with safeguarding peace.

There is only one Chinese state, and it is in China, not elsewhere; and Taiwan and the other Chinese islands where the Chiang Kai-shekites have entrenched themselves are a part of China.

Only the government whose seat is in the capital of China—Peking— and whom the many millions of Chinese people have charged with the administration of the country has the right and actual possibility to represent China in international relations. Only the unrealistic position of the United States government, which still prefers to close its eyes to the real state of affairs in China, prevents the United Nations members from taking the only correct decision—of evicting from this organisation the political corpse of the Chiang Kai-shek impostor and of giving the representatives of great China their lawful seat in the United Nations.

Will any one deny that China is striving to liberate its territory which has been turned into a foreign war base that is a constant threat to the peaceful life of the Chinese people? China has every legitimate right to take all the necessary measures against the traitor Chiang Kai-shek. It is taking these measures on its own soil and is not dispatching troops to the territories of other countries. These actions of the Chinese People's Republic are nothing but a lawful measure of self-defence stipulated by the United Nations Charter. Absolutely different are the actions of the United States government, which is striving to assume the right to send its armed forces many thousands of kilometres away from the United States to retain the Chinese islands it has captured. It is not without reason that even the allies of the United States under military groupings criticise rather loudly American policy towards China and point out that it is unrealistic and dangerous.

I believe that every person who is really concerned for the fate of the world cannot but speak up in support of ending the abnormal and dangerous situation which has developed as a result of the present political line of the United States government in the Far East. The Soviet government is convinced that, for this purpose, it is necessary to give up, above all, the narrow-minded and absolutely unrealistic approach to the great historical changes which have taken place in China, it is necessary to recognise the lawful rights and interests of the Chinese People's Republic and to end once and for all the policy of provocations and blackmail against the Chinese people.

There can be no lasting peace in the Far East until the American naval forces are withdrawn from the Taiwan straits, until the American soldiers are recalled home from Taiwan. We are convinced that this view is shared not only by the Soviet Union and the other socialist states, but also by all the other nations which highly prize the cause of peace in the Far East and throughout the world.

Mr. President, in closing this message, which is dictated by the awareness of the great responsibility which our countries bear for safeguarding world peace, I wish to emphasise strongly that it fully depends on the further actions of the United States government whether peace will prevail in the Far East or whether this area will remain a dangerous breeding ground of war. I should like to hope that you will receive this message of the Soviet government with due understanding. I also permit myself to express the conviction that this message will be correctly understood by all the American people who, we are convinced, as all the other peoples, want peace and do not want war.

If the United States government takes the road of respecting the lawful and sovereign rights of the great Chinese people, this will undoubtedly be assessed with satisfaction by all the nations as a big contribution by the United States to the cause of consolidating universal peace.

Respectfully yours,

N. KHRUSHCHOV

6. Address by President Eisenhower on the communist threat to peace in Formosa, 11 September 1958[1]

My friends: Tonight I want to talk to you about the situation, dangerous to peace, which has developed in the Formosa Straits in the Far East. My purpose is to give you its basic facts and then my conclusions as to our Nation's proper course of action.

To begin, let us remember that traditionally this country and its Government have always been passionately devoted to peace with honor, as they are now. We shall never resort to force in settlement of differences except when compelled to do so to defend against aggression and to protect our vital interests.

This means that, in our view, negotiations and conciliation should never be abandoned in favor of force and strife. While we shall never timidly retreat before the threat of armed aggression, we would welcome in the present circumstances negotiations that could have a fruitful result

[1] D.S.B., 29 September 1958, pp. 481–4. President Eisenhower was speaking to the nation over radio and television.

in preserving the peace of the Formosa area and reaching a solution that could be acceptable to all parties concerned, including, of course, our ally, the Republic of China.

On the morning of August 23d the Chinese Communists opened a severe bombardment of Quemoy, an island in the Formosa Straits off the China coast. Another island in the same area, Matsu, was also attacked. These two islands have always been a part of Free China—never under Communist control.

This bombardment of Quemoy has been going on almost continuously ever since. Also, Chinese Communists have been using their naval craft to try to break up the supplying of Quemoy with its 125,000 people. Their normal source of supply is by sea from Formosa, where the Government of Free China is now located.

Chinese Communists say that they will capture Quemoy. So far they have not actually attempted a landing, but their bombardment has caused great damage. Over 1,000 people have been killed or wounded. In large part these are civilians.

This is a tragic affair. It is shocking that in this day and age naked force should be used for such aggressive purposes.

But this is not the first time that the Chinese Communists have acted in this way.

In 1950 they attacked and tried to conquer the Republic of Korea. At that time President Truman announced the intention of protecting Formosa, the principal area still held by Free China, because of the belief that Formosa's safety was vital to the security of the United States and the free world. Our Government has adhered firmly ever since 1950 to that policy.

In 1953 and 1954 the Chinese Communists took an active part in the war in Indochina against Viet-Nam.

In the fall of 1954 they attacked Quemoy and Matsu, the same two islands they are attacking now. They broke off that attack when, in January 1955, the Congress and I agreed that we should firmly support Free China.[1]

Since then, for about 4 years, Chinese Communists have not used force for aggressive purposes. We have achieved an armistice in Korea which stopped the fighting there in 1953. There is a 1954 armistice in Viet-Nam; and since 1955 there has been quiet in the Formosa Straits area. We had hoped that the Chinese Communists were becoming peaceful— but it seems not.

So the world is again faced with the problem of armed aggression. Powerful dictatorships are attacking an exposed, but free, area.

[1] For background and text of the joint resolution on the defence of Formosa, see D.S.B., 7 February 1955, p. 211.

What should we do?

Shall we take the position that, submitting to threat, it is better to surrender pieces of free territory in the hope that this will satisfy the appetite of the aggressor and we shall have peace?

Do we not still remember that the name of 'Munich' symbolizes a vain hope of appeasing dictators?

At that time the policy of appeasement was tried, and it failed. Prior to the Second World War, Mussolini seized Ethiopia. In the Far East Japanese warlords were grabbing Manchuria by force. Hitler sent his armed forces into the Rhineland in violation of the Versailles Treaty. Then he annexed little Austria. When he got away with that, he next turned to Czechoslovakia and began taking it bit by bit.

In the face of all these attacks on freedom by the dictators, the powerful democracies stood aside. It seemed that Ethiopia and Manchuria were too far away and too unimportant to fight about. In Europe appeasement was looked upon as the way to peace. The democracies felt that, if they tried to stop what was going on, that would mean war. But, because of these repeated retreats, war came just the same.

If the democracies had stood firm at the beginning, almost surely there would have been no World War. Instead they gave such an appearance of weakness and timidity that aggressive rulers were encouraged to overrun one country after another. In the end the democracies saw that their very survival was at stake. They had no alternative but to turn and fight in what proved to be the most terrible war that the world has ever known.

I know something about that war, and I never want to see that history repeated. But, my fellow Americans, it certainly can be repeated if the peace-loving democratic nations again fearfully practice a policy of standing idly by while big aggressors use armed force to conquer the small and weak.

Let us suppose that the Chinese Communists conquer Quemoy. Would that be the end of the story? We know that it would not be the end of the story. History teaches that, when powerful despots can gain something through aggression, they try, by the same methods, to gain more and more and more.

Also, we have more to guide us than the teachings of history. We have the statements, the boastings, of the Chinese Communists themselves. They frankly say that their present military effort is part of a program to conquer Formosa.

It is as certain as can be that the shooting which the Chinese Communists started on August 23d had as its purpose not just the taking of the island of Quemoy. It is part of what is indeed an ambitious plan of armed conquest.

This plan would liquidate all of the free-world positions in the Western

Pacific area and bring them under captive governments which would be hostile to the United States and the free world. Thus the Chinese and Russian Communists would come to dominate at least the western half of the now friendly Pacific Ocean.

So aggression by ruthless despots again imposes a clear danger to the United States and to the free world.

In this effort the Chinese Communists and the Soviet Union appear to be working hand in hand. Last Monday I received a long letter on this subject from Prime Minister Khrushchev.[1] He warned the United States against helping its allies in the Western Pacific. He said that we should not support the Republic of China and the Republic of Korea. He contended that we should desert them, return all of our naval forces to our home bases, and leave our friends in the Far East to face, alone, the combined military power of the Soviet Union and Communist China.

Does Mr. Khrushchev think that we have so soon forgotten Korea?

I must say to you very frankly and soberly, my friends, the United States cannot accept the result that the Communists seek. Neither can we show, now, a weakness of purpose—a timidity—which would surely lead them to move more aggressively against us and our friends in the Western Pacific area.

If the Chinese Communists have decided to risk a war, it is not because Quemoy itself is so valuable to them. They have been getting along without Quemoy ever since they seized the China mainland 9 years ago.

If they have now decided to risk a war, it can only be because they, and their Soviet allies, have decided to find out whether threatening war is a policy from which they can make big gains.

If that is their decision, then a Western Pacific 'Munich' would not buy us peace or security. It would encourage the aggressors. It would dismay our friends and allies there. If history teaches anything, appeasement would make it more likely that we would have to fight a major war.

Congress has made clear its recognition that the security of the Western Pacific is vital to the security of the United States and that we should be firm. The Senate has ratified, by overwhelming vote, security treaties with the Republic of China covering Formosa and the Pescadores, and also the Republic of Korea. We have a mutual security treaty with the Republic of the Philippines, which could be next in line for conquest if Formosa fell into hostile hands. These treaties commit the United States to the defense of the treaty areas. In addition, there is a joint resolution which the Congress passed in January 1955 dealing specifically with Formosa and the offshore islands of Free China in the Formosa Straits.

At that time the situation was similar to what it is today.

[1] For Mr. Khrushchev's letter to President Eisenhower of 7 September 1958, see above, pp. 182–9.

Congress then voted the President authority to employ the armed forces of the United States for the defense not only of Formosa but of related positions, such as Quemoy and Matsu, if I believed their defense to be appropriate in assuring the defense of Formosa.

I might add that the mandate from the Congress was given by an almost unanimous bipartisan vote.

Today, the Chinese Communists announce, repeatedly and officially, that their military operations against Quemoy are preliminary to attack on Formosa. So it is clear that the Formosa Straits resolution of 1955 applies to the present situation.

If the present bombardment and harassment of Quemoy should be converted into a major assault, with which the local defenders could not cope, then we would be compelled to face precisely the situation that Congress visualized in 1955.

I have repeatedly sought to make clear our position in this matter so that there would not be danger of Communist miscalculation. The Secretary of State on September 4th made a statement to the same end.[1] This statement could not, of course, cover every contingency. Indeed, I interpret the joint resolution as requiring me not to make absolute advance commitments but to use my judgment according to the circumstances of the time. But the statement did carry a clear meaning to the Chinese Communists and to the Soviet Union. There will be no retreat in the face of armed aggression, which is part and parcel of a continuing program of using armed force to conquer new regions.

I do not believe that the United States can be either lured or frightened into appeasement. I believe that, in taking the position of opposing aggression by force, I am taking the only position which is consistent with the vital interests of the United States and, indeed, with the peace of the world.

Some misguided persons have said that Quemoy is nothing to become excited about. They said the same about South Korea—about Viet-Nam, about Lebanon.

Now I assure you that no American boy will be asked by me to fight *just* for Quemoy. But those who make up our armed forces—and I believe the American people as a whole—do stand ready to defend the principle that armed force shall not be used for aggressive purposes.

Upon observance of that principle depends a lasting and just peace. It is that same principle that protects the Western Pacific free-world positions as well as the security of our homeland. If we are not ready to defend this principle, then indeed tragedy after tragedy would befall us.

But there is a far better way than resort to force to settle these differences, and there is some hope that such a better way may be followed.

[1] See above, p. 177.

That is the way of negotiation.

That way is open and prepared because in 1955 arrangements were made between the United States and the Chinese Communists that an ambassador on each side would be authorized to discuss at Geneva certain problems of common concern. These included the matter of release of American civilians imprisoned in Communist China and such questions as the renunciation of force in the Formosa area. There have been 73 meetings since August 1955.

When our ambassador, who was conducting these negotiations, was recently transferred to another post, we named as successor Mr. [Jacob D.] Beam, our Ambassador to Poland. The Chinese Communists were notified accordingly the latter part of July, but there was no response.

The Secretary of State, in his September 4th statement, referred to these Geneva negotiations. Two days later, Mr. Chou En-lai, the Premier of the People's Republic of China, proposed that these talks should be resumed 'in the interests of peace.' This was followed up on September 8th by Mr. Mao Tse-tung, the Chairman of the People's Republic of China. We promptly welcomed this prospect and instructed our Ambassador at Warsaw to be ready immediately to resume these talks. We expect that the talks will begin upon the return to Warsaw of the Chinese Communist Ambassador, who has been in Peiping.[1]

Perhaps our suggestion may be bearing fruit. We devoutly hope so.

Naturally, the United States will adhere to the position it first took in 1955, that we will not in these talks be a party to any arrangements which would prejudice rights of our ally, the Republic of China.

We know by hard experiences that the Chinese Communist leaders are indeed militant and aggressive. But we cannot believe that they would now persist in a course of military aggression which would threaten world peace, with all that would be involved. We believe that diplomacy can and should find a way out. There are measures that can be taken to assure that these offshore islands will not be a thorn in the side of peace. We believe that arrangements are urgently required to stop gunfire and to pave the way to a peaceful solution.

If the bilateral talks between ambassadors do not fully succeed, there is still the hope that the United Nations could exert a peaceful influence on the situation.

[1] In its diplomatic initiative to follow up the military offensive against Quemoy, Peking ignored the Nationalists as a party to the conflict, and treated it simply as an issue between the United States and China. The United States maintained that they had not invaded or occupied Formosa, but were helping the Nationalist Government, which they continued to recognize *de jure*, to defend its territory; therefore it was difficult for the United States to negotiate on the future of the Nationalist territory bilaterally with Peking without indirectly endorsing the allegation that the United States was in some sense in possession of it. It was a considerable diplomatic success for Peking that the negotiations between China and the United States about the rights of the Nationalist régime, should take place at all.

In 1955 the hostilities of the Chinese Communists in the Formosa area were brought before the United Nations Security Council. But the Chinese Communists rejected its jurisdiction.[1] They said that they were entitled to Formosa and the offshore islands and that, if they used armed force to get them, that was purely a 'civil war' and that the United Nations had no right to concern itself.

They claimed also that the attack by the Communist north Koreans on south Korea was 'civil war' and that the United Nations and the United States were 'aggressors' because they helped south Korea. They said the same about their attack on Viet-Nam.

I feel sure that these pretexts will never deceive or control world opinion. The fact is that Communist Chinese hostilities in the Formosa Straits area do endanger world peace. I do not believe that any rulers, however aggressive they may be, will flout efforts to find a peaceful and honorable solution, whether it be by direct negotiations or through the United Nations.

My friends, we are confronted with a serious situation. But it is typical of the security problems of the world today. Powerful and aggressive forces are constantly probing, now here, now there, to see whether the free world is weakening. In the face of this there are no easy choices available. It is misleading for anyone to imply that there are.

However, the present situation, though serious, is by no means desperate or hopeless.

There is not going to be any appeasement.

I believe that there is not going to be any war.

But there must be sober realization by the American people that our legitimate purposes are again being tested by those who threaten peace and freedom everywhere.

This has not been the first test for us and for the free world. Probably it will not be the last. But as we meet each test with courage and unity, we contribute to the safety and the honor of our beloved land—and to the cause of a just and lasting peace.

7. Letter from President Eisenhower to Mr. Khrushchev, 12 September 1958[2]

Dear Mr. Chairman: I have your letter of September 7. I agree with you that a dangerous situation exists in the Taiwan area. I do not agree with you as to the source of danger in this situation.

The present state of tension in the Taiwan area was created directly by Chinese Communist action, not by that of the Republic of China or by the United States. The fact is that following a long period of relative

---

[1] See *Documents* for 1955, pp. 448–50.   [2] *D.S.B.*, 29 September 1958, pp. 498–9.

calm in that area, the Chinese Communists, without provocation, suddenly initiated a heavy artillery bombardment of Quemoy and began harassing the regular supply of the civilian and military population of the Quemoys. This intense military activity was begun on August 23rd— some three weeks after your visit to Peiping.[1] The official Peiping radio has repeatedly been announcing that the purpose of these military operations is to take Taiwan (Formosa) as well as Quemoy and Matsu, by armed force. In virtually every Peiping broadcast, Taiwan (Formosa) and the offshore islands are linked as the objective of what is called the 'Chinese Peoples Liberation Army'.

The issue, then, is whether the Chinese Communists will seek to achieve their ambitions through the application of force, as they did in Korea, or whether they will accept the vital requisite of world peace and order in a nuclear age and renounce the use of force as the means for satisfying their territorial claims. The territory concerned has never been under the control of Communist China. On the contrary, the Republic of China— despite the characterizations you apply to it for ideological reasons—is recognized by the majority of the sovereign nations of the world and its government has been and is exercising jurisdiction over the territory concerned. United States military forces operate in the Taiwan area in fulfillment of treaty commitments to the Republic of China to assist it in the defense of Taiwan (Formosa) and the Penghu (Pescadores) Islands. They are there to help resist aggression—not to commit aggression. No upside down presentation such as contained in your letter can change this fact.

The United States Government has welcomed the willingness of the Chinese Communists to resume the Ambassadorial talks, which were begun three years ago in Geneva, for the purpose of finding a means of easing tensions in the Taiwan area. In the past, the United States representative at these talks has tried by every reasonable means to persuade the Chinese Communist representative to reach agreement on mutual renunciation of force in the Taiwan area but the latter insistently refused to reach such agreement. The United States hopes that an understanding can be achieved through the renewed talks which will assure that there will be no resort to the use of force in the endeavour to bring about a solution of the issues there.

I regret to say I do not see in your letter any effort to find that common language which could indeed facilitate the removal of the danger existing in the current situation in the Taiwan area. On the contrary, the description of this situation contained in your letter seems designed to serve the ambitions of international Communism rather than to present the

[1] Mr. Khrushchev visited Peking from 31 July until 3 August 1958. See below, pp. 516–19, for the joint communiqué signed by Mr. Khrushchev and Mao Tse-tung on 3 August 1958.

facts. I also note that you have addressed no letter to the Chinese Communist leaders urging moderation upon them. If your letter to me is not merely a vehicle for one-sided denunciation of United States actions but is indeed intended to reflect a desire to find a common language for peace, I suggest you urge these leaders to discontinue their military operations and to turn to a policy of peaceful settlement of the Taiwan dispute.

If indeed, for the sake of settling the issues that tend to disturb the peace in the Formosa area, the Chinese Communist leaders can be persuaded to place their trust in negotiation and a readiness to practice conciliation, then I assure you the United States will, on its part, strive in that spirit earnestly to the same end.

Sincerely,

DWIGHT D. EISENHOWER

8. Letter from Mr. Khrushchev to President Eisenhower, Moscow, 19 September 1958[1]

On receiving your letter of September 12, and on studying it, I was sorry to note that, as I see it, you have failed to appreciate the essential meaning of my message to you. My message was meant to show the full extent of the danger that will face mankind unless the United States of America abandons its aggressive policy, which is creating centres of grave conflict, now in one area of the world, now in another, and has brought about the present particularly tense situation in the Far East.

While admitting in your reply that a dangerous situation has developed in the Taiwan area, you are at the same time seeking to absolve the United States government of the responsibility for the tension there which is endangering peace. Moreover, to whitewash the aggressive actions of the United States, your message completely distorts the actual state of affairs and draws a picture which has nothing in common with the realities.

If the existing situation is viewed soberly and on the basis of the actual facts, one is bound to admit that the only real source of the tension in that part of the world consists in the fact that the United States has seized inalienable Chinese territory—Taiwan and a number of other islands— and is maintaining under its armed protection the Chiang Kai-shek clique thrown out by the Chinese people, and encouraging its attacks and provocations against People's China.

The recent events are some of the numerous manifestations of this general aggressive policy of the United States with respect to China.

I am surprised at your remark that, while sending a message to you, I

[1] *Soviet News*, 22 September 1958. This letter was rejected by the United States and returned to the Soviet Government. For the White House statements of 20 September 1958 in which Mr. Khrushchev's letter is described as 'abusive and intemperate', see *D.S.B.*, 6 October 1958, pp. 530–1.

did not send any communication to, as you put it, China's communist leaders, with respect to whom and to the Chinese People's Republic your message in a number of instances has a slighting and hostile tone. First of all, Mr. President, I should like to say the following in this connection:

No party or its leaders, and not a single government throughout the whole of China's history have enjoyed such confidence and boundless support of the entire Chinese people as are enjoyed by the great Communist Party of China and its leaders, and also by the government of the Chinese People's Republic. Yes, the Communist Party leaders are, indeed, the recognised leaders of the Chinese people.

It is they who are today not only at the head of the Chinese Communist Party but also at the head of the entire Chinese people and of the new people's democratic state—the Chinese People's Republic.

I addressed my message on the Taiwan events to the President of the United States and not to the government of the Chinese People's Republic for the simple reason that it is not China that is interfering in the internal affairs of the United States of America, but the United States which, trampling underfoot all the standards of behaviour of civilised nations, has grossly interfered in China's affairs and is trying by force of arms to have things all its own way in someone else's house, in this way creating a grave threat to peace in the Far East.

Moreover, Mr. President, to urge us, as you do, to exert some influence on the government of the Chinese People's Republic in connection with the Taiwan events, means trying to induce the Soviet Union to interfere in the internal affairs of China. The Soviet Union would never be a party to such a shameful affair, as that would be fundamentally contrary to its peaceful foreign policy and would be incompatible with the relationship of unbreakable friendship and fraternal co-operation between the Soviet and the Chinese peoples.

As you found it fit to mention in your letter, I have been to Peking lately and had a chance to exchange views with the leaders of the government of the Chinese People's Republic on all matters of interest to the Soviet Union and the Chinese People's Republic. I can tell you frankly and straightforwardly that the full unanimity of views of the U.S.S.R. and the Chinese People's Republic on the main thing, that is, on the necessity of continuing to struggle resolutely against all forces of aggression and of supporting the forces working for peace all over the world, was reaffirmed during our discussions in Peking.

The Chinese people are determined to develop their economy and advance their standards of living, which can only be done in conditions of peace and security. It is quite natural, therefore, that the people of China should feel grave concern at the situation which has developed in the Taiwan area.

It is solely because the United States government, interfering in the internal affairs of China, has taken the venal Chiang Kai-shek clique under its armed protection that the intolerable situation could persist in which a general, expelled by the Chinese people, who has defied the legal government of China and taken possession of some offshore islands lying within a few kilometres of big centres in China's coastal areas, has been ensconced in Taiwan for a number of years.

Who can deny that, but for United States support, there would long since have been no Chiang Kai-shek clique or the so-called Taiwan problem, and that but for United States interference the peoples of the whole area would have long since been living in peace and security. It is clear to all that the reason why the United States has illegally seized those islands is that by keeping Chiang Kai-shek's clique in being on Taiwan it is able to maintain its own armed forces in the area and threaten the Chinese People's Republic with war. Only Chiang Kai-shek, traitor and betrayer of the Chinese people as he is, could let a foreign power—the United States of America—range its armed forces against China, against the Chinese people.

You are trying to substantiate the untenable claim that the United States government has some kind of moral and legal right to keep its armed forces in the Taiwan area. Everyone is free to interpret the facts to suit his own moral principles. But you cannot get away from the facts. They speak for themselves.

The facts are that the United States government has forcibly seized islands belonging to the Chinese people—islands which are 10,000 kilometres away from the American continent—and that it is bent on keeping them. Moreover, you want China to give up that part of her territory and resign herself to it being in foreign hands and used as a base for extending aggression against the Chinese People's Republic and other peaceloving countries of Asia.

But is it not obvious—and is it, indeed, not shown by the entire experience of the peoples' struggle for national liberation and independence— that such a great world power as the Chinese People's Republic will never agree to part of its territory being alienated and used as a place for massing foreign armed forces for aggression against it.

The United States government wants to maintain this situation as it is, as may be seen from your letter. What else can be meant by your remark to the effect that I did not address a letter to the leaders of the Chinese People's Republic urging them to moderation? Had we agreed with your point of view, we would, in fact, have been contributing to the preparations for a war against China, our great friend and ally. To imagine this possibility for a moment is enough to see how utterly absurd it is. How can one expect us, Mr. President, to lull the vigilance of our

Chinese friends and abet the aggressive forces in their preparations for an attack on the Chinese People's Republic, and thereby in their preparations for an attack on the Soviet Union? It is futile to expect us to do so.

In your letter state you that Taiwan and the offshore islands have never been under the control of communist China. This statement seems to be meant to justify the attempt to alienate these islands from the Chinese People's Republic.

However, the United States of America solemnly recognised China's sovereignty over those islands in the Cairo Declaration of 1943. This was reaffirmed in the Potsdam Declaration of 1945, which was signed by the United States and certain other great powers. These declarations bear the signatures of your predecessors—Franklin D. Roosevelt and Harry S. Truman.

But have these territories ceased to be Chinese since the victory of the people's revolution in China resulted in the creation of a government which represents the will of the entire Chinese people and guides itself by the ideas of communism? Of course they have not. To deny this is to interfere in the internal affairs of other peoples and to arrogate to oneself certain police functions.

It appears from your statement that the United States government does not, unfortunately, intend to desist from interference in the internal affairs of China and from an aggressive policy towards the Chinese People's Republic, and this is a very dangerous policy, fraught with the threat of an armed conflict in the Far East and in other areas. Indeed, if Britain, for instance, were to build her policy on such a concept, she might, if she could, start a war against the United States for the simple reason that what is now the territory of the United States was once a colony of the British Empire.

Nor can one fail to note that in opposing Taiwan and the offshore islands to the whole of China, as you do in your letter, an undisguised attempt is being made to create a situation of 'two Chinas.' Such attempts, which are aimed at the dismemberment of China, are resolutely rejected by the people and government of the Chinese People's Republic, just as by all those who respect the sovereign rights of the peoples and the territorial integrity of states.

You seem, Mr. President, to be still proceeding from the assumption that Chiang Kai-shek represents something in China. In reality, however, he is no more than a hated shadow of the past in the eyes of China's 600 million people. And they want this shadow to disappear once and for all as soon as possible. There is only one government of China. That is the government of the Chinese People's Republic. To fail to see this means to base one's actions on illusions, which certainly cannot serve as a basis for any country's foreign policy.

Also unfounded is the assertion in your letter that the American armed forces are operating in the Taiwan area in pursuance of the United States' contractual commitments to a handful of traitors to the Chinese people, with Chiang Kai-shek at the head of these traitors. And this notwithstanding the fact that this handful of people—whom former U.S. Secretary of State Acheson described as early as 1949 as corrupt individuals who had forfeited the confidence of the people—have long represented no one but themselves. Today Chiang Kai-shek has no more reason to act as a representative of China than, say, Kerensky would have to act as a representative of the Soviet people. But to follow the logic of your letter one would say that so long as Kerensky is alive and is kept somewhere in the United States, and with whom, as the head of Russia's one time provisional government, you could also conclude a treaty, the United States might start a war against the Soviet Union, basing itself on such a treaty just as it is basing itself today on its treaty with Chiang Kai-shek. Is it not clear from this example that all references to contractual commitments like those the United States has as regards Chiang Kai-shek are absurd? It is for the purpose of covering up aggressive designs that treaties of this kind are conceived and concocted.

You maintain in your letter that Chiang Kai-shek—who is in the pay of the United States government—is recognised by the majority of states. I would not engage in such arithmetics, Mr. President, for it can lead to serious miscalculations. But I must point out that the Chinese People's Republic has by now been recognised by more than 30 states with a population of over 1,000 million. As for the fact that the Chiang Kai-shek clique is recognised by a number of governments, you are very well aware of how hard it has been and is for the United States to keep this recognition alive. Your Secretary of State, Mr. Dulles, is equally well aware of this. I will not be divulging any secret if I say that the states still maintaining relations with the Chiang Kai-shek clique are disturbed by this recognition and that it is in its final hour.

Surely, the majority of the states which, under pressure from the United States, still maintain diplomatic relations with Chiang Kai-shek will be glad when this situation—which is obviously contrary to common sense and the interests of the peoples of these countries—comes to an end and when China occupies her rightful place in international organisations.

You are, of course, aware of the fact that even those countries which do not dare to recognise the Chinese People's Republic, lest they evoke the displeasure of the United States, feel serious anxiety over the possible consequences of the present policy of the United States towards the Chinese People's Republic. This is only natural because the threats uttered by American statesmen against the Chinese People's Republic, and also the build up of American armed forces and other military preparations by the United States in the Taiwan area, actually create the danger of an armed conflict breaking out, with all the dangerous consequences that would entail.

As for blackmail and threats with regard to People's China, one must say that they have not achieved and cannot achieve their purpose. As I noted in my previous message, certain American military leaders are even trying to threaten China with atomic weapons. Press reports say that units of the American air force, equipped with nuclear weapons, have been rushed to Taiwan together with various rockets and guided missiles of the 'Nike-Hercules' type, and that missile-launching ramps are being built and so on.

Such actions by the United States government cannot, naturally, reduce tension in that area, cannot improve the general climate or create the conditions for greater confidence. On the contrary, these actions tend to aggravate the situation and increase the danger of an outbreak of war involving the use of the most devastating modern weapons.

I must tell you outright, Mr. President, that atomic blackmail with regard to the Chinese People's Republic will intimidate neither us nor the Chinese People's Republic. Those who harbour plans for an atomic attack on the Chinese People's Republic should not forget that the other side too has atomic and hydrogen weapons and the appropriate means to deliver them, and if the Chinese People's Republic falls victim to such an attack, the aggressor will at once suffer a rebuff by the same means.

A war against China on the pretext of defending the security interests of the United States, or on any other equally artificial pretext, will gain nothing for the United States. To touch off a war against People's China means to doom sons of the American people to certain death and to spark off the conflagration of a world war. It means to assume a grave responsibility before mankind, before history. The responsibility for this will also rest with you personally, Mr. President.

Need one say that such an act by the American government would be unanimously condemned by the peoples of the whole world, including, I am convinced, the American people?

I told you earlier, and feel it necessary to stress once more, that an attack on the Chinese People's Republic is an attack on the Soviet Union. We have a Treaty of Friendship, Alliance and Mutual Assistance with this great friend, ally and neighbour of our country, a treaty meeting the fundamental interests of the Soviet and Chinese peoples, the interests of peace, and let no one doubt that we shall fully honour our commitments.

Therefore I would like to appeal to you once more not to bring the atmosphere to red heat, not to create conditions which would trouble mankind, craving for peace as it is, and to weigh up all the circumstances before taking steps which might have disastrous consequences.

The governments, above all the governments of our countries, are duty bound to do everything necessary to ensure that international developments move in the direction of increasing peaceful co-operation, developing trade, economic ties and cultural relations among states, so that all the fruits of man's labour may go to improve the well-being of the peoples and to ensure continued progress.

After your election as President of the United States of America, Soviet statesmen pinned great hopes on you. Remembering the experience of excellent co-operation between the Soviet Union and the United States when you were the commander-in-chief of the armed forces of the United States, Britain and France in the war against fascism, against Hitler Germany, we hoped that this co-operation would also be possible after the war, in the present period, in the interests of preserving and consolidating peace.

However, the policy you are now pursuing as President has largely undermined these good feelings, and to an increasing extent strengthens our belief that the 'brink of war' policy of Mr. Dulles is in fact inseparable from your name, is associated with it. This is highly regrettable.

In our times 'the positions of strength' policy, the policy of balancing 'on the brink of war,' cannot be successful. In contrast to the time when Hitler unleashed world war, the peace forces have now grown immeasurably and, what is more important, the international balance of forces has changed radically in their favour.

History will pass stern judgment on those statesmen who, against all common sense and the interests of the peoples of the whole world, embark on the road of military adventures.

It is universally known that the government of the Chinese People's Republic has repeatedly taken the initiative in putting forward proposals aimed at relaxing tension in the Far East, and at settling outstanding international problems in that area peacefully. Contrary to the contention in your message, in the course of the Chinese-American Ambassadorial talks in Geneva the representative of China repeatedly suggested that both parties, on the basis of the principles of mutual respect for sovereignty, territorial integrity and non-interference in one another's internal affairs, should make a statement concerning their readiness to solve disputes between the Chinese People's Republic and the United States in the Taiwan area by peaceful negotiation and not to rely on force or the threat of force. The Chinese-American talks in Geneva failed to yield positive results only because the United States refused to adopt this attitude and later on unilaterally broke off negotiations.

Mr. President, you declare in your message that you welcome the resumption of talks between the United States and the Chinese People's Republic. We also welcome the initiative taken by the Chinese People's

Republic and are glad that the efforts of the Chinese people's government in this direction found a response on the United States government's part.

We also hope that at these talks the United States will at last take a reasonable, realistic attitude. The only reasonable and realistic attitude on the United States government's part would be to approach the present situation with due consideration for the historic changes which have occurred in China, to stop supporting the Chiang Kai-shek clique and to draw the necessary conclusions from the fact that China is the Chinese People's Republic, whose government represents the Chinese state, the entire Chinese people.

If one does not wish to engage in a policy of preparing war, but really wishes to be guided by the ideal of peaceful co-operation, then the most important thing is to recognise the government of the Chinese People's Republic. Such a step by the United States government would clarify the international situation at once and would be welcomed everywhere as a highly valuable contribution to the cause of maintaining peace.

This approach to the solution of international problems from the standpoint of peaceful co-operation also makes it imperative to discontinue the tactics of obstruction in the United Nations and to refrain from raising obstacles to the solution of the most urgent problem of restoring China's rights in the United Nations. All the member-states of the United Nations would welcome such a decision, since without the Chinese People's Republic the United Nations cannot be a completely representative international body for maintaining international peace and security in conformity with the United Nations Charter.

An end must be put once and for all to intervention in China's internal affairs. The American fleet must be recalled from the Taiwan Strait and American troops must leave Taiwan and go home. Without these steps there can be no lasting peace in the Far East. If the United States does not do that now, People's China will have no other recourse but to expel the hostile armed forces from its own territory which is being converted into a bridgehead for attacking the Chinese People's Republic.

We fully support the Chinese government and the Chinese people. We have supported and will continue to support their policy.

However, if the United States government adopts the course of respecting the sovereign rights of the great Chinese people and will be guided in its policy towards China by the principles of peaceful co-existence, we do not doubt that this will not only enable the present tension in the Taiwan area to be removed, but will also create the necessary conditions for reliably strengthening peace in the Far East and throughout the world.

Respectfully yours,

N. KHRUSHCHOV

9. Statement by the Foreign Minister of the People's Republic of China, refuting Mr. Dulles's speech at the United Nations General Assembly on 18 September, Peking, 20 September 1958[1]

The Chinese people are profoundly enraged by the statement on the situation in the Taiwan Straits area made by U.S. Secretary of State Dulles at the United Nations General Assembly on September 18.[2] The United States has invaded and occupied our territory Taiwan, and in addition has recently concentrated large numbers of armed forces to interfere with the recovery by the Chinese people of Quemoy, Matsu and other coastal islands, and has thus gravely threatened peace in the Far East and the world. In order to disguise these aggressive activities of the United States, Dulles has gone so far as to accuse our country of being an 'aggressor' and to propose a so-called 'ceasefire.' This is indeed extremely preposterous. Actually, the current armed provocations and war threats directed against our country by the U.S. imperialists have met with strong opposition and condemnation from the peace-loving countries and people throughout the world. Dulles' statements which turn the facts upside down can deceive no one.

The Chinese people are determined to recover Quemoy and Matsu, and no force on earth can stop them. The Chiang Kai-shek clique, repudiated by the Chinese people, has been using Quemoy and Matsu all along to carry out all sorts of harassing military activities against our mainland and coastal areas with the support of U.S. imperialism. In the last two months, these military activities have become even more unbridled. The facts show that so long as Quemoy and Matsu are not recovered, the immediate threat to our mainland and coastal areas will not be removed. The punitive military operations conducted by the Chinese people against Chiang Kai-shek's troops entrenched on Quemoy and Matsu are therefore entirely proper and necessary. But the U.S. imperialists have described as 'aggression' this action of the Chinese people in exercising their sovereign right and used this as a pretext to intervene, in an attempt to bring Quemoy, Matsu and other islands in our inland waters under their direct armed control and turn them into springboards for further aggression

---

[1] *Peking Review*, 23 September 1958, pp. 5–6.

[2] Mr. Dulles was speaking on 'the problems of peace', and 'the opportunities for progress' in the world. He accused the Soviet Union of supplying the artillery used by the Communists to bombard the Quemoy Islands. He then listed two 'undisputed' facts: 'First the Chinese Communist régime has never during its nine years of existence exercised authority over Taiwan, the P'eng-hu islands, or the islands of Quemoy and Ma-tsu. Secondly, the Chinese Communists are now attempting to extend their authority to these areas by the use of naked force.' For Mr. Dulles's statement on the situation in Formosa, see G.A.O.R., Thirteenth Session, 749th plenary meeting, pp. 8–9.

against the Chinese mainland. The Chinese people have not forgotten the historical lesson that the Japanese militarists first invaded and occupied Taiwan and northeast China and converted them into springboards for aggression against the whole of China. They will never allow the U.S. imperialists to repeat the old tricks of the Japanese militarists.

The tension in the Taiwan Straits area is entirely the result of U.S. imperialist aggression against our country. The key to eliminating the tension in the Taiwan Straits area is not a so-called 'ceasefire,' but the withdrawal of U.S. forces from the Taiwan area. There is no fighting between China and the United States, so the question of a so-called 'ceasefire' does not arise at all. As to the armed conflict between the Chinese people and the Chiang Kai-shek clique, it has never ceased since the Chinese People's War of Liberation and has never brought about any international tension. The liberation by the Chinese people of their territory, whether by peaceful means or by armed struggle, is the affair of the Chinese people themselves. The point at present is that the United States is playing with fire on the brink of war and is attempting to extend its aggression against China. The imminent danger at present in the situation in the Taiwan Straits area is that the United States, ignoring our repeated grave warnings and the strong protests of the people of the world, persists in its armed provocations and war threats against our people. To ease and eliminate the tension in the Taiwan Straits area, the United States must at once stop its armed provocations and war threats against China and withdraw all its armed forces from Taiwan and the Taiwan Straits. The tension in the Taiwan Straits area will continue as long as the U.S. armed forces are not withdrawn.

The Chinese Government has time and again indicated its willingness to settle the Sino-American disputes in the area of Taiwan and other areas in the Far East through peaceful negotiations without resorting to the threat or use of force. If the United States has any sincere desire to settle the disputes between the two countries peacefully, it should respect China's sovereignty and territorial integrity, and stop interfering in China's internal affairs. The liberation of Taiwan by the Chinese people is China's internal affair—this was publicly acknowledged by the U.S. Government in 1950, and is an undeniable fact no matter how forgetful Dulles is. All sober-minded people in the world agree that Quemoy, Matsu and other coastal islands have always belonged to China, only those who are obsessed with ideas of aggression, like Dulles, refuse to do so. Dulles described the Chinese people's liberation of their own territory as 'armed conquest.' Actually it is precisely the United States itself that has conquered China's territories by force. The United States has concentrated the largest amount of naval and air power in the Taiwan Straits area to engage in war provocations against our people. Yet Dulles parades as an advocate of the renunciation of the use of force and the elimination of provocations. If these statements of Dulles' are not designed to fool other people, the U.S. armed forces must be withdrawn from Taiwan and the Taiwan Straits. This is precisely the urgent question to be settled in the current Sino-American ambassadorial talks. The Chinese Government places hope in the Sino-American ambassadorial talks now in progress, but Dulles said he would bring the Sino-American disputes to the United Nations. It is well known, however, that the People's Republic of China has been unjustifiably deprived of its rightful place in the United Nations.[1] Therefore, one cannot but doubt whether the United States is sincere about Sino-American negotiations.

The Chinese people ardently love peace, but they will never succumb to the war threat of the imperialists. No amount of war threats by the U.S. imperialists can cow the Chinese people. The mighty demonstrations against U.S. aggression held by 300 million Chinese people in the cities and the countryside testify to the Chinese people's firm will. Should the U.S. aggressors, despite the repeated warnings of the Chinese people and the firm opposition of the people of the world, dare to impose war on us, our 600 million people, united as one, will certainly spare no sacrifice and will, under the sacred banner of defending our great motherland, fight against aggression, fight for the preservation of our sovereignty and territorial integrity, and fight for the safeguarding of peace in the Far East and the world! Ours is a just struggle. With the help of the socialist camp headed by the Soviet Union and with the sympathy and support of all the peace-loving countries and people of Asia, Africa and the rest of the world, we will certainly win complete victory.

10. Extracts from Mr. Dulles's press conference, 30 September 1958[2]

Q. Mr. Secretary, in referring to the previous question on the renunciation of force, is it the position of this Government that the United States expects or supports the idea that the Nationalist Chinese Government is someday going to return to the mainland either by force or some other means?

A. Well, that is a highly hypothetical matter. I think it all depends upon what happens on the mainland. I don't think that just by their own steam they are going to get there. If you had on the mainland a sort of

[1] On 23 September 1958 the United Nations General Assembly rejected an Indian request for the inclusion, in the agenda of the thirteenth session, of the item entitled 'Question of the representation of China in the United Nations', by 44 votes to 28 with nine abstentions. G.A.O.R., Thirteenth Session, Supplement No. 18 (A/4090), Resol. 1239 (XIII). The United States released a statement on 11 August 1958, before hostilities broke out, on United States non-recognition policy towards China, see D.S.B., 8 September 1958, pp. 385–90.
[2] D.S.B., 20 October 1958, pp. 599–600 and 602–4.

unrest and revolt, like, for example, what broke out in Hungary, then the presence of a free China with considerable power a few miles away could be a very important element in the situation. I think that we would all feel that, if there had been a free government of Hungary in existence within a few miles of Hungary at the time when that revolt took place, the situation might have developed in a different way from what it did.

So I wouldn't want to exclude any possibility of a situation developing on the mainland of China, or on parts of the mainland of China, which might not lead to reunification of some sort between mainland China, or that part of mainland China, and the free Government of China, the Republic of China, now on Formosa. I do not exclude it.

Q. Would that have to be entirely on the strength of the Government on Formosa, or is there any American commitment, explicit or implied, to aid in the kind of situation that you have described?

A. No. There is no commitment of any kind to aid in that. As I think you know, the only commitment that there is in this connection is the agreement involved in the exchange of letters between the Chinese Foreign Minister and myself which says that no force will be used from the treaty areas except in agreement between us.[1] So neither of us is free to use force from the areas of the treaty against the mainland except, I think it says, in the case of emergency requirements of self-defense. But that exception would not cover the kind of a situation that you are speaking of.

Q. Mr. Secretary, if there were a rebellion or revolt in China, would you expect its leaders to, if they wanted to, turn over their mandate to Chiang Kai-shek?

A. Well, I really don't think that is a question that I can answer very well. It all—it depends upon the nature of the revolution. I would think that it would probably be primarily under local auspices and local leadership. And while outside cooperation and assistance might be sought, it would be hypothetical and problematical as to whether or not it would involve the going back of Chiang as the head of the government. I don't exclude that as a possibility. On the other hand, the situation is so hypothetical at the present time that it is almost unwise, I think, to try to guess about it.

Q. Mr. Secretary, what is the exact status of our negotiations in Warsaw?

A. A meeting was held today. I have had no word on what the outcome of the meeting was. You know, I think, that the meetings are held with the understanding on both sides that information will not be given out as to what transpired at those meetings, and under those circumstances I can't give you information as to what the exact status is.

Q. Mr. Secretary, would you be willing to meet with Chou En-lai if such a meeting appeared to offer any prospect of progress toward settlement of the tensions in the Far East?

[1] See *D.S.B.*, 24 January 1955, p. 152.

A. Well, President Eisenhower has said that, as far as he was concerned, there was nothing he would not do, no place to which he would not go, if he thought that it would really promote the prospects of a just and durable peace. Certainly, if that applies to him, it would equally apply to me. On the other hand, we all, I think, realize that, while there are sometimes some advantages in raising the level, there are also disadvantages in raising the level. It tends to bring matters into a sharp focus and to a climax. So unless there is reason in advance to believe that something positive, constructive, will come out of such a meeting, it would probably be a disadvantage to have it.

The meetings at the ambassadorial level can go on more or less indefinitely. The previous series of meetings went on for 3 years and perhaps served a useful purpose in helping to keep the situation free of hostilities during that period. These present talks that are now going on at Warsaw have been going on—I forget just how long—between 2 and 3 weeks, I think. Any meeting at a higher level, such as the foreign-ministers level, would have to be a short meeting. The matter would almost automatically come to a head, to a climax. Therefore, unless there were reason to think that something positive would come out of it, it might do more harm than good, because it would compel rapid and definitive decisions at a time when perhaps a slower pace will better serve the cause of peace.

Q. Mr. Secretary, you mentioned a few minutes ago an exchange of letters between yourself and Foreign Minister Yeh in December 1954. In that exchange it was agreed that military elements which are the product of joint effort of the two countries would not be removed from the treaty area without mutual consent. Did we agree, as President Chiang said yesterday, to the fortification of the offshore islands and their buildup?

A. The United States did not feel that it was sound to make the major commitment of force to those areas that the Chinese Government wished to make. In view, however, of the very strong views of the Republic of China, we were acquiescent in that. We did not attempt to veto it. The result is, I might say, one of acquiescence on the part of the United States, not of approval. Nor did we attempt to veto it after having used persuasion.

Q. Mr. Secretary, you spoke of the Warsaw talks going on indefinitely, or the possibility of their going on indefinitely. Does that mean you do not foresee the crisis in the Far East would go to the U.N. in any form at any time soon?

A. The talks could go on in Warsaw for a considerable time. I did not use the word 'indefinitely' as implying 'forever.' But they could go on for some little time. I think if they tended to break down, or if the situation in the area became more acute, and if the level of military activity was substantially raised, that that might be an occasion for bringing the situation to the United Nations. Of course, as you recall, the view of the

Chinese Communists and, indeed, of the Nationalists, for that matter, is that this is essentially a civil war and is not properly within the jurisdiction of the United Nations. The Communists took that same position as regards Korea in 1950 when they came temporarily to the United Nations and then walked out. They took the same position in early '55 when the Formosa matter was before the Security Council. They take the same position now. Nevertheless, if, as I say, the level of military activity increased and the likelihood of a general war increased with it, I believe that the matter ought to be brought to the United Nations. The United Nations is the agency which we have agreed is the agency which should be called upon in the event of a real threat to international peace. I do not think that the situation should be allowed to deteriorate without at least an effort in the United Nations.

Q. Mr. Secretary, in that connection the Chinese Communists are claiming that the United States supply of sidewinder guided missiles to Nationalist planes is an act of bad faith while the talks are going on because it is increasing their military potential. First, is it true that they do have the sidewinders, and, secondly, what is your view on that concept?

A. It is true they have the sidewinders. The sidewinders are nothing that was just injected into the situation during the Warsaw talks. That has been a part of the effort on the part of the United States to train better, to equip better, the Chinese Nationalist Air Force. If it happens to coincide with the Warsaw talks that is purely accidental. If there had not been any Warsaw talks this would have happened just the same.

*   *   *

Q. Mr. Secretary, inasmuch as you say you do not think it was sound for the Nationalist Chinese to have built up their forces on Quemoy and Matsu, I would like to ask you if you now think it would be sound to work out some arrangement for the withdrawal of those forces from those two islands?

A. It all depends upon the circumstances under which they would be withdrawn. I think to withdraw as a retreat under fire would not be a wise step to take because of the probable impact of that upon other peoples, other countries, and upon the morale, indeed, on Formosa itself.

Q. Would you state, sir, the circumstances under which you think a withdrawal could be achieved?

A. If there were a cease-fire in the area which seemed to be reasonably dependable, I think it would be foolish to keep these large forces on these islands. We thought that it was rather foolish to put them there, and, as I say, if there were a cease-fire it would be our judgment, military judgment even, that it would not be wise or prudent to keep them there.[1]

[1] At a press conference on 1 October 1958, President Chang Kai-shek said he was 'incredulous' at Mr. Dulles's statement. He went on: 'Mr. Dulles must know that wishes for a cease fire will never materialize. . . . Granted that Mr. Dulles made the statement attributed, it would be

Q. Mr. Secretary, you seem to emphasize the need for a dependable cease-fire. Could you tell us how you can get a dependable cease-fire with the Communists, whose promises you don't like to accept?

A. That is certainly a fair question and a difficult one to answer. I believe that promises of the Communists are never dependable merely because they are promises. They are only dependable if there are unpleasant consequences in case the Communists break their promises. And I believe that circumstances could be created where it would be felt that the consequences of breaking this promise would be so undesirable to the Communists that we could assume that they would probably live up to their promise, not because of the sanctity of the given word—which they do not believe in—but because of expediency.

Q. Mr. Secretary, would it be necessary for a cease-fire to be written or unwritten? Could it be a de facto *cease-fire gained simply by the cessation of shooting without anything being written?*

A. I think it could be *de facto.*

Q. Mr. Secretary, some Senators seem to believe that the administration is extending the area of the security treaty with the Republic of China, and they are recalling that in February when you went before the Senate Foreign Relations Committee and said if you had any intention of extending the area you would return to the Senate. Is this a proper construction, you think, that is being put upon our activity there?

A. No, I do not. The situation is that we do not have any legal commitment to defend the offshore islands. We do not want to make any such commitment. We do not have it today. What we are acting under is the authority of the joint resolution,[1] which is equally the law of the land, which says that, if the President believes that the defense of those offshore islands is necessary or appropriate for the defense of the treaty area, then he can use the forces of the United States for that purpose. And that is the way it was understood, and that is the way we want it. I would say today, if the United States believed that these islands could be abandoned without its having any adverse impact upon the potential defense of Formosa and the treaty area, we would not be thinking of using forces there. It's because there is that relationship, under present conditions, conditions primarily of the Communists' making, that there is the tie-in there.

They say this is a push which is designed not merely to push the Chinese Nationalists out of Quemoy and Matsu but to push the United States out of Formosa. And when you have the edge, the front edge, of a wedge that is driving in, and where they say they are not going to stop at the first

only a unilateral declaration and my Government would be under no obligation to accept it.' For an account of President Chiang Kai-shek's reactions, see *New York Times,* 2 October 1958. For the text of a statement by the Nationalist Foreign Ministry, of 1 October 1958, which defends the fortification of Quemoy and Matsu Islands, see ibid.

[1] For text, see *D.S.B.,* 7 February 1955, p. 213.

obstacle but to go on, then you have to decide whether by allowing the wedge to gather momentum and go on you are strengthening or weakening the defense of the area you are committed to defend. That is the problem we have to think about.

Q. Mr. Secretary, do you see any progress so far in a little more than 2 weeks of negotiation and crisis that now has gone on for more than a month? Do you see any progress at all toward a peaceful settlement either on an agreed basis or on a de facto *basis?*

A. I feel that there is a slight tendency toward a stabilization of the situation, and I feel on the whole that there is less likelihood of the hostilities intensifying and enlarging than I thought was the case a couple of weeks ago.

Q. Mr. Secretary, what do you have in mind when you say you think the circumstances could be created which would make breaking a cease-fire commitment by the Communists unpleasant? Were you talking about some joint allied commitment for Formosa itself, or something else?

A. I am thinking of sanctions that might be applied, perhaps by other nations in addition to the United States. For example, possible trade sanctions and the like.

Q. Have you made any effort with other nations to work out something like that?

A. I would not think that what we have done could be elevated to the role of what you might call an effort. There have been very widespread general discussions that have taken place between me and the Foreign Ministers of 15 or 20 countries about this whole situation.[1] There are very few ideas that have not been batted back and forth on a tentative basis. I would not say that there has been any real effort to organize such a program because so far the premise of it does not seem to be sufficiently likely as to make it worth while. But we have a good many thoughts in our minds about such possibilities.

Q. Mr. Secretary, you said that the renunciation of force, if it occurs, should be reciprocal. Would you consider that under this reciprocal agreement would come renunciation by Chiang to intervene in a Hungarian-type revolt, or would you say that the reciprocal agreement to renounce force ceases the minute there is a revolution in China?

A. Well, you see, in Hungary you had, at least for a time, a govern-

---

[1] In his press conference on 9 September 1958, Mr. Dulles said that although the United States had not sought or obtained any assurances from the allies of support in the event of war with China over the Taiwan Straits, there was 'very general agreement among not only our allies but among so-called neutralists to the proposition that, whatever the merits of this case, it ought not to be resolved by recourse to force.' Later Mr. Dulles said: 'I do not believe that we should seek to require that all of our allies should agree with everything we do in an area of the world where we have the primary responsibility.' See *D.S.B.*, 29 September 1958, pp. 489 and 491. President Eisenhower, in his press conference on 1 October 1958, said that he found the fact that the allies did not all share the United States attitude towards Taiwan 'puzzling'. See *New York Times*, 2 October 1958.

ment which sought assistance from outside and which asked the Soviet Union to withdraw. If there should be a recognized government in China which called for help, I would not consider that that involved an armed intervention in China.

Q. Under Secretary Herter said in a speech yesterday that the Quemoy and Matsu Islands are 'not defensible in the defense of Formosa' and that the Chinese Nationalists' very devotion to them is 'almost pathological.' Do you subscribe to those views?

A. I didn't hear the first sentence that you read. Are not defensible?

Q. Are not defensible in the defense of Formosa. It is phrased rather awkwardly, but it is a direct quote.

Q. In the New York Times it says, 'not strategically defensible in the defense of Formosa.'

A. Well, I don't like to comment on isolated quotations from a speech. I'd rather see what the full text said. I'm not familiar with it.

Q. Mr. Secretary, you said twice at the outset this morning that the United States policy has not changed. Yet during the course of the news conference you have seemed to clarify at least two major points that, so far as I know, have not been publicly clarified by the Department before, to wit: the reciprocal aspect of renunciation of force and the fact that the United States considered it foolish to build up military force on the islands and that under certain circumstances they should be withdrawn. If these two points are major and important, as they seem to be, why haven't they been expressed publicly before?

A. Well, there is nothing really new in our attitude on either of those propositions. I think, if you will go back, for example, to study the record of our prior talks with the Chinese Communists, we have assumed that the renunciation of force should be reciprocal if it occurs and that it would be obviously quite impractical and quite wrong to ask the Chinese Communists to abandon use of force if they were being attacked by the Chinese Nationalists. I might say that when we speak about renunciation of force it has always been a renunciation of force except for purposes of self-defense. Perhaps I did not make that clear before. So that if anybody is attacked, then the renunciation of force would, of course, not apply.

Q. Mr. Secretary, is it fair to say that, while United States policy has not changed as of now, there is a possibility of some important changes, provided there is some give on the Chinese Communist side?

A. Yes, I would say so. Our policy in these respects is flexible and adapted to the situation that we have to meet. If the situation we have to meet changes, our policies change with it.[1]

---

[1] There were unconfirmed reports that Mr. Dulles had been encouraged to take this line by indications from Peking that the Chinese would not be quite as uncompromising as their attitude in Warsaw suggested. See *U.S. in World Affairs* 1958, p. 327. At his press conference on 1 October 1958, President Eisenhower denied that Mr. Dulles's remarks were evidence of a strong modification in policy amounting to appeasement. For the transcript of the President's press conference, see *New York Times*, 2 October 1958.

Q. Mr. Secretary, the Chinese Communists say that to renounce force in what they considered an internal affair is practically to renounce sovereignty and is tantamount, if one considered an American example, to renouncing the right of the United States Government to use, say, troops in Little Rock to prevent disorder. Is there any way that you think you could put this renunciation of force so that the Chinese Communists do not feel they are thereby renouncing their claim on Formosa?

A. Well, we have always made clear that renunciation of force, except for self-defense, on a reciprocal basis did not involve a renunciation of claims. You have comparable situations, I might say, all around the world. This is not a unique situation. In Korea, Viet-Nam, India, Pakistan, and Indonesia you might say that certain governments claim that a territory held by others is rightfully theirs. They could claim that to take it is purely a civil-war operation.

Now you have got to use, you might say, a rule of reason in trying to decide whether, in fact, a situation is a civil war or whether it involves a threat to international peace. And the Communists, as you know, made the argument in the case of Korea that that was purely a civil war, an effort by the north Koreans to reunite their country, that they had a right to do it, and that the United Nations and the United States were aggressors when they came in there to stop this effort of the Korean people to reunite their own country. Similar positions could be made in the case of other countries. You could say if the Federal Republic of Germany tried to reunite Germany that it was a civil operation. But none of us treat it that way.

You have a very practical situation to take into account, which is, will it, in fact, involve world peace? When you apply that test, I think there is no possible doubt but what this effort to take not just the offshore islands but Formosa and the Penghu Islands (the Pescadores) that that will involve world peace.

Here you have the Chinese Communists, with a treaty alliance with the Soviet Union, making these claims, and the Soviet Union saying they are prepared to back them up to the hilt. Here you have the Republic of China, which has a treaty of collective self-defense with the United States, which we are prepared to live up to. Now when those two forces come to clash, nobody in his senses could say, 'This is purely a civil war and doesn't affect international peace.' It does. And therefore it is properly a matter to be dealt with from the standpoint of international peace and the welfare of the world. You cannot treat it purely as a civil-war matter. You can say, 'Well, the United States should stop helping the Nationalists, and the Soviet Union should stop helping Communist China.' That is quite impractical. As far as we can tell, every plane, every piece of artillery, and practically all the ammunition that is being shot there today is of Soviet origin.

Q. Mr. Secretary, Chiang Kai-shek yesterday made statements about a cease-fire and the importance of Quemoy and Matsu which would seem to be quite different from some that you have made here this morning. My question is: Have you discussed your ideas about the cease-fire and possible withdrawal of the bulk of the forces from Quemoy and Matsu with the Nationalist Chinese?

A. Yes. We keep in pretty close touch with each other. We express our views.[1] I wouldn't want to imply that they accept our views. And we don't accept their views in all respects, just as they don't accept ours. But we have a friendly exchange, and I think that, if it ever came down to a point where it was important practically to carry out these things, we would find a way to agree. At least I hope so.

Q. Thank you, sir.

11. Message from the Minister of National Defence of the People's Republic of China to the people of Formosa, 6 October 1958[2]

All compatriots, military and civilian, in Taiwan, Penghu, Quemoy and Matsu! We are all Chinese. Of all choices, peace is the best. The fighting round Quemoy is of a punitive character. For quite a long time, your leaders have been far too wild. They have ordered aircraft to carry out wanton raids on the mainland, dropping leaflets and secret agents, bombing Foochow and harassing Kiangsu and Chekiang, reaching as far as Yunnan, Kweichow, Szechuan, the Kangting area and Chinghai. How can this be tolerated? Hence the firing of a few shells, just to call your attention. Taiwan, Penghu, Quemoy and Matsu are Chinese territory. To this you agree, as proved by documents issued by your leaders, which confirm that they are decidedly not territory of the Americans. Taiwan, Penghu, Quemoy and Matsu are part of China, they do not constitute another country. There is only one China, not two, in the world. To this, you also agree, as proved by documents issued by your leaders. The military agreement signed between your leaders and the Americans is unilateral; we do not recognize it. It should be abrogated. The day will certainly come when the Americans will leave you in the lurch. Do you not believe it? History will bear witness to it. The clue is already there in the statement made by Dulles on September 30. Placed in your circumstances, how can you help but feel dismayed? In the last analysis, the American imperialists are our common enemy. It is hard for the 130,000 troops and civilians in Quemoy to stand for long the lack of supplies and

---

[1] Discussions took place between Mr. Dulles and President Chiang Kai-shek between 21 and 23 October 1958. See below, pp. 370–2, for the joint communiqué issued after the talks, on 23 October 1958.

[2] *Peking Review*, 7 October 1958, Supplement.

the pestering hunger and cold. Out of humanitarian considerations, I have ordered the bombardment to be suspended on the Fukien front for a tentative period of seven days, starting from October 6. Within this period, you will be fully free to ship in supplies on condition that there be no American escort. This guarantee will not stand if there should be American escort. It is not good that fighting between you and us have been in progress for 30 years and have not yet ended. We propose that talks be held to effect a peaceful settlement. You were notified of this by Premier Chou En-lai several years ago. This is China's internal problem involving your side and our side; it is no issue between China and the United States. The issue between China and the United States is U.S. invasion and occupation of Taiwan, Penghu and the Taiwan Straits, and this should be settled through negotiations between the two countries, which are now being held in Warsaw. The Americans will have to pull out. It won't do if they don't. For the United States, the sooner they go the better, because in this way it can have the initiative. Otherwise, it will be to its disadvantage, because it will then be always on the defensive. Why should a country in the East Pacific have come to the West Pacific? The West Pacific belongs to the people in this region, just as the East Pacific belongs to the people over there. This is common sense which the Americans should have understood. There is no war between the People's Republic of China and the United States of America, and so the question of cease-fire does not arise. Is it not a farce to talk about a cease-fire when there is no fire? Friends in Taiwan! There are flames of war between us. They should be stopped and extinguished. To achieve this, talks are needed. Of course, it would not matter so much even if the fighting should continue for another 30 years. It is, however, better to secure an early peaceful settlement. The choice is up to you.

PENG TEH-HUAI

Minister of National Defence

12. Order of the Ministry of National Defence of the People's Republic of China, regarding the suspension of the shelling of Quemoy, 13 October 1958[1]

Comrades of the People's Liberation Army at the Fukien front: Suspend the shelling of Quemoy for another two weeks starting from today, so as to see what the opposite side is going to do and to enable our compatriots on Quemoy, both military and civilian, to get sufficient supplies, including food and military equipment, to strengthen their entrenchment. Nothing is too deceitful in war. But this is no deceit. This

---

[1] *Peking Review*, 14 October 1958, Supplement.

is directed against the Americans. This is a noble national cause, and a clear-cut line must be drawn between the Chinese and the Americans. Taken as a whole, this action on our part does ourselves no harm, but benefits others. Whom does it benefit? It benefits the 10 million Chinese in Taiwan, Penghu, Quemoy and Matsu; it benefits the 650 million people of our whole nation; it only hurts the Americans. Some Communists may not yet understand this for the time being. How comes such an idea? We don't understand! We don't understand! Comrades! You will understand after a while. The Americans in Taiwan and the Taiwan Straits must go home. They have no reason to hang on there; refusing to go will not do. Among the Chinese in Taiwan, Penghu, Quemoy and Matsu, the majority are patriots, only a few are traitors. Therefore, political work must be done to enable the great majority of the Chinese over there to wake up gradually, and to isolate the handful of traitors. The effect will be felt with the accumulation of hours and days of work. So long as the Kuomintang in Taiwan has not yet entered into peaceful negotiations with us and a reasonable solution has not been worked out, the civil war still continues. The spokesman of Taiwan said that stop-fight-stop-fight . . . is but a trick of the Communists. It is quite true that fighting has been going off and on. But this is no trick. If you are not willing to hold peace talks, fighting is unavoidable. So long as you take such a stubborn attitude as you are doing at present, we are free to fight when we want to fight and stop when we want to stop. The Americans want to take a hand in our civil war. They call it cease-fire. This cannot but make one laugh in one's sleeve. What right have the Americans got to raise this question? Whom do they represent, it may be asked. They represent none. Do they represent the Americans? There is no war between China and the United States, and hence no fire to cease. Do they represent the people in Taiwan? The Taiwan authorities have not given them any credentials. The Kuomintang leaders are completely opposed to the Sino-American talks. The American nation is a great nation, and American people are well-meaning. They don't want war. They welcome peace. But among the U.S. government workers, there are some people, like Dulles and his ilk, who are indeed not so smart. Take, for instance, the talk about a cease-fire. Is this not lacking in common sense? To recover Taiwan, Penghu, Quemoy and Matsu as a whole and complete the unification of the motherland is the sacred task of our 650 million people. This is China's internal affair, and no foreigner has any right to meddle with. The United Nations has no right to meddle with, either. The time is not far away when the aggressors and their running dogs in the world will all of them be buried. There can be no escape for them. It won't do even if they take to hiding in the moon. Where the enemy can go, we also can go, and drag them back anyway. In a word, victory belongs to the people of the world. The

Americans must not conduct escort operations in the Quemoy water area. If there should be any escort, shelling shall start at once. This order is to be strictly observed.

PENG TEH-HUAI

Minister of National Defence

13. Order of the Ministry of National Defence of the People's Republic of China, regarding the suspension of the shelling of Quemoy, 20 October 1958[1]

Comrades of the People's Liberation Army at the Fukien front: The order for our army to suspend the shelling of Quemoy is hereby annulled because the Taiwan authorities introduced American military escorts to the Quemoy water area from the night of the 19th to the morning of the 20th. Twice our army has suspended shelling, yet the Taiwan authorities have not shown any repentance. The Taiwan authorities have persisted in their obstinate attitude, refused to hold peace talks, stepped up war preparations and clamoured loudly for an attack to return to the mainland. Now, on the eve of the arrival of Dulles in Taiwan, whom they have invited to plan further implementation of the U.S.-Chiang 'Treaty,' they introduced U.S. naval vessels to provide escort for as long as five hours. This is an open violation of the condition for our temporary suspension of shelling. If this can be tolerated, what is intolerable? Shelling must therefore be resumed as a punitive measure.

It is our sacred national duty absolutely not to permit the Americans to meddle in Chinese affairs. Those who obstinately refuse to come to their senses are after all very few. It appears that some time will have to pass before the Taiwan authorities wake up to the necessity of turning back from the wrong road and accept a peaceful settlement, and we continue to hold hope for such an eventuality. It will not do for the Americans to hang on in Taiwan and the Taiwan Straits. It is absolutely impermissible for the Americans to interfere in China's internal affairs. And we absolutely will not accept any American machinations to utilize the Taiwan authorities to infringe on our country's sovereignty. Patriotic military men and civilians in Taiwan, Penghu, Quemoy and Matsu should wake up. Taiwan, Penghu, Quemoy and Matsu must return to the embrace of the motherland.

PENG TEH-HUAI

Minister of National Defence

[1] *Peking Review*, 28 October 1958, p. 6. Before Mr. Dulles left for Taipei on 20 October 1958, he made a statement on the resumption of firing in the Formosa area, see *D.S.B.*, 10 November 1958, p. 722.

D. KOREA

1. Statement by the Ministry of Foreign Affairs of the People's Republic of China, Peking, 7 February 1958[1]

On February 5, 1958 the Government of the Korean Democratic People's Republic issued a statement on the question of peaceful unification of Korea, proposing that all foreign forces be withdrawn from North and South Korea simultaneously, that within a definite period following the withdrawal of all foreign forces nation-wide free elections be held under the supervision of a neutral nations organisation, that consultations be held between North and South Korea on an equal footing on the economic and cultural intercourse between them, the holding of nation-wide elections and other problems, and that the armed forces of North and South Korea be reduced to the minimum within a short period of time.[2] This is another major effort made by the Government of the Korean Democratic People's Republic for a peaceful settlement of the Korean question. These proposals not only are in full accord with the eager desire of all Korean people for the peaceful unification of their motherland, but also will open up a new practicable avenue for easing the tension in the Far East. The Chinese Government fully endorses and supports this important peace proposal made by the Government of the Korean Democratic People's Republic.

The Chinese Government and people, starting from the fundamental position that the Korean question should be settled by the Korean people themselves, have consistently opposed foreign interference in Korean affairs, and firmly held that all foreign forces should be withdrawn from Korea. At the very beginning of the Korean war, the Chinese Government and people maintained that the United States aggression forces should be withdrawn from Korea immediately. It was only when the warning served by the Chinese Government and people had been spurned by the United States, and when the United States forces had not only invaded the Korean Democratic People's Republic but at the same time occupied China's Taiwan and seriously jeopardized the security of China that the Chinese people organised their volunteers to proceed to Korea to resist United States aggression together with the Korean people. During the Korean armistice negotiations and after the realisation of the armistice, the governments of China and the Korean Democratic People's Republic again proposed continuously that all foreign forces should be withdrawn from North and South Korea simultaneously, and maintained that this

---

[1] *H.N.A.*, 10 February 1958. The statement was handed to the United Kingdom *Chargé d'Affaires* in Peking for communication to the countries which had contributed troops to the United Nations Command.   [2] For the text, see ibid., 7 February 1958.

was the primary condition for the holding of free elections throughout Korea and the realisation of the peaceful unification of Korea. The United States, however, not only rejected all along this reasonable proposal of the Chinese and Korean side, but violated the Korean Armistice Agreement again and again, and recently even openly introduced atomic weapons into South Korea thus further converting South Korea into its colony and atomic base. As pointed out in the statement by the government of the Korean Democratic People's Republic, the continued occupation of South Korea by United States forces is the basic cause for the indefinite putting-off of the peaceful unification of Korea and for the increasingly serious threat to peace in Korea.

The Chinese people have always been concerned about peace in Korea. The Chinese Government has never spared its efforts in promoting a peaceful settlement of the Korean question. Now when the aspirations of the peoples of Asia and the world for peace have risen to unprecedented heights and there are greater possibilities for a peaceful settlement of major international issues, the Chinese Government holds that the Korean situation should not be allowed to deteriorate further.

In order to break the deadlock on the Korean question, promote a peaceful settlement of the Korean question and relax tension in the Far East, the Chinese Government deems that all foreign forces should be withdrawn from Korea within a set period of time; and the Chinese Government is prepared to discuss with the Government of the Korean Democratic People's Republic on the question of withdrawal of the Chinese People's Volunteers from Korea. The Chinese Government asks the governments of the United States and of other countries participating in the United Nations forces also to take measures to withdraw from South Korea United States and all other foreign forces. The Chinese Government hopes that all countries concerned about peace in the Far East and the world would take positive steps to urge the withdrawal of all foreign forces from Korea so as to create a favourable condition for a peaceful settlement of the Korean question and the safeguarding of peace in the Far East and the world.[1]

2. Note from the United Kingdom Government to the Ministry of Foreign Affairs of the People's Republic of China, 9 April 1958[2]

Her Majesty's Charge d'Affaires presents his compliments to the Ministry of Foreign Affairs and, on instructions from Her Majesty's Principal

[1] A Government delegation of the People's Republic of China, led by Premier Chou En-lai, visited the Democratic People's Republic of Korea, from 14 to 21 February 1958. For the text of the joint statement issued on 19 February, see below, pp. 477–82.

[2] Text supplied by the Foreign Office.

Secretary of State for Foreign Affairs, has the honour to state that, as requested by the Vice-Minister for Foreign Affairs on 7 February, the statement on Korea made on that date by the Government of the People's Republic of China has been communicated to the Governments of the countries which have contributed forces for the United Nations force in Korea, who, after consultation, have requested Her Majesty's Government to reply on their behalf.

The Governments of the countries which have contributed forces for the United Nations force in Korea have noted the statement made by the North Korean authorities on 5 February and that made by the People's Republic of China and communicated to Her Britannic Majesty's Charge d'Affaires in Peking on 7 February. They have given careful study to these statements and to the proposals made therein.

The Governments concerned reaffirm that their aim in Korea is to see the establishment of a unified, independent and democratic Korea, in accordance with relevant United Nations resolutions. To this end, as they have often stated, they wish to see free elections held under United Nations supervision for the constitution of a National Assembly. They are glad to note that the North Korean authorities and the People's Republic of China also favour free elections and they welcome the announcement that Chinese forces are to be withdrawn from North Korea.

There appears, however, to be some doubt as to the precise interpretation to be placed on the North Korean proposals. A variety of statements is reported to have been made, for example, by North Korean representatives in Peking and Moscow, to the effect that the 'purpose of supervision by a neutral nations organization was to see that all political parties and public figures in both North and South Korea would have freedom of action, speech, publication, assembly and association' but that 'such supervision should not intervene in the elections'. These interpretations appear to call for some clarification and the Governments of the countries concerned would be glad to know whether, when the North Korean authorities speak of a 'neutral nations organization' to supervise the elections, they accept that these should be held under United Nations auspices and that there should be adequate supervision not only of the preliminaries but also of the elections themselves. They would also be glad to know whether it is accepted that representation in the new National Assembly shall be in proportion to the indigenous population.

If the People's Republic of China will seek from the North Korean authorities clarification of the points mentioned above with such other details of the Korean proposals as may be relevant, they will be given careful consideration.

A copy of this reply is being transmitted to the United Nations.[1]

[1] Circulated to all members of the U.N. (Doc. A/3821).

3. Note from the Ministry of Foreign Affairs of the People's Republic of China to the Government of the United Kingdom, Peking, 6 May 1958[1]

The Ministry of Foreign Affairs of the People's Republic of China presents its compliments to the Office of the British Charge d'Affaires in China, and asks it to communicate the following to the British Government and through the British Government to the Governments of the other countries on the United Nations Command side.

On April 9, 1958, the British Government, on behalf of the Governments of the countries on the United Nations Command side, delivered to the Chinese Government Note No. 35 as a reply to the statements made by the Government of the Democratic People's Republic of Korea and the Government of the People's Republic of China respectively on February 5 and 7, 1958.

The Chinese Government, in its own name and entrusted by the Government of the Democratic People's Republic of Korea, hereby replies to the note of the British Government as follows:

The Korean and Chinese Governments, reviewing the situation in the past three months, are glad to note that the proposals of the Korean and Chinese Governments for the withdrawal of all foreign forces from Korea and the peaceful settlement of the Korean question have won the warm support and approval of many countries and people. Particularly, the fact that the Chinese People's Volunteers have decided to withdraw completely from Korea by stages and in groups and are carrying out the withdrawal has opened up a new and practical way for the peaceful settlement of the Korean question. However, the Korean and Chinese Governments cannot but point out with regret that, while the peace-loving countries and people throughout the world have expected the United States and the other countries on the United Nations Command side also to withdraw all United Nations forces from Korea, just as the Chinese People's Volunteers are being withdrawn, the United Nations Command side has up to now failed to take any positive measure on the question of withdrawal of forces. Furthermore, in their reply to the Korean and Chinese statements, which took as long as two months, the Governments of the United States and the other countries on the United Nations Command side have by-passed the question of withdrawal of forces which is the most urgent and practical step in the peaceful settlement of the Korean question, and, for ulterior purposes, have diverged to the question of so-called 'clarification' on the supervision of elections to entangle the issue, although a clear-cut attitude on this question was set out by the Korean Government in its

[1] *Peking Review*, 13 May 1958, pp. 21–22.

statement of February 5. The Korean and Chinese Governments see in this behaviour of the Governments of the countries on the United Nations Command side an obvious attempt to divert the attention of the people of the world, to escape from its inevitable responsibility of withdrawing its forces from Korea, and to cover up the scheme of the United States to prolong its occupation of South Korea, to continue to obstruct the peaceful unification of Korea and to further create tension in the Far East.

The Korean and Chinese Governments deem it necessary once again to call on the Governments of the countries on the United Nations Command side to face squarely the present situation favourable for the peaceful settlement of the Korean question brought about by the initiative of the Chinese People's Volunteers in withdrawing from Korea, as well as their responsibility before the Korean people and the people of the world. Facts are more eloquent than words. If the Governments of the United States and the other countries on the United Nations Command side are averse to proving themselves to be persistently obstructing the peaceful unification of Korea and relaxation of tension in the Far East, they should show good faith by the actual withdrawal of their forces. All attempts to find pretexts to evade this will be of no avail. The Korean and Chinese Governments would like to know when the Governments of the United States and the other countries on the United Nations Command side intend to withdraw all their forces from South Korea. Whether all United Nations forces will withdraw speedily from Korea will be evidence of the presence or absence of good will on the part of the Governments of the countries on the United Nations Command side for a peaceful settlement of the Korean question.

The Korean people eagerly desire an early realization of the peaceful unification of their motherland, and the peoples of the world are anxious for relaxation of tension in the Far East and the world. The Korean and Chinese Governments have done much in the past for the fulfilment of these desires, and will continue to make untiring efforts in the future. The Korean and Chinese Governments consistently maintain that only a complete withdrawal of all foreign forces from Korea will provide the necessary condition for a peaceful settlement of the Korean question, including the question of holding free elections. Provided that the Governments of the United States and the other countries on the United Nations Command side will clearly decide to withdraw all United Nations forces from South Korea within a definite time limit and put the decision into practice, as proposed by the Korean and Chinese Governments, the Korean and Chinese Governments are going to propose a conference with the countries concerned to carry out negotiations on the peaceful settlement of the Korean question following the withdrawal of all foreign forces from Korea.

4. Note from the Government of the United Kingdom to the Ministry of Foreign Affairs of the People's Republic of China, 2 July 1958[1]

Her Majesty's Charge d'Affaires presents his compliments to the Ministry of Foreign Affairs and, on instructions from Her Majesty's Principal Secretary of State for Foreign Affairs, has the honour to refer to the Ministry's Note of 6 May 1958, communicated to the Governments of the countries which have contributed forces for the United Nations force in Korea, who, after consultation, have requested Her Majesty's Government to reply again on their behalf.

The Governments concerned, noting that the greater part of the forces sent to Korea in accordance with resolutions of the United Nations have already been withdrawn,[2] reiterate that they welcome the announcement by the Government of the Peoples' Republic of China that Chinese troops are also to be withdrawn from North Korea.

The Governments concerned are disappointed, however, that the Note handed to Her Majesty's Charge d'Affaires on the sixth of May does not provide the clarification asked for in the Note delivered by Her Majesty's Charge d'Affaires on the ninth of April and brushes aside the question of the principles on which elections should be held. The Governments concerned consider that these principles, which were set forth in the Note of the ninth of April, lie at the heart of the matter. It was for this reason that they sought the clarification requested in Her Majesty's Charge d'Affaires' Note under reference. They cannot agree that the further withdrawal of United Nations forces without any provision for a proper settlement of the Korean question would be calculated to lead to a reduction of tension in the Far East; indeed they believe that such action would remove one necessary guarantee which exists against further aggression in Korea pending a final settlement.

The Governments concerned wish to see a genuine settlement of the Korean question in accordance with United Nations resolutions and are at all times willing to further the consideration of measures designed to effect reunification on this basis. United Nations forces are in Korea at the instance of the United Nations. In accordance with the existing recommendations of the General Assembly of the United Nations, the Governments concerned are prepared to withdraw their forces from Korea when the conditions for a lasting settlement laid down by the General Assembly have been fulfilled.

A copy of this reply is being transmitted to the United Nations.[3]

[1] Text supplied by the Foreign Office.

[2] A spokesman of the U.S. State Department said in February 1958 that more than 80 per cent of U.N. forces in Korea had been withdrawn since the armistice. The Chinese force in Korea outnumbered the U.N. force by five or six times.

[3] Circulated to all members of the U.N. (Doc. A/3845).

5. Note from the Ministry of Foreign Affairs of the People's Republic of China to the Government of the United Kingdom, Peking, 10 November 1958[1]

The Ministry of Foreign Affairs of the People's Republic of China presents its compliments to the Office of the British Chargé d'Affaires in China and requests it to communicate the following to the British Government and, through it, to the Governments of the other countries on the United Nations Command side.

The Chinese Government, in its own name and entrusted by the Government of the Democratic People's Republic of Korea, replies as follows to Note No. 64 delivered to the Chinese Government on July 2, 1958 by the British Government on behalf of the Governments of the countries on the United Nations Command side:

The Chinese People's Volunteers have already withdrawn completely from Korea. This initiative taken by the Korean and Chinese side has broken the stalemate on the Korean question and provided a favourable condition for a peaceful settlement of the Korean question. Should the United Nations Command side take corresponding measures to withdraw their forces from Korea, too, the prospects for a peaceful settlement of the Korean question would undoubtedly improve greatly. The Korean and Chinese Governments cannot but point out with regret, however, that the United Nations Command side has up to now not only failed to take any corresponding measure but has, in continuous violation of the Armistice Agreement, unlawfully introduced new-type weapons into Korea and established guided missile bases in the southern part of Korea. These facts once again provide living proof as to who wants peace and who is carrying out aggression, as to who is working for a peaceful settlement of the Korean question and who is obstructing it. One cannot help asking: If the United Nations Command side believes their stand to be in conformity with the interests of the Korean people, why don't they withdraw from south Korea and let the Korean people settle their own questions by themselves free from all interference of outside force?

Regarding the question of elections raised in the Note of the United Nations Command side, the Korean Government already set forth its views clearly in its statement of February 5, 1958, namely, that within a definite period after the withdrawal of all foreign forces from north and south Korea, all-Korean free elections should be held and that these elections can be conducted under the supervision of a neutral nations organization. Should the Governments of the countries participating in the United Nations forces actually desire to see a 'unified, independent and democratic Korea' brought about by peaceful means, it will not be

[1] *Peking Review*, 18 November 1958, pp. 15–16.

difficult to attain a reasonable solution to specific questions concerning the elections through further consultation between the countries concerned following the complete withdrawal from Korea of the forces of the United States and other countries participating in the United Nations forces. From the two Notes of the United Nations Command side, however, it is very difficult for one to believe that they have such a desire. The United Nations Command side has repeatedly insisted on the settlement of the Korean question on the unilateral terms of the United Nations. But it is known to all that, under the domination of the United States, the United Nations has been reduced to a belligerent in the Korean war and lost all competence and moral authority to deal fairly and reasonably with the Korean question. Having failed by means of war to impose on the Korean people the unilateral terms of the United Nations for the settlement of the Korean question, the United Nations Command now still persists in these terms—what other interpretation can there be than that it is bent on obstructing the peaceful settlement of the Korean question and maintaining and aggravating the tension in Korea and the Far East?

The Korean and Chinese Governments are of the opinion that the continued presence in the southern part of Korea of the forces of the United States and other countries taking part in the United Nations forces is at present the main obstacle to a peaceful settlement of the Korean question. So long as they do not withdraw from Korea, they will not escape the opposition and condemnation of the Korean people longing for peaceful unification and that of the peace-loving peoples throughout the world. The Korean and Chinese Governments hope that the Governments of the countries on the United Nations Command side would reconsider their rigid stand and take positive measures in conformity with the national aspirations of the Korean people and the desire of the people of the world for peace.

6. Note from the Government of the United Kingdom to the Ministry of Foreign Affairs of the People's Republic of China, 5 December 1958[1]

The Office of Her Britannic Majesty's Chargé d'Affaires present their compliments to the Ministry of Foreign Affairs and, on instructions from Her Majesty's Principal Secretary of State for Foreign Affairs, have the honour to refer to the Ministry's Note of 10 November 1958, communicated to the Governments of the countries which have contributed forces for the United Nations Command in Korea, who, after consultation, have requested Her Majesty's Government to reply again on their behalf.

[1] Text supplied by the Foreign Office. The note was circulated to members of the U.N. (Doc. A/4077).

The Governments concerned have noted the various questions raised in the Note under reference and wish to call to the attention of the People's Republic of China and the North Korean authorities the Notes delivered by Her Majesty's Chargé d'Affaires on 9 April 1958 and 2 July 1958 in which these questions were answered in detail. Answers to all the questions raised in the Ministry's Note again were given in detail and were restated and reaffirmed in the resolution on Korea which was endorsed at the conclusion of the United Nations General Assembly discussion on 14 November 1958, by the overwhelming vote of 54 to 9. The text of that resolution[1] is as follows:

THE GENERAL ASSEMBLY,

Having received the report of the United Nations Commission for the Unification and Rehabilitation of Korea,[2]

Reaffirming its resolution 112 (II) of 14 November 1947, 195 (III) of 12 December 1948, 293 (IV) of 21 October 1949, 376 (V) of 7 October 1950, 811 (IX) of 11 December 1954, 910 A (X) of 29 November 1955, 1010 (XI) of 11 January 1957 and 1180 (XII) of 29 November 1957,

Noting the exchange of correspondence between the communist authorities and the United Kingdom of Great Britain and Northern Ireland on behalf of the Governments of countries which have contributed forces to the United Nations Command in Korea, in which these Governments expressed their wish to see a genuine settlement of the Korean question in accordance with United Nations resolutions, their willingness at all times to further the consideration of measures designed to effect reunification on this basis, and stated that, in accordance with the existing recommendations of the General Assembly of the United Nations, the Governments concerned are prepared to withdraw their forces from Korea when the conditions for a lasting settlement laid down by the General Assembly have been fulfilled,[3]

Noting further that in this exchange the Governments concerned, observing that the greater part of the forces sent to Korea in accordance with resolutions of the United Nations have already been withdrawn, welcomed the announcement that the Chinese communist troops were also to be withdrawn from North Korea,

1. *Calls to the attention* of the communist authorities concerned the continued determination of the United Nations to bring about by peaceful means establishment of a unified, independent and democratic Korea under a representative form of government, and the full restoration of international peace and security in the area;

---

[1] Resol. 1264 (XIII). The resolution was passed by 54 votes to 9 (the Soviet bloc) with 17 abstentions.

[2] G.A.O.R., Thirteenth Session, Supplement No. 13 (A/3865).   [3] U.N. Doc. A/3845.

2. *Calls upon* these authorities to accept the established United Nations objectives in order to achieve a settlement in Korea based on the fundamental principles for unification set forth by the nations participating on behalf of the United Nations in the Korean Political Conference held at Geneva in 1954, and reaffirmed by the General Assembly;

3. *Urges* these authorities to agree at an early date on the holding of genuinely free elections in accordance with the principles endorsed by the General Assembly;

4. *Requests* the United Nations Commission for the Unification and Rehabilitation of Korea to continue its work in accordance with the relevant resolutions of the General Assembly;

5. *Requests* the Secretary-General to place the Korean question on the provisional agenda of the fourteenth session of the General Assembly.

II. THE MIDDLE EAST

A. UNION AND REVOLUTION

1. Proclamation of the United Arab Republic, Cairo, 1 February 1958[1]

On February 1, 1958, in a historic session held at Kubbah Palace in Cairo, His Excellency President Shukry El-Kuwatly of Syria, and President Gamal Abdel-Nasser of Egypt, met the representatives of the Republics of Syria and Egypt, El-Sayed, Sabry El-Assaly, El-Sayed Abdel-Latif El-Baghdady, El-Sayed Khaled El-Azm, El-Sayed Zakaria Mohieddin, El-Sayed Hamed El-Khoga, El-Sayed Anwar El-Sadat, El-Sayed Fakher El Kayyaly, El-Sayed Maamoun El-Kozbary, El-Sayed Hussein El-Shaffei, El-Sayed Assaad Haroun, General Abdel-Hakim Amer, El-Sayed Salaheddin El-Bittar, El-Sayed Kamaleddin Hussein, El-Sayed Khalil El-Kallas, El-Sayed Noureddine Tarraf, El-Sayed Saleh Akeel, El-Sayed Fathy Radwan, General Afif El-Bizry, El-Sayed Mahmoud Fawzy, El-Sayed Kamal Ramzi Stino, El-Sayed Aly Sabri, El-Sayed Abdel-Rahman El-Azm and El-Sayed Mahmound Riad.

The purpose of this meeting was to discuss the final measures to be taken for the realisation of the Arab peoples' will, and the execution of what the Constitutions of both republics stipulate, namely that the people of each of them form a part of the Arab Nation. They, therefore, discussed the decisions unanimously approved by the National Assembly of Egypt and the Syrian House of Representatives that unity should be established between the two countries as a preliminary step towards the realisation of complete Arab unity. They also discussed the clear signs manifest in the

[1] *Basic Documents of the Arab Unifications*, Arab Information Center, New York (June 1958), pp. 5–6. Hereafter cited as *Basic Documents*. Although discussed for some time, the union of Egypt and Syria was decided quickly. On 5 July 1956 the Syrian Chamber of Deputies unanimously approved a resolution providing for the formation of a governmental committee to negotiate the outline of a union with Egypt. A similar resolution was passed on 18 November 1957 by the Syrian Assembly together with a delegation of Egyptian parliamentarians. Serious negotiation only began, however, on 12 January 1958 when General Bizri, Syrian C-in-C, visited Cairo with a delegation of senior officers. The next day he announced, that as a result of his discussions with the Egyptian Chiefs of Staff, the Egyptian and Syrian armies would be one. Salah Bitar, the Syrian foreign minister, arrived in Cairo on 16 January, returned to Damascus on 21, and returned to Cairo again from 25 to 28 January. President Quwatli led a Syrian delegation which arrived in Cairo on 31 January, and the next day, with little time for discussion, the union was signed. This proclamation was read by Sabri al-Asali, Syrian Prime Minister, and followed by speeches by President Quwatli and President Nasser. For the text of these speeches, see *S.W.B., Part IV* 3 February 1958, pp. 2–4.

past few years, that Arab nationalism was the inspiring spirit that dominated the history of Arabs in all their different countries, their common
present and the hoped-for future of every Arab.

They came to the conclusion that this unity which is the fruit of Arab
nationalism is the Arabs' path to sovereignty and freedom, that it is one
of humanity's gateways to peace and co-operation, and that it is therefore
their duty to take this unity with persistence and determination staunch
and unwavering, out of the circle of wishes and aspirations to where it
can be converted into a reality. They came out of this with the conviction
that the elements conducive to the success of the union of the two republics
were abundant, particularly recently after their joint struggle—which
had brought them even closer to one another—made the meaning of
nationalism considerably clearer, stressed the fact that it was a movement
for liberation and rehabilitation and that it was a faith in peace and
co-operation.

For all this, the participants declare their total agreement, complete
faith and deeply rooted confidence in the necessity of uniting Egypt and
Syria into one state to be named 'The United Arab Republic.'

They have likewise decided to declare their unanimous agreement on
the adoption of a presidential democratic system of government for the
Arab Republic. The executive authority shall be vested in the head of
the state assisted by the ministers appointed by him and responsible to him.

The legislative authority shall be vested in one legislative house. The
new republic shall have one flag, one army, one people who shall remain
joined in a unity where all will share equal rights and duties, where all
will call for the protection of their country with heart and soul, and com-
pete in the consolidation of its integrity and the insurance of its invulner-
ability.

His Excellency President Shukry El-Kuwatly and President Gamal
Abdel-Nasser will each deliver a statement to the people in the Syrian
and the Egyptian Parliaments respectively on Wednesday, February 5,
1958 in which they will announce the decisions reached in this meeting
and explain the principals of the unity on which this rising young republic
shall stand.

The peoples of Egypt and Syria shall be called upon to participate in a
general plebiscite on the principles of this unity and the choice of the head
of the state within thirty days.[1]

In proclaiming these decisions, the participants feel great pride and
overwhelming joy in having assisted in taking this positive step on the
road to Arab unity and solidarity—a unity which had been for many an
epoch and many a generation the Arabs' much cherished hope and greatly

---

[1] President Nasser announced in his speech of 5 February, see below, that the date of the
plebiscite would be 21 February 1958.

coveted objective. In deciding on the unity of both nations, the participants declare that their unity aims at the unification of all the Arab
peoples and affirm that the door is open for participation to any Arab
state desirous of joining them in a union or federation for the purpose of
protecting the Arab peoples from harm and evil, strengthening Arab
sovereignty, and safeguarding its existence.

May God protect this step we have taken and those which are to follow
with His ever vigilant care and benevolence so that the Arab people under
the banner of unity may live in dignity and peace.

2. Speech by President Nasser to the Egyptian National Assembly announcing the principles on which the new republic would be based, 5 February 1958[1]

Compatriots, Members of the National Assembly: There are generations which are chosen by destiny to be turning points in history. These
generations are afforded the opportunity to witness decisive stages in the
development of life. These stages resemble the advent of sunrise when the
great transition from the darkness of night to the light of day takes place.

These generations are living through splendid moments. They are witnessing a great victory which they alone did not bring about and for which
they alone have not made sacrifices. They are witnessing the glorious
results of many other factors which continued to work during the darkness
and loneliness of night. They worked and stayed awake, awaiting the
moment of the great transition at the hour of sunrise.

Compatriots, Members of the National Assembly: This generation of
the Egyptian people is one of those generations with which destiny has
covenanted that they shall live through the events of a great transition
which resembles the advent of sunrise. We lived through the hour of dawn;
we saw the coming light erase long hours of darkness; we lived through
the dawn of independence, freedom, and dignity and respect; we lived
through the dawn of force and the dawn of the hope of building a happy
life. Today, compatriots, Members of the National Assembly, we live at a
time of a new and splendid dawn. The sunrise of unity has begun.

Compatriots, Members of the National Assembly: The breaking of the
dawn which we have witnessed was preceded by a long night. The dawn
of independence, freedom, dignity and respect, power, and hope were

---

[1] *S.W.B. Part IV*, 7 February 1958, pp.1–6. After President Nasser had spoken the National
Assembly unanimously passed resolutions expressing full support for the policy outlined in
the speech, and for President Quwatli's nomination of Nasser as first President of the U.A.R.
President Quwatli addressed the Syrian Chamber of Deputies on 5 February; his 14-point
outline of the principles forming the basis of the U.A.R., agreed on in Cairo, was different
in arrangement from President Nasser's 17 points (see below, pp. 235–6) but identical in substance. For the text of President Quwatli's speech, see ibid., pp. 8–13.

preceded by long nights—hundreds of years of continuous struggle with the darkness of imperialism, domination, tyranny, and weakness. People before us lived through these long nights, suffered their terror, and bore their burden in order to bring the splendid moments of the great transition nearer us.

This dawn of unity which we witness[1] preceded the night of one of the longest struggles of our Arab people. The hope being realised today is of our oldest hopes. The history of unity is the life of our people. Both began together. They grew up on the same soil, lived through the same events, and proceeded toward the same objectives. When our people had succeeded in establishing the basis of their existence in this area and strengthening this basis, it became certain that unity was impending.

Compatriots, Members of the National Assembly: The struggle for unity was the struggle for strength and existence. The link between strength and unity is the most outstanding factor in the history of our people. Each time unity was achieved, it was followed by strength. Each time strength was realised, unity came as a natural result. There is no doubt that separation and the establishment of boundaries would be the first steps taken by those who wanted to dominate the area. There is no doubt that efforts to achieve unity in the region have not ceased in the course of 4,000 years, seeking strength and, as I have said, existence.

Methods of achieving unity and efforts to realise it have varied according to the periods. However, the aim remained the same: namely, these events through which we are passing at present. The region was united by the force of arms when arms were the means of expression during ancient times. The region was united by its belief in the Prophet when messages came from heaven to lead the people.

The area was united under the influence of faith when the banners of Islam moved forward carrying the new divine message, conforming messages which had preceded it, and relaying God's latest word which called the people to righteousness. The area was united as a result of the merger of various elements into a single Arab nation. The area became united in language when Arabic alone was uttered from every tongue. The area became united through the urge for peace when it faced the imperialism of Europe advancing towards it and attempting to raise the Cross in order to conceal its ambitions behind the guise of Christianity. The meaning of unity was complete when Christianity in the Arab East participated in resisting the Crusaders side by side with the legions of Islam.

The area was united in sharing tribulation when the assaults of the Ottoman invasion swept over it and encircled it with curtains of ignorance, hindering its progress and preventing it from entering an era of renaissance at a time when the renaissance had begun in Europe. Indeed, the area

---

[1] Presumably: was preceded by . . .

was united under the domination of imperialism to which it was subjected; its unity was then the revolt against this imperialism in all its forms and resistance to these forms. Together with unity in the revolt there was unity in sacrifice. The gallows which Jamal Pasha erected in Damascus, the capital of Syria, did not differ much from those which Lord Cromer erected at Dinshaway in Egypt.

Compatriots, Members of the National Assembly: Thus, you see unity, a reality being sought or actually existing. Thus, you see that the struggle for strength and existence is achieved through unity. You see that unity is only achieved through the strength of existence. You see that the history of Cairo is generally the same as that of Damascus. The details might be different, but the prominent milestones are the same—the same forces, invaders, kings, heros, and martyrs.

When it appeared at certain times that Egypt had abandoned the Arab concept and had severed links between it and the area—following the French campaign against Egypt and then under the Muhammad Ali dynasty—the real position was not as it appeared on the surface. Remoteness was only superficial, and separation existed only in words. However, the truth is that what God has brought together cannot be separated, and what nature has joined cannot be severed.

Facts prove that the army of peasants under the command of Ibrahim Pasha that set out to liberate Syria from the Ottoman tyranny called itself the Arab Army. Facts also show that Cairo, which in the second half of the 19th century hastened to open its windows to the currents of the renaissance, became a bastion of free-thinking in the Arab East. The seekers of freedom in Syria and in all the Arab region came to it to take refuge within its strong walls, and in turn to send the rays of thought to fill men's minds and to inspire.

Cairo in the beginning of the 20th century, together with Damascus, became the headquarters of secret organisations which struggled with youthful self-sacrifice against the tyrannical Sultans of Istanbul to liberate the Arab people. Thus unity was a truth and everything else was artificial. It was clear that if the region was left alone to be its own inspiration and to listen to the beats of its heart, then its inclination towards unity would become irresistible. This is what happened.

Compatriots, Members of the National Assembly: When Syria achieved its complete independence it looked towards Egypt. When Egypt achieved its complete independence it looked towards Syria. The coming together —or rather the friendship—was complete before the signing of the Arab League Charter, and after it was signed then certain Powers wanted it to remain ink on paper. To every action in Egypt there was a reaction in Syria. Every noise in Damascus echoed in Cairo. In Egypt and Syria, unrest followed the second world war, and the great liberation movements in Africa and Asia started. In Syria and Egypt there were the attempts to improve the situation—Egypt and Syria which rushed to the war in Palestine armed with chivalry and faith, but no weapons.

Then came the results of the Palestine war. Foremost was the awakening, an awakening that was much like that of a man roused from his sleep by being burned. In Syria and Egypt there were the same battles. If we take into consideration the recent months alone, we can note that the battles which Damascus waged were the same battles as Cairo waged. These were the battles of military pacts, the battle of weapons, the battle of non-alignment, the battle of conspiracies, the battle of economic liberation.

Syria entered the Suez Canal struggle with the same force and strength that Port Said entered the Suez Canal battle. In turn, Egypt joined in the battle against threats to Syria. All its attention was directed towards Damascus—and even more important was the fact that soldiers of a part of its army occupied posts side by side with their brothers the Syrian soldiers. All that was splendid, and it was not coincidental. Many elements —great, noble and deeply-rooted—paved the way to the linking of Egypt and Syria: nature, history, language, religion, belief, joint security and freedom paved the way to it; something else that paved the way was the pains and sufferings caused by the three horsemen of treachery—prison, exile, and the scaffold. All this paved the way to this dawn, which we view today after the long night.

Citizens, Members of the National Assembly: The forerunner of dawn was the resolution of the Syrian Chamber of Deputies, adopted by your Assembly, calling for immediate action to achieve unity between Egypt and Syria. This resolution of yours was an expression of a great reality which could not be ignored. It was a response to a holy call, which we could not close our ears to. This call did not exist only in Damascus alone, but in all parts of the Arab homeland. The call was a stormy current that had been whipped up and shaped by Arab nationalism. Thus, final talks were held in Cairo to draw up the formal structure of the accomplished fact.

These Cairo talks constituted a new and historic test. The Cairo meetings were held because of the wishes of politicians or rulers, but were brought about by pressure and insistence, and because of the stubborn, determined desires emanating from the hearts of the peoples. In any case, we have done well to let matters reach this point. Peoples must make full use of opportunity and be sure of their convictions first. In the course of days the peoples' faith will grow deeper and deeper, and both events and developments will give assurance to the people that the road of unity (wahdah) is the road of strength and life.

Compatriots, Members of the National Assembly: The meaning of our Cairo talks and the arrival in Egypt of the pioneer and hero of unity, the bearer of its banner, the mujahid, Shukri al-Quwatli, with a delegation of his brothers in the struggle, was that the time had come. It also means that the bells marking the hour which our grandfathers looked for, and our fathers worked for, have rung. It has happened that in our age, after the long night the morning has come. It means that what they aspired to is a reality and the thing for which they tasted death has come alive itself; it means that the thing which scaffolds were built to oppose has acquired for itself alone the power of law and might; it means that what was divided has returned to its natural, God-given condition of a whole and united body. It means that the chains have been broken, the barriers destroyed, and that the scattered parts are about to join each other, or the whole. It means that Syria and Egypt have decided to shoulder the historic responsibility placed on them in their capacity as two Arab countries whose own affairs have been put into the hands of their own people, and on whose territory there is true sovereignty and full independence. That was the meaning of the Cairo discussions. Citizens, Members of the National Assembly: Our discussions have ended in declaring unity officially and in signing this declaration on Saturday, 1st February 1958.

This memorable proclamation has been deposited in your Assembly's office. Its principal result is the unification of Egypt and Syria in one State, called the United Arab Republic (long applause). The system of government will be democratic and presidential; executive power will be exercised by the President of the State, assisted by Cabinet Ministers appointed by, and answerable to, him. The legislative authority will be exercised by a unicameral legislative assembly. It will have one flag and one army—a unity providing equality of rights and obligations to its sons.

Afterwards, we reached agreement on the following principles on which the Republic will be based during the transition period:

(1) The United Arab State is a democratic, independent, and sovereign republic. Its people are part of the Arab nation.
(2) Public freedoms are guaranteed.
(3) General elections are a right of citizens, in accordance with the provisions of the law. Participation in public life is a national duty of citizens.
(4) The legislative authority shall be undertaken by an assembly to be called the National Assembly. Its membership shall be fixed, and members shall be chosen by decree of the President of the Republic. At least half the members shall be members of the Syrian Chamber of Deputies and Egyptian National Assembly.
(5) Executive authority shall be vested in the President of the Republic.

(6) Private ownership is inviolable, and the law shall regulate the manner in which such ownership will fulfil its social function. Expropriation will be undertaken only in the public interest and be justly compensated in accordance with the law.

(7) The imposition, amendment, or repeal of public taxes shall be valid only by law, and no person shall be exempt from payment of taxes except in cases stipulated by law.

(8) Judges shall be independent, and only the law shall have authority over them in the judicial sphere.

(9) All provisions of laws in force in Syria and Egypt shall remain effective within the territorial spheres stipulated at the time of their promulgation. These laws may be repealed or amended.

(10) The United Arab Republic shall consist of two regions—namely, Syria and Egypt.

(11) Each region shall have an Executive Council (majlis tanfidhi), presided over by a president appointed by decree of the President of the Republic, and assisted by Ministers appointed by the President of the Republic on the recommendation of the President of the Executive Council.

(12) The powers of the Executive Council shall be fixed by order of the President of the Republic.

(13) Provisions of international treaties and agreements concluded by Syria and Egypt with other States shall remain in force with regard to the territorial spheres stipulated at the time of their conclusion, in accordance with the provisions of international law.

(14) Public departments and administrative networks at present in existence shall remain in operation in both Syria and Egypt until such time as they are reorganised and unified by decrees of the President of the Republic.

(15) Citizens shall form a National Union (ittihad qawmi), which will endeavour to achieve national aims and stimulate efforts to build the nation on a sound political, social, and economic foundation. The method of forming this union shall be laid down by decree of the President of the Republic.

(16) Steps shall be taken to draw up the permanent constitution of the United Arab Republic.

(17) The referendum on unity and the President of the United Arab Republic shall be held on 21st February 1958.

Compatriots, Members of the National Assembly: Here I must talk about the constitution of 16th January,[1] the greatest result of which was your Assembly. This constitution is immortal. It is not reasonable that the

[1] 1956.

Revolution, which formulated it and proclaimed it as having resulted from the people's will and experience, should agree that this constitution be cast aside. As I told you when I had the honour of speaking to you here on 16th January, the constitution does not merely consist of dry provisions, but represents a perpetual, progressive movement towards the future to which we aspire; it has moulded this movement and united its ranks. A great movement has united two peoples of the same nation into a united republic. Consequently, the mould had to be enlarged in order to include this new development. Thus the constitution of 16th January had to be adapted to wider and more extensive experiences in life. Similarly, your Assembly, which was the greatest result of the constitution of 16th January, had to undergo the same change.

Compatriots, Members of the National Assembly: I told you once that we consider you the new Revolution Council; that the revolution continues; and that it is hoped that the experience of the few months which have passed since your Assembly began to function will augur full cooperation aimed at safeguarding the interests of the people and building the new society. It is our duty to tell you during these decisive moments in the history of our people that you have lived up to our best hopes and expectations, and that your sharing of the responsibilities with us greatly assisted us.

It gives me pleasure that the great events which are taking place will not end our friendship. On the contrary, they will strengthen bonds between us, increase our determination, and make us more united in the course upon which we have embarked.

Compatriots, Members of the National Assembly: I consider it my duty at this time to tell you frankly, and all people of the United Arab Republic, that the road which we are taking is a long and difficult one. Our journey is not a picnic; it is one of hardship, difficulties, struggle, and strife. However, this is a fair price to pay for the great hope to which we aspire. The difficulties we shall encounter on the road will be doubled, because those who are not pleased with the union of Syria and Egypt, and whose objectives do not coincide with ours, will not accept it with satisfaction and in silence. There will be endeavours, attempts, manoeuvres. I tell you therefore that from now on we must keep our eyes open and be alert.

Compatriots, Members of the National Assembly: We are living during a magnificent period—but we must realise that this period also has its dangers. Possibly our personal ambitions are the greatest danger confronting us. Centuries have passed during which our dreams, hopes, desires, and objectives were blocked by barriers and obstructions which imperialism has made. These barriers and obstructions fell when imperialism disappeared from our countries. Thus, these dreams, hopes, desires, and objectives began to emerge and rushed forward in a torrent.

This is the real explanation of the rapid rush of events of our generation. This is a natural development after many centuries of pressure. However, this, too, serves as a warning. It is a warning that one of our first duties is to be reasonable in our hopes—and then so to open the tap that the current flows as a controlled stream and not as a flood.

Compatriots, Members of the National Assembly: I am confident that our experience of today will enable us to achieve everything which those who have worked for it throughout the savage and dark night wished it to achieve. My confidence is borne out by the fact that God Almighty has united our hearts with the hearts of a good travelling companion, reliable in battle, and a good kinsman, brother, and dear one. After successive experiences, the people of Syria have affirmed that they are in the front rank of Arab nationalism, a spearhead of its drive, and that they loyally guard its glorious traditions.

Compatriots, Members of the National Assembly: A new hope has appeared on the horizon—a new State has been born; a great State has been conceived. It is not an intruder or usurper; it is not an aggressor or attacker; it is a State which guards not threatens; gathers, not disperses; strengthens, not weakens; unites, not divides; makes peace and not war; supports it friends, crushes the enemy, shows impartiality and is not fanatical; does not swerve or align itself; fosters justice, consolidates peace, and ensures both its own prosperity and the prosperity of those surrounding it and of as many people as it can sustain.

Compatriots, Members of the National Assembly: God bless you and your unity. May He protect your United Arab Republic. Peace be with you.

3. Proclamation of the Arab Union of Iraq and Jordan, Amman, 14 February 1958[1]

Whereas: the great Arab Revolt led by His Majesty the great savior Ai Hussein Ibn Ali was a proclamation of a new dawn for the Arab nation

---

[1] *Basic Documents*, pp. 7–9. Unofficial translation. This agreement was unanimously ratified by the Iraqi Chamber and Senate on 17 February, and by the Jordanian Chamber of Deputies on 18 February. On 19 March 1958, the Constitution of the Arab Union, worked out by a joint Iraqi-Jordanian commission, was promulgated simultaneously in Baghdad and Amman. For the Constitution of the Arab Union, see *Orient*, 6, pp. 168–81. On 26 March the Jordanian Parliament unanimously approved the Constitution of the Union. On the same day the Iraqi Chamber of Deputies unanimously decided to amend the Iraqi constitution of 1924 in order to authorise the King to participate in a union with one or more Arab states. The Chamber was then dissolved to allow the approval by a new assembly of the second reading of the same amendment. In the elections held on 5 May, 125 out of 145 deputies were elected unopposed. On 10 May the Chamber reassembled and approved the constitutional amendment unanimously. On the 12 May it unanimously approved the Constitution of the Union; one vote was cast against the Constitution in the Senate. On 13 May Nouri as-Said, President of the Iraqi Council, resigned and was charged by the King to form the first federal government; the Cabinet was announced on 19 May and the first session of the Assembly of the Union opened in Amman on 27 May 1958.

advanced by the sacrifices of martyrs for the liberation of the Great Arab Nation and unification of its peoples; an attempt to regain the prestige of Arabs among the nations of the world; and a contribution to the progress of human civilization;

Whereas: the blessed revolution emanated from the surge of Arabs toward liberty and unity based upon the glorious past of the Arab World, faith in itself and its old and eternal mission;

Whereas: the mission of the Arab Revolt, for which its leader has striven, passed to the sons and grandsons and was inherited by generation after generation to remain always as a flame illuminating the path of the Arab nation toward the realization of its hopes and aspirations for the complete unity which integrated all the elements leading to liberty, happiness and strength; the regaining of the glories and preservation of its heritage, and its sacred aims; and the assurance of a happy future under the auspices of this blessed unity;

Therefore: the two Hashemite states decide to form a federation between themselves based upon these sublime aims.

I

An Arab Federation is established on February 14, 1958 between the Hashemite Kingdom of Jordan and the Kingdom of Iraq to be called the Arab Union. This Union is open to other Arab States which wish to join it.

II

Each of the two States reserves its integral State entity, its sovereignty, and its existing form of government.

III

The international treaties, pacts and agreements which bound each of the two states before the establishment of the Union will remain valid with respect to the state which concluded them, without binding the other state. But the international treaties, pacts and agreements which will be concluded after the establishment of the Union and which will involve Union matters will come under the authority and responsibility of the Union Government.

IV

Directly after the official declaration of the Union, measures for complete unity between the two Union States will be taken in the following matters:

a. Unity of foreign policy and diplomatic representation.
b. Unity of the Jordanian and Iraqi armies under the name of the Arab Army.
c. Elimination of customs barriers between the two countries and unification of customs laws.
d. Unification of educational curricula.

V

The two parties agree to carry out, as quickly as possible, the necessary measures for unifying the currency and coordinating the financial and economic policy of the two countries.

VI

Whenever necessity and interest requires the unification of any other matter other than those mentioned in Article Four, the necessary measures will be undertaken according to the Constitution of the Union to put that matter under the competence and authority of the Union Government.

VII

The Arab Revolt flag will be the flag of the Union and the flag of each of the two states.

VIII

a. Union affairs will be undertaken by a Union Government composed of a legislative council and an executive authority.

b. Each of the national Jordanian and Iraqi parliaments elects the members of the legislative council from among their members. Each state will have the same number of representatives.

c. The members of the executive authority will be appointed according to the rules of the Union Constitution to carry out matters under the authority of the Union Government.

IX

The King of Iraq will be the Head of the Union Government. In case of his absence for any reason the King of Jordan will be the Head of the Union Government. Each of the two Kings reserves his constitutional authority in his Kingdom and when another state joins the Union, the question of the Head of state will be reviewed according to circumstances.

X

The capital of the Union will be Baghdad for six months and Amman for the other six months consecutively.

XI

a. The Union Government will prepare the Union Constitution according to the basis indicated in this agreement and the constitution of each of the two states will be amended to the extent required, and within the limits expressed by the Union Constitution.

b. The necessary steps and measures required for the establishment of the Union Government and the enactment of a Union Constitution will be carried out within a period not exceeding three months from the date of the signing of this agreement.

XII

This agreement is to be concluded according to the constitutional principles of each of the two states.

4. Telegram sent by President Nasser to King Faisal on the occasion of the proclamation of the Arab Union, 14 February 1958[1]

His Majesty King Faysal II, King of Iraq. The Arab Federation which unites Iraq and Jordan today is a blessed step to which the entire Arab nation looks with great hope, for the reason that it is a trend which derives its power from the depth of the Arab conscience. We are fully confident that the Arab Federation will be a source of strength to all the Arabs against all enemies of the Arabs.

The days which the Arab nation is now living are immortal and glorious days. There is no doubt that the events lived by our nation in this recent period signify that the dawn of the unity which shines on all Arab horizons is the start of a new history for the struggling Arab nation. Arab nationalism feels glorious and proud of the step you took in Amman today, feeling confident that it brings near the day of the greater unity.

Without doubt your Majesty's youth, faith and sincere devotion will be a driving force toward the realisation of the great dream of the Arabs. In congratulating your Majesty I pray from the depth of my heart that God may make you successful, guide your steps, and bless your great people.

[1] *S.W.B. Part IV*, 17 February 1958. The Union was not mentioned in Arabic commentaries broadcast from Cairo on 14 February 1958, and the only reference from Damascus radio that day to the Union were reports without comment of the agreement. Ibid., pp. i and ii.

5. Letter from Mr. Osman to the Secretary-General of the Security Council, containing a communication from the Prime Minister of the Sudan, 20 February 1958[1]

I have the honour, upon instruction from my Government, to request you to call an urgent meeting of the Security Council to discuss the grave situation existing on the Sudan-Egyptian border, resulting from the massed concentrations of Egyptian troops moving towards the Sudanese frontiers.

As a party to this dispute, I request that I be heard when the meeting is convened.

I attach herewith a communication received from H.E. Prime Minister Abdulla Khalil of the Sudan.

YACOUB OSMAN
Permanent Representative of the Sudan
to the United Nations

20 February 1958

On 1 February 1958, the Egyptian Government sent a note to the Government of the Sudan wherein she claimed sovereignty over the following Sudanese territories:

(a) The north-eastern part of the Sudan, north of latitude 22 north;

(b) That part of the Sudan which is situated north of the town of Wadi Halfa, comprising the Sarra, Debeira and Faras region.

The Egyptian note demanded the handing over of these two territories to Egypt. Egypt alleges that the said two territories belong to Egypt under the 1899 Agreement concluded between Great Britain and Egypt. These two territories belong to the Sudan by virtue of agreements and treaties concluded between the Egyptian Government and the Government of the Sudan in 1902 and 1907. Since then, the said territories have been under the exclusive administration and sovereignty of the Sudan. The inhabitants of these territories are of Sudanese nationality. At no time did they vote in any Egyptian parliamentary election or plebiscite. Moreover, they have voted as Sudanese nationals in the Sudanese parliamentary elections in 1953 on the strength of the self-government statute which had been enacted under the Agreement concluded between Great Britain and Egypt in February 1953.

On 9 February, reports were received by the Government of the Sudan that Egyptian troops were being sent to the north-eastern part of the Sudan north of latitude 22 north. The Government of the Sudan inquired from the Egyptian Government about the truth of these reports. Egypt denied them. On 13 February, the Egyptian Government sent a note,

[1] S.C.O.R., Thirteenth year, Supplement for January, February, and March 1958, Doc. S/3963.

dated 9 February, demanding that the Sudanese inhabitants of the said Sudanese territory should vote in the Egyptian plebiscite which will be held on 21 February. Several representations were made to the Egyptian Government to allow sufficient time for the Government of the Sudan to study such an intricate matter—a matter which the Egyptian Government had chosen to raise at a time when the Government of the Sudan and the Sudanese people are busy with their parliamentary general elections which will be held on 27 February.

The Egyptian Government, on 16 February, informed the Government of the Sudan that it had decided to send into the said territory plebiscite officials accompanied by frontier troops to conduct the Egyptian plebiscite. The Sudanese Government asked twice for time to negotiate with the Egyptian Government.

On 18 February, the Egyptian Government sent a note to the Government of the Sudan insisting to include the said territory in the Egyptian plebiscite and asking the Sudanese Government to withdraw therefrom a platoon which the latter had stationed there, to maintain law and order during the Sudanese parliamentary election—as has been done in other parts of the country. The Sudanese Government refuse to accept this demand which constitutes an infringement of its sovereignty. The Sudanese Government, being eager for an amicable settlement of this dispute, had sent its Minister for Foreign Affairs to Cairo on 18 February to discuss the matter with the Egyptian Government. Unfortunately, no settlement was reached. Reports reveal huge infiltration of Egyptian troops on the border.[1] The Egyptian Government insist on conducting a plebiscite in this Sudanese territory.

The Sudanese Government, though restrained in its action, views with deep concern this unprovoked and illegal attitude of the Egyptian Government which constitutes a breach of Sudanese sovereignty. Since the Sudan is determined to defend its territory, the situation would result in a breach of the peace and, if uncontrolled, may develop into armed conflict. As a peace-loving nation, the Sudan requests the Secretary-General of the United Nations to ask the Security Council to meet immediately and use its good offices to stop the impending Egyptian aggression. The Government of the Sudan will be submitting a note giving full evidence of its unquestionable right to the territories now claimed by Egypt.

ABDULLA KHALIL
Prime Minister

[1] An official Egyptian spokesman stated that: 'This is the second time in three days that the Sudanese Government has announced that the Egyptian army is invading the Sudan or that large Egyptian forces have infiltrated across the Sudanese borders. The fact is that there are no Egyptian forces along the southern borders, either in large or in small numbers, except the Egyptian Frontier Corps, which has been carrying out its duty in these regions for decades past.' S.W.B. Part IV, 22 February 1958, p. 1.

6. Statement by the Egyptian Government regarding the Egyptian-Sudanese frontier dispute, 21 February 1958[1]

For the sake of the ties between the Egyptian and the Sudanese people, the Egyptian Government decided to postpone a settlement on the question of the frontiers between the two countries until after the Sudanese elections, on the understanding that talks on the unsettled questions between the two countries will begin after the new Sudanese Government takes office. Egypt, which co-operated with the Sudan for freedom and independence, in taking this decision aims at cutting the lines of retreat for those who are exploiting the opportunity in order to damage relations between the two brotherly peoples. Egypt has not responded to the provocations which have attempted to portray the situation as an armed intervention or as an invasion of Sudanese territory at a time when Egypt has no forces on the southern borders except the known border patrols. The Egyptian Government announces once more that the Egyptian armed forces were not established to invade the Sudan. They will always be an arm to support the Sudan against the common enemy.

7. Speech by President Nasser on the Provisional Constitution of the United Arab Republic, Damascus, 5 March 1958[2]

Brethren: Today from this place we announce the provisional Constitution of the United Arab Republic.[3] This Constitution will be applied until the permanent Constitution of the United Arab Republic is drawn up and approved by the people.

Brethren: Today, when you were determined to have the unity, when you expressed your will to apply the unity between the Arab people in Syria and Egypt, and when these aspirations were but dreams and you were desirous of accomplishing them, things progressed quickly, and the need arose for a provisional Constitution to organise the relations between the various authorities. This Constitution which will be announced today is the first Constitution for Arab unity. It is the first Constitution, indeed the first fruit of the long struggle for the accomplishment of Arab unity and for the unification of the Arab Nation.

[1] *S.W.B. Part IV*, 22 February 1958, p. 1. For Mr. Loufti's statement to the Security Council, in which he refuted the Sudan's charges, and in which he read the above statement, see S.C.O.R., Thirteenth Year, 812th meeting, paras. 35–47.

[2] *S.W.B. Part IV*, 7 March 1958, pp. 7–13. This speech was made from the balcony of the Guest Palace in Damascus. President Nasser arrived in Damascus three days after his election as President of the U.A.R. In the elections, held on 21 February, 99·98 per cent of Syrian electors and 99·99 per cent of Egyptian electors had approved the formation of the U.A.R., and the choice of President Nasser as the head of the new state.

[3] For the text of the Provisional Constitution of the U.A.R. of 5 March, see Press Release 51, 5 March 1958, Information Department, Cairo.

This Constitution which we shall announce today may be simple in words and articles, but it is very profound in its meaning. It means that your wishes have come true, that the fruits of the long struggle and bitter strife have begun to appear and take shape, that the efforts made by the fathers and forefathers for the sake of the unification of the Arab nation have borne fruit, and that the free peoples who were determined to unite have united.

O brethren and citizens: This also means a hope—a great hope for our Arab brethren everywhere who are struggling against oppression, tyranny, and foreign domination. This is because the implementation of this unity after the long struggle, and the announcement of this Constitution which is simple in words but great in meaning, strengthen the hopes in the souls— the souls of these brethren who are struggling everywhere for the sake of real freedom, for the sake of ridding themselves of imperialism and the lackeys of imperialism, and for the sake of Arab unity.

You have won, brethren, and your brethren will win, God willing. You won because you had determination. You won despite the plots and intrigues. You won despite the imperialist attempts, the imperialist underlings, and the enemies of Arab nationalism who tried to prevent the union. You won as a result of a long and bitter struggle. You won in the battle of freedom. You won in the battle of independence. You won in the battle of alignment and alliances. You won in the battle of positive neutrality.

You won when you decided to have an independent policy for yourselves emanating from your own country, land, and conscience. You won, O brethren, when you faced the fleets and countered the aggression. You won when you countered the war of nerves and the cold war. You won in all battles and at all times. You have won and you have established this unity.

We must know, however, that those who opposed this unity and fought against the independence—those who fought freedom and independent policy—will not calm down or rest, but will work always and by all means and methods to accomplish their aims. The battle of our struggle continues. The battle of strife is long, because we were fighting to accomplish freedom and accomplish independence. We must now struggle to preserve freedom and to preserve our independence.

Brethren: We fought for the sake of establishing an independent policy. We fought for the establishment of an independent policy which would emanate from our conscience and our land. Today, brethren, we must fight and be on the alert in order to preserve this independent policy. We fought and struggled for the sake of unity. Today we must struggle, and if necessary fight as well, in order to preserve unity, this unity.

Brethren: We are still only at the beginning of the road. You have established the United Arab Republic. You have now to preserve the United Arab Republic. You have established Arab unity. It is the duty of all of us to preserve this unity.

Brethren: On this day, which I consider to be the fruit of long struggle and the fruit of bitter strife, I wish to tell you that we must be confident, and we must be well informed and sure that the enemies of Arab nationalism will not slacken, and that imperialism and the enemies of freedom and independence will not slacken, and that the enemies of the Arab power (Arabic: al-quwwat al-Arabiyah) will not slacken. Every one of you must be a soldier for the defence of these ideals and principles which have been won thanks to you, Arab people, and thanks to your determination. These ideals and principles which have been won in this part of the world must be protected by us.

Brethren: We must work to see those ideals and principles victorious everywhere. This is our road to the future. The factors and means which help us to achieve this must be well understood and known by us. We must unite. Unity is the basic force with which you defeated imperialism and won the battle for freedom. Unity is the main weapon which routed the aggression in Port Said and in Sinai. Unity is the main weapon which accomplished unity. Unity is your weapon; with it you established the United Arab Republic.

All of us know what dissension means and what division means. All of us remember what happened in Palestine in 1948. All of us remember these lessons and examples. All of us remember, too, that there are people who are lurking about in order to defeat our principles, to defeat our belief, and to defeat the high ideals to which we cling.

This battle is a continuous one. It is a long battle, but everyone of you will preserve these ideals and these principles. Brethren: Our weapon is unity—no partisanship and no parties. For all of us, citizens, are one man. All of us are one man working for the sake of the people, for the interests of the people, for the aims of the people, and for the high ideals advocated by the people. There is neither dissension, malice nor hatred, but love joining the sons of the one homeland.

We shall forget the past and open a new page in this homeland and in this Republic.[1] We shall learn lessons from the events of the past. We were divided. We were divided into parties and groups. And the imperialist benefited from this to foment hatred and dissension among us and to destroy the confidence in our souls, to destroy the confidence of

---

[1] On 6 March President Nasser nominated by decree the members of the central Government, and the executive councils of the two provinces (out of 34 ministers, 20 were Egyptian and 14 Syrian). Decrees were published on 12 March providing for the assumption by President Nasser of all powers hitherto exercised by the Syrian President, Premier and Cabinet, the dissolution of Syrian political parties and organisations, and an amnesty for some Syrian prisoners. For the texts of the decrees see *S.W.B. Part IV*, 14 March 1958, pp. 4–5.

the individual in himself and in his brother, and to foment dissession and hatred among the parties, groups, and various bodies and communities. These are weak points through which the imperialist can infiltrate.

It was for this reason that the parties in the Syrian sector declared their dissolution. The people believed that the parties must be dissolved, so that we might proceed forward.[1]

Brethren: We all follow one aim, namely the protection of the United Arab Republic and the creation of a society in which justice, prosperity, and equality shall prevail. All of us, O brethren, will work for the accomplishment of this aim. In my capacity as one of you, I shall be the first to work for the accomplishment of this aim. With the help of God we shall destroy the hatred—we shall destroy all hatred and dissension.

I have spent nine days among you. You, as well as I, know that there are grievances and there are hatreds. There are also accusations. The imperialists may have tried to cast accusations among the people, may have tried to cast accusations with the purpose of making us lose confidence and to destroy the spirit of confidence. They have exploited partisanship and dissension in order to accomplish this aim. Despite all this, however, you have won.

Brethren: Today we face the great responsibility of building up this United Arab Republic and creating a happy Arab society where prosperity and equality prevail.

Today, brethren, you have defeated the plots. But have the plots stopped? The plots have not ended. You have won, and the sons of the people have always set the great examples of nobility, honour, sacrifice, and love of the homeland. There was no treason, and they could not use treason to destroy your aims, to thrust against your freedom and your high ideals. But they did not give up at all.

Brethren: They are still conspiring. They are trying by every means to split the army from the people. But the army is nothing but a servant of this people. Brethren: The army consists of individuals from among you who have taken the pledge to the homeland to sacrifice their lives and to sacrifice their blood to save you and to defend your land.

They have resorted to all means. They tried in Egypt also to split the army from the people. Here, too, they tried to divide the army from the people.

Brethren and citizens: The army is nothing but the protective shield which serves the aims of the people, protects the interests of the people, and works for the sake of the people. Citizens and brethren, the army is

---

[1] The Communist Party was the only Syrian party which had not already dissolved itself. The attitude of the Communists in Syria was confused; they started by favouring a federal type of union as opposed to the organic union of 1 February, but then welcomed the creation of the U.A.R. On 4 February Mr. Bagdache, the leader of the Syrian Communist Party, left Syria together with other members of the party.

nothing but your sons and brethren. They [the soldiers] have no alternative but to sacrifice their souls and their blood for the sake of defending you, your independence, and your freedom.

Brethren: They wanted to foment hatred and dissension among the sons of this homeland in this sector and to divide the army and the people. They were sure of themselves and wanted to carry it out. But when you determined to unite, and when you decided to enforce your will and impose your wishes, they tried also to plot, to stab you, and to destroy your aims. They wanted to use the army towards this end. They wanted to use the army towards this end.[1] They wanted to use the army, which is of you and for you. They wanted to use the army, which represents the masses of this people. They wanted to use the army, which undertook to protect you with its soul and with its blood.

They were sure of themselves, but they forgot that this army believed in the people and believed in its homeland. They forgot that this army has sworn to sacrifice its blood for the sake of the people and for the sake of the homeland.

Brethren: When unity was effected, they—the imperialists—wanted, and their underlings—the underlings of imperialism—wanted, and the enemies of Arab nationalism wanted, to find any crack through which to infiltrate and destroy your aims. But they failed.

They believed their biased propaganda and wanted to contact the army to make it strike against the people. They contacted the army and offered to pay it all the money it wanted in return for the destruction of the unity and the staging of a coup d'etat to rule the country.

They contacted a senior army personage in the Syrian army. They contacted him through a third party. They told him: 'We are prepared to pay; we are prepared to pay 2 m. pounds or 5 m. pounds to the army in order to stage a coup d'etat and prevent the unity'.

Brethren, citizens: This senior army officer immediately contacted Gen. Abd al-Hakim Amir and informed him of the matter. I believe that you remember that I said in my speech at Port Said that on some occasions we also nationalise plots. Our plan in regard to this plot was to nationalise it, just as we nationalised the plot hatched against the Arab people in Egypt. The third party contacted this officer and offered him 2 m. pounds—20 m. Syrian pounds—so that he might carry out their plot.

Naturally, they did not make this contact until they became desperate and until all roads were closed in their faces. When this officer contacted Gen. Abd al-Hakim Amir, his colleagues in the army, and myself, we decided to go along to get the money which they offered.

Contacts began. Promises began to flow about the sums of money they would pay. They forgot that there are some people who cannot be bought

[1] Repeated in text.

with money. They forgot that there is something called honour, which cannot be estimated in money. They forgot that there are men who do not sell their peoples, who do not sell their colleagues for any sum, no matter how high. They forgot these ideals and principles. They thought that the peoples are goods which can be bought and sold. They thought that all men can sell their peoples and dispose of them for five or six million dollars. They forgot all these values, because they were dominated by their malice.

They forgot all these feelings which prevail among all the people—men, women, and children. They forgot that some people sacrificed their lives to accomplish these aspirations and sacrificed their blood, of their own accord and with satisfaction and contentment. They forgot that among the members of the army whom they asked to sell you to them, to sell out the people, they forgot that among those members of the army there are some who had a father, brother, or friend martyred for the sake of the accomplishment of these aims which we now demand.

They forgot all these ideals. They remembered only one thing: that everything can be bought for money. Bargains began. Plots began. The first million pounds were delivered—10 m. Syrian pounds. Of course, they demanded that the army stage a coup d'etat. This army, which they on the outside make propaganda about, and which they say interferes in politics—the army which they say in the newspapers carried out coups d'etat in the past, the army against which they make propaganda and about which they spoke with the purpose of dividing it from you—they went and paid money to it, so that it might stage a coup d'etat against the aims of the people. The army, pledged to defend this people with its blood and life!

Contacts continued. They demanded that the coup d'etat be staged after the delivery of the first million pounds. But the officer they contacted asked for the other million. As they were in a hurry and wanted it before the establishment of the Republic, they said they were ready to pay the second million and the third million, but the matter must be carried out.

They began to pay the second million in instalments. The first million they paid by cheque.

Brethren: Naturally, in such matters it is difficult. In this matter there are full documents, because they did not deliver the money in cash: they made payments by cheque.

The first million was delivered by a cheque on the Arab Bank. The cheque bore the number 85902, and was from Riyadh, 20th February 1958, payable to bearer £1,000,000 sterling (Arabic: miliun jinayh istarlini).

The second cheque: The Arab Bank—700,000; payable to bearer £700,000 sterling. The cheque bears the number 85903.

The third cheque: £200,000 sterling—the Arab Bank. It bears the number 85904, payable to bearer £200,000 sterling.

Of course, the money was transferred to the bearer and placed in the Arab Bank here in Damascus with receipts from that bank. The money was put into the account of A.S. [Arabic letters: Ayn Sin]. The sums were : first, £750,000 sterling; second, £250,000 sterling; and third, £200,000 sterling and £700,000. And these initials A.S., of course, stand for Abd al-Hamid as-Sarraj.

Abd al-Hamid as-Sarraj, whom they found to be the one who uncovered the plots they attempted to carry out.[1] They wanted to take the shortest cut and said: This man used to discover the plots, therefore let us buy him with money in order that he may betray his colleagues, and so that with the help of his colleagues in the army he may betray the people and stage a coup d'etat to accomplish the aims of the lackeys of imperialism and the enemies of Arab nationalism. Of course, Abd al-Hamid as-Sarraj told the matter to his colleagues.

Ideals are being manifested these days, O citizens. There are people who (?do not own anything), but still they are not prepared to sell their honour at any price, no matter how many millions of pounds are offered. On the other hand, there are people who own millions of pounds and yet are prepared to sell their honour. There are people who do not own any money but who possess honour and dignity, and who have faith in the people and the value of the people.

Brethren: These days they are trying to make the army the enemy of the people, after having attempted to separate the army from the people. But, as I have already told you, the army is but the servant of the people. The army has taken upon itself to swear to sacrifice its soul and blood for the sake of the people and this good land.

Today we the people and the army will unit together. There will be no parties. We will be one man in order to protect this Republic, these principles and ideals. Neither the foreigner nor the imperialists, neither the collaborators of imperialism nor the enemies of Arab nationalism will be able to divide us and create out of us parties and groups. Our policy is clear and well-known—freedom, independence, a policy emenating from our conscience, a policy of non-alignment, positive neutrality, and Arab nationalism. All these are very clear principles, and not in any way intricate.

The army serves the people and defends them. The army is but a part of you. They are your sons and brothers. The army, which is prepared to sacrifice its blood for the sake of the people, cannot sell the people for one

---

[1] In a press conference held on the evening of 5 March, Colonel Sarraj gave details of alleged Saudi telegrams on the conspiracy, of contacts with a father-in-law of King Saud and of Saudi payments. For the text of his statement, see *S.W.B. Part IV*, 7 March 1958, pp. 13-15.

million, two million, 10 million, or even for millions and millions of pounds. For the army represents the people, and there is no difference between the army and the people, because the army is but the sons of these people.

Imperialism will try to divide you and create parties and groups, and will try to instil hatred. But we should always remember that our course to success is union. There should be union from inside, we should be as one man—no partisanship, or parties, organisations, or groups. We should all work for the sake of the people. Imperialism, the collaborators of imperialism, the enemies of Arab nationalism, and also world Zionism, will all try to separate the army from the people. But we should always remember that the army is but the servant of the people, and that the people themselves are but the great army who support the army in the event of any attack on the homeland.

These, O brethren, are our ideals and our course in the future.

These days we are witnessing examples of honour and dignity. These cheques are in the bank, and photostats of these cheques will be distributed to the papers so that everyone will acquaint himself with the truth and see them with his own eyes. The amount is £1.9m. One hundred thousand pounds have not yet arrived, and I do not think that this money will arrive after I have spoken today.

In other words, these 19m. Syrian pounds this amount which they wanted to use for evil, treachery and treason—this oil money (fulus al-batrul) will be used for the establishment of heavy industry here, in this sector. This amount will be the initial support for the five-year industrialisation plan, and for the establishment of heavy industry in this homeland so that we may turn evil into good. For good may come out of evil.

Brethren: We will work and unite solidly for the sake of protecting this Republic. Our only support is God and the people. We will preserve our independence and freedom, and will always be the highest example for the entire world. With the help of God, brethren, we will be able to build up this Republic.

Today, on this occasion, we give the entire world the highest example of dignity, honour, and pride. Today we should be confident in ourselves, and should have confidence in one another. This confidence is the basic weapon. With union and confidence we shall conquer the plots, imperialism, and the collaborators of imperialism. With union and confidence we shall conquer the enemies of Arab nationalism. With union and confidence we shall strengthen the pillars of the United Arab Republic. With union and confidence, God willing, we shall build, establish, and work, despite plots and intrigues, until we have built the society of which we dream.

This is our course: Union. We should be united as one man—no partisanship, no hatreds. There should be mutual confidence. We have a clear policy of non-alignment and positive neutrality. We should work for the sake of Arab nationalism and for the sake of helping our Arab brethren in every enslaved country, and should help every country which tries to gain its freedom.

This is our course. We seek the aid of God. For we depend only on God. May God make us all successful. May peace and the blessings of God be upon you.

8. Statement summarizing the press conference held by the Tunisian Secretary of State for the Interior, regarding Egyptian connivance in a recent plot against President Bourguiba, 5 March 1958[1]

The press conference held at the office of the Secretary of State for the Interior, M. Taieb Mehiri, was summoned in order to inform public opinion about certain details of the plot discovered recently on the southern border of Tunisia and which aimed at the overthrow of the present Tunisian regime and of President Bourguiba. M. Mehiri first stated that the activities of Salah Bin Yusuf against the regime and President Bourguiba himself had not ceased since Tunisia gained her independence, but that it was for the first time that Salah Bin Yusuf, in his letters and message addressed to his real or supposed supporters in Tunisia, had gone further than giving advice and directives (one word indistinct) to that of inciting murder.[2]

Actually, this plot is important from three points of view: firstly, from the point of view of the fact that the documents, that is the passport or pass, which were found on the young man by the name of Salah Najjar who was arrested at (place name indistinct) was a pass issued by the Egyptian authorities in Cairo on 9th January, and bore the visa of the Libyan Consul in Cairo permitting the transit of Salah Najjar by night. This fact is extremely serious in itself. The Tunisian Government would not wish to draw definite conclusions from this as to the attitude of the Egyptian Government towards the Tunisian regime but, all the same,

---

[1] *S.W.B. Part IV*, 7 March 1958, p. 17. This statement was recorded by the Secretary of State for Information, Mustafa Filali.

[2] President Bourguiba was reported as commenting on the Salah Bin Yousef plot as follows: 'We will not allow any State bound to us by diplomatic relations to hatch a plot to overthrow the regime in our country. We have asked for explanations on this subject, and if we do not obtain a convincing statement then we do not see any need to maintain diplomatic ties between ourselves and Egypt. We agree with President Jamal Abd an-Nasir when he says "We are friendly with those who are friendly with us, and at enmity with those who are at enmity with us".' *S.W.B. Part IV*, 8 March 1958, p. iii.

considers this matter as very serious—the fact that the Egyptian authorities have thus issued a safe-conduct document to a person who (several words indistinct) criminal designs.

The second aspect of this important plot is the tenor of the documents themselves, which were discovered on the young man, Salah Najjar. In fact, Salah Najjar was the bearer of letters addressed to a certain number of Tunisians, various people in Tunisia, and particularly to (names indistinct). The letters asked the people to whom they were addressed to do away with President Bourguiba, to kill him. They also reveal a previous exchange of correspondence between these people in Tunisia and Salah Bin Yusuf in which these people reproached Salah Bin Yusuf for not having, for some time, conducted propaganda for their cause and against the Bourguiba regime abroad. Salah Bin Yusuf replies to this criticism by saying that the fault lies with them for being silent. The fact that they had not made any move, that they had not made a show of opposition in the country, do not allow him personally to stir up propaganda or to turn international opinion against the Bourguiba regime through the international press.

The third important point is precisely the criminal means with which Salah Bin Yusuf is seeking today to get rid of President Bourguiba himself. The Secretary of State for the Interior was led to draw a lesson from these facts, this plot. In fact, this plot takes shape at a time when the Tunisian people are waging a struggle to save the integrity of the country. It is all the more peculiar to see that it is precisely this moment—this particular period after Saqiyat Sidi Yusuf, that the enemy of the regime in the Middle East has chosen to show himself, and to do with such criminal designs. Thus, a certain alliance, whether intentional or not, but an alliance which is a fact links together the two sects, the two categories of ultra-extremists, the French ultra-extremists and the extremists of Salah Bin Yusuf. It will be easy to prove a common identity from the expressions used by one or the other of these two categories.

9. Statement by the Government of Saudi Arabia denying President Nasser's allegations of 5 March, 6 March 1958[1]

The President of the United Arab Republic delivered a speech in Damascus on Wednesday 15th Shaban 1377 AH[2] on the occasion of the proclamation of the Constitution of the Republic in which he said that cheques to the value of £1,700,000 sterling had been drawn by the Arab Bank in Riyadh for the Syrian Lt. Col. Abd al-Hamid as-Sarraj in order to prevent the establishment of the United Arab Republic.

The Saudi Government, which was astonished by this report, declares

[1] *S.W.B. Part IV*, 8 March 1958, p. 4.   [2] 5 March 1958.

that it does not know anything about this and does not acknowledge it. This act in no way agrees with the neutral policy laid down by HM the King and approved by his Government and broadcast all over the world. Nor does it agree with any of the principles which His Majesty has laid down.

This Government believes that this matter can only be the result of one of two things. It is either an intrigue (indistinct word) to cause hostility among the leaders of the Arab world, or it is a fabricated part of a plot aimed at harming Arab interests.

Consequently His Majesty has ordered the immediate formation of a high commission to investigate this matter in order to ascertain its meaning and purpose. The Government will consider the results immediately after the investigations.

10. Constitution of the United Arab States, Damascus, 8 March 1958[1]

CHARTER

of the

CREATION OF THE UNITED ARAB STATES

PART I: THE UNION

ARTICLE I

A Union named the United Arab States is hereby created. It includes the United Arab Republic, the Kingdom of Yemen and those Arab states which will agree to join this Union.

ARTICLE 2

Each State will preserve its international personality and its system of government.

[1] Press Release, Information Department, Cairo, 8 March 1958. On 2 February 1958, it was reported that the Iman of the Yemen had sent an urgent cable to Presidents Quwatli and Nasser 'expressing the Yemen's desire to join the Arab unity on the principle of federal union', S.W.B. Part IV, 4 February 1958, p. 1. The Crown Prince of the Yemen, Saif al-Islam Mohammad al-Badr, arrived in Cairo on 5 February to begin negotiations. He met President Nasser on 6 February and subsequently it was announced that 'complete agreement on the question of the Yemen's adherence to the UAR' had been reached. On 11 February it was stated that the agreement would be signed after the announcement of the plebiscite results, S.W.B. Part IV, 13 February 1958, p. ii. It was reported in Cairo, on 6 February, that Prince al-Badr was returning to the Yemen to submit the completed draft agreement to the Iman for his approval. The Charter, creating a federal relationship between the Yemen and the U.A.R., was signed by President Nasser and Prince al-Badr on 8 March in Cairo.

ARTICLE 3

Citizens of the Union are equal in public rights and obligations.

ARTICLE 4

Each citizen in the Union has the right to work and to occupy public functions in the united countries without discrimination and within the limits prescribed by Law.

ARTICLE 5

Freedom of movement in the Union is guaranteed within the limits prescribed by law.

ARTICLE 6

Member States shall pursue the unified foreign policy drawn by the Union.

ARTICLE 7

Diplomatic and consular representation of the Union abroad shall be assumed by a single mission in those cases specified by the Union.

ARTICLE 8[1]

The Union shall have unified Armed Forces.

ARTICLE 9[2]

Economic Affairs in the Union are organised according to plans aimed at the development of production, the exploitation of natural resources, and the coordination of economic activities.

ARTICLE 10[3]

Currency Affairs in the Union shall be determined by Law.

ARTICLE 11

A Customs Union shall be established between United countries. It will be governed by the conditions and regulations prescribed by Law.

[1] For the text of the Federal Law No. 5 regarding defence, see *S.W.B. Part IV*, 15 March 1958, pp. 4–6.
[2] For the text of the Federal Law No. 3 establishing a Yemeni currency board, see ibid., pp. 3–4.
[3] For the text of the Federal Law No. 4 regarding the co-ordination of the currency system, see ibid., p. 4.

ARTICLE 12

The Law organises the stages and means of coordination of Education and Culture in the Union.

PART II: AUTHORITIES

ARTICLE 13

The Control of Union Affairs shall be assumed by a council named the 'Supreme Council'. It shall be composed of the Heads of the member states.

ARTICLE 14

The Supreme Council shall be assisted in its functions by a council named 'The Union Council'.

ARTICLE 15[1]

The Union Council shall include an equal number of Representatives from Member States. The number of Members, the duration of Membership and the regulations to which they are subject shall be defined by Law.

ARTICLE 16

Presidency of the Union Council shall be assumed alternatively by each member state for a period of one year. The State which is to assume presidency of the Council shall appoint the President, who shall have one or more Vice-Presidents from the Member State or states.

ARTICLE 17[2]

The Supreme Council defines the higher policy of the Union with regard to political, defense, economic and cultural matters. It enacts the laws which are necessary to this effect. It is the supreme authority to which the determination of attributions shall be referred.

The decisions of the Council shall be issued with the unanimous approval of the Council.

ARTICLE 18

The Supreme Council shall enact the Union laws falling within its competence in accordance with this Charter, after the agreement of the competent authorities in each state.

[1] For the text of the Federal Law No. 1 establishing this Council, see *S.W.B. Part IV*, 15 March 1958, pp. 2–3.

[2] See footnotes for articles 9 and 10 above.

ARTICLE 19[1]

The Supreme Council appoints the Commander-in-Chief of the Armed Forces of the Union.

ARTICLE 20[2]

The General Budget of the Union shall be issued by Decree of the Supreme Council. The Law shall determine its resources and the contribution of each Member State.

ARTICLE 21

The Union Council is the permanent authority of the Union. It shall assume the examination of political affairs and shall set down the unified yearly programme which includes the regulations and measures leading to the achievement of Union.

ARTICLE 22

The Decisions and the yearly programme elaborated by the Union Council are to be submitted to the Supreme Council for ratification. It decides on the decisions taken by the Union Council which have been subject of an opposition from one of the two states or more.

ARTICLE 23[3]

The following bodies are attached to the Union Council:

a. The Defense Council
b. The Economic Council
c. The Cultural Council

The decisions taken by these bodies shall be submitted to the Union Council for ratification.

ARTICLE 24

The Law defines the manner of the formation of these bodies attached to the Union Council and their attributions.

---

[1] For the text of Decree No. 2 regarding the C-in-C, see ibid., p. 7.
[2] For the text of the Federal Law No. 2 regarding Budget Revenue, see ibid., p. 3.
[3] For the text of the Federal Law No. 6 regarding the cultural and economic councils, see ibid., pp. 6–7.

PART III: GENERAL AND INTERIM RULES

ARTICLE 25[1]

A Decree shall be issued by the Supreme Council determining the permanent seat of the Union of Arab States, its limits and the city in which the Union Council and the bodies attached to it shall hold their meetings by rotation.

ARTICLE 26

The Law determines the rules to be applied to the region of the permanent seat of the Union.

ARTICLE 27

Union Laws shall have full force in the United countries. They come into effect fifteen days after their publication in the Official Gazette of the Union unless otherwise specified by Law.

ARTICLE 28

The Head of each State shall appoint a minister to the United Arab States to supervise the enforcement of the Union's decisions in respect of the region he belongs to.

ARTICLE 29

The Head of each State shall appoint a minister to represent him before the head or heads of the other states. This minister shall have the capacity of local ministers.

ARTICLE 30

Diplomatic representation between Member States of the Union shall be abolished.

ARTICLE 31

The customs regulations observed in each member state shall remain in effect until the establishment of the Customs union between them. Meanwhile the Law may prescribe a special customs system to be observed by all Member States.

ARTICLE 32

The present charter shall come into effect on the day of its approval, pending the establishment of the permanent system for the Union.

[1] For the text of Decree No. 1 regarding the seat of Government, see *S.W.B. Part IV*, 15 March 1958, p. 7.

11. Foreign policy statement by the Amir Faisal, Saudi Arabian Crown Prince and Prime Minister, Mecca, 18 April 1958[1]

(Indistinct word) the Cabinet decision which has received the approval of HM the King:

(1) The policy of His Majesty's Government has been and is to befriend every State which does not attack it. This Government believes in positive neutrality, operates within its own framework, endeavours to deal with every State in the world in accordance with its interests and the general Arab interests, and is bound to no agreement or obligation towards any foreign State which does not conform with its interests and the general Arab interests. This Government has joined no foreign pacts because of its belief that accession to foreign pacts conflicts with Arab interests, and that pacts should arise from the Arab States themselves.

(2) As there is no diplomatic representation between Saudi Arabia and the Eastern States, relations between us and these States are based on the UN Charter. At the same time His Majesty's Government does not allow any creed which differs from the principles of Islam to enter our country.

(3) Saudi Arabia's relations with the Western Powers differ in so far as Saudi interests, safety, security and the general Arab interests are concerned. His Majesty's Government has therefore found itself in duty bound to define its attitude towards certain Western Powers, to notify them of this (indistinct word):

(a) *Relations with Britain:* The relations between His Majesty's Government and the British Government deteriorated following the British Government's violation of the partition agreement, and its aggression against the Buraimi region and the other disputed areas located in the SE of Saudi Arabia.[2] His Majesty's Government endeavoured by peaceful means to solve this problem, but in vain. Britain and France then followed Israel in committing aggression against Egypt. His Majesty's Government found it necessary, in defence of Arab interests and in upholding collective security, to sever its diplomatic relations with Britain and France, and to prohibit oil supplies to them.

When the British aggression against Egypt was halted and the aggressor forces withdrew from Egyptian soil the direct cause for the severance of

[1] *S.W.B. Part IV*, 21 April 1958, pp. 8–9. For a detailed summary of this policy statement see *Le Monde*, 20–21 April 1958.

[2] On 28 July 1954 agreement was reached in principle between the Saudi Arabian and United Kingdom Governments regarding the terms on which the frontier dispute on the Trucial Coast should be put to arbitration. The agreement divided the disputed area into three districts for the purposes of oil operations, pending the findings of the tribunal. The United Kingdom companies were to operate in one area, the Arabian American Oil Company in another, and no one in the third. (See *The Times*, 29 July 1954.) On 4 October 1955 the Foreign Office issued a statement describing 'the breaches of the conditions of arbitration which were agreed upon by the parties in an exchange of Notes'. For the text of this statement, see *The Times*, 5 October 1955.

diplomatic relations ceased to exist. But there is still another British aggression against Buraimi and other disputed areas. If this dispute is settled by the withdrawal of the British aggressor forces from Buraimi and other disputed areas, and if this solution occurs through arbitration— which His Majesty's Government still agrees to—or through any other means agreed upon, the Saudi Government does not see any objection to re-establishing its relations with Britain.

(b) *The situation with France:* Relations were severed with the French Government following its aggression against Egypt. After its withdrawal from Egyptian soil, talks were held between the two parties leading to the return of certain sums of money which have been handed over to certain French quarters as the price of (indistinct word) which the French Government banned (indistinct words). As a result also of (indistinct words) some of the French employed at the (indistinct word) factories (indistinct words). An agreement was later reached to recoup the (indistinct word) of electricity. After all this, there is nothing to prevent the Saudi Government from re-establishing relations with the French Government at any time (indistinct words).

(c) *Relations with the USA:* His Majesty's Government undoubtedly seeks to strengthen friendly relations with the American Government in view of the (indistinct words). HM the King has endeavoured to (indistinct words). The Saudi Government regrets the USA's attitude towards the question of the Gulf of Aqaba, an attitude which HM the King described during his (?meeting with) President Eisenhower as being one of support of the triple aggression against Egypt. The aggressors have withdrawn from Egypt, but the aggression still exists in the Arab territorial waters in the Gulf of Aqaba. His Majesty's Government hopes that (indistinct passage). However, if (indistinct words) in (?Eilat) which do not (?conform) with legal principles, the US backing of Israel in this situation shall be considered a ratification of the triple aggression and (indistinct words) a threat to the Holy Land and (indistinct words).

However, the other relations between Saudi Arabia and the USA, in certain economic affairs, have been included in the letters exchanged on 18th June (?1955)[1] and those exchanged on 2nd April 1957, letters which have been published in both (indistinct word). His Majesty's Government takes this opportunity to declare that there is no American base in Dahran, and that Dahran airport is a Saudi airport and a Saudi base.[2] All that is (indistinct words) is to facilitate the passage of certain aircraft (indistinct word) and (?refuelling).

---

[1] 1951.

[2] King Saud had been accused by Cairo of converting his kingdom into a vast nuclear depot, *Le Monde*, 20–21 April 1958. For a statement on Dahran airport in February 1957, and for the note of 2 April 1957, see *Documents* for 1957, p. 265, and pp. 281–83; for the agreement of 18 June 1951, see *U.S. Documents* for 1951, pp. 594–601.

(Indistinct passage) of the Arab countries, and that the cause of this problem is the (indistinct words) with all the Arab States and all justice-loving States which oppose (?oppression) and aggression.

(5) His Majesty's Government has several obligations in the Arab League, and is also a party to several other obligations involving member States of the Arab League. The Saudi Government is anxious to honour and carry out all its obligations and undertakings. It is also anxious to co-operate with the States with which it has signed these undertakings, with the idea of implementing them.

(6) (?Our brethren) in Syria and Egypt have agreed to unite. Our brethren in the Yemen have also wished to join their union. Our brethren in Iraq and Jordan have also wished to unite (indistinct words).

(7) His Majesty's Government regrets the storm which is blowing over a group of Arab States (indistinct words). Only the enemy benefits from this. (Indistinct words) His Majesty's Government desires very much to restore the concord between (indistinct words) when it senses a repercussion (indistinct words).

12. *Tass* statement regarding the situation in the Lebanon, 1 May 1958[1]

In connection with the events in recent days in Lebanon reports have been coming in about the attempts by certain foreign powers to make use of these events to interfere in the internal affairs of Lebanon and to exert pressure anew on the Arab states of the Middle East.

The facts prove that the powers concerned, making use of the Lebanese events, are weaving the web of another plot against peace and security in the Middle East. This time they have chosen Lebanon, a small Arab country, as the objective of their schemes.

Foreign press reports say that this is being manifested primarily in the fact that the Embassies of certain western powers in Beirut have come to resemble, not so much diplomatic representations in charge of the relations of their countries with the sovereign Lebanese state, as colonialist headquarters which enter into collusion with reactionary anti-national elements within the country, flagrantly interfere in the internal affairs of that country and try to order it about as if it were a colony.

The United States Sixth Fleet has been ordered to sail at full speed for Lebanese shores. The landing forces of the American command in the Mediterranean area are being hastily increased and preparations are being made for landing American units of Marines on the Lebanese coast. According to statements by representatives of the U.S. State Department, American arms are being sent to Lebanon to massacre the Arab civilian

[1] *Soviet News*, 19 May 1958.

population in accordance with the tried and tested methods of the colonialists.

Press reports and statements by responsible officials make it clear that all this is being done under the false pretext that the present mass demonstrations of the Lebanese population against foreign interference in the country's affairs and in defence of its independence and its constitution, have been inspired by the United Arab Republic.

All these are well-known methods of the colonialists, who have repeatedly strangled the freedom and independence of small countries merely because those countries have refused to submit to the yoke of foreign oppression. In the past such methods were used to unleash colonial robber wars. Today they are being used to impose on some of the small countries systems which are alien to the interests of their peoples, but advantageous to foreign capitalist monopolies and in line with the strategic plans of aggressive military blocs.

What is the reason for this intervention being prepared against a country whose government had given way to foreign pressure and declared its acceptance of the notorious 'Dulles-Eisenhower doctrine'?[1]

The answer is easily found if an examination is made of the real motives, rather than the false assertions circulated by official American propaganda in order to justify the inadmissible actions of the United States and some of the other western powers with regard to Lebanon. It is common knowledge that the 'Dulles-Eisenhower doctrine'—that clear-cut programme for colonial plunder—has been rejected by the Arab peoples, who rightly regard it as being foreign to their real national interests and sovereignty.

Every day makes it clear that the authors of that doctrine are suffering new defeats in their attempts to stifle the national liberation movement of the peoples of the East and to retard the irresistible process of the peoples' complete liberation from the hated colonial domination.

Judging by all this, attempts are being made to revive this moribund doctrine, to 'give it a shot in the arm.' As for the choice of means to which the colonialists—both old and new—are resorting in order to attain this end, well, they have no little experience in such matters. But there is one thing they obviously do not take into account. They do not reckon with the fact that the time has passed when the old imperialist slogan: 'Divide and conquer'—a slogan which was for many centuries the watchword of colonialists—could be successfully used.

The peoples who have secured their political independence want to use their riches at their own discretion and to pursue an independent policy in keeping with their national interests without referring back to London or Washington.

[1] See *Documents* for 1957, pp. 233–40.

In short, the peoples of the East want to live as the complete masters of their own homes, in peace and friendship with all peoples, and not in the way the organisers of N.A.T.O., S.E.A.T.O. and the Baghdad Pact—bound up as they are in their politics with the 'cold war,' the arms race and unrestrained expansion in relation to small countries and nations—would like them to live.

The actions of some western powers, and above all the United States, with regard to Lebanon, whose peaceful people want only one thing—to live in peace and friendship with their neighbours, the Arab states—is an expression of just this policy.

But it is precisely this that is in contradiction with the calculations of the colonialists, who want to bind Lebanon hand and foot, politically and economically.

The present developments in Lebanon permit us to draw another important conclusion.

It stands out that these events have started at a time when the dangerous hotbed of foreign interference in the internal affairs of Indonesia has not yet been eliminated, and when, before the eyes of the whole world, the imperialists are striving by means of blackmail and pressure, developing into open aggression, to suppress the resistance of the Indonesian people who are upholding their independence.

Now the imperialists have chosen Lebanon as a new objective of their intrigues and dangerous provocations, in an attempt to establish a colonialist regime in Lebanon and to deal a blow at the national liberation movement of all the Arab East.

Leading circles in the Soviet Union believe that the solution of questions relating to the Lebanese state is an inalienable right of the Lebanese people, and no other states have the right to interfere in these affairs. All attempts to use these or other internal developments in Lebanon for outside intervention create a dangerous situation in the Middle East and may have serious consequences, not only for the future of the Lebanese state and its independence, but also for peace in the Middle East.

Leading circles in the Soviet Union express confidence that no powers will resort to interference in the internal affairs of Lebanon, no matter in what form, or permit the creation of a dangerous hotbed of war in this area.

13. Statement by Dr. Malik at a press conference regarding the United Arab Republic's interference in the internal affairs of the Lebanon, Beirut, 13 May 1958[1]

Beirut: Foreign Minister Dr. Charles Malik stated at a press conference this evening that the United Arab Republic's interference in Lebanon's

[1] *S.W.B. Part IV*, 15 May 1958, pp. 11–12. Text of a dispatch broadcast by the Arab News Agency.

internal affairs was directly responsible for the present disturbances. He said that 24 persons, all foreigners, had been arrested in Beirut in the past two days and that many of them carried identity cards showing that they had been or still were in the Syrian army. A number of these persons were inquiring about the streets leading to the residences of Lebanese leaders.

Dr. Malik quoted other examples of foreign interference, including the arrest of the former Belgian Minister to Syria and the present Consul-General in Damascus. He said that the Consul-General had been arrested while smuggling a large quantity of weapons and ammunition into the Lebanon. The Belgian Consul-General, whose name was given as Louis De San, was also carrying papers containing instructions to unknown persons with the purpose of carrying out murder and other terrorist activities.

The Lebanese Foreign Minister went on to say that as an act of retaliation for the arrest of the Consul-General, about 500 armed persons crossed the Lebanese borders and attacked the customs post at Al-Masna, where De San had been arrested. They occupied part of the post, burned cars and killed six officials who were carrying out their duties. Dr. Malik added that the attackers did not withdraw from Lebanese territory until the Lebanese Army was summoned.

The Lebanese Foreign Minister said that the authorities had intercepted a boat which was carrying weapons, ammunition and 11 Palestinians from the Gaza strip. Several thousand Egyptian pounds were found on these persons. He added that 11 other Palestinians from the Gaza strip were arrested today near Tabarja, south of Juneh, after five Lebanese boats had pursued them for about two hours. Dr. Malik said that 11 other Palestinians from the Gaza strip had been arrested at Barja, near As-Sadiyat south of Beirut, near the President's private residence. He added that two or three boats had been seen near the Lebanese coast and that the Lebanese air force aircraft and coastguard vessels were keeping them under observation.

The Lebanese Foreign Minister said that the Press and broadcasts of the United Arab Republic had launched intensive campaigns against the Lebanon and its Government. After referring once again to the smuggling of weapons into the Lebanon, the Foreign Minister said that these were the latest incidents connected with the secret movement started years ago which aimed at exposing the Lebanon to destruction and changing its independent policy.

The Lebanese Foreign Minister added that a protest had been sent today to the Government of the United Arab Republic. He said: 'I am authorised to state that the Lebanese President and Government are firm and determined to defend the Lebanon's unity, freedom and independence, and that they will not give way or be lenient towards those who wish to destroy the Lebanon.'

Dr. Malik concluded by saying: 'While we have good intentions towards all, we call on our brethren in the United Arab Republic to refrain from interfering in our internal affairs. We call upon all those with good intentions to understand the circumstances in which the Lebanon (a few words indistinct).'

After reading his press statement, Dr. Malik replied to a number of questions from correspondents. In reply to a question as to whether the Lebanon had requested the withdrawal of the United Arab Republic's Ambassador to the Lebanon he said that he could not reply to that question. The Foreign Minister also declined to reply to a question on whether relations with the United Arab Republic would be severed.

In reply to a question about the identity of those who had attacked the Lebanese customs posts and whether they were Syrians, the Minister said that this matter was being investigated.

The Minister was also asked whether consultations with foreign States, and especially the States of the tripartite declaration, had been held in connection with preserving the prevailing situation in the Middle East. He replied that discussions with several foreign States took place, including the (?State) of the tripartite declaration.

The Foreign Minister was asked whether the question had been referred to the Security Council. To this he replied: 'We are studying the problem and we have not decided to refer it to the Security Council.' Dr. Malik declined to comment whether the Eisenhower doctrine could be applied in such cases. In conclusion the Lebanese Foreign Minister expressed his belief that Belgium had no connection with the arms smuggling carried out by its Consul-General.

14. Joint statement on the talks between Mr. Khrushchev and President Nasser, Moscow, 15 May 1958[1]

Gamal Abdel Nasser, President of the United Arab Republic, has made an official visit to the Soviet Union, at the invitation of the Presidium of the Supreme Soviet of the Union of Soviet Socialist Republics and the Soviet government.

During his stay in the U.S.S.R. friendly talks were held between leaders of both governments which took place in an atmosphere of mutual confidence and friendship. These discussions touched upon questions of

---

[1] *Soviet News*, 16 May 1958. President Nasser left Cairo for Moscow on 29 April in a TU104 placed at his disposal by the Soviet Government. This journey had been announced 2 years earlier, but had been repeatedly postponed. President Nasser was accompanied by Vice-Presidents Baghdadi and Hourani, Dr. Fawzi, Minister for Foreign Affairs, other Ministers, and journalists.

common interest to the two countries and on a number of international problems and events which are now in the centre of world public attention.

The Soviet Union was represented in these discussions by K. E. Voroshilov, President of the Presidium of the Supreme Soviet of the U.S.S.R.; N. S. Khrushchov, Chairman of the Council of Ministers of the U.S.S.R.; A. I. Mikoyan, First Vice-Chairman of the Council of Ministers of the U.S.S.R.; F. R. Kozlov, First Vice-Chairman of the Council of Ministers of the U.S.S.R.; A. I. Kirichenko, member of the Presidium of the Supreme Soviet of the U.S.S.R.; N. A. Mukhitdinov, chairman of the Foreign Affairs Commission of the Soviet of Nationalities of the U.S.S.R. Supreme Soviet; and A. A. Gromyko, Minister of Foreign Affairs of the U.S.S.R.

The United Arab Republic was represented in the discussions by President Gamal Abdel Nasser; Vice-President Abdel Latif Mahmud el Bogdadi; Vice-President Akram el Haurani; Minister of Education Kamaleddin Hussein; Minister of Foreign Affairs Dr. Mahmud Fawzi; Minister of State for Presidential Affairs Ali Sabri; Minister of Rural and Municipal Affairs for the Syrian region of the United Arab Republic Ahmed Abdel Karim; director of the General Information Service, Minister Salah Mohammed Nasr; and Ambassador of the United Arab Republic to the U.S.S.R. Mohammed A. el Kouni.

As a result of the talks both governments drew the following conclusions:

The two governments express their profound satisfaction with the development of the close and steadily expanding relations between the two countries; they will strive for the further development and consolidation of these relations, guided by the following principles:

Mutual respect for the sovereignty and territorial integrity of all states;

Non-intervention in any way in the domestic affairs of any state;

Solution of international problems exclusively by peaceful means and renunciation of the use of force against the sovereignty and independence of any state;

Rejection of the use of political or economic pressure;

Equality in relations between states and between nations.

Both governments adhere to the principle of peaceful co-existence among states irrespective of their social systems, considering that this principle is the cornerstone for the development of friendly relations between states and accords with the interests of world peace. They believe that an end to the 'cold war' accords with the vital interests of all peoples, will promote friendly and good-neighbourly relations between them and strengthen mutual confidence between states.

They denounce colonialism in all its manifestations and aspects and support the right of the peoples to self-determination and independence. The two governments denounce the existence of military bases of some countries on the territories of others. Such bases constitute a serious threat to world peace and infringe the independence of those states on whose territories they are situated; these bases must be abolished.

The two governments examined the question of the rights of the Palestinian Arabs and of their expulsion from their homes. They also examined the question of the violation of human rights and the threat to peace and security in that area which this entails. Both governments re-affirm their full support for the legitimate rights of the Palestinian Arabs.

Both governments denounce the colonial aggression against the Yemen and the attempts to intervene in the internal affairs of the Yemen. Both governments fully support the independence, sovereignty and territorial integrity of the Yemen.

Both governments deplore the savage war France is waging against the Algerian people and the crimes the French armed forces are committing against this heroic Arab country. They call the attention of world public opinion to the actions of the French authorities, which have forcibly ex-pelled hundreds of thousands of Algerians from the Algerian-Tunisian border area, actions which, in violation of human rights, have left people homeless, women and children among them, and have led to the de-struction of whole villages. Both governments fully support the right of the Algerian people to self-determination and independence. They insistently call for a settlement of the Algerian issue on this basis by peaceful means and they are confident that this will promote the interests of the two sides.

Both governments express their deep anxiety at the acts of interference by certain foreign states in the internal affairs of Indonesia. They regard this interference as a threat to world peace and security and as a breach of the United Nations Charter; they declare that this has to be stopped and that the independence and sovereignty of Indonesia must be respected.

Both governments believe in the importance of the United Nations and its role in the maintenance of peace and security and in the peaceful settlement of international problems. They consider that efforts should be made to strengthen this organisation by every means, to make it more effective in carrying out its tasks. Both governments equally believe that the Chinese People's Republic must be given its seat in the United Nations, in order to rectify the present abnormal situation and to further inter-national co-operation and decrease tension in the Far East and all over the world.

Both governments reaffirm their support for the principles enunciated at Bandung, which continue to unite the peoples of Asia and Africa and are attracting increasing world public attention, and which have been re-asserted by the Afro-Asian Solidarity Conference which met in Cairo in

1957 and expressed the hopes and aspirations of these two continents. Both governments likewise declare their support for the principles enunciated at the Conference of Independent African States in Accra in April 1958.[1]

Both governments express their deep anxiety at the arms race, which is one of the greatest perils threatening world peace and which may lead to a devastating nuclear war. Both governments hereby declare that the testing of atomic and hydrogen weapons must be ended by all states possessing such weapons, pending the necessary agreement or agreements on the final and unconditional prohibition of all types of nuclear weapons, up to and including the ending of the manufacture of these weapons, the withdrawal of nuclear weapons from national armaments and the destruction of the stocks of such weapons.

Both governments declare that atomic and hydrogen energy must be used for peaceful purposes only and that all countries should co-operate in this field in order to improve the living standards of the peoples, particularly those of the underdeveloped countries.

Both governments consider that the states must redouble their efforts towards the eventual conclusion of an agreement on a substantial reduction of national armed forces and armaments.

Both governments are of the opinion that the conclusion of non-aggression pacts between the states is one of the ways to reduce international tension, considering that the conclusion of such pacts would be consistent with the peaceful objectives and principles of the United Nations.

It is the firm conviction of both governments that the furtherance of economic and cultural relations between the states must be encouraged as a way to the establishment of mutual understanding between the peoples for the sake of reducing tension and as a way to preserve peace. Such relations should not be accompanied by any conditions or motives designed to allow one state to dominate another.

Both governments declare that the economic and cultural agreements concluded between the Soviet Union and the United Arab Republic are consistent with these requirements and are based on sound principles. They likewise express their complete satisfaction with the development of economic and cultural co-operation between their respective countries and with commercial exchanges between them. In this connection the government of the United Arab Republic has expressed gratitude for the Soviet Union's sizable contribution to the United Arab Republic's industrialisation programme.[2] Both governments reaffirm their determina-

---

[1] See below, Chapter IV, pp. 579–81.

[2] A Soviet-Egyptian Agreement on economic and technical co-operation was signed in Moscow on 29 January 1958. See *Soviet News*, 30 January 1958. It was reported that by this agreement the U.S.S.R. was to provide Egypt with technical assistance, equipment and machinery up to value of $178m. to be repaid over a 12-year period at 2·5 per cent interest. See *Sino-Soviet Economic*

tion to seek a further expansion of economic and cultural co-operation between the two countries to their common good.

Both governments consider that the artificial barriers to world trade must be removed.

Both governments express their complete satisfaction with the results of the present discussions. They regard the meeting of the leaders of the two states as a useful opportunity for an exchange of opinion to the common good of their peoples, and also as an important factor for the consolidation of their economic, cultural and social relations, contributing to universal peace.

Both governments regard as important meetings and contacts between government leaders, in the belief that mutual understanding and mutual trust will thus be strengthened and the chances of settling differences increased.

Both governments consider that the summoning of a summit conference with the participation of the great powers as well as·certain other states would be of paramount importance and must be expedited.

Both governments are deeply satisfied to note the close and developing co-operation between the two countries in every field of activity, which is to their common advantage and promotes universal peace and progress.

President Gamal Abdel Nasser of the United Arab Republic has invited K. E. Voroshilov, President of the Presidium of the Supreme Soviet of the U.S.S.R., N. S. Khrushchov, Chairman of the Council of Ministers of the U.S.S.R., and other leaders of the Soviet Union to visit the United Arab Republic. The invitation has been gratefully accepted.

N. Khrushchov
Chairman of the Council of Ministers of the Union
of Soviet Socialist Republics

Gamal Abdel Nasser
President of the United Arab Republic

15. Statement, in reply to questions in the House of Commons, by Mr. Lloyd regarding the situation in the Lebanon, 19 May 1958[1]

Mr. A. Henderson asked the Secretary of State for Foreign Affairs what discussions are taking place with the Government of the United States of America under the Tripartite Declaration in view of the recent incidents on the Lebanon-Syrian frontier;[2] and whether he will make a statement.

Offensive in Under-Developed Countries (Dept. of State U.S.G.P.O. Washington, 1958). For the general conditions of implementing the agreement see *Egyptian Economic and Political Review*, May 1958.

[1] H.C. Deb., vol. 588, coll. 871–2.　　　　[2] See *D.S.B.*, 5 June 1955, p. 886.

Mr. E. Fletcher asked the Secretary of State for Foreign Affairs what steps he is taking to protect British interests in the Lebanon.

Mr. Shinwell asked the Secretary of State for Foreign Affairs what official consultations have taken place with the United States of America with regard to the movement of North Atlantic Treaty Organisation forces in the vicinity of the Lebanon.

Viscount Hinchingbrooke asked the Secretary of State for Foreign Affairs what steps are being taken to meet a request from the Iraq Petroleum Company for the evacuation of British personnel from the Lebanon.

Mr. du Cann asked the Secretary of State for Foreign Affairs what consultations have taken place with the signatories to the Tripartite Declaration of 1950 with regard to its validity and effectiveness; and what alteration is proposed.

Mr. Zilliacus asked the Secretary of State for Foreign Affairs whether he will call the present situation in Lebanon to the attention of the Security Council as a circumstance tending to cause international friction.

Mr. Selwyn Lloyd: The responsibility for protecting British and all other foreign interests in the Lebanon is in the first place that of the Lebanese Government. From the information at my disposal, I believe that the Lebanese Government will be able to discharge their responsibility in this respect. Her Majesty's Government have received no request for evacuation from the Iraq Petroleum Company, with whom they are in touch, or from anyone else. Her Majesty's Government are however taking routine precautions.

Her Majesty's Government are in close touch with the United States Government, and with their other Allies, with regard to the situation. In reply to the Question of my honourable Friend the Member for Taunton,[1] Her Majesty's Government have recently consulted the other signatories of the Tripartite Declaration, and we are all agreed that it remains valid as a declaration of policy. The situation does not however at present seem to be the sort which the Tripartite Declaration was designed to meet.

The recent announcement of the Lebanese Foreign Minister indicates that subversion and incitement from outside the Lebanon is playing an important part in the current disorders.

On the question of referring the situation to the Security Council, I consider that that is primarily a matter for the Government of the Lebanon, but I am having discussions on this matter at the present time. There is much to be said for this course.

With regard to the movement of North Atlantic Treaty Organisation forces, as far as Her Majesty's Government are concerned, there are no plans. If other forces assigned or earmarked to the North Atlantic Treaty Organisation were to be moved, it would be necessary for the Government

[1] Mr. du Cann.

concerned to notify the North Atlantic Council. No such notification has been made of which I am aware.

Mr. Henderson: In view of the allegations which are contained in the Soviet statement with regard to the Middle East, will the right hon. and learned Gentleman make it quite clear that the Western Governments have no intention of intervening militarily in the situation in the Lebanon?

Mr. Lloyd: The situation is uncertain and obscure, and I cannot make a statement such as that for which the right hon. and learned Gentleman asks. What I will certainly say is that no action will be taken contrary to the Charter or the established rules of international law.

16. Speech by the Premier of the Arab Union, Nuri as-Said, regarding the Arab Union, Baghdad, 19 May 1958[1]

On this blessed day of the formation of the Arab Federal Government, I wish to extend a warm greeting to the memory of the great saviour and martyred hero, His Late Majesty King Husayn, who planned for us the road to unity, inspired us with national agreement, and taught us a great lesson in sacrifice and self-denial. We praise, magnify and exalt his hallowed soul.

Today, while we glorify the message of the saviour, we also remember his blessed and noble sons who bore arms under his command and who proceeded along the road indicated by him to realise the freedom, independence, and comprehensive unity of the Arab nation in its various countries and lands. We pray to God, the Almighty and Omnipotent, to reward them with the best reward for the good they did to us.

I do not forget to greet the heroes, both dead and alive, who bore either arms or pens and struggled under the command of Husayn and his sons for the accomplishment of the Arab nation's aims, and who continued the struggle with patience and forebearance to achieve this day on which we are working under the patronage and guidance of the exalted grandsons of the saviour.

The road of comprehensive unity is a long and thorny way, which cannot be covered except through continuous work, great patience, and sincerity. The unity of Jordan and Iraq which we celebrate today is only the start of the road. It is our duty, as well as the duty of the future generations, to continue the work no matter what the difficulties may be.

In our union we shall proceed slowly and wisely, in order to avoid faults and mistakes. We have begun with the unification of the armed forces so that we may make them a force and protective shield not only for the Arab Federal State alone, but also for the entire Arab nation, which will respond to the call of fraternity at any time it is asked. We have

[1] *S.W.B. Part IV*, 21 May 1958, pp. 7–8.

also unified the diplomatic service, so that we shall have one foreign policy and so that we may have an effective voice in the world in defence of the Arabs' rights and for the realisation of their national aspirations.

The policy of the Arab Federation provides for close co-operation with all the Arab countries and non-interference in the internal affairs of any country. We shall also strengthen our co-operation with the Islamic and friendly States, and shall seek more such friends so that they may support us in the international field for the accomplishment of our national aspirations, particularly as regards the just settlement of the Palestine question and the settlement of the Algerian problem in a way which will realise the aspirations of its people.

As for the other aspects, we shall unify them gradually.

Finally, we pray to God Almighty to support us, bless our unity, and guide us under the command of the two exalted Kings.

17. Extract from a press conference by Mr. Dulles regarding the application of the Eisenhower Doctrine to the situation in the Lebanon, 20 May 1958[1]

Q. Mr. Secretary, during the earlier phases of the Lebanese crisis there seemed to be some non-understanding as to whether the Eisenhower doctrine applied in this case. However, it seems that later we came to feel that we liked Lebanon, although the Eisenhower doctrine probably did not specifically apply, and therefore would aid her if requested. I wonder if you could clear up this confusion that some of us have, sir?

A. I suppose that by the Eisenhower doctrine you refer to the Middle East resolution that was adopted by the Congress.[2] That resolution contains several provisions. It is not just one thing. It authorizes the United States to assist economically and militarily nations which want such assistance in order to preserve their independence. It says that the independence and integrity of these nations of the Middle East is vital to world peace and the national interest of the United States. It says that, if they are attacked from a country under the control of international communism, then the President is authorized, upon request, to send forces to resist that attack.

Now we do not consider under the present state of affairs that there is likely to be an attack, an armed attack, from a country which we would consider under the control of international communism. That doesn't mean, however, that there is nothing that can be done. There is the provision of the Middle East resolution which says that the independence of these countries is vital to peace and the national interest of the United

---

[1] *D.S.B.*, 9 June 1958, p. 945. [2] See *Documents* for 1957, pp. 233–40.

States. That is certainly a mandate to do something if we think that our peace and vital interests are endangered from any quarter.

There is the basic right, and almost duty, at the request or with the consent of a government, to assist in the protection of American life and property. There is the program of military assistance which we render to many countries, including Lebanon, in terms of giving them equipment and certain measures of military training and techniques and helping them train technicians to use this equipment. So that there are a number of areas of possible action if the situation calls for it.

I would say that we are not anxious to have a situation which would be in any sense a pretext for introducing American forces into the area. We hope and believe that that will not be called for, and the situation, to date, does not suggest that it would be called for.

18. Statement by President Chamoun at a press conference, Beirut, 21 May 1958[1]

The Lebanon is undergoing a difficult ordeal. It is a test of our maturity. It is a test which will determine if we are real men who can withstand pressure, no matter how strong it may be, and remain free. I can declare to you now that we shall withstand the pressure, no matter how strong it may be, and we shall remain free.

The issue at present is not the Government. The issue at present is not this person or that. It is not this high post or that in the country. The present issue is the issue of the existence of the Lebanon as a free country in the Near East in which Muslims and Christians live in peace and harmony—a country capable of determining its life and fate freely and independently.

We believe that a Near East country such as this is not only worth living for, but also worth dying for. This country is a country of freedom— freedom of thought, freedom of expression, freedom of conscience and freedom of economic activity. All our national institutions are based on and imbued with this spirit of freedom. We want to preserve these institutions as a heritage for our children. This is because we believe that unless life is free with the deepest and most responsible (masuliyah) sense of freedom, it is not worth living. Yet, if our opponents, whether internal or external, accomplish what they want of us, we shall lose this precious freedom, which is our most priceless heritage.

[1] *S.W.B. Part IV*, 23 May 1958, p. 10. President Chamoun's answers to questions were not reported. Dr. Malik told the Foreign Affairs Committee of the Lebanese Chamber of Deputies that a complaint had been sent to the Arab League on the evening of 20 May, and that the Government were preparing a similar one for the Security Council. The Lebanese Embassy in Cairo had been instructed to request an early meeting of the Arab League Council in the Sudan or Libya. Ibid., p. ii.

The United Arab Republic is still strongly interfering in our internal affairs, with the aim of effecting a radical change in our basic political policy. It seems that our love of freedom and insistence upon remaining a free people do not suit it. The United Arab Republic wants our national policy to be in accord with its policy, or parallel to it. This is a thing which we cannot do. This is because our basic course and friendships are deep, and we cannot change with ease.

Our political life and trends do not harm the United Arab Republic. This is all that the United Arab Republic can reasonably ask of us. However, we are determined not to be subservient to its policy or basic trend. In other words, we are determined to remain independent.

The facts of this strong interference which I mentioned are now being submitted to the judgment of world public opinion.

We fully realise that this battle is not ours alone. It is the battle of small people everywhere to preserve their freedom and security. It is the battle for true freedom—social freedom, personal freedom, freedom of thought and spiritual freedom in the Near East.

For this reason, we pass through these critical days knowing that the eyes of the Middle East—indeed, the eyes of the entire world—are upon us. We pray to God Almighty that there will be nothing in our actions or statements which will make us unworthy of associating with free men.

If the Lebanon wins—and we are certain that it will—and if our basic freedoms weather this ordeal—and we are certain that this will be the case —then not only will our children bless our memory, but the sons of those who are trying to destroy us will do likewise. Perhaps it is the wish of Providence that we should wage this battle on their behalf, since they are yet unable to enter it. Thus on doomsday we will be judged as having replaced evil with good. If it is possible to replace evil with good, then it will be the greatest reward to the Lebanese people for their present ordeal.

19. Letter from the permanent representative of the Lebanon to the United Nations, Mr. Azkoul, to the President of the Security Council, 22 May 1958[1]

Upon instructions from my Government, I have the honour to request you, in your capacity as President of the Security Council, to call an urgent meeting of the Council to consider the following question:

---

[1] S.C.O.R., Supplement for April, May, and June 1958, Doc. S/4007. The Security Council included the Lebanese complaint on its agenda, but postponed further consideration of the item, until 3 June, as the League of Arab States was to consider the matter on 31 May. After a further postponement, to allow the Arab League to complete its consideration of the matter, the Security Council began its discussions on 6 June 1958.

'Complaint by Lebanon in respect of a situation arising from the intervention of the United Arab Republic in the internal affairs of Lebanon, the continuance of which is likely to endanger the maintenance of international peace and security.'

The said intervention consists, *inter alia*, of the following acts: the infiltration of armed bands from Syria into Lebanon, the destruction of Lebanese life and property by such bands, the participation of United Arab Republic nationals in acts of terrorism and rebellion against the established authorities in Lebanon, the supply of arms from Syria to individuals and bands in Lebanon rebelling against the established authorities, and the waging of a violent radio and press campaign in the United Arab Republic calling for strikes, demonstrations and the overthrow of the established authorities in Lebanon, and through other provocative acts.[1]

KARIM AZKOUL

20. Letter from the Minister of Foreign Affairs of the U.A.R. to the Secretary-General of the United Nations, transmitting the text of Heads of Agreement in connection with the compensation of Suez stockholders, 29 May 1958[2]

With reference to my letter to you on 24 April 1957, relating to the Declaration on the Suez Canal and the arrangements for its operation,[3] I have the honour, with particular reference to paragraph 8 of that Declaration, to enclose the text of Heads of Agreement in connexion with the compensation of the Suez stockholders, which was signed on 29 April 1958 in Rome by the representatives of the United Arab Republic and of the Suez stockholders.

It is with pleasure and gratitude that I avail myself of this opportunity to recall Your Excellency's, the Secretariat's and the International Bank's co-operation in this connexion.

MAHMOUD FAWZI

Minister of Foreign Affairs of the United Arab Republic

[1] For Dr. Malik's statement in the Security Council on 6 June 1958 amplifying the Lebanese complaint, see S.C.O.R., Thirteenth Year, 823rd meeting, paras. 7–73. Mr. Loufti, representative of the U.A.R. to the U.N. refuted the Lebanese allegation in his speech of 6 June, see ibid., paras. 74–125.

[2] S.C.O.R., Thirteenth year, Supplement for April, May, and June 1958, Doc. S/4014. An Extraordinary Meeting of the shareholders of the Suez Canal Company was held on 4 July 1958 in Paris, in the course of which these proposals were accepted. The text was signed at Geneva on 13 July 1958, after a delay over the interpretation of the exchange rate in Article 6 of the Agreement, see *The Times*, 14 July 1958.

[3] See *Documents* for 1957, pp. 222–6.

HEADS OF AGREEMENT

The representative of the Government of the United Arab Republic as successor to the Government of Egypt, and the representatives of the Suez stockholders, namely, the shareholders, the holders of founder shares, and the holders of the Parts Civiles (Société civile pour le recouvrement des 15 pour 100 des produits nets de la Compagnie universelle du canal maritime de Suez attribués au Gouvernement égyptien), hereinafter referred to as 'the stockholders', have agreed upon the following Heads of Agreement:

1. As a full and final settlement of the compensation due to shareholders and holders of founders shares as a consequence of the nationalization law No. 285 of 1956, and in full settlement of claims of the holders of the Parts Civiles, the Government of the United Arab Republic will make a payment equivalent to £E28.3 million (twenty-eight million and three hundred thousand Egyptian pounds) and will leave all the external assets to the stockholders.

2. In consideration of the above, the stockholders will accept responsibility for all liabilities outside Egypt as of 26 July 1956, including liability for the service of the outstanding debentures (principal and interest) and for pensions in accordance with paragraph 4 (*b*) below.

3. The Government of the United Arab Republic continues to assume responsibility for all liabilities within Egypt as of 26 July 1956, including liability for pensions in accordance with paragraph 4 (*a*) below.

4. (*a*) The Government of the United Arab Republic will assume liability for pensions as follows:

(i) Pensions already granted as of 26 July 1956 and being paid by Egypt to pensioners resident in Egypt on the date of signature of the present Heads of Agreement;

(ii) Pensions accruing to staff who were employed in the service on 26 July 1956 and who are still in the service of the Suez Canal Authority, or who, having remained in the Authority's service, retired on pension after that date in accordance with the regular pensions regulations.

(*b*) The stockholders will assume liability for all pensions other than those specified in (*a*) above.

(*c*) Each party to these Heads of Agreement will afford facilities for the preparation of lists of individual pensioners falling within the various categories mentioned in the present paragraph 4 in order that the liability for payment of pensions to each individual may be properly determined.

(*d*) The stockholders will pay to the Government of the United Arab Republic the capital value of the pensions payable to persons who, having remained in the Authority's service after 26 July 1956, retired on pension after that date in accordance with the regular pensions regulations, but ceased to reside in Egypt prior to the date of the signature of these Heads of Agreement, and who, at the date of signature of these Heads of Agreement, do not receive their pension from the stockholders.

(e) Liability for pensions after the date of signature of these Heads of Agreement will not be affected by any subsequent change of residence by a pensioner.

5. The payment specified in paragraph 1 will be made as follows:

(a) An initial payment of £E5.3 million (five million and three hundred thousand Egyptian pounds), through the retention by the stockholders of the transit tolls collected in Paris and in London since 26 July 1956.

(b) The balance in instalments, as follows (in millions of Egyptian pounds):

1 January 1959	4 (four)
1 January 1960	4 (four)
1 January 1961	4 (four)
1 January 1962	4 (four)
1 January 1963	4 (four)
1 January 1964	3 (three)

6. The instalments specified in paragraph 5 (b) above will be free of interest and will be payable in pounds sterling in London or in French francs in Paris, calculated at the fixed rate of US$2.8715576 to £E1. Not less than 40 per cent of each instalment shall be payable in pounds sterling.

7. (a) If the Government of the United Kingdom provides a special release from Egypt's No. 2 sterling account for the specific purpose of making advance payments on the instalments specified in paragraph 5 (b), amounts so released will be paid over forthwith by the Government of the United Arab Republic for application to the payment in advance of the two next maturing instalments specified in paragraph 5 (b).

(b) In the event of a release by the Government of the United Kingdom of the total of Egypt's No. 2 sterling account, the Government of the United Arab Republic will pay over forthwith an appropriate amount of the funds so released for application to the payment in advance of the two next maturing instalments specified in paragraph 5 (b).

(c) If either of the releases under (a) or (b) above takes place before the effective date of the final agreement referred to in paragraph 9 below, the appropriate amounts will be paid over forthwith on the effective date.

8. The conclusion and implementation of the final agreement referred to in paragraph 9 below will be done in such a way that the rights and liabilities attributed to the stockholders under the present Heads of Agreement are effectively exercised and assumed by an entity acceptable to both parties as representing regularly all the stockholders and duly

qualified to give full and final discharge to the Government of the United Arab Republic.

9. In view of the fact that the present Heads of Agreement have been negotiated under the good offices of the International Bank for Reconstruction and Development, the Bank having accepted the capacity of the signatories for the purposes of concluding the present Heads of Agreement, the parties hereby request the Bank to continue its good offices until the conclusion and documentation of a final agreement implementing these Heads of Agreement and to act as fiscal agent for the purpose of receiving and paying out the monies provided for in paragraphs 4 (*d*), 5 (*b*) and 7 above.

Done in triplicate at Rome on 29 April 1958 in the presence of a Vice-President of the International Bank for Reconstruction and Development, one copy to be retained by the Government of the United Arab Republic, one copy to be retained by the representatives of the Suez stockholders, and one copy to be deposited in the archives of the Bank.

On behalf of the Government of the United Arab Republic:

ABDEL GALIL EL EMARY

On behalf of the Suez stockholders:

J. GEORGES-PICOT

Witnessed by:

W. A. B. ILLIF
Vice-President
International Bank for Reconstruction and Development

21. Resolution adopted by the Security Council regarding the Lebanon, 11 June 1958[1]

THE SECURITY COUNCIL,

Having heard the charges of the representative of Lebanon concerning interference by the United Arab Republic in the internal affairs of Lebanon and the reply of the representative of the United Arab Republic,

1. *Decides* to dispatch urgently an observation group to proceed to Lebanon so as to ensure that there is no illegal infiltration of personnel or supply of arms or other matériel across the Lebanese borders;

2. *Authorizes* the Secretary-General to take the necessary steps to that end;

3. *Requests* the observation group to keep the Security Council currently informed through the Secretary-General.

---

[1] S.C.O.R., Supplement for April, May, and June 1958, Doc. S/4023. The Swedish draft resolution was adopted by 10 votes in favour, with one abstention (U.S.S.R.).

22. First report by the Secretary-General, Mr. Hammarskjold, on the implementation of the Security Council resolution of 11 June 1958, 16 June 1958[1]

1. The Security Council, in its resolution of 11 June 1958 concerning the complaint by Lebanon, requests the Observation Group authorized by that resolution 'to keep the Security Council currently informed through the Secretary-General'. The Observation Group, two of whose members have not yet arrived in Lebanon, will hold its first meeting in Beirut this week, probably on 19 June. As no information may be expected from the group prior to that date, this report is submitted as an interim measure, to inform the Security Council of the steps that have been taken to date by the Secretary-General, under the authority given to him, toward implementing its resolution.

2. The three members of the Observation Group have been appointed. They are: Mr. Galo Plaza of Ecuador, Mr. Rajeshwar Dayal of India and Major-General Odd Bull of Norway. The Observation Group will constitute itself and determine its own procedures. Military officers in the capacity of observers are assisting the Group. Major-General Bull has been designated as 'executive member of the Observation Group, in charge of military observers'. Major-General Bull arrived in Beirut early on the morning of the fifteenth, Mr. Galo Plaza is scheduled to arrive on the seventeenth and Mr. Dayal is expected on the same day.

3. On 11 June, I appointed Mr. David Blickenstaff as Secretary of the Observation Group, and Mr. Shiv K. Shastri as Assistant Secretary. Mr. Blickenstaff arrived in Beirut on 12 June and Mr. Shastri on 14 June. In the days immediately following, the operation was provided with the secretariat staff required. The United Nations Relief and Works Agency for Palestine Refugees in the Near East, from the beginning, on an emergency and temporary basis, has readily afforded all necessary administrative assistance and other co-operation. This has in no way involved an association of UNRWA with the operation. The headquarters of the Group was established in a Beirut hotel, close to its telecommunications facilities, where all of the staff members, including the observers, are housed.

4. On 11 June, I requested the Chief of Staff of the United Nations Truce Supervision Organization in Palestine, Major-General von Horn, to afford temporary assistance toward the execution of the Security Council's action by detaching ten United Nations military observers from Truce Supervision Organization duty to the Observation Group operation in Lebanon, five of whom were to arrive on the twelfth and another five

[1] S.C.O.R., Thirteenth Year, Supplement for April, May, and June 1958, Doc. S/4029.

not later than the fourteenth, under the command of an officer of sufficient rank. The first five military observers arrived in Beirut on the afternoon of the twelfth and a second group of five arrived there on the afternoon of the thirteenth. They were under the command of Lieutenant-Colonel W. M. Brown. On 14 June, the Chief of Staff in Jerusalem agreed to provide another five United Nations military observers.

5. The United Nations observers, in vehicles painted white with United Nations insignia, began active reconnaissance on the morning of 13 June in Beirut and its environs. Officials of the Group in Beirut, from the beginning, requested of the Lebanese authorities that the United Nations observer teams be accorded complete freedom of movement throughout government-held areas. Beirut Headquarters informs us that in a few initial trips 'of uncertain and dangerous nature', pilot jeeps manned by Lebanese troops have been used to check roads half an hour in advance of the United Nations teams and half an hour behind them. The observer teams have in each subsequent instance proceeded without pilot vehicles. We are also advised that the initial purpose of the patrols and road reconnaissances was to have United Nations observers and vehicles appear in as many areas as possible as soon as possible. In consequence, the observer teams have covered most main road areas in government-held regions, and have reached and entered areas not held by government forces. The observer teams are now working according to a schedule, and the plan being followed is to have them probe further each day in the direction of the frontier. Their observation task in connexion with any 'illegal infiltration of personnel or supply of arms or other *matériel* across the Lebanese borders' is greatly complicated by the fact that, as reported by the Observation Group headquarters in Beirut, only a small part of the total frontier appears to be controlled by government forces. The observer teams are composed of two observers, each with a radio-equipped vehicle, and one radio officer with a communication jeep. The three members of the team in their vehicles operate in a convoy at safe intervals and keep in constant communication with each other.

6. As of 15 June, the observer teams had proceeded as far as Tripoli, Baalbek, the Syrian border on the main Beirut-Damascus road, Marjayoun and Rashaya, some places having been visited several times and some twice daily. The immediate aim, we are informed, is to establish field stations: one to be at Tripoli, for the northern border areas, in the expectation that freedom of movement will be obtained in the area not under the control of government forces; one in the Baalbek area, and one at Marjayoun. From each of these places the observers are attempting to proceed into the frontier areas. In the initial and unavoidably hazardous stage, it has been of great value to have the services of the experienced observers of the Truce Supervision Organization. It is reported that so

far the United Nations observers have generally met with a good reception, particularly in Beirut.

7. Communication and transportation for the immediate needs are adequate but will have to be considerably expanded. The operation thus far has received from the Truce Supervision Organization fourteen jeeps, thirteen of which are radio-equipped, and a military observer-base radio system, which has been in operation since 13 June. For communications beyond Lebanon, Truce Supervision Organization radio facilities in Beirut are employed.

8. On the basis of a careful assessment of needs by the members of the operation now in Beirut, and in view of the planned method of operation of the observers, as described above, the number of military observers is being increased to one hundred, and an urgent request has been made of fourteen Governments to provide officers for the purpose.

9. Immediately upon arrival in Beirut, the United Nations representatives in the operation, both civilian and military, established contact with the appropriate Lebanese authorities with a view to facilitating its work. The Lebanese Government has designated a minister to be in charge of relations between the Government and the Observation Group, and has set up a five-man commission to assist in this purpose, as indicated in the letter of 15 June from the Prime Minister of Lebanon to Major-General Bull (annex I).

10. The status of the United Nations Observation Group in Lebanon, its privileges and immunities, etc., have been defined in a letter of 13 June from the Secretary-General of the United Nations to the Foreign Minister of Lebanon (annex II).

11. Members of the operation have indicated from Beirut the need for a small number of light aircraft of reconnaissance type, together with helicopters. Steps have been taken to meet this need.

12. In view of the urgency of the situation in Lebanon, I considered that it would involve an unwarranted loss of time to request the three members of the Observation Group to assemble in New York prior to their arrival in Lebanon. For only one of them was it convenient to visit United Nations Headquarters en route. The other two were to proceed directly to Beirut. In view of all the circumstances and the character of the task of the Observation Group, I have decided that I should give assistance to the Group by being present when the three members assemble in Beirut and by attending the Group's first meetings there.

Annex I

*Letter dated 15 June 1958 from the Prime Minister of Lebanon
to Major General Odd Bull*

I have the honour to inform you that the Lebanese Government, at a meeting held on 12 June 1958, has taken a decision nominating His

Excellency Dr. Albert Moukheiber, Minister of Health, as Minister in charge of relations between the Government of Lebanon and the United Nations Observation Group.

A Commission has also been formed to assist Dr. Moukheiber in the fulfillment of this mission, composed of: Emir Farid Chehab, Director General of the Sûreté générale, Edward Chorra, Director of International Relations in the Ministry of Foreign Affairs, Captain François Ginadrh, Representative of the Lebanese Army Headquarters, Mr. Raja Hamady, representative of the Ministry of Finance.

The mission of this Commission is to take all necessary measures to facilitate the task of the United Nations Observation Group, to supply said Group with all information coming to the knowledge of the Lebanese Government about the infiltration of arms and armed men and other material from across the Lebanese border, and to assure the contact between the various sections of the Lebanese administration and your Group.

The office of this Commission will be in the Ministry of Foreign Affairs. I would be very grateful if you would channel all communications with the various departments of the Lebanese Government through this Commission which stands ready at all times to answer your requests and to facilitate your work.

Annex II

Letter dated 13 June 1958 from the Secretary-General to the Foreign Minister of Lebanon concerning the status of the United Nations Observation Group in Lebanon

Sir, I have the honour to refer to the resolution of 11 June 1958, by which the United Nations Security Council decided to dispatch urgently an 'observation group to proceed to Lebanon so as to ensure that there is no illegal infiltration of personnel or supply of arms or other material across the Lebanese borders', and authorized the Secretary-General to take the necessary steps to that end.

In view of the special importance and difficult nature of the functions which this Observation Group will perform, I would propose that, with the operation as now envisaged, your Government might agree to extend to the Observation Group consisting of three senior members, the United Nations military observers and members of the United Nations Secretariat—over and above the status which they enjoy under the Convention on the Privileges and Immunities of the United Nations—the privileges and immunities, exemptions and facilities which are enjoyed by diplomatic envoys in accordance with international law. The privileges and immunities necessary for the fulfilment of the functions of the Observation Group also include freedom of entry, without delay or hindrance, of property, equipment and spare parts; freedom of movement of personnel, equipment and transport; the use of United Nations vehicle registration plates; the right to fly the United Nations flag on premises, observation posts and vehicles; and the right of unrestricted communication by radio, both within the area of operations and to connect with the United Nations radio network, as well as by telephone, telegraph or other means.

It is my understanding that the Lebanese Government will provide at its own expense, in agreement with the representative of the Secretariat, all such premises as may be necessary for the accommodation and fulfilment of the functions of the Observation Group, including office space and areas for observation posts and field centres. All such premises shall be inviolable and subject to the exclusive control and authority of the Observation Group. I likewise understand that your Government will, in consultation with the Observation Group, provide for necessary means of transportation and communication.

If these proposals meet with your approval, I should like to suggest that this letter and your reply should constitute an agreement between the United Nations and Lebanon, to take effect from the date of the arrival of the first members of the Observation Group in Lebanon.

Accept, Sir, the assurances of my highest consideration.

DAG HAMMARSKJOLD

23. Second report by Mr. Hammarskjold on the implementation of the Security Council resolution of 11 June 1958, 28 June 1958[1]

1. This progress report on the implementation of the resolution of the Security Council of 11 June 1958, is further to my first such report of 16 June. It is submitted by the Secretary-General, but is based on information received from the Beirut headquarters of the United Nations Observation Group in Lebanon.[2] The Observation Group itself has in preparation a first report on findings, in discharge of its responsibilities under the Security Council resolution, and this may be expected before long.[3]

[1] S.C.O.R., Thirteenth Year, Supplement for April, May, and June 1958, Doc. S/4038 (incorporating S/4038/Corr. 1).

[2] Known as UNOGIL.

[3] UNOGIL submitted its first report to the Security Council, on 3 July, S.C.O.R., Supplement for July, August and September 1958, Doc. S/4040 and Corr. 1, and Add. 1. The report covered problems of observation methods adopted, and observations carried out by the Group. It was noted that the areas of primary concern to the Group were those where the problems of access were the greatest. Details were given on the establishment of a system of permanent observation posts and regular patrols. Finally the report said that the patrols had reported substantial movements of armed troops within the country and concentrations at various places. It had not been possible to establish where the arms had been acquired from, or whether any of the armed men had infiltrated from outside; there was little doubt, however, that the vast majority of the armed men were Lebanese. On 8 July 1958, the Lebanese representative submitted his Government's comments by letter on UNOGIL's first report: the positive conclusions drawn in the

2. With the arrival of Mr. Rajeshwar Dayal in Beirut on 18 June, the organization of the Observation Group was completed. On that date, the Group met informally and was briefed by its secretary on developments since the arrival on 12 June in Beirut of the first secretariat members and military observers. At the same time, attention was also given to administrative arrangements, and the activities of the military observers.

3. On 19 June, the Group held a further informal meeting, with the Secretary-General presiding. Later the same day, it held its first formal meeting and organized its work. At this meeting, Mr. Galo Plaza was designated Chairman of the Group. The first meetings of the Group were devoted to an exchange of views on the methods and procedures which it would follow in carrying out its mandate with regard to illegal infiltration of personnel or supply of arms or other *matériel* across the Lebanese borders, under the resolution of the Security Council, and in keeping the Security Council 'currently informed through the Secretary-General'. The Secretary-General was in close consultation with the Group throughout his stay in Beirut.

4. As of 26 June, ninety-four officers from eleven countries were serving as military observers in Lebanon. They have established a regular patrolling system of areas accessible and, since the report of 16 June on the implementation of the resolution have advanced further into areas outside government control. Areas being regularly patrolled by the observer teams are the following: around Tripoli and south of that city; the coastal road from Nakoura to Damour, and roads branching off toward the interior; the Marjayoun area; the Chtaura area and northeast beyond Baalbek; the area north and east of Beirut and south of the city, except in the vicinity of Beit el Dine.

5. Observer outstations have been established in the following areas: Tripoli (with a sub-station at the Cedars), Chtaura, Zahle, Marjayoun, Saida, and at Saghbine south-east of Beirut. From these outstations, patrol activities are extended into the surrounding countryside. Outstations in several other places are now being established or are under consideration.

6. In visting areas outside government control, the observers have met local leaders and have discussed with them freedom of movement in the Bekaa area north of Baalbek, the Chouf area south of Beit el Dine, and the area north of Tripoli. It was reported from the headquarters of the Group on 25 June that for the time being further efforts at moving deeper into such areas were deferred at the following main points: the area north and north-east of Tripoli (where firing is in close vicinity and the roads are mined), the Beit el Dine area, and the north Bekaa area.

report were inconclusive or misleading or unwarranted, and that the information contained in the Report fully substantiated the Lebanese Government's charge that illegal infiltration of armed men and smuggling of arms was a reality. See S.C.O.R., Thirteenth Year, Supplement for July, August, and September 1958, Doc. S/4043.

7. The basic items of equipment for the observer teams are transport and communications. Arrangements have worked well for the delivery of jeeps and supporting transport at a rate compatible with the arrival in the area of the military observers. Thus, as of 26 June, there were seventy-four vehicles to ninety-four observers. A fully operating radio communication system has been installed for contact between group headquarters, observer outstations and jeeps circulating within the areas assigned for observation.

8. At the request of the Group, United Nations Headquarters has obtained two small helicopters. The helicopters arrived in Beirut on 23 June and, with Norwegian pilots, are now in operation. Four light observation planes have also been requested and will be on hand soon. These, as the helicopters, will be used solely for aerial observation in pursuance of the Group's task under the Security Council resolution. The Governments of neighbouring countries have been notified by the Secretary-General of these observation flights over Lebanese territory in the proximity of the borders.

9. Arrangements have been made by the Group for receiving from the ministry in charge of relations between the Government of Lebanon and the Group, written communications on cases which the Lebanese Government desires to bring to the attention of the Group. The Group in turn submits these to independent study through its own means and in the light of supporting evidence provided. The Group has received information concerning prisoners, said to be Syrians, taken by Lebanese authorities. Such prisoners, when made available to the Group, are being interrogated by the Executive Member of the Group, Major-General Bull, with the assistance of qualified military observers, concerning matters covered by the Security Council resolution.

10. Since the date of the first report, additional personnel have been added to the secretariat of the Group and the basic staffing requirements for the secretariat and administrative services to meet the needs of an operation involving one hundred military observers are about to be completed. The headquarters of the Group continues to be located in the Biarritz Hotel in Beirut, although consideration is being given to the acquisition of new quarters in that city affording more adequate physical conditions.

24. Proclamation on the revolution in Iraq, Baghdad, 14 July 1958[1]

Noble Iraqi people, relying on God and the support of the loyal sons of the people and the national armed forces, we have begun to liberate the

[1] *S.W.B. Part IV*, 15 July 1958, pp. 5–6. The Proclamation was signed by the acting C.-in-C. of the national armed forces.

beloved homeland from the domination of the corrupt clique installed by imperialism to rule the people, trifle with their fate and serve imperialist interests and personal aims.

Brethren, the army which is from you and of you has risen to do as you wished it to do and has removed the tyrannical clique that flouted the rights of the people. Your duty is to support the army, its bullets, its bombs, and its rising against Rihab Palace and the palace of Nuri as-Sa'id. Know that victory can be achieved only by (word indistinct) and by preserving it from the plots of imperialism and its agents. We therefore appeal to you to inform the authorities of anyone concerned in doing harm or guilty of corruption or treason. We hope that you will be united from Sulaymaniyah to (?Rutbah) and from Baqah to (name indistinct). Iraq is united to destroy the corruptors and to get rid of their evil.

Citizens, while we admire your surging national spirit and glorious deeds, we call upon you to keep calm and quiet and to maintain order, unity and co-operation for the good and interest of the homeland. One homeland and one people.

People, we have sworn to sacrifice our blood and all that is precious to us for your sake. So be confident and rest assured that we shall continue to work for you. The affairs of the country must be entrusted to a government emanating from the people and working under its inspiration. This can only be achieved by the formation of a popular republic to uphold complete Iraqi unity, to bind itself with bonds of fraternity with Arab and Muslim countries, to work in accordance with the UN principles to honour all pledges and treaties in accordance with the interests of the homeland, and to act in compliance with the Bandung conference resolutions. This national government shall therefore be known from now on by the name of the Iraqi Republic.

In response to the desire of the people, we have provisionally entrusted the presidency to a Council of State enjoying the powers of the President of the Republic until such time as the people are asked in a plebiscite to elect a President.

We pray God to bring success to our work in the service of our beloved homeland. God hearkens and responds to our prayers.

B. LANDINGS IN THE LEBANON AND JORDAN

1. Statement by President Eisenhower announcing the dispatch of United States forces to the Lebanon on 14 July, 15 July 1958[1]

Yesterday morning, I received from President Chamoun of Lebanon an urgent plea that some United States forces be stationed in Lebanon to help maintain security and to evidence the concern of the United States for the integrity and independence of Lebanon. President Chamoun's appeal was made with the concurrence of all of the members of the Lebanese Cabinet.

President Chamoun made clear that he considered an immediate United States response imperative if Lebanon's independence, already menaced from without, were to be preserved in the face of the grave developments which occurred yesterday in Baghdad whereby the lawful government was violently overthrown and many of its members martyred.

In response to this appeal from the government of Lebanon, the United States has dispatched a contingent of United States forces to Lebanon to protect American lives and by their presence there to encourage the Lebanese government in defense of Lebanese sovereignty and integrity. These forces have not been sent as any act of war. They will demonstrate the concern of the United States for the independence and integrity of Lebanon, which we deem vital to the national interest and world peace. Our concern will also be shown by economic assistance. We shall act in accordance with these legitimate concerns.

The United States, this morning, will report its action to an emergency meeting of the United Nations Security Council.[2] As the United Nations charter recognizes, there is an inherent right of collective self-defense. In conformity with the spirit of the charter, the United States is reporting the measures taken by it to the Security Council of the United Nations, making clear that these measures will be terminated as soon as the Security Council has itself taken the measures necessary to maintain international peace and security.

The United States believes that the United Nations can and should take measures which are adequate to preserve the independence and integrity of Lebanon. It is apparent, however, that in the face of the tragic and

---

[1] *D.S.B.*, 4 August 1958, pp. 181–2. President Eisenhower sent a message to Congress on 15 July and also made a radio and television statement on the same evening. See ibid., pp. 182–6.

[2] The Security Council called an emergency meeting at the request of the United States, on 15 July. The debate continued until 22 July 1958.

shocking events that are occurring nearby, more will be required than the team of United Nations observers now in Lebanon. Therefore, the United States will support in the United Nations measures which seem to be adequate to meet the new situation and which will enable the United States forces promptly to be withdrawn.

Lebanon is a small peace-loving state with which the United States has traditionally had the most friendly relations. There are in Lebanon about 2,500 Americans and we cannot, consistently with our historic relations and with the principles of the United Nations, stand idly by when Lebanon appeals itself for evidence of our concern and when Lebanon may not be able to preserve internal order and to defend itself against indirect aggression.

2. Statement in the House of Commons by Mr. Lloyd regarding the situation in Iraq and the Lebanon, 15 July 1958[1]

The Secretary of State for Foreign Affairs: With your permission, Mr. Speaker, and that of the House, I wish to make a statement on Iraq and the Lebanon.

In my statement yesterday afternoon I promised to keep the House informed about the situation in Iraq.

The general situation in Bagdad and in Iraq as a whole is still obscure, but I have received today a message from Her Majesty's Ambassador. I regret to inform the House that it appears from this message that Colonel Graham, the Comptroller of the Household, has been killed and two other members of the Embassy staff injured. The relatives of these two members of the staff are being informed.

With these exceptions all British members of the staff of the Embassy, of the British Council, of the British Loan Personnel, Iraq, and of the Bagdad Pact Secretariat, are, as far as can be ascertained, safe and well.

The Embassy buildings in Bagdad have been looted and the residence of the Ambassador burned out. The buildings are now guarded by troops, with members of the British staff in occupation.

There is no report of any injury to members of the British community in Bagdad.

[1] H.C. Deb., vol. 591, coll. 1013–14. When Mr. Bevan asked for 'an assurance that no British troops will, in fact, be used and that they will not be sent either to Iraq or to the Lebanon until the House of Commons has had an opportunity of considering the whole situation' Mr. Lloyd replied that: 'On the use of British troops I have no more to say than I have already said. No British troops are being used in this operation.' The Opposition called for a debate on the situation in the Middle East for 16 July, as 'the day after tomorrow [i.e. 17 July] will be too late, especially in view of the fact that no assurance has been given that British troops will not be moved into action either in Iraq, the Lebanon or Jordan before the House has had an opportunity of debating the matter'. The debate took place on 16 July but as Mr. Ross (Member for Kilmarnock) pointed out after Mr. Macmillan's closing speech, the Prime Minister gave no 'indication whatsoever of the Government's policy towards Jordan'. Ibid., col. 1371.

The Iraq Petroleum Company has had news from Kirkuk that all is well, and operations are proceeding as usual. Basra, too, is quiet, and operations there continue.

There is no change in the situation at Habbaniya.

Her Majesty's Ambassador has requested assurances regarding the protection of British lives and property.

I am also arranging for the authorities at present in control in Bagdad to be informed that Her Majesty's Government protest vigorously against the destruction of Her Majesty's Embassy and the treatment of its staff, and hold them responsible for the safety of British lives and property.

There is still no reliable news of the whereabouts of King Feisal, the Crown Prince, and Nuri Said.

I wish now to refer to the Lebanon.

United States forces are landing at Beirut this afternoon at the request of the President of the Lebanon.

Mr. Ellis Smith: Shame.

Mr. Lloyd: The Security Council is also meeting this afternoon, at the request of the United States Government, to discuss the situation.

The President has issued a statement, which has just been published in the last few minutes, giving the reasons for the United States action.

Her Majesty's Government have been in close consultation with the United States Government throughout the present crisis. They were informed in advance of the United States Government's intentions. They believe that the United States action is necessary to preserve the independence and integrity of the Lebanon in this very uncertain situation. This action has Her Majesty's Government's full support.

Mr. Brockway: Shame.

Mr. Lloyd: British troops are not taking part in this operation. British forces in the area have, however, been alerted.

3. Statement by the Government of the Soviet Union regarding the events in the Middle East, 16 July 1958[1]

On July 15 the whole world learned with indignation of the armed intervention by the United States of America in Lebanon. Ships of the United States Sixth Fleet entered the port of Beirut and landed marines on the territory of Lebanon.

On the same day the White House—in the name of the President of the United States—issued a statement attempting somehow to justify this flagrant military intervention in Lebanon's internal affairs. The statement alleges that the United States has sent its troops to Lebanon to demonstrate

---

[1] *Soviet News*, 17 July 1958. Soviet and foreign correspondents were given the text of this statement at a press conference held in the Soviet Foreign Ministry.

United States concern for the integrity and independence of Lebanon, which, so it claims, are being threatened from without, and also to protect American citizens in that country.

The complete absence of any grounds for this contention is self-evident, for no one is threatening Lebanon's integrity and independence. Abundant evidence of this is provided, for example, by the statement of the United Nations Secretary-General, Mr. Hammarskjöld, and by the report of United Nations observers on the situation in Lebanon.[1] As for 'concern' for the safety of American citizens, one may be permitted to ask what standards of international law allow foreign powers to send their armed forces to the territories of other states for such purposes. There are no such standards in international law. It is common knowledge, however, that references to the need to protect their citizens have, from time immemorial, been a favourite device of all colonialists to justify gangster-like attacks on small countries.

The real reason for United States armed intervention in Lebanon is the desire of the oil monopolies of the United States and other western powers to retain their colonial hold on countries of the Middle East, and also the obvious bankruptcy of their policy in the Arab East and the collapse of the Baghdad Pact and of the notorious Dulles-Eisenhower doctrine.

This is borne out in a striking way by the latest events in Iraq, which the White House statement regards as a reason which speeded up armed intervention by the United States. However, the events in Iraq are fresh proof of the Arab peoples' unflinching determination to rid themselves of colonial dependence and to take their destiny into their own hands.

It is well known that on the night of July 13 to 14, the monarchy in Iraq was overthrown by the army, supported by the people; a republic was proclaimed and a government of the Republic of Iraq was set up.[2]

The first acts of this government, led by General Abdel Kerim Kassem, in the sphere of foreign policy were statements expressing full support for the principles of the Bandung Conference, withdrawal from the aggressive military Baghdad Pact, and recognition of the United Arab Republic.

The government of the Republic of Iraq declared that it would 'act in accordance with the principles of the United Nations,' would 'follow an Arab policy and strictly abide by the decisions of the Bandung Conference,' and that it was prepared 'to honour commitments and treaties springing from the interests of the motherland.' It also announced that it guaranteed the security of foreign nationals and their property.

These actions are evidence of the government's intention to defend the country's national independence and to strive, together with the other

[1] See fn. 3 on p. 283, above.
[2] The Soviet Government recognized the new republic of Iraq on 16 July, *Soviet News*, 17 July 1958.

freedom-loving Arab peoples, to overcome the grievous aftermath of colonialism, to develop the national economy and to raise the living standards of the people.

It is natural that the policy statements of the government of the Republic of Iraq, being in accordance as they are with the desires of the Iraqi and all other Arab peoples, should meet with unanimous support, both in Arab countries and in all peaceloving countries which regard the establishment of a republic as an entirely internal affair of the people of Iraq.

This turn in events in the Middle East obviously does not suit the colonial powers, which received the news of the establishment of the Republic of Iraq with undisguised hostility. Feverish activity began immediately in Washington, London and Ankara.

The existence of plans for large-scale intervention by the colonial powers in the internal affairs of countries of the Arab East is also borne out by the statement by the British Foreign Secretary, Mr. Selwyn Lloyd, that the British government had been informed in advance of the United States government's intention to land its troops in Lebanon, that the British government fully supported this action of the United States and that the British armed forces in the area were being kept ready.[1]

In order to provide a pretext for armed intervention in the internal affairs of the Arab countries a statement by the Lebanese President Chamoun asking the governments of the United States, Britain and France to send troops to Lebanon, was inspired. It is well known, however, that the present events in Lebanon are a result of purely internal causes and that only interference by countries of the Baghdad Pact and the United States, seeking to preserve an anti-national régime at any cost, has led to civil war and to a worsening of the entire situation in the area.

It should be noted that the landing of American troops in Beirut is an act of armed intervention, not only against Lebanon, but also against all the freedom-loving Arab countries. No bones are made about this in, for instance, the aforementioned White House statement, which—certainly not by accident—links the dispatch of troops to Lebanon directly with the events in Iraq. This is also borne out by the fact that King Hussein of Jordan, obviously on advice from his patrons, has proclaimed himself the head of the now non-existent Iraqi-Jordanian federation in place of King Feisal, deposed by the Iraqi people, even though he had neither substantive nor formal grounds for this. The provocative nature of this step if self-evident, and the fact is being ignored that the government of the Republic of Iraq, supported by the whole of the people, has officially announced Iraq's withdrawal from the Iraqi-Jordanian federation.

Armed intervention by the United States in Lebanon shows clearly that

[1] See above, p. 289.

the imperialists have cast off their disguise and have begun open aggression against peaceloving Arab peoples. In this connection it becomes particularly clear why the government of the United States did not accept the Soviet government's proposal of February 11, 1957, concerning non-interference by the great powers in the internal affairs of the countries of the area.[1] The government of the United States refused to undertake commitments which would have ensured peace and eased the tension in that part of the world.

It wanted to keep its hands free for aggression in the area.

United States armed intervention in Lebanon creates a grave threat to peace and is fraught with far-reaching consequences. The peoples cannot remain unconcerned in face of this brazen imperialist aggression, this gross encroachment on the sovereignty and national independence of the Arab countries and this unceremonious violation of the principles of the United Nations.

The White House plea that American troops are being sent to Lebanon for purposes of self-defence and in the national interests of the United States is open mockery of these principles. Who does not know that the United States lies thousands of kilometres from Lebanon and that the people of Lebanon and other Arab countries can in no way threaten either the national interests or the security of the United States? As for Lebanon, it is precisely American armed intervention that is the main threat to the security of this small Arab country.

Having taken to the road of flagrant violation of the United Nations Charter, the government of the United States is now attempting to confront the Security Council and the whole of the United Nations with a *fait accompli* and to bring pressure to bear on the United Nations to make it approve the unilateral aggressive actions of the U.S.A.

The Soviet government considers that the situation in the Middle East —a situation created by open aggression on the part of the United States, supported by other colonial powers—is an alarming one and is dangerous to world peace. In these circumstances, the Security Council and the United Nations General Assembly should take urgent and vigorous measures to curb aggression and to protect the national independence of Arab states which have fallen victim to an unprovoked attack.

The Soviet government urges the government of the United States to cease its armed intervention in the internal affairs of Arab countries and to withdraw its troops from Lebanon immediately.[2]

The Soviet government declares that the Soviet Union cannot remain

[1] See *Documents* for 1957, pp. 69–70.

[2] In the course of the debate in the Security Council the representative of the U.S.S.R. submitted a draft resolution by which the Council would, among other things, call upon the United States 'to cease armed intervention in the domestic affairs of the Arab States and to remove its troops from the territory of Lebanon immediately'.

indifferent to events creating a grave menace in an area abutting on its frontiers, and reserves the right to take the necessary measures dictated by the interests of peace and security.

4. Statement by the Government of the People's Republic of China demanding the withdrawal of United States forces from the Lebanon, 16 July 1958[1]

On July 15, the United States, in flagrant violation of the fundamental principles of the United Nations Charter, landed its armed forces in the Lebanon and launched armed intervention in the Lebanon's internal affairs under the pretext of 'protecting American lives' and 'defending Lebanese sovereignty.' This is an extremely grave warlike adventure on the part of the United States to suppress the national independence movements of the Arab peoples and to create world tension. The Government of the People's Republic of China and the Chinese people strongly condemn and protest against this United States act of aggression.

The United States and other Western countries craved for long to carry out armed intervention against the Lebanon, but failed to do so because of the resolute opposition of the Arab peoples and the peace-loving countries and people throughout the world. Now, with colonial rule in the Middle East shaken by the great victory of the national independence movement in Iraq, the United States Government, in a sudden rage and panic, has brazenly launched armed intervention against the Lebanon in defiance of universal censure and also attempts to invade Jordan to menace the Republic of Iraq. This act of aggression on the part of the United States is not only an outrageous provocation against the peoples of the Arab states, but also constitutes a grave threat to the peace of western Asia and the world. The pretexts of 'protecting American lives' and 'defending Lebanese sovereignty' absolutely cannot cover up this naked act of aggression on the part of the United States. All peace-loving countries and peoples of the world must firmly demand the immediate withdrawal of United States forces from the Lebanon and stop the United States' war provocation.

The people of all countries have the right to choose their own governments, in which no intervention is allowed. The armed intervention against the Arab peoples carried out by the United States imperialists is doomed to failure.

In their struggle for independence and freedom, the peoples of the Lebanon, Iraq and other Arab countries by no means stand alone! Together with the peoples of the Asian and African countries and other peace-loving countries and peoples the world over, the 600 million Chinese

[1] *Peking Review*, 22 July 1958, p. 7.

people, will give all-out support to the Arab peoples' just struggle. Should the United States fail to withdraw its forces of aggression from the Lebanon at once, it will have to face the consequences of its action.

5. Statement on the resolution calling for foreign military aid, adopted at the extraordinary meeting of the Jordanian Parliament, 16 July, Amman, 17 July 1958[1]

His Exalted Majesty the King presided over an important extraordinary session held by the Jordanian Parliament at 20.00 hours on the evening of Wednesday 16th July 1958, in the presence of the Senators, Deputies, and all members of the Jordanian Cabinet, as well as the President and members of the Arab Union's Council in Jordan.

His Majesty opened the meeting with a full review of the events and plots which have afflicted the Arab States in general and Jordan and the Arab Union in particular. His Majesty then informed those present of the Government's decision, which was approved by His Majesty, demanding military aid from friendly Powers in accordance with Article 51 of the UN Charter. His Majesty explained the reasons that had led to the adoption of this decision.

After a number of Senators and Deputies had spoken in support of this wise step which provides Jordan with the means to strengthen itself, makes it able to preserve its unity and independence in the face of surrounding dangers, and helps it to continue to shoulder its huge responsibilities in defence of the great Arab homeland, Parliament unanimously adopted a resolution fully supporting the aforesaid Governmental decision and approving it and all measures taken by the Government in this respect.

6. Letter from the permanent representative of Jordan to the United Nations to the President of the Security Council, 17 July 1958[2]

Upon instructions from my Government, I have the honour to request you, in your capacity as President of the Security Council, to inscribe the following item on its agenda for urgent consideration:

[1] *S.W.B. Part IV*, 18 July 1958, p. 12. On 16 July King Hussein had appealed to Iraqis to 'nip the insurrection in the bud', and on 17 July in a broadcast to his own people, he stated that 'the past month has witnessed many convoys crossing the borders from Gaza and Syria, laden with arms and equipment in order to sow the seeds of sedition in this country', and that in view of the crisis, he and his Government would 'resort to the friendly countries and seek their actual military assistance in protecting our borders from our enemies, who surround us on all sides'. *S.W.B. Part IV*, 18 July 1958, pp. 9–12.

[2] S.C.O.R., Thirteenth Year, Supplement for July, August, and September 1958, pp. 37–38, Doc. S/4053. On 17 July the Security Council decided to consider the Lebanese and Jordanian complaints concurrently, and invited the Jordanian representative to participate in the debate.

'Complaint by the Hashemite Kingdom of Jordan of interference in its domestic affairs by the United Arab Republic'.[1]

BAHA UD-DIN TOUKAN

7. Joint communiqué on the Baghdad Pact talks, Ankara, 17 July 1958[2]

1. At the invitation of HE the President of Turkey, meetings were held in Ankara and Istanbul between 14th and 17th July with the participation of HM the Shahinshah of Iran and HE the President of Pakistan.

2. The three Heads of State considered the current situation in the Middle East and dwelt in particular on the events taking place in the Lebanon and Iraq. They noted with deep concern the latest manifestation of subversive activities, inspired from outside, in an allied country, resulting in the bloodthirsty murder of distinguished personalities whose valuable guidance in inter-allied discussions will always be remembered with gratitude.

3. In expressing their profound sorrow at the loss of their loyal and honourable friends, the Heads of State take this opportunity of expressing their most sincere condolences to the mourning families of their dead friends, and generally to the friendly nation. The Heads of State, who are determined to support in all possible ways the measures which are necessary to stop international banditry in this region, denounce this manifestation of savagery inspired from outside.

In this connection, the Heads of State declare that they welcome with satisfaction the initiative taken by the USA for upholding the integrity and the independence of free and peace-loving countries, and in particular the practical support given to the legally-constituted Government of the Lebanon. The Heads of State believe that this initiative will be extended to countries similarly threatened.

4. Being convinced that the recent events in the Middle East have proved, more than at any other time, the necessity of taking joint measures in a most practical and effective way, the Heads of State intend to strengthen their co-operation. They are sure that in their efforts in this respect they will enjoy the full support of other countries who are closely interested in the peace, security and stability of the Middle East.

---

[1] See S.C.O.R., Thirteenth Year, 831st meeting, paras. 18–26, for Mr. Toukan's speech amplifying Jordan's complaint against the U.A.R.

[2] S.W.B. Part IV, 19 July 1958, p. 15. For the text of a letter sent by the heads of the Governments of Turkey, Persia, and Pakistan to President Eisenhower welcoming United States intervention in the Lebanon, see D.S.B., 4 August 1958, p. 183. The other documents on the Baghdad Pact are included in Chapter IIIA.

8. Statement in the House of Commons by Mr. Macmillan regarding military assistance to Jordan, 17 July 1958[1]

The Prime Minister: With permission, Mr. Speaker, I will make a statement on the situation in Jordan.

Within a matter of minutes after the end of the debate yesterday I was given a telegram from Her Majesty's Representative in Jordan. This contained the first news that we had had that King Hussein and the Prime Minister of Jordan had made a request for the immediate despatch of British forces to Jordan.

In making this request, the King and the Prime Minister said that Jordan was faced with an imminent attempt by the United Arab Republic to create internal disorder and to overthrow the present régime, on the pattern of recent events in Iraq.

Mr. Ellis Smith: Are we expected to believe that?

The Prime Minister: They went on to say that Jordan's territorial integrity was threatened by the movement of Syrian forces towards her northern frontier and by the infiltration of arms across it. They had information that a *coup* organised by the United Arab Republic would be attempted today.

I asked the Cabinet to meet late last night to consider this request.

From our own sources we had received up to date intelligence which clearly showed that the apprehensions of the Jordan Government were well founded, and that an attempt was indeed being organised for today.

The Government accordingly decided to accede to the request, and British forces are, in fact, being sent by air to Jordan from Cyprus.

The purpose of this military assistance is to stabilise the situation in Jordan by helping the Jordanian Government to resist aggression and threats to the integrity and independence of their country.

Our troops will be under the orders of the local British commander who will act with the agreement of the King and Government of Jordan.

The Jordan Government have made a similar request for help to the United States Government, who are considering it urgently in the light of their other commitments in the area. Her Majesty's Government's decision was taken after full consultation with the United States Government, and our action has the full support and approval of the United States Government.

The decision of Her Majesty's Government is being reported to the United Nations, and we are making it clear to the United Nations that if arrangements can be made by the Security Council to protect the lawful Government of Jordan from the external threat, and so maintain inter-

[1] H.C. Deb., vol. 591, coll. 1438–9.

national peace and security, the action which we have taken will be brought to an end.

We have informed the other Commonwealth countries, and also the North Atlantic Treaty Organisation Council, of the action we have taken and the reasons which have led to the Government's decision.

9. Statement by the Government of the People's Republic of China demanding the withdrawal of United Kingdom forces from Jordan, Peking, 18 July 1958[1]

Following the United States' armed intervention in the Lebanon, the British Government, fabricating an absurd pretext, openly sent troops to Jordan on July 17 to suppress the people of Jordan; at the same time it concentrated its forces in the eastern Mediterranean and in the area of the Persian Gulf, in an attempt to invade the Republic of Iraq from several directions. These British moves have aggravated the tension in the world situation and brought with them a grave danger of spreading the war. This is flagrant aggression against the Arab peoples as a whole by the British Government in league with the U.S. Government, an open provocation against the peace-loving countries and peoples of the world and a grave menace to world peace. The Chinese Government and people strongly condemn and protest against these acts of aggression and war provocations on the part of the British Government.

There is absolutely no ground for the British Government to send troops to Jordan on the pretext of helping the Jordanian Government to resist aggression and stabilize the situation, because there is no aggression against Jordan at all, and the situation in Jordan is purely a matter for the people of Jordan themselves. Jordan's affairs should be managed by the people of Jordan themselves, and the affairs of the Arab countries should be managed by the Arab peoples themselves, in which no foreign intervention is allowed. Not only do the Arab peoples oppose the British war provocations in invading Jordan and threatening the Republic of Iraq, but the peace-loving countries and peoples throughout the world will certainly not look on with folded arms.

The Chinese Government deems it necessary to warn the British Government that it must immediately stop its armed aggression against Jordan, withdraw all its armed forces from Jordan, and discontinue its acts of provocation in concentrating forces around the Republic of Iraq. Should the British Government refuse to come to its senses and heed the just condemnation and reasonable demand of the people of the world and obstinately refuse to stop its acts of aggression and abandon its aggressive schemes, this will certainly give rise to extremely grave consequences.

[1] *Peking Review*, 22 July 1958, pp. 7–8.

10. Statement by the Government of the Soviet Union regarding United States and United Kingdom aggression in the Middle East, Moscow, 18 July 1958[1]

On July 17, the government of the United Kingdom committed an act of armed aggression against Jordan—British airborne units landed in the Jordan capital, Amman.

Attempting to justify this open armed intervention in the internal affairs of this Arab state, the Prime Minister of the United Kingdom, Mr. Macmillan, insisted in the House of Commons that it was undertaken to help the Jordan government to resist aggression, although it is common knowledge that Jordan is threatened by no one, and the British Prime Minister was unable to give any facts or instances testifying to the existence of such a danger. The British Prime Minister said further that these actions of the British government were fully supported and approved by the government of the United States. Thus, the British government has supported the United States' aggression, while the government of the United States supports Britain's aggression.

Britain's intervention in Jordan, undertaken right after the American invasion of Lebanon, shows that the governments of the United States and the United Kingdom have a broadly conceived plan of aggressive actions to suppress the national liberation movement in the Arab East. They want to impose the yoke of colonialism on the peoples once again and to retain the possibility for American and British monopolies to continue plundering the natural resources and manpower of these countries.

By their decision on armed intervention in Jordan, the ruling circles of Britain, pretending to help King Hussein, are attempting to regain their colonialist positions in the country, which were forfeited to a considerable extent in 1956 when, on the demand of the Jordan people, the British military advisers, headed by Glubb Pasha, who actually controlled the Jordan army, were expelled from the country.

It can be seen from the British Prime Minister's statement that the purpose of Britain's armed intervention in Jordan is not only to suppress the movement of the Jordan people for their independence, but to entrench itself in Jordan and use this country, along with American-occupied Lebanon, as a military base for the suppression of the popular revolution in Iraq. At present the United States and Britain are hastily conditioning

---

[1] *Soviet News*, 21 July 1958. On 15 July 1958 President Eisenhower issued a statement, see above [p. 287], announcing the landing of United States marines in the Lebanon, following on an appeal from President Chamoun of the Lebanon that some United States forces should be stationed in the Lebanon to help maintain security. On 17 July 1958 a contingent of United Kingdom troops was flown into Jordan after a request on the 16 July from King Hussein and the Prime Minister of Jordan, see above [p. 296].

public opinion to the further extension of the American-British armed intervention against the nations of the Arab East.

One cannot fail to see that the governments of the United States and Britain have embarked upon the road of armed interference in the internal affairs of other countries, a practice categorically prohibited by international law and the United Nations Charter.

This path of military ventures is fraught with the gravest consequences for peace, and those who embark upon it must realise that the peoples will make them answer for these aggressive actions. Who better than the British government should realise, particularly after the shameful failure of the military venture against Egypt, that the time has gone forever when the fire of colonialist gunboats and the landing of armed detachments in this or that colonial or dependent country could crush the uprisings of the oppressed peoples and save the colonialist regimes.

Today, when hundreds of millions of formerly oppressed colonial peoples have started a struggle for their national rights, any attempts to prevent these nations from achieving their independence are doomed to failure. The sacred right of the peoples to shape their life as they think fit is proclaimed in the Charter of the United Nations, which was signed also by the United States and Britain.

The United States and British governments have broken their commitments to the United Nations and have come out as violators of peace.

The aggressors should bear in mind that all the peoples, particularly the Moslem population in the Middle East and the adjacent areas, will not be indifferent to the fate of the peoples who have fallen victim to foreign armed intervention. The peoples of the Arab East are not alone in their struggle for independence and freedom, against the criminal actions of the American and British colonialists.

The peoples of the entire world condemn with wrath and indignation the American and British aggressors. A wave of protest against the bloody venture of the United States and British ruling circles in the Middle East has surged throughout the world, including Britain herself. The peoples demand an immediate end to the armed intervention of the United States and Britain, they demand the withdrawal of the American and British troops from Lebanon and Jordan.

The governments of the United States and the United Kingdom have committed hostile acts against peace and they bear the responsibility for the consequences of their acts of aggression against Lebanon and Jordan.

The governments of the United States and the United Kingdom must end their armed intervention in the internal affairs of the Arab States and withdraw their troops at once from Lebanon and Jordan.

The Soviet government believes that at this crucial moment the

Security Council and the United Nations General Assembly must fulfil their duty of safeguarding peace, must curb the aggression, uphold the national independence of the Arab states which have fallen victim to an unprovoked attack, and must stamp out the hotbed of war.

The Soviet government declares that the Soviet Union will not remain indifferent to the acts of unprovoked aggression in an area adjacent to its frontiers, and that it will be compelled to take the necessary steps dictated by the interests of the Soviet Union's security and of safeguarding world peace.

11. Proclamation by Brigadier Kassem, Prime Minister of Iraq, on oil policy, Baghdad, 18 July 1958[1]

In view of the importance of oil to world economy, the Government of the Iraqi Republic wishes to declare its anxiety to see the continuation of the production and flow of oil to the markets where it is sold, because of its importance to national wealth and the national and international economic and industrial interests. The Government of the Iraqi Republic respects its commitments with the parties concerned. It has taken all necessary steps to protect the oil wells, pumping stations, pipe-lines and all other installations within the borders of the Iraqi Republic. The Government of the Iraqi Republic will, at the same time, work for the preservation of its sublime national interests, and hopes that those concerned will respond to its desire to see the continual existence of this vital resource for the good of the national economy as well as the international economy.

12. Letter from Mr. Khrushchev to Mr. Macmillan proposing an immediate meeting on the crisis in the Lebanon and Jordan, Moscow, 19 July 1958[2]

Mr. Prime Minister, At this historic hour the world is on the brink of war catastrophe and any imprudent move, however slight, may entail irreparable consequences.

At this hour, when British and American forces have already invaded the small Arab states, Jordan and Lebanon, when a danger of intervention is hanging over Iraq and other Arab states upholding their independence

---

[1] S.W.B. Part IV, 19 July 1958, p. 13.

[2] Soviet News, 21 July 1958. Similar messages were sent to President Eisenhower, General de Gaulle, and Mr. Nehru, see Soviet News, 22 July 1958. The Soviet permanent representative to the United Nations forwarded the texts of the four letters to the Secretary-General of the United Nations, and requested that the texts should be circulated among all United Nation members as documents of the United Nations Organisation.

and freedom, I wish to address you, as head of the government of the United Kingdom.

You, as a man with a vast knowledge of life and experience of statesmanship, know well what modern war means. Having broken out at one point, it can easily flare up, like a fire in a strong wind, and grow into a world conflagration. All talk of 'little' or 'local' wars in these conditions is no more than a naive illusion and all hope for a limited nature of military operations is deception or self-deception.

Those who are at the helm at this juncture have no right to forget the past. The first links in the chain of events that led up to the Second World War were also 'little' and 'local' wars and the seizure of alien territories.

We, as wartime allies in the past, know what the blood and ruins of the last war looked like, and we know how the aggressors' attempts to impose their will on other nations by force of arms ended. The lessons of history must not be forgotten, and we have no right to forget them.

The armed intervention, launched by Britain in Jordan and by the United States in Lebanon, and the danger hanging over Iraq and other Arab states can entail extremely dangerous and unpredictable consequences and set off a chain reaction which it will be impossible to arrest.

We address you, not from positions of intimidation, but from positions of reason. If there can be any talk of intimidation, then we should say that it is what high-ranking military leaders of the United States are so assiduously engaged in now. The Commander of the United States Sixth Fleet and the Secretary for Defence are making such provocative and warmongering speeches that, if they were citizens of the countries which have banned war propaganda, they would have long ago been put on trial or, if they had gone mad, confined in a lunatic asylum.

Intimidation is, however, a useless means of carrying on international relations. We know that Britain and the United States have atom and hydrogen bombs, aircraft and navies. But you are also well aware that the Soviet Union also has atom and hydrogen bombs, aircraft and a navy, plus ballistic missiles of all types, including intercontinental ones. However, we believe that the atmosphere, which is sufficiently inflammable as it is, should not be brought to flash point. It is necessary to seek different solutions, realistic ways, guided not by military gambles but by common sense and negotiations. The interests of Britain herself, in our view, demand this by no means to a lesser degree than the interests of all mankind craving for peace and tranquillity.

You explain the military intervention in Jordan as a request of the King of Jordan to render him support in resisting aggression. But you know very well that no one is threatening Jordan and there are no facts which would indicate the existence of a threat.

The military invasion of Jordan by Britain has been launched at the request of an irresponsible monarch who does not enjoy the support of the people and acts against the will of the people. And such a request was enough for British troops to be sent into Jordan, in circumvention of the United Nations, which was informed *post factum* of this aggressive act.

Thus, the unprovoked aggression against Jordan is being concealed, in a rather crude manner, by the request of a government which—and this is no secret to anyone—is dependent upon Britain.

Prime Minister, you should be well aware that it is not yet two years since the time when under pressure of the Jordan people, British troops were turned out of Jordan under the same reigning king. Now he is asking for Britain's troops to be moved in again. One can imagine how indignant the population was at the reappearance of British officers and men in Jordan.

Prime Minister, you often make public speeches in support of the United Nations, but by their actions in Jordan and Lebanon the governments of Britain and the United States are dealing a grave blow at this international organisation. At this hour, so vital to the lives of the peoples, the United Nations is, in effect, put off the scene by the bayonets of British and American troops.

Britain and the United States are trying to justify the armed invasion of the Arab states by referring to the need to protect the lives and property of British subjects and American nationals there. But this method of covering up aggression and seizing alien territories is not new.

The powers which have started the aggression are playing with fire. It is always easier to kindle the fire than to put it out. But once it has been kindled, it is better to put it out at the very outset, rather than let the flames flare up and envelope neighbouring houses. The only correct decision in the present circumstances would be to withdraw British and American troops from the Middle East at once to afford the peoples of the countries of that area the opportunity of settling their own destinies.

In this crucial hour of history, when there is not a minute to be lost, the Soviet Union, invariably acting for world peace and peaceful co-existence, cannot be indifferent to what is happening in the Middle East, which is in direct proximity to its frontiers. The Soviet Union cannot be indifferent at a time when the question whether there will be war or peace is being decided.

I think, Prime Minister, that the bitter and grave experience which Britain had as a result of her unprovoked attack on Egypt has left a mark on the heart of every Briton deep enough to make it clear what grave consequences Britain's participation in the new military adventure can entail for the people of Britain.

The government of the Soviet Union proposes an immediate meeting of the heads of government of the U.S.S.R., the United Kingdom, the United States, France and India, with the participation of the United Nations Secretary-General, in order to take immediate measures for ending the armed conflict which has broken out. We propose that we should meet on any day and at any hour, the sooner, the better. You certainly understand that history has allotted us little time to prevent war, to prevent the annihilation of millions of human beings, to prevent the destruction of immense material and cultural values.

In its statements the government of the Soviet Union has already made its position clear enough as regards the peaceful solution of the pressing problems of the Middle East. The Soviet Union considers that solutions to these problems can and must be found such as would meet the vital interests of the peoples of the Middle East and ensure respect for their sovereign rights, with due regard for the interests of all nations associated with the countries of that area.

The governments of the western powers say that they are interested in using oil and other raw material resources of that part of the world. But the peoples of those countries do not deny them that opportunity. The only thing they want is to have this problem solved on terms of equality and on a mutually beneficial commercial basis, which is the most reasonable one.

The Soviet government considers that a conference of the heads of government of the U.S.S.R., the United Kingdom, the United States, France and India could also take up the question of ending arms deliveries to the countries of the Middle East, as the U.S.S.R. had suggested earlier.

We consider it necessary that a conference of the heads of government of the U.S.S.R., the United Kingdom, the United States, France and India, having drawn up concrete recommendations on ending the armed conflict in the Middle East, should submit these recommendations to the Security Council and that this United Nations body should consider them, with the participation of representatives from Arab countries.

The question of the date and place of the conference cannot constitute any obstacle. The Soviet government is willing to have the conference held anywhere, should Geneva or the capital of some other neutral nation prove unsuitable to the western powers for some reason or other. The most important thing is to waste no time, for time is precious, as the guns are already beginning to fire. We propose that we should meet in Geneva on July 22.

A conference of the heads of government of the great powers to resolve the armed conflict which has broken out in the Middle East would be the most reasonable act for the governments of our countries to undertake in the present conditions. It would be an inestimable contribution to the cause of strengthening international peace and security. It would be incontestable evidence that the idea of peaceful and not military solutions can and must prevail throughout the world. An end to the aggression in the Middle East would be enthusiastically welcomed by the peoples of all countries, whatever their colour, creed or political convictions.

I should like to close by emphasising that whether the Middle East conflict will be resolved by war or by peaceful means now depends on the government headed by you, Prime Minister, on yourself and on the President of the United States.

The Soviet government expects that the government of the United Kingdom will understand this message of the Soviet government correctly and that it will have a positive response from the United Kingdom and she will be ready to turn the tide of events radically from the road of war to the road of peace.

On the foregoing subject I have simultaneously addressed the President of the United States, Mr. Eisenhower, the Prime Minister of France, General de Gaulle, and the Prime Minister of India, Mr. Nehru.

Respectfully yours,

N. Khrushchov

13. Agreement concluded between the Republic of Iraq and the United Arab Republic, Damascus, 19 July 1958[1]

On 2nd Muharram 1378, equivalent to 19th July 1958, the delegations of the UAR and the Republic of Iraq agreed on the following:

1. To affirm treaties and pacts binding the two countries, foremost of these being the Arab League Pact and the joint defence pact among the Arab countries.

2. To affirm the strong solidarity between the Government of the two countries regarding the international situation, and that they are determined to stand as one country in defence against any aggression directed against both of them or either of them. Positive steps demanded by this should be taken immediately.

3. To co-operate fully in the international sphere for preservation of the rights of both countries, and to participate positively in supporting the UN Charter and promoting peace in the Middle East and the world.

4. To take positive and immediate steps to promote economic and cultural co-operation between the two countries.

5. To maintain constant contact and deliberations between the two countries in all matters of concern to them.

Jamal Abd an-Nasir, on behalf of the United Arab Republic, and Col. Abd as-Salam Muhammad Arif, on behalf of the Republic of Iraq.

---

[1] *S.W.B. Part IV*, 21 July 1958, p. 12. This agreement was read by the Iraqi Deputy Premier, Abd as-Salam Arif, from the balcony of the Guest Palace in Damascus.

14. Letter from Mr. Macmillan to Mr. Khrushchev regarding the Soviet proposal for a meeting of heads of Government on the crisis in the Lebanon and Jordan, 22 July 1958[1]

Dear Mr. Prime Minister, I am now able to send you a considered reply to your message of July 19 about the situation in the Middle East. As I explained in my interim reply,[2] which will have reached you earlier to-day, this is a matter which Her Majesty's Government have considered in consultation with our allies.

2. I shall come quickly to the point of your letter. First, however, I wish to make it plain that I do not share your judgment that the world is on the verge of a military catastrophe. I say this in full and certain knowledge of the pacific intentions of the Western Powers and in the belief that the Soviet Government would not themselves take a step which would lead to world war.

3. I also wish to forestall any misunderstanding by saying at once that I cannot accept in any particular your description of the action which we have taken in sending troops to Jordan, of our motives, or of the situation in Jordan itself. As has been made abundantly clear the sole reason for our action in Jordan was to protect a small and independent country which had appealed for help against the threat of aggression and subversion stimulated from without.

4. However, although I reject your premises, it by no means follows that I reject your conclusion. Indeed I agree with you that it would be useful if Heads of Government could find an early opportunity to meet and discuss the Middle East. I should certainly be glad to explain to you face to face how Her Majesty's Government view the problems which beset the area.

5. I was glad to see that in your message you referred, with marked disapproval, to the idea of 'circumventing the United Nations'. As you know, the Security Council already has under consideration certain

---

[1] Cmnd. 516, pp. 6–7. Mr. Nehru replied on 21 July 1958, and while he welcomed 'a peaceful approach by negotiation through the United Nations or its Security Council', accepted Mr. Khrushchev's invitation to attend the conference of heads of governments which he understood to be 'different and separate from the proposal for a high level or summit conference which has been under discussion for some time'. For the text of Mr. Nehru's letter see *The Times*, 22 July 1958. Gen. de Gaulle replied on 22 July 1958 that the French Government would be willing to attend a summit meeting if the United Nations was unable to reach a conclusion on the situation in the Middle East, for the text of the French reply, see *Le Monde*, 24 July 1958. President Eisenhower replied on 22 July that the Security Council was 'already dealing with certain phases of the problem' and discussion should continue there; Mr. Khrushchev's proposal for a 5 power conference outside the United Nations seemed 'further calculated to derogate from the authority and prestige of the United Nations'. Also a 5 power conference would omit many countries 'which are deeply concerned with the Near and Middle East'. For the text of the President's letter, see *D.S.B.*, 11 August 1958, pp. 229–31.

[2] Cmnd. 516, pp. 5–6.

questions concerning the Middle East. I hope that you will agree that the proceedings in the Security Council should not be circumvented, but that the discussions for which you have asked should take place in that forum, thus providing continuity. Article 28(2) of the United Nations Charter enables the Security Council to hold meetings at which each of its members may, if it so desires, be represented by a member of the government or by some other specially designated representative. I would certainly be ready to go to New York for such a meeting if you would also go; and I take it from the terms of your message that you would.

6. It would not be the intention of Her Majesty's Government that any resolutions should be put forward at this special meeting of the Security Council unless they arose out of previous agreement. In other words the object would be to reach fruitful agreements rather than to register differences by votes. I hope that this spirit will prevail.

7. You had hoped that we might meet in Geneva to-day. I hope that we may meet soon in New York in accordance with the plan I have suggested.

Yours sincerely,

HAROLD MACMILLAN.

15. Statement by Mr. Hammarskjold regarding the failure of the Security Council to take additional action over the situation in the Lebanon and Jordan, 22 July 1958[1]

The Security Council has just failed to take additional action in the grave emergency facing us. However, the responsibility of the United Nations to make all efforts to live up to the purposes and principles of the Charter remains.

11. The Council now has before it two proposals[2] for the calling of an emergency special session of the General Assembly. I cannot anticipate its decision on those proposals. However, time is of the essence, and, whatever the outcome of the further consideration in this Council, there is need for practical steps to be taken without any delay. That is the background against which I would like to make the following declaration.

12. In a statement before this Council on 31 October 1956, I said that the discretion and impartiality imposed on the Secretary-General by the character of his immediate task must not degenerate into a policy of expediency.[3] On a later occasion—it was 26 September 1957—I said in a statement before the General Assembly that I believed it to be the duty of the Secretary-General 'to use his office and, indeed, the machinery of the Organization to its utmost capacity and to the full extent permitted at

---

[1] S.C.O.R., Thirteenth Year, 837th meeting, paras. 10–17.
[2] An American proposal (S/4056) and a Russian proposal (S/4057).
[3] S.C.O.R., Eleventh Year, 751st meeting, para. 4.

each stage by practical circumstances'.[1] I added that I believed that it is in keeping with the philosophy of the Charter that the Secretary-General also should be expected to act without any guidance from the Assembly or the Security Council should this appear to him necessary towards helping to fill any vacuum that may appear in the systems which the Charter and traditional diplomacy provide for the safeguarding of peace and security.[2]

13. It is my feeling that, in the circumstances, what I stated in those two contexts, on 31 October 1956 and 26 September 1957, now has full application.

14. I am sure that I will be acting in accordance with the wishes of the members of the Council if I, therefore, use all opportunities offered to the Secretary-General, within the limits set by the Charter and towards developing the United Nations effort, so as to help to prevent a further deterioration of the situation in the Middle East and to assist in finding a road away from the dangerous point at which we now find ourselves.

15. First of all—the continued operation of the United Nations Observation Group in Lebanon being acceptable to all members of the Council —this will mean the further development of the Observation Group so as to give it all the significance it can have, consistent with its basic character as determined by the Security Council in its resolution of 11 June 1958[3] and the purposes and principles of the Charter.

16. The Council will excuse me for not being able to spell out at this moment what it may mean beyond that. However, I am certain that what I may find it possible to do, acting under the provisions of the Charter and solely for the purposes of the Charter, and guided by the views expressed around this table to the extent that they have a direct bearing on the activities of the Secretary-General, will be recognized by you as being in the best interests of the Organization and, therefore, of the cause of peace.

17. The Security Council would, of course, be kept fully informed on the steps taken. Were you to disapprove of the way these intentions were to be translated by me into practical steps, I would, of course, accept the consequences of your judgement.

16. Letter from Mr. Khrushchev to Mr. Macmillan regarding a meeting of heads of Government on the crisis in the Lebanon and Jordan, Moscow, 23 July 1958[4]

Mr. Prime Minister, I have received your reply to my message of July 19. I have also received replies from Mr. Nehru, Mr. Eisenhower and M. de Gaulle to my messages of the same date.

[1] G.A.O.R., Twelfth Session, plenary meetings, 690th meeting, para 72.
[2] Ibid., para. 73.   [3] See above, p. 278.
[4] *Soviet News*, 24 July 1958. Mr. Khrushchev sent similar letters on 23 July 1958 to President Eisenhower, General de Gaulle, and Mr. Nehru; for the texts see ibid.

I should not like to enter into polemics at the present time about the reasons for the tension and the threat to peace in the Middle East area. The Soviet government's point of view on these questions has been outlined in my message of July 19.

The Soviet government considers that the threat to world peace is at present so serious that it is most urgently necessary to take all possible steps to prevent a world conflict. We cannot minimise the danger of such a conflict, as there are forces which are in favour of extending the zone of aggression in the Middle East and, in the first place, are harbouring plans for an armed attack on Iraq.

It is precisely in order to prevent the outbreak of such a conflict that the Soviet Union has proposed the immediate calling of a meeting of the heads of government of the U.S.S.R., the United Kingdom, the United States, France and India, with the participation of the United Nations Secretary-General.

We are pleased to note that the Soviet government's proposal concerning a meeting of heads of government has been favourably received by you. It is evident from your message that the government of the United Kingdom is in favour of a meeting of the heads of government for the purpose of discussing, within the framework of the United Nations Security Council, the situation that has now arisen in the Middle East. The Soviet government, in its message of July 19, has already pointed out that the Security Council should not be by-passed. From the replies received from the United States government and from the Prime Minister of France, it follows that they, too, are in favour of such a meeting.

Taking into consideration the need for urgent decisions in the interests of preserving peace, the Soviet government considers that the form in which the meeting of the heads of government takes place cannot be of decisive significance in this particular case. The important thing is that this meeting should be held as soon as possible, so as to find most expeditiously a correct solution which will help to preserve and strengthen peace, will bring tranquillity to the Middle East area, and will promote the relaxation of tension in the relations among states.

We agree with your considerations with regard to the approach to the discussion of this question at a special session of the Security Council with the heads of government taking part. We agree that no resolutions whatsoever should be introduced unless they arise from previous agreement and that the aim of our joint work should be to achieve fruitful agreement and not to record disagreement by means of a vote.

The Soviet government assumes that in order to arrive as quickly as possible at constructive decisions in the interests of preserving and strengthening peace, the heads of government will, as can also be seen from your letter, have the opportunity for joint consultations not only of a formal nature.

Inasmuch as in this case what is involved is a discussion in the Security Council, not of ordinary current questions, but of problems of special importance from the point of view of preserving peace and ensuring security, we consider that in this case it would be useful to invite India, one of the biggest Asian countries and universally recognised as a state which stands for strengthening peace, to take part in the work of the Security Council. Her participation would really be beneficial, in contrast to the participation of one of the so-called permanent members who does not in fact represent anyone. We consider it necessary that the representative of India, in the person of her Prime Minister Jawaharlal Nehru, who has agreed to take part in the meeting of the heads of government—for which we express our gratitude to him—should participate in the work of the Security Council.

We have learned with satisfaction that you, Mr. Prime Minister, are ready to go to New York for a special meeting of the Security Council with the participation of the heads of government. As far as the U.S.S.R. is concerned, taking into account your agreement and the agreement of M. de Gaulle, the Prime Minister of the French Republic, of Mr. Nehru, the Prime Minister of India, and of President Eisenhower of the United States, as is evident from his message of July 22, the Soviet Union will be represented at this meeting by the Chairman of the U.S.S.R. Council of Ministers.

Naturally representatives of the interested Arab states should be invited to take part in the discussion of the problems in the Security Council with the participation of the heads of government of the abovementioned five powers.

The Soviet government would like to know as soon as possible the views of the United Kingdom government regarding the date for convening the Security Council with the participation of the heads of government. For our part, we propose that this work in the Security Council should begin in New York on July 28.

Respectfully yours,

N. KHRUSHCHOV

17. Letter from Mr. Macmillan to Mr. Khrushchev regarding a meeting of heads of Government on the crisis in the Lebanon and Jordan, 26 July 1958[1]

Dear Mr. Prime Minister, Thank you for your message of July 23.

2. I am sorry that in spite of your statement that you do not want to

[1] Cmnd. 516, pp. 8–9. General de Gaulle replied on 26 July, that as the Security Council meeting had reached no conclusion, the French Government would prefer 'une conférence des chefs de Gouvernement des principales puissances', preferably in Europe, to a special meeting of the

enter into polemics you should still have felt it necessary to repeat accusations of Western aggression which have no foundation. Nevertheless, I have noted with satisfaction the main point of your letter which is that you have accepted my view that certain Middle East problems should be discussed at a Security Council meeting in New York under the provisions of Article 28 of the United Nations Charter which permits Heads of Government to be present. I repeat that I would certainly be ready to go to New York for such a meeting if you would also go.

3. I suggest that the necessary arrangements should be made through the Permanent Representatives of the members of the Security Council and that they should be requested to reach agreement about the date of the Council's first meeting under Article 28 and to decide what other States should be invited to be represented. The work could begin without delay in close consultation with the Secretary-General.

Yours sincerely,

HAROLD MACMILLAN.

18. Letter from Mr. Khrushchev to Mr. Macmillan regarding a meeting of heads of Government on the crisis in the Lebanon and Jordan, Moscow, 28 July 1958[1]

Mr. Prime Minister, I have received your message of July 26 in reply to my message concerning a meeting of the heads of government.

I regret your failure not only to consent to have the special meeting of the Security Council with the participation of the heads of government, which you suggested on July 22,[2] held already on July 28, but also to suggest on your part any early date for this meeting. Instead, you now suggest that the permanent representatives of the members of the Security Council should hold discussions about the date for an ordinary meeting of the Security Council.

This position of yours is clearly a digression from the proposal made in your message of July 22. At that time you definitely recognised the desirability of an early meeting of the heads of government to discuss Middle Eastern problems, and declared your willingness to go to New York for a

Security Council. For the text of the French reply, see Le Monde, 29 July 1958. President Eisenhower replied on 25 July 1958. The United States Government welcomed the Soviet suggestion that the meeting should be held at a special session of the Security Council; should the attendance of Foreign Ministers or heads of Governments be 'generally desired, the United States would join in following that orderly procedure'. For the text of President Eisenhower's letter, see D.S.B., 11 August 1958, pp. 233-4.

[1] Soviet News, 29 July 1958. For the text of Mr. Khrushchev's almost identical letter to President Eisenhower, see also ibid., and for Mr. Khrushchev's similar letter to General de Gaulle, see Soviet News, 30 July 1958.   [2] See above, p. 305.

special meeting of the Security Council if the head of the Soviet government also went there.

Expressing your considerations concerning the approach to the discussion of this question by the heads of government at a special meeting of the Security Council, you said that no resolutions should be submitted unless arising from previous agreement and that the purpose of our joint work should be the attainment of fruitful agreement and not the recording of disagreements by taking a vote. The Soviet government fully agreed with your proposals.

It is now clear that the government of the United Kingdom is delaying the convocation of a conference of the heads of government and does not want this conference to take urgent measures for a peaceful solution of the military conflict that has arisen in the Middle East.

One cannot help pointing out that your proposal of July 22 concerning a meeting of the heads of government within the framework of the United Nations Security Council has been welcomed in all countries. Agreement among the U.S.S.R., the United Kingdom, the United States, France and India concerning a meeting of the heads of government had a certain calming effect and the peoples had every reason to expect that this conference would be held in the near future and would ensure the maintenance and strengthening of peace in the Middle East.

Your present reply is a step backward from the agreement reached and, of course, cannot fail to cause serious anxiety among the peoples. The government of the United Kingdom now suggests that the situation in the Middle East, a situation which is a danger to peace, should again be referred to the ordinary session of the United Nations Security Council instead of being discussed by the heads of government of the five powers. But what results can be obtained from this? You are well aware that the Security Council has been discussing the situation in Jordan and Lebanon for a long time without arriving at any decision.

The question of cutting short the armed aggression in the Middle East is now so acute that the Security Council, as the experience of its latest meetings has shown, is not able to take an urgent and effective decision on this question at ordinary sessions. Armed forces are being ceaselessly concentrated in this area, which is increasingly becoming a powder barrel which may be set off by the smallest spark and cause a world disaster. Under such conditions it is imperative to convene with the utmost urgency a meeting of the heads of government of the five powers—the U.S.S.R., the United Kingdom, the United States, France and India, with the participation of the United Nations Secretary-General, who, having full powers, could agree on an immediate discontinuation of the military conflict in the Middle East and on measures for the maintenance and consolidation of world peace.

It is quite obvious that if we in all sincerity want to explore ways for reducing tension, we shall have to agree that in this case it is precisely these five powers that, above all, must come to terms on the necessary measures for the maintenance and consolidation of peace. Can anyone doubt that if these powers succeeded in reaching agreement on the immediate ending of the armed conflict in the Middle East, any other state really concerned for strengthening peace would welcome it and endorse such a decision?

Your proposal of July 22 concerning the holding of a conference of the heads of government within the framework of the Security Council envisaged a meeting of the heads of government such as would provide opportunities for joint consultations not only of an official nature. We agreed to your proposal with the object of bringing about an early solution of the pressing problem of discontinuing the armed conflict in the Middle East. But, as I have already pointed out, Prime Minister, you are now going back on this proposal.

It is necessary to point out that Britain's stand on arranging a meeting of the heads of government is affected by her alliance with certain powers and by the fact that she herself is a party to the armed intervention in the internal affairs of the Arab states, and that is why the British government is passive and does not strive for a solution designed to reduce tension in the Middle East. It can be said that your proposal of July 22 concerning a conference of the heads of government within the framework of the Security Council could have been really effective had it been carried out. But the point is that you are going back on this proposal and we are getting the impression that you are trying to find a pretext for burying your own proposal and are using the discussions of procedure as a screen to cover up a further expansion of aggression.

One cannot help noting that the course is thus set towards burying the agreement reached on an early meeting of the heads of government of the U.S.S.R., the United Kingdom, the United States, France and India within the framework of the Security Council.

We cannot accept this.

The Soviet government firmly adheres to the positions of fighting for the maintenance and consolidation of peace, the positions of peaceful co-existence between states, irrespective of their social and economic systems. The Soviet government is consistently advocating the settlement of conflicts by peaceful means, through negotiations. That is why we insist on an immediate end to the aggression, on the urgent withdrawal of the invading forces from the territories of Jordan and Lebanon.

It is our firm conviction that a meeting of the heads of government of the five powers, given the sincere desire for this by all parties, would help to find ways and means of eliminating the military conflict and bringing tranquillity to the Middle East.

In this context the Soviet government expresses its satisfaction at the view expressed by General de Gaulle, the head of the French government, in his message of July 26,[1] that he endorses the proposal for an immediate conference of the heads of government of the five powers, an opinion which, as we understand it, does not differ from the Soviet government's proposal on this matter. We consider, as we have declared before, that this would be the most correct way to ensure the early accomplishment of the urgent task of ending the armed conflict in the Middle East.

I do not conceal, Prime Minister, that the line taken by the governments of the United Kingdom and the United States in virtually rejecting a conference of the heads of government cannot but alarm the peoples, who are impatiently waiting for an end to the armed conflict in the Middle East and for measures towards the maintenance and consolidation of world peace.

The public of all countries is asking: Do the governments of the countries responsible for the present tension in the Middle East want to lull the vigilance of the peoples and secretly prepare fresh acts of aggression? This is borne out by the landing of more British military contingents in Jordan, the concentration of more and more British troops on Cyprus which are being prepared for dispatch to the countries of the Arab East. The government of the United Kingdom knows full well that American troops continue to land in Lebanon, that United States naval forces are being concentrated in the Eastern Mediterranean, that American reinforcements are being flown from Europe to the Middle East, in particular to Turkey, in the Adana area. In this connection most noteworthy is the recent largescale preparations in Turkey for armed intervention in the affairs of the countries of the Arab East. King Hussein of Jordan, who has lost the support of his people and relies on outside assistance, dares to brandish arms and threatens a march on Baghdad. The tendency towards enlarging the area of aggression is obvious. The threat of a military attack hangs over the Republic of Iraq.

Thus, the dragging out of the discussions about a meeting of the heads of government of the five powers, going hand in hand with an increasing concentration of armed forces in the Middle East, leads to a further aggravation of the tension, the extension of the conflict, and may lead mankind to disaster.

Can one disregard the fact that the government of the United Kingdom, like the government of the United States, while delaying a decision on a heads of government conference, is holding an urgent conference of the members of the Baghdad Pact in London, the capital of your country, at a time when, instead of the withdrawal of the foreign troops from Jordan and Lebanon, preparations are in full swing for armed intervention

[1] See *Le Monde*, 29 July 1958.

in the affairs of the Republic of Iraq? All this looks like a conspiracy against the Arab countries. Is this not being done in order to confront the world, by pursuing a policy of *faits accomplis*, with an increasing extension of the military conflict?

But can one disregard the serious consequences of such a policy, primarily for its sponsors, since in our times the peoples are vigilant enough and cannot tolerate acts of aggression?

At the same time the government of the United Kingdom, following the United States, is seeking to obstruct a solution, awaited by all mankind, of what is now the main problem, the problem of discontinuing the armed intervention by the United Kingdom and the United States in the Middle East, it is seeking to lead the discussions on a meeting of the heads of government into the impasse of endless talk about form and procedure.

Consequently, the governments of the United Kingdom and the United States have not taken the road of settling the military conflict, which has arisen in the Middle East, in the interests of maintaining and strengthening peace, but are working for an extension of the area of the military conflict and are confronting mankind with the threat of a world disaster, although the British government, resorting to all kinds of manoeuvres, seeks to create the impression that it still adheres to its proposal of July 22. Thereby, Prime Minister, you assume a great responsibility before mankind and before history for the consequences of such a policy of the British government.

In view of the extremely tense situation in the Middle East, the Soviet government still considers it indispensable to convene immediately a conference of the heads of government of the U.S.S.R., the United Kingdom, the United States, France and India, with the participation of the United Nations Secretary-General.

The Soviet government urges the governments of the United Kingdom and the United States to revert to the agreement concerning this conference of the heads of government on the basis of the earlier proposal you made on July 22.

As for the venue of the conference, we have noted the statement by General de Gaulle, the head of the government of France, in his message of July 26, to the effect that he prefers the meeting to be held in Europe. The Soviet government had even earlier suggested that the meeting should take place in Europe, and fully supports General de Gaulle's proposal.

The holding of the heads of government conference in a European city should be given consideration, all the more so since it is suggested in the United States press that the American authorities would find it difficult to ensure the safety of the heads of government if the conference were to be held in the United States. We should not like to place the United States government in a difficult position on this score. Without objecting to a conference in New York, the Soviet government therefore agrees to a meeting in Geneva, Vienna, Paris or any other place acceptable to all parties.

We would also welcome agreement on a meeting of the heads of government in Moscow, and the Soviet government guarantees full security to all delegations and the necessary conditions for fruitful work. We are confident that the Soviet people would welcome the envoys who came here to take urgent measures for ending the conflict in the Middle East and for strengthening world peace, and the Soviet people would thereby demonstrate their undeviating allegiance to the cause of peace.

Your message does not say anything about the Prime Minister of India taking part in the heads of government conference. In this context I consider it necessary to re-emphasise that India's participation in the conference would greatly contribute to the taking of constructive decisions for resolving the situation in the Middle East.

As for the date of the conference of heads of government with the participation of the United Nations Secretary-General, we had mentioned the date of July 28. Since it can be understood from your message that the date we suggested did not suit the British government, we are ready to accept any other early date and would like to receive a clear reply to the question when the British government would be ready to take part in a conference of the heads of government of the five powers.

I await, Prime Minister, your earliest possible reply to my message.

Respectfully yours,

N. KHRUSHCHOV

19. Letter from Mr. Macmillan to Mr. Khrushchev regarding a meeting of heads of Government on the crisis in the Lebanon and Jordan, 31 July 1958[1]

Dear Mr. Prime Minister, I have received your letter of July 28. I will not reply to its many accusations against allied policy in the Middle East. None of these has any foundation in fact.

[1] Cmnd. 516, p. 13. General de Gaulle also replied on 31 July 1958. The French Government proposed a summit meeting in Geneva on 18 August 1958; the discussion should not be limited to the problem created by the presence of American troops in the Lebanon, and United Kingdom troops in Jordan, but should consider 'toute l'affaire du Moyen-Orient et l'état continuel de crise qui empêche cette région du monde de vivre et de se développer dans des conditions normales'. Pending a decision by the five powers concerned in the proposed summit conference the French Government had no objection to the American and United Kingdom suggestion to hold a new session of the Security Council, which should not be confused with a conference of heads of Government. For the text of General de Gaulle's letter, see Le Monde, 2 August 1958. On 1 August 1958 President Eisenhower replied that the Security Council should be the place of meeting, and he issued similar instructions to those contained in Mr. Macmillan's letter above (para. 5); the United States Government refused to go to a meeting in Moscow. For the text of the President's letter, see D.S.B., 18 August 1958, pp. 274–5.

2. In my letter of July 22 I proposed a special meeting of the Security Council to be attended by Heads of Government. On July 26 I elaborated this proposal. I said that I was glad that it was acceptable to you and I suggested that the necessary arrangements should at once be made through the Permanent Representatives of Members of the Security Council. I hope that on reflection you will agree that this is the best course; I am encouraged in this hope by the passage in your last letter where you call for a return to my original proposal. From this proposal I have never departed.

3. In addition to meetings of the whole Council under Article 28, it would of course be possible to arrange less formal meetings of Heads of Government on the questions which the Security Council is considering. The procedure would thus be flexible and should promote the chances of making progress. As I said in my message of July 22 it would not be our intention that any resolutions should be put forward at this special meeting of the Security Council unless they arose out of previous agreement.

4. Of course this meeting would not preclude the holding of the Summit meeting for which we have been working for some time.

5. I am now instructing the United Kingdom Permanent Representative at the United Nations to propose to the President of the Security Council a special meeting to take place under Article 28 on August 12. Meanwhile the Permanent Representatives should discuss arrangements for the special meeting and decide where it will take place. If this meeting is agreed I shall be there on August 12. I hope you will be there too. So far as I am concerned New York, Geneva or any other place generally agreeable will do.

Yours sincerely,

HAROLD MACMILLAN.

20. Royal decree regarding the constitutional status of Jordan, Amman, 2 August 1958[1]

A royal decree has been issued approving the following Cabinet decision:

The Cabinet, after taking cognisance of the Premier's note dated 2nd August 1958, has decided the following:

Whereas the Arab Federation which was established by the Hashimite Kingdom of Jordan and the Kingdom of Iraq came into being with regard to its machinery, foundations and entity on the basis of sharing responsibilities and jurisdictions between the two Kingdoms and a mutual partnership with regard to their rights and duties,

[1] S.W.B. Part IV, 4 August 1958, p. 15.

Whereas the treacherous insurrectionist coup which recently took place in Iraq has placed the Iraqi region of the Federation in a position in which it cannot contribute its share to these duties and responsibilities in accordance with the Constitution of the Arab Federation,

Whereas the Constitution of the Arab Federation, in its provisions and context, does not enable the Jordanian region alone to undertake the execution of the duties and jurisdictions, or the executive, legislative and international measures which have been laid down by the provisions of the aforementioned Constitution, particularly with regard to foreign relations and diplomatic representation with all States, in addition to affairs pertinent to the Arab Army,

Whereas the reorganisation of the constitutional status and the State machinery concerned is required by the higher interests of the State,

And whereas the Constitution of the Arab Federation has been rendered invalid and cannot be applied from a realistic and practical point of view,

The Cabinet has decided as follows:

(1) to exercise the constitutional powers of the Hashimite Kingdom of Jordan in accord with the provisions of the Jordanian Constitution, with the provision that the Government shall take urgent measures to amend the articles of this Constitution which was modified in order to bring it in harmony with the Constitution of the Arab Federation;

(2) to retain the assets and properties of the Arab Federation which exist in the Jordanian region, to be deposited with the Government of the Hashimite Kingdom of Jordan;

(3) to regard these arrangements as effective 1st August 1958.

21. Letter from Mr. Khrushchev to Mr. Macmillan regarding the convening of an emergency special session of the General Assembly, Moscow, 5 August 1958[1]

Mr. Prime Minister, I received on July 31 your reply to my message of July 28 concerning the situation now prevailing in the Middle East.

In the earlier messages of the Soviet government we have shown, with facts in hand, that it has been precisely the armed intervention of the United States and the United Kingdom in Lebanon and Jordan that has created an atmosphere dangerous to the cause of peace in the Middle East. Therefore the claim you make in your message about the allegedly groundless nature of the Soviet government's assessment of the actions of the United Kingdom and United States governments is in complete contradiction with the real state of affairs.

In your message of July 31, Mr. Prime Minister, you contend that as

[1] *Soviet News*, 6 August 1958; also for Mr. Khrushchev: letters to President Eisenhower and General de Gaulle, of 5 August 1958.

regards the problem of a meeting of heads of government to discuss the situation that has arisen in the Middle East, your position set forth in your message of July 22 has not altered and that you have never gone back on this position. However, we cannot agree with this, because the proposal which you made in your message of July 26, and which you are making now, signifies the rejection of a meeting of the heads of government, which was supported earlier by the government of the United Kingdom.

You now suggest that a meeting of the Security Council, and not a meeting of heads of government, be called for the aforementioned purposes. The whole world knows, however, that the Security Council, which has been discussing the situation in Lebanon and Jordan for a long time, has so far failed to take effective steps to solve this problem.

The desire of the governments of the United States and the United Kingdom to direct the examination of the problem of the situation in the Middle East precisely into this channel of barren discussions is particularly apparent from Mr. Eisenhower's message of August 1,[1] which I have received and in which the United States President already speaks in quite unambiguous terms about having this question discussed at an ordinary meeting of the Security Council.

While you mention the possibility of organising 'less formal' meetings of the heads of government, it is evident from this message of Mr. Eisenhower that the United States government rejects the very idea of the possibility of a meeting of heads of government outside the procedure for the ordinary meetings of the Security Council, although it is well known that as matters stand in the Security Council at the present time, when most of its members are states which belong to aggressive blocs and when the great Chinese People's Republic is not represented in it, this body cannot draw impartial conclusions with regard to the armed foreign intervention in countries of the Arab world.

From the first days of the intervention by the United States and the United Kingdom in the Middle East, the Soviet Union has been advocating urgent measures for cutting short the aggression, withdrawing foreign troops from Lebanon and Jordan, preventing the extension of the intervention and eliminating the dangerous tension created by the actions of the United Kingdom and the United States. For these purposes the Soviet government suggested that a conference be held of the heads of government of five powers—the U.S.S.R., the United Kingdom, the United States, France and India—with the participation of the United Nations Secretary-General. We regret that you yourself and the United States President have not found it possible to accept this proposal and are continuing to insist on having the Middle East situation discussed, as previously, in the Security Council—a body which is incapable of solving

[1] For the text see *D.S.B.*, 18 August 1958, pp. 274–5.

it in an impartial way. Thus the question of holding a meeting of the heads of government of five powers, with the participation of the United Nations Secretary-General, has not been solved in a positive manner.

Although the governments of the United Kingdom and the United States have made the five-power meeting impossible and are directly responsible for this, it can be pointed out quite definitely at the present time that the demands of the peoples for the immediate convening of such a meeting in order to end the armed intervention in Jordan and Lebanon, and the determination of peaceloving states to put an end to aggression in the Middle East have compelled the initiators of the armed intervention to renounce, for the time being, the plans for extending aggression to other countries, and in the first place to the Republic of Iraq and the United Arab Republic. It is not by chance, therefore, that western powers, including the United Kingdom and the United States, have had to recognise the Republic of Iraq, the emergence of which was at first presented by the aggressors as being a threat to peace in the Middle East. This does not mean, however, that the danger of the conflict in this area being extended and exacerbated has been removed or that the security of the Republic of Iraq and other Arab states has been ensured. The interventionist troops have not yet been withdrawn from Jordan and Lebanon. Moreover, fresh contingents of foreign troops are arriving in this area and new military measures are being taken in the Baghdad Pact countries.

The problem of completely stopping the armed intervention in the Middle East and of providing conditions there for relieving the people of that area of foreign interference, must be solved most urgently. Foreign troops must be withdrawn from Lebanon and Jordan at once, because their presence there is a constant threat to peace and the independence of peoples and a flagrant breach of the United Nations Charter which cannot be tolerated by any member-state of the United Nations.

In these conditions the Soviet government feels itself bound to continue efforts to safeguard and consolidate peace in the Middle East. Since the governments of the United States and the United Kingdom have evaded the convocation of a five-power meeting of heads of government, and the Security Council, as we have previously pointed out, has failed to ensure a solution to the problem of the situation in the Middle East in the interests of peace, the government of the Soviet Union, in order to ensure the speediest measures necessary to end the aggression, has instructed its representative in the United Nations to demand the convocation of an emergency session of the United Nations General Assembly to discuss the problem of the withdrawal of the troops of the United Kingdom from Jordan and of the United States troops from Lebanon. The Soviet government hopes that the discussion of this question in the General Assembly, in which both large states and small ones are represented, will make it possible to find ways to eliminate the war danger that has been created in the Middle East by the actions of the United Kingdom and the United States, and to bring tranquillity to that area.

Mr. Prime Minister, I believe you will agree that the events in the Middle East which have confronted the world with the danger of a general war—with the incalculable suffering that would entail for the peoples—lend special urgency to the question of providing conditions for the peaceful co-existence of states and ending the 'cold war,' which is poisoning the entire international atmosphere. The Soviet Union and all peaceloving countries are doing everything possible to create conditions in which no great power will be able to commit aggression, even against a small country. Precisely for this reason, the great powers must agree not to take steps which would place mankind on the brink of military catastrophes.

We think it necessary to promote in every way contacts and ties between statesmen of all countries. Personal meetings between leaders of states might reduce the existing tension and help to create confidence and mutual understanding among states and to melt the ice of the 'cold war' more quickly. The Soviet government attaches particularly great importance to such contacts and, as you know, as early as last December suggested a top level meeting of statesmen. We are convinced that a summit meeting in the composition we suggested earlier would, given the efforts of all participants, help to find ways and means to put an end to the state of 'cold war' and make it impossible for a shooting war to break out. Let us do everything possible in order to ensure that such a meeting, which all the peoples are awaiting, is not endlessly delayed. We are awaiting your agreement to our proposal for a top level conference, and are prepared to take part in it at any time. It is in the interests of all states, large and small, for a summit meeting to be called as soon as possible.

In conclusion, I should like to express the hope that the government of the United Kingdom will support the proposal for convening an emergency session of the United Nations General Assembly, which could be a useful step towards reducing tension and preparing the ground for an early summit meeting.

Respectfully yours,
N. KHRUSHCHOV

22. Letter from Mr. Macmillan to Mr. Khrushchev regarding the convening of an emergency special session of the General Assembly, 7 August 1958[1]

Dear Mr. Prime Minister, On July 31 I proposed that we should meet on August 12 in New York, Geneva or any other place that might be

[1] Cmnd. 516, pp. 16–17. President Eisenhower acknowledged the letter Mr. Khrushchev wrote to him on 5 August 1958, in a brief statement which expressed similar views to those of Mr. Macmillan, above. For the text of the President's statement, see *D.S.B.*, 1 September 1958,

generally agreeable. I said that I would be there on that date and hoped that you would be there too.

I therefore regret that in your letter of August 5 you have withdrawn your agreement, very clearly set out in your letter of July 23, to a Special Session of the Security Council to be attended by Heads of Government. May I remind you of your words: 'Considering the need for taking urgent decisions in the interests of maintaining peace the Soviet Government considers that the form of meeting of the Heads of Government in these circumstances cannot have any decisive significance. . . . We share your views about the approach to a discussion of this question at a special meeting of the Security Council with Heads of Government participating.'; and of your further words: 'We learnt with satisfaction that you, Mr. Prime Minister, are ready to go to New York for a special meeting of the Security Council with the participation of Heads of Government; so far as the Soviet Union is concerned . . . . the Soviet Union will be represented at this session by the Chairman of the Council of Ministers of the U.S.S.R.'

You now propose instead, that there should be a special meeting of the General Assembly. This had, of course, been proposed by the United States on July 18 but action had been suspended because of your view, which both the United States and United Kingdom Governments approved, that the matter should be discussed by Heads of Government and in a more limited circle.

A special session of the General Assembly would be acceptable to Her Majesty's Government. I do however still think that more progress could have been made on Middle East questions by a meeting of the Security Council, especially one where the Heads of Government could negotiate as well as debate.

As to the 'Summit' meeting of the larger character about which we have corresponded since last January I fail to understand the suggestion in the last paragraph of your letter that you are awaiting a further move from me. On the contrary it is I who am awaiting from you an answer to my letter of July 1.[1] I reminded you in this letter that we had had no response to the suggestions made to you as long ago as May 31 for resolving the difficulty created by the fact that each side had put forward a different set of proposals about which to negotiate. I have always made it abundantly clear that I am anxious for such a meeting under conditions which are acceptable to all of us.

Yours sincerely,

HAROLD MACMILLAN

p. 342. It was reported in *Le Monde*, 14 August 1958, that General de Gaulle would not reply directly to Mr. Krushchev's letter of 5 August 1958; General de Gaulle considered that as the United Nations General Assembly was examining the situation in the Middle East, an exchange of letters between him and Mr. Khrushchev was unnecessary.

[1] See above, pp. 49–50, for the text of this letter.

23. Resolution adopted by the Security Council requesting the convening of an emergency special session of the General Assembly, 7 August 1958[1]

THE SECURITY COUNCIL.

Having considered items 2 and 3 of its agenda as contained in document S/Agenda/838,

Taking into account that the lack of unanimity of its permanent members at the 834th and 837th meetings has prevented the Council from exercising its primary responsibility for the maintenance of international peace and security,

Decides to call an emergency special session of the General Assembly.

24. Statement by the Government of the People's Republic of China supporting the Soviet proposal for an emergency special session of the General Assembly, 8 August 1958[2]

On August 5, 1958 the Government of the Soviet Union proposed the convening of an emergency special session of the United Nations General Assembly to consider the question of immediate withdrawal of United States forces from the Lebanon and of British forces from Jordan. This is yet another major effort for peace made by the Government of the Soviet Union after its proposal for the holding of a conference of the heads of government of big powers to discuss relaxation of the tension in the Near and Middle East was obstructed again and again and rejected obstinately by the United States and British Governments. The Chinese Government fully supports this proposal of the Soviet Government. At the present time, the United States and Britain are still reinforcing their forces and expanding their occupation areas in the Lebanon and Jordan, the situation in the Near and Middle East is still tense, and international peace and security is still in grave danger. The Chinese Government holds that all peace-loving countries have the responsibility to adopt all possible steps to urge the United States and Britain to withdraw their forces of aggression at once from the Lebanon and Jordan so as to restore peace in the Near and Middle East.

The United States and Britain attempt to cover up their naked aggression in the Lebanon and Jordan by falsely accusing the United Arab Republic of so-called indirect aggression against the Lebanon and Jordan.

---

[1] S.C.O.R., Thirteenth Year, Supplement for July, August, and September 1958, pp. 126–7, Doc. S/4083. The resolution was submitted by the United States (S/4056/Rev. 1), and as orally amended in Council, was adopted unanimously by the Council.

[2] *Peking Review*, 12 August 1958, p. 8.

This is like a thief crying 'catch thief!' and can deceive nobody. Even the United Nations Observation Group sent to the Lebanon to carry out investigations has admitted more than once that the charge of so-called indirect aggression is unsubstantiated. Britain had not even the pretext of so-called indirect aggression when, supported by the United States, it carried out aggression against Jordan. It was only when British troops were invading Jordan that the King of Jordan belatedly went through the formality of making the charge of so-called indirect aggression. The United States and Britain hurriedly dispatched their troops to invade the Lebanon and Jordan on the assumption that the Iraqi revolution was so-called indirect aggression. In extending recognition to the Republic of Iraq, they have in effect declared the bankruptcy of this absurd pretext. If they are compelled by the indisputable facts and pressure of a powerful public opinion to recognize the Iraqi people's right to choose their own government, in which case there is no question of indirect aggression at all, then what justification is there for their armed intervention in the internal affairs of the Lebanon and Jordan?

It is the unanimous will of the Arab peoples to oppose the imperialists and their agents and to win and safeguard the independence and freedom of their countries. In describing the struggle of the Arab peoples for independence and freedom as an indirect aggression committed by the United Arab Republic against other Arab countries, the United States and British imperialists not only slander the United Arab Republic but also insult the Arab people as a whole. The Chinese people express extreme indignation at this slander made by the imperialists and give firm support to the United Arab Republic, the Republic of Iraq and all the Arab peoples in their just struggle against colonialist aggression.

The presence of United States and British forces of aggression in the Lebanon and Jordan constitutes a serious threat to the peace and security of the Near and Middle East and the world. The peace-loving countries and peoples of the world unanimously demand the withdrawal of United States and British forces from the Lebanon and Jordan. Only when an emergency special session of the United Nations General Assembly is held in accordance with the Soviet proposal, will it provide an opportunity of urging the United States and Britain to withdraw their forces from the Lebanon and Jordan and easing the tension in the Near and Middle East. The Chinese Government holds that only when the emergency special session of the United Nations General Assembly truly shoulders the noble responsibility of halting aggression and safeguarding peace in conformity with the spirit of the United Nations Charter and the eager desire of the people of the whole world, will it be able to restore to the United Nations its lost prestige. It is another test of historic significance whether an emergency special session of the United Nations General

Assembly will be held in accordance with the Soviet proposal and, if held, whether it will realize the eager desire of the people of the world.

The Chinese Government and people, together with other peace-loving countries and peoples of the world, resolutely demand that the United States and Britain withdraw their forces at once from the Lebanon and Jordan, and so restore peace in the Near and Middle East. Whatever the outcome of an emergency special session of the United Nations General Assembly, as long as the United States and British forces of aggression have not withdrawn from the Lebanon and Jordan completely, the United States and British imperialists will not be able to escape the serious responsibility for endangering the peace and security of the Near and Middle East and the world, nor will they be able to escape being justly condemned and strongly opposed by the Arab people and the peoples of all nations.

25. Letter from Mr. Khrushchev to Mr. Macmillan regarding the convening of an emergency special session of the General Assembly, 10 August 1958[1]

Mr. Prime Minister, I have received your message of August 7 in which you announce the United Kingdom government's consent to the Soviet government's proposal for holding an emergency session of the General Assembly. I could have said no more, Mr. Prime Minister, were it not for the need to reply to two points in your message.

You write that my message of July 23 said that the Soviet government was ready to hold a special session of the Security Council to be attended by heads of government. Indeed, having received your message of July 22, in which you favoured the idea of a meeting of heads of government within the framework of the Security Council to discuss the situation which had arisen in the Middle East, we stated that we were ready to take part in such a meeting.

At the same time, Mr. Prime Minister, I should like to draw your attention to the main point—to the crux of the matter. You will recall that my original message of July 19 to you and to Mr. Eisenhower, M. de Gaulle and Mr. Nehru, contained the proposal for a meeting of the heads of government of the U.S.S.R., the United Kingdom, the United States, France and India, with the participation of the United Nations Secretary-General, to take urgent measures to end the armed conflict which had begun in the Middle East. Now, just as at that time, we are deeply convinced that if we are to make a serious approach to questions of such importance, a meeting of heads of government in the composition

---

[1] *Soviet News*, 12 August 1958.

we suggested might have resulted in the speediest and most effective settlement of the present conflict in the interests of world peace.

If the heads of government of all the powers we addressed had consented to the calling of such a meeting, that would have been evidence of a businesslike approach on the part of the governments to the solution of most important international problems. And we had great hopes that all of them would show precisely such an approach. The Soviet government attached great importance to a meeting of the heads of government of the aforementioned countries also because they are the strongest powers and their attitude would largely determine the direction developments would take—towards peace or towards war. We expected that the leaders of all the countries concerned would display wisdom in their understanding of the present events, of the direction in which they were developing and of the consequences of a war if it were unleashed and the incalculable sufferings it would bring to mankind.

Unfortunately our expectations were not fulfilled. While the Prime Minister of India, Mr. Nehru, and the Prime Minister of France, M. de Gaulle, accepted our proposal for a five-power meeting of heads of government with the participation of the United Nations Secretary-General, the United States President rejected such a meeting and you actually supported him in that.

In circumstances in which the five-power meeting of heads of government suggested by the Soviet government had proved—through no fault of ours—to be impossible, the Soviet government took a positive view of your proposal for a meeting of heads of government within the Security Council to discuss the situation which had arisen in the Middle East, our idea being that this would be nothing else but a five-power meeting of heads of government within the framework of the Security Council.

Moreover, in your message of July 22 you stressed that in the opinion of the government of the United Kingdom no resolutions should be put forward at the special meeting of the Security Council unless they arose out of previous agreement. In other words, you said, the object would be to reach fruitful agreements rather than to register differences by votes. Thus the idea was to hold the principal discussions on the situation in the Middle East between the heads of government of the five states, with the participation of Mr. Hammarskjöld.

However, in your message of July 26 you speak merely of the presence of the heads of government at the meeting of the Security Council, while in your message of July 31 you simply hint at the possibility of arranging less formal meetings of heads of government on the questions under consideration by the Security Council.

It has finally become clear from the messages and explanations of the United States government, and in particular from Mr. Eisenhower's letter of July 25,[1] that for the examination of the situation in the Middle East it was intended to call an ordinary meeting of the Security Council, with all the negative aspects and shortcomings arising from its present composition—shortcomings of which I have spoken in my message of August 5 and which I do not wish to reiterate. And you, Mr. Prime Minister, have actually agreed to those proposals of the United States President.

Moreover, after the press conference held by Mr. Dulles on July 31,[2] it has become absolutely obvious that the government of the United States—and the British government made common cause with it—had decided to have such a meeting of the Security Council with a view to justifying the aggressive actions of the United States and the United Kingdom in the Middle East and, by means of talk about a mythical threat of some indirect aggression, to shift on to other states the responsibility for the dangerous situation in the Middle East arising from the American and British military intervention. Consequently, at the Security Council meeting proposed by the governments of the United States and the United Kingdom there would have been no serious discussion by the heads of government on the situation in the Middle East and it would have amounted to a useless waste of time, as there are no grounds for supposing that, in its present composition, this United Nations body can ensure—as is demanded by the peoples—a correct solution to this question in the interests of peace.

Thus, in pressing for the acceptance of this proposal, the United States, with the backing of the United Kingdom, unquestionably wanted to lure us into a labyrinth of futile discussions. In these circumstances we have come to the conclusion that in order to secure urgent measures to curb aggression it is necessary to convene, not the Security Council, but an emergency session of the United Nations General Assembly.

We also proceeded from the premise that the General Assembly is the most representative body of this international organisation and that both the delegates of member-countries of aggressive military blocs dominated by the United States and representatives of other countries—socialist states and countries which are not committed—will take part in its deliberations. It is, of course, unnecessary to mention that its meetings will be attended by the Arab states which are victims of direct and indirect aggression committed by countries which are members of the aforementioned military blocs. It is absolutely obvious that the present emergency session of the General Assembly will enable all states, both large and small, to give a comprehensive outline of their views in the search for decisions which will help to restore peace and ensure security in the area of the Middle East. The Soviet government is represented at

---

[1] See fn. 1 on pp. 309–10 above.　　　　[2] See *D.S.B.*, 18 August 1958, pp. 265–72.

the Assembly by a delegation led by the Foreign Minister of the U.S.S.R.

As for that part of my message of August 5 in which I speak of the need to resume consideration of the question of a meeting of heads of government in the composition we proposed earlier in order to discuss a wider range of pressing international problems, you in fact evade the crux of the matter by saying that you have not received a reply to your message of July 1 regarding the convocation of a summit meeting. We shall naturally not leave this message of yours unanswered. However, it should not be forgotten that at the time when talks on the calling of a summit conference to ease international tension were in progress between us, the United Kingdom and the United States started armed intervention in the Middle East. That action placed the world on the brink of a world war. Naturally, the main problem, in those circumstances, was to curb aggression and safeguard peace in that area of the world. With this end in view, the Soviet government then raised the question of immediately convening a meeting of the heads of government of the U.S.S.R., the United Kingdom, the United States, France and India, with the participation of the United Nations Secretary-General, in order to discuss the situation existing in the Middle East as a result of the armed intervention of the United States and the United Kingdom.

I should like to hope, Mr. Prime Minister, that the present emergency session of the United Nations General Assembly will cope with its task and thereby to a considerable extent pave the way for the convening of an East-West summit conference, the urgent need for which is becoming increasingly obvious in the light of the latest events in the Middle East.

Respectfully yours,

N. KHRUSHCHOV

C. AFTERMATH

1. Resolution of the General Assembly regarding the situation in the Lebanon and Jordan, 21 August 1958[1]

THE GENERAL ASSEMBLY,

Having considered the item entitled 'Questions considered by the Security Council at its 838th meeting on 7 August 1958',

[1] G.A.O.R., Third Emergency Special Session, Supplement No. 1, (A/3905), Resol. 1237 (ES-III). Fifteen plenary meetings were held from 8 to 21 August 1958. In the course of the debate, the U.S.S.R., on 12 August submitted a draft resolution recommending that the U.S. and U.K. withdraw their troops immediately from the Lebanon and Jordan, that UNOGIL be strengthened and that an Observation Group be despatched to Jordan, with a view to the supervision of the withdrawal of these forces (A/3870 and Corr. 1). On 14 August UNOGIL submitted its Third Report (S/4085), which said, among other things, that since 31 July there

Noting the Charter aim that States should practise tolerance and live together in peace with one another as good neighbours,

Noting that the Arab States have agreed, in the Pact of the League of Arab States, to strengthen the close relations and numerous ties which link the Arab States, and to support and stabilize these ties upon a basis of respect for the independence and sovereignty of these States, and to direct their efforts toward the common good of all the Arab countries, the improvement of their status, the security of their future and the realization of their aspirations and hopes,

Desiring to relieve international tension,

I

1. *Welcomes* the renewed assurances given by the Arab States to observe the provision of article 8 of the Pact of the League of Arab States that each member State shall respect the systems of government established in the other member States and regard them as exclusive concerns of these States, and that each shall pledge to abstain from any action calculated to change established systems of government;

2. *Calls upon* all States Members of the United Nations to act strictly in accordance with the principles of mutual respect for each other's territorial integrity and sovereignty, of non-aggression, of strict non-interference in each other's internal affairs, and of equal and mutual benefit, and to ensure that their conduct by word and deed conforms to these principles;

II

Requests the Secretary-General to make forthwith, in consultation with the Governments concerned and in accordance with the Charter, and having in mind section I of this resolution, such practical arrangements as would adequately help in upholding the purposes and principles of the Charter in relation to Lebanon and Jordan in the present circumstances, and thereby facilitate the early withdrawal of the foreign troops from the two countries;

III

Invites the Secretary-General to continue his studies now under way and in this context to consult as appropriate with the Arab countries of

had been a virtual nation-wide truce in the Lebanon. On 18 August the U.S. and U.K. submitted letters to the President of the General Assembly, stating that their forces would be withdrawn either when requested by the Governments of the Lebanon and Jordan, or when as a result of further action by the U.N. their presence was no longer required (A/3876, A/3877). On 18 August, Canada, Colombia, Denmark, Liberia, Norway, Panama, and Paraguay submitted a 4-part draft resolution, A/3878. On 21 August Sudan introduced the above resolution on behalf of Iraq, Jordan, the Lebanon, Libya, Morocco, Saudi Arabia, Sudan, Tunisia, the U.A.R., and Yemen. It was adopted unanimously.

the Near East with a view to possible assistance regarding an Arab development institution designed to further economic growth in these countries;

IV

1. *Requests* Member States to co-operate fully in carrying out this resolution:

2. *Invites* the Secretary-General to report hereunder as appropriate, the first such report to be made not later than 30 September 1958.

2. Letter from the permanent representative of the United Kingdom to the United Nations to Mr. Hammarskjold, 1 October 1958[1]

I have the honour to inform you that as forecast in the memorandum annexed to your report of September 29[2] Her Majesty's Government in the United Kingdom together with the Jordan Government are today able to announce their decision with regard to the withdrawal of United Kingdom forces from Jordan. The two Governments have reviewed together your report and the arrangements which you have made to assist in giving effect to the General Assembly's resolution of August 21. They have also taken note of the assurances received by you from other Arab Governments concerned that they intend to conduct their relations with Jordan in accordance with this resolution. Taking into account the above factors and the confidence of the Jordan Government that the atmosphere will improve, Her Majesty's Government have agreed with the Jordan Government that the withdrawal of British troops will begin on October 20. This withdrawal will be completed within a period not exceeding such time as may be required for the necessary arrangements for the movement of personnel, stores and equipment.

PIERSON DIXON

3. Letter from the permanent representative of the United States to the United Nations to Mr. Hammarskjold, 8 October 1958[3]

I have the honour to transmit the text of an announcement issued today by the United States Government.

I would be grateful if you would arrange for it to be circulated for the information of all Members of the United Nations.

HENRY CABOT LODGE

---

[1] U.N. Doc. A/3937. The letter was circulated to the members of the United Nations by the Secretary-General.   [2] U.N. Doc. A/3934.

[3] U.N. Doc. A/3942. The letter and memorandum were circulated to the members of the United Nations by the Secretary-General.

Memorandum

The Government of the United States announces that by agreement with the Government of the Republic of Lebanon it has now been decided to complete withdrawal of United States force from Lebanon. It is expected that, barring unforeseen developments, the forces will all be withdrawn by the end of October.

The United States sent forces to Lebanon in response to the urgent appeal of the then Government of that country for assistance in maintaining Lebanese independence and integrity. At the same time, the United States took steps in the United Nations with a view to having it take measures to preserve the independence and territorial integrity of Lebanon and thus facilitate the withdrawal of the United States forces. Subsequently, the United Nations General Assembly unanimously adopted a resolution developed by the Arab States and designed to ensure respect by States for the freedom, independence and integrity of other States, and to establish practical arrangements to uphold the purposes and principles of the Charter in relation to Lebanon.

The steps which have been taken with respect to the situation in Lebanon have led to a substantial improvement in the international aspects of the Lebanese security situation. The current unrest appears to have essentially domestic origins. In view of the progress made toward more stable international conditions in the area, it has been concluded that United States forces can now be totally withdrawn from Lebanon. It is the confident hope of the United States Government that the Republic of Lebanon, its sovereignty and independence strengthened, will move forward in unity, peace and prosperity.

8 October 1958.

4. Soviet statement on Soviet-Persian relations, Moscow, 31 October 1958[1]

The Soviet government considers it necessary to draw the Iranian government's attention to the new situation emerging in Soviet-Iranian relations owing to the latest steps taken by the Iranian government. The point in question is the conclusion by Iran of a new military agreement with the United States which gives the United States armed forces vast possibilities for the even greater subjugation of Iran to American military plans. It is common knowledge that talks between Iran and the United

---

[1] *Soviet News*, 4 November 1958. This statement was handed to the Persian Ambassador in Moscow, Mr. Mustafa Samii, by Mr. Gromyko. Mr. Samii said that he would immediately forward the statement to the Persian Government. It had been stated in the declaration of the Baghdad Pact Council meeting in July 1958, see below, pp. 369–70, that the United States would enter into defence and security arrangements with the countries of the pact.

States on these questions have been conducted, in particular, during the recent visit to Teheran of the American Secretary of Defence, Mr. McElroy.

By further extending its military co-operation with the United States, the Iranian government is overstepping the limit beyond which begins direct support for certain foreign circles in the carrying out of their aggressive plans directed against the U.S.S.R. and other peaceloving states. The conclusion of this military agreement will lead Iran into still greater military and political dependence on the United States and will inevitably increase the danger of Iran being drawn into the military ventures of those foreign circles which have long regarded the Middle East as a potential *place d'armes* for their aggressive plans.

Attempts are being made, as is well known, to justify the new and dangerous step which the Iranian government has taken by references to the needs of Iran's defence. However, these references cannot mislead anyone, because Iran is in no way threatened by her neighbours, and particularly the Soviet Union, which always abides by the policy of good neighbourliness and friendship towards Iran. Moreover, it should be added that if anyone in Iran tries to look for security under the collapsing roof of the Baghdad Pact and under the dubious protection of foreign powers situated thousands of kilometres from Iran, such attempts, as has been shown by the experience of Iran's recent allies under the Baghdad Pact, can least of all serve this purpose.

Actions of this kind by the Iranian government can, of course, only worsen the situation in the Middle East. They are incompatible with the interests of strengthening peace and security in the Middle East.

These steps taken by the Iranian government do not accord with the statements of Iranian government leaders about their desire to develop and improve relations between our two countries. They are also in direct contradiction with the principle of good-neighbourly relations and with Iran's commitments under the existing Soviet-Iranian agreements, and in particular the agreement on guarantees and neutrality of October 1, 1927. Article 3 of this agreement clearly states that both the high-contracting parties undertake not to participate either actually or formally in political alliances or agreements directed against the security of the other high-contracting party on land or at sea.[1]

A strange situation emerges. On the one hand, the official representatives of the Iranian government assure the Soviet Union that they are striving to develop good-neighbourly relations with the U.S.S.R. and to

[1] 'Each of the contracting parties undertakes not to participate, either in fact or in law, in alliances or agreements of a political nature which might be directed against the security of the territory or waters of the other contracting party, or against its integrity, independence or sovereignty. Moreover, each of the contracting parties undertakes not to participate in boycotts or economic blockades organised by third powers against one of the contracting parties.'

prevent the exploitation of Iran by other powers against the Soviet Union. On the other hand, the Iranian government is in a hurry to bind itself to the United States by military agreements of an obviously unfriendly, or, what is more, openly hostile nature in relation to the Soviet Union. It is appropriate to ask how these actions must be judged. They cannot be evaluated otherwise than as an indication of the fact that the Iranian government is embarking on a course of foreign policy which is, above all, dangerous to Iran herself, and that it is obviously giving very little consideration to the possible consequences of all this.

Being concerned for the consolidation of peace and security in the Middle East and throughout the world, the Soviet Union did not remain indifferent in instances in which situations developed in the Middle East during the past years pregnant with military conflicts which could gravely harm the cause of peace in this area and prejudice the security of the U.S.S.R. There is even less reason for the Soviet Union to remain indifferent to the situation that is developing owing to the conclusion by Iran of a new military agreement with the United States—an agreement directly endangering the southern frontiers of the Soviet Union.

In these circumstances the Soviet Union is faced with the need to consider in a new light the present state of Soviet-Iranian relations. The Soviet government believes, for instance, that it is scarcely opportune in the existing situation to proceed with such a step as the visit to Iran of K. E. Voroshilov, President of the Presidium of the U.S.S.R. Supreme Soviet, which had been envisaged recently in connection with the invitation received from the Iranian side and which had been contemplated as a visit of good will and friendship. In conditions in which the Iranian government is taking steps directed against the interests of the Soviet Union, this visit would create a wrong impression of the present state of Soviet-Iranian relations. It is clear from what has been said above that at the present time there seem to be no conditions for such a visit to be undertaken with benefit to Soviet-Iranian relations.

The Soviet government sincerely hopes that the Iranian government will give serious thought to the situation developing in the relations between our two countries in connection with the latest steps of the Iranian side and will consider it appropriate not to take steps directed towards a serious and dangerous worsening of these relations.

In drawing the Iranian government's attention to all these circumstances, the Soviet government is guided solely by the desire to prevent a course of events which might undermine peace in the Middle East and jeopardise the future of Soviet-Iranian relations, for the improvement of which so much has been done in recent years.

5. Report by Mr. Hammarskjold, regarding the withdrawal of troops from the Lebanon and Jordan, 10 November 1958[1]

1. Pursuant to General Assembly resolution 1237 (ES-III) of 21 August 1958, part 4, paragraph 2, the Secretary-General has the honour to submit letters regarding the withdrawal of troops from Lebanon and Jordan received from the Government of the United States of America and the Government of the United Kingdom of Great Britain and Northern Ireland (see Annexes 1 and 2 to the present document). As stated in those letters, the withdrawal of United States troops from Lebanon was completed on 25 October and the withdrawal of United Kingdom troops from Jordan on 2 November 1958.

2. Steps have recently been taken looking towards a normalization of air and overland transport in relation to Jordan.

The development of the special arrangements in relation to Jordan made under the above-mentioned resolution will be the subject of a later report.

ANNEX 1

Letter dated 6 November 1958 from the Representative of the United States of America to the United Nations, addressed to the Secretary-General

New York 6 November 1958

I have the honour to inform you that on 27 September the United States Government made known its intention to complete the withdrawal of United States troops from Lebanon by the end of October, if possible, provided the international security situation with respect to Lebanon continued to improve in the framework of successful implementation of part I of the General Assembly resolution of 21 August 1958. There has been continued improvement. The United States Government has therefore been able to complete the withdrawal of its troops. The last United States troops left Lebanon on 25 October, ahead of schedule.

The United States wishes to express its appreciation for the untiring efforts of the Secretary-General which have contributed to the establishment of conditions making possible the withdrawal of United States forces.

HENRY CABOT LODGE

ANNEX 2

Letter dated 6 November 1958 from the Permanent Representative of the United Kingdom of Great Britain and Northern Ireland to the United Nations, addressed to the Secretary-General

New York, 6 November 1958

In my letter of 1 October I informed you that Her Majesty's Government in the United Kingdom had agreed with the Government of Jordan

[1] U.N. Doc. A/3986.

that the withdrawal of British troops would begin on 20 October and that it would be completed within a period not exceeding such time as might be required for the necessary arrangements for the movement of personnel, stores and equipment. In reaching this decision Her Majesty's Government took into account among other factors the assurances received by you from other Arab Governments concerned that they intended to conduct their relations with Jordan in accordance with the General Assembly's resolution of 21 August.

I now have the honour to inform you that the withdrawal of United Kingdom forces from Jordan was completed on 2 November.

I take this opportunity of conveying to you the appreciation of Her Majesty's Government in the United Kingdom for the contribution which you have made towards giving effect to the purposes of the resolution of 21 August.

PIERSON DIXON

6. Letter from Mr. Hammarskjold to the President of the Security Council regarding the withdrawal of the Lebanese complaint of 22 May from the agenda of the Security Council, 17 November 1958[1]

1. In its letter to you dated 16 November 1958,[2] the Government of Lebanon has asked for the deletion from the list of items of which the Security Council is seized of the Lebanese complaint presented to the Council on 22 May 1958. In its fifth report dated 14 November 1958, the United Nations Observations Group in Lebanon, by way of a conclusion, has stated that since the task assigned to the Group 'may now be regarded as completed, the Group is of the opinion that the withdrawal of the United Nations Observation Group in Lebanon should now be undertaken'.[3] The Group accordingly submits a recommendation to that effect. Both documents are today circulated to the Security Council.

2. In view of the statement of the Government of Lebanon and the recommendation of the Observation Group, I have immediately instructed the Group to present, in consultation with the Government of Lebanon, a detailed plan for the withdrawal. I have taken this step under the authorization given to the Secretary-General in the Security Council resolution of 11 June 1958 to take the necessary steps for implementation of the Security Council's decision. The instruction given to the Observation Group implies that I consider the task of the Group as completed and that my remaining duty under the resolution thus covers only the necessary measures for the liquidation of the operation.

DAG HAMMARSKJÖLD

[1] S.C.O.R., Thirteenth Year, Supplement for October, November, and December 1958, pp. 13-14, Doc. S/4115.   [2] Doc. S/4113.   [3] Doc. S/4114, para. 22.

7. Proclamation by Lieutenant-General Abboud announcing a military *coup d'état* in the Sudan, Omdurman, 17 November 1958[1]

Citizens, I greet you all. You all well know the extent of anarchy, chaos and instability in the country for both individuals and groups. This also extended to Government and public centres without exception. All this was caused by the political crises ruling the country. Everyone wanted gain for himself by all legal and illegal methods, and by using some papers to contact foreign Embassies, not for the sake of reform or to protect the Sudan's independence and progress, nor out of a desire to help the people who lack the necessary means of existence, but in pursuit of authority, influence and domination of the country and its resources.

That lasted a long time. We have been patient with these tendentious Governments, one after the other, and we hoped that things would improve, that stability would reign, that people would be assured and that the hatred latent in their hearts would be removed. But, regretfully, the situation only became worse. Everyone who loved the safety of the Sudan lost patience and everyone complained about the deterioration of the situation and the anarchy and corruption, until the country almost fell into an abyss, the depth of which only God knows.

Consequently it was natural that the army and security men of the country should stop this anarchy and end it and restore peace and stability to all citizens and residents. Thank God, your loyal army accomplished this today, 17th November 1958, and executed this peaceful blessed plan which, with the help of God, will be the turning point from anarchy to stability and from corruption to honesty.

I am sure that everyone who is loyal to this country will receive it gladly.

Citizens, by bringing about a change in the present conditions, we do not seek any gain and we hold no enmity or hatred for anybody. We work for stability. Therefore, I ask all citizens to be calm. I ask everyone to carry out his work in full loyalty to the State—the employee in his office, the worker in the factory, the peasant on his farm, and the merchant in his shop.

As the security forces have taken over the reins of the Government, and in order for them to be able fully to perform their duties, I order the

[1] *S.W.B. Part IV*, 18 November 1958, p. 8. The *coup d'état* took place at three a.m. The Sudanese army occupied all public centres. Later on 17 November, Lieut.-Gen. Abboud, 'in view of the worsening of conditions in the country . . .' declared 'a state of emergency throughout the Sudanese Republic', and 'the suspension of the provisional constitution of the Sudan, and the dissolution of Parliament . . .' and ordered 'the suspension of newspapers, news-sheets, and printing houses until further notice.' Ibid., p. 9. Newspapers were published again on 19 November 1958. On 18 November Lieut.-Gen. Abboud issued decrees proclaiming the Sudan a 'democratic republic' and giving constitutional authority to a 13-man Supreme Council for the Armed Forces, which accorded full 'legislative, executive and judicial powers' to him as its president.

following to be carried out immediately: (1) Dissolution of all political parties; (2) Prohibition of gatherings, processions, and demonstrations in all Sudanese provinces; (3) Suspension of the press pending an order from the Minister of the Interior.

The army authorities ask all citizens to carry this out with good spirit. They also warn those who may think of disturbing the peace that they will not refrain from imposing the severest punishments on them.

Before I end my speech I would like to reassure the foreign Ambassadors, consuls and foreign communities of the safety of their persons, funds and properties. It also pleases me to ascertain that free, independent Sudan will base its relations with all States in general and the Arab States in particular on love, respect and common interest. As to our sister the United Arab Republic, we will do our best to improve relations and solve all pending questions and remove the artificial estrangement which has prevailed between the two sister countries.

8. Soviet-Egyptian Agreement on the Aswan High Dam, Cairo, 27 December 1958[1]

AGREEMENT
CONCERNING THE SUPPLY BY THE U.S.S.R. OF ECONOMIC AND TECHNICAL AID TO THE U.A.R. FOR THE FIRST STAGE CONSTRUCTION OF THE HIGH DAM AT ASWAN.

The Governments of the U.A.R. and the U.S.S.R. drawn by the friendly ties between the two countries and being desirous of increasing and strengthening economic and technical co-operation between them on a basis of equality and non-intervention in internal affairs, and of complete respect of the dignity and national sovereignty of each of the two countries, and in view of the great importance of the construction of the High Dam at Aswan to the national economy of the U.A.R., have agreed to the following:

ARTICLE I

In response to the desire of the Government of the U.A.R. to develop its national economy, the Government of the U.S.S.R. agrees to co-operate with the Government of the U.A.R. in the first stage construction of the High Dam at Aswan.

This stage involves the construction of the front part of the main section of the Dam with a height of 50 metres and a length of 600 metres,

---

[1] *Egyptian Economic and Political Review*, February-March 1959, pp. 48–51. The Vice-President of the U.A.R., Marshal Amer, was invited to visit Moscow, and arrived there on 19 October 1958. On 23 October the Soviet Government held a reception in the Great Kremlin Palace in the course of which Mr. Khrushchev announced that the U.S.S.R.: 'has agreed to commit itself to take part in the construction of the first section of the Aswan Dam . . .' See *Soviet News*, 24 October 1958.

and the construction of the works for water conversion, sluices and the equipment and the machinery necessary for these works, taking into consideration that these dimensions are approximate and will be agreed upon later on making the final details of designs, or when necessary during execution.

The first stage includes also the projects of the basins conversion, the irrigation projects and land reform with a view to utilising the additional water resulting from this stage. The amount of the aid to be supplied by the U.S.S.R., for the execution of these projects, will be fixed by the two parties, after completion of the investigation works for these projects by the U.A.R.

The two parties conceive that all expenses incurred by the Soviet party, whether for the construction of the Dam itself or for the execution of the irrigation works and basin conversion and which will be executed on the account of the loan, will be covered within the limits of the loan offered in conformity with the provisions of Article 5 of this Agreement.

ARTICLE 2

In order to realise the co-operation stipulated in Article 1 of this agreement, the Government of the U.S.S.R. will carry out the following:

a) The preparation, through Soviet organisations, of programmes for executing and accomplishing the necessary investigation and studies to be agreed upon by the two parties to introduce any amendments on the details of the design that may seem necessary, in accordance with the approval of the authorities concerned in the U.A.R., provided all this be accomplished with the least possible delay and in conformity with the hydraulic terms and conditions and the basic details laid down by the U.A.R., on condition that these amendments conform with the Dam designs in its final stage.

b) The supply, in conformity with the agreement of the two parties, of the sluices, machinery and equipment, together with the necessary spare part sets, as well as the necessary materials for the construction and running of the works of the first stage and the projects connected with it, provided these materials are not available in the U.A.R.

c) Offering the necessary technical aid for construction, by sending the necessary number of Soviet specialists, in conformity with the agreement to be approved by the two parties.

ARTICLE 3

A special organisation for the management of the project will be formed by the Government of the U.A.R. for administrative, technical and financial affairs.

The execution of the works demanded by the U.A.R. for the first stage of the High Dam will be entrusted to contractors chosen by the agreement of the two parties, on the basis of the employment of Soviet implements and with the aid of the Soviet specialists and technicians.

The contract to be concluded between the Government of the U.A.R. and the contractors shall include, besides the designs and specifications of the works to be accomplished, all the obligations of the contractors, as well as the services and facilities to be offered by the Government of the U.A.R.

The said organisation will supervise the contractors to ensure of their fulfilling the obligations required of them in conformity with the terms of the contract, and the said organisation, on their part, will offer the facilities and services stipulated in the contract.

ARTICLE 4

The Soviet organisation will be responsible for technical management in the construction of works of the first stage of the High Dam at Aswan and for the accomplishment of these works in a satisfactory manner, and for their safety, and the setting up of machinery and implements, and preparing them for working within the period fixed by the two parties and provided that this special organisation and the contractors referred to in Article 3 of this agreement meet their obligations in the investigation, construction and assembling works in accordance with the programme of execution agreed upon by the two parties.

For this purpose the Soviet authorities will delegate to the U.A.R. a technical expert with high qualifications, together with the necessary number of Soviet engineers, technicians and skilled workers in accordance with the agreement of the two parties.

The Soviet expert, with the aid of the Director of the Organisation referred to in Article 3, will coordinate work among the Soviet specialists and the specialists of the U.A.R., for technical supervision over the said works.

ARTICLE 5

The Government of the U.S.S.R. will supply the Government of the U.A.R. with a loan amounting to 400 million rubles (four hundred million rubles—a ruble equals 0·222168 grammes of pure gold) to cover the expenses of the Soviet organisation, as related to drawing up programmes of execution, activities of investigation and study, and the delivery of machinery, implements and materials on the basis of Soviet F.O.B. rates, as well as the travel expenses of the Soviet specialists in their departure from the Soviet Union to the U.A.R. and vice versa, in accordance with Article 2 of this agreement.

In case the total price of machinery, implements, sluices and materials mentioned above, estimated on the basis of Soviet F.O.B. rates and the travel expenses of the Soviet specialists, as well as the expenses of the Soviet organisations, including the necessary technical aid under this agreement, in case all these exceed the amount of the loan valuing 400 million rubles, the Government of the U.A.R. will remit this increase to the Government of the U.S.S.R., by delivering goods from the U.A.R., in conformity with the Trade and Payments Agreement in force in the U.A.R. (Egypt) and the U.S.S.R.

ARTICLE 6

The Government of the U.A.R. will remit the sums employed out of the loan offered to her in conformity with Article 5 of this agreement, in twelve equal instalments to begin one year after the date of the completion of the works of the first stage of the High Dam at Aswan and the filling of the Dam, provided this does not go beyond 1st January, 1964. The date of employing the loan will be considered the date of consignment of machinery, equipment and materials. As to the remittance of the expenses of designs, research and studies, as well as the expenses of the delegation of Soviet specialists to the U.A.R., the date of employment of the loan will be considered the date of the relative invoices.

The loan interest rate is 2·5%. Date of interest will begin from the date of employing every part of the loan, provided it be paid within the first three months of the year following the year in which it was due.

ARTICLE 7

The Government of the U.A.R. will remit the loan and interest in Egyptian pounds (the rate of one Egyptian pound is equal to 2·55187 grammes of pure gold). The sums due will be recorded in a special account, opened in the Central Bank of the U.A.R. (Egypt), in the interest of the State Bank of the U.S.S.R.

The ruble rate, compared with the Egyptian pound, will be considered on the basis of gold par rate between the two currencies on date of payment.

The Soviet authorities will employ all the sums paid into this account in the purchase of commodities in the U.A.R. (Egypt), in accordance with the Trade and Payments Agreement in force between the U.A.R. (Egypt) and the U.S.S.R.

Any sums paid into this account may be converted into sterling pounds or any convertible currency agreed upon by the two parties.

Should the par rate of the Egyptian pound be altered, the balance of the account of the State Bank of the U.S.S.R. in the Central Bank of the U.A.R. (Egypt) will be re-estimated according to the change in the amount of gold of the Egyptian pound.

ARTICLE 8

Each of the two of the Central Bank of the U.A.R. (Egypt) and the State Bank of the U.S.S.R., will open a special account for recording the operations relating to the employment and remittance of the loan granted, in conformity with this agreement and also the interest due on the same terms.

The two parties will agree to the necessary technical and financial procedures to be followed for the execution of this agreement.

ARTICLE 9

The Government of the U.A.R. will remit to the Soviet Party, all expenses incurred by the Soviet authorities, relating to food and lodging, as well as travel expenses, within the boundaries of the U.A.R., of the Soviet specialists delegated to offer technical aid, according to this agreement and in conformity with the terms of the relative contracts. Remittance of the said expenses will be accomplished by adding these sums, in Egyptian pounds, to the 'proceeds account', opened in the Central Bank of the U.A.R. (Egypt) in the interest of the State Bank of the U.S.S.R., in conformity with the Payments Agreement in force, concluded between the Government of the U.A.R. (Egypt) and the Government of the U.S.S.R.

ARTICLE 10

The supply of equipment, machinery and materials, the execution of projects, studies and research works and the delegation of Soviet specialists to the U.A.R., will be in conformity with the terms of the contracts to be concluded between the authority concerned in the U.A.R. and the competent Soviet authorities in accordance with Article 3 of this Agreement.

The contracts in question will determine, in particular, the amount, date, price and the guarantees relating to types of equipment and machinery and their concurrence with the fixed power, and the responsibility of each of the two parties in case of 'force majeure' circumstances and contravention to copyright law, as well as the provisions and conditions of fulfilling the obligations by the Soviet party in accordance with this agreement.

Prices of equipment, machinery and materials delivered by the U.S.S.R. to the U.A.R., in conformity with this agreement, will be fixed according to the universal market prices.

ARTICLE 11

Without prejudice to the provisions of Article 5, relating to utilising the loan for covering the price of machinery, equipment and materials on the basis of Soviet F.O.B. rates, the supply of machinery, equipment and materials offered by the U.S.S.R. will be shipped, insured, to the ports of the U.A.R., C.I.F.

Shipment and insurance expenses will be remitted apart on the basis of actual prices, in accordance with the Trade and Payments Agreement in force between the U.A.R. (Egypt) and the U.S.S.R.

Marine transport of equipment, machinery and materials, referred to above, will be accomplished in accordance with the Marine Transport Agreement, concluded on 18th September, 1958, between the two countries.

ARTICLE 12

In case any conflict or difference arises between the authorities of the U.A.R. and the Soviet authorities on any subject concerned with this agreement or its execution, the matter will be referred to the representative of the Governments of the U.A.R. and the U.S.S.R. to reach a solution on this conflict or difference referred to above.

This agreement is valid after ratification, which it is anticipated will be made with the least possible delay. It shall have legal force from date of exchange of ratification documents in Moscow.

This agreement has been written in Cairo on   1958, in two copies, one in Arabic and the other in Russian. Each of the two has the same legal force.

For the Government of
the U.S.S.R.
For the Government of
the U.A.R.

Cairo........ 1958

Excellency, In continuation of the agreement signed today and concluded between the Government of the U.S.S.R. and the Government of the U.A.R., relating to the offer of economic and technical aid by the U.S.S.R. to the U.A.R., for construction of the first stage of the High Dam, and with reference to Articel 7, stipulating that the remittance of the loan granted for the above mentioned purpose, will be accomplished by exporting goods from the U.A.R. or in sterling pounds, or any convertible currency, it is understood that the U.S.S.R. shall not utilise the sums remitted to the said account except for the purpose of purchasing goods from the U.A.R. It is also understood, that on utilising the said sums, the U.S.S.R. shall enjoy the same rights, privileges and discounts granted by the U.A.R. for exports in free currency, according to regulations in force during the time of exportation.

The U.S.S.R. shall have the right to request payment in sterling pounds or convertible free currency, agreed upon by the two parties, only in exceptional cases where the U.A.R., on utilising the said sums, cannot apply the same treatment as that applied to exports carried out in free currency, or where the U.A.R. is unable to supply the goods required by the U.S.S.R. within six months.

Will you kindly, therefore, confirm the contents of this letter.

Cairo........ 1958

Field Marshal Abdel Hakim Amer,
Deputy President of the U.A.R.

Dear Sir, I have the honour to acknowledge receipt of your letter of today's date, text as below:

(see letter as above)

and to confirm its contents.

Chief of Russian Delegation

Cairo........ 1958

Excellency, In continuation of the agreement signed today and concluded between the Government of the U.S.S.R. and the Government of the U.A.R., relating to the offer of economic and technical aid by the U.S.S.R. to the U.A.R. for construction of the first stage of the High Dam, I should be much obliged if you would kindly confirm the agreement concluded by our delegations, with regard to the two following points:

1. In the event of the issue of a new currency in the U.A.R., before the date of the termination of this agreement, the balance remaining in the open accounts, in conformity with the text of this agreement, shall be so converted as to guarantee the maintenance of its present value.
2. In the event of the establishment of a new Central Bank in the U.A.R., before the date of the termination of this agreement, this Bank shall replace the Central Bank in the region of Egypt, referred to in the text of this agreement.

Cairo........ 1958

Field Marshal Abdel Hakim Amer,
Deputy President of the U.A.R.

Dear Sir, I have the honour to acknowledge receipt of your letter of today's date, text as below:

(see letter as above)

and to confirm its contents.

Chief of Russian Delegation

Cairo........ 1958

Excellency, In continuation of the agreement signed today and concluded between the Government of the U.S.S.R. and the Government of the U.A.R., relating to the offer of economic and technical aid by the U.S.S.R. to the U.A.R., for the construction of the first stage of the High Dam, and with reference to Article 5, stipulating that the gold par rate of the ruble is 0·222168 grammes of pure gold, it is understood by both of us that, should the ruble gold par rate change before the exhaustion of the loan, the balance of the loan will be amended, following this change, so as to maintain the value of the said balance, estimated by gold, as it had been.

I should be very much obliged if you would kindly confirm the contents of this letter.

Cairo........ 1958

Field Marshal Abdel Hakim Amer,
Deputy President of the U.A.R.

Dear Sir, I have the honour to acknowledge receipt of your letter of today's date, text as below:

(see letter as above)

and to confirm its contents·

Chief of Russian Delegation

III. THE WESTERN ALLIANCE

A. WESTERN RELATIONS

1. Final communiqué of the fourth session of the Baghdad Pact ministerial Council, Ankara, 31 January 1958[1]

The Fourth Session of the Baghdad Pact Council was held in the New Grand National Assembly Building in Ankara from January 27 to January 30, 1958. His Excellency Mr. Adnan Menderes, Prime Minister of Turkey was in the Chair. The Delegations from the member countries were led by:—

   (i) His Excellency Dr. Manouchehr Eghbal—Prime Minister—Iran
  (ii) His Excellency Sayid Nuri Al-Said—Iraq
 (iii) Malik Firoz Khan Noon—Prime Minister—Pakistan
 (iv) His Excellency Mr. Adnan Menderes—Prime Minister—Turkey
  (v) The Right Honourable Selwyn Lloyd—Secretary of State for Foreign Affairs—United Kingdom.

The United States participated through a delegation led by the Honourable John Foster Dulles, Secretary of State.

The Council noted with satisfaction the presence of Mr. Dulles at the session.

The Council, during its four day session, reviewed the work of the Baghdad Pact Organisation and after discussions adopted the reports and recommendations of:—

   (i) The Economic Committee;
  (ii) The Liaison Committee;
 (iii) The Counter Subversion Committee; and
 (iv) The Military Committee.

The Council recalled that the Baghdad Pact arose from the desire of the peoples of the area for security from Communist imperialism or Communist-inspired domination in any shape or form, and noted with satisfaction that despite attacks on the Pact and its members, the Pact had developed into a strong and cohesive organisation representing the best hope for the safeguard of peace, liberty and independence in the area.

The purpose of the Pact, a free alliance between equal partners, is the

[1] *D.S.B.*, 17 February 1958, pp. 255–7.

defence and security of the area. This is as vital to world peace as it is to constructive cooperation for the benefit of the 135 million people of the Pact region who are predominantly Muslim.

The Council recognised that attempts at subversion in the area must be defeated and peaceful conditions maintained.

The Council reaffirmed that the economic progress of the Pact area and the promotion of the social well-being of its people require a speedy implementation of its programme of economic development.

Political

The Council reviewed the international situation in a series of meetings. A number of these meetings were of a private nature in which heads of delegations were able to exchange views and information with that frankness which befits the equal and intimate association of member countries within the Pact. The Council recognised the usefulness of full and candid discussions which have become an invaluable feature of the Baghdad Pact Organisation.

The Council recognised the need for the constant exposure of the familiar Communist technique of subversive penetration falsely presented as friendly co-existence and help for underdeveloped countries.

While the free world has taken bold and important steps in the liberation and granting of independence to many nations in recent years; and while it is striving to settle the problems of the area in a spirit of justice and equality, the Council noted with regret that in pursuit of its aims, the International Communist movement attempts to exploit nationalism, fear of war, economic distress, the plight of Arab refugees, 'colonialism', and Afro-Asian sentiment through propaganda and Communist controlled and influenced organisations. Communist efforts to penetrate the region by means of indirect aggression such as infiltration and subversion continue to be a menace and call for constant vigilance and increased solidarity.

The Council further noted that since its last meeting in Karachi in June, 1957,[1] Communist imperialism had increased its efforts to dominate the Middle East. These efforts, in the form of pressure, threats and false accusations, were particularly directed by the Soviet Union against Turkey, whose calm and courageous stand evoked the admiration of her associates in the Council.

The Council expressed the desirability of cooperation between the Pact and other free world regional collective security organisations, in the belief that closer contacts among free world nations would contribute to

---

[1] For the final communiqué of the Baghdad Council of 6 June 1957, see *Documents* for 1957, pp. 297–300.

their common cause of promoting security and social well-being for their peoples.

The Council noted with concern that areas of conflict which offer a rich opportunity for exploitation by Communist imperialism and constitute a potential threat to international peace continue to exist in various parts of the world. It devoted considerable time to discussing the situations in the Mediterranean region, the Middle East and South Asia and emphasised that situations which imperil the security of the Pact area should be resolved in accordance with the principles of justice and the United Nations Charter.

The Council was of the opinion that the indiscriminate use of the Veto in the Security Council should be given up as an instrument of cold war so that the United Nations can function as an effective force for the pacific settlement of disputes.

The Council believed that the concept of the United Nations Emergency Force as an instrument of the United Nations and its use in areas of disturbance should be recommended for acceptance to members of the United Nations.

While recognising the continuing need for vigilance and therefore for constant improvement in the security and defence of the Pact area, the Council reaffirmed their earnest desire for peace and their determination to spare no efforts to seek it.

Economic

The Council reviewed the work of the Economic Committee and approved resolutions containing recommendations in the fields of health, agriculture, communications, public works, trade and the financing of joint projects.

The Council noted with satisfaction that a firm basis of economic cooperation had been established on which the Pact could continue to build and that, as a result of the work done by the sub-committees, there is now a promising programme of technical assistance which is developing on a cooperative basis. This will be of great benefit to the living standards in the Region.

Technical Assistance already provided or planned covers the following fields:—

Health; Agriculture; Pest-Control; Animal Health; and Animal Production.

In the field of technical assistance the Government of Iran has allocated 10,000,000 rials, the Government of Turkey TL750,000 over a period of 5 years. These are in addition to the offers made at Karachi (namely £1,000,000 over five years by the United Kingdom and RS.500,000 by Pakistan).

The Council noted that progress had been made in the implementation of approved joint projects. It approved the resolution of the Economic Committee for further implementation of these projects. This resolution recommends that the donor governments, members of the Baghdad Pact Economic Committee, give early and favourable consideration to providing assistance for such projects; and that member countries of the region continue their present efforts to implement them.

The Council recognised the need for specific action on approved projects and was pleased to note that the survey for the telecommunications network linking the capitals of the area members was already under way. It received with appreciation the announcement by the United States that it expected to provide an additional $10,000,000, thus ensuring that most of the funds needed for the construction of this network will be available. The United States referred also to the possibility of obtaining additional financing for joint projects from the World Bank, the Export-Import Bank and the recently established Development Loan Fund.

Scientific Cooperation:

The Council noted that cooperation among members of the Economic Committee and the sub-committees and in the Nuclear Centre and its Scientific Council is already making a contribution to the raising of standards of technical and scientific knowledge in the Pact countries. It decided that their Deputies should examine the possibilities of extending the present programme into wider fields.

Military

The Council noted that 'The Combined Military Planning Organisation' had been set up in Baghdad last autumn. This gave considerable impetus to defensive military planning, increased the effectiveness of the defence efforts of the signatory states of the Pact and marked a significant step forward in the determination of member nations by international cooperation to uphold their sovereignty.

The Council approved the designation of the permanent planning organisation as the 'Combined Military Planning Staff', and approved a charter for the Director and his staff. Among the duties of the Combined Military Planning Staff are the planning and coordination of combined staff training exercises.

The Council also accepted a recommendation of the Military Committee to hold combined staff training exercises in the near future.

The Council also accepted the Military Committee's recommendation to appoint Lt. General Ekrem Akalin of the Turkish Army to be Director of the Combined Military Planning Staff for the year 1958. He will be assisted by Major General Daniel S. Campbell of the United States Air

Force, who has been the Deputy Director of the Combined Military Planning Staff since September 1957.

The Council commended the work in 1957 of the first Director of the Combined Military Planning Staff, Major General M. Habibullah Khan of the Pakistan Army.

Next Meeting of the Council

The Council decided to hold its next meeting at the Ministerial level in London in July, 1958. Meanwhile the Council will continue to meet regularly at the Deputy level.

2. Agreement on the supply of ballistic missiles by the United States to the United Kingdom, Washington, 22 February 1958[1]

(a) *Note from the United States Under-Secretary of State to Her Majesty's Ambassador in Washington, enclosing a memorandum*

Excellency: I have the honor to refer to discussions which have taken place between representatives of the Government of the United Kingdom of Great Britain and Northern Ireland and of the Government of the United States of America on the subject of the supply by the United States Government to the United Kingdom Government of intermediate range ballistic missiles.

I also have the honor to record that, pursuant to the agreement in principle reached between the Prime Minister of the United Kingdom and the President of the United States at Bermuda on March 22, 1957, and in support of the purposes of the North Atlantic Treaty and of the obligations of the parties thereto, the representatives of the two Governments have agreed to the terms set out in the memorandum annexed hereto regarding the proposed supply of intermediate range ballistic missiles.

Accordingly, I have the honor to propose that this Note and Your Excellency's reply to that effect shall be regarded as constituting an Agreement between the two Governments in the terms set out in the annexed memorandum and that such Agreement shall have effect from the date of Your Excellency's reply.

Accept, &c.

For the Secretary of State:

CHRISTIAN A. HERTER

Enclosure:

Memorandum.

---

[1] Cmnd. 366. This agreement was concluded in the form of an Exchange of Notes covering a memorandum. Mr. Macmillan and President Eisenhower, at their meeting in March 1957 at Bermuda, see *Documents* for 1957, pp. 381–3, agreed in principle that certain ballistic missiles should be supplied by the United States to the United Kingdom.

Memorandum

1. The Government of the United States shall supply to the Government of the United Kingdom an agreed number of intermediate range ballistic missiles and their related specialized equipment and make available training assistance in order to facilitate the deployment by the Government of the United Kingdom of the said missiles. The missiles shall be located only in the United Kingdom at such sites and under such conditions as may be agreed upon between the two Governments.

2. The United Kingdom Government shall provide the sites and supporting facilities required for the deployment of the missiles.

3. Ownership of the missiles and related equipment shall pass to the United Kingdom Government under established United States Mutual Assistance Program procedures as soon as the United Kingdom Government is in a position to man and operate the missiles.

4. The missiles will be manned and operated by United Kingdom personnel, who will be trained by the United States Government for the purposes of this project at the earliest feasible date.

5. For the purposes of this Agreement, training and test-firing of missiles will normally take place on United States instrumented ranges but by agreement with the United States Government the United Kingdom Government may arrange with the Government of the Commonwealth of Australia for missiles to be test-fired on the Woomera Range in Australia.

6. Material, equipment, and training provided by the United States Government to the United Kingdom Government pursuant to the arrangements recorded herein will be furnished pursuant to the United States Mutual Security Act of 1954, as amended, acts amendatory or supplementary thereto, appropriations acts thereunder or any other applicable United States legislative provisions.

7. The decision to launch these missiles will be a matter for joint decision by the two Governments. Any such joint decision will be made in the light of the circumstances at the time and having regard to the undertaking the two Governments have assumed in Article 5 of the North Atlantic Treaty.[1]

8. References to intermediate range ballistic missiles in this Agreement do not include the nuclear warheads for such missiles. The United States Government shall provide nuclear warheads for the missiles transferred to the United Kingdom Government pursuant to this Agreement. All nuclear

[1] 'The parties agree that an armed attack against one or more of them in Europe or North America shall be considered an attack against them all . . . If such an armed attack occurs, each of them . . . [will take forthwith] individually and in concert . . . such action as it deems necessary, including the use of armed force, to restore and maintain the security of the North Atlantic Area.'

warheads so provided shall remain in full United States ownership, custody and control in accordance with United States law.

9. The arrangements recorded herein are made in consonance with the North Atlantic Treaty and in pursuance of the Mutual Defense Assistance Agreement between the United Kingdom Government and the United States Government, signed January 27, 1950,[1] as supplemented, and related agreements, and are subject to the applicable provisions thereof.

10. This Agreement shall be subject to revision by agreement between the two Governments and shall remain in force for not less than five years from the date of the Agreement but may thereafter be terminated by either Government upon six months' notice.[2]

(b) *Reply from Her Majesty's Ambassador in Washington*

Sir, I have the honour to acknowledge receipt of your Note of to-day's date with reference to discussions which have taken place between representatives of the Government of the United States of America and of the Government of the United Kingdom of Great Britain and Northern Ireland on the subject of the supply to the United Kingdom of intermediate range ballistic missiles, which Note reads as follows:

'Excellency: I have the honor to refer to discussions which have taken place between representatives of the Government of the United Kingdom of Great Britain and Northern Ireland and of the Government of the United States of America on the subject of the supply by the United States Government to the United Kingdom Government of intermediate range ballistic missiles.

I also have the honor to record that, pursuant to the agreement in principle reached between the Prime Minister of the United Kingdom and the President of the United States at Bermuda on March 22, 1957, and in support of the purposes of the North Atlantic Treaty and of the obligations of the parties thereto, the representatives of the two Governments have agreed to the terms set out in the memorandum annexed

---

[1] For the text of the agreement, see *Documents* for 1949–50, pp. 304–8.

[2] On 24 February 1958, Mr. Sandys in a statement to the House of Commons, summarized the terms of the agreement, and then went on: 'The United States will supply the missiles and specialised equipment at their expense and will also pay for the training of British personnel in America. Britain will meet the cost of providing and constructing the sites and supplying certain items of equipment. The British share of this expenditure is estimated at about £10 million. The missiles will be deployed in small numbers on dispersed sites, mostly on active or disused R.A.F. airfields. These sites will be mainly in East Anglia, Lincolnshire and Yorkshire.' In reply to questions Mr. Sandys said that the U.S. had not asked for any facilities to deploy missiles of their own or to man missiles in the U.K., that the missiles would be assigned to Bomber Command, whose operational plans were already being co-ordinated with those of the U.S. Strategic Air Force, and that the U.K. was not planning the development of a British warhead for the U.S. *Thor* missile, but was concentrating on a more advanced rocket. See H.C. Deb., vol. 583, especially coll. 29–32.

hereto regarding the proposed supply of intermediate range ballistic missiles.

Accordingly, I have the honor to propose that this Note and Your Excellency's reply to that effect shall be regarded as constituting an Agreement between the two Governments in the terms set out in the annexed memorandum and that such Agreement shall have effect from the date of Your Excellency's reply.

Accept, &c.
For the Secretary of State:
CHRISTIAN A. HERTER'

I have the honour to inform you that the proposal made in your Note is acceptable to the Government of the United Kingdom and to confirm that your Note, together with this reply, shall constitute an Agreement between the two Governments in the terms set out in the memorandum annexed to your Note, a copy of which memorandum is enclosed, such Agreement to have effect from the date of this Note.

I avail myself, &c.
HAROLD CACCIA

3. Final communiqué of the Council of S.E.A.T.O., Manila, 13 March 1958[1]

The Fourth Annual Meeting of the SEATO Council was held in Manila from 11th to 13th March 1958 under the Chairmanship of the Acting Secretary of Foreign Affairs of the Philippines, the Honourable Felixberto M. Serrano.

The Council reviewed the world situation with special attention to the Treaty Area, approved the work of the Organization since the meeting in Canberra a year ago,[2] and considered reports by the Council Representatives, the Military Advisers and the Secretary-General.

The Council welcomed the appointment of H. E. Nai Pote Sarasin of Thailand as Secretary-General of the Organization. This position was created at last year's meeting.

Security of the Region

The Council considered the continuing Communist threat to the region. The Ministers reaffirmed their determination to maintain national and collective defence against the possibility of Communist and Communist-inspired armed aggression, while at the same time earnestly working

[1] *D.S.B.*, 31 March 1958, pp. 504–6. For a report on the development of S.E.A.T.O. in its third year, by the Secretary-General, Pote Sarasin, see ibid., pp. 509–16.
[2] See *Documents* for 1957, pp. 378–81.

for international disarmament with adequate safeguards covering both nuclear and conventional elements.

SEATO has become a bulwark which has enabled the countries protected hereby to proceed in peace with their programmes of national development.

Members of SEATO recognized that a threat to security or to freedom in any region of the world was a threat to security and freedom everywhere.

Some criticism of the aims and objectives of SEATO continues to be heard. The Council agreed that every country has the right to follow the policy it prefers. The Council noted with regret that some countries nevertheless continue to criticise the collective security arrangements of the free world, though such arrangements are in accordance with the United Nations Charter.

Subversion

The problems of Communist subversion in the Treaty Area were discussed at length. It was recognized that this represented the most substantial current menace.

The Council was of the opinion that collective security measures had resulted in the diversion of the emphasis of Communist activities from the military to the non-military field.

Communist and Communist-inspired activity has continued within the Treaty Area. In countries protected by the Treaty there has been a noticeable change of emphasis by the Communists to activity in the economic, political and cultural fields and also to activity within youth and labour organizations.

The Council welcomed the counter subversion measures being taken by the members and noted particularly the success of the Seminar on Countering Communist Subversion held in Baguio in the Philippines last November.[1]

The Council recognized that in view of the insidious character of Communist subversion there was particular danger arising from some non-Communist governments failing to distinguish between the aims and ideals of the free world and the purposes of international communism.

Economic Activities

The Council heard statements on the economic progress and problems of the Treaty Area and on what further steps could be taken inside and outside SEATO to attain the economic objectives set forth in the Manila Treaty.[2]

[1] For the text of a final communiqué issued on 29 November 1957, at the close of the session, see D.S.B., 23 December 1957, p. 993.
[2] For the text, see Documents for 1954, pp. 153–6.

A principal means of attaining these objectives continues to be through extensive bilateral and other economic arrangements between the SEATO countries. During the past year over $700,000,000 for economic purposes was provided for countries covered by the Manila Treaty, principally by the United States. This aid is a major factor in preserving peace and genuine independence for countries of the region.

Australia announced that it would make available to the Asian members of SEATO a further £A1,000,000 ($2,240,000) for purposes generally related to SEATO defence; this is in addition to £A2,000,000 previously contributed by Australia for these purposes.

The United States announced that $2,000,000 was being made available to the Asian members of SEATO for vocational and on-the-job training. Australia, France, New Zealand and the United Kingdom also offered to help on various aspects of skilled labour training.

The United States also announced that the major portion of its economic aid was now being directed to the region of Asia.

The Council approved in principle a project submitted by Thailand to establish a SEATO Graduate School of Engineering in Bangkok and several members announced that they would be pleased to participate in providing the necessary funds.

Cultural Activities

The Council agreed to continue and expand its programme of cultural activities.

The Council expressed its satisfaction at the holding in Bangkok under SEATO auspices of a Round Table on the impact of modern technology upon traditional cultures in South East Asia. A number of SEATO Fellowships have been awarded and some Members are conducting bilateral cultural exchanges.

The Council agreed to continue its fellowships programmes and to initiate new cultural projects, the most important being a scholarship programme and the appointment of professors at universities of the Asian members and of travelling lecturers.

Relations with other Organizations and Countries

The Council expressed its interest in the development of relations with other collective defence organizations of the Free World as well as the facilitation of an exchange of information and opinion between these organizations on a mutually agreeable basis. The Council authorized the Secretary General to enter into contact with the Secretaries General of other collective security organizations of the Free World.

The Council considered that contacts between SEATO and non-member States had proved useful in many respects and directed that, as circumstances permitted, such contacts be continued and expanded in the coming years.

Work of Military Advisers

The Council noted with approval the work of their Military Advisers and of the Military Planning Office, which has completed its first year's work. Plans in fulfilment of the defensive role of SEATO have been developed to resist aggression in the Treaty Area. Since the last Council meeting four major SEATO military exercises have been held as well as three multilateral or bilateral exercises. These have served effectively to increase the degree of cooperation between the forces of the SEATO powers and to make them more ready for speedy action in the event of any sudden attack. The Council authorized a further programme of combined exercises.

The Council learned with regret the news of the relief of Brigadier General Alfredo M. Santos, who has been the first Chief of the SEATO Military Planning Office. He is returning for reassignment in the Philippines.

The United States and the Philippines announced that they intend to co-sponsor a defence college to be located in the Philippines. This would be open to members and non-members of SEATO. The Council took note of this announcement with particular interest.

1958/59 Budget

The Council approved Budget Estimates totalling $850,360 for the financial year 1958/59, to cover the cost of the Secretariat-General and Military Planning Office in Bangkok and to finance certain joint programmes.

Next Meeting

The Council accepted with pleasure the invitation of the New Zealand Government to hold its next annual meeting in Wellington.

Conclusion

The Council considered that the work of the present meeting had helped to consolidate the work already achieved by SEATO. They placed on record their determination to continue to work together for the security and progress of South-East Asia in accordance with the principles and purposes of the Charter of the United Nations. The Council Members again emphasized the defensive character of SEATO and reaffirmed the principle that international disputes be settled peacefully in accordance with the principles of the United Nations Charter.

The Representatives attending the Fourth SEATO Council Meeting were—Australia—Rt. Hon. R. G. Casey; France—M. Christian Pineau; New Zealand—Rt. Hon. Walter Nash; Pakistan—Hon. Nawab Mozaffar Ali Khan Qizilbash; Philippines—Hon. Felixberto M. Serrano; Thailand —H. R. H. Prince Wan Waithayakon Krommun Naradhip Bongsprabandh; United Kingdom—Rt. Hon. Selwyn Lloyd; United States—Hon. John Foster Dulles.

4. Final communiqué issued at the conclusion of the N.A.T.O. Defence Ministers Conference, Paris, 17 April 1958[1]

In accordance with the decision taken at the Ministerial Meeting of the North Atlantic Council held at the level of Heads of Government on 19th December last,[2] the Defense Ministers of the NATO member countries met at the Palais de Chaillot, under the Chairmanship of the Secretary General, Monsieur P. H. Spaak, on 15th, 16th and 17th April, 1958.

2. The Ministers heard full and valuable reports by the Military Committee, the Standing Group and the Supreme Allied Commanders on the present state of the forces of the Alliance, on the progressive introduction of the most modern weapons and equipment and on the forces needed for NATO defense in the years ahead. They also heard progress reports on projects initiated by the Heads of Government in December. On the basis of these reports a most useful discussion took place between the Ministers and the NATO military authorities.

3. In order to meet the continuing efforts made by the Soviet leaders to equip their large forces with the most modern weapons[3] the Ministers discussed ways and means of making the best of the resources of the

[1] *D.S.B.*, 5 May 1958, pp. 729–30.

[2] For the declaration and communiqué of the N.A.T.O. Council of 19 December 1957, see *Documents* for 1957, pp. 404–10. It was decided at this meeting 'to establish stocks of nuclear warheads, which will be readily available for the defence of the Alliance in case of need'. It was also decided 'that intermediate range ballistic missiles will have to be put at the disposal of the Supreme Allied Commander Europe'. Ibid., p. 408. Mr. Dulles stated on 16 December, at the N.A.T.O. meeting, that the United States was prepared, if the Council wished it, '. . . to participate in a N.A.T.O. atomic stockpile', and 'to make available to other N.A.T.O. countries intermediate range ballistic missiles for deployment in accordance with the plans of SACEUR'. The nuclear warheads of the I.R.B.M.s were to become part of the N.A.T.O. atomic stockpile system. See *D.S.B.*, 6 January 1958, p. 9, for the relevant part of Mr. Dulles's statement.

[3] The strength of Soviet bloc armed forces was estimated at 6 million in April 1958. These forces were said to have undertaken a comprehensive programme of adaptation to atomic warfare. The Soviet army was believed to consist of 175 divisions, 75 of which were tank or mechanized; the satellite ground forces were thought to be organized into about 60 divisions. The Soviet air forces comprised some 20,000 operational aircraft, and the satellite air forces another 2,500, 75 per cent of which were jets. The Soviet naval strength was estimated to include, by 1961, 30 cruisers, 150 destroyers, and 700 submarines. See *Nato Letter*, April 1958, pp. 8–10.

Alliance and of achieving greater effectiveness for its forces. They confirmed their support of the basic NATO strategy for the preservation of peace and for the defense of member countries. This defensive strategy continues to be founded on the concept of a strong deterrent, comprising the shield, with its conventional and nuclear elements, and the nuclear retaliatory forces.

4. The Ministers also were in agreement on certain measures to achieve greater co-ordination and to widen co-operation among member countries, both with respect to defense research, development and production and to the organization of forces.

5. The Ministers are confident after these discussions, which confirmed their unity and common purpose, that the progressive modernization of NATO forces, on the basis of the agreed strategic plans, will enable the Alliance to maintain its defensive strength while efforts continue to be made to re-establish international confidence through effective, controlled disarmament.

5. Final communiqué of the N.A.T.O. Council ministerial meeting, Copenhagen, 7 May 1958[1]

The Foreign Ministers of the 15 NATO countries have deepened and strengthened their mutual understanding and their unity of purpose. NATO, a defensive organization, is now much more than merely a military alliance. It is becoming a true community of free nations. Within this community, to a degree unprecedented in history, countries are carrying out a policy of close co-operation in peacetime without abandoning their independence. This development is one of the most significant and promising events of our time.

The Council reviewed the activities of the Alliance and examined the international situation. For the first subject of discussion, the Council had before it the report submitted by the Secretary General. The Council was in agreement with this analysis of the work of the Alliance in the past year. They agreed in particular that the outstanding achievement had been the remarkable progress made in the strengthening of political consultation. This has been successfully applied to an increasing number of problems and has led to co-ordination of policy on major questions of common interest. The Council also expressed its satisfaction with the results of the recent Conference of Defence Ministers and with the good start made in the field of scientific co-operation.

The Ministers recognized that political unity and the efficient organization of defence were not enough. Economic co-operation is also essential

[1] *Nato Letter*, June 1958, pp. 13–15.

between the members of the Alliance. Every effort should be made to ensure economic prosperity, notably by the expansion of international trade and by aid to underdeveloped countries. Consultations on methods and machinery for such co-operation will take place within the Alliance. The Ministers attach special importance to the successful conclusion of the economic negotiations now being undertaken and to the establishment of close ties between the European countries and the whole free world.

During their consideration of the international situation the Ministers had a discussion on the question of a possible Summit Conference.[1] The Council believe that summit meetings are desirable if they offer prospects of reaching settlements on important questions. The Council considers that conferences at the Summit are not the only way, or necessarily the best way, of conducting negotiations or reducing international tensions. In any event, such conferences must be properly prepared and take place in a favourable atmosphere.

The Ministers regretted that during the last few weeks the Soviet Union has made the preparations for a possible Summit Conference more difficult by posing unreasonable conditions. The Soviet Union has recently aggravated international tension by its veto in the Security Council of the United States proposals to reduce the risks of surprise attack over the Arctic.

Despite the disappointment and doubts to which the Soviet attitude gives rise, the NATO governments will not be discouraged nor give up their attachment to the principle of negotiation.

Should a Summit Conference take place at this time it should consider certain important problems, among others the German problem, which were identified by the Heads of Governments meeting at Geneva in 1955 and on which unfortunately little or no progress towards a solution has been made. Controlled disarmament, desired so ardently by all peoples, should be one of the main questions on the agenda. The proposals made by the Western powers on 29th August, 1957, and approved by a large majority in the United Nations could afford a reasonable basis for this discussion.

The Council expressed the hope that it might yet prove possible, in spite of repeated Soviet refusals to inaugurate expert technical discussions, between representatives of the Soviet Union and of the Western powers principally concerned, on detailed measures of control over disarmament.

[1] The following joint statement was issued by the Foreign Ministers of France, the United Kingdom and the United States:
'The three countries conducting the preliminary diplomatic contacts with the Soviet Union indicated that they did not consider that they would necessarily be the only Western nations to take part in a possible Conference of Foreign Ministers or in a possible Summit Conference. Other countries, as for instance Italy, might then be included.' See ibid., p. 15.

Agreement on measures necessary, for example, to prevent surprise attack or to detect nuclear explosions might go far towards demonstrating the possibility of agreement on disarmament, improving its prospects and accelerating its application when reached. In order to prepare the way for such agreement the Council will consider the possibility of carrying out studies and experiments on the technical problems of inspection and control.

In conclusion, the Ministers confirmed the full agreement of their governments on the basic principles of the Alliance, its goals and the methods of obtaining them.

6. Joint Philippine-United States announcement regarding the establishment of a Mutual Defence Board, 15 May 1958[1]

The Philippine and United States Governments today announced agreement on the establishment of a Philippine-United States Mutual Defense Board and the assignment of a Philippine military liaison officer to the staff of the Base Commander in major United States military bases in the Philippines.

One of a continuing series of actions implementing existing security and defense agreements between the two countries, today's exchange of notes marks a major step in securing effective collaboration between the two countries in the joint effort to improve and enhance the common defense.[2]

As stated in the Exchange of Notes 'the purpose of this (Mutual Defense) Board is to provide continuing inter-governmental machinery for direct liaison and consultation between appropriate Philippine and United States authorities on military matters of mutual concern so as to develop and improve, through continuing military cooperation, the common defense of the two sovereign countries.' The Board will have Philippine and United States co-chairmen.

The Philippine military liaison officer, who will be assigned to a major United States military base, will cooperate with the Base Commander by advice, suggestion and/or other appropriate action to assure observance of Philippine law and regulations within the base, will advise the Base Commander concerning problems involving Philippine nationals and residents on the base, and the day-to-day relationships between the base, Base Commander and such nationals and residents. These officers will be appointed by the Chief of Staff, Armed Forces of the Philippines, will be

---

[1] *D.S.B.*, 2 June 1958, p. 913.

[2] See fn. 1 on p. 484, below, for Soviet and Chinese attacks on President Garcia's pro-Western policy.

under the Administration of the Philippine Co-Chairman of the Mutual Defense Board, and will submit reports to the Board.

The agreements announced today are designed to enable the two governments to carry out more effectively the specified purposes and objectives of the Mutual Defense Agreement, and are part of the continuing effort of both governments to further strengthen their mutual defense and to contribute to international peace and security.

7. Statement by the United Kingdom Foreign Office regarding the maintenance of United Kingdom forces in Germany, 29 May 1958[1]

On 3rd December, 1957, Her Majesty's Government requested the assistance of their NATO partners for a solution of the foreign exchange difficulties which would arise for them in 1958–59 as the result of stationing British forces in Germany. This was under a NATO procedure established in 1957 to deal with currency problems arising from the stationing of forces in other member countries of the Alliance. At the same time Her Majesty's Government invoked Article 6 of Protocol II of the revised Brussels Treaty, whereby, 'if the maintenance of the United Kingdom forces on the mainland of Europe throws at any time too great a strain on the external finances of the United Kingdom', Her Majesty's Government '. . . will invite the North Atlantic Council to review the financial conditions on which the United Kingdom formations are maintained'; Her Majesty's Government accordingly invited the North Atlantic Council to carry out such a review.

2. The United Kingdom case for financial relief was endorsed early last January by three independent experts appointed by the Secretary-General of NATO in accordance with the NATO procedure. They found that the United Kingdom was experiencing serious balance of payments difficulties and that the cost of stationing forces in Germany represented a heavy additional burden on the United Kingdom balance of payments. The North Atlantic Council accepted these conclusions.

3. There have been extensive discussions in the North Atlantic Council and elsewhere. An arrangement in NATO has now been reached on a three-year basis, that is to say, covering the years 1958–59, 1959–60, and 1960–61,

4. Under this arrangement, the German Federal Government have, for their part, undertaken, as a measure of mutual aid under Article 3 of the

---

[1] *Commonwealth Survey*, 10 June 1958, pp. 541–2. For an exchange of notes between the Government of the United Kingdom and the Government of the German Federal Republic regarding local defence costs of United Kingdom forces stationed in the Federal Republic, see Cmnd. 588.

North Atlantic Treaty, to make, in 1958–59 and each of the two following years, an annual payment to Her Majesty's Government of £12 million; to deposit with Her Majesty's Government, interest-free, a sum of £50 million for arms orders and to repay, in 1958–59, £22½ million of their post-war debt which would otherwise be due to be repaid over the years 1962–64 (this will require certain waivers from other parties to the London debt agreements of 1953 and the Federal Government are initiating the necessary action to obtain these waivers). Negotiations are also to take place for reducing the interest rates on the balance of the sum which was deposited with the Bank of England in 1957 to meet the instalments of the post-war debt due to be repaid in the years 1957–66. The annual payment of £12 million and the deposit of £50 million for arms orders will be new money across the exchanges, but the advance repayment of £22½ million of the debt will be made to the Exchequer out of the sum already deposited with the Bank of England.

5. Her Majesty's Government for their part have declared their readiness to continue to maintain a substantial British force on the Continent, not only in 1958–59 but also in 1959–60 and 1960–61 within the limits of what can be afforded in relation to the balance of payments. Under this arrangement, Her Majesty's Government have declared to NATO their intention to maintain the British Army in Germany at the strength of 55,000 men throughout the calendar year 1958, and thereafter up to the end of the financial year 1960–61 to maintain a minimum strength of 45,000. In addition they have declared their intention to maintain the Second Tactical Air Force at its present strength until towards the end of the year 1960–61. They have undertaken to find the balance of the DM costs involved, after taking into account the three annual payments of £12 million to be received from the Federal Government.

6. Discussions are taking place in NATO which it is hoped may lead to further financial arrangements that would enable the British Army in Germany to be maintained at the strength of 55,000 throughout the year 1959. Her Majesty's Government do not themselves feel able to make any additional financial contribution in such further arrangements.

7. Her Majesty's Government are sure that their Allies recognise the importance of the contribution which Her Majesty's Government are making in the arrangement which has been reached, one of whose major advantages is that it should provide stability over a period of at least three years, removing the necessity for annual discussions and the uncertainties which they create within the Alliance. Her Majesty's Government welcome the contribution which is being made by the Federal German Government, who have shown understanding of their difficulties. They also

express their appreciation of the valuable part which has been played in working out the arrangement by the Secretary-General of NATO, M. Spaak, and the NATO international staff.

8. Agreement between the United Kingdom and the United States for co-operation on the uses of atomic energy for mutual defence purposes, Washington, 3 July 1958[1]

The Government of the United Kingdom of Great Britain and Northern Ireland on its own behalf and on behalf of the United Kingdom Atomic Energy Authority and the Government of the United States of America.

Considering that their mutual security and defense require that they be prepared to meet the contingencies of atomic warfare;

Considering that both countries have made substantial progress in the development of atomic weapons;

Considering that they are participating together in international arrangements pursuant to which they are making substantial and material contributions to their mutual defense and security;

Recognizing that their common defense and security will be advanced by the exchange of information concerning atomic energy and by the transfer of equipment and materials for use therein;

Believing that such exchange and transfer can be undertaken without risk to the defense and security of either country; and

Taking into consideration the United States Atomic Energy Act of 1954, as amended, which was enacted with these purposes in mind,

Have agreed as follows:

ARTICLE I

General Provision

While the United States and the United Kingdom are participating in an international arrangement for their mutual defense and security and making substantial and material contributions thereto, each Party will communicate to and exchange with the other Party information, and transfer materials and equipment to the other Party, in accordance with the provisions of this Agreement provided that the communicating or transferring Party determines that such cooperation will promote and will not constitute an unreasonable risk to its defense and security.

[1] Cmnd. 537. The agreement entered into force on 4 August 1958.

ARTICLE II
Exchange of Information

A. Each Party will communicate to or exchange with the other Party such classified information as is jointly determined to be necessary to:

1. the development of defense plans;
2. the training of personnel in the employment of and defense against atomic weapons and other military applications of atomic energy;
3. the evaluation of the capabilities of potential enemies in the employment of atomic weapons and other military applications of atomic energy;
4. the development of delivery systems compatible with the atomic weapons which they carry; and
5. research, development and design of military reactors to the extent and by such means as may be agreed.

B. In addition to the cooperation provided for in paragraph A of this Article each Party will exchange with the other Party other classified information concerning atomic weapons when, after consultation with the other Party, the communicating Party determines that the communication of such information is necessary to improve the recipient's atomic weapon design, development and fabrication capability.

ARTICLE III
Transfer of Submarine Nuclear Propulsion Plant and Materials

A. The Government of the United States will authorize, subject to terms and conditions acceptable to the Government of the United States, a person to transfer by sale to the Government of the United Kingdom or its agent one complete submarine nuclear propulsion plant with such spare parts therefor as may be agreed by the Parties and to communicate to the Government of the United Kingdom or its agent (or to both) such classified information as relates to safety features and such classified information as is necessary for the design, manufacture and operation of such propulsion plant. A person or persons will also be authorized, for a period of ten years following the date of entry into force of this Agreement and subject to terms and conditions acceptable to the Government of the United States, to transfer replacement cores or fuel elements for such plant.

B. The Government of the United States will transfer by sale agreed amounts of U-235 contained in uranium enriched in the isotope U-235 as needed for use in the submarine nuclear propulsion plant transferred pursuant to paragraph A of this Article, during the ten years following the date of entry into force of this Agreement on such terms and conditions as may be agreed. If the Government of the United Kingdom so requests, the Government of the United States will during such period reprocess any material sold under the present paragraph in facilities of the Government of the United States, on terms and conditions to be agreed, or authorize such reprocessing in private facilities in the United States. Enriched uranium recovered in reprocessing such materials by either Party may be purchased by the Government of the United States under terms and conditions to be agreed. Special nuclear material recovered in reprocessing such materials and not purchased by the Government of the United States may be returned to or retained by the Government of the United Kingdom and any U-235 not purchased by the Government of the United States will be credited to the amounts of U-235 to be transferred by the Government of the United States under this Agreement.

C. The Government of the United States shall be compensated for enriched uranium sold by it pursuant to this Article at the United States Atomic Energy Commission's published charges applicable to the domestic distribution of such material in effect at the time of the sale. Any purchase of enriched uranium by the Government of the United States pursuant to this Article shall be at the applicable price of the United States Atomic Energy Commission for the purchase of enriched uranium in effect at the time of purchase of such enriched uranium.

D. The Parties will exchange classified information on methods of reprocessing fuel elements of the type utilized in the propulsion plant to be transferred under this Article, including classified information on the design, construction and operation of facilities for the reprocessing of such fuel elements.

E. The Government of the United Kingdom shall indemnify and hold harmless the Government of the United States against any and all liabilities whatsoever (including third-party liability) for any damage or injury occurring after the propulsion plant or parts thereof, including spare parts, replacement cores or fuel elements are taken outside the United States, for any cause arising out of or connected with the design, manufacture, assembly, transfer or utilization of the propulsion plant, spare parts, replacement cores or fuel elements transferred pursuant to paragraph A of this Article.

ARTICLE IV

Responsibility for use of Information, Material, Equipment and Devices

The application or use of any information (including design drawings and specifications), material or equipment communicated, exchanged or transferred under this Agreement shall be the responsibility of the Party receiving it, and the other Party does not provide any indemnity, and does not warrant the accuracy or completeness of such information and does not warrant the suitability or completeness of such information, material or equipment for any particular use or application.

ARTICLE V

Conditions

A. Cooperation under this Agreement will be carried out by each of the Parties in accordance with its applicable laws.

B. Under this Agreement there will be no transfer by either Party of atomic weapons.

C. Except as may be otherwise agreed for civil uses, the information communicated or exchanged, or the materials or equipment transferred, by either Party pursuant to this Agreement shall be used by the recipient Party exclusively for the preparation or implementation of defense plans in the mutual interests of the two countries.

D. Nothing in this Agreement shall preclude the communication or exchange of classified information which is transmissible under other arrangements between the Parties.

ARTICLE VI

Guaranties

A. Classified information, materials and equipment communicated or transferred pursuant to this Agreement shall be accorded full security protection under applicable security arrangements between the Parties and applicable national legislation and regulations of the Parties. In no case shall either Party maintain security standards for safeguarding classified information, materials or equipment made available pursuant to this Agreement less restrictive than those set forth in the applicable security arrangements in effect on the date this Agreement comes into force.

B. Classified information communicated or exchanged pursuant to this Agreement will be made available through channels existing or hereafter agreed for the communication or exchange of such information between the Parties.

C. Classified information, communicated or exchanged, and any materials or equipment transferred, pursuant to this Agreement shall not be communicated, exchanged or transferred by the recipient Party or persons under its jurisdiction to any unauthorized persons, or, except as provided in Article VII of this Agreement, beyond the jurisdiction of that Party. Each Party may stipulate the degree to which any of the information, materials or equipment communicated, exchanged or transferred by it or persons under its jurisdiction pursuant to this Agreement may be disseminated or distributed; may specify the categories of persons who may have access to such information, materials or equipment; and may impose such other restrictions on the dissemination or distribution of such information, materials or equipment as it deems necessary.

ARTICLE VII

Dissemination

Nothing in this Agreement shall be interpreted or operate as a bar or restriction to consultation or cooperation in any field of defense by either Party with other nations or international organizations. Neither Party, however, shall communicate classified information or transfer or permit access to or use of materials, or equipment, made available by the other Party pursuant to this Agreement to any nation or international organization unless authorized to do so by such other Party, or unless such other Party has informed the recipient Party that the same information has been made available to that nation or international organization.

ARTICLE VIII

Classification Policies

Agreed classification policies shall be maintained with respect to all classified information, materials or equipment communicated, exchanged or transferred under this Agreement. The Parties intend to continue the present practice of consultation with each other on the classification of these matters.

ARTICLE IX

Patents

A. With respect to any invention or discovery employing classified information which has been communicated or exchanged pursuant to Article II or derived from the submarine propulsion plant, material or equipment transferred pursuant to Article III, and made or conceived by the recipient Party, or any agency or corporation owned or controlled thereby, or any of their agents or contractors, or any employee of any of the foregoing, after the date of such communication, exchange or transfer but during the period of this Agreement:

    1. in the case of any such invention or discovery in which rights are owned by the recipient Party, or any agency or corporation owned or controlled thereby, and not included in subparagraph 2 of this paragraph, the recipient Party shall, to the extent owned by any of them:

(a) transfer and assign to the other Party all right, title and interest in and to the invention or discovery, or patent application or patent thereon, in the country of that other Party, subject to the retention of a royalty-free, non-exclusive, irrevocable license for the governmental purposes of the recipient Party and for the purposes of mutual defense; and

(b) grant to the other Party a royalty-free, non-exclusive, irrevocable license for the governmental purposes of that other Party and for purposes of mutual defense in the country of the recipient Party and third countries, including use in the production of material in such countries for sale to the recipient Party by a contractor of that other Party;

2. in the case of any such invention or discovery which is primarily useful in the production or utilization of special nuclear material or atomic energy and made or conceived prior to the time that the information it employs is made available for civil uses, the recipient Party shall:

(a) obtain, by appropriate means, sufficient right, title and interest in and to the invention or discovery, or patent application or patent thereon, as may be necessary to fulfill its obligations under the following two subparagraphs;

(b) transfer and assign to the other Party all right, title and interest in and to the invention or discovery, or patent application or patent thereon, in the country of that other Party, subject to the retention of a royalty-free, non-exclusive, irrevocable license, with the right to grant sublicenses, for all purposes; and

(c) grant to the other Party a royalty-free, non-exclusive, irrevocable license, with the right to grant sublicenses, for all purposes in the country of the recipient Party and in third countries.

B. 1. Each Party shall, to the extent owned by it, or any agency or corporation owned or controlled thereby, grant to the other Party a royalty-free, non-exclusive, irrevocable license to manufacture and use the subject matter covered by any patent and incorporated in the submarine propulsion plant and spare parts transferred pursuant to paragraph A of Article III for use by the licensed Party for the purposes set forth in paragraph C of Article V.

2. The transferring Party neither warrants nor represents that the submarine propulsion plant or any material or equipment transferred under Article III does not infringe any patent owned or controlled by other persons and assumes no liability or obligation with respect thereto, and the recipient Party agrees to indemnify and hold harmless the trans-

ferring Party from any and all liability arising out of any infringement of any such patent.

C. With respect to any invention or discovery, or patent application or patent thereon, or license or sublicense therein, covered by paragraph A of this Article, each Party:

1. may, to the extent of its right, title and interest therein, deal with the same in its own and third countries as it may desire, but shall in no event discriminate against citizens of the other Party in respect of granting any license or sublicense under the patents owned by it in its own or any other country;

2. hereby waives any and all claims against the other Party for compensation, royalty or award, and hereby releases the other Party with respect to any and all such claims.

D. 1. No patent application with respect to any classified invention or discovery employing classified information which has been communicated or exchanged pursuant to Article II, or derived from the submarine propulsion plant, material or equipment transferred pursuant to Article III, may be filed:

(a) by either Party or any person in the country of the other Party except in accordance with agreed conditions and procedures; or

(b) in any country not a party to this Agreement except as may be agreed and subject to Articles VI and VII.

2. Appropriate secrecy or prohibition orders shall be issued for the purpose of giving effect to this paragraph.

ARTICLE X

Previous Agreements for Cooperation

Effective from the date on which the present Agreement enters into force, the cooperation between the Parties being carried out under or envisaged by the Agreement for Cooperation Regarding Atomic Information for Mutual Defense Purposes, which was signed at Washington on June 15, 1955[1], and by paragraph B of Article I bis of the Agreement for Cooperation on Civil Uses of Atomic Energy, which was signed at Washington on June 15, 1955[2], as amended by the Amendment signed at Washington on June 13, 1956[3], shall be carried out in accordance with the provisions of the present Agreement.

[1] Cmd. 9555.   [2] Cmd. 9560.
              [3] Cmd. 9847.

ARTICLE XI

Definitions

For the purposes of this Agreement:

A. 'Atomic weapon' means any device utilizing atomic energy, exclusive of the means for transporting or propelling the device (where such means is a separable and divisible part of the device), the principal purpose of which is for use as, or for development of, a weapon, a weapon prototype, or a weapon test device.

B. 'Classified information' means information, data, materials, services or any other matter with the security designation of 'Confidential' or higher applied under the legislation or regulations of either the United Kingdom or the United States, including that designated by the Government of the United States as 'Restricted Data' or 'Formerly Restricted Data' and that designated by the Government of the United Kingdom as 'ATOMIC'.

C. 'Equipment' means any instrument, apparatus or facility and includes any facility, except an atomic weapon, capable of making use of or producing special nuclear material, and component parts thereof, and includes submarine nuclear propulsion plant, reactor and military reactor.

D. 'Military reactor' means a reactor for the propulsion of naval vessels, aircraft or land vehicles and military package power reactors.

E. 'Person' means:

1. any individual, corporation, partnership, firm, association, trust, estate, public or private institution, group, government agency or government corporation other than the United Kingdom Atomic Energy Authority and the United States Atomic Energy Commission; and

2. any legal successor, representative, agent or agency of the foregoing.

F. 'Reactor' means an apparatus, other than an atomic weapon, in which a self-supporting fission chain reaction is maintained and controlled by utilizing uranium, plutonium or thorium, or any combination of uranium, plutonium or thorium.

G. 'Submarine nuclear propulsion plant' means a propulsion plant and includes the reactor, and such control, primary, auxiliary, steam and electric systems as may be necessary for propulsion of submarines.

H. References in this Agreement to the Government of the United Kingdom include the United Kingdom Atomic Energy Authority.

ARTICLE XII

Duration

This Agreement shall enter into force on the date[1] on which each Government shall have received from the other Government written notification that it has complied with all statutory and constitutional requirements for the entry into force of this Agreement, and shall remain in force until terminated by agreement of both Parties, except that, if not so terminated, Article II may be terminated by agreement of both Parties, or by either Party on one year's notice to the other to take effect at the end of a term of ten years, or thereafter on one year's notice to take effect at the end of any succeeding term of five years.

In witness whereof, the undersigned, duly authorized, have signed this Agreement.

Done at Washington, this third day of July, 1958, in two original texts.

> For the Government of the United Kingdom
> of Great Britain and Northern Ireland:
> Hood

> For the Government of the United States
> of America:
> John Foster Dulles

9. Declaration issued at the ministerial meeting of the Baghdad Pact, London, 28 July 1958[2]

1. The members of the Baghdad Pact attending the Ministerial meeting in London have re-examined their position in the light of recent events and conclude that the need which called the Pact into being is greater than ever. These members declare their determination to maintain their collective security and to resist aggression, direct or indirect.

2. Under the Pact collective security arrangements have been instituted. Joint military planning has been advanced and area economic projects have been promoted. Relationships are being established with other free world nations associated for collective security.

3. The question of whether substantive alterations should be made in the Pact and its organization or whether the Pact will be continued in its present form is under consideration by the Governments concerned. However, the nations represented at the meeting in London reaffirmed

---

[1] 4 August 1958.

[2] *D.S.B.*, 18 August 1958, pp. 272–3. The meeting took place in London from 28 to 29 July. A final communiqué was issued on 29 July, see ibid., p. 273. Iraq did not leave the Pact until 24 March 1959.

their determination to strengthen further their united defence posture in the area.

4. Article I of the Pact of Mutual Co-operation signed at Baghdad on February 24, 1955,[1] provides that the parties will co-operate for their security and defence and that such measures as they agree to take to give effect to this co-operation may form the subject of special agreements. Similarly, the United States, in the interest of world peace, and pursuant to existing Congressional authorisation, agrees to co-operate with the nations making this Declaration for their security and defence, and will promptly enter into agreements designed to give effect to this co-operation.[2]

MANOUCHEHR EGHBAL
Prime Minister of Iran

MALIK FIROZ KHAN NOON
Prime Minister of Pakistan

ADNAN MENDERES
Prime Minister of Turkey

HAROLD MACMILLAN
Prime Minister of the United Kingdom

JOHN FOSTER DULLES
Secretary of State, United States of America

10. Joint communiqué issued by the United States and the Republic of China, Taipei, 23 October 1958[3]

Consultations have been taking place over the past three days between the Government of the United States and the Government of the Republic of China pursuant to Article IV of the Mutual Defense Treaty.[4] These consultations had been invited by President Chiang Kai-shek. The following are among those who took part in the consultations:

For the Republic of China:

President Chiang Kai-shek
Vice President-Premier Chen Cheng
Secretary General to the President Chang Chun
Minister of Foreign Affairs Huang Shao-ku
Ambassador to the United States George K. C. Yeh

---

[1] See *Documents* for 1955, pp. 287–8.

[2] See the Soviet note to Persia of 31 October 1958, p. 330, above.

[3] *D.S.B.*, 10 November 1958, pp. 721–2. Discussions between Mr. Dulles and President Chang Kai-shek took place between 21 and 23 October 1958. For the other documents on the crisis over Formosa, see Chapter I, C, above.

[4] See *D.S.B.*, 13 December 1954, p. 899.

For the United States of America:

Secretary of State John Foster Dulles
Assistant Secretary of State Walter S. Robertson
Ambassador to the Republic of China Everett F. Drumright

The consultations had been arranged to be held during the two weeks when the Chinese Communists had declared they would cease fire upon Quemoy. It had been hoped that, under these circumstances, primary consideration could have been given to measures which would have contributed to stabilizing an actual situation of non-militancy. However, on the eve of the consultations, the Chinese Communists, in violation of their declaration, resumed artillery fire against the Quemoys. It was recognized that under the present conditions the defense of the Quemoys, together with the Matsus, is closely related to the defense of Taiwan and Penghu.

The two Governments recalled that their Mutual Defense Treaty had had the purpose of manifesting their unity 'so that no potential aggressor could be under the illusion that either of them stands alone in the West Pacific Area.' The consultations provided a fresh occasion for demonstrating that unity.

The two Governments reaffirmed their solidarity in the face of the new Chinese Communist aggression now manifesting itself in the bombardment of the Quemoys. This aggression and the accompanying Chinese Communist propaganda have not divided them, as the Communists have hoped. On the contrary, it has drawn them closer together. They believe that by unitedly opposing aggression they serve not only themselves but the cause of peace. As President Eisenhower said on September 11,[1] the position of opposing aggression by force is the only position consistent with the peace of the world.

The two Governments took note of the fact that the Chinese Communists, with the backing of the Soviet Union, avowedly seek to conquer Taiwan, to eliminate Free China and to expel the United States from the Western Pacific generally, compelling the United States to abandon its collective security arrangements with free countries of that area. This policy cannot possibly succeed. It is hoped and believed that the Communists, faced by the proven unity, resolution and strength of the Governments of the United States and the Republic of China, will not put their policy to the test of general war and that they will abandon the military steps which they have already taken to initiate their futile and dangerous policy.

In addition to dealing with the current military situation, the two Governments considered the broad and long-range aspects of their relationship.

The United States, its Government and its people, have an abiding faith

[1] See above, pp. 189–95.

in the Chinese people and profound respect for the great contribution which they have made and will continue to make to a civilization that respects and honors the individual and his family life. The United States recognizes that the Republic of China is the authentic spokesman for Free China and of the hopes and aspirations entertained by the great mass of the Chinese people.

The Government of the Republic of China declared its purpose to be a worthy representative of the Chinese people and to strive to preserve those qualities and characteristics which have enabled the Chinese to contribute so much of benefit to humanity.

The two Governments reaffirmed their dedication to the principles of the Charter of the United Nations. They recalled that the treaty under which they are acting is defensive in character. The Government of the Republic of China considers that the restoration of freedom to its people on the mainland is its sacred mission. It believes that the foundation of this mission resides in the minds and the hearts of the Chinese people and that the principal means of successfully achieving its mission is the implementation of Dr. Sun Yat-sen's three people's principles (nationalism, democracy and social well-being) and not the use of force.

The consultations which took place permitted a thorough study and reexamination of the pressing problems of mutual concern. As such they have proved to be of great value to both Governments. It is believed that such consultations should continue to be held at appropriate intervals.

11. Communiqué on the talks on Berlin, in Paris, between the Foreign Ministers of the United States, United Kingdom, France, and the German Federal Republic, 14 December 1958[1]

The Foreign Ministers of France, the Federal Republic of Germany, the United Kingdom and the United States met on December 14, 1958, in Paris, to discuss developments in the Berlin situation during the past month, including a Note addressed to their several Governments on November 27 by the Soviet Union.[2]

The four Foreign Ministers had the benefit of an oral statement on the situation in Berlin by Herr Brandt, governing mayor of that city.

The Foreign Ministers of France, the United Kingdom and the United States once more reaffirmed the determination of their Governments to maintain their position and their rights with respect to Berlin, including the right of free access.

---

[1] Cmnd. 634, p. 21. This document has not been included in the section in Chapter I, on Germany and the Berlin crisis since it was not an East–West Exchange.

[2] See above, pp. 146–64.

They found unacceptable unilateral repudiation by the Soviet Government of its obligations to the Governments of France, the United Kingdom and the United States in relation to their presence in Berlin and their freedom of access to that city, or the substitution of the German authorities of the Soviet Zone for the Soviet Government in so far as those rights are concerned.

After further discussion of the Soviet notes of November 27, 1958, the four Foreign Ministers found themselves in agreement on the basic issues to be dealt with in the replies to those Notes.

They will consult with their allies in the N.A.T.O. Council following which the four Governments will formulate their replies.

12. Communiqué of the North Atlantic Council regarding Berlin, 16 December 1958[1]

The North Atlantic Council examined the question of Berlin.

2. The Council declares that no State has the right to withdraw unilaterally from its international engagements. It considers that the denunciation by the Soviet Union of the inter-allied agreements on Berlin can in no way deprive the other parties of their rights or relieve the Soviet Union of its obligations. Such methods destroy the mutual confidence between nations which is one of the foundations of peace.

3. The Council fully associates itself with the views expressed on the subject by the Governments of the United States, the United Kingdom, France and the Federal Republic of Germany in their statement of 14th December.

4. The demands expressed by the Soviet Government have created a serious situation which must be faced with determination.

5. The Council recalls the responsibilities which each member state has assumed in regard to the security and welfare of Berlin, and the maintenance of the position of the Three Powers in that city. The member states of N.A.T.O. could not approve a solution of the Berlin question which jeopardised the right of the three Western Powers to remain in Berlin as long as their responsibilities require it, and did not assure freedom of communication between that city and the free world. The Soviet Union would be responsible for any action which had the effect of hampering this free communication or endangering this freedom. The two million inhabitants of West Berlin have just reaffirmed in a free vote their overwhelming approval and support for that position.

6. The Council considers that the Berlin question can only be settled in the framework of an agreement with the U.S.S.R. on Germany as a whole. It recalls that the Western Powers have repeatedly declared

[1] Cmnd. 634, pp. 21–22. See fn. 1 of preceding document.

themselves ready to examine this problem, as well as those of European security and disarmament. They are still ready to discuss all these problems.

13. Final communiqué of the N.A.T.O. Council ministerial meeting, Paris, 18 December 1958[1]

International Situation

In a comprehensive survey of the international situation, the Council gave first place to the question of Berlin. The Member countries made clear their resolution not to yield to threats. Their unamimous view on Berlin was expressed in the Council's Declaration of December 16th.[2] The Council will continue to follow this question with close attention and will shortly discuss the replies to be sent to the Soviet Notes of November 27th.[3]

The member States of NATO sincerely believe that the interests of peace require equitable settlements of the outstanding political issues which divide the Free World from the Communist world. A solution of the German question, linked with European security arrangements, and an agreement on controlled disarmament remain in their view essential. The NATO Governments will continue to seek just settlements of these problems, but regret that Western proposals on these questions have so far been ignored by the Soviet Government.

The Council heard reports on the Geneva discussions on the discontinuance of nuclear weapons tests, and on measures helpful in preventing surprise attack.

The Council's review of the international situation, on the basis of reports prepared by the Political Committee, covered a wide range of problems. Special attention was given to the efforts of the Communist-bloc to weaken the positions of the Free World in different areas.

Political Co-operation

The Council had before it a report by the Secretary General on political co-operation in the Alliance. The Ministers consider that important progress has been made in this field during 1958. They examined the problems inevitably created by the widening of political consultation. There was general agreement that the existing machinery of NATO is well suited to the needs of the Alliance, and that flexible methods would produce better results than any codification of rules. The Ministers agreed that the preparation of political consultation in the Council could be improved, in particular by more systematic study of long-term political

[1] *Nato Letter*, January 1959, p. 9.   [2] See preceding document.
[3] See above, pp. 146–64.

questions.[1] The Council paid tribute to the efforts of the Secretary-General in the field of conciliation between member countries.

Economic Questions

The Ministers reaffirmed the importance they attach to the measures taken both individually and collectively by member countries to stimulate economic activity and to ensure continuing expansion without inflation.

The Council noted the difficulties encountered in the negotiations undertaken for the organization of economic co-operation between the European members of the Alliance who are in the Common Market and those who are not. It considers it necessary that a multilateral association should be established at the earliest possible date and expresses the hope that the efforts now being undertaken with a view to a solution will be successful.

The Council heard a joint statement by the Greek and Turkish Foreign Ministers on the problems of the less developed member countries, and instructed the Permanent Council to undertake a study of this matter.

Military Questions

The Council examined the military situation of the Alliance. After hearing reports by the Standing Group and the Supreme Allied Commanders, the Ministers emphasised the vital need, in view of the continuing increase in Soviet armaments, to sustain without relaxation the effort of member countries to improve the defensive power of the Alliance.[2]

The Council reaffirmed that NATO defensive strategy continues to be based on the existence of effective shield forces and on the manifest will to use nuclear retaliatory forces to repel aggression.[3]

[1] In October 1958 it was widely reported in the press that General de Gaulle (who became Prime Minister of France on 1 June 1958), had sent letters to President Eisenhower and Mr. Macmillan, dated 24 September, Le Monde, 29 October 1958. General de Gaulle was reported to have said that the United States, United Kingdom and France occupy a special position by reason of their responsibilities for territories beyond their frontiers, and that the idea of tripartite planning and consultation, in the military sphere already embodied in the standing group in Washington, should be extended to the political sphere to cover if need be the whole world, The Times, 25 October 1958. For further accounts, see Le Monde, 26–27 October 1958, and New York Times, 21 June 1959. It was then reported that French Government spokesmen denied that General de Gaulle was proposing any changes in the structure of N.A.T.O. as such, but that he was aiming at the regular consultation of the three great Western Powers on world problems. A West German Government official had already rejected the idea of a three-power directorate within N.A.T.O., The Times, 28 October 1958. A Foreign Office spokeman said on 4 December that conversations were being held between the American, French, and United Kingdom Governments on General de Gaulle's proposals, The Times, 5 December 1958.

[2] On 3 November 1958, General Norstad said that the 30 battalions of guided missiles (mostly short-range, but all capable of carrying nuclear warheads) under his command would be increased to more than 100 by 1963. For reports of his press conference, see Manchester Guardian, 4 November 1958, and The Times, 4 November 1958.

[3] See fn. 2 on p. 355, above. There was opposition amongst certain N.A.T.O. countries to the American offer of 16 December 1957. The Prime Minister of Norway stated that Norway would

The Ministers examined the report of the 1958 Annual Review and approved its conclusions. The implementation of the plans agreed in December 1957 by the Heads of Government is being actively pursued, and methods for accelerating their realization were agreed.

The next regular Ministerial meeting of the Council will be held in Washington on April 2nd to 4th, 1959, at the invitation of the United States Government, on the occasion of the tenth anniversary of the signing of the North Atlantic Treaty.

B. CYPRUS

1. Statement by Mr. Macmillan in the House of Commons, 19 June 1958[1]

With permission, Mr. Speaker, I now propose to make the statement on the Government's policy on Cyprus which I had intended to make on Tuesday, but which, with the forbearance of the House, I decided to defer at the request of the North Atlantic Treaty Organisation Council.

The policy of Her Majesty's Government in Cyprus has had four main purposes:

(a) To serve the best interests of all the people of the island.

(b) To achieve a permanent settlement acceptable to the two communities in the island and to the Greek and Turkish Governments.

(c) To safeguard the British bases and installations in the island, which are necessary to enable the United Kingdom to carry out her international obligations.

(d) To strengthen peace and security, and co-operation between the United Kingdom and her Allies, in a vital area.

These are the aims which Her Majesty's Government have consistently pursued and which have guided their efforts in recent months to find

not accept rocket bases for medium-range missiles, nor atomic arms depots, see *Norwegian Press Bulletin*, 21 December 1957. More serious was the French refusal to the establishment of intermediate-range missile bases in France except under French control. The French would not agree to the stockpiling of atomic warheads for the French Air Force under United States control, see *The Times*, 15 December 1958. In a press conference on 23 October 1958 General de Gaulle indicated, not for the first time, that the forthcoming possession of nuclear weapons by France would enable her to *'faire sentir notre action dans les domaines qui nous sont chers et utiles à tous les hommes: celui de la sécurité mondiale et celui du désarmement.' Le Monde*, 25 October 1958.

[1] H.C. Deb., vol. 589, coll. 1315–18. Mr. Macmillan went on to say: 'I have myself sent a personal appeal to the Prime Ministers of Greece and Turkey asking them to approach this policy in a spirit of co-operation and moderation . . .' The statement was to have been made on 17 June but the announcement was postponed 48 hours at the special request of M. Spaak, on behalf of the N.A.T.O. Council, see ibid., coll. 897–8. Sir Hugh Foot, the Governor of Cyprus, broadcast the statement to the people of Cyprus on 19 June 1958.

common ground on which an agreed settlement might be reached. It is deeply regretted that all attempts in this direction have hitherto proved unsuccessful.

In view of the disagreement between the Greek and Turkish Governments and between the two communities in Cyprus, and of the disastrous consequences for all concerned if violence and conflict continue, an obligation rests with the United Kingdom Government, as the sovereign Power responsible for the administration of the island and the well-being of its inhabitants, to give a firm and clear lead out of the present deadlock. They accordingly declare a new policy which represents an adventure in partnership—partnership between the communities in the island and also between the Governments of the United Kingdom, Greece and Turkey.

The following is an outline of the partnership plan:

Cyprus should enjoy the advantages of association not only with the United Kingdom, and, therefore, with the British Commonwealth, but also with Greece and Turkey.

Since the three Governments of the United Kingdom, Greece and Turkey all have an interest in Cyprus, Her Majesty's Government will welcome the co-operation and participation of the two other Governments in a joint effort to achieve the peace, progress and prosperity of the island.

The Greek and Turkish Governments will each be invited to appoint a representative to co-operate with the Governor in carrying out this policy.

The island will have a system of representative Government with each community exercising autonomy in its own communal affairs.

In order to satisfy the desire of the Greek and Turkish Cypriots to be recognised as Greeks and Turks, Her Majesty's Government will welcome an arrangement which gives them Greek or Turkish nationality, while enabling them to retain British nationality.

To allow time for the new principle of partnership to be fully worked out and brought into operation under this plan in the necessary atmosphere of stability, the international status of the island will remain unchanged for seven years.

A system of representative government and communal autonomy will be worked out by consultation with representatives of the two communities and with the representatives of the Greek and Turkish Governments.

The essential provisions of the new constitution will be:

(a) There will be a separate House of Representatives for each of the two communities, and these Houses will have final legislative authority in communal affairs.

(b) Authority for internal administration, other than communal affairs and internal security, will be undertaken by a Council presided over by the Governor and including the representatives of the Greek and Turkish Governments and six elected Ministers drawn from the Houses of Representatives, four being Greek Cypriots and two Turkish Cypriots.

(c) The Governor, acting after consultation with the representatives of the Greek and Turkish Governments, will have reserve powers to ensure that the interests of both communities are protected.

(d) External affairs, defence and internal security will be matters specifically reserved to the Governor acting after consultation with the representatives of the Greek and Turkish Governments.

(e) The representatives of the Greek and Turkish Governments will have the right to require any legislation which they consider to be discriminatory to be reserved for consideration by an impartial tribunal.

If the full benefits of this policy are to be realised it is evident that violence must cease. Subject to this, Her Majesty's Government intend to take progressive steps to relax the Emergency Regulations and eventually to end the state of emergency. This process would include the return of those Cypriots at present excluded from the island under the Emergency Regulations.

A policy based on these principles and proposals will give the people of the island a specially favoured and protected status. Through representative institutions they will exercise authority in the management of the island's internal affairs, and each community will control its own communal affairs. While the people of the island enjoy these advantages, friendly relations and practical co-operation between the United Kingdom, Greece and Turkey will be maintained and strengthened as Cyprus becomes a symbol of co-operation instead of a cause of conflict between the three Allied Governments.

Her Majesty's Government trust that this imaginative plan will be welcomed by all concerned in the spirit in which it is put forward, and for their part they will bend all efforts to ensuring its success. Indeed, if the Greek and Turkish Governments were willing to extend this experiment in partnership and co-operation, Her Majesty's Government would be prepared, at the appropriate time, to go further and, subject to the reservation to the United Kingdom of such bases and facilities as might be necessary for the discharge of her international obligations, to share the sovereignty of the island with their Greek and Turkish Allies as their contribution to a lasting settlement.[1]

---

[1] These proposals for a solution to the Cyprus problem were debated in the House of Commons on 26 June 1958. The principal proposal put forward by the Opposition was that the Constitution of Cyprus should make provision for a legislative assembly, ideally based on a common roll, where Greek and Turkish Cypriots could meet to discuss the common affairs of the island. Their main criticism was that the United Kingdom Government's plan tended to emphasize the separation of the two communities rather than their unity. For a report of the debate see H.C. Deb., vol. 590, coll. 611–731.

2. Statement by Mr. Zorlu, Turkish Foreign Minister, regarding the United Kingdom proposals for Cyprus, 19 June 1958[1]

The Turkish Government has been aware since June 10 of the main lines of the British plan which has been announced today. The Turkish Government has had the opportunity of discussing the plan, as well as the Cyprus question, in the NATO Permanent Council, as well as to explain our attitude towards the plan in the Committee on Foreign Affairs (of the G.N.A.) and in a closed session of the Turkish Grand National Assembly on June 16.

Let me point out before all else that the Turkish Government continues to maintain its conviction and decision that the best solution for a final settlement of the Cyprus question is partition. It is positively impossible to accept any proposal which does not contain this final solution, particularly in view of the recent resolution of the Turkish Grand National Assembly on this question.

The views of the Turkish Government on the plan, which has been communicated to us and which has been disclosed in the North Atlantic Council and the British Parliament today, and on the discussions which took place in the Council with respect to the solution of the Cyprus question in relation to this plan, may be summarized as follows:

The British Government, in announcing this plan with regard to the provisional administration of the island, also dwelt on certain basic points with regard to the final international status of Cyprus. Among these Mr. Selwyn Lloyd has confirmed to our Ambassador in London the statement made by Mr. Lennox-Boyd on December 19, 1956, with regard to the application of the principle of self-determination including partition among eventual options.[2] The British Government also mentioned the fact that effective measures are being taken with a view to putting an end to terrorism in the island. These points have had favourable effects on the Turkish Government, which is convinced that partition is the best radical solution and that terrorism should never be tolerated and should be eliminated in the island.

On the other hand, the views of the Turkish Government on the proposed means to solve this dispute may be stated as follows:

1. It is advisable to hold a conference on the Cyprus dispute among the interested parties with the shortest possible delay. The Turkish Prime Minister has already answered in the affirmative to this suggestion which was referred to in the message from Mr. Macmillan.
2. The Turkish Government is convinced that it is perfectly clear that

---

[1] *Turkish News*, 24 June 1958. (Unofficial translation.)
[2] See *Documents* for 1956, pp. 690–1.

the question is above all else a dispute among three governments, one of claims and counter claims. It is impossible to hide Turkey and Greece behind the communities in the island, and it is certain that to use such tactics in order to disguise specific aims would in no way help solve the problem, but, on the contrary, would complicate it further.

3. It is essential that negotiations should take the form of a conference among the three interested Governments. To refuse this would be tantamount to ignoring realities, and it is certain that indirect negotiations, which would not bring the parties face to face, always lead to, and increase misunderstandings. The Turkish Government considers that it would be advantageous if the Conference were to be held at the highest level, as has been suggested by the British Prime Minister.

4. It is essential that the final international status of the island should be determined at the Conference. As for the British Government's plan, in the view of the Turkish Government, this plan should not be taken as the basic document at the Conference, but may be acceptable as a Conference paper. Naturally, any plan submitted by the Turkish Government should also be accepted as such.

Again, in the view of the Turkish Government it is quite possible to fuse together the principles of partition and partnership, and only thus can a perfected plan emerge.

After thus setting forth the Turkish Government's views on the new plan, let me point out that it appears that the purpose of the British Prime Minister in disclosing the plan is no doubt to show that the British Government is making every effort to solve this question. It is certainly gratifying to note that these efforts are being made with a view to the solution of a dipute among three governments which are allies within N.A.T.O. If these efforts had been made, as they were some time ago, in consultation with the interested parties, and particularly with Turkey, there is no doubt that they would have produced more positive and constructive results.

May I also point out that if the British Government had taken the necessary measures, as it is doing now, at the time when the Turkish Government first drew its attention to the need to take such measures, or had it not relaxed such measures in spite of the warning of Turkey, the regrettable incidents on the island would not have taken place.

I shall for the time being confine myself to the foregoing explanation of the Turkish views on the British plan. It is, of course, impossible to leave our public opinion in the dark, even for one day, on this question which rightly interests it so closely. I wish to assure the Turkish people that our just cause in the Cyprus question will in the end be realized.

3. Letter from Mr. Karamanlis, Greek Prime Minister, to Mr. Macmillan regarding the United Kingdom proposals for Cyprus, 21 June 1958[1]

I have very carefully studied the message that Your Excellency conveyed to me through Sir Roger Allen in the evening of June 10th. I entirely agree with Your Excellency's appreciation of the gravity of the present situation and know from experience the consequences which the dispute over Cyprus bears upon our alliances. I draw my experience from my endeavours during the past two years to avert these consequences.

While making efforts to contain public opinion in this country, which was justly aroused, I had declared myself ready to discuss any solution of the problem which would give satisfaction to the just claim of the Cypriot people, would safeguard the interests of Great Britain and, through constitutional and international guarantees, would cover the legitimate interests of the Turkish minority and the strategic preoccupations of Turkey.

The British response to my endeavours did not correspond to my expectations. From the Turkish side we have met only with provocations. I have nevertheless insisted on this policy because I believed that justice and the ideals for which our two peoples have gone through so many sacrifices would prevail.

The publication of the British plan, coming after the horrible acts of violence committed by the Turks in Cyprus which the administration of the island ought to have prevented, renders my persistent efforts even more difficult.

I had conveyed in time to Your Excellency through Her Majesty's Ambassador in Athens our views on your plan and was hoping until yesterday that those views would influence the thoughts of the British Government. Unfortunately, Your Excellency's statement in the House of Commons has widened the divergence between our position and your plan. Cyprus is a British Crown Colony by virtue of international treaties. Turkey has relinquished all rights and titles on the island. Greece, supporting the right of the Cypriots to self-determination, has declared that she does not aim at the annexation of Cyprus. Those entitled to determine the future of the island are, therefore, principally the people of Cyprus and the United Kingdom since, according to the Treaty of Lausanne, this right was reserved to the 'interested parties'.[2] Turkey is certainly not an 'interested party', having relinquished her rights of whatever nature by the same Treaty.

---

[1] Press Release, Greek Embassy, London, 23 June 1958. Archbishop Makarios rejected the United Kingdom proposals for Cyprus in a short statement of 20 June 1958, see Press Release, 20 June 1958.   [2] Treaty of Peace signed at Lausanne, 24 July 1923.

The United Kingdom is now inviting Greece and Turkey to participate in the administration of the island for a period of seven years, thus tending to create a sort of de facto condominium upon the island. This virtually amounts to upsetting the prevailing legal status. Allow me to draw your attention to this point as through their plan, Her Majesty's Government tend to disregard the principle of the sanctity of treaties, a principle so valuable to us all. I am aware that it is sometimes argued that practical solutions must not be hindered by legal considerations, but in the present case I, at least, believe it is possible to find practical solutions which would also be in accordance with justice and existing international treaties.

May I point out that it is inconceivable to invoke the provocative attitude and the intransigence of Turkey as a decisive factor barring any just and practical solution. Great Britain has been exercising sovereignty over Cyprus for many years. She has the privilege of being a great power. Hers is the responsibility to determine the future of the island in accordance with the principles of the Charter of the United Nations as well as with the provisions of other international agreements. I do not think it possible that Great Britain can dismiss this responsibility by diverting the whole issue into the limited and artificial frame of a so-called Greco-Turkish dispute.

In examining the outline of your plan from a practical point of view, it is apparent that the whole system is based on an entirely ephemeral situation, i.e. on tension in the relations between the Greek and Turkish Cypriots who have lived for centuries in peace on a united and indivisible territory. I sincerely believe that this tension has been artificially created during the last months and, therefore, can be brought to an end. Consequently, the administrative machinery which the plan sets up is unjustified and, owing to its intricate nature and to the friction which it is bound to cause, will prove inoperative. I do not believe that the system set up by the British plan will be an instrument of appeasement. On the contrary, because of its structure and of the conditions temporarily created, it will help in maintaining the present tension.

But, apart from the above considerations, and even if we were to disregard that, owing to its provisional character it does not provide for a final solution of the problem through the application of the right of self determination, the plan itself has very serious disadvantages, as for instance, the composition of the Council. The way the Council is constituted disregards the principle of true representation at the expense of the vast Greek majority. Thus, the only democratic institution set up by the proposed administrative system is falsified.

For the reasons stated above, the Greek Government, prepared as they are to face this problem in a realistic way, are unable to agree with the British Government's proposals, being convinced that this plan would only add new complications to those already existing. Since the main issue, namely the right of the Cypriot people to decide their own future, is being put aside for a period of seven years, the plan would have been more constructive in proposing a temporary solution on the basis of democratic self government under British sovereignty and postponing the settlement on the main issue until a more appropriate time. This would be a matter between the British Government and the Cypriot people. The Greek Government would be prepared to help wherever they could usefully act in a mediatory way.

I agree with Your Excellency that personal contact would be more useful to our efforts of finding a solution than the interchange of messages. I, therefore, consider your proposal as a useful one, provided that the ground is sufficiently cleared through diplomatic channels. A tripartite meeting, however, which you also suggest, would not, in my opinion, lead to any constructive results under the present circumstances.

In conclusion, I believe that a way of promoting the Cyprus issue, in view of present difficulties, would be for the British Government to reconsider their plan and make a new effort to find a solution which could be considered satisfactory. I believe that, if the British Government were prepared to make this new effort, appeasement in the island would follow, thus making it possible to reach through various stages a final solution.

On our side we shall do our best to contribute to the success of this effort.

4. Statement by Mr. Macmillan, London, 15 August 1958[1]

On 19th June, 1958, the Prime Minister presented to Parliament a statement of the policy which Her Majesty's Government intend to pursue in regard to the Cyprus problem for a period of seven years. This policy was explained by the Prime Minister to the House of Commons in broad terms, and its outline and main practical features were described in the Parliamentary statement of policy of 19th June, 1958.[2] As Parliament was informed, the policy has been the subject of friendly and confidential consultation and discussion within the North Atlantic Treaty Organisation. In the last few days, the Prime Minister has had the opportunity of personal meetings, in Athens and Ankara with the Prime Ministers of Greece and Turkey, which have enabled him to acquaint himself, at first hand, with the views of their respective Governments.

After the most careful consideration of the views expressed to him by the Prime Ministers of Greece and Turkey, and in the light of the advice tendered by the Governor of Cyrpus regarding the situation in the island, Her Majesty's Government have decided to proceed to give effect to the policy as announced to Parliament in the following manner.

---

[1] *Commonwealth Survey*, 19 August 1958, pp. 789–90. This statement was accepted by the Turkish Government, but rejected by the Greek Government, see following document.

[2] See above, pp. 376–78.

An order-in-council has already been approved, authorising the preparation of electoral rolls in the island. This is expected to take two or three months. Meanwhile, in accordance with the spirit of the decision whereby the communities are encouraged to order their own communal affairs, the Governor will, where local circumstances make this desirable, authorise the establishment of separate Greek and Turkish Cypriot municipal councils. When the electoral rolls are complete, it will be possible to hold elections for the two Houses of Representatives. The preparations for the elections should involve consultations between the Governor and leaders of the two communities. If, as Her Majesty's Government earnestly hope, violence ceases,[1] this will make possible the return of those at present excluded from the island, in order that they may play their part in these electoral processes, and in consultations on the details of the system of representative government and communal autonomy set out in the statement of policy. As soon as the Houses of Representatives have been elected, they will be asked to elect their representatives to the Governor's Council, which will then become the authoritative body to deal with all matters not specifically devolved upon the Houses of Representatives or reserved to the Governor at his discretion.

With regard to the representatives of the Greek and Turkish Governments as proposed in the statement of policy, Her Majesty's Government feel, on reflection, that the representatives of other sovereign powers could not suitably sit as members of the council under the chairmanship of the Governor. It would be more correct to regard them as specially appointed representatives of their countries with direct access to the Governor and such other facilities as they need to carry out their functions. Accordingly, Her Majesty's Government invite the Governments of Greece and Turkey to appoint their representatives with effect from 1st October.

The establishment of this system of communal assemblies charged with certain specific functions, and of the Governor's Council, charged with other more general duties, does not exclude and should, with general goodwill, facilitate the development of some form of representative institution serving the interests of the island as a whole.

As regards the proposal for dual nationality, it does not appear that there is need for urgent action in this matter. Further enquiries have revealed that any special provision of this kind would require carefully devised legislation in view of the complexities of international law. It is,

---

[1] In a statement to the House of Commons on 24 July 1958, Mr. Lennox Boyd, the Secretary of State for Colonial Affairs, said: '. . . Between 1 June and 22 July, 95 people have been killed in Cyprus and over 170 wounded . . .' See H.C. Deb., vol. 592, coll. 676–7. On 31 July Mr. Macmillan made an appeal for a cessation of violence in Cyprus, see *Commonwealth Survey*, 5 August 1958, p. 745. A similar appeal was broadcast by Mr. Karamanlis on 30 July, see *Daily Telegraph*, 1 August 1958, and by Mr. Menderes on 1 August, see *Turkish News*, 8 August 1958.

therefore, wiser to defer action pending the consideration of the legal and other aspects.

Finally, Her Majesty's Government appeal with confidence for support from all concerned for the two major concepts which underlie their policy. The first, is a period of calm and the cessation of violence in the island. The second is the deferring, for a period of seven years, of any final solution without prejudice to the future or to the views and aspirations of any parties concerned. At the same time such a period cannot be a period of stagnation. Her Majesty's Government feel that the form of growth and development which they propose is one suited to the needs of the moment and in conformity with the two principles which appear to be generally accepted by all concerned.

5. Letter from Mr. Karamanlis to Mr. Macmillan, 19 August 1958[1]

My dear Prime Minister, I have carefully studied the contents of your letter of August 14th. During our recent meeting in Athens, you had the opportunity of ascertaining our goodwill and sincere desire to reach a solution of the Cyprus question acceptable to all. You will thus appreciate the disappointment and regret which the contents of your letter have caused us.

The position of Greece on the Cyprus issue is well known to Your Excellency. We are claiming the right of self-determination for the Cypriots. For that reason, Greece has appealed to the United Nations convinced that the exercise of this right cannot be refused to a European people still living under full colonial status.

In view however of recent complications, mostly of an artificial nature, Greece has accepted to postpone temporarily the final issue and discuss a provisional solution which would leave the future status of Cyprus entirely open and would ensure to the people of Cyprus, during the period of its application, democratic self-government with all possible guarantees in favour of the Turkish minority. Such a solution would lead to the pacification of the island which we all sincerely desire, and would strengthen our alliances in this area so vital to peace.

It is in this spirit that I addressed to Your Excellency my letter of June 21st stating the reasons for which your plan is not conducive to pacification and conciliation.[2] Furthermore, during our talks in Athens, after having stated the basic position of my country on the Cyprus question, I had the opportunity of explaining that your plan ought to be cleared of those elements which deprive it of the agreed provisional character of the solution, and which instead of simplifying the issue complicate it further. Thus I had asked:

---

[1] *News from Greece*, 20 August 1958.   [2] See above, pp. 381–83.

(*a*) That no third Governments be involved in the administration of the island. I notice instead in your recent statement that the provision for two representatives is maintained with capacities which render clear their interference in the administration. This however will create, every day, complications, constant discord and rivalry which would aggravate relations not only between the two sections of the population but also between two allied countries. But above all the very presence of the two representatives within the provisional administration will engender conditions which will in time give rise to claims for permanent rights. This also clearly contradicts the agreed provisional nature of your solution.

(*b*) In regard to the two separate houses of representatives. I had stated my view that a single legislative assembly ought to be instituted to deal with all matters except those reserved to the Governor. Even if the idea of two houses were to be retained and their authority strictly limited to communal affairs only, a single assembly, representative of the whole population ought to be set up. I notice instead that not only are the two houses maintained with the authority of both clearly determined, but that the single assembly which we consider a basic element of the whole system is only vaguely mentioned.

(*c*) You will recall that during our conversations we also raised the question of the numerical composition of the council in order that it should correspond to that of the population. Unfortunately even on that point no modification has been brought to your initial plan.

Not only have the above points not been modified, but a new element has also been added which would disrupt the unity of the population since the Governor can authorize the establishment of separate municipal councils in the towns and villages of Cyprus. I cannot sincerely see why the system of single municipal councils which is in force for many centuries in Cyprus and all over the world need now be abandoned on the island. The dangerous complications which the establishment of separate municipal councils in the towns and villages of Cyprus will provoke are clear to everybody and I must say that whatever doubtful political expediency this measure is destined to serve I am unable to understand how such an unprecedented institution could have been conceived.

In general, our observations, as Your Excellency will notice, seek to remove from your plan those elements which divide the Cypriots in an almost organic way instead of promoting concord and co-operation. The Greek Government, appreciating the situation, thus regret that they are unable to co-operate in the application of your plan. They do not, therefore, intend to appoint a representative to co-operate with the Governor of Cyprus. The Greek Government have never asked to participate in the exercise of sovereignty on the island. Moreover, as I have pointed out, this would serve no purpose.

As regards the attitude of the Greek Cypriots it is for them to decide whether they will co-operate with your plan or not.

I am afraid, Mr. Prime Minister, that the plan put forward by the British Government without the modifications suggested by the Greek Government will not serve the purposes which you have proclaimed of the pacification of the island and of its prosperity. Thus, the plan retains traces of unfortunate solutions which have caused such tragic complications throughout the world at the expense of the prestige of the free world and that because they exceeded the limits beyond which the basic principles in international life cannot be harmlessly sacrificed to ephemeral expediencies.

The Greek Government have not hesitated to make conciliatory moves in view of the pacification of the island and the strengthening of their alliances. If similar moves had been forthcoming from other sides as well, we would have by now overcome the present crisis. I must emphasize that in their conciliatory efforts the Greek Government have been seconded by the people of Cyprus not only through the recent proposals made by their representative, but also through the truce which the Cypriot fighting organisation has offered and kept, although constantly provoked to discontinue it.

We therefore face future developments with a clear conscience since we have done everything possible to render them peaceful and constructive. Since the agreement for a provisional solution has been frustrated, Greece will continue with all legitimate means her efforts towards the freedom of the people of Cyprus.

It is pointed out from various sides to us that, in spite of our moderation, our future will be dark if we do not accept the plan which you propose. The Greek Government are fully conscious of the ordeals which they will eventually have to face. But the Greek Nation is prepared, as in other similar circumstances, to stand these eventual ordeals for it has full confidence in justice.

6. Message from Archbishop Makarios to Mr. Macmillan, 27 September 1958[1]

On 22 September during an interview with Mrs. Barbara Castle, M.P. and Vice-Chairman of the Labour Party,[2] I said that the Cypriot People would accept as a solution of the Cyprus issue, a constitution of self-government for an agreed period, at the end of which a status of

---

[1] *News from Greece*, 30 September 1958.

[2] For the text of the interview between Archbishop Makarios and Mrs. Barbara Castle see *The Times*, 23 September 1958. It was announced on 27 September by Mr. Averoff, Greek Foreign Minister, that he was in full agreement with Archbishop Makarios on the future of the handling of the Cyprus dispute, see *The Times*, 29 September 1958.

independence should be given to the Island. This status of independence should be guaranteed by the U.N. and in no way changed without the consent of the U.N. I now wish to set out these proposals, as above, officially for the consideration of Her Britannic Majesty's Government.

7. Discussion on Cyprus in the N.A.T.O. Council, September–October 1958[1]

INTRODUCTION

The Cyprus question was discussed in the North Atlantic Council at the time of the statement of policy on Cyprus made by the Prime Minister in the House of Commons on June 19, 1958.[2] Further discussions within the North Atlantic Treaty Organisation took place before the Prime Minister's visits to Athens and Ankara for discussions with the Governments of Greece and Turkey, which led up to the further statement of policy issued by Her Majesty's Government on August 15.[3]

2. The Secretary-General of the North Atlantic Treaty Organisation, Monsieur Spaak, after visiting Athens on September 23, put forward to a meeting of the North Atlantic Council on September 24 a paper[4] containing certain proposals on the question of Cyprus. Monsieur Spaak also proposed that an early conference should be held, between the three Governments with the participation of representatives of the two main Cypriot communities and of some neutral party, on the basis of his paper.

3. The North Atlantic Council at a number of subsequent meetings has considered the proposal for a conference in the light of Her Majesty's Government's statements of policy and Monsieur Spaak's paper. The discussions were concerned with the terms of reference and agenda of a conference and also with its composition and the place where it should be held.

4. In the course of the discussions the two following papers were drafted for consideration by the Council and discussed by them:

(a) a minute[5] recording the main points established in the Council's discussions and the attitudes of the three Governments principally concerned;

(b) a covering letter[6] for the Secretary-General to send in transmitting the minute to the Permanent Representatives of Member Governments.

These documents were substantially agreed by the North Atlantic Council. Document No. II still contains two alternative paragraphs 8.

[1] Cmnd. 566.   [2] See above, p. 376.   [3] See above, p. 383.
[4] Document No. I, below.   [5] Document No. II, below.
[6] Document No. III, below.

The United Kingdom Permanent Representative on the Council indicated that Her Majesty's Government could accept either of these alternatives.

6. It will be seen from the documents that Her Majesty's Government agreed that

(a) Her Majesty's Government's policy should be discussed at a conference.

(b) Modifications or additions to the policy agreed upon by the three Governments at the conference could be incorporated.

(c) The discussions of a final solution should also appear on the Agenda of the conference.

(d) Greek and Turkish Cypriot representatives might participate, and if Archbishop Makarios attended as representing the Greek Cypriots, Her Majesty's Government would not object.

(e) While convening the conference themselves, Her Majesty's Government. were ready to invite the Secretary-General of the North Atlantic Treaty Organisation to take the Chair.

(f) If the conference were held in Paris, the Secretary-General could at his discretion report to the North Atlantic Council, or convene the Council to consider the position reached; nevertheless, if it was desired that a representative of the Government of the United States, and of another Member Government, should be present as well as the Secretary-General, Her Majesty's Government would not object.

7. On October 29 the Greek Government confirmed through their Permanent Representative that in the present circumstances they abandoned the attempt to convene the conference.

DOCUMENT No. I

A conference will take place as soon as possible between the British, Greek and Turkish Governments and representatives of the Greek and Turkish Cypriot communities.

The Secretary-General of NATO will offer his good offices.

The document which could serve as a basis for discussion would be as follows:—

PART I

The Cyprus problem must be settled. This must be done for the good of the inhabitants and in order to restore understanding and friendship between Great Britain, Greece and Turkey.

2. It would obviously be highly desirable for the solution reached to settle the problems raised once and for all. This, unfortunately, seems

impossible because of the passions roused by events and because of the political positions recently taken up.

3. It is therefore necessary to make up our minds to finding a provisional solution.

4. But to be acceptable and valid this provisional solution must not prejudge in any way the definitive solution which must be reached later. It is necessary, therefore, that in the application of the provisional solution nothing should favour or hinder either directly or indirectly any of the solutions hitherto envisaged and this without any exception.

5. A provisional solution must, at the same time, mark important progress towards the possibility of the Cypriot community governing itself and must include all necessary guarantees to protect the minority.

6. A provisional solution must equally safeguard the bases and installations necessary for Great Britain to fulfil its international obligations.

PART II

The principles on which the new institutions should be elaborated are as follows:—

(1) Creation of a House of Representatives for each of the two communities having competence in all communal affairs (education, religion, justice—everything to do with the personal status of the individual).

(2) Creation of a representative institution having competence over questions of joint interest (internal affairs).

(3) A governmental council presided over by the Governor with a Greek Cypriot majority having competence to deal with internal affairs.

(4) Foreign affairs, defence and security will remain within the competence of the Governor.

(5) The Governor will be British. He will be assisted in his executive task by the Presidents of the two Houses of Representatives.

(6) Either of the Representative Houses will have the right to submit to an impartial tribunal any measure which it considers to be discriminatory or unfavourable to one or other of the communities.

(7) The provisional solution will be for seven years.

DOCUMENT No. II

The Council, in its examination of the problem of Cyprus, heard statements from the representatives of the countries directly concerned.

It took note:

(1) that the Governments of the United Kingdom, Greece and Turkey accepted the idea of calling a conference at an early date;

and that these three Governments looked with favour on the presence at this conference of representatives of the Greek and Turkish communities of the Island.

It noted that, for the purpose of this conference,

(2) the United Kingdom Government desired that its plan should be examined, and agreed that it could be defined or modified on points over which agreement was reached at the conference;

(3) the Greek Government, for its part, desired that the suggestions put forward by the Secretary-General of NATO on 24th September, 1958,[1] should be discussed.

(4) Finally, the Turkish Government asked that the British Plan should be taken into consideration but agreed that any amendment could be put forward at the conference, and moreover intended itself to present such amendments.

(5) The Council notes,

that while these statements of position each present special points of view, they are neither contradictory nor irreconcilable;

(6) it also notes that,

the three Governments are in agreement that, apart from the discussions proposed above in regard to a temporary solution of the problem of Cyprus, the discussion of a final solution should also appear on the agenda of the conference;

(7) it therefore recommends that the United Kingdom Government should take the initiative in calling a conference in the conditions indicated above;

(8) it further suggests that the conference be held in Paris and that the Secretary-General of NATO should, as representing the Organisation as a whole, extend his good offices to the parties directly concerned.

[*Alternative paragraph 8:*

(8) it further suggests that the Secretary-General of NATO, assisted by one of the Permanent Representatives on the North Atlantic Council, and a Representative of the Government of the United States, should attend the conference in order to help the participants by lending their good offices.]

Document No. III

Mr. Ambassador, I beg to enclose, addressed to your Government, the text of a document relating to the calling of a conference having for its

---

[1] Document I, above.

purpose the discussion of the Cyprus problem, the terms of which have been approved by the North Atlantic Council.

In the course of the discussions which preceded the approval of this document, the Permanent Representatives of the three countries directly concerned clearly expressed their desire that, in addition to the discussion of a provisional solution, a free and fair discussion should also take place to seek a final solution of the Cyprus problem.

The Government of Turkey indicated for its part that the discussion of a final solution could not, however, constitute a prior condition for the discussion of the provisional solution.

The British Government for its part made it clear that, in discussing the elements of a provisional solution of this problem, it would be appropriate to assess these in relation to their effect upon the final solution.

Finally, the Turkish Government emphasised that it could accept discussion of a provisional solution only on the condition that this did not prejudice the final solution.

In transmitting this document to you, I felt it my duty to draw your attention to the above declarations.

8. Resolution of the General Assembly, 5 December 1958[1]

THE GENERAL ASSEMBLY,

Having considered the question of Cyprus,

Recalling its resolution 1013 (XI) of 26 February 1957,[2]

Expresses its confidence that continued efforts will be made by the parties to reach a peaceful, democratic and just solution in accordance with the Charter of the United Nations.

9. Statement by Mr. Macmillan in the House of Commons, 10 December 1958[3]

With permission, Mr. Speaker, I will make a statement on Cyprus.

We have been striving, and we shall continue to strive, for a political settlement which will bring peace to the island. I intend in a few moments to say something on the position now that the debate in the United Nations is over. But I wish, first, to refer to the suggestion arising out of the inquest on Andreas Louca that there should be some form of inquiry into the conduct of British troops in Cyprus.

---

[1] G.A.O.R., Thirteenth Session, Supplement 18 (A/4090), Resol. 1287 (XIII). This resolution was submitted in plenary meeting and adopted by the General Assembly without objection, after consideration of the report of the First Committee. For the text of the report, see G.A.O.R., Thirteenth Session, Annexes, agenda item 68, Doc. A/4029.

[2] See *Documents* for 1957, p. 411.   [3] H.C. Deb., vol. 597, coll. 343-7.

When we consider the crimes which have been committed against our troops and the provocation which they have undergone, I think that we have a right to be proud not only of their high morale but of their discipline and restraint. Of course, there are people in some countries who would wish to discredit Great Britain by wild and unjustified allegations.

At the same time, we are very jealous of the honour of our troops and we have recognised that in the peculiarly difficult circumstances of maintaining order in the face of terrorism and civil disorder vigilance was required and there were bound to be incidents concerning which as full information as possible should be available. The Governor, therefore, some time ago, set up a special investigation group to undertake prompt inquiries into any complaints against the security forces. This has been of considerable value to the Governor and his advisers. It is clear that these reports could not be released for publication without prejudicing the usefulness of this system in the future.

After the murder in Famagusta, on 3rd October, of Mrs. Cutliffe, and the wounding of another soldier's wife, it was hoped that the assailant might be seized and identified in the neighbourhood of the crime. A round-up of the males nearby for possible identification therefore followed. In accordance with normal practice a report of the events was made to the Governor. The searching inquiries which were made have not led to the securing of any evidence to identify any particular individual or individuals of the security forces as having used an unjustified degree of force.

Coroner's inquests were held in two cases. The coroner formed the view that there appeared to have been used on some of those arrested a greater degree of force than was justifiable. The coroner also recognised the horror, disgust and anger that filled the minds and hearts of everyone on that day. Thirdly, he drew attention to the many discrepancies in the evidence of certain witnesses who alleged brutality and he said that certain witnesses seemed more anxious to inculpate the security forces than to help the court with unbiased evidence. He said that he had not sufficient evidence to enable him to conclude when or by whom the blow which led to Louca's death was struck.

In view of the very full inquiries made by the coroner and the group to which I have referred, and to the fact that none of these investigations has produced evidence to identify any particular individual or individuals as having used excessive force, I do not consider that any useful purpose would be served by holding a further inquiry now.

I should mention that there was one case in which misconduct by a particular individual has come to light—it was a case of larceny—and this man has already been tried and sentenced by court-martial.

More generally, I must repeat that even in the suppression of brutal murder the use of undue force is repugnant to the civil and military authorities in Cyprus as well as to the Government here. In any case, where there is evidence of a kind to justify the preferment of charges in respect of such misconduct action will be taken in the future as in the past. In addition, the new Director of Operations has recently seen all the commanding officers and made personal visits to the units to impress upon them the need for the utmost restraint in the use of force, however great the provocation. I feel sure that we can have full confidence both in the troops and in their commanders.

Before passing to the future, I ought perhaps to say a word about the Geunyeli incident, concerning which the Governor of Cyprus published a Report on Tuesday, 9th December, of which copies have been placed in the Library of the House. This Report is of a Commission of Inquiry conducted by the Chief Justice into an incident on 12th June, when eight Greek Cypriots met their deaths at the hands of Turkish Cypriots after they had been detained by the security forces and then released some distance from their village.

A special inquiry was held in this case because the incident occurred at a time of acute intercommunal tension and it was imperative to investigate the allegation that the security forces had intentionally contributed to the death of the unfortunate victims. The Chief Justice's Report, although he had certain criticisms to make, wholly repudiates this baseless suggestion.

I now turn to questions of general policy. After two weeks of debate on the Cyprus question the General Assembly of the United Nations has passed a short resolution in very general terms. At one time there were seven different draft resolutions before the Political Committee. Some of these would have been acceptable to us; others, we thought, pointed too much in the direction of a particular final solution.

The Minister of State for Foreign Affairs took the opportunity, of the debate in the United Nations, to give a full explanation of our policy. He described in detail the British plan with which the House is familiar. He also explained the lengths to which Her Majesty's Government have gone in their endeavours to reach an agreement for the holding of a conference at which the British plan could be discussed and amendments to it agreed, and at which the final solution could also be discussed. We still believe that useful progress could be made through a conference, either confined to the parties directly concerned, including, of course, Cypriot representatives, or with the assistance of others chosen by agreement.

The proceedings in the General Assembly revealed a wide measure of understanding of the complexity of the Cyprus problem and not a little sympathy for the efforts which Her Majesty's Government have made to deal with it. They also, I think, revealed some reluctance on the part of many of those not directly concerned with the problem to try to lay down the conditions on which a settlement should be sought. The resolution finally adopted avoided this and simply expressed confidence that continued efforts would be made by the parties to reach a peaceful, democratic and just solution in accordance with the Charter of the United Nations. That is certainly our hope.

It is right that a little time should now be allowed for the Governments concerned to consider their position in the light of the United Nations' debate. Next week, in Paris, there is a Ministerial meeting of the North Atlantic Council which will be attended by my right hon. and learned Friend the Foreign Secretary and I have every expectation that the Foreign Ministers of Greece and Turkey will be present. No doubt advantage will be taken of this occasion for confidential discussions between those who have been principally concerned. I feel sure that this approach is the most likely to be fruitful.

As we have already made clear, we are ready to discuss with our Greek and Turkish Allies the interim arrangements for the administration of Cyprus described in my statements of 19th June and 15th August; and we are willing, as we have said, to put into effect any amendments to our announced policy on which agreement can be reached. These offers remain open and can be taken up at any time. We regretted that the Greek Government did not feel able to agree to a conference on the lines discussed in N.A.T.O. last October. But the position may now have changed. In any case, we continue to hope that in time the Greek Government will see the advantages to the Greek Cypriots and to Greece of the offers which we have made to them.

Whatever the difficulties, progress has been made in narrowing the area of dispute. For our part, we shall do our utmost to reach agreement.

C. NORTH AFRICA

1. Letter from the representative of Tunisia to the United Nations to the President of the Security Council, 13 February 1958[1]

Upon instructions from my Government, I have the honour to request you to convene the Security Council for the purpose of considering the following question:

'Complaint by Tunisia in respect of an act of aggression committed against it by France on 8 February 1958 at Sakiet-sidi-Youssef.'[2]

[1] S.C.O.R., Thirteenth Year, Supplement for January, February, and March 1958, Doc. S/3952.

[2] The raid had been carried out by the local commander without authority from Paris. It was defended by M. Chaban-Delmas, French Defence Minister, as 'un droit de légitime défense

An explanatory memorandum on this question is attached.

Under Article 31 of the Charter, I have the honour to request you to permit me to participate in the discussion of this question and, accordingly, to inform me of the date on which the Security Council will meet for that purpose.

MONGI SLIM

Ambassador, Permanent Representative of
Tunisia to the United Nations

EXPLANATORY MEMORANDUM

On 8 February 1958, at 10 a.m., the small Tunisian village of Sakiet-sidi-Youssef, near the Algerian border, was subjected to a sudden act of aggression.

Twenty-five bomber and fighter aircraft, in successive waves, subjected the village and the area immediately surrounding it to a massive bombardment with bombs and rockets and continuous strafing by machine-guns.

Many persons had gathered in the village, for it was a market-day and, in addition, the International Red Cross, assisted by the Tunisian Red Crescent, was scheduled to distribute relief supplies to the children of Algerian refugees in the area. The attack lasted for one hour and twenty minutes. Seventy-nine persons were killed, including eleven women and twenty children, and 130 were wounded, among them a large number of women and children.

Most of the village was destroyed, including homes, civilian buildings and the school.

Three Red Cross or Red Crescent trucks, clearly marked with their distinctive insignia, were destroyed or damaged.

This attack, which constitutes an act of armed aggression by France against Tunisia, is one of a series of deliberate violations of the integrity of Tunisian soil committed since May 1957 by French troops coming from Algeria which have on each occasion resulted in material damage, loss of life and, at times, the abduction of Tunisians.

On each violation of its territory, the Government of the Republic of Tunisia made strong protests to the French Government.

Each time these acts of aggression have been deemed to be serious, either because of their frequency over a specific period or because of the size of the losses sustained by Tunisia, the Government of the Republic of Tunisia has not failed to inform the Secretary-General of the United Nations and to draw his attention to the danger they constituted and the

à l'égard d'éléments anti-aériens opérant à partir du territoire tunisien', Le Monde, 11 February 1958. For the Tunisian note to the French chargé d'Affaires at Tunis, of 8 February 1958, ordering restrictions on the movement of French troops in Tunisia, see Le Monde, 15 February 1958.

fact that they were a violation of the Principles of the Charter and the obligations devolving therefrom upon Member States, particularly under Article 2, paragraph 4 (letters MTP 278 of 31 May 1957, MTP 280 of 3 June 1957, MTP 281 of 4 June 1957, MTP 429 of 11 September 1957, MTP 430 of 12 September 1957, MTP 437 of 16 September 1957 and MTP 470 of 8 October 1957).

The permanent representative of Tunisia wishes to point out in particular that, when the constant threat to Tunisian sovereignty resulting from such violations of Tunisia's territory was deemed to be sufficiently serious, he informed the Secretary-General of the United Nations, by letter dated 11 September 1957 (MTP 429), that, in accordance with Article 51 of the Charter, the Tunisian Government proposed to exercise its right of self-defence.

Accordingly, the act of aggression committed on 8 February is of a particularly serious nature, not only because of the number of lives lost and the extent of the damage caused, but also because of the earlier acts of a similar kind committed since May 1957.

The permanent representative of Tunisia draws particular attention to the fact that the intentions expressed by the French Government do not appear to hold out any prospect that these deliberate attacks on Tunisia's sovereignty and flagrant violations of Article 2, paragraph 4, of the United Nations Charter, will cease.

Every effort made by the Government of the Republic of Tunisia, through friendly discussion, to end these numerous and deliberate violations, has proved fruitless.

Accordingly, upon instructions from my Government, I have the honour to seize the Security Council of the situation created by the deliberate act of aggression committed on 8 February 1958 and to request it to take whatever decision it may deem appropriate to put an end to a situation which threatens Tunisia's security and endangers international peace and security in that part of the world.

MONGI SLIM
Ambassador, Permanent Representative of
Tunisia to the United Nations

2. Letter from the representative of France to the United Nations to the President of the Security Council, 14 February 1958[1]

Upon instructions from my Government, I have the honour to request that the Security Council should, at its next meeting, consider the following complaint brought by France against Tunisia:

[1] S.C.O.R., Thirteenth Year, Supplement for January, February, and March 1958, Doc. S/3954.

'Situation resulting from the aid furnished by Tunisia to rebels enabling them to conduct operations from Tunisian territory directed against the integrity of French territory and the safety of the persons and property of French nationals.'

An explanatory memorandum is attached to the present letter.

G. GEORGES-PICOT
Ambassador, Permanent Representative of
France to the United Nations

EXPLANATORY MEMORANDUM

In bringing a complaint before the Security Council, it is the purpose of the French Government to make it clear that the Tunisian Government has not shown itself capable of maintaining order on the Franco-Tunisian frontier, or disposed to do so. Tunisia thus stands in violation of the obligations assumed by it under Article 4 of the Charter upon its admission to the United Nations and is taking a position contrary to the good-neighbourly spirit which Member States must observe if they wish to live at peace with the other States of the international community.

It is in these circumstances that the Algerian rebels, aided and abetted by the Tunisian authorities, have been able in recent months to establish in Tunisia a complete organization enabling them to carry out numerous border violations and incursions into French territory where they commit particularly heinous crimes.

The 'Front de libération nationale' (FLN) has set up a veritable military infrastructure based in Tunis which, from the military point of view, has now become the main centre of rebel activity in view of the fact that, since last July, a general staff, responsible for the conduct of operations carried out in eastern Algeria, has been set up in that city with the Tunisian Government's permission.

Among the facilities available to the FLN in Tunisia are rest camps, bases, and quartering and training centres where the rebel bands receive training and weapons and are quartered for the purpose of military operations.

In addition to the asylum given by the Tunisian Government, Tunisian armed forces and the national guard provide the FLN with direct logistical support (organization of transport, the supplying of arms and equipment, and medical facilities). Tunisia is in fact the chief base for moving supplies to the FLN in the form of military weapons delivered in Tunisia to the FLN which then sends them into Algeria. The Tunisian authorities take part in this traffic and in the movement and delivery of weapons. The latter are generally stored in the premises of the Tunisian national guard which is also responsible for their transport.

The Tunisian authorities tolerate, and sometimes even facilitate, the movement of armed bands on Tunisian territory and incursions effected from Tunisian soil against French territory. Finally, Tunisian radio broadcasts constantly furnish moral support to the rebellion.

In these circumstances, it is not surprising that, in recent months, incidents in the vicinity of the border, resulting in the death of many members of the French armed forces and French civilians often in atrocious circumstances, have steadily increased in number and intensity. On many occasions, French patrols have encountered rebel groups operating from Tunisian territory, to which they returned when pursued; similarly, French aircraft have on several occasions, been fired on by automatic weapons in Tunisian territory.

A particularly serious incident occurred on 11 January last in the vicinity of Sakiet-sidi-Youssef. In the course of an engagement with a rebel band which came from Tunisia, sixteen French soldiers were killed and four were taken prisoner. In addition, aircraft flying over French territory have on several occasions sustained damage caused by automatic weapons, including weapons fired from the building in this village occupied by the Tunisian national guard.

The French Government had warned the Tunisian Government of the heavy responsibility it was assuming by lending its assistance to the rebels. It had suggested measures to prevent the recurrence of such incidents. These warnings have unfortunately been without effect and no positive response has been made to our suggestions.

The reaction of the French Air Force at the time of the incident to which the Tunisian complaint refers was thus the outcome of the many acts of provocation to which our forces have been subjected. While the French Government deplores the losses suffered by the civilian population, and has the question of compensation for those losses under consideration, it cannot isolate this incident from the incidents which were its cause.

For these reasons, the French Government considers that Tunisia has seriously failed in its obligations as a State Member of the United Nations and has directly and indirectly caused very grave injury to the legitimate interests of France. The French Government accordingly asks that the assistance furnished by Tunisia to the Algerian rebels should be condemned by the Council.

3. Statement by the Department of State extending good offices to France and Tunisia, 17 February 1958[1]

After receiving indications from both the Tunisian and French Governments that good offices would be acceptable, the United States Government has decided to extend its good offices, in conjunction with the United Kingdom, in order to assist the Governments of France and Tunisia to settle outstanding problems between them.

4. Communiqué announcing an agreement between France and Tunisia on the settlement of military problems, Paris, 17 June 1958[2]

Un accord est intervenu le 17 juin 1958 en Tunisie, entre le gouvernement français et le gouvernement tunisien, au sujet du règlement des problèmes militaires qui avaient soulevé de graves difficultés durant de longs mois entre les deux pays.

Cet accord assure le maintien des forces françaises de la base stratégique de Bizerte et la reprise sans délai de leur activité normale.

Il contient l'engagement des deux gouvernements d'ouvrir, dans les meilleurs délais, des négociations destinées à fixer les modalités du statut futur de cette base.

Les troupes françaises se trouvant encore en Tunisie, en dehors de la zone de Bizerte, et dont l'effectif est d'environ sept mille hommes, seront retirées dans un délai de quatre mois et deviendront ainsi disponibles pour d'autres tâches.

Dès à présent sont levées les entraves qui avaient été apportées à leur activité.

[1] *D.S.B.*, 10 March 1958, p. 372. On 18 February 1958, Mr. Wadsworth, Deputy United States Representative to the U.N., announced, in the Security Council, that the U.K. and U.S. offer of good offices had been accepted by both France and Tunisia. The Council adjourned without taking any action; the proposals of the good offices team (Mr. Murphy and Mr. Beeley) were presented to M. Gaillard on 8 March 1958. On 15 April, in the debate in the French National Assembly, M. Pineau, the French Foreign Minister, described the four essential proposals to form a basis for discussion as: '*Le régime de la base de Bizerte doit être défini par un accord spécial, ce qui est conforme à l'esprit du protocole du 20 mars 1956: Des mesures seront prises pour aplanir les difficultés concernant les ressortissants français en Tunisie; Un contrôle neutre sera organisé sur les cinq aérodromes de Tunisie où les troupes françaises stationnent actuellement; Nos troupes évacueront— . . . —les régions autres que Bizerte et auront, à cet effet, leur pleine liberté de mouvement.*' See *Journal Officiel*, 16 April 1958, p. 2130. The Assembly refused to accept the proposals, by 321 votes to 255, on 16 April, and M. Gaillard resigned.

[2] *Le Monde*, 19 June 1958. See ibid. for the communiqué issued by the Tunisian Ministry of Information, which stated that agreement had been reached '*sur le retrait de toutes les forces armées françaises stationées en Tunisie, sauf Bizerte, suivant un calendrier*'. The second and last paragraph of the Tunisian announcement stated that negotiations between France and Tunisia to establish '*un régime provisoire de la base aéronavale de Bizerte*' would begin after the withdrawal of the French forces had been completed. On 14 June 1958 agreement was reached on the withdrawal of French forces from Morocco, see *New York Times*, 15 June 1958.

L'accord intervenu va permettre le retour à son poste de M. Georges Gorse, ambassadeur de France, qui engagera aussitôt avec le gouvernement tunisien des pourparlers sur l'ensemble des problèmes en suspens entre les deux pays.

5. Policy declaration by Mr. Ferhat Abbas in the name of the Provisional Government of the Algerian Republic, 26 September 1958[1]

On September 19, 1958, the Provisional Government of the Algerian Republic was proclaimed. This proclamation, made in the name of a people fighting for their independence for the last four years, restores the Algerian state which was brutally and unjustly stricken from the political map of North Africa by the hazard of the military conquest of 1830.

Thus is brought to an end the most scandalous usurpation of the last century, one that which attempted to strip a people of its nationality, divert it from the course of its history and deprive it of the means of survival by reducing it to a pitiful scattering of individuals. Thus, the long night of myths and fictions has come to an end. Thus, too, is ended the time of disdain, humiliation and servility.

A people who through 128 years of domination did not renounce for one instant its personality; a people who suffered bloody defeats yet never knew resignation, nor abandoned the daily rhythm of its own life; a people which has conserved intact its past heritage, its traditions, language and civilization—this people merits respect, and has the right to its liberty.

And it is because, from generation to generation, this liberty has remained the sacred ideal transmitted from father to son, that on November 1, 1954, the Algerian people rose up in a new and this time irresistible movement to affirm their imprescriptible right to independence, liberty and dignity.[2]

Tribute to the Algerian People

For four years, our people have been engaged in this combat. They are facing one of the largest armies in the world. More than 600,000 Algerian victims line the long and glorious route towards liberty. Handed over by France to the discretionary power of the colonialists and the colonels, our people are tortured and massacred each day. But despite this suffering and the thousands of dead, they remain unshakeable in their faith and their certitude of the approaching liberation.

[1] Text issued by the Ministry of Information of the Provisional Government of the Algerian Republic.

[2] The *Front de Libération Nationale*, which is a political organization, came into being in 1954, when an activist minority seceded from the then leading nationalist party, *The Movement for the Triumph of Democratic Liberties*. The Front came into the open on the night of 31 October– 1 November 1954, with surprise attacks on police posts, etc.

Our invincible Army of National Liberation, with limited means, stands up victoriously to a French army equipped with powerful modern armament, artillery, aviation and naval units.

It is this heroism, this courage, these multiple sacrifices—in a word, it is the united will of the Algerian people—which legitimizes the constitution of the Government which I have the honor to head.

The first duty of the Provisional Government of the Algerian Republic is therefore to render a vibrant tribute to the martyred Algerian people who have accepted such enormous sacrifices so that the free Algerian Republic may be born and live. This tribute is also addressed, with the same fervor, to the glorious Army of National Liberation whose courage and sacrifices have definitely placed the cause of the Algerian Revolution on the path of success.

In these historic moments, the Provisional Government of the Algerian Republic, with deep emotion, salutes the memory of all Algerian martyrs. In evoking the imperishable memory of those who were tortured atrociously, of those whose horrible executions were cynically disguised as flight, or attempted escape, of those also whose assassinations were camouflaged as suicide, as if to add the final insult to their supreme sacrifice, to all these, the Provisional Government of the Algerian Republic vows to remain faithful to their ideal of liberty, justice and social emancipation.

The Provisional Government of the Algerian Republic, the emanation of the will of the people, is conscious of its responsibilities on their behalf. It shall assume them all. And firstly, that of leading our people and their Army to the attainment of their national liberation.

The Voice of the Algerian People

Once our liberation is completed, the decisions belong to the Algerian people. The right to found the institutions of the Algerian state belongs to the Algerian people, and only to them. By their complete espousal of the principles of the revolution, the Algerian people have already pronounced themselves before the world, in favor of a democratic and social republic.

The Algerian people are a peaceful people. Having tried in vain all peaceful means to recover their liberty and independence, the Algerian people took up arms under the force of French colonialism. The fiction of French Algeria, and the myth of integration, are founded solely upon the policy of force.

Algeria is not France. The Algerian people are not French. To voice the pretention of 'Frenchifying' our country, constitutes an aberration, an anachronistic and criminal enterprise, condemned by the charter of the United Nations. To force Algerians to pronounce themselves by referendum[1] on purely French institutions is an intolerable provocation against a people who for almost four years, have been fighting precisely for their national independence.

Established in their imperialistic and racist institutions, the French colonialists still entertain the myths of the past, and, by the war in Algeria intend to perpetuate the crime of 1830 and assure the permanence of their domination.

But this epoch no longer exists. Today no nation, however powerful it may be, can assert the liberty of imposing its law upon another nation. This signifies that force will remain powerless before the united will of the Algerians to build their own country and to pick up the strands of their own history.

This signifies that our people will never put down their arms until the day when their rights as a sovereign people shall be recognized.

Algeria Is No Longer Alone in Her Struggle

Algeria is no longer alone in this struggle. May the French authorities reflect upon this. Behind us, there are first of all, Tunisia and Morocco, whose destiny throughout history has always been linked with ours. It is a matter of logic that Algeria, as an integral part of the Arab Maghreb, shall build a North African Federation, together with her two brother countries. The Tangier Conference is a historic event.[2] The Provisional Government of the Algerian Republic remains faithful to the spirit of this conference, for it is more than ever convinced that a Maghreb Federation is the only formula which can provide viable solutions to the problems which we face. It offers us perspectives in harmony with the modern world.

There is also the glorious heritage of the Arab-Islamic civilization. Profoundly attached to this civilization, the Algerian people are a part of the Arab world. This world forms a unity, and it is political nonsense to attempt to divide it. One cannot pretend to be the friend of the Arabs at Tunis, Rabat, and Beirut, and stand against them at Algiers, Cairo, and Baghdad. Arab solidarity is not an empty phrase. It is thanks to the active support of these brother peoples and their governments that the Algerian people stand on the threshold of realizing their objectives. If such a debt

[1] The referendum on the Constitution of the Fifth Republic took place on 28 September 1958. Electors in the overseas territories voted for the most part for those sections of the draft Constitution that directly concerned their future status. In Algeria 76·1 per cent of the electors voted; 96·5 per cent being in favour of the Constitution. For the text of the Constitution, promulgated on 5 October 1958, see *L'Année Politique 1958*, pp. 553–61.

[2] The Front was recognized as the principal organization representing the Algerian people, at the Tangier Conference, 27–30 April 1958. For the Resolution of the Conference of Tangier on the Algerian situation, see below, p. 581. The Front's representatives were treated on a footing of equality by the Moroccan and Tunisian Governments, at the subsequent Governmental conference at Tunis.

could exist between brothers, that of the Algerian people to the Arab peoples would be immense.

I shall refer also to the free countries of the Accra Conference,[1] and to the peoples of the vast African continent still in chains, who aspire to independence. At this decisive moment of their destiny, the Provisional Government of the Algerian Republic salutes the peoples of Africa and Madagascar, linked to the Algerian people in the same community of suffering and of struggle against French colonialism. Africans, Madagascans, and Algerians will aid each other with the faith needed for the liberation and development of the African continent.

Finally, in support of Algeria, there is all of Asia—all the peoples recently freed from the yoke of colonial domination, who are one by one acceding to the responsibilities of power and of modern techniques. In this respect, we regard as very significant the recognition of the Provisional Government of the Algerian Republic by the People's Republic of China, a recognition which will be followed by other countries of Asia.[2] To all the peoples whom the Conference of Bandung united around the principle of the right to self-determination, fighting Algeria addresses its gratitude and assures them of its faithfulness to the principles of Bandung, and its deep recognition of the material and moral aid which they have provided.

Our gratitude goes also to the intellectuals—to the French democrats, and to all those in Europe and in both Americas—who, with a freedom of spirit which does them great honor, have never ceased to support our just cause. These men—the propagators of new ideas, the builders of a world cleansed of all spirit of domination—condemn without reserve, any system of colonization. These men of all religions and origins are our friends and our allies.

Therefore, the Algerian people are upheld by solid support. But, they do not fight for the sake of fighting. The Algerian people are not the enemy of the people of France. Their only enemy is colonialism. However, friendship between peoples can be conceived only in mutual respect for the liberty and sovereignty of each.

We have always affirmed our desire for a peaceful and negotiated solution to the Algerian problem. Only the obstinate refusal of French Governments to accept such negotiations is responsible for the prolongation of the war. In other words, the Algerian war can be brought to a speedy end if such is the desire of the French Government.

---

[1] See below, p. 579.

[2] The People's Republic of China recognized the Provisional Government of the Algerian Republic on 22 September 1958 (*H.N.A.*, 23 September 1958), North Korea on 25 September 1958 (*H.N.A.*, 26 September 1958), Indonesia and North Vietnam on 27 September 1958 (*Egyptian Gazette*, 28 September 1958), and Outer Mongolia on 30 September 1958 (*H.N.A.*, 3 October 1958). The following states extended recognition within 24 hours of the announcement: U.A.R., Libya, Iraq, the Yemen, Pakistan, Morocco, Tunisia (*Daily Telegraph*, 20 September 1958), and Saudi Arabia on 21 September 1958 (*New York Times*, 22 September 1958).

THE POSITION OF PROVISIONAL ALGERIAN GOVERNMENT

Negotiations

For its part, the Provisional Government of the Algerian Republic is ready to begin negotiations. To achieve this, it is ready at any moment to meet with the representatives of the French Government.[1]

European Minority

The presence of Frenchmen and Europeans in Algeria does not pose an insoluble problem. It is certain that Algeria, freed of colonialists, will have neither first nor second class citizens. The Algerian Republic will make no distinction due to race or religion among those who wish to remain Algerian. Fundamental guarantees will be given so that all citizens may participate in the total life of the nation. All legitimate interests will be respected.

Relations With France

Moreover, the independence of Algeria is in no way an obstacle to the establishment of new relations between France and Algeria. These relations will be all the more fruitful for being founded on mutual respect of the sovereignty of the two countries. Furthermore, only this independence can open new perspectives for cooperation with these other countries.

Since its proclamation, the Provisional Government of the Algerian Republic has registered, with satisfaction, its recognition by a certain number of powers. It extends its profound thanks. Others will recognize it in the days to come. To all these nations, we declare that our government is conscious of its responsibilities on the international plane. It shall respect the principles of the charter of the United Nations, and subscribe to the Universal Declaration of the Rights of Man. These principles will remain the lasting base of the policy of the Algerian Republic, and will guide the action of our government.

In this respect, the Provisional Government of the Algerian Republic will welcome with the greatest favor, any international initiative aimed at achieving the application to the Algerian war of the humanitarian arrangements of the Geneva Convention.

In the same way, the Government will welcome all initiatives tending to consolidate peace in the world, to halt the armament race, and to forbid

---

[1] Mr. Abbas repeated this offer to negotiate with the French Government in an interview accorded to *El Moudjahid* on 10 October 1958. He said that the provisional Government was: 'ready to arrange meetings between its representatives and those of the French Government to determine the political and military conditions of a cease-fire'. The full text of the interview is published by the Ministry of Information of the Provisional Government of the Algerian Republic.

the holding of nuclear tests such as France wishes now to extend to Algerian soil.

To conclude this declaration, we wish to recall that the prolongation of the war in Algeria constitutes a permanent menace to world peace. We extend an urgent appeal to all men, to all peoples, to join their efforts to ours with a view to ending this bloody war of colonial reconquest. We express the fervent hope that this appeal will be heard.

6. Speech by General de Gaulle outlining his plan for Algeria, Constantine, Algeria, 3 October 1958[1]

Last Sunday, three and a half million men and women of Algeria, without distinction of community, in complete equality, gave France and myself their vote of confidence.[2] They did this quite simply without any constraint and in spite of the threats that certain fanatics brought to bear against them, their families and their property. This is a fact, as clear as the bright light of day. And this fact is fundamental not only because it mutually and forever pledges, one to the other, Algeria and France, but also because it ties in with what happened that same day in Metropolitan France, in Overseas Departments, in the Territories of the Community.

The least that can be said of this great demonstration is that the French people proved to themselves and to the entire world their determination for renovation, and that, at the same time, a hundred million men decided to build their future together in Liberty, Equality and Fraternity.

With regard to Algeria, what is the future to which France is calling her? Women and men of Algeria, I have come here to tell you what it is.

What must be achieved is the basic transformation of this country, so brave, so alive, but also so full of difficulties and suffering. This means that it is necessary for the living conditions of each man and woman to improve from day to day. This means that, for the benefit of the inhabitants, the resources of the earth and, the ability of the elites must be brought to light and developed. This means that children must be taught. This means that all Algeria must have her share in what modern civilization can and must bring to men in terms of well-being and dignity.

But the loftiest plans call for practical measures. Here are the measures that my Government intends to take in the near future covering the next five years by virtue of the full powers that the new Constitution has just conferred upon it.

During these five years, of the young people in Metropolitan France—

---

[1] Text supplied by the French Embassy, London. General de Gaulle visited Algeria for the fourth time since his investiture as Prime Minister, from 2 to 5 October 1958.

[2] See fn. 1 on p. 402, above, for the results of the referendum in Algeria.

yes, I say in Metropolitan France—that enter the service of the State, in the Administration, in the Army, in education and in the public services, at least a tenth of these young people must be recruited from the Arab, the Kabyle and Mozabite communities, and that without prejudice to an increased proportion of Algerians serving in Algeria.

In the course of these five years, salaries and wages in Algeria will be raised to a level comparable to what they are in Metropolitan France.

Before the end of these five years, 250,000 hectares (617,500 acres) of new land will be allotted to Moslem farmers.

Before the end of these five years, the first phase of the plan for the agricultural and industrial development of Algeria will be brought to its conclusion. This phase includes, in particular, the delivery and the distribution of the oil and gas of the Sahara, the setting up, on this soil, of great metallurgical and chemical complexes, the construction of housing for a million people, the corresponding development of health services, of roads, ports, means of communication—in short, the regular employment of 400,000 new workers.

Gradually in the course of these five years, two thirds of the girls and boys will be enrolled in school and, during the three years after that, complete school enrollment of all Algerian youth will be achieved.

During these five years, the human contact that has been made especially by the French Army—by its career officers, its reserve officers, its fighting men, its young conscripts—will be continued and developed and, in Metropolitan France, the same must be true, in Paris and in our provinces.

What will be the political consequences of this evolution which calls for very extensive and prolonged efforts? I believe it is quite useless to freeze in advance in words, that which, in any event, is going to take shape, little by little, as it is undertaken. But, in any case, two things are certain as of now: the first concerns the present.

In two months, Algeria will elect her representatives under the same conditions as will Metropolitan France. But at least two thirds of her representatives will have to be Moslem citizens.

The other refers to the future. The future of Algeria will in any event —because that is the nature of things—be built on a double foundation: her personality and her close solidarity with Metropolitan France.

In any case, it is absolutely essential that this fruitful transformation be accomplished. This is necessary for the good of the men of Algeria, for the good of the women, for the good of the children who live here; but it is also necessary for the honor of mankind. It is necessary for the peace of the world. For no one has any interest in the stagnation of a people, except the kind of people, who, to serve their ambitions, gamble on the spirit of revolt and the poverty of others.

This transformation, this immense political, economic, social and cultural task—who could effect this transformation, if not France?

Now it happens that France has the will and the means to do so. It also happens that the vote of the Algerians has just proved that they desire this transformation and that it should be carried out with France.

Therefore, turning toward those who are prolonging a fratricidal conflict, who are organizing lamentable attacks in Metropolitan France, or who are spreading—through the chancelleries, through underground dens, by means of the radios and the newspapers of certain foreign capitals— vilifications of France, to those I say: why kill? We must enable people to live. Why destroy? Our duty is to build. Why hate? We must cooperate.

Stop this absurd fighting and you will at once see a new blossoming of hope over all the land of Algeria. You will see the prisons emptying; you will see the opening up of a future big enough for everybody, and for you yourselves in particular. And then, speaking to those States which are throwing oil on the fire here while their unhappy peoples writhe under dictatorships, I say: Could you do what France is in a position to do here, what only France is capable of doing? Could you people do it? No. Then let France carry on, unless you deliberately decide to envenom the conflict in order to distract attention from your own difficulties. But in the present state of the World, where can these bitter incitements lead if not to universal cataclysm? Only two paths lie open to the human race today: war or brotherhood. In Algeria as everywhere, France, for her part, has chosen brotherhood.

Long live the Republic! Long live Algeria and long live France!

7. Statement by the Provisional Government of the Algerian Republic regarding General de Gaulle's cease-fire proposals of 23 October, Cairo, 26 October 1958[1]

The news conference by the head of the French Government contains no new element. The proposals put forth represent in many cases a step backward from those made by his predecessors.[2]

Thus, the declaration of General de Gaulle constitutes a refusal to negotiate. To the efforts of the Provisional Government of the Algerian

---

[1] Text issued by the Ministry of Information of the Provisional Government of the Algerian Republic.

[2] General de Gaulle, in his press conference of 23 October 1958, made a peace offer to the F.L.N. He guaranteed that if the local commanders came forward with '*le drapeau blanc des parlementaires*', they would be received and treated honourably, and he continued: '*Si des délégués étaient désignés pour venir régler avec l'autorité la fin des hostilités, ils n'auraient qu'à s'adresser à l'ambassade de France à Tunis ou à Rabat. L'une ou l'autre assurerait leur transport vers la métropole. Là une sécurité entière leur serait assurée, et je leur garantis la latitude de repartir.*' For the full text of the press conference, see *Le Monde*, 25 October 1958.

Republic to find a peaceful solution through negotiation, he responds with a request for unconditional surrender.

The Provisional Government of the Algerian Republic emphasizes once more the incomprehension and blindness of the French Government. It recalls that it was this same incomprehension and this same blindness that caused, in November, 1954, the start of the present war. Contrary to the contention of the head of the French Government, this was started through the fault of a colonial regime that claimed to be perpetual and that grew so cynical that it violated its own laws to resist the legitimate aspirations of a people who want to be free and independent.

The present French Government, faithful to the traditional policy of France, intends to maintain Algeria by force within the French framework. The organization of a pretended referendum by the colonialist administration and military occupation authorities, while the war continued, constituted a new mystification in the history of French colonialism. The elections that, in the same conditions, the French Government intends to impose on Algeria for the designation of deputies to the French National Assembly aim at consecrating the integration of Algeria with the French nation. For four years the Algerian people has been precisely fighting to get out of this French framework and to recover its national sovereignty and its independence.

As of now, the Government denounces these elections and considers the results worthless. It warns international opinion against this mockery of a popular consultation organized by a colonialist administration under the pressure of a foreign army of occupation of more than 600,000 men.

The Provisional Government of the Algerian Republic, responsible for the future of Algeria, has offered negotiations in its Ministerial declaration last September 26. It is ready to appoint its representatives to meet those of the French Government, but to negotiate a true solution to the whole of the Algerian problem. This meeting can take place only in a neutral country.

The French leaders deceive themselves if they take our desire for peace as a sign of weakness. The pretended progress of the pacification, making it appear that a French military solution is near, is along the same lines as the propaganda of 'the last quarter-hour' that has been repeated continuously for four years.

The French Government will thus continue to bear the responsibility for the war's prolongation.

Supported by the glorious Army of National Liberation, which nothing can defeat, and expressing the sentiments of all the Algerian people, the Provisional Government of the Algerian Republic is determined to carry on the fight to its goal, that is, the independence of the country.

8. Draft resolution recommended by the First Committee to the General Assembly, 13 December 1958[1]

THE GENERAL ASSEMBLY,

Having discussed the question of Algeria,

Recalling its resolution 1012 (XI) of 15 February 1957 by which the General Assembly expressed the hope that a peaceful, democratic and just solution would be found, through appropriate means, in conformity with the principles of the Charter of the United Nations,[2]

Recalling further its resolution 1184 (XII) of 10 December 1957 by which the General Assembly expressed the wish that *pourparlers* would be entered into, and other appropriate means utilized, with a view to a solution, in conformity with the purposes and principles of the Charter of the United Nations,[3]

Recognizing the right of the Algerian people to independence,

Deeply concerned with the continuance of the war in Algeria,

Considering that the present situation in Algeria constitutes a threat to international peace and security,

Taking note of the willingness of the Provisional Government of the Algerian Republic to enter into negotiations with the Government of France,[4]

Urges negotiations between the two parties concerned with a view to reaching a solution in conformity with the Charter of the United Nations.

---

[1] G.A.O.R., Thirteenth Session, Annexes, Agenda item 63, Doc. A/4075. On 16 July 1958 24 Afro-Asian delegations asked that the question of Algeria be put on the agenda of the General Assembly's Thirteenth Session, Doc. A/3853. On 17 September 1958 at a meeting of the Assembly's General Committee the French representative opposed putting the item on the Assembly's agenda, and said that if the item was placed on the agenda, France would not take part in the debate. The Assembly decided to include the item on the agenda on 22 September, and the matter was considered by the First Committee from 8 to 13 December 1958. The draft resolution, submitted on 12 December was adopted by the First Committee on 13 December by a roll-call vote of 32 to 18 (including U.S. and U.K.) with 30 abstentions. In the General Assembly the draft resolution did not obtain the required two-thirds majority and failed of adoption on 13 December 1958 by a roll-call vote of 35 in favour, 18 against (including the U.K.), and 28 abstentions (including the U.S.).

[2] See *Documents* for 1957, p. 417.

[3] See ibid., p. 427.

[4] At the plenary meeting of the Assembly on 13 December 1958, Ceylon proposed, and the Assembly agreed by a roll-call vote of 38 to 0, with 43 abstentions, to delete this paragraph.

D. ICELANDIC FISHERIES DISPUTE

1. Statement by the Government of the United Kingdom, 3 June 1958[1]

On 2nd June, 1958, the Prime Minister of Iceland made a broadcast elaborating upon an official statement, issued the previous day, to the effect that the parties constituting the Government coalition in Iceland had agreed to the issue on 30th June, 1958, of a decree concerning the fishery limits off Iceland.[2] The decree would claim the extension of Icelandic fishery limits to 12 miles as from 1st September, 1958; it would seek to subject fishing within the new limits to Icelandic control, and to reserve the right to alter the base lines from which Icelandic fishery limits are at present measured.

Her Majesty's Government in the United Kingdom have noted with surprise and regret the disregard, both in the Icelandic Prime Minister's broadcast and in the official statement, of the long-established rights of other nations to fish in the high seas around Iceland.

In an *aide mémoire* dated 29th May, 1958, Her Majesty's Ambassador at Reykjavik pointed out to the Icelandic Government that, if the proposed decree were issued, it could not, and would not, in law, in any way restrict the rights of other nations on the high seas, nor could it lawfully prohibit fishing by other nations in areas which have long been regarded as part of the high seas.

Her Majesty's Government, accordingly, will not be able to accept the proposed decree, if issued, as of any effect in law. Claims to exercise exclusive jurisdiction in relation to fishing in areas outside the normal

[1] *Commonwealth Survey*, 10 June 1958, pp. 548–9. In March 1952 the Icelandic Government announced the extension of the fishery limits around Iceland from 3 miles (measured from the low-water mark) to 4 miles (measured from base-lines drawn between widely separated headlands). All fishing by foreigners, and trawling and seine fishing by Iceland nationals was prohibited in those newly enclosed areas. The Icelandic Government maintained that their action was based on the decision of the International Court of Justice in 1951 in the Anglo-Norwegian Fisheries Case, but the validity of this contention was denied by the United Kingdom Government. The protracted dispute was settled after 4 years by a special body set up within O.E.E.C. At the Geneva Conference on the Law of the Sea, documented below, pp. 535–69, no decision was reached on territorial waters or fishery limits, see fn. 1, p. 542. The Government of Iceland publicly stated after the end of the conference that as no agreement had been reached, it regarded itself as entitled to complete freedom of action over its limits, and farther claimed the right to enclose even wider areas than in 1952 by freshly drawn straight base-lines.

[2] For the text of the Regulations concerning the fishery limits off Iceland and a useful map, see *British Aggression in Icelandic Waters* (Ministry of Foreign Affairs, Reykjavik, June 1959), pp. 29–32. A useful account of the dispute is given in the final report of a project on the nature and extent of offshore claims in Northwestern Europe, sponsored by the Research Foundation of the State University of New York and the Office of Naval Research (February 1960), pp. 86–112.

limits of territorial waters are wholly unwarranted under international law. Further, Her Majesty's Government will not be able to recognise base lines beyond those permitted by international law.

Her Majesty's Government find it difficult to believe that the Icelandic Government would use force against British fishing vessels in order to secure compliance with a unilateral decree which the parties of the Government coalition propose to issue without regard for international law.[1] At the same time, Her Majesty's Government must point out that it would be their duty to prevent any unlawful attempt to interfere with British fishing vessels on the high seas.

While one nation, or a number of nations, cannot, by themselves, alter international law, it is, of course, open to nations to enter into bilateral or multilateral agreements waiving or restricting in specified areas some, or all, of the rights which they now enjoy under the law of the sea. Her Majesty's Government, and a number of other friendly Governments, have done their utmost to persuade the Icelandic Government to abstain from unilateral action and to enter into discussions with a view to the negotiation of an appropriate fisheries agreement.

Her Majesty's Government are aware of the importance of fisheries to Iceland. Fisheries are also of great importance to the United Kingdom. Her Majesty's Government adhere to the view that, through negotiation, it should be possible to conclude an acceptable agreement. For that reason, before the announcement of the Icelandic Government's intention, Her Majesty's Government informed the Icelandic Government that they were prepared to enter into negotiations for this purpose. Her Majesty's Government are still prepared to enter into such negotiations in the spirit of goodwill which they showed during the Geneva conference on the law of the sea. They hope that the Icelandic Government will agree that negotiation is, in every respect, preferable to unilateral action, and that the period before 1st September should be used to negotiate a lasting solution acceptable to all concerned.

2. Statement by the Government of the United Kingdom, 31 August 1958[2]

The position of Her Majesty's Government in the United Kingdom concerning the decision of the Government of Iceland to extend Icelandic

[1] Between 1952 and 1957 a total of 28 British trawlers and 34 of other nationalities were arrested and heavily fined for fishing within the 4-mile limit claimed by Iceland.

[2] *Commonwealth Survey*, 2 September 1958, pp. 807–8. See also ibid., pp. 808–9, for a United Kingdom reply of 24 August 1958, to statements made by the Icelandic Ambassador in London at a press conference on 22 August. Among other things Dr. Gudmundsson said that there was a danger of Iceland withdrawing from N.A.T.O. if the United Kingdom persisted in its attitude, but that he sincerely hoped 'in the tradition of British diplomacy and the traditionally good

fishery limits to twelve miles was fully explained in a statement published on 4th June, 1958.[1]

Since that date, Her Majesty's Government, and a number of other Governments concerned, have made prolonged efforts to secure by negotiation an agreement which would have safeguarded the future of the fisheries around Iceland, and taken account of Iceland's dependence on these fisheries, while not prejudicing the consideration, on a world-wide basis, of the questions of territorial waters and fishery limits at a second United Nations conference on the law of the sea.[2]

The holding of such a conference is to be considered at the forthcoming session of the General Assembly of the United Nations.[3]

For application during the interim period before such a conference can be convened, two alternative arrangements concerning the fisheries around Iceland have been under discussion.

The first of these arrangements would have guaranteed to Icelandic fishermen a generous share of the total yield of the fisheries throughout the whole area surrounding the coasts of Iceland, and important areas would have been reserved exclusively for Icelandic small boat fishermen.

After the Icelandic Government had declined to accept an arrangement on these lines, an alternative suggestion was considered.

Under this alternative, a continuous belt outside the limit claimed by Iceland since 1952 would have been reserved to Icelandic fishermen. For most of its length, the line delimiting the new area of exclusive Icelandic fishing would have amounted to a straightforward extension of Icelandic fishery limits for a further two miles, making a six-mile limit, but, in a few areas of importance to Iceland, additional concessions would have been made.

The agreement, which would have been without prejudice to the views of the parties as to the limits in international law of exclusive jurisdiction in fishery matters, would have run for three years, or for a shorter period if, in the meantime, a second United Nations conference on the law of the sea had reached agreement on territorial waters and fishery limits.

The Icelandic Government, however, demanded that the other Governments concerned should recognise the right of the Icelandic Government

---

relations between Iceland and Britain, we will be able to solve this problem in conformity with the findings of the International Law Commission'. See *The Times*, 23 August 1958. The Icelandic Foreign Minister later said that he had never heard the question of Iceland's withdrawal from N.A.T.O. mentioned before, and that 'it had never entered the heads of anyone in Iceland'. See *Commonwealth Survey*, 2 September 1958, p. 808.   [1] Dated 3 June 1958.

[2] On 29 August 1958 the following statement was issued from N.A.T.O. headquarters: 'During recent weeks there have been conversations between fishing experts, aimed at finding a solution to the problem of the Icelandic fisheries. These efforts have not so far met with success. It is expected that the conversations will be resumed shortly.' Ibid., p. 807.

[3] See below, p. 570, for the United Nations Resolution of 10 December 1958, convening the second conference on the Law of the Sea.

to extend their fishery limits to twelve miles on the expiry of the agreement, and was not prepared to consent to the inclusion in the agreement of a reservation of rights by the other parties. Because of this it has not yet been possible to bring the discussion to a successful conclusion.

Her Majesty's Government would have accepted, and would still accept, an agreement of either kind. It is prepared to continue negotiations for an agreement, or for any *modus vivendi*, on an acceptable basis. It hopes that negotiations will continue, but, in default of an agreement or *modus vivendi*, it must preserve the rights of British fishing vessels on the high seas.[1]

E. UNITED STATES AND LATIN AMERICA

1. Speech by Vice-President Richard Nixon to the National Press Club regarding his visit to Latin America, Washington, 21 May 1958[2]

Mr. President, members of the diplomatic corps, my fellow travelers, my fellow members of The Press Club, and ladies and gentlemen, I want to say that this for me is a very special occasion, because although I have stood many times at this rostrum in my capacity as Vice President for a few words, this is the first time that I will be on the griddle.

Now I have been very subtly reminded by your President and others of your Board of Directors that since I am going to be on the griddle today, and am going to have questions submitted, that I remember I was once a member of the House, in which there was a limitation on the opening remarks, rather than a member of the Senate where the filibuster is permitted. Consequently, I am going to limit my opening remarks to a lesser time than the usual 30 minutes, which I understand is standard, so that more of the questions may be responded to during the question period.

There are a few things that I would like to say which might not come up in questions, and which I cannot miss the opportunity of mentioning to this audience today.

First of all, I was particularly interested in your comments with regard to the custom in The Press Club, which I understand is that a Vice President automatically becomes President. I mean I suppose there are some who would, naturally, think that this would be a very good system to be adopted in some other institutions as well. As a matter of fact, I have been

---

[1] From 1 September 1958 United Kingdom trawlers within the disputed area were protected by British naval vessels seconded for fisheries protection.

[2] *Vital Speeches of the Day*, 15 June 1958, pp. 514–19. Mr. Nixon visited Latin America from 27 April to 13 May 1958. He visited Argentina, Bolivia, Columbia, Ecuador, Paraquay, Peru, Uruquay, and Venezuela. There were serious disorders during his visits to Peru and Venezuela.

thinking of my South American trip in those terms. You know, when we think of democracy and political institutions we sometimes have a tendency to think that democracy is just one typical, rigid form of government. Now this is true of Communism; it is certainly not true of democracy where there is a great deal of deviation. And all over Latin America where we find a very encouraging development toward political institutions in a climate of freedom, we find variations of the system that we have in the United States. I am not sure that some of those variations might not be beneficial for some of us here in the United States.

I recall, for example, in Colombia they worked out a system, because of the difficulties they have had, where for the next 12 years they are going to divide the legislative seats equally between the Conservative Party and the Liberal Party, each gets half regardless of how the votes are cast in an election. And I can say that there are some Republicans that might be willing to make that deal now with the Democrats. Of course, about six months from now maybe the Democrats are going to want to make that deal with us. But, be that as it may, this does indicate the differences that we do have in our democratic systems. The question is whether they work; whether they do provide the climate of freedom which we all desire for the American communities of which we are all proud to be members.

Now, turning to some specific comments with regard to people who were on this trip, may I mention one group which seldom gets mentioned and get their pictures in the paper usually only when their backs are to the camera, I speak of the Secret Service. In both Peru and in Venezuela there was a very small number of Secret Servicemen, six men I believe in both instances.

And I think that one of the greatest tributes to the Secret Service and the performance of these men is the fact that where there was a possibility that someone might have been injured—despite the provocation, in neither of these countries was anybody killed nor seriously injured. The greatest credit goes not to me, not to the members of our party, but to the Secret Service who showed tremendous restraint, who took a great deal of abuse, and who handled themselves magnificently.

Of course, I have a personal interest—the Secret Service is there to protect me. I didn't want to get killed. But, on the other hand, as most of you can imagine, there were the international repercussions and the national repercussions, in the event that one of them had found it necessary to use a weapon. You can see what the results would have been from the standpoint of the United States.

Now I turn to the same group that I have referred to as my fellow travelers who are seated here at this table, the members of the press. The members of the press in this instance also had great provocation. I can't testify as to whether they responded to that provocation with the same admirable restraint in every instance, but I can assure you that I always felt they were a great credit not only to the press corps but to the United States of America every place that we went.

I was proud to have them with me. They worked very hard, I can assure you.

You know, I have talked to some of my good friends in the Ambassadorial corps here from Latin America about the difference in customs with regard to hours for dining. And one thing that you find when you visit Latin America is that dinner begins at ten o'clock rather than eight o'clock. It usually ends around one-thirty. Now this is fine if you have your day regulated. But our American Ambassadors in the countries that I visited, who were making up my schedule, just assumed that we would have the United States-type of schedule during the day, and the Latin American-type of schedule at night. Now this gave me very little sleep, as you can probably see from my appearance today. But imagine the problem of the press corps! The press corps had to write after one or one-thirty at night, night after night. I don't know whether any bonus can be given to people of the press who worked as hard as they did. I want to put in a word to any publishers that may be listening on television or radio, and suggest this: I realize that reporters always have a little problem with expense accounts, what will be allowed and what will not be allowed, the matter of precedents and the like. I do happen to know that at least three or four members of the press corps, who were in some of the milling mobs had their pockets picked. I think they ought to be reimbursed for the cost of the purse as well as the money that they had stolen.

Incidentally, I also heard this comment about La Paz, which is a magnificently striking city. Ambassador Andrade, who, as you know, is one of the best golfers in Washington, tells me that the golf balls go 50 yards farther there (La Paz) than they do in the United States—and I didn't even get a chance to see the golf course. But one of the press men who heard this conversation with the Ambassador said, 'I don't want to go to the moon. I have been half way there, and I don't like it there.'

May I say in that connection, Mr. Ambassador (Andrade), though, that everybody who lives in La Paz from the United States, once they get used to altitude of 13,000 feet, like both the altitude and the people of Bolivia.

Another point that I might mention: As far as my staff was concerned, my personal staff, the State Department staff headed by Mr. Rubottom, Mr. Bernbaum, Mr. Waugh—I think they all did an admirable job throughout this trip, and I wanted to pay my respects to them. I want to say also there was one man here who was indispensable. He is sitting right in front of me, Colonel Walters. Colonel Walters is an amazing man. He knows seven languages as well as he knows English, and he knows Spanish so well that many people used to ask him, in the various countries where he translated for me without ever making a note (had it all in his head), where he learned such perfect Spanish. He pointed out that he learned his Spanish in France, which, of course, made quite an impression on our friends in Latin America. After the events in Venezuela we were all concerned by the possibility that somebody might have been injured. But some of the less, shall we say, considerate members of the press corps suggested to me afterwards that the only thing that I was worried about was that Colonel Walters got a mouthful of glass and I was afraid that he wouldn't be able to translate after this accident. I can say he did a splendid job, and without him we couldn't have gotten across the messages that we were able to get across through his being my dictionary and constant aide.

I have been asked whether the Communists, who in some instances inspired, as you know, the incidents which occurred made any mistakes. I think I can best answer that question by pointing out what Munoz Marin, the very capable Governor of Puerto Rico, a man all of us can be immensely proud of in the United States—for not only his leadership of his own commonwealth, but all of Latin America—said on our way back to the United States. He said, 'Mr. Vice President, there were several particular incidents and actions in the various demonstrations against you which indicated they were controlled by Communists, and were not simply the action of Latin American Liberals.' And he is an expert on this particular subject. He said some of their slogans, of course, were the usual slogans that a Latin American Liberal might use. But in some instances they had slogans which were slogans of the International Communist Party, but were not typically Latin American. For example, 'Freedom for Puerto Rico,' 'Freedom for Mr. Campos', the man who tried to kill Mr. Truman. Incidentally, this is one instance where I think Mr. Truman might even have agreed with me on this particular matter.

Another example were the slogans with regard to the banning of the bomb; and other international slogans which are not typically Latin American, because in these international issues we find that Latin Americans of all political hues, with the exception of the Communists, stand shoulder-to-shoulder with the United States.

The second thing he pointed out—a mistake that they made—was in the denial of freedom of speech which occurred at San Marcos, and which, also, occurred as a result of the riots in Venezuela. Because one of the arguments that the Communists had been using against the dictatorships in Latin America was that freedom was denied, and particularly freedom of speech. And then, he said, when this opportunity was presented for them to show that they could use speech, and use slogans, but not resort to violence, they resorted to violence. By denying freedom of speech, by going to excess, they exposed themselves for the very tactics that they would use if they came to power. This, he said, needed to be done, and, therefore, it served a useful purpose. He also pointed out that not only did they continue to conduct their demonstrations, their cat calls and so forth, during the playing of the National Anthem of the United States; they also did the same when the National Anthem of their own country was played, which showed that they were not Venezuelan in their loyalty, not Peruvian in their loyalty, but that they were loyal to another system which was neither Venezuelan nor Peruvian.

Then Mr. Munoz Marin pointed out a very significant thing, and this brings me to the other point that I would like to make, I think with pardonable pride, today. He said perhaps the greatest error they made, from the standpoint of eliciting support throughout Latin America, was when they insulted Mrs. Nixon. Because, he said, one thing about the people of Latin America is that they have great respect for women. A man, in politics, is fair game, but to a woman courtesy is always shown. These people when they insulted Mrs. Nixon showed that they were truly not Venezuelan, not Peruvian, in their attitude, and this was a major mistake.

I can say in that respect, with some pride, that long after the incidents are forgotten, long after the commendations that are made after this trip are forgotten, there will be literally thousands of people in all the eight countries we visited who will remember the visits that Mrs. Nixon paid to orphanages, to hospitals, to various institutions in these countries. I can say, as I have said on many previous occasions; there is no question about the Vice President being controversial; but I am happy to say that, except for a very small Communist minority, Mrs. Nixon is not controversial in Latin America.

Now there is just one other point that I want to cover, and then we will go to the questions. I said when I returned that we must not allow incidents to obscure the total picture of this trip. We must not allow incidents of this type to obscure the real feeling of friendship and affection that the majority of the people of Latin America have for the people of the United States. There is no question in my mind that in the end the results of this trip will prove to be beneficial, but the trip will be remembered, not in terms of what is said now, today; not in terms of the stories that were written while it was going on—its success or failure will be measured in terms of what is done and what happens in the relationships between the United States and Latin America in the months ahead.

And, if as a result, some people, who did not previously recognize the true character and nature of the Communist conspiracy, now recognize it, it will have served a useful purpose. If, as a result, some people, who may not have recognized the tremendous importance of Latin America to the United States, now realize it, the trip will have been worthwhile. If, as a result, the Latin American story, not just the story of the revolution which usually gets on the first page, but the great constructive story of a continent which is on the way to economic progress and freedom, gets from page 8 onto page 1 in the nation's great newspapers—the trip will have been worthwhile. All of these things I think should be said.

And may I say, too, that as we consider this part of the world we should realize the tremendous stake we have in the future as far as Latin America is concerned. Population-wise today we are approximately equal—180 million here; 180 million there. The rate of growth in Latin American population is two and one-half times as great as it is in the United States. And by the year 2,000, if the current rates of population increase continue, Latin America will have 500 million people; we will have 250 million people.

I can point out, also, that Latin America, next to Europe, provides the best market that the United States has. I could point out other ties that we have: The fact that in the United Nations we have stood shoulder-to-shoulder, time after time, on the great issues affecting the Western Community, and the principles of freedom and democracy in which we believe.

But all of this, perhaps, will be elicited in the question period. I will not go further at this point along these lines.

I would just like to add one final note that I think is worth covering, and that is, despite what you may have read about this trip, as you look at the whole picture we must not forget that in the last 10 years Latin America has experienced great economic progress. They need a great deal more, but the record in the last 10 years has been encouraging.

And another area in which we find real encouragement when you look at the last 10 years—you find steady progress toward democracy and toward freedom. What has happened in Argentina, Colombia, and Venezuela, are symbols of the progress to which I refer. We are witnessing changes for the good taking place, and we should not overlook these changes for the good as we consider the problems.

The final word is that any of you who have the idea that this trip was put on for partisan purposes, or any of you that might have the idea that as far as Latin America is concerned we must look at this problem from either a Republican or a Democratic standpoint, I can say that there certainly is no partisanship so far as our friends south of the border are concerned. Some of you may have noted the names I was called. I was called a 'dog,' a 'viper,' a 'shark.' You may not have noticed another name that I was called, which proves that this trip was completely non-partisan, bi-partisan, and will remain so—'Nixon is a donkey.'

MR. HORNER: Thank you Mr. Vice President.

As you know, the form of these question and answer periods is not quite like a news conference. The questions are submitted in writing from the members of the audience and are read by the presiding officer.

Q. Mr. Vice President, how do you explain what happened in Venezuela?

A. Well, explaining what happened in Venezuela, of course, requires a longer analysis than this question period will permit. In so far as security was concerned, it can be explained primarily from the standpoint that there has been a revolution in Venezuela. In January a completely new police force took over from the police force that had been in control of the City of Caracas for ten years. The Venezuelan Government had no reason to expect, in my opinion, that the police force would be unable to handle the demonstrations which they had been warned, and which we had been warned, might occur. As far as the trip to Venezuela was concerned, we were in the position where we had to go for a variety of reasons: One, the Venezuelan Government had invited us to come; two, after we had received the warnings and they had received the warnings, there were checks made with them as to whether or not they thought the situation could be controlled, and, of course, as to whether or not they considered that it would be advisable for us to change our plans. And so, under the circumstances, the trip was made. And I can say that we are particularly happy that no violence occurred to the extent of causing death or serious injury to those who had the responsibilities for protecting me and the members of our party.

I can say also that when we consider what happened in Venezuela we have to consider some much more basic problems than the violence we have read about and seen through the use of the photographic medium. It would be a great mistake just to attribute what happened in Venezuela to Communism. It is true that the Communists spearheaded the attack. But you have to remember that they had a lot of willing spear carriers along with them. Now why did this happen? We must really get at the cause of it. This was because there happened to be in Venezuela at the time that we visited some real problems with regard to the relations between Venezuela and the United States. One of them was their feeling that the United States, both on the part of Government and as far as private enterprise was concerned, supported dictatorship, including the dictatorship of Perez Jimenez. Another was the feeling among many in Venezuela that we had made a mistake in providing refuge for Perez Jimenez, and the head of the Venezuelan Police, Estrada.[1]

Another factor was related to economic problems. In Venezuela, which

[1] On 1 January 1958 the Venezuelan air force rebelled against General Pérez Jiménez. The uprising was suppressed but was followed by popular demonstrations against the régime. A general strike took place on 21 January and a committee of officers of the armed forces compelled Pérez Jiménez to resign on 23 January 1958. He fled to the Dominican Republic, and then to Miami, U.S.A.

depends to a great extent as you know, on its oil exports to the United States, there had been some dropping down of those exports from the high reached during the Suez crisis, and also some dropping down because of the economic decline in the United States.

Now, all these issues were played upon by the Communists—played upon very effectively and used to stir up the people—people who were noncommunists in such a way that they would resort to violence against a visitor from abroad, something which is completely out of character for the Venezuelan people generally.

The significant thing we should remember about Venezuela is that they have experienced the greatest economic progress in any country in Latin America. Through the tremendous development of its oil resources it has been able to embark on a program of public works and some programs in the field of public housing which were astounding to all members of our party. The question which comes to the minds of observers trying to get beneath the surface is this: How is it that a country experiencing the greatest economic progress is the one where you had the most violent demonstration?

I have given some of the reasons already—the fact, as I pointed out in my news conference in Venezuela, we were seeing there the residue of dictatorship. Dictatorship breeds violence. It leads to it, the great lesson for the United States in so far as its policy is concerned toward Latin America generally—is that economic progress in itself is not enough.

The idea exists among many people in Latin America that when private enterprise comes to a country it means providing and sustaining a good life for the few rather than providing a better life for the many. This idea exists in too many quarters.

What we must prove and what we must do is to show that when private enterprise comes into Latin America—when the United States comes in with its programs of assistance, Point-Four, Export-Import Bank loans, and the like, we do so not for the purpose of simply keeping in power a group of the elite who have had a great deal of the world's goods for many many years. Not for the purpose of making the rich richer and keeping the poor poorer. But that we believe, and our policies are designed to carry out the objective that the best way for economic progress, which will raise the standards of living of the miserably poor people all over Latin America, is through a program of private enterprise of the Twentieth Century enlightened type that we enjoy in the United States combined with government assistance in those areas where private enterprise cannot do the job.

Only if we approach the problems of Latin America in this way, and only if in our information programs we get across this message, will we be able to combat the communist theme—which is that the only way for the poor—the 'have-nots' to get a better way of life is to turn to communism. We know that this is not the case but what we have to do by action and by words is to prove that isn't the case.

Q. Sir, are you glad to be home?

A. I am very glad to be home. But may I say I would not have missed this trip for anything.

Q. Mr. Vice President, did you receive advice before the trip not to go?

A. The other part which you did not read: 'If so, why did you go anyway?' I don't want your President to be easy on me simply because I am a member of the Press Club. The answer is that on every trip I have made abroad, including the first one to the Far East, the one to Africa, the first one to Central America, and this trip, I have received varied advice from friends as to whether I should or should not go.

In this instance there were those who said there were more important issues being undertaken in the United States that we should be paying attention to. And there were suggestions there might be demonstrations. But I want to say also that I have never taken a trip yet in which I have not been warned that there would be demonstrations. I have never taken a trip yet in which I have not had at least some warning somebody was going to try to kill me or members of my party. I can only say that if we allowed what I would call a bunch of blackmailing bullies to keep the officials of the Government of the United States from doing what we think needs to be done to carry out our foreign policy, then we better get off the face of the earth.

Q. I was going to ask that second question but I wanted to see what you said to the first question. Then I was going to edit it.

Sir, does any of the blame for the violence in Lima and Caracas lie at the feet of Governor Faubus and his actions in Little Rock?

A. I can assure you that as far as the communists are concerned, and some noncommunists, in Latin America they seize upon every anti-American issue which is convenient. This one was seized upon in some places although it wasn't brought up in the various question and answer periods that I had with labor leaders and university students to the extent that I thought it might.

There may have been a residue of opposition to the United States because of the stories with regard to Little Rock which appeared in Latin America. It wasn't on this trip, however, a major problem as far as answering the charges that I tried to answer in the conversations I had.

Q. Which South American liberation movement do you prefer, the Rumba, Samba, or Cha-Cha-Cha?

A. I want to make very clear here that I was raised as a Quaker. Consequently, my father and mother were violently opposed to dancing. As

Pat will tell you, I am a very poor dancer. I cannot even do a waltz and I wouldn't try these tough dances.

I would like to add something in a serious vein. This question I know was suggested from a facetious standpoint. Perhaps as we consider our problems in Latin America one of the best ways I could capsule how our attitude should change toward this tremendously vital continent is to say we have to quit thinking of Latin America in terms of siestas, manana, Rumba, Samba, and Cha-Cha-Cha. We must think of Latin America as it is, a great powerful force in the free world and as a place where changes are taking place, a great revolutionary change. A change in which we in the United States should be proud to participate because we should never forget that the people of Latin America would rather have economic progress with freedom than slavery. They like the people of the United States. They prefer our machinery to Russian machinery. They prefer having American technical advisers coming into their country rather than inviting Russian technical advisers.

The problem is there and if we take it seriously and act effectively on it there isn't any question that the American family, as we like to call it, has a great future in store for it.

Q. Mr. Vice President, can you confirm or deny the news story which said the plot was to trample you to death?

A. I can say that some of those teenagers who tried to break my window were not just playing around. Whether the plot was to trample me to death is of course something that would simply be second guessing. What probably happened in these cases and from my analysis of similar situations is that a mob gets out of hand and the violence probably becomes much greater than those who planned the demonstration would have liked. I personally believe, for example, that the group at the University of San Marcos in Lima who planned the demonstration regretted very much that stones were thrown. They would have preferred to block the entrance with slogans if they could.

The best evidence that they made a mistake is that the non-communists at this, the oldest university in the Western Hemisphere, got up a movement to remove the communists from the student body. This shows they made a mistake by the use of violence.

As far as Venezuela was concerned, there was no question once the mob reached a fever pitch, had we not been able to break the road block, there would perhaps have been violence worked upon me and other members of the party. Whether it was planned in the first instance, I don't know.

Q. Sir, what were your thoughts as you sat inside that car in Caracas?

A. Well, as I have already pointed out, I was greatly worried about Colonel Walters because he received a mouthful of glass and I knew I couldn't get along without his fine interpretations. In addition to that my

thoughts were primarily these; one, the hope that it would not be necessary for the police, or for our Secret Service people, to use violent means
in order to keep the mob from carrying out its objective, and, two, my
thoughts were 'what are you going to do in the next minute—the next five
minutes.' You don't think in terms of world politics or hemisphere problems when somebody is banging on your window.

I might say that I realize that all the decisions I made on this trip, and I
take the responsibility for all of them—although I received advice, my
decision to go to San Marcos, my decision to go on to Caracas, all those
decisions were questions of judgment—sometimes very close judgment.

I don't claim I am infallible. That may have been a mistake. I personally
feel that they were right and I think I would make the same decisions if I
had to make them again, but one decision we made that was correct was
that once we broke the road block I decided that we would not go to the
Pantheon to lay the wreath. We were out of radio contact with it but I
have learned from experience that in dealing with a mob, particularly a
communist directed mob, you must always try to outguess them and do the
unexpected. They expected us at the Pantheon in ten minutes and if we
had arrived at that time, as we later learned, the mob would probably
have taken over the place. So we shot down a side street and went to the
Embassy residence arriving there an hour before the communists and mob
expected. Five minutes after we arrived at the Embassy residence, the
mob started up the hill, which indicated that decision was perhaps
correct.

Beyond that, my thoughts obviously were the usual ones that anybody
has, of course, my personal safety, the safety of my wife and the members
of our party in the car immediately behind and I can say again that I have
often given thanks to my lucky star that we had six courageous Secret
Service boys who, when some of the police evaporated, stayed on the job
and with their bare hands kept the damage from being worse than it was.

Q. What the American people read of your South American trip was
written by reporters in this audience. Will you tell us what you meant
when you said your reception in Peru and Venezuela wasn't as bad as it
may have read in the papers.

A. What I meant by that, Mr. Horner, very simply, is that the reception, it is true, was violent in the extreme in Venezuela. It could have
reached overtones of violence in Peru. But I would point out the side of
the story which perhaps has never been adequately told, and not because
of the fault of the newsmen. Violence makes news; controversy makes
news, whereas the constructive side ends up on the back page rather than
on the front page. The story that is not told, for example, in Peru, in
scores of scores of scores of places that we visited, we received a very
friendly welcome.

The story that isn't told is that after we left the University of San Marcos we went next door, and this is a shift our friends on the other side did not expect, to the Catholic University. They didn't know we were coming. I walked in. I stood before a group of three or four hundred students and answered questions about the United States policies with regard to Peru, as I hoped to do at San Marcos. They were tough questions.

At the conclusion of that question period I think even the objective reporters would say that the audience was overwhelmingly friendly, and as the Ambassador from Peru, who was with us, will agree, the next day after this occurred, the crowds everywhere we went were overwhelmingly friendly. I was particularly touched by the fact that student groups, labor groups, and groups from government and people in all walks of life came to see us at the hotel and protested this wasn't the attitude of the great majority of the Peruvians and that the Peruvians essentially were very friendly to the people of the United States.

In Caracas I could repeat this—not to the same extent because we did not have the opportunity to move through the town. But, as the Ambassador well knows, in Caracas, the day after this event occurred we had delegations calling on us all day long, delegations from the various women's societies calling on Mrs. Nixon, delegations from three of the universities of Caracas. The Rector and students as well called, protesting although they had some disagreement with some of the policies of the United States, that they believed the use of violence was completely out of character with the attitude of Venezuela toward any visitor, particularly a visitor from the United States, apologizing for what happened, and then sitting down and discussing seriously the problems that we had. So what I am trying to say when I say it isn't as bad as it appears in the papers is perhaps this: Yes, there was danger and we are fortunate nothing worse happened but don't let the danger obscure the fact that as far as Venezuela and Peru are concerned, there is still a tremendous amount of friendship for the United States and for the other countries which we visited. I can repeat this in many, many instances.

Q. Sir, the point has been made that it is beneath the dignity of the Vice President of the United States to go around debating with radical students. Why did you feel impelled to do it?

A. Mr. Horner, I have had that question asked me after every trip that I have taken. I have had it asked by some of our Ambassadors before the debates, as you call them, occurred—the discussions—but usually not afterwards. I think this very question points up one of the grave problems that we confront in our relations not only with Latin America but with Africa, and with Asia, in which you have what I call newly developed societies moving toward political democracy.

Now, there was a time in the history of Latin America, and it isn't too

distant—when a revolution in Latin America was simply a way to transfer power from one section of the elite to another, It had no mass base
whatever. When you consider what happened in Argentina, Colombia, and
Venezuela, you look at the new leaders that are arising on the Latin
American scene. Frondizi, for example; Lleras in Colombia, one of the
great leaders of the world today, not only in Latin America but in world
quarters as well; when you consider some of the fine men I met and
visited with in the government Junta in Venezuela; when you consider
Siles in Bolivia, you have a new group of leaders.

Where do they come from? These are people coming from what I call
the class of intelligentsia, not the very wealthy and the usual ruling class
but a new group.

This brings me to the key question: Why do you go to universities? Why
do you go, as I did, in every country where possible, to labor union halls?

I want to point out the format we used. First, we went only when we
were invited, and the universities generally issued the invitations because
they were most anxious to have the opportunity of seeing a visiting digni-
tary from abroad and submitting questions to him. Second, these were not
debates in the sense you think of debates. I went to the university and made
a few opening comments and then submitted myself to questions.

I will tell you why I used that format. When you don't know the language the question and answer technique is far more effective. You can
punctuate the problems. So we had these question and answer sessions
and, believe me, we covered every difficult, tough problem that you could
possibly imagine because the labor leaders and the university students who
asked questions were not diplomats. They really wanted to get down to
brass tacks, and so what did I find? First, it was good for me. I learned a
lot about Latin America; secondly, I believe it is essential from the standpoint of American foreign policy that we talk to these groups.

I can assure you it is a lot easier to run one of these trips as some people
want them run, a round of cocktail parties and white-tie dinners. We had
a lot of those too, but I can also assure you that if that is what we do in
Latin America—if we continue to concentrate primarily on that area, we
might as well figure right now we are going to lose the battle. Because,
although the people in the universities don't run these countries now, they
will in the future and although the people in the universities don't control
policy now, they affect policy now.

The same is true of the incipient labor movement too. It is weak at the
present time but growing stronger.

The other point I should make is what are the communists doing?
They are concentrating on the universities and the labor union movements. Why? Because they know it is the wave of the future and they are
trying to control it in the communist direction. So, do we leave the field

to them or go in and debate these issues with this rising new force, which within five or ten years is going to be a terribly important factor in Latin America and in the free world?

I have already talked too long in answer to this question but I think it is fundamental.

I would just like to add this word with regard to it. In instance after instance I think that it was possible during the course of going to these groups to answer some of the difficult questions about the United States policy that ought to be answered before university students, before labor union groups: Does the United States really favor dictatorships? The answer is no. Does the United States in its private enterprise policy really want to make the rich richer and the poor poorer? The answer is no. I haven't time to give the answers today but over and over again I tried to get this message across.

I repeat that it is easier to do it the other way but I also repeat in all of our foreign policy activities at the diplomatic level, at the USIA level, at the economic level, it is high time we paid attention to the university student and the rising labor leaders, more attention to the people in the press, the radio, the opinion-making people than we have in the past. If we don't, as I said, we are going to leave the field to the other side and that we cannot do. If I had to do it over again I would certainly do the same thing. I would urge any other visitors who go there to do the same thing.

In that connection one final word. I think one of the problems in our relations with Latin America is that sometimes there is too much of a tendency to think that you can smother a burning issue with sweet words. This may have been possible in times past but it isn't possible now. You have to get these issues out on the table and you have got to discuss them with the people who are advocates and you have got to meet them, call it debate, discussion, or whatever you will. I would say being a representative of the United States, a representative of democracy, of free enterprise, I am proud to present our position. I don't think a lot of these people have had it adequately presented to them and I want them to see that there is an alternative to what the communists offer. That is what I was trying to offer in going to these groups.[1]

---

[1] Following Vice-President Nixon's visit to Latin America and his reception in Peru and Venezuela, the Senate Foreign Relations and House Foreign Affairs Committee scheduled full-dress inquiries into U.S.-Latin American relations. Dr. Milton Eisenhower went on a 3-week fact-finding and goodwill mission to Central America, and on his return on 1 August 1958, urged a 3-point programme for Latin America: 'bankable loans', action on commodity prices, promotion of better understanding of U.S. aims and capabilities, see *D.S.B.*, 25 August 1958, pp. 309–10. Mr. Foster Dulles's visit to Brazil in August 1958 was followed by the announcement of a balance of payments credit to Brazil of $158m., extended by the Export-Import Bank and 12 private banks. Further economic action included: emergency credits to Columbia, Chile, and Peru, and an emergency programme of stabilization and development loans for Argentina, totalling $329m., see *D.S.B.*, 19 January 1959, pp. 105–6.

Q. Sir, are you still planning a good will tour of Europe?

A. We don't have any trip planned to Europe at the present time. We have a number of invitations and I can say that no final plans will be made on this trip until we see when Congress adjourns, whether or not there will be a summit conference and whether or not other considerations can be worked out. I understand we are having an election this fall and I will have to take that into any decisions I make.

Q. One final question. Are you planning to run for a third term as Vice President of the United States?

A. I can only say that we Republicans have always been against the third term.

MR. HORNER: Mrs. Nixon, I present to you a token of appreciation on behalf of the National Press Club.

Mr. Vice President, we are grateful for your address and your answers and I am happy to present to you this certificate of appreciation from The Press Club.

2. Proposal 'Operation Pan America' put forward by the Government of Brazil, Rio de Janeiro, 9 August 1958[1]

(a) *Note accompanying the Brazilian aide-mémoire, 12 August 1958*

Dear Mr. Ambassador: I have the honor to transmit to Your Excellency, in order that it may be submitted for consideration by the Government of the United States, the enclosed *aide mémoire*, which describes in detail the views of the Government of Brazil with respect to the nature, characteristics, objectives, and functioning of Operation Pan America.

2. The Government of Brazil is completely convinced that the Pan America movement as now initiated will only achieve tangible and specific results if it can count on the positive support of all the American Republics by means of the fullest and most unrestricted exchange of views on matters of fundamental interest to the cause of hemispheric solidarity.

3. The Government of Brazil is now consulting the governments of its sister republics in the hemisphere on whether they would be in agreement that informal contacts for initial understandings should be carried out in Washington, through diplomatic missions accredited to the Government of the United States, with a view to preliminary study and analysis of the problem of underdevelopment in Latin America. These understandings reached in Washington, in which missions accredited to the Organization

---

[1] *Special Committee to study the Formulation of New Measures for Economic Cooperation*, vol. 1: Report and Documents (Council for the Organization of American States, Washington, D.C., 1959), pp. 28–32. Hereafter cited as *New Measures for Economic Cooperation*, The *aide-mémoire*, and note were sent by the Government of Brazil to the Governments of the other American states, through their diplomatic representatives in Rio de Janeiro.

of American States would also participate, might ultimately attain a more coordinated form and expression if a Committee of Twenty-one, were created for the purpose of determining the bases of an agreement to be approved in a final meeting. The question of the level, place, and time of such a meeting would only be defined and determined in the light of the progress achieved by the said Committee of Twenty-one.

4. In the enclosed *aide mémoire*, the Government of Brazil suggests that the first meeting in Washington might be held during the latter half of September or the first half of October, if that period is considered adequate for the necessary preliminary work of preparing documents and defining the problems of economic development. The Government of Brazil conceives Operation Pan America as a multilateral undertaking and not merely an interweaving or juxtapositioning of bilateral operations. Moreover, the Government of Brazil is the first to recognize that each American country has its own distinctive characteristics on which only its government, statesmen, and technicians can pass judgment with certainty and authority. At the same time, it is indispensable that each American Republic express its own point of view concerning the most adequate practical manner for considering the multilateral problem.

5. In formulating the present proposal, the Government of Brazil expresses the firm belief that the fight for democracy in the hemisphere is closely linked to the struggle against economic underdevelopment itself, and that this struggle cannot be carried to a successful conclusion without the joint effort of all American Republics, through the fullest utilization of a system of mutual consultations concerning the problems that are common to our peoples and nations.

6. Included in the *aide mémoire*, in addition, is a draft of a basic agenda for the informal discussions to be held at Washington. That agenda would be modified or amplified in accordance with the points of view expressed by the various American Republics and constitutes only the first attempt to bring order and direction to the work.

7. I would appreciate very much Your Excellency's kindness in transmitting to me as soon as possible the views of the United States Government concerning this matter, which is so significant and timely in our current effort to reformulate Pan American ideas.

(b) *Aide-mémoire 'Operation Pan America', 9 August 1958*

I. DEFINITION AND OBJECTIVES

The Brazilian Government considers that a clearer definition of the objectives of Operation Pan America is necessary in order that this movement, which has been initiated at the right time and under the best auspices, may not be impaired or lose its impact.

A. *General definition:* Operation Pan America is not an undertaking limited by time, with objectives to be attained in a short period; rather it is a reorientation of hemispheric policy, intended to place Latin America, by a process of full appraisement, in a position to participate more effectively in the defense of the West, with a growing sense of vitality and a greater development of its capacities. Thus, Operation Pan America is more than a mere program; it is an entire policy.

B. *Strategic political concept:* Operation Pan America must be understood as a corollary of the general strategy of the West, and among its fundamental purposes the following are particularly outstanding: preservation of the democratic system, based on political and religious freedom and on respect for private ownership and free enterprise, and the defense of all areas that concern the security of the free world. Because of its intrinsic, political, economic, social and strategic importance, and because 'a threat to the peace in any part of the world is now a threat to the peace of the entire world,' it is opportune to re-examine, with a view to strengthening it, the contribution to the resources of the free world that may be made by the nations that are signatories of the Treaty of Rio de Janeiro.

C. *Economic concept:* The more rapid development of Latin America's economic strength will result in a growing sense of vitality and will enable it to increase its contribution to the defense of the West.

II. CHARACTERISTICS

A. *Joint multilateral action:* Operation Pan America is conceived as involving the joint action of the twenty-one republics of the Western Hemisphere, the preservation of its strictly multilateral nature being indispensable. Bilateral matters will continue to be handled through the channels normally followed in such cases, without becoming part of the aforesaid Operation.

B. *Struggle for democracy:* Within the framework of Operation Pan America, the struggle for democracy becomes identified with the struggle against stagnation and underdevelopment. The underdevelopment that prevails in this Hemisphere morally and materially involves the cause that we are defending. Underdeveloped areas are open to the penetration of antidemocratic ideology. From many standpoints and in all of its implications, the battle of the West is the battle for development. Materialist ideologies feed upon the poverty and misery that give rise to them in the first place; to combat these factors is the only sure way to combat those ideologies. Where there is poverty, our cause will always be in danger. It is illusory to expect positive action on behalf of a cause embracing such complex factors from peoples whose isolation in the rigors of extreme poverty prevents them from thinking or feeling anything beyond the narrow limits of their urgent needs for survival.

C. *Latin America's participation in world policy:* According to the Brazilian concept, Operation Pan America is a reflection of the need for more active and more vigorous participation and cooperation by the Latin American countries in international policy, and it reveals these countries' full awareness of their moral, political, and demographic importance. Latin America's contribution may become highly significant in the struggle for a balance of power.

III. WESTERN POSTWAR POLICY

A. *Inter-American political reorientation:* The Brazilian Government believes that the time has come for a revision of inter-American policy, with a view to strengthening hemispheric unity in the face of the increasing common danger. A stronger, more courageous, creative, and dynamic initiative is urgently needed in the Western Hemisphere at this time.

It is imperative that the West become ever more conscious of its mission in the modern world. The principal objective of this mission is to defend and to perfect man's spiritual and moral achievements. Spiritual and moral forces should be the ones to guide and regulate a world expanded and profoundly transformed by technology. This is what is important to the West; this is its own Cause.

B. *Economic reorientation of Pan Americanism:* The reasons for underdevelopment are many and complex. One could not in good faith fix responsibility for Latin America's chronic anemic condition and the consequent organic weakening of Pan Americanism. Although it is understood that efforts toward economic development devolve primarily upon each country individually, it is now understood better than ever before that there must be cooperation on international bases.

IV. THE OPERATION'S COURSE OF ACTION

A. *Advance preparation:* The Brazilian Government wishes to clarify the fact that it was never its intention or plan to hold a conference of American Chiefs of State without the most careful advance preparation. Furthermore, the Brazilian Government is not committed to any rigid plans for carrying out the Operation in question, and it believes that only after a series of contacts and consultations among the countries of our community will it be possible to make a definitive determination of the best methods for achieving the common objective.

B. *Preliminary inquiries:* The Brazilian Government would now be willing to assume responsibility for making diplomatic inquiries with a view to the preparation of a basic agenda and toward ascertaining whether the American governments would agree with the idea of reaching informal understanding and carrying out preliminary negotiations in

Washington through the embassies accredited to the Government of the United States.

C. *Initiation of the Operation:* The preparatory work could be done at the diplomatic or technical level, and it is anticipated that the participation by members of the delegations accredited to the Organization of American States would be desirable. These informal understandings would become more clearly defined and be better coordinated if a *Committee of Twenty-one* were created. Brazil does not wish to propose any date, but nonetheless it does state that it would be ready to begin its work in the said committee during the latter part of September.

D. *High-level meeting:* Once the bases for an agreement have been established and significant results obtained that might be looked upon as substantial progress, then the competent organs of the Organization of American States could study the idea of a high-level meeting among the republics of the Hemisphere to approve and to sign that group of resolutions and proclamations that could become the plan of action for achieving Pan American unity; among thse would be included, with special emphasis, the preparation of a dynamic and progressive program for the struggle against underdevelopment, and this would be the crowning feature of Operation Pan America.

V. BASIC OBJECTIVES OF THE OPERATION

The following points might be the basic objectives of the Operation:

1. Reaffirmation of the principles of hemispheric solidarity;
2. Recognition of underdevelopment as a problem of common interest;
3. Adaptation of inter-American organs and agencies, if necessary, to the requirements of more dynamic action to carry on the struggle against underdevelopment;
4. Technical assistance for increased productivity;
5. Measures to stabilize the market for basic commodities;
6. Adaptation to present needs and expansion of the resources of international financial institutions;
7. Reaffirmation of private initiative in the struggle against underdevelopment; and
8. Revision by each country, where necessary, of its fiscal and economic policy, for the purpose of assuring means to promote economic development.

VI. AGENDA FOR THE PREPARATORY MEETINGS

By way of example, certain topics that might be analyzed during the preparatory inquiries, consultations, and meetings are appended to this document.

Maximum use should be made of the contribution of various international agencies engaged in research relating to the Latin American economy (Inter-American Economic and Social Council and the Economic Commission for Latin America), as well as of private agencies or organizations that may be in a position to make appreciable technical contributions.

ANNEX

Topics mentioned in Part VI of the Aide-mémoire

1. Study and adoption of measures favoring the use of private capital of the industrialized countries in under or semi-developed areas; more effective mobilization and utilization of available private capital for underdeveloped economies;

2. Increase in the volume and an easing of the terms of loans made by international public credit agencies, or the creation of inter-American financing institutions organized with the same objective in mind;

3. Study and adoption of other measures to strengthen the domestic economies, principally to fight inflation and to encourage savings and the investment of savings;

4. Study and adoption of measures for the equitable regulation of the market in basic commodities;

5. Study of joint measures to be adopted to meet the problems arising from the formation of large economic blocs, such as the so-called 'European Common Market'; studies and measures leading to the establishment of regional markets in the Hemisphere; and

6. Expansion and diversification of technical assistance programs, using all available resources in the field.

3. Memorandum presented by the Brazilian delegation at the meeting of American Foreign Ministers, Washington, 24 September 1958[1]

The time has come to give a real meaning to Pan Americanism, to translate into concrete accomplishments, into plans for action, the sentiments of solidarity that have been reiterated over the years in inter-American conferences.

2. The initiative taken by President Kubitschek, in asserting the need for transforming Pan American ideals into a live and active reality, merely envisaged starting, on a hemispheric scale, a discussion of common problems and of their solutions sought by the peoples of Latin America.

3. That clarion call is today bringing together the American Foreign Ministers, at the seat of the OAS, for the first contact, for a thorough exchange of ideas, in an informal manner.

[1] *New Measures for Economic Co-operation*, pp. 33–41.

4. It is unnecessary to recapitulate the origins of this movement. They are not far behind us, but they have roots in all our countries, whose Chiefs of State, foreign ministers, or delegates to meetings of the United Nations or the OAS have made statements or have taken clear positions to the same effect as that which is today known as 'Operation Pan America.'

5. There are, therefore, no priorities to discuss or nations acting as interpreters of Latin American thought. What we want to outline is a coordinated and effective action by all the nations of the Hemisphere in order to arrive at a solution of the serious problems that make Latin America one of the most vulnerable points in the western world.

6. The greatest, the most pressing of these problems is, without doubt, underdevelopment, which limits the significance and the scope of the innumerable proclamations of Pan American solidarity.

7. It is the proposal of Brazil, exclusively by way of collaboration, to submit for discussion by all the other foreign ministries of the Hemisphere a number of preliminary definitions that might serve as a starting point for a study of common action to be taken against underdevelopment.

8. The Government of Brazil also wishes to outline, in the same spirit of collaboration, the kind of economic reasoning that is adopted, as an experiment, for a 'plan' of growth for the Brazilian economy, in accordance with alternative 'working hypotheses.'

9. It would be well to make it quite clear that Brazil is not animated by any other intention than to keep the organs of the OAS itself, or any special working groups that are set up, informed as to the direction taken by the basic studies in preparation in Brazil. The methodology followed, may be altered, adapted, or corrected, or other paths may even be taken, other 'models' or growth, with a frank and faithful readiness to adopt the line of thought and action that will lead most quickly to the elimination of the affliction of underdevelopment.

FIVE POINTS

10. Brazil believes that this taking of a collective position should be preceded by agreement as to certain basic points that might guide common action.

11. The first of these is, naturally, the definition of '*development*' itself, in absolute and relative terms, for the purposes of 'Operation Pan America.'

12. '*Development*' *may be defined as obtaining a per capita income level that will make possible the beginning of a cumulative and self-acting process of growth with one's own resources, at a satisfactory rate, without sudden or serious institutional changes.* Unless they reach this level, the Latin American countries

would continue to depend greatly on outside economic assistance, and be exposed to the hazards of stagnation and pauperism, aggravated by an increase in population.

13. According to studies made by the United Nations, such a level would be approximately about $400 per capita, on the basis of 1950 values, or that is, about 480 dollars in present-day values. This latter figure might, perhaps, come to be adopted as the minimum objective to be attained during the period set for the full execution of 'Operation Pan America.'

14. In *relative* terms, satisfactory *development* would be the quantitative projection of a rate of economic development that would allow the Latin American countries to decrease the distance separating them from the great economic powers, in terms of per capita income.

15. The projection of the present trends of the different economies shows the present economic and institutional aggregate of the world leaves, for Latin America, on the whole, prospects so limited that they become extremely dangerous for the security of the West, when compared with the propensities for increase of the great economies, above all the planned economies.

16. As to the time required for the transformation of the Latin American economies into 'developed' economies, according to the quantitative criterion referred to above, the Brazilian plan adopted as a goal the year 1980, and extended all its projections to that year.

17. A period of two decades, sufficiently long to permit an over-all view of the objectives to be attained, makes it necessary to divide the efforts into shorter periods by setting partial goals for intermediate years. In this way, some idea as concrete as possible will always be available as to the next efforts to be made, within the general framework of procedures and objectives, avoiding the contradiction between short and long periods, so common in underdeveloped countries.

18. We should emphasize that the selection of an index as simple as per capita income was not made without an understanding of the methodological limitations implied therein. However, other indices, such as well-being and progress, are difficult to define, and above all, require complex measurement, which would be detrimental to the ends that should be sought in this phase of the task, that is, the acceptance of clear and well-defined objectives in relation to what can be done to formulate together an effective minimum of Pan American joint action.

19. Although exceptional conditions, generated by certain sectors of Latin American production, have raised the per capita income above this level in two or three countries, the average for the region is still extremely low, around a bare 270 dollars. As has been noted, the level of 480 dollars is indicated as the general objective, not as a limit, for any individual

country, inasmuch as international comparisons of income do not authorize uniform conclusions applicable in all cases.

20. *The second point would consist of fixing, by hemisphere agreement, the rate
of cumulative increase for the gross production of the Latin American countries,
taken as a whole, necessary to overcome the increase in population and bring about
the beginning of the self-acting process of development at a satisfactory pace.*

21. If there should be adopted, as the basis of reasoning, the two-decade
period indicated in the Brazilian plan and the index accepted by the
experts of the United Nations, planning for the development of Latin
America would have as a goal the raising of the gross production of the
whole community in such a way as to permit the attainment by 1980 of a
per capita income equal to or above 480 dollars.

22. In the case of Brazil, for example, within its present institutional
system, this rate is not, presumably, attainable by that date, on the basis
of domestic resources, in the face of the present aggregate of international
prices and if the present levels of international cooperation are maintained. Such levels would enable us to attain, probably, a rate of increase
of 4·5 percent per annum and 400 dollars per capita by 1980. Consequently, 'Operation Pan America' should represent, for Brazil, the adoption and maintenance of a higher rate, in accordance with details explained
below, when the alternatives adopted for the Brazilian 'model' are outlined.

23. Hence, one of our specific tasks would be to analyze the Latin American
economies and their needs, in order to fix the annual rate of increase
required to ensure the economic emancipation, in fact, of the Latin
American community.

24. *The third point would be the determination of the sources and the amount
of international funds, public and/or private, required to supplement domestic savings.*

25. The relationship between rates of increase in population and the
increase in national income necessary to attain rates of development compatible with the aims to be set by 'Operation Pan America' would indicate
the gross investment required. Once the possible extent of the efforts to
accumulate savings has been estimated, there would be an idea of the size
of the supplementation necessary from international funds, public or
private, or both.

26. This study should embrace, throughout the period under consideration, a rational plan for increasing the imports necessary for maintaining
the progress of development, which implies a corresponding expansion of
Latin American capacity to export.

27. As the process of development of any country means, in turn, an
appreciable intensification of the demand for imported goods, it does not
seem possible, at least in short or medium periods, to pay for what is
required as the result of the increased demand, and to import only from

the revenues derived from sales abroad. Thus a supplementary entry of capital is made necessary, on a scale sufficient to compensate for the disequilibrium in the balance of payments and to permit an acceleration in the process of development.

28. Not only public capital, governmental or from international credit institutions, but also private capital, in all its different forms, would have a relevant role to play in this field.

29. The studies to be made should include a quantitative geographical separation of the possibilities for increasing exports for different areas, that is, those of free economies, with convertible or inconvertible currencies, and those of planned economies, bearing in mind the determination of the most suitable levels for trade and for obtaining credit.

30. *The fourth point would consist of the identification of the principal bottlenecks in the Latin American economies that should be removed by individual and/or collective action.*

31. This is one of the topics of greatest interest, which opens up wide possibilities of effective cooperation between the American nations. The enumeration that follows does not pretend to be complete, but only suggests some of the bottlenecks that, especially in the case of Brazil, are shown to be crucial. It should be noted that there is a growing awareness of this kind of problem, on both national and international levels, and this will greatly facilitate the study and planning of common action.

1. *Expansion of the importing capacity of the Latin American countries*

32. This is, no doubt, in most cases, the most serious bottleneck, above all because of the severe limitations it imposes on the machinery of international credit and transfers, necessary for the process of accumulation of capital and for obtaining critical goods and raw materials.

33. The fields in which Pan American action might first be exercised include:

a. Cooperation in the expansion of international markets;
b. Cooperation for the establishment of a broad Regional Market;
c. Creation of financial institutions intended to mobilize and facilitate intra-regional transfers;
d. Stabilization of the markets for primary products on bases that will ensure a fair remuneration to producers;
e. Installation and expansion of industries that will replace imports.

2. *Development and correction of dynamic deficiencies, above all in the following internal sectors:*

a. Power;
b. Transportation and communications;

c. Food supply and agriculture;

d. Basic industries,

e. Education.

34. With respect to this last point, we believe that education, for the over-all goals sought by 'Operation Pan America,' should be included not only in its typically economic aspects (the supply of skilled and trained manpower) but in its broadest sense, since the incorporation of sectors of the population still living on a marginal basis is essential to the process of development.

35. *The fifth point would be a description of the alternatives open to Latin America to assure its attaining the rates of growth adopted as goals of 'Operation Pan America.'*

36. It is evident that the Latin American countries are called upon to make most serious choices that can hardly be postponed, since the whole future of these countries does, in fact, depend upon the decisions made.

37. The fact is that a re-examination of the international system, especially its economic aspects, has been sorely needed since the First World War.

38. It became evident at the end of World War II, after the hardships of the depression and the ideological and military conflict it produced, that man should not be a pawn of history but rather should play a meaningful, wise, and active role in order to achieve the highest possible levels of progress and well-being for the greatest number.

39. It is well to note the great role of the United States, which, in that period, made marked changes not only in its national economic and social policy but also in its international relations, outstanding among which is the extent of its reconstruction and development programs, especially in Europe, whose net value, including military aid, wartime and other, amounted to more than $80 billion.

40. The timely action of the United States, when the Western European economic system seemed on the point of collapse, with the very survival of Europe at stake, implied recognition of two important principles: first, that historical responsibility is exercised not only on the national level but on the international as well, and on a long-term as well as on a short-term basis; second, that, unless man takes reasonable action, the spontaneous or normal unfolding of history does not automatically ensure the achievement of the goal of the greatest good for the greatest number.

41. In view of the direct and indirect sacrifices brought about by world upheavals—and, in the case of some countries, like Brazil, by its active participation in the conflict—Latin America hoped that United States leadership would result in a common effort to improve general conditions and initiate a process of economic growth that would be the counterpart,

on a regional level, of the adequate, wise, and much needed action of the United States in Europe.

42. The following question arose in the Latin American countries: Did the great western economic powers, especially the United States, believe that their responsibilities were restricted to European recovery?

43. World events seem to leave little doubt that to win the peace those responsibilities increased just when the most pressing work of reconstruction and defense was completed.

44. Latin America's experience teaches that its development requires them to choose great objectives and to decide to play a reasonable and active role in history in order to remove the obstacles to its economic and social progress.

45. In a general way, no process of growth in the less-developed countries has been found to compare with that which took place during the industrial revolution in Western Europe and the United States. On the contrary, the economic development of Latin America, which is markedly cyclical, is largely the result of fluctuations in its capacity to import, redistribution caused by inflation, and, finally, state action to facilitate the accumulation of capital, create foreign markets, and introduce new techniques.

46. For various reasons, the flow of private capital to Latin America has not, in general, been sufficient. Furthermore, a study of the impact on the balance of payments of the Latin American countries and of the earnings of foreign private capital does not always give a clear idea of its unconditional advantage.

47. In the last century, certain countries were able to make great strides in the formation of capital, thanks to the sacrifices imposed upon large segments of their respective populations. The truth is that the historical and socio-cultural conditions prevailing at that time made possible such a distribution of the share of the national product of those countries that funds naturally were concentrated in the hands of those who were best able to accumulate and reinvest them. Meanwhile, the needs of today's masses are greater and growing. They have a higher level of education and consumption and they are spurred on in their demands by forceful advertising techniques. Today those masses would hardly be willing to make burdensome sacrifices unless they had a clear understanding of their need and fairness.

48. Experience shows, however, that most people yield to the measures dictated wholly by consideration of the welfare of all, like the self-imposed sacrifices of the allies to win the war and assure the peace.

49. These facts certainly have not escaped notice by the United States, the very democratic and fully developed country where the systematization of the economic process is extended to the mechanics of parity prices

for dozens of products and achieves the redistribution of income with tax rates affecting the most privileged sector of the population in a way that is more extreme than any ever put into practice in a Latin American country. The effort at systematization assumes the proportions of a complex and forceful anticyclical policy.

50. Further, it is well to note another characteristic phase of the problem of economic development requiring action that transcends national borders: the extremely limited basic resources of most underdeveloped countries. To a great extent, the United States undoubtedly owes its tremendous growth during the last century and this one, to the wealth of its natural resources. In the same way, the nations that made the most progress in Europe owed their growth to the abundance of essential materials, especially fuels and iron. There is no doubt that, although not as well endowed as the United States in terms of topography and power resources, Latin America, as a whole, still has sufficient materials to form the basis of a great civilization. But considered individually, few Latin American countries could achieve a spontaneous and progressive growth under current conditions, which have been aggravated by the obstacles to international economic relations.

51. The countries that are larger and better endowed with natural resources could, if necessary, carry out a process of development to a large extent independently, that is, even without any change in present levels of international cooperation. But the position of small nations or those with less-diversified resources is, obviously, less favorable for guaranteeing the process of development with their own resources alone.

52. Brazil has presented these considerations in detail, since its experience, in a certain sense, seems to reflect many of the outstanding characteristics of Latin American problems. The Brazilian economy is really a complex composed of a relatively highly developed region in the south, where there is an important industrial concentration, and marginal and even submarginal regions in the north and west, which are our relatively underdeveloped areas. Brazil is now carrying out a systematic program, continually being improved, which has its roots in a close initial cooperation with the United States through the Brazilian-American Mixed Economic Development Commission.

53. The Government of Brazil is sure that the Brazilian people are ready to make the necessary sacrifices in consumer goods and social discipline in order to continue the development of the country. But it believes that it is preferable to lessen the amount of immediate sacrifice so that the present generation, especially the less-privileged sectors of the population, will be able to enjoy now some of the advantages to which all aspire.

SOME DETAILS OF THE BRAZILIAN PLAN

54. The studies now in progress in Brazil were based at the outset on a series of hypotheses of an increase in the per-capita gross national product. At the same time information was gathered and reports were prepared on the rates of growth achieved in other areas, undeveloped as well as under-developed, for purposes of reference and comparison with the alternatives arbitrarily adopted in Brazil.

55. Brazil has a very high rate of population growth, some 2·5% per year. Taking this into consideration, the rate of increase in the national product would have to be quite high in order to permit substantial increases in per capita income. For example, rates of increase of 4·5%, 5·5%, and 6·5% would bring about, in 1980, a per capita gross product of 400, 497, and 619 dollars respectively, for a population of 110 million. In line with these three hypotheses would be a total gross product of 43, 55, and 68 billion dollars.

56. Even though those rates of growth are higher than the average of the last 27 years, they would not be unreasonable if certain bottlenecks in the Brazilian economy were removed.

57. The gross investments required in the three cases considered would have to amount to 14·4%, 17·6%, and 20·8% of the gross national product.

58. Even though investment levels as high as 17% have been reached at times in the last ten years, a rate of 20·8% would require an unprecedented accumulation of national savings or the supplementation of national savings with international funds, public or private, or both.

59. The greatest bottleneck to be removed is, undoubtedly, the matter of the capacity to import, still excessively low in the case of Brazil. Even if a strict program of reducing and substituting imports should be instituted whereby our relative dependence on foreign goods would be slightly lessened, the unavoidable need to import would increase rapidly under any of the three hypotheses considered. The value of imports would exceed 3, 4·5, and even 7 billion dollars by 1980, as contrasted with 1·65 billion in 1957.

60. A realistic examination of the Brazilian economy reveals that, by strenuous and continuing efforts, it would be possible to reach the level of the first alternative. The other two, because they are slightly higher than historical trends in the expansion of international trade, are con-sidered difficult to reach unless the country could count upon substantially greater outside help or an appreciable expansion of foreign markets, or even a judicious combination of both.

61. While all long-range estimates should be assessed with the necessary caution, it is possible to determine, at the intermediate stages, how much

foreign capital would be required to attain the highest rates of growth mentioned above.

62. The *aide mémoire* that Brazil sent to the other Latin American Foreign Offices and to the Department of State contains a list of six topics that frequently have been the subject of international study.

63. Prompt attention to those matters might enable the countries in the Hemisphere to begin to put into practice now the principles and the philosophy of Pan American economic cooperation that they should jointly delineate.

64. The truth, however, is that, in the long run, for 'Operation Pan America' to be completely successful, the governments and the peoples of the Hemisphere should rally behind a well-planned program, to be carried out in specific periods and with specific values, a program that would reverse the present trend toward growing impoverishment in Latin America in comparison with the great economic powers.

4. Communiqué of the Foreign Ministers of the Twenty-one American Republics, Washington, 24 September 1958[1]

The Foreign Ministers of the 21 American Republics met informally in Washington on September 23 and 24, at the invitation of the Secretary of State of the United States, and discussed important current questions of common interest. In three sessions, the Foreign Ministers exchanged views regarding inter-American relations and problems, particularly those of an economic nature, and also reviewed the international scene.

The Ministers recognize that in the history of the world, the solidarity of the American States has been of great importance, and that at the present time it acquires special significance. They reaffirm that solidarity, which is founded on the principles of the Charter of the Organization.[2] The present period of evolutionary change in the political, economic and social structure of society calls for a renewed dedication to the inter-American ideals of independence, political liberty, and economic and cultural progress, and for a reaffirmation of the faith of the American nations in their capacity to proceed dynamically toward the realization of those high ideals.

The Ministers are confident that their exchange of views and informal conversations will have fruitful results. They agree to recommend that their governments instruct their representatives on the Council of the Organization of American States to consider the desirability of holding

---

[1] *New Measures for Economic Co-operation*, pp. 42–44.
[2] Of American States.

more frequently similar informal meetings of Foreign Ministers and other high-ranking government representatives.

The Ministers are of the opinion that, in keeping with the aspirations and needs of the peoples of America expressed on numerous occasions, action to promote the greatest possible economic development of the continent must be intensified. They are certain that a harmonious and carefully planned joint effort to that end will contribute enormously to strengthening the solidarity of the hemisphere and to the well-being of all Americans.

The Foreign Ministers are deeply gratified at the affirmation made by President Eisenhower, that the Government of the United States is prepared to lend its full cooperation in achieving concrete results in the common effort to promote the economic development of the American countries, for it considers that peace, prosperity and security are in the end, indivisible.

They furthermore consider that this is the proper time to review and strengthen inter-American cooperation in the economic field, as has been suggested by President Kubitschek and in the proposals of various American Governments.[1] The Ministers recommend that, during the coming period before the Eleventh Inter-American Conference, special attention be given to working out additional measures of economic cooperation taking as the point of departure the six topics proposed by the Government of Brazil in its memorandum of August 9, 1958 concerning the plan known as 'Operation Pan America', any other specific topics that the other governments of the Republics of the hemisphere may wish to submit in connection with the general topic under consideration, namely, the promotion of economic development, and the following topic proposed by the Foreign Minister of Argentina:

Preparation and immediate execution of a broad hemispheric program to train experts for economic development, chiefly in the fields of engineering, agronomy, industrial engineering, economics, public administration, and business administration.

For this purpose and to facilitate other informal talks, the Ministers are of the opinion that the Council of the Organization of American States should set up a Special Commission of the Council on which the governments of the 21 American Republics would be represented.[2] As the Commission reaches conclusions regarding measures that might be taken, it should submit its reports to the Council of the Organization. Then the necessary action may be taken to have those proposals or measures carried

[1] See for example President Frondizi's letter of 4 June 1958 to President Eisenhower, and President Eisenhower's reply of 1 July 1958, in *D.S.B.*, 4 August 1958, pp. 209–10.

[2] The Committee known as the Committee of Twenty-one was inaugurated on 17 November 1958 by the Chairman of the Council of O.A.S., Dr. José Gutierrez Gomez; it held its first meeting from 17 November to 12 December 1958.

out through the organs of the Organization, or directly by the government, as may be appropriate.

Also, the Ministers are of the opinion that practical measures may be taken now in connection with certain specific proposals. These are:

1. The establishment of an inter-American economic development institution in which all the American countries would participate. For this purpose the Inter-American Economic and Social Council should convene as soon as possible a specialized committee of government representatives, as recommended in Resolution XVIII of the Buenos Aires Economic Conference. It is recommended that this committee meet in continuous session until it completes draft articles of the agreement for the proposed institution, which will be signed at a later date.[1]

2. Intensification of efforts to establish regional markets in Latin America. It would be well for the governments directly concerned and the international organizations directly interested, chiefly the Organization of American States, the Economic Commission for Latin America, and the Organization of Central American States, to expedite their studies and concrete measures directed towards the establishment of regional markets in Central and South America. The Ministers suggest that a report on this important project be submitted to the members of the OAS not later than the Eleventh Inter-American Conference. In this connection the Ministers note that the United States Government has made known that it is prepared to assist financially in the establishment of solvent industries, through appropriate agencies, under suitable conditions, with a view to promoting enjoyment of the benefits of regional markets through public and private investment.

The Ministers again express their constant concern about the problems of markets for basic products. They are in agreement that the economic structure of the majority of the American Republics requires that solutions to these problems be sought urgently, for which purpose consultations should be carried out between the interested members of the Organization of American States, on bilateral and multilateral bases, as well as with the producer and consumer countries of other geographic areas.

In concluding this communiqué, the Ministers expressed that there prevailed at this meeting an atmosphere of frankness, sincerity, and

---

[1] On 12 August 1958, Under-Secretary Dillon stated before the Inter-American Economic and Social Council of O.A.S. in Washington, that: 'the United States Government is prepared to consider the establishment of an inter-American regional development institution which would receive support from all its member countries'. *D.S.B.*, 1 September 1958, pp. 347–8. Negotiations were concluded on 8 April 1959 for the establishment of an inter-American Bank to provide development funds for Latin and Central America, see *Agreement Establishing the Inter-American Development Bank* (Pan American Union, Washington, 1959). The bank came into being on 30 December 1959.

understanding which contributed greatly to the establishment of a feeling of confidence that the important tasks being started at this time will be completed successfully.

F. EUROPEAN INTEGRATION

1. Franco-German communiqué following the meeting of General de Gaulle and Dr. Adenauer, Colombey-les-Deux-Eglises, 14 September 1958[1]

Le chancelier de la République fédérale d'Allemagne, M. Konrad Adenauer, et le général de Gaulle se sont rencontrés dimanche 14 septembre 1958 dans la propriété de campagne du chef du gouvernement français à Colombey.

Ils ont eu un échange de vues approfondi sur les problèmes communs intéressant leurs deux pays. L'entretien, qui a duré plusieurs heures et auquel ont été invités à se joindre les deux ministres des affaires étrangères, MM. von Brentano et Couve de Murville, s'est déroulé en toute franchise et dans un esprit d'entente sincère.

A l'issue de leurs conversations, le chancelier Adenauer et le général de Gaulle ont fait la déclaration commune suivante:

Nous nous sommes longuement, librement, cordialement, entretenus de beaucoup de choses.

Nous sommes tous deux profondément conscients de l'importance et de la signification que revêt notre rencontre. Nous croyons que ce doit en être fini à jamais de l'hostilité d'autrefois et que Français et Allemands sont appelés à vivre d'accord et à travailler côte à côte.

Nous avons la conviction que la coopération étroite de la République fédérale d'Allemagne et de la République française est le fondement de toute œuvre constructive en Europe. Elle contribue à renforcer l'alliance atlantique et elle est indispensable au monde.

Nous pensons que cette coopération doit être organisée et, en même temps, inclure les autres nations de l'Europe occidentale avec lesquelles nos deux pays ont des liens étroits.

Nous désirons qu'elle s'exerce à l'avantage de tous les peuples dans le domaine des grands problèmes du monde. Nous souhaitons qu'elle puisse s'étendre au plus grand nombre possible d'Etats européene.

[1] *Le Monde*, 16 September 1958.

D.I.A.—30

2. Anglo-German communiqué following the meeting of Mr. Macmillan and Dr. Adenauer, Bonn, 9 October 1958[1]

The Prime Minister of the United Kingdom of Great Britain and Northern Ireland, Mr. Harold Macmillan, visited Bonn at the invitation of the Federal Government from October 8 to 9, 1958 for talks with the Federal Chancellor and the Federal Foreign Minister. The Prime Minister was accompanied by Mr. Ormsby-Gore, Minister of State for Foreign Affairs. The purpose of the visit was to enable the Heads of Government to maintain the regular personal contacts which they had last renewed when Dr. Adenauer visited London from April 16 to 19, 1958. During the visit, the Prime Minister paid a courtesy call on the Federal President, who is due to make a State Visit to England later this month as guest of Her Majesty The Queen.

The talks, which, as before, took place in a friendly atmosphere, were especially valuable in view of the many important developments in the Middle East, the Far East and elsewhere during the period since the previous meeting. The two Heads of Government agreed on the necessity for close co-operation in their joint efforts for the maintenance of world peace.

They regretted that the Soviet Government had failed to reply to the Western proposals designed to enable the preparations for a Summit Conference to be resumed. Nevertheless, they agreed that no opportunity should be lost for reducing tension between East and West by any available means.

In the field of disarmament they looked forward in particular to the negotiations on the suspension of nuclear weapons' tests under effective international control which are due to take place shortly between the United Kingdom, United States and Soviet Governments.

As regards the German problem, the Federal Chancellor expressed his growing anxiety about developments in the Soviet Zone and thanked the Prime Minister for the support which the United Kingdom Government had given, in their note of September 30 to the Soviet Government, to the German proposal for the establishment of a Four Power Commission for the discussion of this problem. At the same time he expressed his satisfaction at the declaration which the United Kingdom Foreign Minister had made on the German problem at the Thirteenth General Assembly of the United Nations in New York. The Prime Minister confirmed that Her Majesty's Government were ready to enter into discussion with the Soviet Government at any time and in any appropriate forum on the basis of proposals genuinely designed to ensure the reunification of Germany in freedom. He informed Dr. Adenauer of the sympathy of the British people for the sufferings of the population of the Soviet Zone in face of new measures of repression.

[1] Text supplied by the Foreign Office.

The two Heads of Government agreed that it was essential, in the interests of European unity, to bring the negotiations for a Free Trade Area to an early and satisfactory conclusion.

The Prime Minister and the Federal Chancellor resolved to continue to maintain their personal contacts by means of further meetings in the future.

3. Text of an agreement for co-operation between the United States and Euratom regarding the peaceful uses of atomic energy, Brussels, 8 November 1958[1]

Whereas the Government of the United States of America and the European Atomic Energy Community (EURATOM) on May 29 and June 18, 1958 signed an agreement[2] which provides a basis for cooperation in programs for the advancement of the peaceful applications of atomic energy;

Whereas the Government of the United States of America and the European Atomic Energy Community (EURATOM) recognize that it would be to their mutual benefit to cooperate by establishing a joint program:

(a) To bring into operation within the European Atomic Energy Community (EURATOM) large-scale power plants using nuclear reactors of types on which research and development have been carried to an advanced stage in the United States, having a total installed capacity of approximately one million kilowatts of electricity by December 31, 1963 (except that two reactors may be selected to be in operation by December 31, 1965), and under conditions which would approach the competitive range of conventional energy costs in Europe;

(b) To initiate immediately a joint research and development program centered on these types of reactors;

The Parties agree as follows:

ARTICLE I

A. Under the joint program, reactor projects may be proposed, constructed and operated by private or governmental organizations in the Community engaged in the power industry or in the nuclear energy field. Such projects will be selected in accordance with technical standards, criteria (including those relating to radiation protection and reactor safety), and procedures developed by the United States Atomic Energy Commission (hereinafter referred to as the 'United States Commission') and the Commission of the European Atomic Energy Community

<hr/>

[1] *D.S.B.*, 12 January 1959, pp. 69–74.
[2] For text, see ibid., 14 July 1958, p. 70.

(hereinafter referred to as the 'EURATOM Commission'). In the evaluation and selection of such reactor projects, the technical and economic
features will be considered and approved jointly by the United States
Commission and the EURATOM Commission. Other features of such
reactor projects will be considered and approved by the EURATOM
Commission. Reactors now being planned or constructed in Member
States of the Community will be eligible for, and will receive, early
consideration under the criteria established pursuant to this paragraph.

B. The total capital cost, exclusive of the fuel inventory, of the nuclear
power plants with an installed capacity of approximately one million
kilowatts of electricity to be constructed under the program is estimated
not to exceed the equivalent of $350,000,000 to be financed as follows:

1. Approximately $215,000,000 to be provided by the participating
utilities and other European sources of capital, such financing to be
arranged with the appropriate assistance of the Community; and

2. Up to $135,000,000 to be provided by the Government of the United
States of America to the Community in the form of a long-term line of
credit on terms and conditions to be agreed, including terms and conditions satisfactory to the Parties regarding security for such loan, such
funds to be re-lent by the Community for the construction of facilities
under this program.

C. The United States Commission and the EURATOM Commission
will enter into special arrangements with respect to the fuel cycle of
reactors to be constructed and operated under the joint program according
to the principles set forth in Annex 'A' to this Agreement.

ARTICLE II

A. The United States Commission and the EURATOM Commission
under mutually agreed arrangements intend to initiate a program of
research and development to be conducted both in the United States and
in Europe on the types of reactors to be constructed under the joint
program. This research and development program will be aimed primarily
at the improvement of the performance of these reactors, and at lowering
fuel cycle costs. It will also deal with plutonium recycling and other
problems relevant to these reactors.

B. The research and development program will be established for a
ten (10) year period. During the first five (5) years the financial contribution of the Government of the United States of America and the Community will amount to about $50,000,000 each. Prior to the completion
of the first five-year period the Parties will determine the financial
requirements for the remaining five-year period and will undertake to
procure funds necessary to carry out the program. Funds for the second
five-year period may be in the same order of magnitude.

C. The administration of this program will be conducted under arrangements to be mutually agreed.

ARTICLE III

A. The United States Commission will sell to the Community uranium enriched in the isotope U-235 for use in projects designated by the Parties pursuant to the joint program up to a net amount of thirty thousand (30,000) kilograms of contained U-235 in uranium. This net amount shall be the gross quantity of contained U-235 in uranium sold to the Community less the quantity of contained U-235 in recoverable uranium which has been resold or otherwise returned to the Government of the United States of America or transferred to any other nation or international organization with the approval of the Government of the United States of America. The United States Commission will also from time to time sell to the Community such quantities of special nuclear material, in addition to the quantities of enriched uranium set forth above, as may be agreed.

B. Contracts for the sale of special nuclear materials will specify the quantities to be supplied, composition of material, compensation for material, delivery schedules and other necessary terms and conditions. Such contracts for the sale of enriched uranium for fueling power reactors under the joint program may also provide, under terms and conditions to be agreed, that payment for such enriched uranium may be made on a deferred basis. Such terms and conditions will include an obligation that the Community return to the United States Commission enriched uranium to the extent that there is default in payment. The Community will grant no rights to third parties that may be inconsistent with such obligation. The uranium supplied hereunder for use in reactors designed for production of electric power may be enriched up to twenty percent (20%) by weight in the isotope U-235. The United States Commission, however, may, upon request and in its discretion, make a portion of the foregoing enriched uranium available as material enriched up to ninety percent (90%) for use in materials testing reactors and research reactors, each capable of operating with a fuel load not to exceed eight (8) kilograms of contained U-235 in uranium, and as highly enriched material for use for research purposes.

C. It is agreed that the Community may distribute special nuclear material to authorized users in the Community; the Community will retain, pursuant to the Treaty establishing the European Atomic Energy Community, title to any special nuclear material which is purchased from the United States Commission.

D. The United States Commission is prepared to perform while such services are available from the Commission to its licensees in the United

States, and on terms and conditions to be agreed, chemical reprocessing services with respect to any source or special nuclear material received by the Community from the United States under this program. It is agreed that such reprocessing will be performed at established United States domestic prices in effect upon delivery of such material. It is understood except as may be otherwise agreed, that the form and content of any irradiated fuel elements shall not be altered after their removal from reactors and prior to delivery to the United States Commission or to other facilities. Special nuclear material and other material recoverable from material returned to the United States for reprocessing will be returned to the Community unless otherwise agreed. It is anticipated that any withdrawal by the United States Commission of chemical reprocessing services will be based upon the availability of commercial facilities to meet requirements for such services at reasonable prices, including the requirements of projects in the joint program. The United States Commission will give written notice to the Community of non-availability of its chemical reprocessing services twelve (12) months prior to such non-availability.

E. With respect to any special nuclear material produced in reactors fueled with materials obtained from the United States under this Agreement which is in excess of the need of the Community for such material for the peaceful uses of atomic energy, the International Atomic Energy Agency is granted the right of first option to purchase such material at the announced fuel value price in effect in the United States at the time of purchase. In the event this option is not exercised by the International Atomic Energy Agency, the Government of the United States of America is prepared to purchase such material at the United States announced fuel value price in effect at the time of purchase. However, with respect to plutonium produced in any reactor constructed under the joint program, no purchase commitment shall extent for a period beyond ten (10) years of operation of such reactor, or December 31, 1973 (or December 31, 1975, for not more than two reactors selected under Article I, A), whichever is earlier. Extension of such period will be the subject of negotiation on the request of either Party.

ARTICLE IV

The United States Commission will assist the EURATOM Commission in obtaining reactor materials other than special nuclear material from private organizations located in the United States if the EURATOM Commission desires such assistance. If no commercial sources are available, specific arrangements may be made by the Parties, from time to time, under terms and conditions to be agreed, for the transfer of such materials.

ARTICLE V

Persons under the jurisdiction of the Government of the United States of America or within the Community will be permitted to make arrangements to transfer and export material, including equipment and devices, to, and perform services for, the other Party and such persons under the jurisdiction of the Government of the United States of America or within the Community (as the case may be) as are authorized by the appropriate Party to receive and possess such material and utilize such services, subject to applicable laws, directives, regulations and license requirements of the Government of the United States of America, the Community and the Member States of the Community.

ARTICLE VI

A. 1. Under mutually agreed arrangements, all non-patentable information developed in connection with the joint program of research and development, and all non-patentable information developed in connection with the selected projects, concerning designs, plans and specifications, construction costs, operations and economics, will be delivered currently to the Parties as developed and may be used, disseminated, or published by each Party for any and all purposes as it sees fit without further obligation or payment. There will be no discrimination in the dissemination or use of such information for the reason that the proposed recipient or user is a national of the United States or of any Member State of the Community.

2. Both Parties shall have access to the records of the participating contractors pertaining to their participation in research and development projects under the joint research and development program, or pertaining to the performance of fuel elements that are the subject of United States guarantees.

B. The United States Commission and the EURATOM Commission shall also exchange other unclassified information in fields related to the peaceful uses of atomic energy to further the joint program. Such exchange of information shall include technical advice in the design and construction of future reprocessing plants which the Community may decide to design and construct or sponsor.

C. The Parties will expedite prompt exchange of information through symposia, exchange of personnel, setting up of combined teams, and other methods as may be mutually agreed.

D. Except as otherwise agreed, the application or use of any information (including designs, drawings and specifications) and any material, equipment, and devices, exchanged or transferred between the Parties under this Agreement, shall be the responsibility of the Party receiving it, and the other Party does not warrant the accuracy or completeness of such information, nor the suitability of such information, materials, equipment, and devices for any particular use or application.

ARTICLE VII

A. As to any invention made or conceived in the course of or under the joint program of research and development:

1. The Government of the United States of America shall without further obligation or payment be entitled to assignment of the title and rights in and to the invention and the patents in the United States subject to a non-exclusive, irrevocable, and royalty-free license, with the right to grant sublicenses, to the Community for all purposes.

2. The Community shall without further obligation or payment be entitled to assignment of the title and rights in and to the invention and the patents in the Community subject to a non-exclusive, irrevocable, and royalty-free license, with the right to grant sublicenses, to the Government of the United States of America for all purposes.

3. With respect to title and rights in and to the invention and patents in third countries:

a. The Government of the United States of America, if the invention is made or conceived within the United States, or the Community, if the invention is made or conceived within the Community, shall be entitled to assignment of such title and rights, subject to a non-exclusive, irrevocable, and royalty-free license, with the right to grant sublicenses, to the other Party for all purposes.

b. If the invention is made or conceived elsewhere, the Party contracting for the work shall be entitled to assignment of such title and rights, subject to a non-exclusive, irrevocable and royalty-free license, with the right to grant sublicenses, to the other Party for all purposes.

B. As to inventions and patents under paragraph A of this Article neither Party shall discriminate in the granting of any license or sublicense for the reason that the proposed licensee or sublicensee is a national of the United States or of any Member State of the Community.

C. As to patents used in the work of the joint program, other than those under paragraph A, which the Government of the United States of America owns or as to which it has the right to grant licenses or sublicenses, the Government of the United States of America will agree to grant licenses or sublicenses, covering use either in or outside the joint program, on a non-discriminatory basis to a Member State and to industry of a Member State, if the Member State has agreed to grant licenses or sublicenses as to patents used in the work of the joint program which it owns or as to which it has the right to grant licenses or sublicenses, on a non-discriminatory basis to the Government of the United States of America and to industry of the United States, covering use either in or outside the joint program.

D. The respective contractual arrangements of the Parties with third parties shall contain provisions that will enable each Party to effectuate the provisions of paragraphs A and B of this Article as to patentable information.

E. It is recognized that detailed procedures shall be jointly established to effectuate the foregoing provisions and that all situations not covered shall be settled by mutual agreement governed by the basic principle of equivalent benefits to both Parties.

ARTICLE VIII

The United States Commission and the EURATOM Commission will work closely together to develop training programs to satisfy requirements of the joint program. The Parties may under mutually agreeable terms and conditions make available their facilities for use by the other, including facilities to satisfy training needs.

ARTICLE IX

The Government of the United States of America and the Community recognize that adequate measures to protect equipment manufacturers and other suppliers as well as the participating utilities against now uninsurable risks are necessary to the implementation of the joint program. The EURATOM Commission will seek to develop and to secure the adoption, by the earliest practicable date, of suitable measures which will provide adequate financial protection against third party liability. Such measures could involve suitable indemnification guarantees, national legislation, international convention, or a combination of such measures.

ARTICLE X

The EURATOM Commission will take all action open to it under the Treaty establishing the European Atomic Energy Community to minimize the impact of customs duties on goods and products imported under the joint program.

ARTICLE XI

The Community guarantees that:

1. No material, including equipment and devices, transferred pursuant to this Agreement to the Community or to persons within the Community,

will be used for atomic weapons, or for research on or development of atomic weapons, or for any other military purpose;

2. No such material will be transferred to unauthorized persons or beyond the control of the Community, except as the Government of the United States of America may agree to such transfer and then only if the transfer of the material is within the scope of an Agreement for Cooperation between the Government of the United States of America and another nation or group of nations;

3. No source or special nuclear material utilized in, recovered from, or produced as a result of the use of materials, equipment or devices transferred pursuant to this Agreement to the Community or to persons within the Community will be used for atomic weapons, or for research on or development of atomic weapons, or for any other military purpose;

4. The Community will establish and maintain a mutually satisfactory system of safeguards and control as provided in Article XII, to be applied to materials, equipment and devices subject to the guarantees set forth in paragraphs 1 through 3 of this Article.

ARTICLE XII

A. The Community undertakes the responsibility for establishing and implementing a safeguards and control system designed to give maximum assurance that any material, equipment or devices made available pursuant to this Agreement and any source or special nuclear material derived from the use of such material, equipment and devices, shall be utilized solely for peaceful purposes. In establishing and implementing its safeguards and control system, the Community is prepared to consult with and exchange experiences with the International Atomic Energy Agency with the objective of establishing a system reasonably compatible with that of the International Atomic Energy Agency. The Government of the United States of America and the Community agree that the principles which will govern the establishment and operation by the Community of a mutually satisfactory safeguards and control system under this Agreement are those which are set forth in Annex 'B' to this Agreement. The Community shall be responsible for establishing and maintaining a mutually satisfactory and effective safeguards and control system which is in accord with the principles set forth in Annex 'B' to this Agreement.

B. As has been requested by the Community, the Government of the United States of America will provide assistance in establishing the Community's safeguards and control system, and will provide continuing assistance in the operation of the system.

C. The Parties agree that there will be frequent consultations and exchanges of visits between the Parties to give assurance to both Parties that the Community's safeguards and control system effectively meets the responsibility and principles stated in paragraph A of this Article and that the standards of the materials accountability systems of the Government of the United States of America and the Community are kept reasonably comparable.

D. In recognition of the importance of the International Atomic Energy Agency, the Government of the United States of America and the Community will consult with each other from time to time to determine whether there are any areas of responsibility with regard to safeguards and control and matters relating to health and safety in which the Agency might be asked to assist.

E. It is understood by the Parties that a continuation of the cooperative program between the Government of the United States of America and the Community will be contingent upon the Community's establishing and maintaining a mutually satisfactory and effective safeguards and control system which is in accord with the principles set forth in Annex 'B' to this Agreement.

ARTICLE XIII

The Government of the United States of America and the Community reaffirm their common interest in fostering the peaceful applications of atomic energy through the International Atomic Energy Agency and intend that the results of the joint program will benefit the Agency and the nations participating in it.

ARTICLE XIV

A. The Parties anticipate that from time to time they may enter into further agreements providing for cooperation in the peaceful aspects of atomic energy.

B. Article 106 of the Treaty establishing the European Atomic Energy Community contemplates that Member States which before the date of entry into force of that Treaty have concluded agreements with third countries for cooperation in the field of nuclear energy shall jointly with the EURATOM Commission enter into the necessary negotiations with third countries in order as far as possible to cause the rights and obligations arising out of such agreements to be assumed by the Community. The Government of the United States of America is prepared to enter into such negotiations with reference to any agreement to which it is a party.

C. Existing agreements for cooperation in the field of nuclear energy between Member States and the Government of the United States of America are not modified by the joint program. Modifications may be made as necessary by mutual agreement between the Member States concerned and the United States to permit transfers of reactor projects now contemplated under existing agreements that qualify for and are accepted under the joint program.

For the purposes of this Agreement:

(a) 'Person' means any individual, enterprise, corporation, partnership, firm, association, trust, estate, public or private institution, group, government agency, or government corporation, but does not include the Parties to this Agreement.

(b) 'Special nuclear material' means (1) plutonium, uranium enriched in the isotope 233 or in the isotope 235, and any other material which either Party determines to be special nuclear material; or (2) any material artificially enriched by any of the foregoing.

(c) 'Source material' means (1) uranium, thorium, or any other material which is determined by either Party to be source material; or (2) ores containing one or more of the foregoing materials, in such concentration as either Party may determine from time to time.

(d) 'Parties' means the Government of the United States of America, including the United States Atomic Energy Commission on behalf of the Government of the United States of America, and the European Atomic Energy Community (EURATOM), acting through its Commission. 'Party' means one of the Parties.

ARTICLE XVI

A. The Parties agree that the establishment and initiation of the joint program and the undertakings of the Parties under this Agreement are subject to appropriate statutory steps, including authorization by competent bodies of the Government of the United States of America and the Community, and the provisions of applicable laws, regulations and license requirements in effect in the United States and in the Community and within the Member States.

B. This Agreement shall enter into force on the day on which each Party shall have received from the other Party written notification that it has complied with all statutory and constitutional requirements for the entry into force of such Agreement and shall remain in force for a period of twenty-five (25) years.

In witness whereof, the undersigned representatives duly authorized thereto have signed this Agreement.

Done at Brussels on November 8, 1958, in duplicate, in the English, French, German, Italian, and Netherlands languages, each language being equally authentic.

For the Government of the United States of America:
Pour le Gouvernement des Etats-Unis d'Amerique:
Für die Regierung der Vereinigten Staaten von Amerika:
Per el Governo degli Stati Uniti d'America:
Voor de Regering van de Verenigde Staten van Amerika:

W. W. Butterworth

John A. McCone

For the European Atomic Energy Community (EURATOM):
Pour la Communaute Europeenne de l'Energie Atomique (EURATOM):
Für die Europäische Atomenergiegemeinschaft (EURATOM):
Per la Comunità Europea dell'Energia Atomica (EURATOM):
Voor de Europese Gemeenschap voor Atoomenergie (EURATOM):

L. Armand

Enrico Medi

Paul de Groote

Heinz L. Krekeler

Sassen

Annex 'A'

With the objective of assuring the success of the joint program, the United States Commission will offer guarantees designed to limit certain financial risks associated with the fuel cycle.

These guarantees will be extended in the form of maximum charges for fabrication of the fuel elements and minimum integrity of the fuel elements under irradiation. They will be offered only to the extent that equivalent or better guarantees are not available commercially.

The liability of the United States Commission under these guarantees will be limited to meeting guaranteed maximum charges for fabricated fuel elements and to the adjustment of charges for fabrication, chemical reprocessing, and transportation of fuel elements when required by failure to meet guaranteed integrity.

The guarantees will provide for equitable sharing of decreases in costs realized through fuel performance in excess of guaranteed levels, the United States share not to exceed costs experienced by the United States Commission under these guarantees.

The guarantees provided by the United States Commission will be applicable to all loadings made in reactors under the joint program during ten (10) years of operation or prior to December 31, 1973 (or December 31, 1975, for not more than two reactors selected under Article I, A, of this Agreement for Cooperation), whichever is earlier.

Annex 'B'

Principles for Establishing the Safeguards and Control System Under This Agreement

The principles which will govern the establishment and operation of the safeguards and control system are as follows:

The EURATOM Commission will:

1. Examine the design of equipment, devices and facilities, including nuclear reactors, and approve it for the purpose of assuring that it will not further any military purpose and that it will permit the effective application of safeguards, if such equipment, devices and facilities:

(a) are made available pursuant to this Agreement; or

(b) use, process or fabricate any of the following materials received from the United States: source or special nuclear material, moderator material or any other material relevant to the effective application of safeguards; or

(c) use any special nuclear material produced as the result of the use of equipment or material referred to in subparagraphs (a) and (b).

2. Require the maintenance and production of operating records to assure accountability for source or special nuclear material made available, or source or special nuclear material used, recovered, or produced as a result of the use of source or special nuclear material, moderator material or any other material relevant to the effective application of safeguards, or as a result of equipment, devices and facilities made available pursuant to this Agreement.

3. Require that progress reports be prepared and delivered to the EURATOM Commission with respect to projects utilizing material, equipment, devices and facilities referred to in paragraph 2 of this Annex.

4. Establish and require the deposit and storage, under continuing safeguards, in EURATOM facilities of any special nuclear material referred to in paragraph 2 of this Annex which is not currently being utilized for peaceful purposes in the Community or otherwise transferred as provided in the Agreement for Cooperation between the Government of the United States of America and the Community.

5. Establish an inspection organization which will have access at all times:

(a) to all places and data, and

(b) to any person who by reason of his occupation deals with materials, equipment, devices or facilities safeguarded under this Agreement, necessary to assure accounting for source or special nuclear material subject to paragraph 2 of this Annex and to determine whether there is compliance with the guarantees of the Community. The inspection organization will also be in a position to make and will make such independent measurements as are necessary to assure compliance with the provisions of this Annex and the Agreement for Cooperation.

It is the understanding of the Parties that the above principles applicable to the establishment of the Community's inspection and control system are compatible with and are based on Article XII of the Statute of the International Atomic Energy Agency, Chapter VII of Title Two of the Treaty establishing the European Atomic Energy Community, and those adopted by the Government of the United States of America in its comprehensive Agreements for Cooperation.

4. Franco-German communiqué following the meeting of General de Gaulle and Dr. Adenauer, Bad Kreuznach, 26 November 1958[1]

Poursuivant les entretiens qui ont eu lieu de 14 septembre 1958, à Colombey-les-Deux-Eglises, le général de Gaulle, président du conseil des ministres de la République française, et le Dr Konrad Adenauer, chancelier fédéral, se sont rencontrés à Bad-Kreuznach le 26 novembre 1958.

Les chefs de gouvernement étaient accompagnés des ministres des affaires étrangères, M. Maurice Couve de Murville et le Dr Heinrich von Brentano, ainsi que de M. Antoine Pinay, ministre des finances et des affaires économiques, du Pr Ludwig Erhard, ministre fédéral de l'économie, et de M. Franz Etzel, ministre fédéral des finances.

Les entretiens des deux chefs de gouvernement ont donné l'occasion de discuter, d'une manière approfondie et dans un esprit amical, un certain nombre de questions d'intérêt commun aux deux pays. L'évolution de la situation mondiale au cours des deux dernières semaines a également été examinée.

Les premières questions discutées ont été celles que posent l'entrée en vigueur du Marché commun et les récentes difficultés nées des discussions relatives à la création d'une zone de libre-échange.

Les chefs de gouvernement ont affirmé de nouveau leur volonté de poursuivre, en accord avec les gouvernements belge, italien, luxembourgeois et néerlandais, leur collaboration dans le domaine économique et dans le domaine politique.

Cette collaboration n'est nullement en contradiction avec le coopération de ces Etats européens dans le cadre de l'O.E.C.E., qu'il importe de maintenir et de développer.

Les deux chefs de gouvernement ont discuté des mesures qui pourraient être prises le 1er janvier 1959 à la suite de la mise en vigueur du Marché commun pour ce qui concerne les relations commerciales avec les autres pays, et en particulier avec les pays membres de l'O.E.C.E.

[1] *Le Monde,* 28 November 1958.

Ces mesures seront soumises à l'examen des autres membres de la Communauté économique européenne. Des suggestions communes leur seront également présentées pour l'étude d'une association multilatérale entre la Communauté économique européenne et les autres pays membres de l'O.E.C.E.

Parmi les questions politiques qui ont été examinées ensuite figure notamment la situation de Berlin. Les deux chefs de gouvernement ont confirmé l'importance qu'ils attachent à ce problème, c'est-à-dire au maintien du statut de Berlin tel qu'il est défini par les accords internationaux en vigueur et tel qu'il est garanti par les gouvernements de la France, des Etats-Unis et du Royaume-Uni, auxquels se sont associés les gouvernements des autres Etats membres de l'O.T.A.N.

Les entretiens prolongés auxquels a donné lieu la rencontre ont permis de constater de nouveau l'accord fondamental des deux gouvernements sur les grands problèmes internationaux et de souligner le prix qu'ils attachent à leur entente.

5. Decision adopted by the Council of the European Economic Community regarding relations with non-member countries, Brussels, 4 December 1958[1]

A. TARIFS

A la date du 1er janvier 1959, les six Etats membres réduiront de 10%, sur les produits industriels,[2] les droits de douane dont le taux est supérieur à celui du tarif extérieur commun, sans pour autant ramener ces droits à un taux inférieur à ce tarif.

Cette réduction tarifaire interviendra à l'égard des Etats membres de l'O.E.C.E., des Etats membres du G.A.T.T. ainsi que des Etats non membres du G.A.T.T. qui bénéficient de la clause de la nation la plus favorisée.

Cette réduction revêt un caractère provisoire et intervient pour une durée non déterminée.

Les Etats membres ne mettent pas comme condition à cette réduction tarifaire une réciprocité de la part des Etats tiers, mais ils accueilleraient avec satisfaction des gestes similaires de leur part.

N.B.—En ce qui concerne les produits pour lesquels le tarif extérieur commun n'est pas encore connu, ainsi que pour les produits de la Liste G, chaque Etat membre déterminera, en application des dispositions cidessus, la réduction éventuelle à opérer, après en avoir informé la Commission.

[1] *Chronique de Politique Etrangère*, vol. XII, No. 5–6, pp. 747–8.
[2] A l'exclusion des produits relevant de la C.E.C.A. et des produits pour lesquels la réduction ne s'applique pas entre les six Etats membres en vertu des dispositions du Traité de Rome [footnote in original].

B. Contingents

1. Sous réserve de réciprocité, les Etats membres de la Communauté feront bénéficier, pour les produits industriels, leurs partenaires de l'O.E.C.E. d'une augmentation des contingents subsistant au-delà du niveau de libération réalisé en application des décisions du Conseil de l'O.E.C.E. en date du 14 janvier 1955.

Cette augmentation portera sur 20% de la valeur totale des contingents ouverts, par chaque pays à chacun des autres partenaires (contingents normaux et faibles).

Dans le cadre de cette augmentation, une augmentation de 10% sera nécessairement opérée pour chaque contingent.

La deuxième tranche de 10% ne s'appliquera pas nécessairement à chacun des contingents, mais pourra être affectée à tous produits qui intéressent plus particulièrement les pays en cause et notamment ceux qui font l'objet de contingents faibles ou nuls.

Les dispositions ci-dessus seront notifiées au Conseil de l'O.E.C.E. Les Etats membres de la C.E.E. seraient d'accord pour que celui-ci en discute si les autres Etats membres de l'O.E.C.E. le désireraient.

2. Le Conseil a pris acte en outre d'une déclaration du Gouvernement français suivant laquelle celui-ci, en dehors des mesures sub 1) ci-dessus, se propose de porter à la date du 1er janvier 1959 ses mesures de libération dans le cadre de l'O.E.C.E. à 40% de ses importations. Pour la tranche se situant entre ces 40% et les 82% de libération antérieurement atteint, la France procédera à une augmentation de 20%.

C. Produits agricoles

Pour ces produits, compte tenu du caractère particulier de la production agricole, les Etats membres procèderont à une réduction de 10% des droits de douane dans les mêmes conditions que pour les produits industriels, au moins pour les produits non libérés.

D. Mesures d'application

Les mesures d'application des dispositions ci-dessus seront prises par chaque Etat membre dans les délais les plus rapides.

Le principe de la réciprocité étant admis, les négociations bilatérales devraient comporter une certaine coordination par l'intermédiaire de la Commission.

6. Report to the Chairman of the Council of O.E.E.C. by the Chairman of the Inter-Governmental Committee on the establishment of a Free Trade Area, Paris, 12 December 1958[1]

The Inter-Governmental Committee was established by Resolution C(57)221 of the Council dated 17th October, 1957. The text of this Resolution is as follows:

The Council

Having met at Ministerial level, considered the progress achieved hitherto and having taken account of the aims of the Organisation, of the interests of its individual Member countries and of the need to find means of reinforcing the economic solidarity of the Member countries of the O.E.E.C.;

Declares its determination to secure the establishment of a European Free Trade Area which would comprise all Member countries of the Organisation, which would associate, on a multi-lateral basis, the European Economic Community with the other Member countries, and which, taking fully into consideration the objectives of the European Economic Community, would in practice take effect parallel with the Treaty of Rome;

Declares, also, its determination to reach agreement at the same time on methods of further co-operation between all Member countries in agricultural matters with a view to ensuring the expansion of trade in agricultural products;

Declares, equally, its determination in the establishment of the European Free Trade Area to take full account of the interests of the economically less developed Member countries in the light of the reports by the Chairman of Working Party No. 23;

Decides, to these ends, to convene forthwith an Inter-Governmental Committee at Ministerial level.

2. It is now apparent that the Committee has been unable to secure the establishment of a European Free Trade Area, which would, in practice, take effect parallel with the Treaty of Rome. It is therefore my duty, in accordance with our terms of reference as a Committee, to inform you, as Chairman of the Council, of this fact.

3. I have asked the Secretariat to prepare a report on the progress we have made, and this is attached to my Report.

4. We shall all have to explain to our national Parliaments what has taken place during the negotiations. This cannot be done adequately without the declassification of the relevant documents a list of which is attached to the Secretary-General's note. I propose that in particular the following documents be de-restricted:

[1] Cmnd. 641, pp. 1–3.

The Report by the Secretariat (attached).

The Annotated Agenda [CIG(57)1].

The Papers on Agriculture [CIG(58)4, 25, 47 and 62].

The Memorandum of the Six [CIG(58)60].

The Reports on Origin from the Trade Experts and the Steering Board [CIG(58)12, 33, 35, 44 and 57].

The Chairman's Proposals on External Commercial Policy [CIG(58)29 and 69].

The United Kingdom Paper on Institutions [CIG(58)61].

The Managing Board's Reports [CIG(58)1 and 41].

The United Kingdom's Compromise Proposals on Harmonisation of Social Policies [CIG(58)7].

THE WORK OF THE INTER-GOVERNMENTAL COMMITTEE ON
THE ESTABLISHMENT OF A EUROPEAN FREE TRADE AREA
(Note by the Secretariat)

1. It was in July, 1956, that the Council of O.E.E.C. decided to establish a Working Party to 'study the possible forms and methods of association, on a multilateral basis, between the proposed Customs Union [of the Six] and Member countries not taking part therein'.[1] As a possible method of association, the Working Party was to consider the creation of a Free Trade Area which would include the Customs Union and these Member countries. In its Report, published in January, 1957, the Working Party concluded that 'it is possible to conceive of a system which takes account of the characteristics of a Free Trade Area and which would ensure satisfactory operation of the latter'.[2]

2. This Report was considered by the Council in February, 1957, together with a memorandum by the United Kingdom Government [C(57)27], and the Council then decided [C(57)30] to continue the discussion further and to organise negotiations between the Governments. These discussions and negotiations took place in a number of Working Parties which were specially created for the purpose. The Chairmen of the principal Working Parties reported to the Council in July, 1957 [FTA(57)51; FTB(57)7; FTC(57)1 and 2] and these reports, together with a Memorandum by the Chairman of the Council [C(57)168], were considered by the Council in October. The Council then decided [17th October—C(57)221 and 222] to set up the Inter-Governmental Committee.

3. This Committee, which has been assisted by a large number of other bodies, of which a list is given in Annex II, has held nine sessions extending

---

[1] Cmnd. 641, p. 7 (C(56)196).

[2] The Report on the possibility of creating a Free Trade Area in Europe, prepared for the Council of O.E.E.C., published January 1957.

over twenty-three days. It began its work on the basis of a Joint Note by the Governments of the Six [CES/7.117] and an Annotated Agenda prepared by its Chairman [CIG(57)1]. At an early stage of its deliberations, the Six Member States of the European Economic Community decided to present a paper setting forth their common views on the questions under discussion. A paper by the Six on agricultural questions [CIG(58)47] was presented on 25th July, 1958, and considered by the Committee in the same month. A further paper, covering other questions [CIG(58)60], was presented on 20th October, 1958, and considered by the Committee at the end of that month and again in the middle of November.

4. Summaries of the results achieved by the Committee up to 7th October, 1958, have been prepared by the Secretariat [CIG(58)54 and 56]. These show that, subject to agreement being reached on the main issues, a wide measure of agreement seems to have been achieved on a number of questions such as, for example, the methods whereby tariffs and quotas could be gradually eliminated within a Free Trade Area, the rules regarding the right of establishment, rules for freeing movements of capital and permitting the international exchange of services, transport problems, and rules relating to restrictive business practices and state aid. At the same time, progress has been made, and differences between national points of view have been reduced, on a number of other questions. These include: agriculture, movements of workers, the inclusion of coal and steel in a Free Trade Area, trade in products used in the production of nuclear energy, and the special arrangements required for countries in the process of economic development.

5. The Inter-Governmental Committee and the various other bodies listed in Annex II have thus made some progress; but the agreement or near-agreement reached on the points mentioned above has always been conditional upon agreement being reached on certain more fundamental issues, and this has so far proved to be impossible to achieve. These issues may be conveniently summarised in three groups:

(a) external tariffs and external commercial policy—this includes the principal aspects of the problems of definition of origin and the relations between the Free Trade Area and the preferential trading system of the Commonwealth;

(b) the harmonization and co-ordination of internal economic and social policies; and

(c) the institutional system and voting rules, including the rules which should apply to the use of escape clauses.

6. Some compromise proposals have been made from time to time in regard to the first of these issues. There were, for example, proposals for introducing a difference between the timing of the transition period for

the Free Trade Area and that established for the transition period of the Common Market. In the same context, it has been proposed that the arrangements for the passage from the first to the second stage of this period should, for the Free Trade Area, be different from those laid down for the Common Market; this could involve differing treatment for imports under the two systems. Again, the proposals which bear the name of Signor Carli were put forward. They had, as their principal feature, the institution of a special system of internal taxes designed to offset differences between Members (in tariff and other matters) and thereby to provide an incentive for harmonization. Suggestions have also been made for instituting different systems of defining origin for different products or groups of products. These proposals, some of which have not yet been fully investigated, have not provided the basis for a compromise. It is not to be inferred from this survey of an uncompleted task that a multilateral association between the Community of the Six and the rest of Western Europe is impossible.

7. Report on the course of negotiations for a European Free Trade Area, up to December 1958[1]

1. This Command Paper describes the history up to the end of 1958 of the negotiations to establish a European free trade area.

2. For an understanding of the circumstances in which these negotiations started reference may be made to the following:—

(a) the statements made by the Chancellor of the Exchequer (Mr. Macmillan) and by the President of the Board of Trade (Mr. Thorneycroft) during the debate in the House of Commons on 26th November, 1956;[2]

(b) the Report on the possibility of creating a free trade area in Europe prepared for the Council of the Organisation for European Economic Co-operation (O.E.E.C.) by a special working party;

(c) the United Kingdom Memorandum to the O.E.E.C. of February, 1957.[3]

The principal documents, other than the above, relating to the negotiations are reproduced in a separate Command Paper[4] which is being presented simultaneously to Parliament.

I

3. Six Member countries of the O.E.E.C.—Belgium, France, Germany, Italy, Luxembourg and the Netherlands—had already in 1951 signed a Treaty establishing the European Coal and Steel Community. In 1956 the

---

[1] Cmnd. 648. [2] H.C. Deb., vol. 561, coll. 35–54 and 154–64.
[3] See *Documents* for 1957, pp. 433–41 (Cmnd. 72). [4] Cmnd. 641.

idea that the customs union then under discussion and since established by the six countries might be accompanied by free trade area arrangements with certain other countries was put forward in the Report to the Foreign Ministers of the Six, dated 21st April of that year, by a group of their officials under the chairmanship of M. Spaak, then Belgian Minister for Foreign Affairs. This Report was the basis of the negotiations which led up to the Treaties of Rome.

4. The Council of the O.E.E.C., in July, 1956, decided[1] to 'study the possible forms and methods of association, on a multilateral basis, between the proposed Customs Union and Member countries not taking part therein', and set up a working party under the chairmanship of Baron Snoy (Belgium) to do this.

5. This working party, on which all the seventeen Member countries of O.E.E.C. were represented, concluded in its report published in January, 1957, that it was technically possible to operate a free trade area in Europe which would include the customs and economic union of the Six.

6. Her Majesty's Government had for some time been considering these developments in Europe. The Chancellor of the Exchequer (Mr. Macmillan) and the President of the Board of Trade (Mr. Thorneycroft) had discussed the subject with Commonwealth Finance Ministers at the time of the annual meetings of the International Bank and the International Monetary Fund in September, 1956. Thereafter the Government continued to maintain the fullest and closest consultation with other Commonwealth Governments.

7. In the course of a debate in the House of Commons on 26th November, 1956,[2] the Government explained the conclusion which they had reached: that it was desirable and consistent both with their Commonwealth relationships and with their other international obligations to enter into negotiations for the establishment of an industrial free trade area in Europe. Subsequently their general attitude on some of the questions on which broad decisions of principle needed to be taken, in order that negotiations might proceed, was described in a memorandum circulated to O.E.E.C. on 7th February, 1957.[3]

8. The O.E.E.C. Council met at Ministerial level on 12th/13th February, 1957, to consider the report of Baron Snoy's working party. A resolution[4] was unanimously adopted stating that the Council:

'Decides to enter into negotiations in order to determine ways and means on the basis of which there could be brought into being a European Free Trade Area, which would, on a multilateral basis, associate the European Common Market with other Member countries of the Organisation, and to prepare the necessary instruments. It draws special

---

[1] Cmnd. 641, p. 7 (C(56)196). [2] See para. 2a, above.
[3] See para. 2c, above. [4] See ibid., pp. 7–8 (C(57)30).

attention to the objective of finding ways to ensure the expansion of trade in agricultural products on a non-discriminatory basis between all member countries of the Organisation. It also draws attention to the need to deal with the special situation of Member countries in the course of economic development.'

9. At a further Council meeting on 8th March three working parties were set up.[1] The first was to determine the conditions under which a European free trade area could be brought into being. The second was to deal with trade in agricultural products. The third was to examine the cases of certain member countries who declared that the state of their economic development would not allow them to accept the general obligations of a European free trade area, and to examine the conditions in which they could take part in or be associated with the free trade area.

10. The Six countries had meanwhile been completing their negotiations for a customs and economic union. The Treaties establishing the European Economic Community and the European Atomic Energy Community were signed in Rome on 25th March, 1957.

11. Her Majesty's Government welcomed the signing of these treaties and opened discussions with the French and German Governments in order to secure the speediest possible development of the free trade area project.

12. This question, among others, was discussed during a meeting in Paris between the Prime Minister (Mr. Macmillan) and the French Prime Minister (M. Mollet) on 9th March, 1957. It was announced in a communiqué issued after this meeting that:

'Questions arising out of the Customs and Economic Union on the one hand, and the proposed Free Trade Area on the other, were discussed, in particular the problems resulting from the decision of the Brussels Conference to associate overseas territories within the Customs Union. While recognising that there were differences between the concept of the Customs Union and that of the Free Trade Area, Ministers agreed that both were of great importance in order to maintain the economic unity of Western Europe as a whole. They agreed that the objective of both was the expansion of world trade, not the creation of a protective grouping. They decided that there should be further detailed study and discussions of these problems between experts.'[2]

13. On 6th May, 1957, the Minister of State for Foreign Affairs in the French Government (M. Maurice Faure), visited London for discussions with the Chancellor of the Exchequer (Mr. Thorneycroft) as Chairman of the O.E.E.C. Council. It was announced at the time that:—

[1] Ibid., pp. 8–9 (C(57)42).
[2] For the text of the communiqué, see *Documents* for 1957, pp. 377–8.

'The meeting discussed the stage now reached in the negotiations for the European Common Market and the Free Trade Area. The United Kingdom representatives welcomed the signature of the Treaty of Rome and emphasised the importance which they attached to its ratification. The French representatives on their side emphasised their support for the association in a Free Trade Area of the United Kingdom and other countries of the O.E.E.C. with the European Economic Community.

There. was a satisfactory exchange of views and it was agreed that the two Governments would do what they could to ensure that the negotiations in the O.E.E.C. for the creation of the Free Trade Area should be carried forward to a satisfactory conclusion.'

14. On 8th May, 1957, the Prime Minister had talks with the Chancellor of the Federal Republic of Germany at Bonn. It was stated in the communiqué issued after the meeting that:—

'The British Government welcomes the treaties signed in Rome on 25th March as a further step towards a united Europe and a contribution to strengthening the European economy. Both Heads of Government agreed that the interests of Europe would best be served by the early ratification of the Rome Treaties. They further agreed that it was necessary to establish as soon as possible a Free Trade Area as a complement to the Common Market. They therefore resolved to do all in their power to ensure that the negotiations to this end are carried forward with a view to their successful conclusion at the appropriate time.'[1]

15. At the meeting on 6th May a request was made by the French Government for a delay in the free trade area negotiations until there had been substantial progress with the ratification of the Treaties of Rome. This request was supported by the German Government at the meeting on 8th May. Her Majesty's Government agreed to the proposed delay, while reiterating the importance they attached to bringing the free trade area negotiations to an early and successful conclusion.

16. The Chancellor of the Exchequer (Mr. Thorneycroft), as Chairman of the O.E.E.C. Council, thereupon arranged that the Chairmen of the three working parties should prepare personal reports on the progress made since they had been set up in March. These were to provide a basis for discussion when negotiations were restarted in the Autumn. These reports[2] were submitted in July, 1957, and showed that much useful preparatory work had been done. The Chancellor circulated them with a memorandum[3] of the points which needed immediate consideration by Governments.

[1] For the text of the communiqué, see *Documents* for 1957, pp. 386–7.
[2] Cmnd. 641, pp. 10–22, 22–29, and 30–38 (FTA(57)51, FTB(57)7, FTC(57)1).
[3] Ibid., pp. 42–44 (C(57)168).

17. When the Council met again on 17th October, 1957, a resolution was unanimously passed declaring the Council's

'determination to secure the establishment of a European Free Trade Area which would comprise all Member countries of the Organisation; which would associate, on a multilateral basis, the European Economic Community with the other Member countries; and which, taking fully into consideration the objectives of the European Economic Community, would in practice take effect parallel with the Treaty of Rome.'[1]

The Council also decided to establish an Inter-Governmental Committee at Ministerial level,[2] on which all seventeen member countries of O.E.E.C. were represented, to carry on the negotiations. There was agreement that the negotiations should be pressed forward so that the free trade area could be established in time for the first steps in the removal of tariffs and quotas to be taken on 1st January, 1959, simultaneously with the first measures to reduce tariffs and quantitative restrictions in the European Economic Community.

18. The Inter-Governmental Committee held its first meeting on the following day, with the Paymaster General (Mr. Maudling) in the Chair. The Paymaster General undertook to prepare a paper on the basis of which the Committee could discuss the substantive problems with which they had to deal. He circulated this paper to the Committee on 30th October, 1957, in the form of an annotated agenda[3] covering the wide range of subjects to be dealt with in the course of the negotiations.

19. The Inter-Governmental Committee met at frequent intervals until the end of March 1958. It began by working through all the subjects listed in the Chairman's annotated agenda, with the object of reaching agreement on as many of them as possible. It was understood that all expressions of readiness to accept particular points were provisional in the sense that no country would be finally committed on any point until agreement had been reached over the whole field.

20. The range of subjects under discussion had by this time been greatly enlarged beyond the original concept, which had been related primarily to the elimination of tariffs and quantitative restrictions. Throughout the second half of 1957, including the period when negotiations at the political level were suspended, experts had continued to examine the technical and trade policy aspects of the free trade area. Several important documents emerged from these discussions, in particular a comprehensive report to the Inter-Governmental Committee on the problems of defining the origin of the goods to benefit from the tariff reductions and of avoiding trade deflections resulting from differences in external tariffs.[4] Other subjects

[1] Ibid., pp. 48–49 (C(57)221). [2] Ibid., pp. 49–50 (C(57)222).
[3] Ibid., pp. 50–59 (CIG(57)1).
[4] Ibid., pp. 104–47 (CIG(58)12 and Annexes).

which were discussed up till March 1958 either in the Inter-Governmental Committee or in working parties or groups reporting to it included:— the length and stages of the transitional period, the removal of quantitative import restrictions, rules for the reduction of tariffs, rules for administering the definition of origin, rules of competition, agriculture and fisheries, co-ordination of economic policy, harmonisation of legislation, payments questions, coal and steel, nuclear materials, invisibles and capital movements, movement of workers, freedom of establishment, inland transport and transport charges, and the problems of the less developed countries. In addition the Inter-Governmental Committee had preliminary discussions on escape clauses and institutions and looked briefly at the position of overseas territories associated with O.E.E.C. countries. All countries concerned actively participated in the work of the Committee.

21. Although coal and steel and nuclear materials fell within the competence of the European Coal and Steel Community and the European Atomic Energy Community, and not of the European Economic Community, it was agreed at an early stage that they should be included among the subjects to be dealt with in the free trade area negotiations.

22. As regards trade in agricultural products, a statement[1] was made on behalf of the United Kingdom at the O.E.E.C. Council meeting on 17th October, 1957. The ideas set out in this statement formed the basis of more detailed proposals[2] which the Paymaster General later circulated.

23. On 15th January, 1958, the French Government, who had already indicated the difficulties which they feared in a free trade area of the type under discussion, announced their intention of preparing an alternative approach. The members of the European Economic Community subsequently agreed that any proposals to the Inter-Governmental Committee arising from this plan should take the form of a joint memorandum by the Community.

24. At the meeting of the Inter-Governmental Committee in March, 1958, the Italian Minister for Foreign Trade (Signor Carli) made a proposal for a comprehensive solution to the difficulties arising from differences in external tariffs. This proposal was the subject of detailed examination by experts.[3]

25. It had become increasingly clear during successive meetings of the Inter-Governmental Committee that little further progress could be made on the main issues of principle until the memorandum by the European Economic Community had been circulated. In consequence a meeting of the Committee which had been fixed for 2nd May, 1958, was cancelled at

---

[1] The text of this statement was circulated in H.C. Deb., vol. 575, coll. 27–29, by the Prime Minister in answer to a parliamentary question on 29 October 1957.

[2] Cmnd. 641, pp. 190–6 (CIG(58)4).

[3] Ibid., pp. 147–9, 149–52, 153–63, 163–4, 165–75 (CIG(58)27, 30, 33 and 35, and SBR(58)6).

the request of the Council of Ministers of the Community. On 23rd May a pause in the negotiations in the Inter-Governmental Committee was agreed to in view of the French constitutional crisis, though technical studies continued at the official level.

26. The Inter-Governmental Committee resumed its activities with a further series of meetings on 24th–25th July, 23rd–24th and 28th–30th October and 13th–14th November, 1958. The fundamental issues which had emerged from the technical studies at official level, and which required decisions by the Inter-Governmental Committee to enable further progress to be made, were:—the principles for establishing what goods, partly derived from third countries' materials or components, would be entitled to free trade area treatment ('origin problems'), the means for preventing deflections of trade as a result of differences in external tariffs, arrangements about commercial policy towards third countries, harmonisation of social policies, the nature, functions and voting procedures of the institutions, and the conditions on which countries could escape or be excused from their obligations under the Convention. The question of agriculture was discussed further on the basis of the papers circulated by the United Kingdom, Switzerland, the European Economic Community and the Scandinavian countries[1]; here the problem was to secure reasonable reciprocity, from the point of view both of importers and exporters, between agricultural exporting countries and industrial exporting countries.

27. The Memorandum[2] setting out the agreed views of the European Economic Community (paragraph 23 above) was circulated on 20th October. In this Memorandum the Community reaffirmed that it was determined, both for economic and political reasons, to arrive at an agreement which would make it possible to associate with the Community, on a multilateral basis, the other members of the O.E.E.C. in a European Economic Association to come into force on 1st January, 1959. The Memorandum set out in some detail the Community's views on most of the important issues to be dealt with in the course of the negotiations. Discussion proceeded on these subjects but without reaching decisions on the major issues. The Progress Report[3] by the Secretariat of the O.E.E.C. records in detail the development of discussion on all these subjects. New procedures, involving detailed examination, sector by sector, of origin and related problems were agreed upon at the October meetings to facilitate decisions on these matters by 31st December, 1958.

28. The latest meeting of the Inter-Governmental Committee was held on 13th–14th November, 1958. On 14th November an announcement was

---

[1] Ibid., pp. 190–6, 196–8, 199–204, 204–6 (CIG(58)4, 25, 47 and 62).
[2] Ibid., pp. 96–104 (CIG(58)60), the so-called Ockrent Report.
[3] Ibid., pp. 59–96 (C(58)287).

made to the Press on behalf of the French Government that it did not seem possible to them to establish the free trade area as it had been proposed and that they were looking for a new solution. As the Paymaster General informed Parliament on 17th November, 1958,[1] the further meetings in Paris which had been arranged could not take place in these circumstances, because the whole basis on which the Inter-Governmental Committee had been operating, namely the unanimous determination of all Governments to secure the establishment of a free trade area, seemed to have been brought into question.

29. Accordingly the Paymaster General, as Chairman of the Inter-Governmental Committee, submitted to the Chairman of the O.E.E.C. Council on 12th December, 1958, a Report[2] to which was attached a Note by the Secretariat summarising the progress made by the Committee. In his Report the Paymaster General said that the Committee had been unable to secure the establishment of a European free trade area to take effect parallel with the Treaty of Rome.

30. In these circumstances the Council of O.E.E.C., at its meeting on 15th December, considered the immediate problems which would arise between members of O.E.E.C. in view of the fact that no free trade area would be in existence when the provisions of the Treaty of Rome, as regards tariffs and quotas, came to be implemented on 1st January, 1959.

31. Throughout the negotiations recorded in the preceding paragraphs there was continuous transmission of information and frequent exchange of views between Her Majesty's Government and other Commonwealth Governments. The negotiations were discussed at a series of Commonwealth conferences. The first of these was the Commonwealth Prime Ministers Conference in London in June–July 1957. Following this meeting a conference of senior Commonwealth officials on 8th–9th July, 1957, was devoted to discussion of the whole free trade area project in detail. Subsequent developments formed the subject of discussion at the Commonwealth Finance Ministers' Meeting at Mont Tremblant in September, 1957, at the Second Preparatory Meeting of officials for the Commonwealth Trade and Economic Conference in June, 1958, and at the Commonwealth Trade and Economic Conference itself at Montreal in September, 1958. It was stated in the agreed Report of the Montreal Conference[3] that:—

'It is our conviction that an outward-looking Free Trade Area, in which trade would be increased rather than merely re-channelled, would contribute to the objective of an expanding world economy. It is our hope that closer economic association in Europe will not be per-

---

[1] H.C. Deb., vol. 595, coll. 845–6.   [2] Cmnd. 641, pp. 1–6 (C(58)267).
[3] Cmnd. 539, para. 6; see also para. 10.

mitted to result in a contraction of trading opportunities or in an extension of protection.'

II

32. The United Kingdom Memorandum of February, 1957,[1] set out Her Majesty's Government's general attitude to the proposal for a free trade area at the time when serious negotiations were first in immediate prospect. Since then there have been important developments in this original attitude during the course of negotiation.

33. Two years ago Her Majesty's Government's concept of a free trade area related primarily to the removal of barriers to trade in industrial goods within Europe. The scope of the project was limited to what was needed to carry out this objective—the removal of tariffs and quantitative import restrictions, and the formulation of rules and procedures to prevent the frustration of the objective by other forms of Government intervention or by restrictive business practices.

34. In the rest of the economic field Her Majesty's Government recognised the great and continuing importance of extended co-operation, for political as much as economic reasons, but believed that this could be achieved best through the existing procedures of O.E.E.C. More particularly in relation to foodstuffs, which they proposed should be excluded from the free trade area, Her Majesty's Government expressed their intention to continue to play a full part in the work of the Ministerial Food and Agriculture Committee and other organs of O.E.E.C. concerned with trade in agricultural products.

35. It proved to be the general wish of the participating countries that the scope of negotiations should cover the whole range of these subjects—so embracing most of the subject-matter of the Rome Treaty—and Her Majesty's Government gladly modified their original attitude to meet the views of their O.E.E.C. partners. In the case of agriculture Her Majesty's Government suggested that there should be a simultaneous but separate agreement[2] to strengthen European co-operation and to expand trade in agricultural products. All concerned accepted the obligation to work towards these objectives.

36. Moreover, once the Treaty of Rome had been signed Her Majesty's Government recognised the importance of reducing to a minimum divergencies between its provisions and those of the free trade area. They therefore readily undertook to modify their original proposals to meet this situation. The starting point of the detailed negotiations was the annotated agenda,[3] circulated by the Chairman of the Inter-Governmental Committee, not a British plan; it covered a wide field and drew extensively on the provisions of the Treaty of Rome.

[1] Cmnd. 72.   [2] Cmnd. 641, pp. 190–6 (CIG(58)4).
                    [3] Ibid., pp. 50–59 (CIG(57)1).

37. The report dated 12th December, 1958,[1] by the Chairman of the Inter-Governmental Committee to the O.E.E.C. Council contains an analysis by the Secretariat of the work achieved on the basis of this agreed agenda. The Secretariat summarised in paragraph 5 of this analysis the fundamental matters on which agreement could not be reached under three heads: namely, external tariffs and external commercial policy; the harmonisation and co-ordination of internal economic and social policies; and the institutional system. The attitude of Her Majesty's Government on these fundamental issues is set out below.

38. *External tariffs and external commerical policy.*—Her Majesty's Government have always taken the view, which was accepted in January, 1958, by representatives of the great majority of negotiating countries,[2] that a system of certificates of origin is practicable and that, given a will to work together and a code of good conduct[3] to prevent abuse and provide for adjustments in the origin rules, any deflections of trade that may arise in practice could be dealt with by institutional means. Experience of the working of the Commonwealth Preference system provides practical proof that the certificate of origin system can be used successfully, and the United Kingdom's experience in this matter has been made available to other O.E.E.C. countries. Her Majesty's Government accepted the principles set out in July in the Report of the O.E.E.C. Steering Board for Trade[4] for a settlement of the problem of origin and proposed to meet the wishes of some other countries that there should be an examination sector by sector of the practical application of these principles. They were very disappointed that this examination, which was to begin immediately after the July meeting, should have made little or no progress by October.

39. The attitude of Her Majesty's Government on the problem of external commercial policy was indicated in the draft articles[5] circulated by the Paymaster General. It will be seen from this draft that over a substantial part of the field there was agreement between the United Kingdom point of view and the proposals of the European Economic Community, as set out in the Community's memorandum.[6]

40. The existence of Commonwealth Preference has never caused difficulty in the development of the O.E.E.C., and there has been a very great and welcome extension in recent years of trade between Europe and the Commonwealth. Her Majesty's Government do not therefore believe that in practice any risk of disequilibrium in the conditions of competition could arise in a European free trade area as a result of Commonwealth Preference, as was suggested in the Memorandum from the European Economic Community.

[1] Ibid., pp. 1–6 (C(58)267).   [2] Cmnd. 641, pp. 104–47 (CIG(58)12).
[3] Ibid., pp. 152–3 (CIG(58)29).   [4] Ibid., pp. 175–7 (CIG(58)44).
[5] Ibid., pp. 189–90 (CIG(58)69).   [6] Ibid., pp. 96–104 (CIG(58)60).

41. The question came before the Inter-Governmental Committee at the meeting of 13th November, when discussions took place on the relevant passage in the Community's Memorandum. It was then explained on behalf of Her Majesty's Government that the preferences which United Kingdom exports enjoy in certain parts of the Commonwealth had been negotiated with the Commonwealth Governments concerned and were not therefore under the sole control of the United Kingdom Government: they were part of a balanced system of rights and obligations, and it was wholly misleading to consider the question of Commonwealth Preference by calling attention simply to the benefits it confers and ignoring the obligations: the two must be taken together.

42. Her Majesty's Government expressed willingness to consider any difficulties which their partners in the negotiations might wish to bring forward in this connection, on the understanding that not only Commonwealth Preference but all preferential arrangements enjoyed by any member country would be subject to similar scrutiny. After a brief discussion it was left to the Community to raise any practical example they wished during the sector-by-sector studies of the origin problem.

43. *Internal economic and social policies.*—Her Majesty's Government have always recognised that a closer co-ordination of internal economic policies would be a necessary accompaniment of a free trade area.

44. For co-ordination of social policies, Her Majesty's Government made certain definite proposals[1] in January, 1958, to meet the point of view expressed by some members of the Community. These compromise proposals, which represented a substantial move by the United Kingdom and the maximum to which a number of countries felt they could possibly go, were considered to be inadequate by the French Government. In its Memorandum,[2] which came before the Committee in October, 1958, the Community as a whole took its stand on the original provisions of the Treaty of Rome in their entirety. After discussion, the spokesman of the Community agreed that the subject should be reconsidered in the light of the proposals that had been made. Her Majesty's Government remain convinced that a compromise, satisfactory to the interests of all concerned, can be found along the lines of their proposal.

45. *Institutional arrangements.*—Her Majesty's Government had started from the assumption that all decisions in the free trade area institutions should be taken by unanimity, though by the time the Memorandum of February, 1957,[3] was produced they were prepared to concede that some departure from the unanimity rule would be necessary in certain carefully defined matters. Their concept of the free trade area was still at that time more strictly limited to the removal of trade barriers and action immedi-

---

[1] Ibid., pp. 216–17 (CIG(58)7).   [2] Ibid., pp. 96–104 (CIG(58)60).
[3] Cmnd. 72.

ately consequent thereon. In the course of negotiations it became apparent, first, that this conception should be widened to cover the whole field of economic relations as has been explained above, and that, if the necessary decisions were to be reached, more discretion would have to be left to the institutions, because exceptions and escape clauses would be more numerous than was at first expected. In these circumstances Her Majesty's Government indicated in the spring of 1958 that they would accept the principle of majority voting on a number of matters. This proposal was at the time warmly welcomed by a number of delegates including members of the European Economic Community. Her Majesty's Government continued to believe that, if the free trade area agreement were to be effective, either there must be very tightly defined rules or, if the rules were to be loose and the escape clauses numerous, recourse to them must be subject to strict control in order to ensure that all members felt confident that the rules would be universally and impartially observed.

46. Her Majesty's Government are firmly convinced of the over-riding importance for the future of Europe of finding a multilateral solution which will provide for freedom of trade including the removal of tariffs and quantitative restrictions among all members of the O.E.E.C. The outstanding points are indeed of considerable significance. But Her Majesty's Government do not believe that they are incapable of solution by further negotiation in an atmosphere of common determination to succeed and agreement on the ultimate objective.

IV. THE COMMUNIST POWERS AND ALLIES

1. Joint statement of the Government of the People's Republic of China and the Government of the Democratic People's Republic of Korea, Pyongyang, 19 February 1958[1]

The Government Delegation of the People's Republic of China led by Chou En-lai, Premier of the State Council of the People's Republic of China, is paying a friendly visit to the Democratic People's Republic of Korea from February 14 to 21, 1958 at the invitation of the Government of the Democratic People's Republic of Korea.

The Government Delegation of the People's Republic of China toured Pyongyang, Hamheung, Heungnam, Wonsan and other cities, and visited factories, an agricultural co-operative, and cultural and educational establishments.

During its friendly visit in the Democratic People's Republic of Korea, the Government Delegation of the People's Republic of China was accorded a hearty welcome and warm reception by the Korean people and Government.

During the visit, talks were held between the Government Delegations of the People's Republic of China and the Democratic People's Republic of Korea.

Taking part in the talks on the side of the People's Republic of China were Chou En-lai, Premier of the State Council; Chen Yi, Vice-Premier of the State Council and Minister of Foreign Affairs; Chang Wen-tien, Vice-Minister of Foreign Affairs; Su Yu, Chief of General Staff of the Chinese People's Liberation Army; and Chiao Hsiao-kuang, Ambassador Extraordinary and Plenipotentiary of the People's Republic of China to the Democratic People's Republic of Korea.

Taking part in the talks on the side of the Democratic People's Republic of Korea were Kim Il Sung, Premier of the Cabinet; Kim Il, Vice-Premier of the Cabinet; Nam Il, Vice-Premier of the Cabinet and Minister of Foreign Affairs; Kim Kwang Hyup, Minister of National Defence; and Li Young Ho, Ambassador Extraordinary and Plenipotentiary of the Democratic People's Republic of Korea to the People's Republic of China.

The talks proceeded throughout in an atmosphere of cordiality and friendship.

[1] *Peking Review*, 4 March 1958, pp. 21–23. See Chapter I, D, for the exchange of letters between the People's Republic of China and the United Kingdom regarding the reunification of Korea.

In the course of the talks views were exchanged on the expansion and development of friendly relations between the two countries, the strengthening of the friendship and solidarity between the socialist countries, the present international situation and the peaceful settlement of the Korean question.

The two government delegations reached fully identical views on the above-mentioned questions.

In the talks, the two parties pointed out unanimously that the all-round friendly relations being strengthened and developed between the People's Republic of China and the Democratic People's Republic of Korea fully conform with the interests of the peoples of the two countries and have a significant bearing on the safeguarding of peace in the Far East and the world. The two peoples had undertaken protracted joint struggles against aggression, through which, and particularly through the struggle against the aggression of U.S. imperialism, their traditional friendship was cemented and developed with the blood of their best sons and daughters. In order to promote their respective socialist constructions, the two countries have developed an extensive co-operation in the economic, cultural, scientific, technical and other fields, and given each other brotherly assistance. In international affairs, they have also closely co-operated with and supported each other. This friendly co-operation between the two countries not only accords with the five principles of peaceful co-existence but is based on the Marxist-Leninist principles of national equality and proletarian internationalism. Both parties affirmed their determination to continue to exert all their efforts to develop and strengthen this great and unbreakable friendly co-operation.

The Government Delegation of the People's Republic of China noted with satisfaction and admiration the great achievements in post-war rehabilitation and socialist construction made by the Korean people who, rallying round the Korean Workers' Party and the Government of the Democratic People's Republic of Korea, have displayed a high degree of patriotic labour enthusiasm. During the talks, the two parties also exchanged information concerning their socialist construction work, and warmly congratulated each other on their achievements. Both parties believed that these achievements not only strengthened the material foundation of socialism in their respective countries, but also constituted a major contribution to the common cause of the socialist camp headed by the Soviet Union.

Both parties pointed out that, as the forces of socialism have surpassed those of imperialism, and the forces of peace those of war, a new turn has taken place in the international situation definitely in favour of the cause of peace, democracy and socialism.

Both parties pointed out with satisfaction that tremendous achievements have been gained by the socialist countries in building socialism and communism, and that the Soviet Union, in particular, is now in the forefront of the world in certain important fields of science and technology. In November 1957, representatives of Communist and Workers' Parties met in Moscow and issued two declarations of great historic significance, ushering in a new stage in the solidarity of the socialist countries and that of the international communist movement. Both parties stressed that solidarity of the socialist countries loyal to proletarian internationalism and Marxism-Leninism is an important guarantee of the national independence and construction of the socialist countries, as well as of world peace and the progress of mankind. Both parties pledged that they will, as they did in the past, exert unswerving efforts to increase the strength and solidarity of the socialist camp headed by the Soviet Union.

Both parties reaffirmed that the foreign policy of peace consistently pursued by them and the other socialist countries is designed to bring about relaxation in the international situation and peaceful co-existence among nations with different social systems. A concrete expression of this foreign policy of peace is the recent proposals of the Government of the Soviet Union for a summit East-West conference, immediate cessation of atomic and hydrogen weapons tests, prohibition of the use of atomic and hydrogen weapons, a non-aggression agreement between parties to the Warsaw Treaty and those to the North Atlantic Treaty, and for ensuring the independence and peace of the countries in the Near and Middle East, etc. Both parties expressed full support for these proposals of the Government of the Soviet Union. At the same time, both parties expressed active support for the proposal put forward by the Polish Government for the establishment of a zone free of atomic armaments in central Europe. They agreed that the German Democratic Republic's consistent opposition to the revival of militarism in West Germany is an important contribution to the peace and security of Europe. They expressed full support for the position of the German Democratic Republic that the two Germanys seek a peaceful unification of Germany through negotiation on an equal footing.

Both parties unanimously praised the faithful implementation of the Geneva Agreements by the Democratic Republic of Viet-nam and gave full support to the Democratic Republic of Viet-nam in its untiring efforts to bring about the peaceful unification of Viet-nam.

Both parties pointed out that a main characteristic of our age is the high upsurge of national independence movements. They expressed firm support for the Indonesian people, the Arab peoples and other Asian and African peoples in their struggles against colonialism and for winning and safeguarding national independence, and considered these just struggles as being at the same time struggles in defence of peace. Both parties warmly hailed the increasingly important role played by the Asian and African nationalist countries in international affairs, as well as the development of peaceful and friendly co-operation between them and the socialist countries on the basis of equality. The recent Asian-African Peoples' Solidarity Conference played a great role in strengthening and furthering the unity of the Asian and African peoples in their struggles against imperialism and colonialism. Both parties expressed agreement with India's propositions against the establishment of guided missiles bases in Europe and Asia and for the establishment and expansion of an area of peace free of weapons of mass destruction. Both parties were glad to see the world peace movement forging ahead in full swing and becoming more and more a people's movement in all countries.

The two parties could not but note with regret that the Japanese Government still pursued an unfriendly policy towards China and Korea in spite of the Japanese people's growing demand for strengthening solidarity with other Asian and African countries and establishing and developing friendly relations with China and Korea.

The two parties unanimously condemned the rigid policy of the U.S. aggressive circles and their followers of carrying on arms expansion and war preparations, rejecting peaceful negotiation and aggravating international tension. They particularly condemned the United States for its continued occupation of China's territory of Taiwan and its scheme to actively create 'two Chinas,' and for its introducing of atomic weapons into South Korea in violation of the Korean Armistice Agreement in an attempt to turn South Korea into a U.S. atomic base. Both parties pointed out that the policy of the United States Government of relying on so-called 'strength' did not succeed in the past, and that today when its 'strength' has gone bankrupt, continuation of this policy will fare no better. Both parties stressed that with the forces in defence of peace growing stronger than ever, so long as all peace-loving countries and peoples strengthen their confidence, keep up vigilance and carry on unremitting struggle, war can be prevented and peace can be safeguarded.

During the talks, the two parties exchanged views especially on the withdrawal of all foreign troops from both North and South Korea and on the peaceful settlement of the Korean question. They agreed that the proposals made in the statement of the Government of the Democratic People's Republic of Korea of February 5, 1958 not only represent the national aspiration of the Korean people for the peaceful unification of their motherland, but are also timely and realistic proposals in the present international situation. In line with its consistent stand of actively promoting the peaceful settlement of the Korean question, the Chinese Government in a statement issued on February 7, 1958 expressed full support for the Korean Government's proposals and now, in addition, after consultations with the Korean Government, has proposed to the Chinese People's Volunteers that they take the initiative in withdrawing from Korea. The Chinese People's Volunteers have fully concurred in this proposal of the Chinese Government and have decided to withdraw completely from Korea by stages and to complete the withdrawal before the end of 1958. The first stage of the withdrawal will be completed before April 30, 1958. The Government of the Democratic People's Republic of Korea has agreed to this decision of the Chinese People's Volunteers and is willing to assist in their complete withdrawal.

The two parties pointed out that the initiative in withdrawing all Chinese People's Volunteers from Korea is yet another proof of the sincere desire of the Korean and Chinese side for the peaceful settlement of the Korean question and relaxation of tension in the Far East. Now is a time when the United States and the other countries participating in the United Nations forces are faced with a serious test. If they have any sincerity for the peaceful settlement of the Korean question, they should likewise withdraw all their forces from Korea. Otherwise, the whole world will see even more clearly that it is they who have all along been obstructing the peaceful unification of Korea. Should the United States Government and the Syngman Rhee clique in South Korea go so far as to interpret this initiative of the Korean and Chinese side as a sign of weakness and think that it is a chance to take advantage of, they will certainly meet with unthinkable consequences. The people of the whole world are now even more determined not to allow the imperialists to start a new war. The Korean people's power to resist aggression is also stronger than ever before. The Chinese and Korean peoples have common vital interests. The Chinese people did not supinely tolerate any imperialist aggression on the Democratic People's Republic of Korea, nor will they ever do so in the future.

In the talks, the Korean Government Delegation expressed once more heartfelt thanks to the Chinese people for the material and moral assistance given to the Korean people during and after the war and for dispatching their best sons and daughters to Korea to support with their own blood the Korean people's just Fatherland Liberation War. The Chinese People's Volunteers, after defeating the U.S. imperialist aggression in Korea together with the Korean People's Army, have in the post-war period continued to guard the peace front and actively helped in the peaceful construction of Korea; the Government of the Democratic People's Republic of Korea and the Korean people, cherishing brotherly sentiments and profound friendship for the Chinese People's Volunteers, praise highly and will always remember their immortal deeds. The Chinese Government Delegation considers that the Korean people, by defeating the armed aggression of the U.S. imperialists, have made an extremely important contribution to the safeguarding of peace in the Far East and the world, and that it was not only for the purpose of saving their homes and defending their country, but also to fulfil an internationalist obligation due to the Korean people that the Chinese people resisted American aggression and aided Korea. The Chinese Government Delegation expressed deep gratitude to the Korean Government and people for the support and concern they have accorded the Chinese People's Volunteers in the past seven years and more.

Both parties expressed thanks to the Neutral Nations Supervisory Commission for its great efforts and good role in supervising and stabilizing the Korean armistice under various difficult conditions. They held that all parties concerned are still under the obligation to give all possible assistance to the Neutral Nations Supervisory Commission in its continued performance of functions as provided for in the Korean Armistice Agreement.

Both parties are deeply convinced that the visit to Korea by the Government Delegation of the People's Republic of China and the talks between the two government delegations not only have strengthened the friendship and solidarity of the two countries, but also will further consolidate and develop their relations of mutual help and co-operation.

2. Statement by the Government of the People's Republic of China regarding the S.E.A.T.O. meeting in Manila, 10 March 1958[1]

A Council session of the South-east Asia Treaty Organization will begin in Manila on March 11. Through this session the Western colonial powers headed by the United States attempt to interfere further in the internal affairs of the South-east Asian countries, step up arms expansion and war preparations, set up U.S. bases for nuclear and rocket weapons on the territories of the Asian member states of this bloc, expand the sphere of activity of this aggressive bloc, and aggravate tension in Asia and the Pacific region. These aggressive designs of the United States are diametrically opposed to the present fervent desire of the peace-loving countries and people throughout the world and, first of all, those in Asia for an end to the cold war and for a further relaxation of international tension.

Making use of the aggressive Manila bloc, the United States has all along been interfering in the internal affairs of many South-east Asian countries under the pretext of combating so-called Communist subversive activities, and recently it has directed its spearhead against Indonesia in particular. Not long ago, U.S. Secretary of State Dulles made statements against the President and Government of Indonesia, crudely

[1] *Peking Review*, 18 March 1958, pp. 22–23.

intervening in the domestic affairs of a sovereign state. At the same time, as everybody knows, Manila and Singapore have become the main bases through which the rebel elements of Indonesia get their supplies and contact others. The United States Seventh Fleet made a show of force and posed a threat by moving to the vicinity of the territorial waters of Indonesia under the pretext of manoeuvres. At the current Manila meeting the United States is attempting to muster more countries to interfere further in the internal affairs of Indonesia. This cannot but attract the serious attention of all countries and peoples who love peace and treasure their own sovereignty. The Chinese Government and people fully support the Government and people of Indonesia in their just struggle to safeguard their national independence and sovereignty against outside intervention and subversive plots, and are firmly convinced that this struggle will triumph ultimately. The Chinese Government holds that the Asian member states of the Manila bloc should honour the obligations they undertook at the Bandung Asian-African Conference and refuse to follow the United States in interfering in the internal affairs of another Asian country; they should know that it will bring them no good to pull chestnuts out of the fire for the United States. The Chinese Government deems it necessary to point out that the U.S. interference in Indonesia has already aroused ever-mounting censure and opposition from the people of Indonesia and Asia, and that any further action will certainly lead to serious consequences. The United States must immediately stop its interference in the internal affairs of Indonesia, or else bear full responsibility for all consequences arising therefrom.

As it did at the NATO Paris conference and the Bagdad treaty Ankara meeting held not long ago, the United States also attempts at the present Manila meeting to enlarge its network of bases for nuclear and rocket weapons in Asia and the Pacific region. The setting up by the United States of bases for launching rockets with nuclear wearheads on China's territory of Taiwan which it occupies, and in South Korea and Japan has aggravated tension in the Far East and has already met with the strong opposition of the Chinese people and the peoples of other Asian countries. The setting up of such bases in more countries not only will tighten U.S. control over these countries and increase the danger of war, but will bring incalculable disaster upon these countries first of all should war be started by the United States. The Chinese Government and people are firmly opposed to the deployment by the United States of nuclear and rocket weapons in any part of Asia, and are all out for the establishment throughout Asia of an area of peace free from atomic weapons and the conclusion of a treaty of collective peace. We believe these to be in full accord with the vital interests of the peoples of all Asian countries. But in the Asian member states of the Manila bloc there are actually certain leaders who, in disregard of the interests of their own countries and in defiance of the opposition of the people all over the world, have openly welcomed the setting up of bases for nuclear and rocket weapons on the territories of their countries by the United States.[1] Itself an Asian country, China and these countries have the common duty to observe the resolution of the Bandung Asian-African Conference on the ten principles of peaceful co-existence. As a neighbour of these countries, the Chinese Government cannot but express serious concern over the establishment of U.S. bases for nuclear and rocket weapons on their territories.

The people of the whole world are eager for peace and ardently desire negotiations between the Eastern and the Western countries, prohibition of atomic and nuclear weapons, and peaceful co-existence among all peoples. To realize these desires, the Soviet Union, China and other peace-loving countries have put forward a series of peace proposals and took the initiative in measures which have met with universal welcome and support. However, the United States ruling circles have tried hard to obstruct the development of this mainstream in the international situation, press on with arms expansion and war preparations, and bolster up their aggressive blocs which are finding themselves in an increasingly critical situation. The present Manila meeting is precisely part of this struggle put up by the United States. This perverse line of action of the United States will only make it more isolated, and will by no means be able to stem the advance of the powerful current of peace throughout the world. So long as the people of the Asian countries strengthen their unity, heighten their vigilance and persist in their struggle, all conspiratorial activities carried out by the United States and other Western colonial powers through the Manila bloc are doomed to failure.

3. Joint statement on talks between Party and Government delegations of the Soviet Union and the Hungarian People's Republic, Budapest, 9 April 1958[2]

From April 2 to April 10 a party and government delegation of the Soviet Union led by N. S. Khrushchov, first secretary of the central

---

[1] The *Tass* statement of 8 March 1958 on the forthcoming S.E.A.T.O. meeting was more specific on this point. 'Noteworthy in this respect was a statement by President Garcia of the Philippines in which he came out for the building of rocket-launching bases in Asian S.E.A.T.O. countries and welcomed, in particular, the siting of American missile bases in the Philippines. Similar statements have been made by Thai officials as well.' See *Soviet News*, 11 March 1958. For a report of a press conference given by President Garcia on 7 March, see *Japan Times*, 8 March 1958. President Garcia said that there had been no discussion between the Philippines and the United States about the setting up of atomic or missile bases in the Philippines either inside or outside S.E.A.T.O.

[2] *Soviet News*, 11 April 1958.

committee of the Communist Party of the Soviet Union and Chairman of the U.S.S.R. Council of Ministers, paid a return visit to the Hungarian People's Republic at the invitation of the central committee of the Hungarian Socialist Workers' Party and the Hungarian Revolutionary Workers' and Peasants' Government. During the visit talks were held between the Soviet party and government delegation and the party and government delegation of the Hungarian People's Republic.

The Soviet delegation consisted of N. S. Khrushchov, first secretary of the central committee of the C.P.S.U. and Chairman of the U.S.S.R. Council of Ministers (head of the delegation); F. R. Kozlov, member of the presidium of the central committee of the C.P.S.U. and First Vice-Chairman of the U.S.S.R. Council of Ministers; A. A. Gromyko, U.S.S.R. Foreign Minister; V. V. Grishin, chairman of the All-Union Central Council of Trade Unions; P. E. Shelest, first secretary of the Kiev regional committee of the Communist Party of the Ukraine; A. P. Boikova, second secretary of the Leningrad city committee of the C.P.S.U., and E. I. Gromov, U.S.S.R. Ambassador to the Hungarian People's Republic.

The Hungarian delegation was composed of Janos Kadar, first secretary of the central committee of the Hungarian Socialist Workers' Party (head of the delegation); Dr. Ferenc Münnich, member of the political bureau of the central committee of the Hungarian Socialist Workers' Party and Chairman of the Hungarian Revolutionary Workers' and Peasants' Government; Gyorgy Marosan, member of the political bureau of the central committee and secretary of the central committee of the H.S.W.P.; Gyula Kallai, member of the political bureau and secretary of the central committee of the H.S.W.P.; Karoly Kiss, member of the political bureau and secretary of the central committee of the H.S.W.P.; Miklos Somodyi, member of the political bureau of the central committee of the H.S.W.P. and chairman of the Hungarian Council of Trade Unions; Jenö Fok, member of the political bureau and secretary of the central committee of the H.S.W.P., and Endre Sik, Foreign Minister of the Hungarian People's Republic.

The talks were held in an atmosphere of friendship and complete mutual understanding.

The party and government delegation of the Soviet Union took part in the nationwide celebrations on the occasion of the Hungarian national day—the 13th anniversary of Hungary's liberation from the fascist yoke—and visited industrial enterprises, scientific institutions and co-operative farms and travelled to various towns and villages of the country.

During its stay in the Hungarian People's Republic the party and government delegation of the Soviet Union had many friendly meetings and talks with party, government and public leaders, workers, peasants and intellectuals. In the course of these meetings and talks a frank exchange of views took place on a wide range of problems concerned with the further promotion and strengthening of the friendly and fraternal relations between the two countries.

The party and government delegation of the Soviet Union had the opportunity to see for itself the noble spirit displayed in labour and in political life by the working people of Hungary, who demonstrated their unshakable faith in the great ideas of socialism and their determination to build a happy future for their country in close co-operation with the other countries of the socialist camp. The delegation saw for itself how deep is the Hungarian working people's feeling of friendship for the Soviet people and how great is their desire to develop and strengthen Hungarian-Soviet relations based on fraternal mutual assistance and the great principles of proletarian internationalism.

During its stay in the Hungarian People's Republic, the party and government delegation of the Soviet Union had the opportunity to witness the great postwar achievements of the Hungarian people and their success in eliminating the aftermath of the counter-revolutionary uprising and in strengthening the people's power in the country.

The party and government delegation of the Hungarian People's Republic, for its part, considers it necessary to emphasise that the political and moral support of the Soviet Union helped to a great extent to eliminate most rapidly the consequences of the counter-revolutionary uprising and that the Soviet Union's economic aid enabled the government of the Hungarian People's Republic, within a short space of time, to overcome economic difficulties, eliminate the danger of unemployment and avoid inflation in the country.

During the talks the two delegations informed each other of the internal problems of their parties and countries and exchanged views on measures to develop further the friendly relations between the Soviet Union and the Hungarian People's Republic, and also on the international situation and the pressing problems of the struggle for the consolidation of peace. The exchange of opinions revealed the complete identity of views of the two delegations on all the problems under discussion.

Both sides noted with satisfaction that the implementation of the Joint Declaration of the governments of the Soviet Union and the Hungarian People's Republic of March 28, 1957,[1] had helped to extend further the fraternal relations between the two countries and to strengthen the friendship between the Soviet and Hungarian peoples. For the purpose of strengthening friendly ties and extending co-operation between the Soviet Union and the Hungarian People's Republic a number of important agreements were signed: an agreement on the legal status of Soviet troops temporarily stationed in Hungary, a convention on settling

[1] See *Documents* for 1957, pp. 484–97.

the problem of persons with dual citizenship, and a consular convention. Other conventions pertaining to the relations between the two countries are in the preparatory stage.

Both sides note with great satisfaction that economic co-operation between the Soviet Union and the Hungarian People's Republic is effectively developing on the basis of the principles set forth in the Joint Declaration of March 28, 1957.

In conformity with this declaration a long-term agreement on goods deliveries has been signed for the period from 1958 to 1960. The agreement ensures full-capacity operation for Hungarian industry and the supplying of the Soviet Union with corresponding industrial goods for Hungary.

The long-term trade agreement provides for a further increase in reciprocal goods deliveries. In conformity with the request of the Hungarian government and guided by the desire to assist a further rise in Hungary's economy, the Soviet government has extended to Hungary additional economic aid in the building and reconstruction of enterprises of the metallurgical, machine-building, electrical engineering, chemical, oil, consumer goods and other industries, and also transport.

A long-term agreement has been reached on extending scientific and technical co-operation between the Soviet Union and the Hungarian People's Republic, including co-operation in the production of heavy current and weak current equipment, instruments and diesel engines.

Both delegations stressed that in order to bring about a further rise in the level of the economy and the living standards of the peoples of their countries, it was necessary to co-ordinate to a greater degree the plans for the development of the national economies, with due regard for the possibilities and prospects for developing the economy of each of the two countries.

Both delegations note with deep satisfaction that scientific and cultural contacts between the two countries are developing fruitfully and successfully. The successes in the sphere of scientific and cultural contacts have greatly helped to strengthen Soviet-Hungarian friendship and mutually to enrich the cultures of the two peoples. In 1957 many representatives of Hungarian science and culture visited the Soviet Union. At the same time many people prominent in Soviet science and culture visited Hungary. These visits provide opportunities for mutual acquaintance with the rich scientific and cultural heritage of both countries and the boundless horizons opening up before them under socialism. A cultural co-operation plan for 1958 and an agreement between the Academies of Sciences of the two countries have been signed for the purpose of promoting further cultural and scientific ties.

Both sides greatly appreciate the work of the friendship societies in the Soviet Union and the Hungarian People's Republic in further extending the cultural ties between the two countries and declare that they will give every support to these organisations.

The talks revealed a complete identity of views on the role and significance of the defensive Warsaw Treaty, which is an important factor ensuring the security of the countries which are parties to it, in face of the continually mounting military preparations of the aggressive North Atlantic bloc.

It was unanimously noted that the close cohesion of the socialist states in a single camp on the basis of the principles of fraternal mutual assistance, complete equality, respect for territorial integrity, state independence and sovereignty, and non-interference in one another's internal affairs is a reliable guarantee of the national independence and sovereignty of every socialist country. The solidarity of the socialist states is not directed against any other countries but serves the interests of all peoples by containing the aggressive aspirations of the imperialist circles and supporting the forces of peace and progress which are growing stronger every day.

In the sphere of foreign policy the Soviet Union and the Hungarian People's Republic will continue to be guided by the aim of further strengthening and welding together the mighty socialist camp in the interests of consolidating world peace. No power on earth can disrupt this unity based on common adherence to the great ideas of Marxism-Leninism, on unity of purpose in building a communist society, and on the determination of the socialist states to rebuff any attempt to violate the peaceful constructive efforts of their peoples.

The talks revealed the identity of the views of both sides on all problems concerning the present international situation.

Loyal to the principles and ideas of the Declaration and Peace Manifesto of the Communist and Workers' Parties signed in Moscow in November, 1957,[1] the Soviet Union and the Hungarian People's Republic believe that their major task is to aid in every way the consolidation of all the forces of peace in the struggle for genuine security of the peoples, for the removal of the danger of a new war.

The Soviet Union and the Hungarian People's Republic note that the principal problem of the present international situation is still that of achieving an agreement on concrete and urgent measures to reduce international tension, end the arms race and remove the danger of war, which in our age is fraught with grave consequences for mankind. Both delegations expressed their deep conviction that an early meeting of leading statesmen with the participation of heads of government would be an important step in this direction.

A positive solution to the problems proposed by the Soviet government

[1] See *Documents* for 1957, pp. 527–39.

for discussion at a summit meeting would offer a good basis for establishing an effective system of collective security in Europe, which is especially important for the preservation of peace, since it has been in Europe that bloody wars have broken out twice within half a century, bringing incalculable disasters to the European nations.

Especially important in this connection would be a non-aggression agreement between the member-states of the North Atlantic bloc and the signatories to the Warsaw Treaty. Under the present conditions, with the peoples insistently demanding that steps be taken to settle major international problems, such an agreement could be a beginning towards easing international tension and achieving the required turn in the development of international relations in general.

The Soviet Union and the Hungarian People's Republic proclaim their determination to work for the settlement, among other pressing international problems, of such urgent questions as the immediate and universal ending of atomic and hydrogen weapon tests, the reduction of the numerical strength of the foreign troops stationed in Germany and in other member-states of N.A.T.O. and the Warsaw Treaty, and the establishment in Central Europe of a zone free from nuclear and rocket weapons.

The delegation of the Hungarian People's Republic stresses the historic significance of the decision of the Supreme Soviet of the U.S.S.R. on the unilateral ending of nuclear tests by the Soviet Union.[1] This extremely humane act, prompted by concern for peace among the nations, for removing the hazards to human health involved in nuclear tests, accords with the vital interests of all peoples and is an invaluable contribution to the establishment of the necessary international confidence. This decision provides an opportunity for the universal ending of nuclear tests by all countries for all time.

Both sides express the hope that other powers possessing nuclear weapons will also end test explosions of atomic and hydrogen weapons at once and make their own contribution to the great cause of strengthening peace.

The Soviet Union and the Hungarian People's Republic stand for the realisation of concrete disarmament measures and resolutely condemn the arms race and the military preparations conducted by N.A.T.O. member-states. They condemn all attempts of N.A.T.O. member-countries to impose, during the examination of disarmament problems, conditions such as would give an ever freer hand to the participants in the North Atlantic bloc in carrying out their aggressive policy of military preparations. Now as in the past, they resolutely stand for the ending of the 'cold war' in all its forms, for the ending of the war propaganda which is being conducted in some countries, and for the free development of

[1] For the text of the Resolution of 31 March 1958, see above, pp. 59–60.

international economic relations and international trade, which are the most stable foundation for strengthening international confidence.

The Soviet Union and the Hungarian People's Republic stand resolutely for the dismantling of military bases on the territories of other countries, since the existence of such bases is one of the main causes of the suspicion and mistrust which poison international relations.

Both sides cannot but express grave concern over the decision of the Bundestag of the Federal Republic of Germany which has given the Federal Government a mandate to equip the West German army with atomic and hydrogen weapons.[1] They also express concern over the preparations for setting up foreign atomic and rocket bases in Western Germany, since this policy of Western Germany leads to a situation in Europe which resembles in many respects the situation when Nazi Germany began preparations for unleashing the Second World War. The two sides express the hope that there are forces in Western Germany which will not allow her to be pushed on to the dangerous fatal road of preparing a nuclear war whose devastating flames would sweep the territory of Western Germany first of all.

Both delegations point out that the question of unifying Germany lies entirely within the competence of the two sovereign German states—the German Democratic Republic and the Federal Republic of Germany—and that the setting up of a German confederation as proposed by the government of the German Democratic Republic would be the first step towards the peaceful reunification of Germany. The Soviet Union and the Hungarian People's Republic fully support this proposal of the German Democratic Republic.

The Soviet Union and the Hungarian People's Republic consider that the immense achievements in science and technology, as expressed in the launching by the Soviet Union of the first artificial earth satellites, open up new, hitherto non-existent possibilities for international co-operation in studying the laws of nature for the benefit of all mankind.

Both sides believe that an agreement banning the use of outer space for military purposes and eliminating foreign military bases on the territories of other countries, as the Soviet Union has suggested, would not only open up broad avenues for international co-operation in the study of outer space but would also, at the same time, be a major step towards the solution of the disarmament problem as a whole.

---

[1] A foreign affairs debate was held in the Bundestag between 20 and 25 March 1958, on a Government motion calling for the equipment of the West German forces with 'the most modern weapons'. The motion was approved by 267 votes to 194, *Commonwealth Survey*, 1 April 1958, p. 310. Herr Strauss, the West German defence minister, is reported to have said that there was no intention of equipping the Bundeswehr with tactical atomic weapons (i.e. complete with warheads). 'We do not want this, and we will not do it so long as N.A.T.O. can give us security.' For a report of the debate in the Bundestag, see *The Times*, 26 March 1958.

Both delegations have once again declared the firm determination of the Soviet Union and the Hungarian People's Republic to wage a resolute struggle against every attempt of the circles concerned in fomenting hostility among states to poison the international political atmosphere by bringing to the fore such provocative issues as the question of the situation in the East European countries. The Soviet Union and the Hungarian People's Republic firmly declare that the question of the state system in the people's democracies, as in any other sovereign state, cannot be the subject of discussion at international conferences, because it has long since been settled by the peoples of these countries who have firmly and irrevocably taken the road of building socialism.

Both sides regard the attempts to impose a discussion of the question of the situation in the people's democracies as being incompatible with the principles of the United Nations Charter and as inadmissible interference in the affairs of sovereign states. They resolutely brush aside such attempts as being hostile to the cause of peace.

The raising of the question of the situation in the East European people's democracies, like the demand to discuss at an international conference the question of German unification, that is to say, an issue within the competence of the two sovereign German states, cannot be viewed otherwise than as an attempt to frustrate agreement on eliminating the 'cold war' and ending the arms race. It cannot be viewed otherwise than as an attempt to frustrate the convocation of a summit conference to discuss the most pressing questions of ending the frenzied arms race and remove the threat of war, as well as being an attempt to keep the peoples in a state of fear regarding their future, to increase hostility and suspicion in relations between states, to foment war hysteria, and at the same time to reap enormous and increasing profits on war deliveries.

Both delegations declare that the Soviet Union and the Hungarian People's Republic express complete solidarity with the peoples of the colonies and dependencies who are waging a struggle for their national liberation, being convinced that the fall of the colonial system—that system of the domination of certain countries over others—is an inevitable historical process.

The party and government delegation of the Hungarian People's Republic has proclaimed the desire of the government of the Hungarian People's Republic to resume or establish normal relations with states that so desire. It regards as very important the steps which the Hungarian People's Republic has been taking to improve relations with neighbouring Austria, because co-operation between Hungary and Austria based on mutual recognition of each other's sovereignty and consistent observance of the principle of non-interference in internal affairs would be a contribution to the cause of establishing peace and security in Europe. This view of the government of the Hungarian People's Republic has met with complete understanding on the part of the party and government delegation of the Soviet Union.

The party and government delegations of the Soviet Union and the Hungarian People's Republic are firmly convinced that the noble goals of preserving and strengthening peace among the peoples, ending the 'cold war', stopping the arms race and extending co-operation among all states, large and small, can be reached by observance of the principles of the peaceful co-existence of states, regardless of their social systems—principles which have already won wide international recognition.

During the stay of the Soviet party and government delegation in the Hungarian People's Republic, a broad exchange of views on mutual party relations was held between the representatives of the Communist Party of the Soviet Union and the representatives of the Hungarian Socialist Workers' Party. The talks, which were held in a spirit of friendship and cordiality, revealed the complete unanimity of views of the two parties on all the issues discussed.

The representatives of both parties stated that co-operation between the C.P.S.U. and the Hungarian Socialist Workers' Party was developing in complete conformity with the statement on the talks between the delegations of the Communist Party of the Soviet Union and the Hungarian Socialist Workers' Party signed in Moscow on March 28, 1957. Since that time relations between the two parties have been further strengthened and at present the C.P.S.U. and the H.S.W.P. are maintaining constant contacts with each other for the purpose of keeping each other informed on all important questions of mutual interest.

The representatives of the C.P.S.U. and the H.S.W.P. unanimously note that the rapid normalisation of the economic and political situation in the Hungarian People's Republic was achieved owing to the correct policy pursued by the Hungarian Socialist Workers' Party—a policy based on the unshakable principles of Marxism-Leninism. This policy, which is in line with the vital interests and aspirations of the Hungarian working people, is a creative fusion of the general laws governing the socialist revolution and socialist construction with the concrete historical conditions of development in the Hungarian People's Republic.

The fruitful exchange of views between the representatives of the C.P.S.U. and the H.S.W.P. testifies to the fact that bilateral meetings between representatives of fraternal Communist and Workers' Parties are unquestionably useful. Both sides reaffirm their desire to continue meetings for the purpose of jointly discussing questions of interest to both parties. At the same time, the representatives of the two parties are of the opinion that in the interests of the international working-class and communist movement periodical multilateral meetings of the representatives of fraternal Communist and Workers' Parties would also be beneficial.

Both delegations believe that the Moscow meetings of representatives of fraternal parties held in November, 1957, were a major contribution to the cause of strengthening the unity and cohesion of the international communist movement and the cause of peace among the peoples.

The representatives of both parties note the great importance of the struggle against opportunist trends in the working-class and communist movement and of the struggle for the ideological purity of the Marxist-Leninist teaching.

Today, when imperialist reaction is making special efforts to weaken the Communist and Workers' Parties, to undermine their unity and weaken their cohesion and staunchness, one of its main weapons in the efforts to put a brake on the growing influence of communist ideas among the peoples of the world is to support every kind of revisionist trend within the Communist and Workers' Parties. That is why both parties regard it as their duty to continue the resolute struggle against revisionism as the main danger jeopardising the unity of the parties.

The representatives of the C.P.S.U. and the H.S.W.P. also note the danger presented within the working-class and communist movement by dogmatism and sectarianism, which hamper the development of Marxist-Leninist theory and its creative application to concrete conditions and which substitute a scholastic approach for the study of the concrete conditions existing in this or that country. Dogmatism and sectarianism result in divorcing the party from the masses, which can in no case bring victory to the cause of the working class, the cause of socialism.

The Communist Party of the Soviet Union and the Hungarian Socialist Workers' Party have emphasised their unswerving loyalty to the Leninist principles of proletarian internationalism and have declared that both parties will continue to wage a resolute struggle against the attempts of the enemy to make use of nationalism in order to foment hostility and hatred among the peoples.

In the course of the talks the representatives of the two parties also discussed concrete steps for the further extension of fraternal ties between the C.P.S.U. and the H.S.W.P.

The party and government delegations of the Soviet Union and the Hungarian People's Republic have expressed profound satisfaction with the results of the talks and have noted that there is every possibility of further developing friendly co-operation between the two countries in every sphere of politics, economy and culture. They declare their firm determination to continue developing existing relations for the benefit of their peoples, which will be conducive to the further fraternal cohesion of the countries of the socialist camp and the strengthening of world peace.

N.KHRUSHCHOV
First Secretary of the Central Committee
of the Communist Party of the Soviet
Union and Chairman of the U.S.S.R.
Council of Ministers

JANOS KADAR
First Secretary of the Central Committee
of the Hungarian Socialist Workers'
Party and Minister of State of the Hun-
garian Revolutionary Workers' and
Peasants' Government

4. Communiqué regarding the question of foreign representation at the Seventh Congress of the League of Communists held in Ljubljana, 19 April 1958[1]

In connection with the holding of the Seventh Congress of the League of Communists of Yugoslavia, the Central Committee of the League of Communists of Yugoslavia sent invitations to Communist, Socialist and other Labour Parties and progressive movements in a number of countries with which the League of Communists and the Socialist Federation of Working People of Yugoslavia co-operate or have contact. Fifty-one Parties were invited.

During March and April most of the parties accepted these invitations and informed the Central Committee of the League of Communists of Yugoslavia of the composition of their delegations.

A group of Social Democratic Parties in Western Europe did not accept the invitation and gave notice that they would not send their delegations to the Seventh Congress. Some of these Parties gave as their reason for not accepting the invitation principled differences with the League of Communists of Yugoslavia.

But most of the Communist Parties later also withdrew their decision to send delegations to the Seventh Congress.

Thus, the Communist Party of the Soviet Union in its letter of 5th April 1958 withdrew its decision to send its delegation, and later, the Communist and Workers' Parties of the following countries also withdrew their decisions to send delegations: China, Bulgaria, Czechoslovakia, Hungary, Mongolia, Poland, Sweden and Great Britain.

[1] *S.W.B. Part IIB*, 22 April 1958, pp. 38–39.

As the principal reason for changing their decision on sending delegations to the Seventh Congress of the League of Communists of Yugoslavia, the leaderships of these parties cited disagreement with the draft programme of the League of Communists of Yugoslavia.[1]

The Central Committee of the League of Communists of Yugoslavia has been informed by the Albanian Workers' Party, the Rumanian Workers' Party and the Socialist Unity Party of Germany that they would not send their delegations for the same reason.

Some of the Communist and Workers' Parties of the socialist countries have authorised their Ambassadors in Belgrade to attend the Seventh Congress of the League of Communists of Yugoslavia as observers.

Owing to this situation, the exact number of foreign delegations which will attend the Seventh Congress is as yet unknown.

From a number of Parties which have notified their intention to send their delegations and their composition no subsequent information has been received of any possible change in their decision, nor has any confirmation been given of the arrival of their delegations.

At present it is known that the Seventh Congress will be attended by a Delegation of the Indonesian Communist Party, headed by Njoto, the Assistant Secretary-General; a delegation of the Italian Socialist Party, headed by Giovanni Alassia; a delegation of the Algerian Front of National Liberation, headed by Benkhedda Ben Youssef; a delegate of the Asian Socialist Conference and Social Democratic Party of Japan, Tadataka Sata, a member of the Party leadership; a delegate of the Socialist Party of Chile, Salamon Corbalan, Secretary-General of the party; a delegate of the Union of Peoples of the Cameroons, Ernest Oulandie, Vice-President of the Union of Peoples of the Cameroons.

The National Union of the United Arab Republic is sending four members of its leadership to the Seventh Congress as observers.

Some Communist and Socialist Parties have sent greetings letters and greetings telegrams to the Seventh Congress.

The Congress will also be attended by over 60 foreign journalists.[2]

---

[1] According to press reports, the Programme had already been revised in an unsuccessful effort to meet Russian criticism, see, for example, *New York Times*, 18 and 20 April 1958, and *Le Monde*, 19 April 1958. In April, *Kommunist* (No. 6) attacked the programme as 'unscientific, non-Marxist and anti-Marxist', and accused the Yugoslavs of levelling at the Communist countries all the accusations that 'peace-lovers rightly make against the imperialist policies of the ruling circles of the Western Powers', see *The Times*, 21 April 1958. An English version of the *Programme of the League of Yugoslav Communists* has been published by the International Society for Socialist Studies (London 1959).

[2] For a summary of President Tito's four-hour speech on the tasks of the League in the international situation and the internal developments in Yugoslavia, on 22 April 1958, see *Tanjug*, 23 April 1958. On 23 April Vice-President Rankovic concluded a speech devoted largely to internal Party questions, by alluding to a country (unnamed) which, instead of concerning itself with the affairs of its own people, '. . . lays down as its chief task' the settlement of 'accounts with the Yugoslav communists, interfering in this way in the internal affairs of Yugoslavia'. The

5. Communiqué of the Conference of representatives of Communist and Workers' Parties of member-countries of the Economic Mutual Assistance Council, Moscow, 23 May 1958[1]

A conference of representatives of the Communist and Workers' Parties of the member-countries of the Economic Mutual Assistance Council met in Moscow from May 20 to 23, 1958.

It was attended by representatives of the Albanian Party of Labour, the Bulgarian Communist Party, the Hungarian Socialist Workers' Party, the Socialist Unity Party of Germany, the Polish United Workers' Party, the Rumanian Workers' Party, the Communist Party of the Soviet Union, and the Communist Party of Czechoslovakia. Representatives from the Viet Namese Party of Labour, the Communist Party of China, the Korean Party of Labour and the Mongolian People's Revolutionary Party were also invited to take part in the conference.

The conference considered the further promotion of economic co-operation between the socialist countries on the basis of the consistent implementation of the principle of international socialist division óf labour and rational industrial specialisation and co-ordination, and heard reports on the work of the government planning agencies of the socialist countries in drawing up long-term plans for the basic sections of the national economy.

The members of the conference were unanimous in noting that economic contacts between the socialist countries were steadily being consolidated and were acquiring an increasingly many-sided character. Considerable progress has been made in recent years, in specialisation and co-ordination of production, notably in machine-building.

The Economic Mutual Assistance Council and its standing committees have carried out a considerable amount of work in preparing recommendations in connection with the drafting of long term plans for the development of the economy of the socialist countries.

The many-sided co-operation among the socialist countries, founded on the principles of complete equality, respect for one another's national interests and socialist inter-assistance, serves the cause of building socialism and communism and makes it possible to use to the full the advantages of the world socialist system of economy for developing the productive forces of every socialist country individually and for strengthening the economic might of the socialist camp as a whole.

The conference holds that now that the economic ties among the

diplomatic representatives of the Soviet *bloc* countries, who attended the Congress as observers, absented themselves, with the exception of the Polish ambassador, during the latter part of Vice-President Rankovic's speech. For a summary of the first part of the speech and a full report of the concluding section, see *Tanjug*, 24 April 1958.

[1] *Soviet News*, 27 May 1958.

socialist countries have been considerably strengthened and have become all-embracing, it is becoming particularly important further to develop and improve the forms of economic co-operation among them, further to specialise and co-ordinate the production in the inter-related branches of national economy of the countries of the socialist camp.

The correct organisation of co-ordination and specialisation in production within the socialist camp ensures an economy of material resources and a rise in the productivity of social labour, the most rational use of the natural resources and the economic conditions in the socialist countries for speeding up the expansion of socialist reproduction. The conference drew attention to the need for the utmost development of the raw material branches of the national economy and the power industry and for the further development and introduction of new machinery and techniques. Particular attention was drawn to the necessity of further co-ordination and specialisation in machine-building, making it possible to go over to the more rational mass and serial production, which sharply reduces production expenditures per unit of output.

The representatives of the Communist and Workers' Parties unanimously reaffirmed the need for the utmost utilisation of the vast possibilities and the greatest possible consideration for the interests of all socialist countries in the preparation of long-term plans, and also for expanding the mutually advantageous forms of co-operation with a view to raising the level of industrialisation in countries with a less developed industry.

The conference found it necessary further to enhance the role of the Economic Mutual Assistance Council and its agencies in the organisation of economic co-operation.

The conference worked out and approved agreed recommendations on the further development of economic co-operation among the socialist countries, the co-ordination and specialisation of production, and on the preparation of long-term national economic development plans. The conference decided to refer these recommendations to the Economic Mutual Assistance Council for the elaboration of the required practical measures.

The representatives of parties of the countries which do not belong to the Economic Mutual Assistance Council expressed readiness to take an active part in the economic co-operation of the socialist countries and to strengthen this co-operation in due form by measures conforming to the specific conditions in their countries.

The discussion of the questions on the conference's agenda took place in a friendly and cordial atmosphere, in the spirit of fraternal mutual understanding, and revealed the complete community of views of the parties represented on all the questions discussed.

6. Communiqué on the meeting of the political consultative committee of the Warsaw Treaty Organization, 24 May 1958[1]

A meeting of the Political Consultative Committee of the states, parties to the Warsaw Treaty of Friendship, Co-operation and Mutual Assistance, was held in Moscow on May 24, 1958.

The following representatives attended the meeting of the Political Consultative Committee:

From the People's Republic of Albania—Mehmet Shehu, Chairman of the Council of Ministers; Enver Hodja, first secretary of the central committee of the Albanian Party of Labour; Behar Shtylla, Minister of Foreign Affairs; and Arif Hasko, Chief of the General Staff of the People's Army of the Albanian People's Republic.

From the Bulgarian People's Republic—Anton Yugov, Chairman of the Council of Ministers; Todor Zhivkov, first secretary of the central committee of the Bulgarian Communist Party; Karlo Lukanov, Minister of Foreign Affairs; and Pyotr Panchewski, Minister of National Defence.

From the Hungarian People's Republic—Janos Kadar, Minister of State and first secretary of the central committee of the Hungarian Socialist Workers' Party; Endre Sik, Minister of Foreign Affairs; and Colonel-General Geza Revesz, Minister of Defence.

From the German Democratic Republic—Otto Grotewohl, Chairman of the Council of Ministers; Walter Ulbricht, first secretary of the central committee of the Socialist Unity Party of Germany; Colonel-General Willi Stoph, Minister of National Defence; Bruno Leuschner, Vice-Chairman of the Council of Ministers; and Otto Winzer, Deputy Minister of Foreign Affairs.

From the Polish People's Republic—Josef Cyrankiewicz, Chairman of the Council of Ministers; Wladislaw Gomulka, first secretary of the central committee of the Polish United Workers' Party; Adam Rapacki, Minister of Foreign Affairs; and Colonel-General Marian Spychalski, Minister of National Defence.

From the Rumanian People's Republic—Chivu Stoica, Chairman of the Council of Ministers; Gheorghe Gheorghiu-Dej, first secretary of the central committee of the Rumanian Workers' Party; Emil Bodnaras, Vice-Chairman of the Council of Ministers; Avram Bunaciu, Minister of Foreign Affairs; and Colonel-General Leontin Salajan, Minister of the Armed Forces.

From the Union of Soviet Socialist Republics—N. S. Khrushchov, Chairman of the Council of Ministers and first secretary of the central committee of the Communist Party of the Soviet Union; A. A. Gromyko, Minister of

Foreign Affairs; Marshal of the Soviet Union R. Y. Malinovsky, Minister of Defence.

From the Czechoslovak Republic—Viliam Siroky, Prime Minister; Vaclav David, Minister of Foreign Affairs; and Colonel-General Bohumir Lomsky, Minister of National Defence.

As observers from the People's Republic of China—Chen Yun, Vice-Premier of the Government Council; and Li Fuchun, Vice-Premier of the Government Council.

Anton Yugov, Chairman of the Council of Ministers of the People's Republic of Bulgaria, presided over the session.

In conformity with Article 3 of the Warsaw Treaty, envisaging consultations between the states, parties to the treaty, on all major international questions affecting their interests, an exchange of opinion on the present international situation took place at the meeting of the Consultative Committee. The Political Consultative Committee noted with satisfaction the complete unanimity of the socialist countries, parties to the meeting, both in assessing the international situation and their common tasks in the struggle for peace and the security of the peoples. The Political Consultative Committee unanimously adopted a declaration of the states, parties to the Warsaw Treaty, which is published in the press.[1]

The Political Consultative Committee heard a report by Marshal of the Soviet Union I. S. Koniev, Commander-in-Chief of the Joint Armed Forces of the states, parties to the Warsaw Treaty, on a further reduction in the armed forces of the Warsaw Treaty countries, and on the withdrawal of the Soviet forces from the territory of the Rumanian People's Republic.

Besides the further cut in the armed forces of the Soviet Union in 1958 by 300,000 men, which was announced earlier, the states, parties to the Warsaw Treaty, resolved to effect in 1958, in addition to the earlier substantial reduction in their armed forces, another cut in the armed forces by a total of 119,000 men, including: the Rumanian People's Republic by 55,000 men, the Bulgarian People's Republic by 23,000 men, the Polish People's Republic by 20,000 men, the Czechoslovak Republic by 20,000 men and the Albanian People's Republic by 1,000 men. Thus the Warsaw Treaty member-countries will have reduced their armed forces by 419,000 men in 1958.

The Political Consultative Committee approved a proposal of the government of the Soviet Union, agreed with the government of the Rumanian People's Republic, on the withdrawal in the near future from the Rumanian People's Republic of the Soviet troops stationed there in conformity with the Warsaw Treaty.

The Soviet government, by agreement with the Hungarian govern-

---

[1] For the text of the Declaration signed on 24 May 1958, by the representatives of the countries which are signatories of the Warsaw Treaty, see *Soviet News*, 28 May 1958.

ment, resolved to reduce, in 1958, the Soviet troops stationed in Hungary by one division and to withdraw it from Hungarian territory.

The Political Consultative Committee approved this decision of the Soviet government.

Decisions were also taken on certain organisational matters involved in the activity of the Joint Armed Forces of the states, parties to the Warsaw Treaty.

The Political Consultative Committee resolved to address to the member-states of the North Atlantic Treaty (N.A.T.O.) a proposal concerning the conclusion of a non-aggression pact between the states, parties to the Warsaw Treaty, and the N.A.T.O. member-states. The text of the draft of the aforesaid non-aggression pact is published separately.[1]

The proceedings of the meeting of the Political Consultative Committee of the states, parties to the Warsaw Treaty, demonstrated the complete unity, unbreakable fraternal friendship and co-operation of the socialist countries, which are concentrating their efforts on a relaxation of international tension, the creation of an atmosphere of mutual confidence and businesslike co-operation between all states, for the further consolidation of peace.

7. Note from the Soviet Ministry of Foreign Affairs to the Yugoslav Government regarding Soviet-Yugoslav economic relations, Moscow, 27 May 1958[2]

The Ministry of Foreign Affairs of the Union of Soviet Socialist Republics presents its compliments to the Embassy of the Federal People's Republic of Yugoslavia and, on the instructions of the government of the U.S.S.R., has the honour to address itself to the government of the Federal People's Republic of Yugoslavia in connection with the economic agreements of January 12 and August 1, 1956.

These agreements envisage that the Soviet Union will grant Yugoslavia credits for the period from 1957 to 1964 to finance the construction of an aluminium plant and to pay for equipment for fertiliser and other enterprises and also for designing and other work enumerated in the agreements.

At the present time there is a need to revise the period of the credits granted to Yoguslavia in accordance with the abovementioned agreements. This need has arisen in connection with the decision recently taken

[1] See *Soviet News*, 28 May 1958.
[2] Ibid., 2 July 1958. On 9 May 1958, *Pravda* published an editorial article dealing with the draft programme of the League of Communists of Yugoslavia. The article denounced President Tito for trying to weaken the unity of the Socialist countries, and indicated that the ideological dispute between the U.S.S.R. and Yugoslavia might spread into the political arena. The article, summarised in *Soviet News*, 12 May 1958, hinted at a cancellation of economic aid to Yugoslavia.

in the Soviet Union to speed up the development of the chemical industry, and particularly the production of synthetic materials and goods to satisfy the requirements of the population and the needs of the national economy, the implementation of which will require large new capital investments in the chemical industry of the U.S.S.R. in the next few years. The Soviet government is therefore making changes in its financial plans with a view to ensuring that financial resources are used in the most effective way from the economic standpoint.

Owing to this circumstance, the government of the U.S.S.R. is faced with the necessity of proposing some later periods for the use of the credits granted to Yugoslavia, namely:

> Under the agreement of January 12, 1956, in the part relating to the further use of the credit, to establish that this credit will be used in the period from 1962 to 1969;
> Under the agreement of August 1, 1956, to establish that the credit will be used in the period from 1963 to 1969.

The time for the delivery of equipment and the fulfilment of designing and other work provided for by the agreements should be made to accord with the changes in the period for the use of the credits.

However, Soviet foreign trading organisations, should the government of the Federal People's Republic of Yugoslavia so desire, could deliver equipment to Yugoslav organisations and carry out designing and other work in the period established by the protocols of July 29, 1957, and could deliver equipment of various kinds in accordance with the protocol of August 2, 1956, not, however, on credit but to be paid for under current trade turnover.

As regards the time of the postponement of the putting in operation of the enterprises envisaged by the agreements, including enterprises for the production of fertilisers, the Soviet side, should the Yugoslav side so desire, could by way of mutual trade turnover deliver to Yugoslavia a definite quantity of mineral fertilisers and also industrial goods by agreement between the parties.

The proposals stated above are, in the opinion of the Soviet government, in keeping with the principles of economic co-operation between states which is profitable to both sides. The government of the U.S.S.R. expresses confidence that the government of the Federal People's Republic of Yugoslavia will correctly understand the proposals made in the present Note and will adopt a positive attitude to them.

The proposed changes in the agreements of January 12 and August 1, 1956, could be effected, depending on the desire of the government of the Federal People's Republic of Yugoslavia, either by an exchange of Notes or by signing additional protocols to these agreements.

The proposal with regard to the agreement of August 1, 1956, has been co-ordinated with the government of the German Democratic Republic, which is one of the parties to this agreement.

8. Note from the Yugoslav State Secretariat for Foreign Affairs to the Soviet Government regarding Soviet-Yugoslav economic relations, Belgrade, 3 June 1958[1]

The State Secretariat for Foreign Affairs of the Federal People's Republic of Yugoslavia presents its compliments to the Embassy of the Union of Soviet Socialist Republics and, on behalf of the government of the Federal People's Republic of Yugoslavia, in connection with the U.S.S.R. government's Note of May 27, 1958, concerning the agreements between the two governments of January 12 and August 1, 1956, has the honour to state the following to the government of the U.S.S.R.:

The government of the Federal People's Republic of Yugoslavia cannot accept the proposals of the U.S.S.R. government put forward in the above Note and establishing a period of credits for Yugoslavia later than that fixed by the agreement of January 12, 1956, the protocol to this agreement of July 29, 1957, the agreement of August 1, 1956, and the protocol to this agreement of July 29, 1957, as it cannot accept the proposals concerning the delivery of equipment and the fulfilment of designing and other work which would be paid for under current trade turnover.

On this point the government of the Federal People's Republic of Yugoslavia would like to emphasise that the rights and duties of the two countries in this sphere are clearly defined by the above agreements, not only as regards an understanding on the agreements in general, but also as regards the methods and conditions for the fulfilment of these agreements.

Both the agreements mentioned are the product of a prolonged and all-round study of mutual economic relations, as well as of the mutual possibilities for fulfilment of the obligations ensuing from these agreements.

The proposals put forward in the U.S.S.R. government's Note of May 27, 1958, would lead to changes in the current and long-term national economic plans of the Federal People's Republic of Yugoslavia in the sense that they would change the distribution of the national income already adopted, particularly at the expense of investments, and, accordingly, the living standards of the population. Furthermore, in view of the fact that the construction of certain enterprises, envisaged under the above

---

[1] *Soviet News*, 2 July 1958. On 22 December 1958 the United States signed an agreement with Yugoslavia for the sale of $94·8 million worth of American surplus agricultural commodities for domestic dinar funds, see T.I.A.S., 4153. On 8 January 1959 an agreement was signed between the United States and Yugoslavia to establish a Development Loan Fund of up to $22·5 million, to finance the foreign-exchange costs (estimated at half the total cost of the project) of a nitrogenous fertilizer plant to be built near Pancevo, Yugoslavia, see *D.S.B.*, 26 January 1959, p. 136.

agreements, has been partly begun, and that the Yugoslav side has assigned an organisation which is to work in this direction, and that considerable manpower and resources are engaged in this, any postponement of the periods provided for under the agreements would do direct harm to Yugoslavia and to the Yugoslav economy.

Proceeding from what has been said, and also from the fact that in its international relations the government of the Federal People's Republic of Yugoslavia is guided by the principles of consistent respect for, and implementation of, international agreements and obligations, and that in accordance with this it can with every right count on respect for such obligations on the part of the Soviet Union as well, it cannot accept as valid the reasons put forward in the Note of the U.S.S.R. government.

The government of the Federal People's Republic of Yugoslavia cannot but note the fact that the Soviet side has already on one occasion raised the question of postponing the periods of fulfilment of these agreements and that then, with the aim of displaying maximum good will and in spite of considerable material losses, the Yugoslav side went as far as possible to meet the suggestions of the Soviet side half way and accepted the proposed postponement.

In its Note of May 27, this year, the government of the Soviet Union again proposes, after nearly 10 months, to postpone the period of fulfilment, and this would mean that, as regards the initial agreements, the period of fulfilment would accordingly be postponed from six to 10 years for the first agreement and from seven to 12 years for the second agreement.

The government of the Federal People's Republic of Yugoslavia is obliged to declare that such acts on the part of the U.S.S.R. government introduce a lack of confidence in the economic relations between the Federal People's Republic of Yugoslavia and the U.S.S.R., and this can only do harm to the general normal relations between our countries. The government of the Federal People's Republic of Yugoslavia would also like to draw the attention of the Soviet government, in so far as it adheres to its positions, to the responsibility which the U.S.S.R. government is taking upon itself as regards losses inflicted on the Yugoslav economy. In this case the Federal People's Republic of Yugoslavia reserves the right to demand just compensation.

On the basis of what has been said above, the government of the Federal People's Republic of Yugoslavia expects that the U.S.S.R. government will reconsider its attitude as expressed in the Note of May 27, 1958, from the standpoint of strict observance of the obligations it has undertaken in the abovementioned agreements.

The State Secretariat for Foreign Affairs takes the opportunity to express its respect to the Embassy of the Union of Soviet Socialist Republics.

9. Announcement by the Hungarian Ministry of Justice regarding the criminal proceedings taken against Imre Nagy and his associates, Budapest, 16 June 1958[1]

The judiciary authorities have completed proceedings in the case of the group of leading persons who with the active co-operation of the imperialists brought about the outbreak of an armed counter-revolutionary uprising on 23rd October 1956, aimed at the overthrow of the lawful order of the Hungarian People's Republic.

In his indictment, the Supreme Prosecutor of the Hungarian People's Republic accused Imre Nagy and his accomplices—Ferenc Donath, Miklos Gimes, Zoltan Tildy, Pal Maleter, Sandor Kopacsi, Jozsef Zzilagyi, Ferenc Janosi and Miklos Vasarhelyi—of the crime of conspiracy to overthrow the State order of the Hungarian people's democracy. In addition, Imre Nagy was charged with high treason and Sandor Kopacsi and Pal Maleter with the crime of military mutiny.

Criminal proceedings against the accused Geza Losonczy were dropped by the Prosecutor's Office following his death after an illness.

The People's Court Bench of the Supreme Court having heard the testimony of the accused, the evidence of 29 witnesses, the indictment and the case for the defence and after the examining of the extensive material submitted in evidence, found as follows in the criminal case of Imre Nagy and his associates:

Imre Nagy and his closest accomplices—Geza Losonczy, Ferenc Donath, Miklos Gimes and Jozsef Szilagyi—set up a clandestine anti-State organisation in December 1955 to seize power by force and to overthrow the Hungarian People's Republic. In the course of the hearings of the criminal case, it was established that Imre Nagy and his accomplices had taken a leading role in the preparation and outbreak of the October 1956 counter-revolutionary rising.

Zoltan Tildy and Pal Maleter were acquainted with the hostile aims of Imre Nagy and his associates in October 1956, approved of them, and actively joined the counter-revolutionary rising. In alliance with foreign imperialists, the members of the group of conspirators heading the reactionary forces at home staged a putsch attempt to overthrow the Hungarian People's Republic.

The court established that to seize power by force, Imre Nagy had set up a small illegal group consisting of his closest supporters as far back as the end of 1955. This illegal group pursued its hostile activities both by illegal means and by exploiting legal opportunities. To carry out their aim of overthrowing the people's power, they mobilised, and associated

[1] *S.W.B. Part IIB*, 19 June 1958, pp. 1–5.

with their activities, all types of people who were enemies of the people's democratic State order.

By demagogically and mendaciously concealing their real aims and by proclaiming socialist slogans, they temporarily misled a number of well-meaning people as well, and used them for their own anti-State purposes. The conspirators' group, and its leader, Imre Nagy himself in the first place, worked out the political platform of the movement against the people's democracy: its immediate purposes, methods and more remote aims.

The person representing the prosecution submitted to the Court secret documents in this connection, for the most part in Imre Nagy's own handwriting. In the document headed 'Morality and Ethics', written in December 1955, Imre Nagy described the people's democratic State order as a power which had degenerated into Bonapartism and appealed for its overthrow by force. In another document entitled 'On some Topical Questions', written in January 1956, he advocated an alliance with forces opposing the people's democracy.

Abandoning the working class power, he set out to restore the multi-Party system. In an essay headed 'Five Principles of International Relations', also dated January 1956, he said that the annihilation of the country's defensive pact—the Warsaw Treaty—and handing over the country to the imperialists on the pretext of eliminating the policy of blocs were among the aims of the group of adventurers.

On the basis of the evidence and of confessions, the Court established that Imre Nagy had these writings duplicated and clandestinely distributed in the circle of his immediate accomplices and among elements whom they considered trustworthy. In the course of the hearings it was proved that the illegal organisation set up by Imre Nagy and his associates pursued planned subversive activities to undermine the worker-peasant power, to cause the legal order of the people's democracy to disintegrate and later to seize power by force. They drew Gabor Tanczos, as well as Balazs Nagy, who later escaped to the West, into their illegal activities. Working through these two men, they turned the Petoefi Circle into a meeting place for hostile elements and a forum of attacks against the Party and the State.

On the pretext of arranging debates, they themselves organised the Petoefi Circle's moves against the people's democracies. A number of hostile speeches were prepared in advance, including the speech made by Tibor Dery in the so-called debate on the Press, which incited young people to engage in counter-revolutionary activities. This speech was prepared jointly by Geza Losonczy, Sandor Haraszti and Dery. Another of their methods was to publish inciting articles in the Press, making use of Tibor Dery, Gyula Hay, Tamas Aczel, and elements who like them were opposed to the People's Republic. In these articles, mistakes made in the course of socialist construction were magnified out of proportion and unbridled slanders were uttered against the system.

The aim of all these activities was to undermine the power of the State, to run down its authority and to set into motion elements hostile or opposed to the people's democracy, and in this atmosphere to seize power by force. In September 1956, Geza Losonczy publicly told Amos Klon, an Israeli journalist staying in Budapest at the time: 'If it comes to it, we shall oppose the Government by force.'

On 20th October 1956, Jozsef Szilagyi announced at an illegal meeting arranged by him that Imre Nagy and his associates were ready to seize power. The notorious demonstration of 23rd October was initiated by Imre Nagy and his group, using the contacts they had established in the Petoefi Circle and the universities. For instance, at a meeting held in the Technical University on the night of 22nd October, Jozsef Szilagyi personally called for demonstrations on behalf of Imre Nagy. The demonstration on 23rd October was directed by Imre Nagy's group through Gabor Tanczos and his companions. At this period, the conspirators held clandestine meetings almost daily and on some days the group met several times. On Imre Nagy's initiative, Geza Losonczy, Ferenc Donath and Miklos Gimes, helped by other members of the organisation, began on 19th, 20th and 22nd October 1956 to draft the programme of the government they were to set up.

During a secret discussion held in Geza Losonczy's flat on the morning of 23rd October 1956, which was presided over by Imre Nagy and attended by Miklos Gimes, Miklos Vasarhelyi, Ferenc Janosi, and Sandor Haraszti, the list of the Government with which they intended to assume power after the overthrow of the legal Hungarian Government was drawn up. In this secret Government list, Imre Nagy had himself designated as Premier. The Ministerial posts were distributed by members of the group of conspirators among themselves.

To take over the direction of the armed rising which started simultaneously with the demonstration serving as its legal screen, the members of the conspiracy set up several illegal groups. One of the centres, consisting of Sandor Kopacsi, Jozsef Szilagyi, Miklos Gimes, Gyoergy Fazekas, and Tamas Aczel, was organised in the Budapest Central Police Command.

Betraying his oath, abusing his post as Chief of Police and deceiving his subordinates, Sandor Kopacsi carried out the duties assigned to him by the illegal centre. To arm the insurgent anti-people's democratic forces and at the same time to disband the armed forces loyal to socialism, he gave orders to the City District police commands not to put up any resistance to the rebels but on the contrary to hand their arms and the police building over to them. In this fashion Kopacsi caused over 20,000 rifles to be distributed to the rebels from police stores. This group was in close co-operation with another sub-centre, set up on 24th October 1956, which consisted of Geza Losonczy, Ferenc Donath and Ferenc Janosi. This group directed the activities designed to incite disaffection in the ranks of the Army. At the same time, it kept the rebels continuously informed of the military plans of the armed forces defending the People's Republic.

Well before the October uprising, Imre Nagy and his accomplices had established secret relations and conducted talks with the representatives of bourgeois 'restoration', with whom they allied themselves so as to seize power by force. In the course of these talks, Geza Losonczy and Sandor Haraszti had personally agreed with Anna Kethly as early as July 1956 and later through the mediation of Istvan Erdei on her participation in a future Nagy Government.

In December 1955, Imre Nagy decided to restore the former so-called 'coalition parties', and to form a Government together with them. But when, relying on the counter-revolutionary forces, he became Premier by force and fraud, he went much further. Being without scruple, he connived at the setting-up of 70 different Parties and organisations in contravention to the Constitution during the few short days of the counter-revolution, including such notorious bourgeois-fascist parties as the Party of Hungarian Life, the Christian Democrat Party, the Hungarian Christian Party, the Hungarian People's Party, the National Camp, the Christian Front, the Catholic People's Party, the Christian People's Party and—in Gyoer—the Arrow Cross Party. These parties are proscribed in the Peace Treaty. To secure power, Imre Nagy's group of conspirators concluded an alliance with the most extreme reactionary groups. They even rehabilitated the former Prince Primate, Jozsef Mindszenty, who had been legally and justly sentenced, and produced him against the People's Republic. Having reached an agreement with them through Zoltan Tildy, Mindszenty proclaimed a programme of capitalist restoration on the radio on 3rd November.

Imre Nagy and his associates also reached agreement with the imperialist-paid bourgeois-fascist Hungarian emigration. This is proved by a statement made on 28th October 1956 by Bela Varga, Chairman of the so-called National Commission, in which he said: 'Members of the Council are in constant touch with leaders of the Hungarian rising.' Zoltan Tildy later came to an agreement by telephone with Ferenc Nagy, who had arrived in Vienna to support the counter-revolution. The agreement was that the emigration would give the Imre Nagy Government its support.

In the course of his activities as Prime Minister, Imre Nagy in contravention of this oath illegally excluded from leadership the constitutional directing organs of the country: the National Assembly, the Presidential Council and the Government, and set up his own Government organ: a so-called Cabinet. He picked this Cabinet in such a way that although persons loyal to socialism were included in it for purposes of deception, the majority of its members were reactionaries. On 2nd November he reorganised even this Cabinet and included in it further fanatical extremist representatives of bourgeois restoration and leaders of the counter-revolutionary uprising. At this time the Cabinet, apart from Imre Nagy, included Geza Losonczy, Zoltan Tildy, Anna Kethly, Istvan Szabo, Istvan Bibo, and—as Minister of Defence—Pal Maleter, the commander of the counter-revolutionary armed forces.

After either disbanding or setting aside the central organs of the power of the People's Republic, Imre Nagy and his associates set out to annihilate the local organs of power. The legal administrative bodies—the Councils —were liquidated, as were the organs of economic management. They were replaced by so-called Revolutionary Committees—most of which consisted of bourgeois-fascist elements—and the so-called Workers' Councils, which were designed to mislead the workers.

With their treasonable and disruptive activities, Imre Nagy and his accomplices eventually paralysed the armed forces defending the People's Republic with the cease-fire order they enforced. At the same time, they organised, armed and eventually legalised, the insurgent counter-revolutionary forces. They recruited into the so-called National Guard war criminals, persons who had committed crimes against the people, convicts released from prison and all sorts of enemies of the people's democracy.

A White Terror began in Budapest and throughout the country after this. According to data so far examined, during the few short days of the rule of Imre Nagy and his associates terrorist detachments murdered 234 defenceless citizens. In the same period they imprisoned 3,000 progressive persons loyal to the people's democratic system, intending to execute them within a few days. They had in addition prepared a 'death-list' by 4th November. This included the names of over 10,000 persons who were to be massacred.

While rallying round themselves the country's reactionary forces, Imre Nagy and his accomplices established relations and co-operation on a broad basis with various imperialist circles, organs and representatives. Laszlo Kardos, a member of the group of conspirators, was in contact with Cope, a former official of the British Legation in Budapest, with whose help they smuggled abroad Imre Nagy's anti-State political writings. Through Pal Maleter they were in contact with Cowley, the British Military Attache, who took a direct part in the military direction of the insurrection. Through Geza Losonczy, they made contact and established co-operation with Prince Loewenstein, a representative of West German imperialists who had been sent to Hungary. Following negotiations, Prince Loewenstein assured the counter-revolutionary insurgents of the support of West German big capital in a speech over Kossuth Radio.

Certain imperialist circles, led by the US imperialists, had for years been throwing in their whole propaganda apparatus and their news and intelligence services in support of the Imre Nagy group—the representatives in Hungary of the counter-revolutionary trend which they called national communism. The American intelligence organ known as the University of Strasbourg had drafted the programme of the counter-revolutionary uprising as early as September 1956. This was illegally disseminated in the country. At the time of the counter-revolution they sent considerable quantities of small arms, smuggled in as Red Cross gifts, into the country. The imperialist Press and radio had meanwhile started a campaign to popularise Imre Nagy personally.

They declared that it would suit the Western Powers better if Hungary's breakaway from the socialist camp were carried out by a group which was Communist in name. The notorious Radio Free Europe incited the counter-revolutionary rising and after its outbreak helped and guided it with military instructions in its Hungarian broadcasts and with its notorious balloon scheme. These instructions were carried out by the conspirators.

To realise its aims and to leave the road quite free for imperialist intervention, Imre Nagy and his group of traitors attempted to denounce the country's defensive pact—the Warsaw Treaty—illegally and unilaterally. The culmination of this attempt was the radio broadcast by Imre Nagy on 4th November, in which he appealed to the Western imperialists for an open armed intervention against the Revolutionary Worker-Peasant Government and the Soviet troops it had called in.

After the fall of the armed counter-revolutionary insurrection, individuals and groups belonging to the Imre Nagy conspiracy sought refuge where they had formerly received support. Among the participants of the coup, Bela Kiraly, Anna Kethly, Jozsef Koevago and others escaped to the West to evade being taken to task; Jozsef Mindszenty—according to information available to the Hungarian authorities—went into hiding in the US Legation; Istvan Szabo tried to escape to the British Legation in Budapest; the Imre Nagy group, which had come forward under the pirate flag of national communism, escaped to the Yugoslav Embassy in Budapest to evade being held responsible for what they had done.

It is characteristic of the infamy of the conspirators that they continued with their counter revolutionary activities as before even after the Hungarian people had, under the guidance of the Revolutionary Worker-Peasant Government, begun to re-establish law and order, to ensure peaceful life for the people, and to repair the grave damage done by the counter-revolution. Anna Kethly, Bela Kiraly, Jozsef Koevago and their companions issued their instructions for the continuation of armed resistance, the organisation of strikes to paralyse life, and the reorganisation of underground subversive work from the West. Imre Nagy, Geza Losonczy and others did so from the Yugoslav Embassy in Budapest. For instance, Nagy and Losonczy established links from the Yugoslav Embassy building with the Central Workers' Council of Budapest and with Radio Free Europe through Miklos Gimes and other accomplices of theirs, and even published a new illegal paper called '23rd October'.

All this has been proved by irrefutable facts, by investigations conducted subsequently, and by the Court proceedings now instituted. The material of the case, produced during the Court proceedings, has also shown and proved that Imre Nagy and his companions, as a result of their earlier revisionist and bourgeois nationalist political attitude, were bound to arrive at an alliance with the most reactionary and imperialist bourgeois forces and were bound to become traitors to the workers' power, the people's democratic system, the working Hungarian people and the socialist homeland.

During the Court hearing, the accused Ferenc Donath, Miklos Gimes, Zoltan Tildy, Sandor Kopacsy, Ferenc Janosi and Miklos Vasarhelyi showed repentance and fully admitted their guilt. Imre Nagy, Jozsef Szilagyi and Pal Maleter denied that they were guilty. But as a result of the damning evidence of their accomplices and of witnesses, as well as of the material evidence produced, they were unmasked in the course of the hearing and partially admitted the facts incriminating them.

On the basis of its hearing, having weighed the gravity of the criminal acts and taken both aggravating and extenuating circumstances into account the People's Court Bench of the Supreme Court found the accused guilty of the acts on which the indictment was grounded and sentenced:

> Imre Nagy to death;
> Ferenc Donath to 12 years' imprisonment;
> Miklos Gimes to death;
> Zoltan Tildy to six years' imprisonment;
> Pal Maleter to death;
> Sandor Kopacsy to life imprisonment;
> Dr. Jozsef Szilagyi to death;
> Ferenc Janos to eight years' imprisonment; and
> Miklos Vasarhelyi to five years' imprisonment.

The sentences are final. The death sentences have been carried out.

10. Yugoslav note to the Hungarian Government protesting against the secret trial and execution of Imre Nagy, 23 June 1958[1]

On 17th June 1958, the Ministry of Justice of the People's Republic of Hungary published a statement on the pronouncing of the sentence on Imre Nagy and his companions and on its execution. The statement alleges, among other things, that 'certain groups of conspirators of the type of Imre Nagy have sought asylum where they had earlier received support', that Imre Nagy, Geza Losonczy and others 'were sending their instructions from the building of the Yugoslav Embassy in Budapest for the continuation of the armed resistance, for organising of strikes to paralyse life and for reorganising underground subversive activity', that they have 'from the building of the Yugoslav Embassy established, through Miklos Gimes and other accomplices, contacts with the Central Workers' Council of Budapest, with the "Free Europe" radio station and, what is more, that they published a new illegal paper "23rd October".'

The Yugoslav Government and our people have received the sudden news about the secret trial and execution of the death sentence on Imre Nagy with profound indignation. The assertions of an alleged activity of the mentioned persons after their arrival in the Yugoslav Embassy building are untrue, and invented from beginning to end. The Hungarian Government knows very well that those persons, while staying in the Yugoslav Embassy building, did not commit any of the acts mentioned in the statement of the Hungarian Ministry of Justice. As soon as they came to the Yugoslav Embassy building, the mentioned persons made, as a normal condition for using asylum, a statement to the effect that they renounced any political activity during the term of their asylum, to which they strictly adhered. The President of the Revolutionary Worker-Peasant Government, Comrade Janos Kadar, was also informed of their statement soon after his arrival in Budapest on the fourth day after Imre Nagy and his companions came to the Yugoslav Embassy.

Apart from this, the Embassy building was, during the whole time, under the strictest supervision of Soviet military detachments and the Hungarian security service. In that same period, on 5th November 1956, a Yugoslav diplomat Milovanov was killed in the Embassy building from shots fired from the street by tanks.

Judging by the staged accusations against Yugoslavia, and by the circumstances in which the trial was held—the statement contains no data of the time when the trial was held and when the sentences were executed —there is justified doubt in the accuracy of the other material evidence as well, certainly in all that is directly or indirectly imputed to Yugoslavia.

[1] S.W.B., Part II B, 26 June 1958, pp. 26–28.

The Yugoslav Government stresses this finding all the more resolutely, as the past has also seen similar trials, such as the trial of Rajk, in which Yugoslavia was accused, and as allegations were at that time also made that reliable evidence was available on Yugoslavia's guilt and interference, and then later, when much innocent blood had been shed, it was established that this evidence, along with the explicit admission of responsible Hungarian men, was invented. Such attacks had, at that time, as is known, inflicted great difficulties to us, but the chief victims were the peoples of the countries in which these trials were staged.

Therefore, the Yugoslav Government does not consider it at all necessary to prove its uprightness in this matter. It has never interfered in the internal affairs of Hungary, nor is it doing so now. The facts about this stand of the Yugoslav Government are known not only to the Hungarian Government but to the whole international public as well. Thus, it is generally known that precisely at the time for which she is accused, Yugoslavia was making considerable efforts, selfless efforts, to contribute towards the stabilisation of conditions in Hungary, for which she was often paid tribute by the Hungarian leaders themselves.

From the above, it follows that the quoted assertions given in the mentioned statement constitute a harsh and completely unprovoked attack on the Federal People's Republic of Yugoslavia, with the obvious aim of sharpening and justifying, by again using the most sinister methods from the recent past, the existing organised and merciless anti-Yugoslav action, of fundamentally vitiating Hungarian-Yugoslav relations, and of trying to cast the responsibility for those events in Hungary on to Yugoslavia.

This is undeniably confirmed by the fact that the allegations in the Hungarian statement were immediately made use of in the Press of certain Governments which are taking part in this action. This attack, regardless of whether it was made by free will, is all the more deplorable and to be condemned, as relations between the Yugoslav and Hungarian peoples have been developing favourably, which could only be of interest both ways, as well as in the interest of all the factors who really want the consolidation of peace in this part of the world. It is obvious that by this act the Government of the People's Republic of Hungary has inflicted a heavy blow on relations between the Federal People's Republic of Yugoslavia and the People's Republic of Hungary.

In connection with the statement of the Hungarian Ministry of Justice, the Government of the Federal People's Republic of Yugoslavia considers it necessary to recall the following facts: By the exchange of letters between the Governments of the Federal People's Republic of Yugoslavia and the People's Republic of Hungary of the 18th and 21st November 1956 respectively, agreement was reached on the solution of the question of the asylum of Imre Nagy and other persons who were given asylum in the

Yugoslav Embassy in Budapest, in that the Hungarian Government had guaranteed personal security and free departure of those persons to their homes, after leaving the Yugoslav Embassy building, obliging itself that 'it would not apply any sanctions against them for their past activities'.

As the Hungarian Government did not ensure the implementation of the mentioned agreement, by which it is violated, the Yugoslav Government lodged a protest with the Hungarian Government in its Note of 24th November 1956. In its reply, set out in a Note of 1st December 1956, the Hungarian Government, rejecting the Yugoslav Government protest, asserted that the fact that the mentioned persons had not returned to their homes was 'a secondary question of technical importance', and that it was otherwise keeping to the obligations of the agreement between the two Governments, reaffirming that 'it was prepared to guarantee the personal security of the mentioned persons', and declaring that it 'did not intend to apply any punishments for their past activities'.

Whereas in this political situation in Hungary there was danger of counter-revolutionary elements organising attempts against Imre Nagy and other persons belonging to his group with the object of turning over responsibility for the consequences to the Revolutionary Worker-Peasant Government, further, 'bearing in mind that their personal security is threatened by possible revenge on the part of their political opponents, Imre Nagy and companions, on the basis of an agreement on this issue concluded between Governments of the People's Republic of Hungary and the People's Republic of Rumania, have left for the People's Republic of Rumania until such time as appropriate conditions of security are brought about in the People's Republic of Hungary.'

It is obvious that the Government of the People's Republic of Hungary has on two occasions harshly offended the obligations, given by it to the Government of the Federal People's Republic of Yugoslavia: by not making possible the free return of Imre Nagy and other persons to their homes, but instead sending them to a compulsory stay to the People's Republic of Rumania, and by the fact that, contrary to the given guarantees regarding personal security and non-application of punishment because of their past action, it brought some of these persons to a secret trial, and sentenced Nagy and some of his companions to death, which punishment was executed, whereby the fully valid agreement was served beyond repair.

The Government of the Federal People's Republic of Yugoslavia most energetically protests to the Government of the People's Republic of Hungary because, in addition to harshly violating the above-mentioned agreement between the two Governments reached by the exchange of letters of 18th and 21st November 1956 respectively, and confirmed by the Hungarian Note of 1st December 1956, in the statement of the Hungarian Ministry of Justice of 17th June 1958, which announced the pronouncement and execution of the death sentence on Imre Nagy and his companions, the Hungarian Government lays a number of heavy accusations against the Federal People's Republic of Yugoslavia which are groundless, whereby it inflicted a heavy blow on the relations between the Federal People's Republic of Yugoslavia and the People's Republic of Hungary, thus taking upon itself before its people and the world public opinion full responsibility for the consequences issuing from this.

11. Note from the Soviet Ministry of Foreign Affairs to the Yugoslav Government regarding Soviet-Yugoslav economic relations, Moscow, 28 June 1958[1]

The Foreign Ministry of the Union of Soviet Socialist Republics presents its compliments to the Embassy of the Federal People's Republic of Yugoslavia and, on the instruction of the Soviet government, in connection with the Note of the State Secretariat for Foreign Affairs of the Federal People's Republic of Yugoslavia of June 3, 1958, has the honour to communicate the following:

In its Note of May 27, this year, the U.S.S.R. government submitted to the government of the Federal People's Republic of Yugoslavia a proposal for revising the periods for the use of the credits granted by the Soviet Union to Yugoslavia under the economic agreements of January 12 and August 1, 1956. In so doing, the U.S.S.R. government outlined the motives which had prompted it to make this proposal and expressed confidence that the government of the Federal People's Republic of Yugoslavia would correctly understand this step by the Soviet government.

The government of the Federal People's Republic of Yugoslavia, however, has not expressed consent even to discuss the substance of the Soviet Union's proposal and has taken a stand which cannot but cause surprise.

[1] *Soviet News*, 2 July 1958.

The content and the tone of the Note of June 3, this year, like the entire approach of the Yugoslav side to this question, and in particular the groundless allegation that the U.S.S.R. has torn up these agreements, indicate an attempt to present the Soviet Union's position on Soviet-Yugoslav economic relations in a wrong light and at the same time to cast doubt on the fulfilment by the Soviet Union of its commitments under international agreements.

There is no need to say that the Soviet Union, pursuing a policy designed to strengthen peace and develop co-operation among all states, strictly abides by its international commitments.

It is common knowledge that a change in certain terms of agreements as a result of negotiations between the parties does not go beyond the bounds of the normal, generally recognised practices of states in relation to international treaties, and that agreements as such do not deprive the parties of the right to raise the question of changing particular terms of the agreements.

The Soviet government, in making the aforementioned proposal, also took into account the interests of the Yugoslav side. This is seen from the fact that in proposing to defer the periods for the use of the credits and, correspondingly, the periods for the delivery of equipment and the carrying out of designing and other work envisaged in the agreements, the Soviet side expressed readiness, for the period for which the putting into operation of enterprises would be postponed, to supply to Yugoslavia, by way of current trade, the industrial goods these enterprises were to produce. It was meant, of course, that the deliveries would be made at mutually advantageous world prices. At the same time, in case this might prove more acceptable to Yugoslavia, the Soviet government expressed willingness to continue, also on the basis of current trade, the deliveries of equipment in the periods specified earlier and to carry out designing and other work envisaged in the agreements. This alone shows that the Soviet government approached this question in a spirit of good will.

As was pointed out in the Soviet Note of May 27, the Soviet government, in proposing to change the periods for the use of the credits, proceeded on the basis of the new requirements which have arisen in the Soviet Union for large capital investments for the development of the chemical industry. At the same time it took into account the statement of the Yugoslav side that relations between the Soviet Union and the Federal People's Republic of Yugoslavia must be based on the principles of mutual benefit. The Soviet side proceeds from the premise that these statements reflect the well thought out position of the Yugoslav government and its desire to base the economic relations between our two countries on the aforementioned principle. Thus, it is a question of bringing the terms of the economic agreements between the U.S.S.R. and Yugoslavia closer to the principles upon which mutually advantageous agreements between states are concluded.

In submitting the proposal to defer the period for the use of the credits, which to some extent would balance the advantageous character of the agreement for both sides, and not only for Yugoslavia, the Soviet government does not propose to change the other terms of the agreements, although these terms, too, are exceptionally easy for the Federal People's Republic of Yugoslavia and are not applied in cases in which the parties proceed only from the purely commercial aspects of mutual benefit. This, too, cannot but be taken into account in discussing the Soviet proposal.

Proceeding from what has been stated above, the Soviet government would consider it correct for representatives of the two governments to meet in the immediate future, discuss in a businesslike way the questions raised in the Soviet Note of May 27, and reach understanding on introducing changes in the agreements of January 12 and August 1, 1956, as proposed by the government of the U.S.S.R.

The Soviet government, for its part, has entrusted the negotiations to the State Committee for Foreign Economic Relations.

12. Communiqué on the meeting between Mr. Khrushchev and Mao Tse-tung in Peking from 31 July to 3 August, 3 August 1958[1]

Meetings took place in Peking, over the period July 31 to August 3, between N. S. Khrushchov, first secretary of the central committee of the Communist Party of the Soviet Union and Chairman of the Council of Ministers of the U.S.S.R., and Mao Tse-tung, chairman of the central committee of the Communist Party of China and Chairman of the Chinese People's Republic.

The meeting was attended, on the Soviet side, by Marshal R. Y. Malinovsky, U.S.S.R. Minister of Defence, V. V. Kuznetsov, acting Foreign Minister of the U.S.S.R., and B. N. Ponomarev, member of the central committee of the Communist Party of the Soviet Union; the Chinese side was represented by Chou En-lai, Premier of the State Council, Marshal Peng Teh-hwai, Vice-Premier and Minister of Defence, Chen Yi, Vice-Premier and Foreign Minister, and Wang Chia-haiang, member of secretariat of the central committee of the Communist Party of China.

In an exceedingly warm and cordial atmosphere, the two parties held all-round discussions and recorded complete identity of views on the

[1] *Soviet News*, 5 August 1958. Following Mr. Khrushchev's visit to Peking an agreement was signed in Moscow on 8 August 1958, between the U.S.S.R. and the People's Republic of China, on technical assistance to China for the construction or expansion of 47 metallurgical, chemical, coal, machine-building, wood-working and building materials enterprises and power stations. For a report of the agreement, see *Soviet News*, 20 August 1958. Moscow had extended no new credits to China since 1954.

urgent and important problems of the present international situation, on further strengthening the relations of friendship, alliance and mutual assistance between the U.S.S.R. and the Chinese People's Republic, and also on problems concerning the joint struggle for a peaceful settlement of international questions and concerning the safeguarding of world peace.

The two parties were unanimous in considering that the U.S.S.R. and the Chinese People's Republic, together with the other countries of the socialist camp, and with all peaceloving countries and peoples, have achieved great successes in the struggle to ease international tension and to defend peace. The peaceful policy of the U.S.S.R. and the Chinese People's Republic is receiving growing support and sympathy from the peoples of all countries. India, Indonesia, the United Arab Republic and other countries and peoples of Asia, Africa, America and Europe are playing an ever-growing role in strengthening peace. Everywhere, the forces of peace have grown immeasurably.

In contrast to this clear and consistent policy—a policy which corresponds to the vital interests of our two countries and of all peoples—aggressive imperialist circles, headed by monopolist groups in the United States, continue to reject peaceful co-existence and co-operation, stubbornly oppose the easing of international tension, obstruct the holding of a conference of the heads of government of the great powers, and intensify their preparations for a new war, threatening the peace and security of the peoples. These imperialist forces are acting as enemies of peace, democracy, national independence and socialism. They are knocking together aggressive military and political blocs, enmeshing the world in their network of military bases, and interfering more often, and more brazenly, in the domestic affairs of other countries.

The armed aggression recently undertaken against Lebanon and Jordan by the United States and Britain, and the threats of force against the Republic of Iraq and the United Arab Republic, have sharply increased the tension in the Middle East and have made the war danger still more serious; they have aroused the protest and condemnation of the peoples of all countries. The U.S.S.R. and the Chinese People's Republic strongly condemn the flagrant aggression by the United States and Britain in the Middle East; they demand the immediate summoning of a conference of the heads of government of the great powers, to discuss the Middle East situation; and they firmly insist on the immediate withdrawal of United States troops from Lebanon and of British forces from Jordan.[1]

The Soviet Union and the Chinese People's Republic give firm support to the just struggle of the peoples of the United Arab Republic, the Republic

---

[1] For a statement by the Government of the People's Republic of China, of 8 August 1958, supporting the Soviet proposal for an emergency special session of the United Nations, see above, pp. 322-4.

of Iraq and the other Arab countries, as well as to the national liberation movements of the peoples of Asia, Africa and Latin America.

The events in the Middle East and other parts of the world confirm that the national liberation movement is indomitable, that the age of colonialism has gone, never to return, and that any attempt to preserve or restore colonial domination, running counter to the course of history, is harmful to peace and is doomed to failure.

The all-round exchange of views on a number of important questions of the present international situation, facing both parties in Asia and Europe, led to the reaching of complete agreement on measures to be taken to combat aggression and preserve peace.

The Soviet Union and the Chinese People's Republic will do everything possible to ease international tension and prevent the horrors of a new war. Both parties declare once again that the right of the peoples of all countries to choose their own social and political systems must be respected; countries with different social systems must co-exist peacefully, in accordance with the well-known Five Principles, which have received wide international recognition; all controversial international issues must be settled peacefully, by means of negotiation; the development of economic and cultural relations among countries, on the basis of mutual benefit and peaceful competition—relations which promote mutual understanding and are fully in line with the aim of easing international tension and preserving peace—must be encouraged.

The major task in preserving and consolidating peace at the present time is the achievement of agreement among states to reduce armaments, to end the tests and ban the use of atomic and hydrogen weapons, to abolish all military groupings and bases on foreign territories, and to conclude a pact of peace and collective security.

Whether war can be averted does not, however, depend solely on the good intentions of the peaceloving peoples and their unilateral efforts. Right up to the present moment, aggressive circles of the western powers are refusing to take any genuine measures to preserve peace; on the contrary, they are senselessly aggravating the international tension, putting mankind on the brink of the catastrophe of war. If the sabre-rattling imperialist maniacs dare to force war on the peoples, however, they should realise that all the peaceloving and freedomloving countries and peoples, closely united in a single unit, will put an end to the imperialist aggressors once and for all, and establish everlasting peace the world over.

Both parties note with great satisfaction that the fraternal relations of friendship, all-round co-operation and mutual assistance between the Communist Party of the Soviet Union and the Communist Party of China, between the Soviet government and the Chinese government and between the peoples of the two countries, are being developed successfully and are becoming more firmly established. The economic development of both countries is proceeding at a rapid pace and their strength is increasing daily. The unity and co-operation between the two countries, based on complete equality and comradely mutual assistance, has great vitality. This unity and co-operation promotes not only the rapid progress of both countries along the road of socialism and communism, but also increases the strength of the socialist camp as a whole. Both parties have decided to ensure the continued all-round development of the comprehensive co-operation between their two countries and to strengthen still further the unity of the socialist camp and the solidarity of all peaceloving countries and peoples; they have expressed wholehearted agreement on all questions which came under consideration.

Both parties are in complete accord in assessing the tasks facing the Communist Party of the Soviet Union and the Chinese Communist Party. The unshakable unity of our two Marxist-Leninist parties will always provide a firm guarantee of the triumph of our common cause.

The Soviet Communist Party and the Chinese Communist Party will defend this sacred unity untiringly; they will fight for the purity of Marxism-Leninism; they will defend the principles of the Moscow Declaration of the Communist and Workers' Parties, and will wage an uncompromising struggle against revisionism—the principal danger in the communist movement. This revisionism has found its clearest manifestation in the programme of the League of Communists of Yugoslavia.

Both parties have expressed their full confidence that the steadily growing forces of peace and socialism will, beyond doubt, overcome all obstacles on the road ahead and will win a great victory.

N. Khrushchov
First Secretary of the Central Committee
of the C.P.S.U. and Chairman of the
U.S.S.R. Council of Ministers

Mao Tse-tung
Chairman of the Central Committee of
the Communist Party of China and
Chairman of the Chinese People's
Republic

13. Joint statement by Premier Chou En-lai and the Prime Minister of Cambodia, Prince Norodom Sihanouk, Peking, 24 August 1958[1]

At the invitation of Chou En-lai, Premier of the State Council of the People's Republic of China, on the occasion of the establishment of

[1] *Peking Review*, 2 September 1958, pp. 14-15.

normal diplomatic relations between the Government of the People's Republic of China and the Government of the Kingdom of Cambodia, His Royal Highness Prince Norodom Sihanouk, Premier of the Government of the Kingdom of Cambodia, leading a state delegation of the Kingdom of Cambodia, arrived in China on August 14, 1958 as the state guest of the Government of the People's Republic of China.

The members of the Cambodian delegation are:

Head of the delegation: His Royal Highness Premier Norodom Sihanouk,

Members: His Excellency Leng-Ngeth, Member of the King's High Council; His Excellency Kou-Roun, Member of the King's High Council; Mr. Tim-Nguon, Minister of National Defence, Surface Defence and National Security; Mr. Touch-Kim, Minister of Economic and Financial Affairs; Mr. Chheng-Hak, Secretary General of the King's High Council; Mr. Phuong Magain, Deputy Secretary General of the King's High Council; Mr. Ang-Kim-Khoan, Member of the National Assembly.

His Royal Highness the Premier and the members of the delegation visited Kunming, Peking, Anshan, Shenyang, Lushun and Dairen, Chinhuangtao and the Special Administrative Region of Tientsin. Wherever they went they were accorded a very warm welcome and grand reception by the Chinese Government and people. They will proceed to visit Wuhan and Canton. The friendly visit of the Premier and the delegation and the welcome and reception they received in China were a clear reflection of the long-existing, profound friendship between the two peoples which has undergone a new development and the relations of friendship and co-operation between the two countries.

The Prince and the delegation, deeply impressed by the steady progress made by the Chinese people in their peaceful construction, expressed their heart-felt admiration and warm congratulations to them. The Chinese Government sincerely thanked the Prince and the delegation for their congratulations and considered them as a great encouragement to the Chinese people.

During their visit, Chairman Mao Tse-tung of the People's Republic of China received Prince Norodom Sihanouk and the delegation, and held sincere and cordial talks with them.

Many talks were held between Premier Sihanouk and Premier Chou En-lai. Also participating in the talks were among the members of the Cambodian delegation: Leng-Ngeth and Kou-Roun, Members of the King's High Council; Tim-Nguon, Minister of National Defence, Surface Defence and National Security; Touch-Kim, Minister of Economic and Financial Affairs; etc.; and, on the Chinese side: Ho Lung and Chen Yi, Vice-Premiers of the State Council; Yeh Chi-chuang, Minister of Foreign Trade; Lo Kuei-po, Vice-Minister of Foreign Affairs; Wang Yu-ping,

Ambassador of the People's Republic of China to the Kingdom of Cambodia; etc.

During the talks which were held in an atmosphere of perfect understanding and sincere co-operation, the two Premiers exchanged views on questions of common interest to the two countries and reviewed the current international situation.

The two parties recalled the happy development of Sino-Cambodian relations which were established on the basis of the five principles of peaceful co-existence following the Bandung Conference and were solemnly confirmed in the two statements signed in 1956 during His Royal Highness Prince Sihanouk's visit to Peking and Premier Chou En-lai's visit to Phnom-Penh.

The peoples of the two countries have always scrupulously observed the five principles of peaceful co-existence, and in particular the principles of non-interference and respect for each other's sovereignty. As a natural result of the development of these relations between the two countries, the Kingdom of Cambodia proposed recently to establish normal diplomatic relations with the People's Republic of China and to exchange representatives of ambassadorial rank. The People's Republic of China accepted this proposal with great pleasure.

The two parties expressed satisfaction over the successful implementation of the agreement on economic assistance concluded on June 21, 1956 and studied in detail various problems concerning the implementation of the trade agreement concluded on April 24, 1956. With a view to achieving a better implementation of the trade agreement the two parties agreed that, in accordance with Article 1 of the trade agreement, which stipulates the principle of import-export balance, the two Governments should work out, with the least delay, concrete measures designed to develop trade between the two countries. In order to promote Cambodia's economic prosperity and industrialization, the Chinese side expressed its readiness, apart from supplying the aid specified in the agreement on economic assistance concluded on June 21, 1956, further to assist Cambodia without any compensation or conditions, according to the needs and capabilities of Cambodia, in building small-sized iron and steel works, prospecting for underground fuel resources, the construction of other enterprises and the search for other materials deemed to be necessary, etc.

The two parties were satisfied with the progress already made in the fields of cultural intercourse and friendly contacts. They agreed to take appropriate measures to further the cultural exchanges and friendly contacts between the two countries.

The two parties were satisfied with the fact that the overseas Chinese in Cambodia have always lived in friendship and fraternity with the Cambodian people. On behalf of the Chinese Government, Premier Chou

En-lai reiterated that the Chinese residing in Cambodia should strictly abide by the laws and regulations of the Kingdom of Cambodia and respect the customs of the Cambodian people, refrain from all political activities in their host country, and assist the Cambodian people in their efforts for the prosperity of the country and the development of its economy. Premier Sihanouk expressed satisfaction with this statement of Premier Chou En-lai's and indicated on behalf of the Government of the Kingdom of Cambodia the desire to protect the legitimate rights and interests of the Chinese residing in Cambodia.

The two parties pointed out unanimously that the policy of peace and neutrality pursued by the Kingdom of Cambodia which was not only conducive to the maintenance of the independence of Cambodia, but also to the consolidation of peace in Asia and the world, should be respected by all nations. Premier Chou En-lai expressed the regret of the Chinese Government at the fact that Cambodian territory was often invaded and blockaded by some of its neighbours, and deemed these to be extremely unfriendly acts. The Chinese Government hopes that the Asian countries concerned will live in peace with the Kingdom of Cambodia in accordance with the resolutions of the Bandung Conference, and not allow themselves to be influenced by the policy of foreign colonialists. Premier Chou En-lai further stressed that the Kingdom of Cambodia is one of the examples of the pursuance of a policy of peace and neutrality and that the Chinese Government fully respects and firmly supports this policy of peace and neutrality pursued by the Kingdom of Cambodia. Premier Sihanouk accepted with satisfaction Premier Chou En-lai's above statement.

Premier Sihanouk declared that the Government of the Kingdom of Cambodia holds that the participation of the Government of the People's Republic of China, representing 600 million people, in international organizations and conferences would be an important and necessary factor in the settlement of international issues and hence also in the maintenance of peace in Asia and the world. Premier Chou En-lai expressed thanks to Premier Sihanouk for this expression of friendship.

The two parties expressed the unanimous opinion that the independence, sovereignty and territorial integrity of all nations must be fully respected, that the national independence movement is an irresistible current in our present epoch, that colonialism in all its manifestations is against the trend of history and is an evil which must be uprooted speedily. All international differences should be settled by the peaceful means of negotiation · in accordance with the principles of co-existence, instead of by means of war and the threat of armed force.

Finally, the two parties expressed their desire to develop continuously the economic and political relations between the two countries on the basis of the five principles of peaceful co-existence for the mutual benefit of the two peoples and of the peace of Southeast Asia and the world.

14. Statement by the Government of the People's Republic of China regarding the extension of Chinese territorial waters, 4 September 1958[1]

The Government of the People's Republic of China declares:

1) The breadth of the territorial sea of the People's Republic of China shall be twelve nautical miles. This provision applies to all territories of the People's Republic of China, including the Chinese mainland and its coastal islands, as well as Taiwan and its surrounding islands, the Penghu Islands, the Tungsha Islands, the Hsisha Islands, the Chungsha Islands, the Nansha Islands and all other islands belonging to China which are separated from the mainland and its coastal islands by the high seas.

2) China's territorial sea long the mainland and its coastal islands takes as its baseline the line composed of the straight lines connecting base-points on the mainland coast and on the outermost of the coastal islands; the water area extending twelve nautical miles outwards from this baseline is China's territorial sea. The water areas inside the baseline, including Pohai Bay and the Chiungchow Straits, are Chinese inland waters. The islands inside the baseline, including Tungyin Island, Kaoteng Island, the Matsu Islands, the Paichuan Islands, Wuchiu Island, the Greater and Lesser Quemoy Islands, Tatan Island, Erhtan Island and Tungting Island, are islands of the Chinese inland waters.

3) No foreign vessels for military use and no foreign aircraft may enter China's territorial sea and the air space above it without the permission of the Government of the People's Republic of China.

While navigating Chinese territorial sea, every foreign vessel must observe the relevant laws and regulations laid down by the Government of the People's Republic of China.

4) The principles provided in paragraphs 2) and 3) likewise apply to Taiwan and its surrounding islands, the Penghu Islands, the Tungsha Islands, the Hsisha Islands, the Chungsha Islands, the Nansha Islands, and all other islands belonging to China.

The Taiwan and Penghu areas are still occupied by the United States by armed force.[2] This is an unlawful encroachment on the territorial integrity and sovereignty of the People's Republic of China. Taiwan, Penghu and such other areas are yet to be recovered, and the Government of the People's Republic of China has the right to recover these areas by

---

[1] *Peking Review*, 9 September 1958, p. 21. For the documents on the Conference on the Law of the Sea, 24 February–27 April 1958, see below, pp. 535–69.

[2] See Chapter I, C, for documents on the crisis over Formosa.

all suitable means at a suitable time. This is China's internal affair, in which no foreign interference is tolerated.

15. Soviet note to the Government of the People's Republic of China regarding the extension of Chinese territorial waters, 9 September 1958[1]

The Embassy of the Union of the Soviet Socialist Republics sends its compliments to the Foreign Ministry of the People's Republic of China and, entrusted by the Government of the Soviet Union, has the honour to make the following notification concerning the note of the Foreign Ministry, dated September 4, which contained the statement of the Government of the Chinese People's Republic on China's territorial sea:

The Government of the Soviet Union has learned and fully respects the decision contained in the statement of the Government of the Chinese People's Republic, that is: The breadth of the territorial sea of the People's Republic of China shall be 12 nautical miles and that no foreign vessels for military use and no foreign aircraft may enter the Chinese territorial sea and the air space above it without the permission of the Government of the People's Republic of China. At the same time, it takes note of the method of defining the territorial sea of the People's Republic of China stipulated in the statement.

The Government of the Soviet Union understands that this decision of the Government of the People's Republic of China applies to all the territories of the People's Republic of China, including the Chinese mainland, Taiwan and its surrounding islands, the Penghu Islands and other islands belonging to the People's Republic of China.

The Embassy has the honour to notify the Foreign Ministry that the organisations concerned of the Soviet Union have already been instructed strictly to abide by the 12 nautical mile line of the territorial sea of the People's Republic of China laid down by the Government of the People's Republic of China.

16. Joint Soviet-Polish statement on the Polish visit to the Soviet Union, Moscow, 10 November 1958[2]

All aspects of the question of further strengthening friendly relations, co-operation and mutual assistance between the Union of Soviet Socialist Republics and the Polish People's Republic, and also problems of the present international situation concerning both sides and questions arising

---

[1] *H.N.A.*, 11 September 1958, p. 7.

[2] *Soviet News*, 12 November 1958. The introductory paragraphs of the statement were not reproduced in full.

from the common struggle of the two countries for peace, were discussed during the talks, which took place in a cordial atmosphere and were marked by a spirit of complete mutual understanding.

The two delegations noted the complete identity of their views on all questions under discussion.

I

The two sides, following a wide exchange of views on major international problems, emphasised the steadily growing influence of the socialist system and its countries, and also the forces of socialism and peace, on the international situation. The idea of socialism is embracing ever broader masses of people. The countries of the socialist camp threaten no one and are striving for a peaceful settlement of all disputes; they uphold the principle of peaceful co-existence between countries with differing social and political structures; they advocate peaceful competition between the socialist and capitalist systems. They are confident that this competition will be won by the socialist system, which is demonstrating in practice its superiority over the capitalist system.

The Union of Soviet Socialist Republics and the Polish People's Republic will continue to spare no efforts to avert the threat of another war and, together with the entire socialist camp, will support all forces that cherish the cause of peace and desire peaceful co-existence between all peoples. The stubborn efforts for peace made by the Union of Soviet Socialist Republics and the other countries of the socialist camp have met with a wide response throughout the world. The forces of peace are growing and becoming more active, embracing wide sections of the public in all countries; the tendency to seek for ways of easing international tension is becoming more pronounced among political circles in the capitalist world.

The most aggressive imperialist circles, however, do not want to abandon the 'policy of strength.' They are causing a worsening of international tension; they are supporting reactionary anti-peace forces in various parts of the world.

A most dangerous symptom of this tendency, in the opinion of the delegations, is the policy of the ruling circles of the North Atlantic Pact and its dominant force—the United States of America—aimed at converting Western Europe into an arsenal of atomic weapons.

The imperialist circles of the United States, seeking to subject most countries to their domination, are rallying all the reactionary forces of the capitalist world.

A mainstay of this policy in Europe is the stand taken by the government of the Federal Republic of Germany. The imperialist circles are using the revenge-seeking policy of the government of the Federal Republic of Germany for their own ends. The rapid militarisation of that country, the stepping up of the arming of the Bundeswehr with atomic and rocket weapons, the desire of the Federal Republic of Germany to take a leading place among the European members of the Atlantic Pact, the support given by the Adenauer government to the militarist and revenge-seeking elements who are openly making territorial claims on other countries—all this is a threat to the peace and security of the European countries which are primarily affected by the consequences of such a policy.

Both sides emphasise the growing role of the German Democratic Republic—the first workers' and peasants' state in the history of Germany —as an important factor for peace in Europe. They support the proposals made by the German Democratic Republic with the object of beginning the preparations for the conclusion of a German peace treaty which would considerably ease present-day tensions in Europe.

The expansion of the armaments of the Federal Republic of Germany adds significance to the proposal of the government of the Polish People's Republic for an atom-free zone in Central Europe, a proposal which has enlisted the full support of the member-states of the Warsaw Treaty and has met with a wide response in various circles in the West.

The two delegations express the conviction that this proposal, which can successfully facilitate the elimination of the threat of atomic war and the strengthening of the security of an area in Europe which is fraught with conflicts, will continue to enlist support, notwithstanding the obstacles created by the circles that oppose any, even partial, measures aimed at solving the disarmament problem.

The Soviet Union and the other socialist countries have put forward, and are continuing to put forward numerous proposals aimed at a relaxation of international tension and a solution to the main problem of the security of the world—the ending of the arms race, and first and foremost the nuclear arms race.

The Soviet Union and the Polish People's Republic declare that they will continue to do everything possible for an early solution to the problem of disarmament and the strengthening of peace between nations.

These important aims are being well served by the proposals submitted by the socialist countries to the United Nations for the prohibition of atomic and hydrogen weapons and for the cessation of tests of those weapons, for the reduction of armed forces, armaments and military budgets, for the abolition of foreign military bases, and on other aspects of disarmament.

The socialist countries have, by practical action, demonstrated their readiness to contribute to the removal of the danger of a new world war.

Being guided by the policy of peace and friendship among the peoples and by the desire for a relaxation of international tension, the countries of the socialist camp have unilaterally made substantial cuts in their armed forces.

The delegation of the Polish People's Republic resolutely supports the Soviet Union's proposal for a summit conference to examine and solve the most pressing problems of disarmament and to decide on steps to be taken to reinforce the security of Europe and the rest of the world. However the policy of delaying and dodging talks, pursued, in the first place, by the government circles of the United States of America, is preventing agreement on issues on which world peace depends.

In these circumstances, both delegations consider it necessary to strengthen the defensive Warsaw Treaty, which is designed to safeguard the security of all the countries of the socialist camp.

Along with this, they will continue their efforts to reduce international tension by various means, including partial agreements, and declare themselves ready to co-operate with all states and forces pursuing this goal.

The Polish delegation, supporting as it does the measures taken by the Union of Soviet Socialist Republics to achieve the complete stopping of the tests of nuclear weapons, shares the view that the most urgent task of the moment should be for the great powers to achieve agreement on the immediate and universal ending of these tests for all time, the more so since the Geneva conference of experts acknowledged the perfect feasibility of control over test explosions.

Both sides declare their complete solidarity with the striving of the peoples fighting to liberate themselves from the yoke of imperialism and colonialism and to win the right freely to shape their own destinies. They enthusiastically support the struggle of the Arab peoples against imperialism, which is seeking to maintain or restore its domination in those countries by new methods of colonialism.

The resolute attitude adopted by the socialist countries and all peace-loving states with regard to the national liberation struggle of the Arab peoples, prevented the extension of American and British aggression in the Middle East. Under pressure from the peace forces of the world, the United States and Britain have had to withdraw their troops from Lebanon and Jordan, which is a great victory over the forces of war.

The Union of Soviet Socialist Republics and the Polish People's Republic have been following with anxiety the situation brought about by the United States' aggression against the Chinese People's Republic in the Taiwan Straits, where there is continued evidence of armed intervention by the United States of America in the internal affairs of China and of determination to turn China's domestic problem into an international conflict.

Both delegations fully support the just and sovereign right of the great Chinese people to liberate and unite all their lands, including Taiwan and the offshore islands. They are at one with the government of the Chinese People's Republic in its demand for the withdrawal of the American troops from the Taiwan area.

II

The leaders of the Communist Party of the Soviet Union and the Polish United Workers' Party exchanged information on the work of the two parties and discussed relations between them, as well as topical problems of the international working-class movement.

Both parties attach great importance to the all-round development and strengthening of fraternal relations between the members of the great community of socialist states united by the common ideas of Marxism-Leninism and by the common aim of building socialism and communism.

The unbreakable unity of the socialist camp, the strength of the Soviet Union, the first and most advanced socialist country, the Chinese People's Republic and of all the states building socialism, is the surest guarantee of the security of the socialist countries. It is also one of the major factors representing an effective force against the threat of a new war and exerting a decisive influence on the cause of strengthening peace and consolidating the forces of peace.

The unity and solidarity of the countries of the socialist camp, based on the Leninist principles of proletarian internationalism and the all-round fraternal co-operation of the socialist countries, is an inalienable factor facilitating the successful building of socialism and the all-round development of their productive forces.

In the interests of socialism and peace, both countries are determined to continue strengthening the bonds of brotherhood and solidarity uniting the community of socialist states in keeping with the principles enunciated in the Declaration of 12 Communist and Workers' Parties. Both parties, true as they are to the principles of the 12-party Declaration and the Peace Manifesto adopted in Moscow in November 1957, will continue to defend the principles laid down in those documents, for the sake of strengthening the unity of the socialist countries and of all of the world's forces working for peace.

An indispensable condition for success in building socialism lies in an uncompromising struggle against revisionism, which represents the main danger at the present moment and which is seeking to undermine the fundamental principles of the ideology of Marxism-Leninism and to break the unity of the great family of socialist states and the international working-class movement.

The cause of socialism requires a further creative enrichment of the Marxist-Leninist teaching, adherence to the common laws governing the building of socialism and their bold embodiment by methods suiting the conditions of each individual country, as well as opposition to the practices of dogmatism.

There was a discussion on concrete steps for the further exchange of experience in party work and on the extension of contacts between the Communist Party of the Soviet Union and the Polish United Workers' Party. It has been recognised with satisfaction that co-operation between the Communist Party of the Soviet Union and the Polish United Workers' Party has become still closer, witness, for instance, the exchange of visits by party delegations for joint discussion on a number of exceedingly important issues and also the exchange of delegations between individual towns and regions of the Soviet Union and the Polish People's Republic.

The Communist Party of the Soviet Union and the Polish United Workers' Party are determined to go on developing and extending fraternal co-operation between the two parties and the reciprocal exchange of experience of party work. They are convinced that this is helping towards the successful development of both countries and assisting their advance towards socialism and communism, and at the same time is a contribution to the theory and practice of Marxism-Leninism.

Both parties will oppose any attempts to break the unity of the socialist camp. They will continue to extend and strengthen international contacts with all the Communist and Workers' Parties and with the entire international revolutionary movement, for the sake of the triumph of the cause of peace, progress and socialism.

III

Both sides note with satisfaction that friendship between the Soviet and Polish peoples, which has ever-living, deep-rooted traditions in the common struggle of Russian and Polish revolutionaries, which was reinforced in the common struggle against nazism and which found expression in the Treaty of Friendship, Mutual Assistance and Postwar Co-operation between the Union of Soviet Socialist Republics and the Polish People's Republic, concluded on April 21, 1945, is gaining in strength and scope thanks to the all-round political, economic and cultural co-operation and to the numerous contacts and links uniting the two equal and sovereign peoples.

Soviet-Polish friendship and alliance between the Union of Soviet Socialist Republics and the Polish People's Republic, supported by the will of the peoples and representing today a powerful material force, constitute an important factor for peace in Europe and the best guarantee of the inviolability of Poland's western frontier on the Oder and the Neisse. This is of special importance in view of the growing activity of the

West German revenge-seeking forces and also in view of the western powers' continued refusal to take up a clear-cut stand on this indisputable matter.

Vain have been the hopes cherished by certain reactionary and imperialist circles of setting the Polish people at loggerheads with the peoples of the Union of Soviet Socialist Republics and of undermining their fraternal friendship. The Soviet and Polish peoples know full well that any weakening of the bonds that unite them, just as of those uniting the two peoples with the rest of the great socialist community, could only harm the cause of socialism and peace and would be exploited by the imperialist forces, and especially the revenge-seeking and chauvinist elements in Western Germany, which are hostile to both peoples.

The Soviet-Polish joint statement of November 18, 1956,[1] the purpose of which was the strengthening and further expansion of the relations between the Union of Soviet Socialist Republics and Poland, resting on the immutable Leninist principles of proletarian internationalism, has fully passed the test of life and has promoted the further strengthening of the unbreakable solidarity and friendship uniting the two countries. This friendship, based on the most reliable principles of proletarian internationalism, respect for one another's sovereignty, mutual fraternal assistance and solidarity, and on the community of interests and aspirations, is today stronger than ever before.

The common class foundations of the state structure of the two countries, one of which, the Polish People's Republic, has been building socialism for 14 years, and the second, the Soviet Union, having victoriously accomplished the building of socialism, is now building a communist society, the common theoretical foundations of the immortal teaching of Marxism-Leninism—these are the firm foundation on which Soviet-Polish friendship and co-operation are developing.

Both countries support each other in the international field in measures having a single purpose—to avert the threat of war and to establish firm peaceful international co-operation.

Both sides find that the economic co-operation based on long-term agreements covering the period up to 1965 is developing successfully.

The agreements on reciprocal goods deliveries and economic co-operation, concluded in 1958, are evidence of the further expansion and strengthening of mutual economic ties on the basis of co-ordination and co-operation of production and the international socialist division of labour.

The delegation of the Polish People's Republic proposed to the Soviet government that the Soviet Union render technical assistance to the Polish People's Republic in the development of some major branches of

---

[1] For the text, see *Documents* for 1956, pp. 517-23.

the Polish national economy, and in particular in the prospecting of new deposits of oil and natural gas and in the preparations for the exploitation of those deposits, in the building of an oil refinery, the expansion of the Lenin Steel Mills and the expansion of the copper ore mining industry. The government of the U.S.S.R., having in view the further extension of the economic co-operation between the two countries, agreed to render assistance to the Polish People's Republic in these matters.

The two sides pointed out that scientific and cultural co-operation is developing extensively between the Soviet Union and the Polish People's Republic, as is shown by the expansion of contacts between Soviet and Polish scientists and writers and artists, the exchange of students and a wider exchange of specialists and technical documentation, and also by the establishment of permanent contacts between a number of Soviet and Polish enterprises.

A great contribution to the development of Soviet-Polish relations and the further strengthening of fraternal friendship between the two peoples was made by the conference of representatives of Communist and Workers' Parties of the states represented on the Council for Mutual Economic Assistance, held in May, 1958, and by the conference of the Political Consultative Committee of the member-states of the Warsaw Treaty of Friendship, Co-operation and Mutual Assistance, which considerably facilitated the further development of co-operation and mutual relations between countries building socialism and communism.

Both sides expressed their firm resolve to continue to expand to the utmost the political, economic and cultural co-operation between the two countries, to develop and strengthen the unbreakable fraternal friendship and alliance between the Union of Soviet Socialist Republics and the Polish People's Republic resting on the principles of Marxism-Leninism, on the principles of proletarian internationalism.

The friendship visit by the delegation of the Polish People's Republic to the Union of Soviet Socialist Republics will promote the further strengthening of the brotherhood and friendship between the peoples of both countries, will make another contribution to the unity of the great family of the socialist states and will promote the cause of strengthening world peace.

While in the Soviet Union the delegation of the Polish People's Republic invited N. S. Khrushchov, first secretary of the central committee of the Communist Party of the Soviet Union and Chairman of the U.S.S.R. Council of Ministers, together with other party leaders and statesmen of the Soviet Union, to visit the Polish People's Republic.

This invitation was gladly accepted.

17. Resolution of the General Assembly regarding the situation in Hungary, 12 December 1958[1]

THE GENERAL ASSEMBLY,

Having considered the supplementary report, dated 14 July 1958, of the United Nations Special Committee[2] established by resolution 1132 (XI) of 10 January 1957 to report on the problem of Hungary,

Having considered the report, dated 9 December 1957, of the Special Representative of the General Assembly, His Royal Highness Prince Wan Waithayakon,[3] who was appointed by Assembly resolution 1133 (XI) of 14 September 1957 to take steps to achieve the objectives of Assembly resolutions 1004 (ES-11) of 4 November 1956, 1127 (XI) of 21 November 1956, 1131 (XI) of 12 December 1956 and 1132 (XI) of 10 January 1957,

1. *Expresses its appreciation* to its Special Representative, Prince Wan Waithayakon, for the efforts he has made to enter into consultation with the appropriate authorities with a view to achieving the objectives of the resolutions referred to above;

2. *Endorses* the unanimous report of the Special Committee on the Problem of Hungary, dated 14 July 1958, and expresses its thanks to the Committee for its objective and efficient discharge of the tasks entrusted to it;

3. *Deplores* the continued refusal of the Government of the Union of Soviet Socialist Republics and the régime in Hungary to co-operate with the Special Representative and with the Committee in their efforts to achieve the objectives of the United Nations in accordance with the pertinent resolutions of the General Assembly;

4. *Deplores* the continuing repression in Hungary of fundamental rights of the Hungarian people and of their freedom of political expression under the shadow of the continuing presence of Soviet armed forces;

5. *Denounces* the execution of Mr. Imre Nagy, General Pál Maléter and other Hungarian patriots;

6. *Condemns* this continued defiance of the resolutions of the General Assembly;

7. *Again calls upon* the Union of Soviet Socialist Republics and the present authorities in Hungary to desist from repressive measures against the Hungarian people and to respect the liberty and political independence

---

[1] G.A.O.R., Thirteenth Session, Supplement No. 18 (A/4090), Resol. 1312 (XIII). The resolution, as recommended by 37 powers, was adopted by the Assembly without reference to a committee, by a roll-call vote of 54–10 (Albania, Bulgaria, Byelorussian SSR, Czechoslovakia, Hungary, Poland, Rumania, Ukranian SSR, U.S.S.R., Yugoslavia), with 15 abstentions (Afghanistan, Ceylon, Ethiopia, Finland, Ghana, Greece, India, Indonesia, Iraq, Lebanon, Libya, Morocco, Saudi Arabia, Sudan, United Arab Republic).

[2] G.A.O.R., Thirteenth Session, Annexes, agenda item 69, Doc. A/3849.

[3] Ibid., Twelfth Session, Annexes, agenda item 63, Doc. A/3774.

of Hungary and the Hungarian people's enjoyment of fundamental human rights and freedoms;

8. *Declares* that the United Nations will continue to be seized of the situation in Hungary in view of the fact that the Government of the Union of Soviet Socialist Republics and the present authorities in Hungary are disregarding the above-mentioned resolutions of the General Assembly;

9. *Decides* to appoint Sir Leslie Munro to represent the United Nations for the purpose of reporting to Member States or to the General Assembly on significant developments relating to the implementation of the Assembly resolutions on Hungary;

10. *Requests* the Secretary-General to provide the necessary facilities to assist Sir Leslie Munro in the performance of his duties.

18. Joint communiqué of the Government of the People's Republic of China and the Provisional Government of the Algerian Republic, Peking, 20 December 1958[1]

At the invitation of the Government of the People's Republic of China, a delegation of the Provisional Government of the Republic of Algeria composed of Mahmoud Cherif, Minister of Armaments and Supplies, Benyoussef Benkhedda, Minister of Social Affairs, and Saad Dahlab, Director of the Office of the Ministry of Information, visited China from December 3 to 13 and from December 16 to 20, 1958.

Mao Tse-tung, Chairman of the People's Republic of China, and Chou En-lai, Premier of the State Council, received the Delegation of the Provisional Government of the Republic of Algeria.

Chen Yi, Minister of Foreign Affairs of the People's Republic of China, Lei Jen-min, Acting Minister of Foreign Trade, and Chi Peng-fei, Vice-Minister of Foreign Affairs, held talks with the Delegation of the Provisional Government of the Republic of Algeria.

The talks were held in an atmosphere of sincerity and friendship. During the talks, the two parties exchanged views on questions concerning the present international situation, and particularly the situation of the struggle in Algeria and the development of Sino-Algerian relations, and reached unanimity of views.

The two parties were of the common opinion that the present international situation is favourable to the struggle of the peoples of the world for the maintenance of world peace. Cessation of the testing, and prohibition of the use of atomic and thermo-nuclear weapons are the general

---

[1] *Peking Review*, 23 December 1958, p. 24. For the policy statement made by Mr. Ferhat Abbas on 26 September 1958, and other documents regarding Algeria, see above, pp. 401–10. The People's Republic of China recognised the Provisional Government of the Algerian Republic on 22 September 1958, see fn. on p. 404 above.

demands of the peoples of the world. Both parties expressed their resolute support for these demands.

The two parties pointed out with pleasure that the movement of the peoples of Asia and Africa to safeguard and win national independence has already become an irresistible historical trend. The two parties expressed their firm support for the Asian and African peoples in their struggle against colonialism and were of the opinion that all foreign troops should withdraw from Asian and African countries.

During the talks, the Chinese Government reiterated the just stand it solemnly expressed at the Bandung Conference of supporting resolutely the Algerian people in their just struggle for national independence. Algeria belongs to the Algerians. The two parties were convinced that, supported by the Arab states and peoples and all peace-loving countries and peoples of the world, the heroic Algerian people persisting in their struggle against colonialism will certainly win final victory in national liberation.

During the talks, the two parties studied concrete methods to strengthen relations between the two countries and affirmed the principle of establishing diplomatic and cultural relations between the two countries. The two parties indicated their determination to further strengthen friendly co-operation between the two countries.

CHEN YI
Minister of Foreign Affairs of the
People's Republic of China

MAHMOUD CHERIF
Minister of Armaments and Supplies of the Provisional Government of the Republic of Algeria

V. SIX CONFERENCES

A. CONFERENCE ON THE LAW OF THE SEA

1. Conventions and resolutions adopted by the Conference on the Law of the Sea, 23–29 April 1958[1]

(a) *Convention on the Territorial Sea and the Contiguous Zone*[2]

The States Parties of this Convention
Have agreed as follows:

PART I

TERRITORIAL SEA

SECTION I. GENERAL

ARTICLE I

1. The sovereignty of a State extends, beyond its land territory and its internal waters, to a belt of sea adjacent to its coast, described as the territorial sea.

2. This sovereignty is exercised subject to the provisions of these articles and to other rules of international law.

ARTICLE 2

The sovereignty of a coastal State extends to the air space over the territorial sea as well as to its bed and subsoil.

---

[1] U.N. Doc. A/Conf. 13/38, Annexes, pp. 132–45. The conference, held in Geneva from 24 February until 27 April 1958 under the presidency of Prince Wan Waithayakon of Thailand, was attended by some 700 delegates from 86 countries and from seven specialized agencies, and observers from nine non-governmental organizations, see the Final Act of the conference, ibid., pp. 146–7 (Doc. A/Conf. 13/L.58). The conference was convened in accordance with the General Assembly Resolution 1105 (XI) of 21 February 1957, and its work was based on 73 draft articles prepared by the International Law Commission, and on relevant debates of the General Assembly early in 1957. In addition to the four conventions and the resolutions, an optional protocol was adopted by the conference. All countries signing the optional protocol agreed to recognize the compulsory jurisdiction of the International Court of Justice in disputes arising out of the conventions of the Law of the Sea, except with respect to measures for the conservation of resources of the high seas. For the text of the optional protocol see ibid., pp. 145–6 (Doc. A/Conf. 13/L.57). The four conventions were subject to ratification and all required a minimum of 22 ratifications or accessions to come into force. They were closed for signature on 31 October 1958. For the dates of the signatures to the conventions and the optional protocol by members of the conference, see Cmnd. 584, pp. 45–46.

[2] Ibid., pp. 132–5 (Doc. A/Conf. 13/L.52). Adopted by the conference at its 20th plenary meeting, 29 April 1958, by 61 votes to 0, with two abstentions.

Section II. Limits of the Territorial Sea

ARTICLE 3

Except where otherwise provided in these articles, the normal baseline for measuring the breadth of the territorial sea is the low-water line along the coast as marked on large-scale charts officially recognized by the coastal State.

ARTICLE 4

1. In localities where the coastline is deeply indented and cut into, or if there is a fringe of islands along the coast in its immediate vicinity, the method of straight baselines joining appropriate points may be employed in drawing the baseline from which the breadth of the territorial sea is measured.

2. The drawing of such baselines must not depart to any appreciable extent from the general direction of the coast, and the sea areas lying within the lines must be sufficiently closely linked to the land domain to be subject to the régime of internal waters.

3. Baselines shall not be drawn to and from low-tide elevations, unless lighthouses or similar installations which are permanently above sea level have been built on them.

4. Where the method of straight baselines is applicable under the provisions of paragraph 1, account may be taken, in determining particular baselines, of economic interests peculiar to the region concerned, the reality and the importance of which are clearly evidenced by a long usage.

5. The system of straight baselines may not be applied by a State in such a manner as to cut off from the high seas the territorial sea of another State.

6. The coastal State must clearly indicate straight baselines on charts, to which due publicity must be given.

ARTICLE 5

1. Waters on the landward side of the baseline of the territorial sea form part of the internal waters of the State.

2. Where the establishment of a straight baseline in accordance with article 4 has the effect of enclosing as internal waters areas which previously had been considered as part of the territorial sea or of the high seas, a right of innocent passage, as provided in articles 14 to 23, shall exist in those waters.

ARTICLE 6

The outer limit of the territorial sea is the line every point of which is at a distance from the nearest point of the baseline equal to the breadth of the territorial sea.

ARTICLE 7

1. This article relates only to bays the coasts of which belong to a single State.

2. For the purposes of these articles, a bay is a well-marked indentation whose penetration is in such proportion to the width of its mouth as to contain landlocked waters and constitute more than a mere curvature of the coast. An indentation shall not, however, be regarded as a bay unless its area is as large as, or larger than, that of the semi-circle whose diameter is a line drawn across the mouth of that indentation.

3. For the purpose of measurement, the area of an indentation is that lying between the low-water mark around the shore of the indentation and a line joining the low-water mark of its natural entrance points. Where, because of the presence of islands, an indentation has more than one mouth, the semi-circle shall be drawn on a line as long as the sum total of the lengths of the lines across the different mouths. Islands within an indentation shall be included as if they were part of the water area of the indentation.

4. If the distance between the low-water marks of the natural entrance points of a bay does not exceed twenty-four miles, a closing line may be drawn between these two low-water marks, and the waters enclosed thereby shall be considered as internal waters.

5. Where the distance between the low-water marks of the natural entrance points of a bay exceeds twenty-four miles, a straight baseline of twenty-four miles shall be drawn within the bay in such a manner as to enclose the maximum area of water that is possible with a line of that length.

6. The foregoing provisions shall not apply to so-called 'historic' bays, or in any case where the straight baseline system provided for in article 4 is applied.

ARTICLE 8

For the purpose of delimiting the territorial sea, the outermost permanent harbour works which form an integral part of the harbour system shall be regarded as forming part of the coast.

ARTICLE 9

Roadsteads which are normally used for the loading, unloading and anchoring of ships, and which would otherwise be situated wholly or partly outside the outer limit of the territorial sea, are included in the territorial sea. The coastal State must clearly demarcate such roadsteads and indicate them on charts together with their boundaries, to which due publicity must be given.

ARTICLE 10

1. An island is a naturally formed area of land, surrounded by water, which is above water at high tide.

2. The territorial sea of an island is measured in accordance with the provisions of these articles.

ARTICLE 11

1. A low-tide elevation is a naturally formed area of land which is surrounded by and above water at low-tide but submerged at high tide. Where a low-tide elevation is situated wholly or partly at a distance not exceeding the breadth of the territorial sea from the mainland or an island, the low-water line on that elevation may be used as the baseline for measuring the breadth of the territorial sea.

2. Where a low-tide elevation is wholly situated at a distance exceeding the breadth of the territorial sea from the mainland or an island, it has no territorial sea of its own.

ARTICLE 12

1. Where the coasts of two States are opposite or adjacent to each other, neither of the two States is entitled, failing agreement between them to the contrary, to extend its territorial sea beyond the median line every point of which is equidistant from the nearest points on the baselines from which the breadth of the territorial seas of each of the two States is measured. The provisions of this paragraph shall not apply, however, where it is necessary by reason of historic title or other special circumstances to delimit the territorial seas of the two States in a way which is at variance with this provision.

2. The line of delimitation between the territorial seas of two States lying opposite to each other or adjacent to each other shall be marked on large-scale charts officially recognized by the coastal States.

ARTICLE 13

If a river flows directly into the sea, the baseline shall be a straight line across the mouth of the river between points on the low-tide line of its banks.

Section III. Right of Innocent Passage

Sub-section A. Rules applicable to all ships

ARTICLE 14

1. Subject to the provisions of these articles, ships of all States, whether coastal or not, shall enjoy the right of innocent passage through the territorial sea.

2. Passage means navigation through the territorial sea for the purpose either of traversing that sea without entering internal waters, or of proceeding to internal waters, or of making for the high seas from internal waters.

3. Passage includes stopping and anchoring, but only in so far as the same are incidental to ordinary navigation or are rendered necessary by *force majeure* or by distress.

4. Passage is innocent so long as it is not prejudicial to the peace, good order or security of the coastal State. Such passage shall take place in conformity with these articles and with other rules of international law.

5. Passage of foreign fishing vessels shall not be considered innocent if they do not observe such laws and regulations as the coastal State may make and publish in order to prevent these vessels from fishing in the territorial sea.

6. Submarines are required to navigate on the surface and to show their flag.

ARTICLE 15

1. The coastal State must not hamper innocent passage through the territorial sea.

2. The coastal State is required to give appropriate publicity to any dangers to navigation, of which it has knowledge, within its territorial sea.

ARTICLE 16

1. The coastal State may take the necessary steps in its territorial sea to prevent passage which is not innocent.

2. In the case of ships proceeding to internal waters, the coastal State shall also have the right to take the necessary steps to prevent any breach of the conditions to which admission of those ships to those waters is subject.

3. Subject to the provisions of paragraph 4, the coastal State may, without discrimination amongst foreign ships, suspend temporarily in specified areas of its territorial sea the innocent passage of foreign ships if such suspension is essential for the protection of its security. Such suspension shall take effect only after having been duly published.

4. There shall be no suspension of the innocent passage of foreign ships through straits which are used for international navigation between one part of the high seas and another part of the high seas or the territorial sea of a foreign State.

ARTICLE 17

Foreign ships exercising the right of innocent passage shall comply with the laws and regulations enacted by the coastal State in conformity with these articles and other rules of international law and, in particular, with such laws and regulations relating to transport and navigation.

Sub-section B. Rules applicable to merchant ships

ARTICLE 18

1. No charge may be levied upon foreign ships by reason only of their passage through the territorial sea.

2. Charges may be levied upon a foreign ship passing through the territorial sea as payment only for specific services rendered to the ship. These charges shall be levied without discrimination.

ARTICLE 19

1. The criminal jurisdiction of the coastal State should not be exercised on board a foreign ship passing through the territorial sea to arrest any person or to conduct any investigation in connexion with any crime committed on board the ship during its passage, save only in the following cases:

(a) If the consequences of the crime extend to the coastal State; or

(b) If the crime is of a kind to disturb the peace of the country or the good order of the territorial sea; or

(c) If the assistance of the local authorities has been requested by the captain of the ship or by the consul of the country whose flag the ship flies; or

(d) If it is necessary for the suppression of illicit traffic in narcotic drugs.

2. The above provisions do not affect the right of the coastal State to take any steps authorized by its laws for the purpose of an arrest or investigation on board a foreign ship passing through the territorial sea after leaving internal waters.

3. In the cases provided for in paragraphs 1 and 2 of this article, the coastal State shall, if the captain so requests, advise the consular authority of the flag State before taking any steps, and shall facilitate contact between such authority and the ship's crew. In cases of emergency this notification may be communicated while the measures are being taken.

4. In considering whether or how an arrest should be made, the local authorities shall pay due regard to the interests of navigation.

5. The coastal State may not take any steps on board a foreign ship passing through the territorial sea to arrest any person or to conduct any investigation in connexion with any crime committed before the ship entered the territorial sea, if the ship, proceeding from a foreign port, is only passing through the territorial sea without entering internal waters.

ARTICLE 20

1. The coastal State should not stop or divert a foreign ship passing through the territorial sea for the purpose of exercising civil jurisdiction in relation to a person on board the ship.

2. The coastal State may not levy execution against or arrest the ship for the purpose of any civil proceedings, save only in respect of obligations or liabilities assumed or incurred by the ship itself in the course or for the purpose of its voyage through the waters of the coastal State.

3. The provisions of the previous paragraph are without prejudice to the right of the coastal State, in accordance with its laws, to levy execution against or to arrest, for the purpose of any civil proceedings, a foreign ship lying in the territorial sea, or passing through the territorial sea after leaving internal waters.

Sub-section C. Rules applicable to government ships other than warships

ARTICLE 21

The rules contained in sub-sections A and B shall also apply to government ships operated for commercial purposes.

ARTICLE 22

1. The rules contained in sub-section A and in article 18 shall apply to government ships operated for non-commercial purposes.

2. With such exceptions as are contained in the provisions referred to in the preceding paragraph, nothing in these articles affects the immunities which such ships enjoy under these articles or other rules of international law.

Sub-section D. Rules applicable to warships

ARTICLE 23

If any warship does not comply with the regulations of the coastal State concerning passage through the territorial sea and disregards any request for compliance which is made to it, the coastal State may require the warship to leave the territorial sea.

PART II

CONTIGUOUS ZONE[1]

ARTICLE 24

1. In a zone of the high seas contiguous to its territorial sea, the coastal State may exercise the control necessary to:

(*a*) Prevent infringement of its customs, fiscal, immigration or sanitary regulations within its territory or territorial sea;

(*b*) Punish infringement of the above regulations committed within its territory or territorial sea.

2. The contiguous zone may not extend beyond twelve miles from the baseline from which the breadth of the territorial sea is measured.

3. Where the coasts of two States are opposite or adjacent to each other, neither of the two States is entitled, failing agreement between them to the contrary, to extend its contiguous zone beyond the median line every point of which is equidistant from the nearest points on the baselines from which the breadth of the territorial seas of the two States is measured.

PART III

FINAL ARTICLES

ARTICLE 25

The provisions of this Convention shall not affect conventions or other international agreements already in force, as between States Parties to them.

---

[1] No provision was included for regulating the breadth of the territorial sea, as none of the various proposals submitted was able to command the necessary two-thirds majority. The United States and the United Kingdom favoured a three-mile limit, regarding it as the only limit valid in international law, and this position was supported by France, Greece, Japan, the Netherlands, and Pakistan. Most states favoured a wider limit. The U.S.S.R. proposed that each state be allowed to fix its own limit at, as a rule, from three to twelve miles. See U.N. Doc. A/Conf. 13/38, p. 126. Twelve-mile limits were favoured by, among other states, Ghana, Guatemala, Saudi Arabia, and Venezuela. The United Kingdom, followed by the United States and Canada, eventually proposed a maximum of six miles, with the United Kingdom calling for the preservation of existing navigation and overflight rules outside the three-mile limit. Both the United Kingdom and the United States indicated that if compromise efforts failed they would revert to the three-mile limit. Another compromise, proposed by the United States on 24 April, provided for six miles of territorial seas and six more miles of exclusive fishing rights. See ibid., pp. 125–6. This proposal eventually received the largest number of votes, 45 to 33 with seven abstentions, but this did not amount to the required two-thirds majority. On 4 September 1958 the Government of the People's Republic of China declared the breadth of territorial water of the People's Republic of China to be 12 miles. See above, pp. 523–4.

ARTICLE 26

This Convention shall, until 31 October 1958, be open for signature by all States Members of the United Nations or of any of the specialized agencies, and by any other State invited by the General Assembly of the United Nations to become a party to the Convention.

ARTICLE 27

This Convention is subject to ratification. The instruments of ratification shall be deposited with the Secretary-General of the United Nations.

ARTICLE 28

This Convention shall be open for accession by any States belonging to any of the categories mentioned in article 26. The instruments of accession shall be deposited with the Secretary-General of the United Nations.

ARTICLE 29

1. This Convention shall come into force on the thirtieth day following the date of deposit of the twenty-second instrument of ratification or accession with the Secretary-General of the United Nations.

2. For each State ratifying or acceding to the Convention after the deposit of the twenty-second instrument of ratification or accession, the Convention shall enter into force on the thirtieth day after deposit by such State of its instrument of ratification or accession.

ARTICLE 30

1. After the expiration of a period of five years from the date on which this Convention shall enter into force, a request for the revision of this Convention may be made at any time by any Contracting Party by means of a notification in writing addressed to the Secretary-General of the United Nations.

2. The General Assembly of the United Nations shall decide upon the steps, if any, to be taken in respect of such request.

ARTICLE 31

The Secretary-General of the United Nations shall inform all States Members of the United Nations and the other States referred to in article 26:

(a) Of signatures to this Convention and of the deposit of instruments of ratification or accession, in accordance with articles 26, 27 and 28;

(*b*) Of the date on which this Convention will come into force, in accordance with article 29;

(*c*) Of requests for revision in accordance with article 30.

ARTICLE 32

The original of this Convention, of which the Chinese, English, French, Russian and Spanish texts are equally authentic, shall be deposited with the Secretary-General of the United Nations, who shall send certified copies thereof to all States referred to in article 26.

In witness whereof the undersigned plenipotentiaries, being duly authorized thereto by their respective governments, have signed this Convention.

Done at Geneva, this twenty-ninth day of April one thousand nine hundred and fifty-eight.

(*b*) *Convention on the High Seas*[1]

The States Parties to this Convention,

Desiring to codify the rules of international law relating to the high seas,

Recognizing that the United Nations Conference on the Law of the Sea, held at Geneva from 24 February to 27 April 1958, adopted the following provisions as generally declaratory of established principles of international law,

Have agreed as follows:

ARTICLE I

The term 'high seas' means all parts of the sea that are not included in the territorial sea or in the internal waters of a State.

ARTICLE 2[2]

The high seas being open to all nations, no State may validly purport to subject any part of them to its sovereignty. Freedom of the high seas is exercised under the conditions laid down by these articles and by the other rules of international law. It comprises, *inter alia*, both for coastal and non-coastal States:

(1) Freedom of navigation;

(2) Freedom of fishing;

(3) Freedom to lay submarine cables and pipelines;

(4) Freedom to fly over the high seas.

---

[1] Doc. A/Conf. 13/38, pp. 135–9 (Doc. A/Conf. 13/L.53). Adopted by the conference at its 18th plenary meeting on 29 April 1958 by 65 votes to 0 with one abstention.

[2] Resolution I on nuclear testing on the high seas was adopted by the conference in connexion with this article, see below, p. 565.

These freedoms, and others which are recognized by the general principles of international law, shall be exercised by all States with reasonable regard to the interests of other States in their exercise of the freedom of the high seas.

ARTICLE 3

1. In order to enjoy the freedom of the seas on equal terms with coastal States, States having no sea-coast should have free access to the sea. To this end States situated between the sea and a State having no sea-coast shall by common agreement with the latter and in conformity with existing international conventions accord:

(a) To the State having no sea-coast, on a basis of reciprocity, free transit through their territory; and

(b) To ships flying the flag of that State treatment equal to that accorded to their own ships, or to the ships of any other States, as regards access to seaports and the use of such ports.

2. States situated between the sea and a State having no sea-coast shall settle, by mutual agreement with the latter, and taking into account the rights of the coastal State or State of transit and the special conditions of the State having no sea-coast, all matters relating to freedom of transit and equal treatment in ports, in case such States are not already parties to existing international conventions.

ARTICLE 4

Every State, whether coastal or not, has the right to sail ships under its flag on the high seas.

ARTICLE 5

1. Each State shall fix the conditions for the grant of its nationality to ships, for the registration of ships in its territory, and for the right to fly its flag. Ships have the nationality of the State whose flag they are entitled to fly. There must exist a genuine link between the State and the ship; in particular, the State must effectively exercise its jurisdiction and control in administrative, technical and social matters over ships flying its flags.

2. Each State shall issue to ships to which it has granted the right to fly its flag documents to that effect.

ARTICLE 6

1. Ships shall sail under the flag of one State only and, save in exceptional cases expressly provided for in international treaties or in these

articles, shall be subject to its exclusive jurisdiction on the high seas. A ship may not change its flag during a voyage or while in a port of call, save in the case of a real transfer of ownership or change of registry.

2. A ship which sails under the flags of two or more States, using them according to convenience, may not claim any of the nationalities in question with respect to any other State, and may be assimilated to a ship without nationality.

ARTICLE 7

The provisions of the preceding articles do not prejudice the question of ships employed on the official service of an intergovernmental organization flying the flag of the organization.

ARTICLE 8

1. Warships on the high seas have complete immunity from the jurisdiction of any State other than the flag State.

2. For the purposes of these articles, the term 'warship' means a ship belonging to the naval forces of a State and bearing the external marks distinguishing warships of its nationality, under the command of an officer duly commissioned by the government and whose name appears in the Navy List, and manned by a crew who are under regular naval discipline.

ARTICLE 9

Ships owned or operated by a State and used only on government non-commercial service shall, on the high seas, have complete immunity from the jurisdiction of any State other than the flag State.

ARTICLE 10

1. Every State shall take such measures for ships under its flag as are necessary to ensure safety at sea with regard *inter alia* to:

(a) The use of signals, the maintenance of communications and the prevention of collisions;
(b) The manning of ships and labour conditions for crews taking into account the applicable international labour instruments;
(c) The construction, equipment and seaworthiness of ships.

2. In taking such measures each State is required to conform to generally accepted international standards and to take any steps which may be necessary to ensure their observance.

ARTICLE 11

1. In the event of a collision or of any other incident of navigation concerning a ship on the high seas, involving the penal or disciplinary responsibility of the master or of any other person in the service of the ship, no penal or disciplinary proceedings may be instituted against such persons except before the judicial or administrative authorities either of the flag State or of the State of which such person is a national.

2. In disciplinary matters, the State which has issued a master's certificate or a certificate of competence or licence shall alone be competent, after due legal process, to pronounce the withdrawal of such certificates, even if the holder is not a national of the State which issued them.

3. No arrest or detention of the ship, even as a measure of investigation, shall be ordered by any authorities other than those of the flag State.

ARTICLE 12

1. Every State shall require the master of a ship sailing under its flag, in so far as he can do so without serious danger to the ship, the crew or the passengers:

(a) To render assistance to any person found at sea in danger of being lost;

(b) To proceed with all possible speed to the rescue of persons in distress if informed of their need of assistance, in so far as such action may reasonably be expected of him;

(c) After a collision, to render assistance to the other ship, her crew and her passengers and, where possible, to inform the other ship of the name of his own ship, her port of registry and the nearest port at which she will call.

2. Every coastal State shall promote the establishment and maintenance of an adequate and effective search and rescue service regarding safety on and over the sea and—where circumstances so require—by way of mutual regional arrangements co-operate with neighbouring States for this purpose.

ARTICLE 13

Every State shall adopt effective measures to prevent and punish the transport of slaves in ships authorized to fly its flag, and to prevent the unlawful use of its flag for that purpose. Any slave taking refuge on board any ship, whatever its flag, shall, *ipso facto*, be free.

ARTICLE 14

All States shall co-operate to the fullest possible extent in the repression of piracy on the high seas or in any other place outside the jurisdiction of any State.

ARTICLE 15

Piracy consists of any of the following acts:

(1) Any illegal acts of violence, detention or any act of depredation, committed for private ends by the crew or the passengers of a private ship or a private aircraft, and directed:

> (*a*) On the high seas, against another ship or aircraft, or against persons or property on board such ship or aircraft;
> (*b*) Against a ship, aircraft, persons or property in a place outside the jurisdiction of any State;

(2) Any act of voluntary participation in the operation of a ship or of an aircraft with knowledge of facts making it a pirate ship or aircraft;

(3) Any act of inciting or of intentionally facilitating an act described in sub-paragraph 1 or sub-paragraph 2 of this article.

ARTICLE 16

The acts of piracy, as defined in article 15, committed by a warship, government ship or government aircraft whose crew has mutinied and taken control of the ship or aircraft are assimilated to acts committed by a private ship.

ARTICLE 17

A ship or aircraft is considered a pirate ship or aircraft if it is intended by the persons in dominant control to be used for the purpose of committing one of the acts referred to in article 15. The same applies if the ship or aircraft has been used to commit any such act, so long as it remains under the control of the persons guilty of that act.

ARTICLE 18

A ship or aircraft may retain its nationality although it has become a pirate ship or aircraft. The retention or loss of nationality is determined by the law of the State from which such nationality was derived.

ARTICLE 19

On the high seas, or in any other place outside the jurisdiction of any State, every State may seize a pirate ship or aircraft, or a ship taken by piracy and under the control of pirates, and arrest the persons and seize the property on board. The courts of the State which carried out the seizure may decide upon the penalties to be imposed, and may also determine the action to be taken with regard to the ships, aircraft or property, subject to the rights of third parties acting in good faith.

ARTICLE 20

Where the seizure of a ship or aircraft on suspicion of piracy has been effected without adequate grounds, the State making the seizure shall be liable to the State the nationality of which is possessed by the ship or aircraft, for any loss or damage caused by the seizure.

ARTICLE 21

A seizure on account of piracy may only be carried out by warships or military aircraft, or other ships or aircraft on government service authorized to that effect.

ARTICLE 22

1. Except where acts of interference derive from powers conferred by treaty, a warship which encounters a foreign merchant ship on the high seas is not justified in boarding her unless there is reasonable ground for suspecting:

(a) That the ship is engaged in piracy; or
(b) That the ship is engaged in the slave trade; or
(c) That, though flying a foreign flag or refusing to show its flag, the ship is, in reality, of the same nationality as the warship.

2. In the cases provided for in sub-paragraphs (a), (b) and (c) above, the warship may proceed to verify the ship's right to fly its flag. To this end, it may send a boat under the command of an officer to the suspected ship. If suspicion remains after the documents have been checked, it may proceed to a further examination on board the ship, which must be carried out with all possible consideration.

3. If the suspicions prove to be unfounded, and provided that the ship boarded has not committed any act justifying them, it shall be compensated for any loss or damage that may have been sustained.

ARTICLE 23

1. The hot pursuit of a foreign ship may be undertaken when the competent authorities of the coastal State have good reason to believe that the ship has violated the laws and regulations of that State. Such pursuit must be commenced when the foreign ship or one of its boats is within the internal waters or the territorial sea or the contiguous zone of the pursuing State, and may only be continued outside the territorial sea or the contiguous zone if the pursuit has not been interrupted. It is not necessary that, at the time when the foreign ship within the territorial

sea or the contiguous zone receives the order to stop, the ship giving the order should likewise be within the territorial sea or the contiguous zone. If the foreign ship is within a contiguous zone, as defined in article 24 of the Convention on the Territorial Sea and the Contiguous Zone, the pursuit may only be undertaken if there has been a violation of the rights for the protection of which the zone was established.

2. The right of hot pursuit ceases as soon as the ship pursued enters the territorial sea of its own country or of a third State.

3. Hot pursuit is not deemed to have begun unless the pursuing ship has satisfied itself by such practicable means as may be available that the ship pursued or one of its boats or other craft working as a team and using the ship pursued as a mother ship are within the limits of the territorial sea, or as the case may be within the contiguous zone. The pursuit may only be commenced after a visual or auditory signal to stop has been given at a distance which enables it to be seen or heard by the foreign ship.

4. The right of hot pursuit may be exercised only by warships or military aircraft, or other ships or aircraft on government service specially authorized to that effect.

5. Where hot pursuit is effected by an aircraft:

(a) The provisions of paragraphs 1 to 3 of this article shall apply *mutatis mutandis*;

(b) The aircraft giving the order to stop must itself actively pursue the ship until a ship or aircraft of the coastal State, summoned by the aircraft, arrives to take over the pursuit, unless the aircraft is itself able to arrest the ship. It does not suffice to justify an arrest on the high seas that the ship was merely sighted by the aircraft as an offender or suspected offender, if it was not both ordered to stop and pursued by the aircraft itself or other aircraft or ships which continue the pursuit without interruption.

6. The release of a ship arrested within the jurisdiction of a State and escorted to a port of that State for the purposes of an inquiry before the competent authorities may not be claimed solely on the ground that the ship, in the course of its voyage, was escorted across a portion of the high seas, if the circumstances rendered this necessary.

7. Where a ship has been stopped or arrested on the high seas in circumstances which do not justify the exercise of the rights of hot pursuit, it shall be compensated for any loss or damage that may have been thereby sustained.

ARTICLE 24

Every State shall draw up regulations to prevent pollution of the seas by the discharge of oil from ships or pipelines or resulting from the exploitation and exploration of the seabed and its subsoil, taking account of existing treaty provisions on the subject.[1]

ARTICLE 25[2]

1. Every State shall take measures to prevent pollution of the seas from the dumping of radio-active waste, taking into account any standards and regulations which may be formulated by the competent international organizations.

2. All States shall co-operate with the competent international organizations in taking measures for the prevention of pollution of the seas or air space above, resulting from any activities with radio-active materials or other harmful agents.

ARTICLE 26

1. All States shall be entitled to lay submarine cables and pipelines on the bed of the high seas.

2. Subject to its right to take reasonable measures for the exploration of the continental shelf and the exploitation of its natural resources, the coastal State may not impede the laying or maintenance of such cables or pipelines.

3. When laying such cables or pipelines the State in question shall pay due regard to cables or pipelines already in position on the seabed. In particular, possibilities of repairing existing cables or pipelines shall not be prejudiced.

ARTICLE 27

Every State shall take the necessary legislative measures to provide that the breaking or injury by a ship flying its flag or by a person subject to its jurisdiction of a submarine cable beneath the high seas done wilfully or through culpable negligence, in such a manner as to be liable to interrupt or obstruct telegraphic or telephonic communications, and similarly the breaking or injury of a submarine pipeline or high-voltage

[1] The International Convention for the Prevention of Pollution of the Sea by Oil, which was signed in London on 12 May 1954, entered into force on 26 July 1958. Under its terms the parties are obliged to prohibit the discharge of oil from ships registered in their territories within certain specified areas (normally 50 miles from land). Any violation of the convention should be prosecuted by the authorities of the state in which the vessel is registered. The practical effects of the convention are limited as, apart from Canada and Mexico, only European states have accepted the obligations. See 'Memorandum on Pollution of the Sea by Oil', U.N. Doc. A/Conf. 13/8, 29 October 1957.

[2] The U.S.S.R., Czechoslovakia, Poland, and Yugoslavia submitted a joint proposal for a new article providing that: 'States are bound to refrain from testing nuclear weapons on the high seas.' See summary records of the Tenth plenary meeting, Doc. A/Conf. 13/38, p. 22. This was opposed by the Western powers and by some Asian delegations, and on the proposal of India, Resolution I, below, p. 565, was adopted by 58 votes to 0 with 13 abstentions. Resolution II, below, p. 566, was also adopted in connexion with this article.

power cable shall be a punishable offence. This provision shall not apply to any break or injury caused by persons who acted merely with the legitimate object of saving their lives or their ships, after having taken all necessary precautions to avoid such break or injury.

ARTICLE 28

Every State shall take the necessary legislative measures to provide that, if persons subject to its jurisdiction who are the owners of a cable or pipeline beneath the high seas, in laying or repairing that cable or pipeline, cause a break in or injury to another cable or pipeline, they shall bear the cost of the repairs.

ARTICLE 29

Every State shall take the necessary legislative measures to ensure that the owners of ships who can prove that they have sacrificed an anchor, a net or any other fishing gear, in order to avoid injuring a submarine cable or pipeline, shall be indemnified by the owner of the cable or pipeline, provided that the owner of the ship has taken all reasonable precautionary measures beforehand.

ARTICLE 30

The provisions of this Convention shall not affect conventions or other international agreements already in force, as between States parties to them.

ARTICLE 31

This Convention shall, until 31 October 1958, be open for signature by all States Members of the United Nations or of any of the specialized agencies, and by any other State invited by the General Assembly of the United Nations to become a Party to the Convention.

ARTICLE 32

This Convention is subject to ratification. The instruments of ratification shall be deposited with the Secretary-General of the United Nations.

ARTICLE 33

This Convention shall be open for accession by any States belonging to any of the categories mentioned in article 31. The instruments of accession shall be deposited with the Secretary-General of the United Nations.

ARTICLE 34

1. This Convention shall come into force on the thirtieth day following the date of deposit of the twenty-second instrument of ratification or accession with the Secretary-General of the United Nations.

2. For each State ratifying or acceding to the Convention after the deposit of the twenty-second instrument of ratification or accession, the Convention shall enter into force on the thirtieth day after deposit by such State of its instrument of ratification or accession.

ARTICLE 35

1. After the expiration of a period of five years from the date on which this Convention shall enter into force, a request for the revision of this Convention may be made at any time by any Contracting Party by means of a notification in writing addressed to the Secretary-General of the United Nations.

2. The General Assembly of the United Nations shall decide upon the steps, if any, to be taken in respect of such request.

ARTICLE 36

The Secretary-General of the United Nations shall inform all States Members of the United Nations and the other States referred to in article 31:

(a) Of signatures to this Convention and of the deposit of instruments of ratification or accession, in accordance with articles 31, 32 and 33;

(b) Of the date on which this Convention will come into force, in accordance with article 34;

(c) Of requests for revision in accordance with article 35.

ARTICLE 37

The original of this Convention, of which the Chinese, English, French, Russian and Spanish texts are equally authentic, shall be deposited with the Secretary-General of the United Nations, who shall send certified copies thereof to all States referred to in article 31.

In witness whereof the undersigned plenipotentiaries, being duly authorized thereto by their respective governments, have signed this Convention.

Done at Geneva, this twenty-ninth day of April one thousand nine hundred and fifty-eight.

(c) Convention on Fishing and Conservation of the Living
Resources of the High Seas[1]

The States Parties to this Convention,

Considering that the development of modern techniques for the exploitation of the living resources of the sea, increasing man's ability to meet the need of the world's expanding population for food, has exposed some of these resources to the danger of being over-exploited.

Considering also that the nature of the problems involved in the conservation of the living resources of the high seas is such that there is a clear necessity that they be solved, whenever possible, on the basis of international co-operation through the concerted action of all the States concerned,

Have agreed as follows:

ARTICLE I

1. All States have the right for their nationals to engage in fishing on the high seas, subject (*a*) to their treaty obligations, (*b*) to the interests and rights of coastal States as provided for in this Convention, and (*c*) to the provisions contained in the following articles concerning conservation of the living resources of the high seas.[2]

2. All States have the duty to adopt, or to co-operate with other States in adopting, such measures for their respective nationals as may be necessary for the conservation of the living resources of the high seas.

ARTICLE 2

As employed in this Convention, the expression 'conservation of the living resources of the high seas' means the aggregate of the measures rendering possible the optimum sustainable yield from those resources so as to secure a maximum supply of food and other marine products. Conservation programmes should be formulated with a view to securing in the first place a supply of food for human consumption.

ARTICLE 3

A State whose nationals are engaged in fishing any stock or stocks of fish or other living marine resources in any area of the high seas where the nationals of other States are not thus engaged shall adopt, for its own nationals, measures in that area when necessary for the purpose of the conservation of the living resources affected.

---

[1] Doc. A/Conf. 13/L.54. Adopted by the conference at its 18th plenary meeting on 29 April 1958, by 45 votes to one with 18 abstentions.

[2] See above, pp. 411–14, for the fisheries dispute between the United Kingdom and Iceland.

1. If the nationals of two or more States are engaged in fishing the same stock or stocks of fish or other living marine resources in any area or areas of the high seas, these States shall, at the request of any of them, enter into negotiations with a view to prescribing by agreement for their nationals the necessary measures for the conservation of the living resources affected.

2. If the States concerned do not reach agreement within twelve months, any of the parties may initiate the procedure contemplated by article 9.

1. If, subsequent to the adoption of the measures referred to in articles 3 and 4, nationals of other States engage in fishing the same stock or stocks of fish or other living marine resources in any area or areas of the high seas, the other States shall apply the measures, which shall not be discriminatory in form or in fact, to their own nationals not later than seven months after the date on which the measures shall have been notified to the Director-General of the Food and Agriculture Organization of the United Nations. The Director-General shall notify such measures to any State which so requests and, in any case, to any State specified by the State initiating the measure.

2. If these other States do not accept the measures so adopted and if no agreement can be reached within twelve months, any of the interested parties may initiate the procedure contemplated by article 9. Subject to paragraph 2 of article 10, the measures adopted shall remain obligatory pending the decision of the special commission.

1. A coastal State has a special interest in the maintenance of the productivity of the living resources in any area of the high seas adjacent to its territorial sea.

2. A coastal State is entitled to take part on an equal footing in any system of research and regulation for purposes of conservation of the living resources of the high seas in that area, even though its nationals do not carry on fishing there.

3. A State whose nationals are engaged in fishing in any area of the high seas adjacent to the territorial sea of a State shall, at the request of that coastal State, enter into negotiations with a view to prescribing by agreement the measures necessary for the conservation of the living resources of the high seas in that area.

4. A State whose nationals are engaged in fishing in any area of the

high seas adjacent to the territorial sea of a coastal State shall not enforce conservation measures in that area which are opposed to those which have been adopted by the coastal State, but may enter into negotiations with the coastal State with a view to prescribing by agreement the measures necessary for the conservation of the living resources of the high seas in that area.

5. If the States concerned do not reach agreement with respect to conservation measures within twelve months, any of the parties may initiate the procedure contemplated by article 9.

ARTICLE 7

1. Having regard to the provisions of paragraph 1 of article 6, any coastal State may, with a view to the maintenance of the productivity of the living resources of the sea, adopt unilateral measures of conservation appropriate to any stock of fish or other marine resources in any area of the high seas adjacent to its territorial sea, provided that negotiations to that effect with the other States concerned have not led to an agreement within six months.

2. The measures which the coastal State adopts under the previous paragraph shall be valid as to other States only if the following requirements are fulfilled:

(*a*) That there is a need for urgent application of conservation measures in the light of the existing knowledge of the fishery;

(*b*) That the measures adopted are based on appropriate scientific findings;

(*c*) That such measures do not discriminate in form or in fact against foreign fishermen.

3. These measures shall remain in force pending the settlement, in accordance with the relevant provisions of this Convention, of any disagreement as to their validity.

4. If the measures are not accepted by the other States concerned, any of the parties may initiate the procedure contemplated by article 9. Subject to paragraph 2 of article 10, the measures adopted shall remain obligatory pending the decision of the special commission.

5. The principles of geographical demarcation as defined in article 12 of the Convention on the Territorial Sea and the Contiguous Zone shall be adopted when coasts of different States are involved.

ARTICLE 8

1. Any State which, even if its nationals are not engaged in fishing in an area of the high seas not adjacent to its coast, has a special interest

in the conservation of the living resources of the high seas in that area, may request the State or States whose nationals are engaged in fishing there to take the necessary measures of conservation under articles 3 and 4 respectively, at the same time mentioning the scientific reasons which in its opinion make such measures necessary, and indicating its special interest.

2. If no agreement is reached within twelve months, such State may initiate the procedure contemplated by article 9.

ARTICLE 9

1. Any dispute which may arise between States under articles 4, 5, 6, 7 and 8 shall, at the request of any of the parties, be submitted for settlement to a special commission of five members, unless the parties agree to seek a solution by another method of peaceful settlement, as provided for in Article 33 of the Charter of the United Nations.

2. The members of the commission, one of whom shall be designated as chairman, shall be named by agreement between the States in dispute within three months of the request for settlement in accordance with the provisions of this article. Failing agreement they shall, upon the request of any State party, be named by the Secretary-General of the United Nations, within a further three-month period, in consultation with the States in dispute and with the President of the International Court of Justice and the Director-General of the Food and Agriculture Organization of the United Nations, from amongst well-qualified persons being nationals of States not involved in the dispute and specializing in legal, administrative or scientific questions relating to fisheries, depending upon the nature of the dispute to be settled. Any vacancy arising after the original appointment shall be filled in the same manner as provided for the initial selection.

3. Any State party to proceedings under these articles shall have the right to name one of its nationals to the special commission, with the right to participate fully in the proceedings on the same footing as a member of the commission, but without the right to vote or to take part in the writing of the commission's decision.

4. The commission shall determine its own procedure, assuring each party to the proceedings a full opportunity to be heard and to present its case. It shall also determine how the costs and expenses shall be divided between the parties to the dispute, failing agreement by the parties on this matter.

5. The special commission shall render its decision within a period of five months from the time it is appointed unless it decides, in case of necessity, to extend the time limit for a period not exceeding three months.

6. The special commission shall, in reaching its decisions, adhere to these articles and to any special agreements between the disputing parties regarding settlement of the dispute.

7. Decisions of the commission shall be by majority vote.

1. The special commission shall, in disputes arising under article 7, apply the criteria listed in paragraph 2 of that article. In disputes under articles 4, 5, 6 and 8, the commission shall apply the following criteria, according to the issues involved in the dispute:

(a) Common to the determination of disputes arising under articles 4, 5 and 6 are the requirements:

(i) That scientific findings demonstrate the necessity of conservation measures;
(ii) That the specific measures are based on scientific findings and are practicable; and
(iii) That the measures do not discriminate, in form or in fact, against fishermen of other States;

(b) Applicable to the determination of disputes arising under article 8 is the requirement that scientific findings demonstrate the necessity for conservation measures, or that the conservation programme is adequate, as the case may be.

2. The special commission may decide that pending its award the measures in dispute shall not be applied, provided that, in the case of disputes under article 7, the measures shall only be suspended when it is apparent to the commission on the basis of *prima facie* evidence that the need for the urgent application of such measures does not exist.

The decisions of the special commission shall be binding on the States concerned[1] and the provisions of paragraph 2 of Article 94 of the Charter of the United Nations shall be applicable to those decisions. If the decisions are accompanied by any recommendations, they shall receive the greatest possible consideration.

---

[1] The scheme for the binding settlement of disputes was opposed by the Soviet *bloc* and certain Latin American states in particular, but the attitude of states, especially those of Western Europe, insisting that the scheme should be an integral part of the Convention prevailed because the conference, by a procedural vote requiring only a simple majority, decided to vote on the first twelve articles as a whole. If a separate vote had been taken on Articles 9–12 they would probably not have obtained the necessary two-thirds majority.

ARTICLE 12

1. If the factual basis of the award of the special commission is altered by substantial changes in the conditions of the stock or stocks of fish or other living marine resources or in methods of fishing, any of the States concerned may request the other States to enter into negotiations with a view to prescribing by agreement the necessary modifications in the measures of conservation.

2. If no agreement is reached within a resonable period of time, any of the States concerned may again resort to the procedure contemplated by article 9 provided that at least two years have elapsed from the original award.

ARTICLE 13

1. The regulation of fisheries conducted by means of equipment embedded in the floor of the sea in areas of the high seas adjacent to the territorial sea of a State may be undertaken by that State where such fisheries have long been maintained and conducted by its nationals, provided that non-nationals are permitted to participate in such activities on an equal footing with nationals except in areas where such fisheries have by long usage been exclusively enjoyed by such nationals. Such regulations will not, however, affect the general status of the areas as high seas.

2. In this article, the expression 'fisheries conducted by means of equipment embedded in the floor of the sea' means those fisheries using gear with supporting members embedded in the sea floor, constructed on a site and left there to operate permanently or, if removed, restored each season on the same site.

ARTICLE 14

In articles 1, 3, 4, 5, 6 and 8, the term 'nationals' means fishing boats or craft of any size having the nationality of the State concerned, according to the law of that State, irrespective of the nationality of the members of their crews.

ARTICLE 15

This Convention shall, until 31 October 1958, be open for signature by all States Members of the United Nations or of any of the specialized agencies, and by any other State invited by the General Assembly of the United Nations to become a Party to the Convention.

ARTICLE 16

This Convention is subject to ratification. The instruments of ratification shall be deposited with the Secretary-General of the United Nations.

ARTICLE 17

This Convention shall be open for accession by any States belonging to any of the categories mentioned in article 15. The instruments of accession shall be deposited with the Secretary-General of the United Nations.

ARTICLE 18

1. This Convention shall come into force on the thirtieth day following the date of deposit of the twenty-second instrument of ratification or accession with the Secretary-General of the United Nations.

2. For each State ratifying or acceding to the Convention after the deposit of the twenty-second instrument of ratification or accession, the Convention shall enter into force on the thirtieth day after deposit by such State of its instrument of ratification or accession.

ARTICLE 19

1. At the time of signature, ratification or accession, any State may make reservations to articles of the Convention other than to articles 6, 7, 9, 10, 11 and 12.

2. Any contracting State making a reservation in accordance with the preceding paragraph may at any time withdraw the reservation by a communication to that effect addressed to the Secretary-General of the United Nations.

ARTICLE 20

1. After the expiration of a period of five years from the date on which this Convention shall enter into force, a request for the revision of this Convention may be made at any time by any contracting party by means of a notification in writing addressed to the Secretary-General of the United Nations.

2. The General Assembly of the United Nations shall decide upon the steps, if any, to be taken in respect of such request.

ARTICLE 21

The Secretary-General of the United Nations shall inform all States Members of the United Nations and the other States referred to in article 15:

(*a*) Of signatures to this Convention and of the deposit of instruments of ratification or accession, in accordance with articles 15, 16 and 17;

(*b*) Of the date on which this Convention will come into force, in accordance with article 18;

(*c*) Of requests for revision in accordance with article 20;
(*d*) Of reservations to this Convention, in accordance with article 19.

ARTICLE 22

The original of this Convention, of which the Chinese, English, French, Russian and Spanish texts are equally authentic, shall be deposited with the Secretary-General of the United Nations, who shall send certified copies thereof to all States referred to in article 15.

In witness whereof the undersigned plenipotentiaries, being duly authorized thereto by their respective governments, have signed this Convention.

Done at Geneva, this twenty-ninth day of April one thousand nine hundred and fifty-eight.

(*d*) *Convention on the Continental Shelf*[1]

The States Parties to this Convention
Have agreed as follows:

ARTICLE I

For the purpose of these articles, the term 'continental shelf' is used as referring (*a*) to the seabed and subsoil of the submarine areas adjacent to the coast but outside the area of the territorial sea, to a depth of 200 metres or, beyond that limit, to where the depth of the superjacent waters admits of the exploitation of the natural resources of the said areas; (*b*) to the seabed and subsoil of similar submarine areas adjacent to the coasts of islands.

ARTICLE 2

1. The coastal State exercises over the continental shelf sovereign rights for the purpose of exploring it and exploiting its natural resources.

2. The rights referred to in paragraph 1 of this article are exclusive in the sense that if the coastal State does not explore the continental shelf or exploit its natural resources, no one may undertake these activities, or make a claim to the continental shelf, without the express consent of the coastal State.

---

[1] Doc. A/Conf. 13/L.55. Adopted by the conference at its 18th plenary meeting on 29 April 1958 by 57 votes to three, with eight abstentions. By 1958 some twenty states and the United Kingdom with respect to a dozen dependent territories had claimed sovereign rights over the continental shelf. Some of them, in particular certain Latin American states, had not limited their claims to the subsoil and the sea-bed, but had assumed sovereignty over the superjacent waters thereby interfering with the freedom of the high seas. The outcome of the Geneva Conference left no doubt that the claim to sovereignty over superjacent waters was unfounded in law. The International Law Commission's draft provision for compulsory judicial settlement of disputes relating to the Continental Shelf was not adopted by the conference.

3. The rights of the coastal State over the continental shelf do not depend on occupation, effective or notional, or on any express proclamation.

4. The natural resources referred to in these articles consist of the mineral and other non-living resources of the seabed and subsoil together with living organisms belonging to sedentary species, that is to say, organisms which, at the harvestable stage, either are immobile on or under the seabed or are unable to move except in constant physical contact with the seabed or the subsoil.[1]

ARTICLE 3

The rights of the coastal State over the continental shelf do not affect the legal status of the superjacent waters as high seas, or that of the air space above those waters.

ARTICLE 4

Subject to its right to take reasonable measures for the exploration of the continental shelf and the exploitation of its natural resources, the coastal State may not impede the laying or maintenance of submarine cables or pipelines on the continental shelf.

ARTICLE 5

1. The exploration of the continental shelf and the exploitation of its natural resources must not result in any unjustifiable interference with navigation, fishing or the conservation of the living resources of the sea, nor result in any interference with fundamental oceanographic or other scientific research carried out with the intention of open publication.

2. Subject to the provisions of paragraphs 1 and 6 of this article, the coastal State is entitled to construct and maintain or operate on the continental shelf installations and other devices necessary for its exploration and the exploitation of its natural resources, and to establish safety zones around such installations and devices and to take in those zones measures necessary for their protection.

3. The safety zones referred to in paragraph 2 of this article may extend to a distance of 500 metres around the installations and other devices which have been erected, measured from each point of their outer edge. Ships of all nationalities must respect these safety zones.

4. Such installations and devices, though under the jurisdiction of the coastal State, do not possess the status of islands. They have no territorial

[1] For example pearl-bearing oysters.

sea of their own, and their presence does not affect the delimitation of the territorial sea of the coastal State.

5. Due notice must be given of the construction of any such installations, and permanent means for giving warning of their presence must be maintained. Any installations which are abandoned or disused must be entirely removed.

6. Neither the installations or devices, nor the safety zones around them, may be established where interference may be caused to the use of recognized sea lanes essential to international navigation.

7. The coastal State is obliged to undertake, in the safety zones, all appropriate measures for the protection of the living resources of the sea from harmful agents.

8. The consent of the coastal State shall be obtained in respect of any research concerning the continental shelf and undertaken there. Nevertheless, the coastal State shall not normally withhold its consent if the request is submitted by a qualified institution with a view to purely scientific research into the physical or biological characteristics of the continental shelf, subject to the proviso that the coastal State shall have the right, if it so desires, to participate or to be represented in the research, and that in any event the results shall be published.

ARTICLE 6

1. Where the same continental shelf is adjacent to the territories of two or more States whose coasts are opposite each other, the boundary of the continental shelf appertaining to such States shall be determined by agreement between them. In the absence of agreement, and unless another boundary line is justified by special circumstances, the boundary is the median line, every point of which is equidistant from the nearest points of the baselines from which the breadth of the territorial sea of each State is measured.

2. Where the same continental shelf is adjacent to the territories of two adjacent States, the boundary of the continental shelf shall be determined by agreement between them. In the absence of agreement, and unless another boundary line is justified by special circumstances, the boundary shall be determined by application of the principle of equidistance from the nearest points of the baselines from which the breadth of the territorial sea of each State is measured.

3. In delimiting the boundaries of the continental shelf, any lines which are drawn in accordance with the principles set out in paragraphs 1 and 2 of this article should be defined with reference to charts and geographical features as they exist at a particular date, and reference should be made to fixed permanent identifiable points on the land.

ARTICLE 7

The provisions of these articles shall not prejudice the right of the coastal State to exploit the subsoil by means of tunnelling irrespective of the depth of water above the subsoil.

ARTICLE 8

This Convention shall, until 30 October 1958, be open for signature by all States Members of the United Nations or of any of the specialized agencies, and by any other State invited by the General Assembly of the United Nations to become a party to the Convention.

ARTICLE 9

This Convention is subject to ratification. The instruments of ratification shall be deposited with the Secretary-General of the United Nations.

ARTICLE 10

This Convention shall be open for accession by any States belonging to any of the categories mentioned in article 8. The instruments of accession shall be deposited with the Secretary-General of the United Nations.

ARTICLE 11

1. This Convention shall come into force on the thirtieth day following the date of deposit of the twenty-second instrument of ratification or accession with the Secretary-General of the United Nations.

2. For each State ratifying or acceding to the Convention after the deposit of the twenty-second instrument of ratification or accession, the Convention shall enter into force on the thirtieth day after deposit by such State of its instrument of ratification or accession.

ARTICLE 12

1. At the time of signature, ratification or accession, any State may make reservations to articles of the Convention other than to articles 1 to 3 inclusive.

2. Any contracting State making a reservation in accordance with the preceding paragraph may at any time withdraw the reservation by a communication to that effect addressed to the Secretary-General of the United Nations.

ARTICLE 13

1. After the expiration of a period of five years from the date on which this Convention shall enter into force, a request for the revision of this

Convention may be made at any time by any contracting party by means of a notification in writing addressed to the Secretary-General of the United Nations.

2. The General Assembly of the United Nations shall decide upon the steps, if any, to be taken in respect of such request.

ARTICLE 14

The Secretary-General of the United Nations shall inform all States Members of the United Nations and the other States referred to in article 8:

(a) Of signatures to this Convention and of the deposit of instruments of ratification or accession, in accordance with articles 8, 9 and 10;

(b) Of the date on which this Convention will come into force, in accordance with article 11;

(c) Of requests for revision in accordance with article 13;

(d) Of reservations to this Convention, in accordance with article 12.

ARTICLE 15

The original of this Convention, of which the Chinese, English, French, Russian and Spanish texts are equally authentic, shall be deposited with the Secretary-General of the United Nations, who shall send certified copies thereof to all States referred to in article 8.

In witness whereof the undersigned plenipotentiaries, being duly authorized thereto by their respective governments, have signed this Convention.

Done at Geneva, this twenty-ninth day of April one thousand nine hundred and fifty-eight.

(e) Resolutions adopted by the Conference[1]

I

NUCLEAR TESTS ON THE HIGH SEAS[2]

The United Nations Conference on the Law of the Sea,

Recalling that the Conference has been convened by the General Assembly of the United Nations in accordance with resolution 1105 (XI) of 21 February 1957,

Recognizing that there is a serious and genuine apprehension on the part of many States that nuclear explosions constitute an infringement of the freedom of the seas,

[1] Doc. A/Conf. 13/L.56.

[2] Adopted at the 10th plenary meeting on 23 April 1958 on the report of the Second Committee in connexion with article 2 of the Convention on the High Seas.

Recognizing that the question of nuclear tests and production is still under review by the General Assembly under various resolutions on the subject and by the Disarmament Commission, and is at present under constant review and discussion by the governments concerned,

Decides to refer this matter to the General Assembly of the United Nations for appropriate action.

II

POLLUTION OF THE HIGH SEAS BY RADIO-ACTIVE MATERIALS[1]

The United Nations Conference on the Law of the Sea,

Recognizing the need for international action in the field of disposal of radio-active wastes in the sea,

Taking into account action which has been proposed by various national and international bodies and studies which have been published on the subject,

Noting that the International Commission on Radiological Protection has made recommendations regarding the maximum permissible concentration of radio-isotopes in the human body and the maximum permissible concentration in air and water,

Recommends that the International Atomic Energy Agency, in consultation with existing groups and established organs having acknowledged competence in the field of radiological protection, should pursue whatever studies and take whatever action is necessary to assist States in controlling the discharge or release of radio-active materials to the sea, in promulgating standards, and in drawing up internationally acceptable regulations to prevent pollution of the sea by radio-active materials in amounts which would adversely affect man and his marine resources.

III

INTERNATIONAL FISHERY CONSERVATION CONVENTIONS[2]

The United Nations Conference on the Law of the Sea,

Taking note of the opinion of the International Technical Conference on the Conservation of the Living Resources of the Sea, held in Rome in April/May 1955, as expressed in paragraph 43 of its report, as to the efficacy of international conservation organizations in furthering the conservation of the living resources of the sea,

Believing that such organizations are valuable instruments for the co-ordination of scientific effort upon the problem of fisheries and for the making of agreements upon conservation measures,

---

[1] Adopted at the 10th plenary meeting on the report of the Second Committee in relation to article 25 of the Convention on the High Seas.

[2] Adopted at the 15th plenary meeting on 25 April 1958 on the report of the Third Committee.

Recommends:

1. That States concerned should co-operate in establishing the necessary conservation régime through the medium of such organizations covering particular areas of the high seas or species of living marine resources and conforming in other respects with the recommendations contained in the report of the International Technical Conference on the Conservation of the Living Resources of the Sea;

2. That these organizations should be used so far as practicable for the conduct of the negotiations between States envisaged under articles 4, 5, 6 and 7 of the Convention on Fishing and Conservation of the Living Resources of the High Seas, for the resolution of any disagreements and for the implementation of agreed measures of conservation.

IV

CO-OPERATION IN CONSERVATION MEASURES[1]

The United Nations Conference on the Law of the Sea,

Taking note of the opinion of the International Technical Conference on the Conservation of the Living Resources of the Sea, held in Rome in April/May 1955, as reported in paragraphs 43 (*a*), 54 and others of its report, that any effective conservation management system must have the participation of all States engaged in substantial exploitation of the stock or stocks of living marine organisms which are the object of the conservation management system or having a special interest in the conservation of that stock or stocks,

Recommends to the coastal States that, in the cases where a stock or stocks of fish or other living marine resources inhabit both the fishing areas under their jurisdiction and areas of the adjacent high seas, they should co-operate with such international conservation organizations as may be responsible for the development and application of conservation measures in the adjacent high seas, in the adoption and enforcement, as far as practicable, of the necessary conservation measures on fishing areas under their jurisdiction.

V

HUMANE KILLING OF MARINE LIFE[1]

The United Nations Conference on the Law of the Sea,

Requests States to prescribe, by all means available to them, those methods for the capture and killing of marine life, especially of whales and seals, which will spare them suffering to the greatest extent possible.

[1] Adopted at the 15th plenary meeting on 25 April 1958 on the report of the Third Committee.

VI

Special Situations Relating to Coastal Fisheries[1]

The United Nations Conference on the Law of the Sea,

Having considered the situation of countries or territories whose people are overwhelmingly dependent upon coastal fisheries for their livelihood or economic development.

Having considered also the situation of countries whose coastal population depends primarily on coastal fisheries for the animal protein of its diet and whose fishing methods are mainly limited to local fishing from small boats.

Recognizing that such situations call for exceptional measures befitting particular needs,

Considering that, because of the limited scope and exceptional nature of those situations, any measures adopted to meet them would be complementary to provisions incorporated in a universal system of international law.

Believing that States should collaborate to secure just treatment of such situations by regional agreements or by other means of international co-operation,

Recommends:

1. That where, for the purpose of conservation, it becomes necessary to limit the total catch of a stock or stocks of fish in an area of the high seas adjacent to the territorial sea of a coastal State, any other States fishing in that area should collaborate with the coastal State to secure just treatment of such situation, by establishing agreed measures which shall recognize any preferential requirements of the coastal State resulting from its dependence upon the fishery concerned while having regard to the interests of the other States;

2. That appropriate conciliation and arbitral procedures shall be established for the settlement of any disagreement.

VII

Régime of Historic Waters[2]

The United Nations Conference on the Law of the Sea,

Considering that the International Law Commission has not provided for the régime of historic waters, including historic bays,

Recognizing the importance of the juridical status of such areas,

[1] Adopted at the 16th plenary meeting on 26 April 1958 on the report of the Third Committee.

[2] Adopted at the 20th plenary meeting on 27 April 1958 on the report of the First Committee.

Decides to request the General Assembly of the United Nations to arrange for the study of the juridical régime of historic waters, including historic bays, and for the communication of the results of such study to all States Members of the United Nations.

VIII

CONVENING OF A SECOND UNITED NATIONS CONFERENCE ON THE LAW OF THE SEA[1]

The United Nations Conference on the Law of the Sea,

Considering that, on the basis of the report prepared by the International Law Commission,[2] it has approved agreements and other instruments on the régime applicable to fishing and the conservation of the living resources of the high seas, the exploration of the continental shelf and the exploitation of its natural resources and other matters pertaining to the general régime of the high seas and to the free access of land-locked States to the sea,

Considering that it has not been possible to reach agreement on the breadth of the territorial sea and some other matters which were discussed in connexion with this problem,

Recognizing that, although agreements have been reached on the régime applicable to fishing and the conservation of the living resources of the high seas, it has not been possible, in those agreements, to settle certain aspects of a number of inherently complex questions,

Recognizing the desirability of making further efforts at an appropriate time to reach agreement on questions of the international law of the sea, which have been left unsettled,

Resolves to request the General Assembly of the United Nations to study, at its thirteenth session, the advisability of convening a second international conference of plenipotentiaries for further consideration of the questions left unsettled by the present Conference.

IX

TRIBUTE TO THE INTERNATIONAL LAW COMMISSION

The United Nations Conference on the Law of the Sea, on the conclusion of its proceedings,

Resolves to pay a tribute of gratitude, respect and admiration to the International Law Commission for its excellent work in the matter of the codification and development of international law, in the form of various drafts and commentaries of great juridical value.

[1] Resolutions VIII and IX were adopted at the 21st plenary meeting on 27 April 1958.
[2] G.A.O.R., Eleventh Session, Supplement 9.

2. Resolution of the General Assembly regarding the convening of a second United Nations Conference on the Law of the Sea, 10 December 1958[1]

THE GENERAL ASSEMBLY,

Having received the resolution adopted on 27 April 1958 by the United Nations Conference on the Law of the Sea,[2] requesting the General Assembly to study at its thirteenth session the advisability of convening a second international conference of plenipotentiaries for further consideration of questions left unsettled by the Conference,

Recalling that the Conference made an historic contribution to the codification and progressive development of international law by preparing and opening for signature conventions on nearly all of the subjects covered by the draft articles on the law of the sea drawn up by the International Law Commission,

Noting that no proposal concerning the breadth of the territorial sea or fishery limits received the two-thirds majority required for adoption by the Conference,

Believing that the desire for agreement on these two vital issues continues, and that agreement thereon would contribute substantially to the lessening of international tensions and to the preservation of world order and peace,

Convinced that to reach such agreement it is necessary to undertake considerable preparatory work so as to ensure reasonable probabilities of success,

1. *Decides* that a second international conference of plenipotentiaries on the law of the sea should be called for the purpose of considering further the questions of the breadth of the territorial sea and fishery limits;

2. *Requests* the Secretary-General to convoke the conference at the earliest convenient date in March or April 1960 at the European Office of the United Nations in Geneva[3];

3. *Invites* all States Members of the United Nations and States members of the specialized agencies to participate in the conference and to include among their representatives experts competent in the matters to be considered;

4. *Requests* the Secretary-General to invite the specialized agencies and

---

[1] G.A.O.R., Thirteenth Session, Supplement 18 (A/4090), Resol. 1307 (XIII). Adopted by roll-call vote of 71 to 0, with six abstentions (Cambodia, Denmark, Finland, Iceland, Norway, Sweden).

[2] Resolution VIII, above.

[3] The second United Nations Conference on the Law of the Sea met at Geneva from 17 March to 26 April 1960. No agreement was reached on the breadth of the territorial sea and fishery limits. For one account of the proceedings, see *The Guardian*, 27 April 1960.

inter-governmental bodies concerned with the matters to be considered to send observers to the conference;

5. *Requests* the Secretary-General to arrange for the necessary staff and facilities which would be required for the conference, and to present to the conference recommendations concerning its methods of work and procedures, and other questions of an administrative nature;

6. *Refers* to the conference for its information the relevant records of the United Nations Conference on the Law of the Sea held in 1958.

B. CONFERENCE ON ANTARCTICA

1. United States note proposing a conference on Antarctica, 3 May 1958[1]

Excellency: I have the honor to refer to the splendid example of international cooperation which can now be observed in many parts of the world because of the coordinated efforts of scientists of many countries in seeking a better understanding of geophysical phenomena during the current International Geophysical Year. These coordinated efforts of the scientists of many lands have as their objective a greatly increased knowledge of the planet on which we live and will no doubt contribute directly and indirectly to the welfare of the human race for many generations to come.

Among the various portions of the globe where these cooperative scientific endeavors are being carried on with singular success and with a sincere consciousness of the high ideals of mankind to which they are dedicated is the vast and relatively remote continent of Antarctica. The scientific research being conducted in that continent by the cooperative efforts of distinguished scientists from many countries is producing information of practical as well as theoretical value for all mankind.

The International Geophysical Year comes to a close at the end of 1958. The need for coordinated scientific research in Antarctica, however, will continue for many more years into the future. Accordingly, it would appear desirable for those countries participating in the Antarctic program of the International Geophysical Year to reach agreement among themselves on a program to assure the continuation of the fruitful scientific cooperation referred to above. Such an arrangement could have the

---

[1] *D.S.B.*, 2 June 1958, pp. 911–12. The note was addressed to the foreign minister of each of the 11 other countries participating in the International Geophysical Year activities in Antarctica (Argentina, Australia, Belgium, Chile, France, Japan, New Zealand, Norway, Union of South Africa, U.S.S.R., and the U.K.). Each note was signed and delivered by the American ambassador to that country. The Antarctic Treaty was finally signed on 1 December 1959 in Washington.

additional advantage of preventing unnecessary and undesirable political rivalries in that continent, the uneconomic expenditure of funds to defend individual national interests, and the recurrent possibility of international misunderstanding. It would appear that if harmonious agreement can be reached among the countries directly concerned in regard to friendly cooperation in Antarctica, there would be advantages not only to those countries but to all other countries as well.

The present situation in Antarctica is characterized by diverse legal, political, and administrative concepts which render friendly cooperation difficult in the absence of an understanding among the countries involved. Seven countries have asserted claims of sovereignty to portions of Antarctica, some of which overlap and give rise to occasional frictions. Other countries have a direct interest in that continent based on past discovery and exploration, geographic proximity, sea and air transportation routes, and other considerations.

The United States for many years has had, and at the present time continues to have, direct and substantial rights and interests in Antarctica. Throughout a period of many years, commencing in the early eighteen-hundreds, many areas of the Antarctic region have been discovered, sighted, explored and claimed on behalf of the United States by nationals of the United States and by expeditions carrying the flag of the United States. During this period, the Government of the United States and its nationals have engaged in well-known and extensive activities in Antarctica.

In view of the activities of the United States and its nationals referred to above, my Government reserves all of the rights of the United States with respect to the Antarctic region, including the right to assert a territorial claim or claims.

It is the opinion of my Government, however, that the interests of mankind would best be served, in consonance with the high ideals of the Charter of the United Nations, if the countries which have a direct interest in Antarctica were to join together in the conclusion of a treaty which would have the following peaceful purposes:

A. Freedom of scientific investigation throughout Antarctica by citizens, organizations, and governments of all countries; and a continuation of the international scientific cooperation which is being carried out so successfully during the current International Geophysical Year.

B. International agreement to ensure that Antarctica be used for peaceful purposes only.

C. Any other peaceful purposes not inconsistent with the Charter of the United Nations.

The Government of the United States is prepared to discuss jointly with the Governments of the other countries having a direct interest in

Antarctica the possibility of concluding an agreement, which would be in the form of a treaty, for the purpose of giving legal effect to these high principles. It is believed that such a treaty can be concluded without requiring any participating nation to renounce whatever basic historic rights it may have in Antarctica, or whatever claims of sovereignty it may have asserted. It could be specifically provided that such basic rights and such claims would remain unaffected while the treaty is in force, and that no new rights would be acquired and no new claims made by any country during the duration of the treaty. In other words, the legal status quo in Antarctica would be frozen for the duration of the treaty, permitting cooperation in scientific and administrative matters to be carried out in a constructive manner without being hampered or affected in any way by political considerations. Provision could likewise be made for such joint administrative arrangements as might be necessary and desirable to ensure the successful accomplishment of the agreed objectives. The proposed treaty would be deposited with the United Nations, and the cooperation of the specialized technical agencies of the United Nations would be sought. Such an arrangement would provide a firm and favorable foundation for a continuation of the productive activities which have thus far distinguished the International Geophysical Year; would provide an agreed basis for the maintenance of peaceful and orderly conditions in Antarctica during years to come; and would avoid the possibility of that continent becoming the scene of international discord.

In the hope that the countries having a direct interest in Antarctica will agree on the desirability of the aforesaid high objectives, and will work together in an effort to convert them into practical realities, the Government of the United States has the honor to invite the Government of _____ to participate in a Conference for this purpose to be convened at an early date at such place as may be mutually agreeable.

Accept, Excellency, the renewed assurances of my highest consideration.

2. Soviet reply to the United States proposal for a conference on Antarctica, 2 June 1958[1]

In connection with the U.S. State Department's letter of May 2, 1958, on the question of the Antarctic, the U.S.S.R. Embassy, on the instructions of the Soviet government, has the honour to communicate the following:

The government of the U.S.S.R., like the United States government, notes with satisfaction that representatives of scientific circles of a number of countries, which are carrying on investigations in the Antarctic under

---

[1] *Soviet News*, 9 June 1958.

the International Geophysical Year programme, are engaging in fruitful scientific co-operation.

The competent Soviet scientific circles which are co-operating with representatives of scientific organisations in the special committee on Antarctic investigations, set up by the International Council of Scientific Unions, approve of the measures, adopted by this committee at the Hague in February, 1958, to continue international co-operation in the Antarctic after the end of the Geophysical Year. Soviet scientific organisations are prepared to continue in the future to co-ordinate their efforts in the Antarctic with scientists of all other countries, considering that this will make it possible to develop the successes achieved in the scientific investigations during the International Geophysical Year.

The Soviet government, for its part, is prepared to render all possible help in the development of international scientific co-operation in the Antarctic in the future, too. In the opinion of the Soviet government, this co-operation should be based, as hitherto, on the following principles:

1. The Antarctic should be used by all countries exclusively for peaceful purposes; this implies, among other things, that no military bases should be set up in the Antarctic, and no military, naval and air manœuvres, or testing of any weapons should be held there.

2. The governments, organisations and citizens of all countries should enjoy freedom of scientific investigation throughout the entire Antarctic on an equal basis.

The Soviet Union considers it useful that these principles, which have in practice developed in the course of scientific co-operation during the International Geophysical Year, should be laid down in an international agreement ensuring the successful development of scientific investigations in the Antarctic for a long time to come.

The Soviet government agrees that an important aim of the projected international agreement should be the prevention of any international misunderstandings that could hinder successful scientific investigations in this area.

With reference to the question of territorial claims in the Antarctic made by some countries, the Soviet government considers it necessary to state again that it has not recognised and cannot recognise as lawful any separate settlement of the question regarding state jurisdiction over the Antarctic. In this connection it is well to recall the outstanding services of Russian explorers in the discovery of the Antarctic and, among other things, the universally known fact that it was precisely the Russian navigators Bellinshausen and Lazarev who, early in the 19th century, were the first to reach the shores of the Antarctic and to circle this continent.

The Soviet Union reserves all rights based on the discoveries and explorations by Russian navigators and scientists, including the right to present appropriate territorial claims on the Antarctic.

At the same time the Soviet government considers it possible and desirable, in the interests of all mankind, and guided by the principles and purposes of the United Nations Charter, to reach an international agreement ensuring the freedom of scientific investigation in the Antarctic and its exclusive use for peaceful purposes.

For the achievement of that aim, it is important, in the Soviet government's opinion, to prevent from the very outset complications that may arise from attempts directly or indirectly to settle or predetermine the question concerning the territorial claims of states in the Antarctic. In this light it would be well for the projected treaty not to include any provisions affecting the question of territorial claims in the Antarctic, which could be regarded as placing some states in an unequal status with regard to other states.

The projected treaty could, in the Soviet government's opinion, envisage such forms of international scientific co-operation in the Antarctic which, taking into account the practice already prevailing, are most expedient.

As regards the proposal, contained in the U.S. State Department's letter of May 2, to convene an international conference, the Soviet government states that it is ready to take part in such a conference to discuss the use of the Antarctic exclusively for peaceful purposes and the freedom of scientific investigations in this area for all countries on an equal basis, and to take part in drafting a respective international treaty.

While agreeing to take part in this conference, the Soviet government considers it necessary to point out that the conference and the projected international treaty on the Antarctic would be much more effective if all states wishing to do so were to take part in the discussion of this question.

There is no doubt that such an important question as the use of the Antarctic exclusively for peaceful purposes transcends the bounds of the interests of the states which are already carrying on scientific investigations in that area. The question of the freedom of scientific investigations in the Antarctic is of interest not only to those states which are already now carrying on this work, but also to those which would like to undertake respective scientific investigations in the future.

Indicative of the interest of other countries in the use of the Antarctic exclusively for peaceful purposes and in the freedom of scientific investigations is, among other things, the well-known initiative taken by India in 1956, when it proposed that this question be discussed within the framework of the United Nations.

Participation of a sufficiently wide range of states in the discussion of the question regarding the Antarctic could, in the opinion of the Soviet government, be ensured by convening a conference of all states which might express a desire to take part in it.

Bearing in mind that the State Department's letter of May 2 says that the question of the time and place of the conference on the Antarctic is to be the subject of a further study so that a mutually acceptable decision may be adopted, the Soviet government awaits proposals on this question and is prepared to take part in discussing them.

C. AFRO-ASIAN AND AFRICAN CONFERENCES

a. Afro-Asian People's Solidarity Conference

1. Declaration of the Afro-Asian People's Solidarity Conference, Cairo, 1 January 1958[1]

We representatives of Asian and African peoples met in Cairo in the period from December 26, 1957, to January 1, 1958, to discuss general international questions with particular attention to causes of interest to Asian and African peoples.

We also reviewed social, economic and cultural problems facing our peoples and declare that the conference has approved the establishment of a permanent body in Cairo whose task will be to implement the resolutions and recommendations of the conference.

Emphasising the unity of purpose and unanimity of the Afro-Asian Solidarity Conference in approving the resolutions and recommendations, this declaration, made at the opening of the final session of the Conference on January 1, 1958, on behalf of all the delegates, continued:

We declare that the principles approved by the Bandung conference in April 1955 should continue to serve as bases for international relations and we are in complete agreement that if the world were to accept them, they would end the state of fear which threatens the world.

These principles are:

1. Respect of basic Human Rights and the aims and principles of the United Nations Charter.

2. Respect of the sovereignty of nations and the safety of their territories.

3. Respect and Equality among all races and all nations, big and small.

[1] Delegates from some 45 states and territories, including the U.S.S.R. and China, attended the conference which met in Cairo from 26 December 1957 until 1 January 1958. The delegations were non-governmental, although some included holders of official posts. The emphasis of the conference was on peace; on the importance of the suspension of nuclear tests; on the right to independence of all colonial territories; and on the right of non-committed countries to be heard in international councils. Israel was vigorously condemned. For the texts of the political, economic and cultural resolutions of the conference, see *Egyptian Gazette*, 3 January 1958.

4. To refrain from any interference in the internal affairs of other countries.

5. Respect of the right of every nation to defend herself individually or collectively in accordance with the United Nations Charter.

6. (a) To refrain from using collective defensive organisations to serve the personal interests of any of the Big Powers.

(b) Each country should refrain from bringing pressure to bear on other countries.

7. To avoid actions, aggressive threats and the use of force against the territorial safety or political independence of any country.

8. The settlement of all international disputes through peaceful means such as negotiations, conciliation, arbitration, judiciary settlement or any other peaceful means to be chosen by the parties concerned in accordance with the United Nations Charter.

9. The development of common interests and mutual cooperation.

10. Respect of justice and international obligations.

We declare that peace cannot be based on stable foundations unless we strive for the removal of tension. We welcome every step in this direction and appeal to all peoples to do all in their power to provide facilities for understanding and rapprochement which will inevitably lead to disarmament and the banning of the production, test and use of nuclear weapons and work for directing scientific efforts and nuclear power to peaceful purposes in order to serve and realise the welfare of humanity in full cooperation among nations on an equal footing and within the framework of the United Nations.

Asian and African peoples believe that domination and foreign exploitation and the evils which result from subjugating peoples to colonialism constitute a transgression on basic human rights and a violation of the United Nations Charter, in addition to the evil they bring to rulers and ruled alike and obstructs the development of peace and world cooperation.

The continuance of colonialism is not in line with new conditions in the world because colonialism neglects human progress and is contradictory to the laws of development. It is also one of the reasons of the anxiety which prevails in the world at present.

Asian and African peoples strongly believe in the right of every people to freedom and independence. Asian and African peoples seek unity and shall work in cooperation to help each other to struggle for the welfare of peoples and the whole human race.

We shall consecrate our efforts until a permanent peace is realised. Peace shall inevitably triumph and humanity shall achieve its aspirations in the shadow of peace.

This is the message of the New Year which the conference sends to the world at large.

2. Declaration of the Afro-Asian People's Solidarity Conference regarding the establishment of a permanent organization, Cairo, 1 January 1958[1]

The Afro-Asian People's Solidarity Conference, realising the importance of continuing and developing the work for solidarity amongst the Afro-Asian Peoples, resolves to establish a permanent organisation to carry out the following tasks:

1. To implement and put into practice the resolutions and recommendations of the Conference.

2. To promote and strengthen the Afro-Asian Solidarity movements in all countries of the two continents.

3. To act as a permanent liaison between the solidarity movements in the various countries.

The Conference resolves that this permanent organisation shall be composed of:—

A. Afro-Asian Peoples' Solidarity Council (A.A.P.S.C.) in which all the countries in the two continents shall be entitled to have one representative nominated by the National Solidarity Committees. This Council shall be convened through its Secretariat at least once every year and more often when necessary.

B. The Permanent Secretariat of the A.A.P.S.C. which will consist of one Secretary-General and ten Secretaries.

The Conference resolves that till the next Conference meeting:

1. The head-quarters of this Permanent Secretariat shall be at Cairo.

2. The Secretary-General shall be nominated by Egypt.

3. The ten Secretaries shall be nominated by the following countries (arranged alphabetically)

        Cameroon,
        China,
        Ghana,
        India,
        Indonesia,
        Iraq,
        Japan,
        Sudan,
        Syria,
  and U.S.S.R.

4. The Secretariat shall divide the responsibilities amongst its members

[1] *Egyptian Gazette*, Afro-Asian Supplement. By the end of 1958 less than half the secretaries had reported for duty. The Chinese and Russians were among the first to arrive, but countries like Ghana had so far not sent their representatives.

as it deem it necessary, and shall be collectively responsible for the world.

The Conference resolves that the Secretariat should take urgent measures to publish a 'Journal' at such regular intervals as it considers it possible.

The Conference appeals to the peoples in all countries of Asia and Africa to establish 'National Afro-Asian Peoples' Solidarity Committees' where they do not exist, and to widen and strengthen the existing committees.

Financial Affairs

The Afro-Asian Peoples' Conference considers it necessary to establish a fund for the running of the organisational bodies created by the Conference.

The Conference calls on all the participating peoples to contribute to this fund in accordance with their capacities. The Conference expresses its gratitude to the 'Egyptian Committee for Afro-Asian Solidarity' for offering to open this fund with a generous donation of 10,000 Egyptian pounds annually and providing the necessary premises for the Permanent Secretariat.

The Conference directs the Permanent Secretariat to prepare a budget in accordance with the amounts of contributions of the various countries.

The Conference resolves that the Secretary-General shall take a special responsibility for the financial affairs, together with such other Secretary as may be appointed for the purpose.

Transitional period

The Afro-Asian Peoples' Conference resolves that the first meeting of the A.A.P.S.C. shall take place on January the 4th, 1958 at Cairo.

The Conference requests all countries which are represented on the Permanent Secretariat to send their representatives to Cairo by March the 1st, 1958.

Till then, the Conference requests the Egyptian Committee for Afro-Asian Solidarity to carry on with the work decided upon by the A.A.P.S.C. and the Cairo Conference.

b. Conference of Independent African States

3. Declaration of the Conference of Independent African States, 15–22 April 1958, Accra, 22 April 1958[1]

We, the African States assembled here in Accra in this our first conference, conscious of our responsibilities to humanity and especially to the

[1] *Ghana Today*, vol. 2, no. 6, 14 May 1958. Convened by Dr. Nkrumah, Prime Minister of Ghana, who presided over its deliberations, the conference was attended by delegations from eight

peoples of Africa, and desiring to assert our African Personality on the side of peace, hereby proclaim and solemnly reaffirm our unswerving loyalty to the Charter of the United Nations, the Universal Declaration of Human Rights and the Declaration of the Asian-African Conference held at Bandung.

We further assert and proclaim the unity among ourselves and our solidarity with the dependent peoples of Africa, as well as our friendship with all nations. We resolve to preserve the unity of purpose and action in international affairs which we have forged among ourselves in this historic conference, and to safeguard our hard-won independence, sovereignty and territorial integrity, and to preserve among ourselves the fundamental unity of outlook on foreign policy so that a distinctive African Personality will play its part in co-operation with other peace-loving nations to further the cause of peace.

We pledge ourselves to apply all our endeavours to avoid being committed to any action which might entangle our countries to the detriment of our interests and freedom; to recognize the right of the African people to independence and self-determination and to take appropriate steps to hasten the realization of this right and to affirm the right of the Algerian people to independence and self-determination and to exert all possible effort to hasten the realization of their independence,[1] to uproot forever the evil of racial discrimination in all its forms wherever it may be found; to persuade the great Powers to discontinue the production and testing of nuclear and thermonuclear weapons, and to reduce conventional weapons.

Furthermore, mindful of the urgent need to raise the living standard of our peoples by developing to the fullest possible advantage the great and varied resources of our lands, We hereby pledge ourselves to co-ordinate our economic planning through a joint economic effort and study the economic potentialities, the technical possibilities and related problems existing in our respective States; to promote co-ordinated industrial planning either through our own individual efforts and/or through co-operation with Specialized Agencies of the United Nations; to take measures to

independent African states: Ethiopia (represented by Prince Sahele-Salassie), Liberia (represented by President Tubman), Morocco, Sudan, Libya, Tunisia, U.A.R. (represented by their foreign Ministers), and Ghana. The participating states agreed to hold similar conferences at least every two years, the next to be held at Abbis Ababa. For the text of the resolutions, see Colin Legum, *Bandung, Cairo and Accra. A Report on the First Conference of Independent African States* (London, 1958), pp. 29–32.

[1] The U.A.R., with some support from Libya, favoured the seating of the uninvited F.L.N. delegation at the conference. The other delegations all opposed this; it was finally agreed that the Algerians be allowed to testify to the conference in closed session. There was general agreement on the Algerian question, but the U.A.R. fought hard for a resolution committing the African states to send aid (including military weapons) to Algeria. This was defeated but the conference took a strong line against France, and designated the F.L.N. as the official group with whom France should negotiate to establish conditions for the independence of Algeria. This proposal was subsequently put forward at the Tangiers Conference, see next document.

increase trade among our countries by improving communications between our respective countries and to encourage the investment of foreign capital and skills provided they do not compromise the independence, sovereignty and territorial integrity of our States.

Desirous of mobilizing the human resources of our respective countries in furtherance of our social and cultural aspirations, we will endeavour to promote and facilitate the exchange of teachers, professors, students, exhibitions, educational and cultural and scientific material which will improve cultural relations between the African States and inculcate greater knowledge amongst us through such efforts as joint youth festivals, sporting events, etc.; will encourage and strengthen studies of African culture, history and geography in the institutions of learning in the African States; will take all measures in our respective countries to ensure that such studies are correctly orientated.

We have charged our Permanent Representatives at the United Nations to be the permanent machinery for co-ordinating all matters of common concern to our States, for examining and making recommendations on concrete practical steps for implementing our decisions, and for preparing the grounds for future conferences.

Faithful to the obligations and responsibilities which history has thrown upon us as the vanguard of the complete emancipation of Africa, We do hereby affirm our dedication to the causes which we have proclaimed.

c. Conference of Tangiers

4. Resolution regarding the situation in Algeria, 30 April 1958[1]

La conférence de l'unité du Maghreb arabe—comprenant le parti marocain de l'Istiqlal, le F.L.N. algérien et le parti du Néo-Destour tunisien—réunie à Tanger les 27, 28, 29 et 30 avril, ayant étudié le développement de la guerre d'Algérie et son effet sur la situation en Afrique du Nord, la nature de la guerre d'Algérie et son inévitable destinée, et ayant également remarqué la puissante solidarité parmi les peuples représentés à cette conférence en ce qui concerne les questions vitales, proclame que le droit du peuple algérien à la souveraineté et à l'indépendance est la seule condition qui puisse être proposée pour résoudre la question franco-algérienne.

Etant donné que les tentatives pour mettre fin à la guerre d'Algérie par des moyens pacifiques n'ont abouti à aucun résultat, et que la médiation offerte par Sa Majesté le roi du Maroc et par Son Excellence le président de Tunisie, a été repoussée par le gouvernement français[2]; et étant donné

[1] La Documentation française, Articles et Documents, 1 July 1958. See Chapter III, C, above for the other documents on Algeria.
[2] See *Documents* for 1957, pp. 424–5.

que la bonne volonté des Nord-Africains s'est heurtée à des mesures croissantes pour la guerre d'Algérie, et à une politique de violence et de provocations vis-à-vis de la Tunisie et du Maroc, comme on en a eu la preuve par l'arraisonnement de l'avion transportant Ben Bella et ses compagnons, ainsi que par l'attaque sur Sakiet Sidi Youssef et d'autres opérations militaires en Afrique du Nord; étant donné que cette guerre coloniale constitue un défi perpétuel aux principes humains et un acte tendant à l'annihilation menaçant l'existence d'un peuple entier, la paix en Afrique du Nord, et la paix mondiale, la conférence a, en conséquence, décidé que les partis politiques devraient offrir au peuple algérien qui lutte pour son indépendance, le plein appui de leurs gouvernements.

Etant donné que la question de l'indépendance algérienne intéresse tous les Nord-Africains et leurs leaders, et qu'elle reçoit entièrement leur aide; étant donné la solidarité du peuple algérien avec le Front de Libération nationale, le suel représentant l'Algérie; étant donné les diverses responsabilités prises par le F.L.N., la conférence recommande la constitution d'un gouvernement algérien après consultation avec les gouvernements marocain et tunisien.

Etant donné l'aide financière et militaire que la France obtient de certaines puissances occidentales dans la guerre coloniale d'Algérie; étant donné que cette aide permet la continuation d'une guerre d'anéantissement contre le peuple algérien; et étant donné que ces puissances soutiennent, directement ou indirectement, une action inhumaine menaçant la paix mondiale, les peuples d'Afrique du Nord, par l'intermédiaire de leurs représentants réunis à la conférence de Tanger les 27, 28, 29 et 30 avril 1958, dénoncent une telle attitude qui, sans aucun doute, les rendra hostiles à ces puissances.

Les peuples d'Afrique du Nord espèrent que ces puissances abandonneront leur politique qui est nuisible à la paix et à la coopération internationale. Ils adressent également un appel public et urgent en faveur de la fin de toute aide politique et matérielle visant à encourager cette guerre coloniale.

5. Resolution regarding the unity of the Maghreb, 30 April 1958[1]

Ayant conscience d'exprimer le désir des peuples de l'Afrique du Nord d'unifier leur destin en vertu de la puissante solidarité de leurs intérêts, la conférence de Tanger de l'unité du Maghreb arabe qui a eu lieu les 27, 28, 29 et 30 avril 1958, décide de s'efforcer de réaliser cette unité et considère la fédération comme plus appropriée à l'état de choses dans les pays participant à cette conférence.

Dans ce but, la conférence propose qu'au cours de la période transitoire

---

[1] La Documentation française, Articles et Documents, 1 July 1958.

un conseil consultatif du Maghreb soit formé au moyen des conseils locaux de Tunisie et du Maroc et du Conseil national de la révolution algérienne. La tâche de ce Conseil sera d'étudier les problèmes sur la base des intérêts communs et d'adresser des recommandations aux autorités exécutives locales.

La conférence recommande qu'il est nécessaire, de temps en temps, toutes les fois que les circonstances l'exigent, que les autorités locales des 3 pays se contactent mutuellement en vue de consultations sur les problèmes du Maghreb arabe et pour l'exécution des recommandations présentées par le Conseil consultatif du Maghreb arabe.

La conférence recommande en outre aux gouvernements du Maghreb arabe de ne pas prendre de décisions séparées sur le destin de la paix de l'Afrique dans le domaine des relations étrangères et de la défense tant que des institutions fédérales ne seront pas établies.

d. All-African People's Conference

6. Resolutions of the All-African People's Conference, Accra, 5-13 December 1958[1]

(a) On Imperialism and Colonialism

Whereas the great bulk of the African Continent has been carved out arbitrarily to the detriment of the indigenous African peoples by European Imperialist, namely: Britain, France, Belgium, Spain, Italy and Portugal.

2. *Whereas* in this process of colonisation two groups of Colonial territories have emerged to wit:

(a) Those territories where indigenous Africans are dominated by foreigners who have their seats of authority in foreign lands, for example, French West Africa, French Equatorial Africa, Nigeria, Sierra Leone, Gambia, Belgian Congo, Portuguese Guinea, Basutoland, Swaziland and Bechuanaland.

(b) Those where indigenous Africans are dominated and oppressed by foreigners who have settled permanently in Africa and who regard the position of Africa under their sway as belonging more to them than to the Africa, e.g. Kenya, Union of South Africa, Algeria, Rhodesia, Angola and Mozambique.

3. *Whereas* world opinion unequivocally condemns oppression and subjugation of one race by another in whatever shape or form.

4. *Whereas* all African peoples everywhere strongly deplore the economic exploitation of African peoples by Imperialist Countries thus reducing Africans to poverty in the midst of plenty.

[1] Records of the All-African People's Conference (Accra, 1959), pp. 1–12.

5. *Whereas* all African Peoples vehemently resent the Militarisation of Africans and the use of African soldiers in a nefarious global game against their brethren as in Algeria, Kenya, South Africa, Cameroons, Ivory Coast, Rhodesia and in the Suez Canal invasion.

6. *Whereas* fundamental human rights, freedom of speech, freedom of association, freedom of movement, freedom of worship, freedom to live a full and abundant life as approved by the All African People's Conference on 13th December, 1958, are denied to Africans through the activities of Imperialists.

7. *Whereas* denial of the franchise to Africans on the basis of race or sex has been one of the principal instruments of colonial policy by Imperialists and their agents, thus making it feasible for a few white settlers to lord it over millions of indigenous Africans as in the proposed Central African Federation, Kenya, Union of South Africa, Algeria, Angola, Mozambigue and the Cameroons.

8. *Whereas* Imperialists are now co-ordinating their activities by forming Military and economic pacts such as NATO, European Common Market, Free Trade Area, Organisation for European Economic Co-operation, Common Organisation in Sahara for the purpose of strengthening their Imperialist activities in Africa and elsewhere.

Be it resolved and it is hereby resolved by the All African People's Conference meeting in Accra 5th to 13th December, 1958 and comprising of over 300 delegates representing over 200 million Africans from all parts of Africa as follows:—

(1) That the All African People's Conference vehemently condemns colonialism and Imperialism in whatever shape or form these evils are perpetuated.

(2) That the political and economic exploitation of Africans by Imperialist Europeans should cease forthwith.

(3) That the use of African manpower in the nefarious game of power politics by Imperialists should be a thing of the past.

(4) That independent African States should pursue in their International policy principles which will expedite and accelerate the Independence and sovereignty of all dependent and colonial African Territories.

(5) That fundamental human rights be extended to all men and women in Africa and that the rights of indigenous Africans to the fullest use of their lands be respected and preserved.

(6) The Universal adult franchise be extended to all persons in Africa regardless of race or sex.

(7) That Independent African States ensure that fundamental human rights and universal adult franchise are fully extended to everyone within their states as an example to Imperial Nations who abuse and ignore the extension of those rights to Africans.

(8) That a permanent secretariat of the All African People's Conference be set up to organise the All African Conference on a firm basis.

(9) That a human rights committee of the Conference be formed to examine complaints of abuse of human rights in every part of Africa and to take appropriate steps to ensure the enjoyment of the rights by everyone.

(10) That the All African People's Conference in Accra declares its full support to all fighters for freedom in Africa, to all those who resort to peaceful means of non-violence and civil disobedience as well as to all those who are compelled to retaliate against violence to attain national independence and freedom for the people. Where such retaliation becomes necessary, the Conference condemns all legislations which consider those who fight for their independence and freedom as ordinary criminals.

(b) On Frontiers, Boundaries and Federations

1. *Whereas* the great mass of African peoples are animated by a desire for unity;

Whereas the unity of Africa will be vital to the independence of its component units and essential to the security and general well-being of African peoples;

Whereas the existence of separate states in Africa is fraught with the dangers of exposure to imperialist intrigues and of resurgence of colonialism even after their attainment of independence, unless there is unity among them;

And whereas the ultimate objective of African nations is a Commonwealth of Free African States,

Be it resolved and it is hereby resolved by the All-African Peoples Conference that the Conference:

(a) endorses Pan-Africanism and the desire for unity among African peoples;

(b) declares that its ultimate objective is the evolution of a Commonwealth of Free African States;

(c) calls upon the Independent States of Africa to lead the peoples of Africa towards the attainment of this objective; and

(d) expresses the hope that the day will dawn when the first loyalty of African States will be to an African Commonwealth.

2. *Whereas*, as a first step towards the attainment of the broad objective of an African Commonwealth, the independent states of Africa should amalgamate themselves into groups on the basis of geographical contiguity, economic inter-dependence, linguistic and cultural affinity,

Whereas linguistic, religious and cultural divisions and national sovereignty should be subordinated to the overriding demands of Pan-African

Unity where common geographical and economic considerations and national interests suggest the grouping of certain states;

Whereas amalgamation, federation or groupings should only take place between independent states governed by Africans;

Whereas each state should decide to which group it wishes to adhere by a referendum based on universal adult suffrage;

Whereas regional federations of groups should be regarded as a means to amend and should not be prejudicial to the ultimate objective of a Pan-African Commonwealth by hardening as separate entities and thereby impeding progress towards a continental Commonwealth;

Whereas the people of North Africa have taken the initiative towards a North African Federation and there is a strong desire in West Africa for a West African Grouping;

Whereas it is desirable that other groups should emerge in Africa provided they are not Federations visualised or constituted by colonial powers against the wishes of the African people, since such Federations are a ready weapon in the hands of Colonial Governments and white settlers for the oppression of the African people;

And whereas countries which do not appear to fall naturally into any geographical group should after their attainment of independence decide by democratic processes whether to adhere to existing groups or to evolve different groups;

Be it resolved and it is hereby resolved by the All-African People's Conference that the Conference;

(a) endorses the desire in various parts of Africa for regional grouping of states;

(b) advocates that such groupings should be based on three principles, namely:

  (i) only independent states and countries governed by Africans should come together;
  (ii) the establishment of groups should not be prejudicial to the ultimate objective of a Pan-African Commonwealth;
  (iii) adherence to any group should be based on the wishes of the people ascertained by referendum on the basis of universal adult suffrage; and

(c) recommends that countries which do not appear to fall naturally within any group should decide by similar means whether to adhere to any group or to evolve different groups.

3. *Whereas* artificial barriers and frontiers drawn by imperialists to divide African peoples operate to the detriment of Africans and should therefore be abolished or adjusted;

Whereas frontiers which cut across ethnic groups or divide peoples of the same stock are unnatural and are not conducive to peace or stability;

Whereas leaders of neighbouring countries should co-operate towards a permanent solution of such problems which accords with the best interests of the people affected and enhances the prospects of realisation of the ideal of a Pan-African Commonwealth of Free States;

Whereas the 20th February, 1959 will be an important date in the history of the Cameroons, when a special session of the United Nations General Assembly will discuss the question of unification and independence of the territory;

Be it resolved and it is hereby resolved by the All-African People's Conference that the Conference:

(a) denounces artificial frontiers drawn by imperialist powers to divide the peoples of Africa, particularly those which cut across ethnic groups and divide people of the same stock;

(b) calls for the abolition or adjustment of such frontiers at an early date;

(c) calls upon the Independent States of Africa to support a permanent solution to this problem founded upon the true wishes of the people;

(d) notes with satisfaction that a special session of the United Nations General Assembly will discuss the question of unification and independence of the Cameroons on the 20th February, 1959 and

(e) invites all Africans to observe that date as Cameroons Day.

4. *Whereas* it is desirable that certain measures should be adopted by Independent African States and Dependent African Countries which are in a position to do so, towards achieving Pan-African unity:

Whereas firstly passports, travel certificates, etc., should be abolished in respect of bona-fide African tourists, visitors and students for the purpose of facilitating the free movement of Africans from one territory to another and thereby promoting intercourse among Africans, provided that this is not used as an excuse by white settlers to indulge in mass movement of cheap labour;

Whereas secondly, it is desirable, for the purpose of promoting intercourse among Africans on a continental basis, that the English language should be taught in the Secondary Schools of French speaking territories and vice versa and that the histories of African nations should be taught in schools throughout Africa:

Whereas thirdly, it should be possible for Africans to enjoy reciprocal rights of citizenship at least in territories within the same regional group and not be subjected to discrimination on grounds of their country of origin, so that ultimately no African shall be considered an alien in any part of Africa;

Whereas fourthly, in order to promote inter-territorial co-operation certain forms of joint activity could be brought into being, such as a common West African Airline, intercommunications system, road and rail transport system, research and scientific institutions, and military organisations;

Whereas, fifthly, regional conferences of political parties, trade unions, youth organisations, journalists and writers, women's organisations, etc., could be held regularly to promote singleness of purpose and community sense;

Whereas, sixthly, Africans wherever they are in control could use radio services, the press and other media of mass communication to promote the ideals of Pan-Africanism;

And whereas seventhly it is desirable that political parties throughout Africa should make provisions in their Constitutions and programmes for promoting African Solidarity;

Be it resolved and it is hereby resolved by the All-African People's Conference that the Conference:

(*a*) calls upon all states and countries in Africa which are in a position to do so to implement the following programme forthwith;

    (i) abolition of passports requirements and other travel restrictions for bona fide African visitors, tourists and students;

    (ii) reciprocal rights of citizenship for Africans from other territories;

    (iii) reciprocal teaching of the English and French languages and the history of other African nations in the Secondary Schools of each territory;

    (iv) organisation of inter-territorial enterprises;

(*b*) urges the organisation of regional conferences respectively of political parties, trade unions, youth organisations, journalists and writers, women's organisations, etc.

(*c*) calls upon all Africans wherever they can to use the radio, the press and other media of mass communication to promote the ideals of Pan-Africanism.

(*d*) urges political parties throughout Africa to provide in their constitutions and programmes for the promotion of African Solidarity.

(c) On Racialism and Discriminatory Laws and Practices

1. PREAMBLE

Whereas having heard shocking accounts of the brutal operation of racialism and discriminatory laws and denial of human rights on the continent of Africa from representatives of the participating organisations,

Whereas racialism is one of the outcomes of colonialism and the independence of states is a pre-requisite for the end of discrimination,

Whereas Africans in the Union of South Africa, the Rhodesias, Nyasaland, Mozambique, Angola, Kenya, the Cameroons, Belgian Congo, Basutoland, South West Africa, and Kamerun are victims of a racialism that has reached alarming proportions;

Whereas racialism in Algeria has caused and is causing race extermination;

Whereas in a colonial country land belongs to a foreign power;

Whereas the problem of land in a colonial territory represents the ugliest form of colonial rule that must be destroyed so that African authorities own the land;

Whereas the Universal Declaration of Human Rights is being flouted in Africa and the Africans are deprived of the rights of man;

Whereas the recognition of, and respect for human dignity are the bases of a decent society;

Whereas those who practise racialism and discrimination are therefore out of step with the law;

Whereas colonial authorities do not respect international conventions;

Whereas democracy needs to be established immediately in Africa;

Whereas the colonial authorities have shown obstinate indifference towards resolutions adopted to set up a democracy;

Whereas the African must find concrete means of effectively reversing the situation;

Whereas Africa's destiny and political constitution must be forged by Africans themselves;

Be it resolved that this Conference registers its vehement protest against this ugly system;

Condemns the pernicious system of racialism and discriminating laws, especially as expressed in its extreme and most brutal forms in the Union of South Africa, Rhodesia, the Portuguese Territories of Angola, Mozambique, Principe, and Sao Thome, where the indigenous populations exist under a regime of apartheid;

Condemns the lack of educational facilities and the denial of social benefits;

Condemns the denial of human democratic rights as enunciated in the charter of the United Nations;

Condemns racial segregation, reserve systems and all other forms of racial discrimination and colour bar;

Condemns the use of forced labour in territories such as Angola, Mozambique, Belgian Congo, South and South-west Africa;

Condemns the political policies of territories like South Africa which base their minority rule of the majority upon apartheid's social doctrines;

Condemns the alienation of the African's best land for the use of European colonisers.

The All-African People's Conference declares that as long as the system of discrimination and racialism remains on this African continent it will arrest the development of the African peoples and stifle their self-expression;

Maintains that while discrimination continues to exist the problems facing Africa cannot be solved;

The All-African People's Conference calls upon the United Nations to reconstitute the Committee on the Racial Situation in the Union of South Africa;

If the United Nations should fail to reconstitute this committee this conference calls upon the Secretariat of the independent States of Africa to set up such a Committee.

The All-African People's Conference declares that the struggle for the freedom of Africa is the task of the Africans themselves, and calls upon the workers, the peasant, and other sections of the toiling masses, together with the intellectuals to unite their forces in common action for a final attack on discrimination and racialism;

Declares that political parties and leaders should recognise the need for a united front in the struggle for freedom and independence.

Convinced further that the overwhelming majority of the populations of the dependent territories have been made conscious of their rights under the Universal Declaration of Human Rights;

The All-African People's Conference *Recommends*:

(1) That the permanent Secretariat to be set up should urge any African independent states which conduct trade with South Africa to impose economic sanctions against the latter country as a protest against racial discrimination which the European minority are practising to the humiliation of the non-European majority. Such economic sanctions should include the boycott of South African goods.

(2) That all African countries which supply South Africa with migrant labour should organise this reservoir of workers for its own use and thus withhold such labour from South African industry which has become the instrument of oppression. The permanent Secretariat should endeavour to give financial aid to any development plan that any country may have to initiate as a result of the diversion of its labour force.

(3) That no African state should have any diplomatic relations with any country on our continent that practises race discrimination.

(4) That April 15 should be set aside and called Africa Freedom Day, which all African countries and all friends of Africa throughout the world shall observe as a rallying point for the forces of freedom.

(5) That the permanent Secretariat should set up a bureau of informa-

tion. Such bureau should appoint correspondents in various African territories who will send factual news items relating to the Liberatory Movement to a central office for publication. The bureau should also be a depot from which liberatory journals in Africa will be circulated. This we believe will be not only a medium through which we shall get to know one another, but also through which we can co-ordinate our struggle.

(6) That the Independent African States should form an 'African Legion' consisting of volunteers who will be ready to protect the freedom of the African peoples.

(7) That this conference insists on immediate independence for all African territories in order to put an end to racial discrimination in the spirit of the United Nations Charter.

(8) That this Conference rejects the claim of Portugal that its colonies constitute part of metropolitan Portugal, and demands immediate independence for countries in Africa under Portuguese rule.

(9) That this Conference, considering that the future of the Mandated Territory of South-west Africa has been debated at the United Nations for 12 successive years, and that the Herero, Nama, and other African inhabitants, who have been petitioning the United Nations during that time, still complain of the loss of their lands, and their humiliating subjection to the apartheid system, in this co-called sacred trust of civilisation; that this Conference call on the Great Powers who entrusted the Mandate to South Africa, especially the United Kingdom, the United States, and France, together with other former members of the League of Nations, to revoke the mandate and take immediate steps to grant independence to South-west Africa.

(10) This Conference regards as unacceptable and discreditable any plan that would allow the incorporation into the Union of South Africa's apartheid system any African land or people whether belonging to the Mandated Territory of South-west Africa, or the British Protectorates of Bechuanaland, Basutoland, and Swaziland.

(11) That this Conference condemns the Central African Federation and all its discriminatory laws and practices which lead to social, cultural, economic and political racial consideration. Therefore calls upon the British Government to honour the declaration of human rights as entrenched in the United Nations Charter and dissolve the Central African Federation in the benefit of all people.

(12) That in respect of Kenya this Conference urges the British Government to end the present state of emergency in Kenya and the release of all political prisoners. Also that this Conference demands the abrogation of all discriminatory laws, the establishment of a common electoral roll based on adult suffrage with provision for one man one vote, and the

insertion of laws in the Statute Books for the transfer of the lands and rights to the African people.

(d) On Tribalism, Religious Separatism, and Traditional Institutions

Whereas we strongly oppose the imperialist tactics of utilizing tribalism and religious separatism to perpetuate their colonial policies in Africa;

Whereas we are also convinced that tribalism and religious separatism are evil practices which constitute serious obstacles to—

    (i) the realisation of the unity of Africa
   (ii) the political evolution of Africa
  (iii) the rapid liberation of Africa

Be it resolved that steps be taken by political, trade union, cultural and other organisations to educate the masses about the dangers of these evil practices and thereby mobilise the masses to fight these evils.

That in addition to any action taken by dependent countries, the independent countries shall:—

    (*a*) allow their governments to pass laws and through propaganda and education, discourage tribalism and religious separatism.
    (*b*) encourage their governments to give the dependent countries and their leaders effective aid in the fight to realise their common objectives rapidly.

RESOLUTION ON TRADITIONAL INSTITUTIONS

Whereas the All-African People's Conference convened in Accra from the 5th December to the 13th December, 1958, realises that some of the African Traditional Institutions especially chieftaincy do not conform to the demands of democracy.

And whereas some of these institutions actually support colonialism and constitute the organs of corruption, exploitation and repression which strangle the dignity, personality and the will of the African to emancipate himself.

Be it resolved that those African traditional institutions whether political, social or economic which have clearly shown their reactionary character and their sordid support for colonialism be condemned.

That all conscientious peoples of Africa and all African political leaders be invited to intensify and reinforce their educational and propaganda activities with the aim of annihilating those institutions which are incompatible with our objectives of national liberations.

And that Governments of independent countries be called upon to suppress or modify these institutions.

(e) On the Establishment of a Permanent Organisation

Whereas the Imperialist Powers of Great Britain, France, Spain, Portugal, Belgium and the Union of South Africa have, between them, deprived various people of Africa of their freedom and liberty,

And whereas the leaders of political parties in Africa gathered in Accra between the 5th day of December, 1958 and the 13th day of December, 1958, are irrevocably resolved to wage a final assault upon the denial of freedom, liberty and fundamental human rights to people of Africa,

Be it resolved that the All-African People's Conference be established with a permanent secretariat in Accra with the following aims and objects:

(*a*) To promote understanding and unity among peoples of Africa

(*b*) To accelerate the liberation of Africa from Imperialism and Colonialism

(*c*) To mobilise world opinion against the denial of political rights and fundamental human rights to Africans

(*d*) To develop the feeling of one community among the peoples of Africa with the object to the emergence of a United States of Africa.

And that the Conference Secretariat should be governed by the rules approved for that purpose at this Conference.

CHRONOLOGICAL LIST OF DOCUMENTS
1958

May

August

September

November

December

SET AND PRINTED IN GREAT BRITAIN
BY HAZELL, WATSON AND VINEY LTD.
AYLESBURY AND SLOUGH
REPRINTED LITHOGRAPHICALLY AT THE
UNIVERSITY PRESS, OXFORD
BY VIVIAN RIDLER
PRINTER TO THE UNIVERSITY